NEW SAT®
Strategies,
Practice &
Review

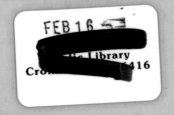

NEW SAT®
Strategies, Practice & Review

KAPLAN)

PUBLISHING

New York

Acknowledgments

Special thanks to those who made this book possible including Laura Aitcheson, Becky Berthiaume, Michael Boothroyd, Matthew Callan, Potoula Chresomales, Kate Fisher, Adam Hinz, Kate Hurley, Brandon Jones, Rebecca Knauer, Celina Lasota, James Radkins, Justin Starr, Bob Verini, Devon Wible, Daniel Wittich, and many others who contributed materials and advice.

SAT® is a registered trademark of the College Board, which was not involved in the production of, and does not endorse, this product.

This publication is designed to provide accurate and authoritative information in regard to the subject matter covered. It is sold with the understanding that the publisher is not engaged in rendering legal, accounting, or other professional service. If legal advice or other expert assistance is required, the services of a competent professional should be sought.

Published by Kaplan Publishing, a division of Kaplan, Inc.
750 Third Avenue
New York, NY 10017

Printed in the United States of America

10 9 8 7 6 5 4 3 2

ISBN-13: 978-1-62523-154-3

Kaplan Publishing books are available at special quantity discounts to use for sales promotions, employee premiums, or educational purposes. For more information or to purchase books, please call the Simon & Schuster Special Sales Department at 866-506-1949.

Table of Contents

Introduction to the SAT

The first step to achieving SAT success is to learn about the structure of the test and why it's so important for your future. The SAT, like any standardized test, is predictable. The more comfortable you are with the test structure, the more confidently you will approach each question type, thus maximizing your score.

SAT STRUCTURE

The SAT is 3 hours long, or 3 hours and 50 minutes long if you choose to complete the optional Essay Test. It is made up of mostly multiple-choice questions that test two subject areas: Math and Evidence-Based Reading and Writing. The latter is broken into a Reading Test and a Writing & Language Test.

Test	Allotted Time (min.)	Question Count
Reading	65	52
Writing & Language	35	44
Math	80	58
Essay (optional)	50	1
Total	180 OR 230 (w/essay)	153 OR 154 (w/essay)

SAT SCORING

SAT scoring can be pretty complex. You will receive one score ranging from 200 to 800 for Evidence-Based Reading and Writing and another for Math. Your overall SAT score will range from 400 to 1600 and is calculated by adding these two scores together. You will receive a separate score for the Essay Test, if you choose to take it.

In addition to your overall scores, you will receive subscores that provide a deeper analysis of your SAT performance. The SAT also gives you a percentile ranking, which allows you to compare your scores with those of other high school students who took the test. For example, a student with a percentile of 63 has earned a score better than 63 percent of test takers.

WHERE AND WHEN TO TAKE THE SAT

The SAT is offered every year on multiple Saturday test dates. Typically, exams are offered in October, November, December, January, March, May, and June. You can take the SAT multiple times. Some states offer special administrations of the SAT on different dates. Sunday tests are available by request for students requiring religious or other exemptions. The SAT is administered at high schools around the country that serve as testing centers. Your high school may or may not be a testing center. Check www.collegeboard.org for a list of testing centers near you. Note that you must register for the SAT approximately one month in advance to avoid paying a late fee. Some SAT test dates also offer SAT Subject Tests. You may not take both the SAT and the Subject Tests in a single sitting.

THE SAT MATH TEST

The SAT Math Test is broken down into a calculator section and a no-calculator section. Questions across the sections consist of multiple-choice, student-produced response (Grid-in), and more comprehensive Multi-Part questions.

	Calculator Section	No-Calculator Section	Total
Duration (minutes)	55	25	80
Multiple-choice	30	15	45
Grid-in	8	5	13
Total Questions	38	20	58

The SAT Math Test is divided into four content areas: Heart of Algebra, Problem Solving and Data Analysis, Passport to Advanced Math, and Additional Topics in Math.

SAT Math Test Content Area Distribution	
Heart of Algebra (19 questions)	Analyzing and fluently solving equations and systems of equations; creating expressions, equations, and inequalities to represent relationships between quantities and to solve problems; rearranging and interpreting formulas
Problem Solving and Data Analysis (17 questions)	Creating and analyzing relationships using ratios, proportions, percentages, and units; describing relationships shown graphically; summarizing qualitative and quantitative data

SAT Math Test Content Area Distribution	
Passport to Advanced Math (16 questions)	Rewriting expressions using their structure; creating, analyzing, and fluently solving quadratic and higher-order equations; purposefully manipulating polynomials to solve problems
Additional Topics in Math (6 questions)	Making area and volume calculations in context; investigating lines, angles, triangles, and circles using theorems; and working with trigonometric functions

A few math questions might look like something you'd expect to see on a science or history test. These "crossover" questions are designed to test your ability to use math in real-world scenarios. There are a total of 16 "crossover" questions that will contribute to subscores that span multiple tests. Eight of the questions will contribute to the Analysis in Science subscore, and eight will contribute to the Analysis in History/Social Studies subscore.

THE SAT READING TEST

The SAT Reading Test will focus on your comprehension and reasoning skills when presented with challenging extended prose passages taken from a variety of content areas.

SAT Reading Test Overview	
Timing	65 minutes
Questions	52 passage-based multiple-choice questions
Passages	4 single passages; 1 set of paired passages
Passage Length	500–750 words per passage or passage set

Passages will draw from U.S. and World Literature, History/Social Studies, and Science. One set of History/Social Studies or Science passages will be paired. History/Social Studies and Science passages can also be accompanied by graphical representations of data such as charts, graphs, tables, and so on.

Reading Test Passage Types	
U.S. and World Literature	1 passage with 10 questions
History/Social Studies	2 passages or 1 passage and 1 paired-passage set with 10–11 questions each
Science	2 passages or 1 passage and 1 paired-passage set with 10–11 questions each

The multiple-choice questions for each passage will be arranged in order from the more general to the more specific so that you can actively engage with the entire passage before answering questions about details.

Skills Tested by Reading Test Questions	
Information and Ideas	Close reading, citing textual evidence, determining central ideas and themes
Summarizing	Understanding relationships, interpreting words and phrases in context
Rhetoric	Analyzing word choice, assessing overall text structure, assessing part-whole relationships, analyzing point of view, determining purpose, analyzing arguments
Synthesis	Analyzing multiple texts, analyzing quantitative information

THE SAT WRITING & LANGUAGE TEST

The SAT Writing & Language Test will focus on your ability to revise and edit text from a range of content areas.

SAT Writing & Language Test Overview	
Timing	35 minutes
Questions	44 passage-based multiple-choice questions
Passages	4 single passages with 11 questions each
Passage Length	400–450 words per passage

The SAT Writing & Language Test will contain four single passages, one from each of the following subject areas: Careers, Humanities, History/Social Studies, and Science.

Writing & Language Passage Types	
Careers	Hot topics in "major fields of work" such as information technology and health care
Humanities	Texts about literature, art, history, music, and philosophy pertaining to human culture
History/Social Studies	Discussion of historical or social sciences topics such as anthropology, communication studies, economics, education, human geography, law, linguistics, political science, psychology, and sociology
Science	Exploration of concepts, findings, and discoveries in the natural sciences including Earth science, biology, chemistry, and physics

Passages will also vary in the "type" of text. A passage can be an argument, an informative or explanatory text, or a nonfiction narrative.

Writing & Language Passage Text Type Distribution	
Argument	1–2 passages
Informative/Explanatory Text	1–2 passages
Nonfiction Narrative	1 passage

Some passages and/or questions will refer to one or more informational graphics that represent data. Questions associated with these graphical representations will ask you to revise and edit the passage based on the data presented in the graphic.

The most prevalent question format on the SAT Writing & Language Test will ask you to choose the best of three alternatives to an underlined portion of the passage or to decide that the current version is the best option. You will be asked to improve the development, organization, and diction in the passages to ensure they conform to conventional standards of English grammar, usage, and style.

Skills Tested by Writing & Language Test Questions	
Expression of Ideas (24 questions)	Development, organization, and effective language use
Standard English Conventions (20 questions)	Sentence structure, conventions of usage, and conventions of punctuation

THE SAT ESSAY TEST (OPTIONAL)

The SAT Essay Test will assess your college and career readiness by testing your abilities to read and analyze a high-quality source document and write a coherent analysis of the source supported with critical reasoning and evidence from the given text.

The SAT Essay Test features an argumentative source text of 650–750 words aimed toward a large audience. Passages will examine ideas, debates, and shifts in the arts and sciences as well as civic, cultural, and political life. Rather than having a simple for/against structure, these passages will be nuanced and will relate views on complex subjects. These passages will also be logical in their structure and reasoning.

It is important to note that prior knowledge is not required.

The SAT Essay Test prompt will ask you to explain how the presented passage's author builds an argument to convince an audience. In writing your essay, you may analyze elements such as the author's use of evidence, reasoning, style, and persuasion; you will not be limited to those elements listed, however.

Rather than writing about whether you agree or disagree with the presented argument, you will write an essay in which you analyze *how* the author makes an argument.

The SAT Essay Test will be broken down into three categories for scoring: Reading, Analysis, and Writing. Each of these elements will be scored on a scale of 1 to 4 by two graders, for a total score of 2 to 8 for each category.

TEST-TAKING STRATEGIES

You have already learned about the overall structure of the SAT as well as the structure of the three tests it entails: Reading, Writing & Language, and Math. The strategies outlined in this section can be applied to any of these tests.

The SAT is different from the tests you are used to taking in school. The good news is that you can use the SAT's particular structure to your advantage.

For example, on a test given in school, you probably go through the questions in order. You spend more time on the harder questions than on the easier ones because harder questions are usually worth more points. You probably often show your work because your teacher tells you that how you approach a question is as important as getting the correct answer.

This approach is not optimal for the SAT. On the SAT, you benefit from moving around within a section if you come across tough questions because the harder questions are worth the same number of points as the easier questions. It doesn't matter how you arrive at the correct answer—only that you bubble in the correct answer choice.

STRATEGY #1: TRIAGING THE TEST

You do not need to complete questions on the SAT in order. Every student has different strengths and should attack the test with those strengths in mind. Your main objective on the SAT should be to score as many points as you can. While approaching questions out of order may seem counterintuitive, it is a surefire way to achieve your best score.

Just remember, you can skip around within each section, but you cannot work on a section other than the one you've been instructed to work on.

To triage the test effectively, do the following:

- First, work through all the easy questions that you can do quickly. Skip questions that are hard or time-consuming

- For the Reading and Writing & Language Tests, start with the passage you find most manageable and work toward the one you find most challenging. You do not need to go in order

- Second, work through the questions that are doable but time-consuming

- Third, work through the hard questions

- If you run out of time, pick a Letter of the Day for remaining questions

A Letter of the Day is an answer choice letter (A, B, C, or D) that you choose before Test Day to select for questions you guess on.

STRATEGY #2: ELIMINATION

Even though there is no wrong-answer penalty on the SAT, Elimination is still a crucial strategy. If you can determine that one or more answer choices are definitely incorrect, you can increase your chances of getting the right answer by paring the selection down.

To eliminate answer choices, do the following:

- Read each answer choice

- Cross out the answer choices that are incorrect

- Remember: There is no wrong-answer penalty, so take your best guess

STRATEGY #3: GUESSING

Each multiple-choice question on the SAT has four answer choices and no wrong-answer penalty. That means if you have no idea how to approach a question, you have a 25 percent chance of randomly choosing the correct answer. Even though there's a 75 percent chance of selecting the incorrect answer, you won't lose any points for doing so. The worst that can happen on the SAT is that you'll earn zero points on a question, which means you should *always* at least take a guess, even when you have no idea what to do.

When guessing on a question, do the following:

- Always try to strategically eliminate answer choices before guessing

- If you run out of time, or have no idea what a question is asking, pick a Letter of the Day

COMMON TESTING MYTHS

Since its inception, the SAT has gone through various revisions, but it has always been an integral part of the college admissions process. As a result of its significance and the changes it has undergone, a number of rumors and myths have circulated about the exam. In this section, we'll dispel some of the most common ones. As always, you can find the most up-to-date information about the SAT at the College Board website (https://www.collegeboard.org).

Myth: **There is a wrong-answer penalty on the SAT to discourage guessing.**

Fact: While this statement was true a few years ago, it is no longer true. Older versions of the SAT had a wrong-answer penalty so that students who guessed on questions would not have an advantage over students who left questions blank. This penalty has been removed; make sure you never leave an SAT question blank!

Myth: **Answer choice C is most likely to be the correct answer.**

Fact: This rumor has roots in human psychology. Apparently, when people such as high school teachers, for example, design an exam, they have a slight bias toward answer choice C when assigning correct answers. While humans do write SAT questions, a computer randomizes the distribution of correct choices; statistically, therefore, each answer choice is equally likely to be the correct answer.

Myth: **The SAT is just like another test in school.**

Fact: While the SAT covers some of the same content as your high school math, literature, and English classes, it also presents concepts in ways that are fundamentally different. While you might be able to solve a math problem in a number of different ways on an algebra test, the SAT places a heavy emphasis on working through questions as quickly and efficiently as possible.

Myth: **You have to get all the questions right to get a perfect score.**

Fact: Many students have reported missing several questions on the SAT and being pleasantly surprised to receive perfect scores. Their experience is not atypical: Usually, you can miss a few questions and still get a coveted perfect score. The makers of the SAT use a technique called scaling to ensure that a SAT score conveys the same information from year to year, so you might be able to miss a couple more questions on a slightly harder SAT exam and miss fewer questions on an easier SAT exam and get the same scores. Keep a positive attitude throughout the SAT, and in many cases, your scores will pleasantly surprise you.

Myth: **You can't prepare for the SAT.**

Fact: You've already proven this myth false by buying this book. While the SAT is designed to fairly test students regardless of preparation, you can gain a huge advantage by familiarizing yourself with the structure and content of the exam. By working through the questions and practice tests available to you, you'll ensure that nothing on the SAT catches you by surprise and that you do everything you can to maximize your score. Your Kaplan resources help you structure this practice in the most efficient way possible, and provide you with helpful strategies and tips as well.

HOW TO USE THIS BOOK

WELCOME TO KAPLAN!

Congratulations on taking this important step in your college admissions process! By studying with Kaplan, you'll maximize your score on the SAT, a major factor in your overall college application.

Our experience shows that the greatest SAT score increases result from active engagement in the preparation process. Kaplan will give you direction, focus your preparation, and teach you the specific skills and effective test-taking strategies you need to know for the SAT. We will help you achieve your top performance on Test Day, but your effort is crucial. The more you invest in preparing for the SAT, the greater your chances of achieving your target score and getting into your top-choice college.

Are you registered for the SAT? Kaplan cannot register you for the official SAT. If you have not already registered for the upcoming SAT, talk to your high school guidance counselor or visit the College Board's website at www.collegeboard.org to register online and for information on registration deadlines, test sites, accommodations for students with disabilities, and fees.

PRACTICE TESTS

Kaplan's practice tests are just like the actual SAT. By taking a practice exam you will prepare yourself for the actual Test Day experience. One practice test is included in this book, and two more can be accessed online. See the Digital Resources section to learn how to access your online practice tests. You can score your test by hand using the score conversion tables in this book, or log into the online companion for easy online scoring.

EXTRA PRACTICE

You need to reinforce what you learn in each chapter by consistently practicing the Kaplan Methods and Strategies. Each chapter contains additional practice problems that reinforce the concepts explained in that chapter. These questions are great practice for the real SAT. Answers & Explanations are provided in the back of the book.

SMARTPOINTS

Each chapter contains a breakdown of SmartPoints. By studying the information released by the College Board, Kaplan has been able to determine how often certain topics are likely to show up on the SAT, and therefore how many points these topics are worth on Test Day. If you master a given topic, you can expect to earn the corresponding number of SmartPoints on Test Day.

SAT EXTRA MATERIALS

The chapters that are in this book will help you answer the most questions on Test Day. However, there is additional content that will be covered on the SAT. We have provided 14 additional chapters online to help you prepare for Test Day. See the note below on Digital Resources to learn how to access these extra materials.

DIGITAL RESOURCES

Register Your Online Companion

To access your online companion:

1. Go to kaptest.com/booksonline.

2. Follow the on-screen instructions. Have this book available.

Join a Live Online Event

Kaplan's SAT Live Online sessions are interactive, instructor-led prep lessons that you can participate in from anywhere you have Internet access.

SAT Live Online sessions are held in our state-of-the-art visual classroom: Actual lessons in real time, just like a physical classroom experience. Interact with your teacher using chat, whiteboards, and polling. Just like courses at Kaplan centers, SAT Live Online sessions are led by top Kaplan instructors.

To register for an SAT Live Online event:

1. Once you've signed in to your student home page, open your syllabus.

2. In the Syllabus window, go to the Live Online Registration menu option.

3. Click on the link. A separate window will appear with registration instructions.

SAT Live Online events are scheduled to take place throughout the year. Please check the registration page with dates and times.

SAT Practice Test

Your SAT online companion includes two additional full-length practice tests. We recommend you complete these practice tests as you make your way through the content of this book. After completing each practice test, you'll receive a detailed online score report. Use this summary to help you focus and review the content areas that comprise your greatest areas of improvement.

Extra Materials

Your SAT online companion includes 14 extra chapters that you can use to prepare for the SAT. If you have additional time to study, it is recommended that you access these chapters and use them to help you prepare for the SAT.

Math

Heart of Algebra

BY THE END OF THIS UNIT, YOU WILL BE ABLE TO:

1. Apply the Kaplan Method for Math to any math question on the SAT
2. Solve linear equations and inequalities
3. Graph linear equations and inequalities
4. Solve systems of equations
5. Translate word problems into math

CHAPTER 1

The Kaplan Method for Math & Linear Equations

CHAPTER OBJECTIVES

By the end of this chapter, you will be able to:

1. Apply the Kaplan Method for Math to Heart of Algebra questions

2. Recognize, simplify, and solve linear equations efficiently

3. Translate complex word problems into equations

4. Interpret the most commonly tested types of linear graphs

SMARTPOINTS

Point Value	SmartPoint Category
Point Builder	Kaplan Method for Math
110 Points	Linear Equations

THE KAPLAN METHOD FOR MATH

Because the SAT is a standardized test, students who approach each question in a consistent way will be rewarded on Test Day. Applying the same basic steps to every math question—whether it asks you about geometry, algebra, or even trigonometry—will help you avoid minor mistakes as well as tempting wrong answer choices.

Use the Kaplan Method for Math for every math question on the SAT. Its steps are applicable to every situation and reflect the best test-taking practices.

The Kaplan Method for Math has three steps:

Step 1: Read the question, identifying and organizing important information as you go

Step 2: Choose the best strategy to answer the question

Step 3: Check that you answered the *right* question

Let's examine each of these steps in more detail.

Step 1: Read the question, identifying and organizing important information as you go

This means:

- **What information am I given?** Take a few seconds to jot down the information you are given and try to group similar items together.

- **Separate the question from the context.** Word problems may include information that is unnecessary to solve the question. Feel free to discard any unnecessary information.

- **How are the answer choices different?** Reading answer choices carefully can help you spot the most efficient way to solve an SAT math question. If the answer choices are decimals, then painstakingly simplifying your final answer as a fraction is a waste of time; you can just use your calculator instead.

- **Should I label or draw a diagram?** If the question describes a shape or figure but doesn't provide one, sketch a diagram so you can see the shape or figure and add notes to it. If a figure is provided, take a few seconds to label it with information from the question.

✔ **Expert Tip**

Don't assume you understand a question as soon as you see it. Many students see an equation and immediately begin solving. Solving math questions without carefully reading can take you down the wrong path on Test Day.

Step 2: Choose the best strategy to answer the question

- **Look for patterns.** Every SAT math question can be solved in a variety of ways, but not all strategies are created equally. To finish all of the questions, you'll need to solve questions as *efficiently* as possible. If you find yourself about to do time-consuming math, take a moment to look for time-saving shortcuts.

- **Pick numbers or use straightforward math.** While you can always solve an SAT math question with what you've learned in school, doing so won't always be the fastest way. On questions that describe relationships between numbers (such as percentages) but don't actually use numbers, you can often save time on Test Day by using techniques such as Picking Numbers instead of straightforward math.

> ✔ **Expert Tip**
>
> The SAT won't give you any extra points for solving a question the hard way.

Step 3: Check that you answered the *right* question

- When you get the final answer, **resist the urge to immediately bubble in the answer**. Take a moment to:

  - Review the question stem

  - Check units of measurement

  - Double-check your work

- The SAT will often ask you for quantities such as $x + 1$ or the product of x and y. **Be careful on these questions!** They often include tempting answer choices that correspond to the values of x or y individually. There's no partial credit on the SAT, so take a moment at the end of every question to make sure you're answering the right question.

LINEAR EQUATIONS

Linear equations and linear graphs are some of the most common elements on the SAT Math Test. They can be used to model relationships and changes such as those concerning time, temperature, or population.

The graphs of these equations are as important as the equations themselves. The graphs you will see most are either linear or lines of best fit. A sample graph is shown:

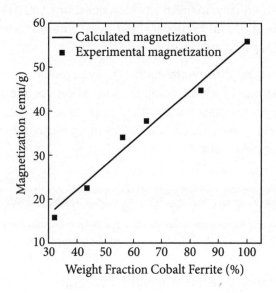

When working with a graph like this, you may not know anything about magnetization or cobalt ferrite, but you do see a graph with a straight line on it. That straight line is your clue that you're dealing with a linear equation.

Being able to work with, understand, and interpret linear equations will make up a substantial part of your Math score. In this chapter, we will explore all of those scenarios so you'll be ready to tackle linear equations in whatever form you encounter them on the test.

Many students inadvertently switch on "math autopilot" when solving linear equations, automatically running through the same set of steps on every equation without looking for the best way to solve the question. On the SAT, however, every second counts. You will want to use the *most* efficient strategy for solving questions. Take a look at the following example:

1. $$\frac{4+z-(3+2z)}{6}=\frac{-z-3(5-2)}{7}$$

   What is the value of z in the equation above?

   A) -61

   B) $-\dfrac{61}{27}$

   C) $\dfrac{61}{27}$

   D) 61

The following below shows Kaplan's strategic thinking on the left, along with suggested math scratchwork on the right. Keeping your notes organized is critical for success on the SAT, so start practicing setting up well-organized scratchwork now.

Strategic Thinking	Math Scratchwork
Step 1: Read the question, identifying and organizing important information as you go This question is straightforward: You're given an equation and need to solve for *z*.	
Step 2: Choose the best strategy to answer the question Straightforward algebra will work well here. Combine like terms on both sides of the equation first, being mindful of negative signs. Once you've combined, cross-multiply to eliminate the fractions, and then isolate *z*.	$$\frac{4+z-(3+2z)}{6}=\frac{-z-3(5-2)}{7}$$ $$\frac{1-z}{6}=\frac{-z-9}{7}$$ $$7-7z=-6z-54$$ $$-z=-61$$ $$z=61$$
Step 3: Check that you answered the *right* question You've determined that *z* is equal to 61; therefore, (D) is correct.	$$z=61$$

You could have approached a question like this in many ways, but remember, the goal is to get the correct answer quickly. The faster you solve algebraic equations, the more time you'll be able to devote to challenging questions, setting you up to earn more points on Test Day.

✔ **Remember**

As you practice, always ask yourself: "Is there a faster way to solve this question?" Use the Answers & Explanations at the back of this book to check!

When solving an equation, always keep in mind the fundamental principles of equality: Because both sides of an equation are equal, you need to do the same thing to both sides so that equality is preserved. Try solving another linear equation for extra practice:

2. $3y + 2(y - 2) = -25$

What value of y satisfies the equation above?

A) $-\dfrac{29}{5}$

B) $-\dfrac{21}{5}$

C) $\dfrac{21}{5}$

D) $\dfrac{29}{5}$

Work through the Kaplan Method for Math step-by-step to solve this question. The following table shows Kaplan's strategic thinking on the left, along with suggested math scratchwork on the right.

Strategic Thinking	Math Scratchwork
Step 1: Read the question, identifying and organizing important information as you go This looks similar to the first question: It's asking you to find the value of y.	$3y + 2(y - 2) = -25$
Step 2: Choose the best strategy to answer the question Straightforward algebra is the fastest route to the answer. Start by distributing the 2. Continue by combining like terms until you isolate y.	$3y + 2y - 4 = -25$ $5y - 4 = -25$ $5y = -21$ $y = -\dfrac{21}{5}$
Step 3: Check that you answered the *right* question You found y, so you're done! Choice (B) is correct.	

Notice that none of the answer choices are integers. The SAT may challenge you by designing questions so that the answer is in a form you do not expect. If you arrive at an answer in an unusual form, don't be dissuaded. Fractions and decimals are often correct on the SAT.

Looking carefully at how the SAT uses fractions and decimals can guide your strategy in solving linear equations. The presence of fractions in the answer choices likely means you'll need to rely on techniques for combining and simplifying fractions to get to the right answer. Seeing decimals in the answer choices, on the other hand, likely indicates that you can rely on your calculator and save time on Test Day.

Try to determine the best strategy for solving the next question.

3. $3(y - 8) + 3(6x + 2) = 24 + 3y$

    Which approximate value of x satisfies the equation above?

    A) 0.80

    B) 1.33

    C) 2.33

    D) The value cannot be determined from the given information.

Work through the Kaplan Method for Math step-by-step to solve this question. The following table shows Kaplan's strategic thinking on the left, along with suggested math scratchwork on the right.

Strategic Thinking	Math Scratchwork
Step 1: Read the question, identifying and organizing important information as you go	
The question is asking you to solve for a variable. Note that there are two variables present.	$3(y - 8) + 3(6x + 2) = 24 + 3y$
Step 2: Choose the best strategy to answer the question	
Before blindly choosing D because there are two variables and only one equation, determine whether the y terms can be eliminated. Divide both sides by 3, and then combine like terms. You'll see that the y terms cancel, leaving one equation with one variable. Isolate x.	$y - 8 + 6x + 2 = 8 + y$ $-8 + 6x + 2 = 8$ $-6 + 6x = 8$
The presence of decimals means your calculator will be a great asset here. Don't worry about reducing the fraction; just punch it into your calculator to find its decimal equivalent.	$6x = 14$ $x = \dfrac{14}{6} = 2.33$
Step 3: Check that you answered the *right* question	
Double-check the question stem. You've found the value of x, which is 2.33, making (C) correct.	$x = 2.33$

Notice in the previous question that careful use of your calculator can eliminate the need to complete time-consuming tasks by hand. Be conscious of the format of the answer choices—decimal answers are a great clue that you can use your calculator.

✔ Note

Many graphing calculators have a built-in function that will let you input and solve algebraic equations like the previous one. Consider learning how to use it ahead of Test Day by reading the instruction manual or searching online.

LINEAR WORD PROBLEMS (REAL-WORLD SCENARIOS)

Another way linear equations can be made to look complicated is for them to be disguised in "real-world" word problems, where it's up to you to extract and solve an equation. When you're solving these problems, you may run into trouble translating English into math. The following table shows some of the most common phrases and mathematical equivalents you're likely to see on the SAT.

Word Problems Translation Table	
English	**Math**
equals, is, equivalent to, was, will be, has, costs, adds up to, the same as, as much as	=
times, of, multiplied by, product of, twice, double, by	×
divided by, per, out of, each, ratio	÷
plus, added to, and, sum, combined, total, increased by	+
minus, subtracted from, smaller than, less than, fewer, decreased by, difference between	−
a number, how much, how many, what	x, n, etc.

Linear word problems are made more difficult by complex phrasing and extraneous information. Don't get frustrated—word problems can be broken down in predictable ways. To keep you organized on Test Day, use the **Kaplan Strategy for Translating English into Math:**

- **Define any variables, choosing letters that make sense.**
- **Break sentences into short phrases.**
- **Translate each phrase into a mathematical expression.**
- **Put the expressions together to form an equation.**

Let's apply this to a straightforward example: Colin's age is three less than twice Jim's age.

- **Define any variables, choosing letters that make sense:** We'll choose C for Colin's age and J for Jim's age.
- **Break sentences into short phrases:** The information about Colin and the information about Jim seem like separate phrases.
- **Translate each phrase into a mathematical expression:** Colin's age = C; 3 less than twice Jim's age = $2J - 3$.
- **Put the expressions together to form an equation:** Combine the results to get $C = 2J - 3$.

This strategy fits into the larger framework of the Kaplan Method for Math: When you get to **Step 2: Choose the best strategy to answer the question** and are trying to solve a word problem as efficiently as possible, switch over to this strategy to move forward quickly.

The Kaplan Strategy for Translating English into Math works every time. Apply it here to a test-like example:

4. Malia and Omar want to find the shortest route from their school to a local burger hangout. Route A is 1.5 times longer than Route B and $\frac{3}{4}$ the length of Route C. If Route C is 3 km, how much longer is Route A than Route B?

   A) 0.75 km

   B) 1.5 km

   C) 2 km

   D) 2.25 km

Work through the Kaplan Method for Math step-by-step to solve this question. The following table shows Kaplan's strategic thinking on the left, along with suggested math scratchwork on the right.

Strategic Thinking	Math Scratchwork
Step 1: Read the question, identifying and organizing important information as you go The question is asking you to solve for the difference between the lengths of Routes A and B.	C is 3 km A is $\frac{3}{4}$ of C and 1.5 times B
Step 2: Choose the best strategy to answer the question This looks like a word problem, so go through each step of the Kaplan Strategy for Translating English into Math. Use the route labels for your variables. Note each comparison of the routes in your scratchwork, and then translate them into math. Work carefully through the algebra to find the lengths of routes A and B.	$A = \frac{3}{4} \times C$ $A = \frac{3}{4} \times 3 = \frac{9}{4}$ km $= 2.25$ km $A = 1.5B$ $2.25 = 1.5B$ $1.5 = B$
Step 3: Check that you answered the *right* question One more step to go. Subtract the length of Route B from the length of Route A to yield (A) as your match.	$A - B = 2.25 - 1.5$ $= 0.75$ km

LINEAR GRAPHS

Working with equations algebraically is only half the battle. The SAT will also expect you to work with graphs of linear equations, which means using lines in slope-intercept form and point-slope form.

One of the most important quantities you'll be working with when graphing a linear equation is the slope. Slope is given by the following equations: $m = \frac{(y_2 - y_1)}{(x_2 - x_1)}$, $m = \frac{\text{rise}}{\text{run}}$, and $m = \frac{\Delta y}{\Delta x}$, where (x_1, y_1) and (x_2, y_2) are coordinates of points on the line, Δy is the change in the y direction and Δx is the change in the x direction.

One of the most common forms of a linear equation is *slope-intercept form*, which is used to describe the graph of a straight line. The formula is quickly recognizable: $y = mx + b$. The variables y and x represent a point on the graph through which the line passes, while m tells us what the slope of the line is and b represents the point at which the line intersects the y-axis.

Remember: A line with a positive slope runs up and to the right ("uphill"), and a line with a negative slope runs down and to the right ("downhill"). In the following figure, lines n and l have positive and negative slopes, respectively.

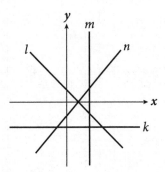

Occasionally, you will encounter a line with a slope of 0—meaning it does not rise or fall from left to right. These lines are easy to spot because they are horizontal and are parallel to the x-axis (line k in the figure shown). Lines that are parallel to the y-axis, such as line m in the figure, have slopes that are "undefined." The lines themselves exist, but their slopes cannot be calculated numerically.

The slope of a graph can also tell you valuable information about the rate of change of numbers and variables associated with the line. A positive slope signifies an increase in a variable, while a negative slope indicates a decrease. *Large* numerical values for slope indicate rapid changes, while *small* numerical values point to more gradual changes. Imagine the balance in your checking account is B, and it changes with the number of days that go by, D. Several proposed models are listed here. Think about how each one would impact your life.

$$B = 100D + 75$$
$$B = 0.25D + 75$$
$$B = -100D + 75$$
$$B = -0.25D + 75$$

The first equation probably looks pretty good. The second equation isn't as great. An extra quarter a day isn't going to do much for you. The third equation would quickly drive you into bankruptcy, while the fourth equation might be cause for concern after a while.

The *y*-intercept, on the other hand, is much less significant, typically representing the initial condition in a number of models—that is, where the model begins. In the checking account example, the beginning balance was $75 in all four models. Notice, the *y*-intercept didn't change at all.

Look at the following question to see how the SAT might test your ability to match a linear equation with its graph.

5. If a line contains the coordinates $(-\frac{2}{5}, 0)$ and $(0, 1)$, which of the following lines will it never intersect?

A)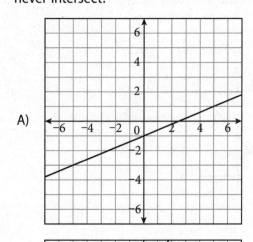

C)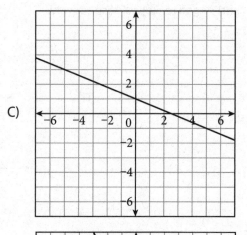

B)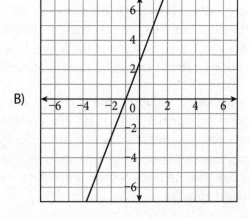

D)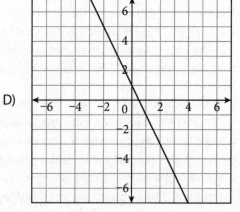

Approach this question by using the Kaplan Method for Math. Try to ask yourself similar questions as you work through questions like this on Test Day.

Strategic Thinking	Math Scratchwork
Step 1: Read the question, identifying and organizing important information as you go This question is asking you to determine which line will never intersect the one that contains the two points provided by the question stem.	
Step 2: Choose the best strategy to answer the question Using your calculator will take too long, so use the slope formula and your critical thinking skills instead. Start by finding the slope of the line in the question stem. Because the slope is positive, you can eliminate C and D, which both contain lines with negative slopes. Two lines that never intersect are parallel and therefore have the same slope, so determine which of the remaining answer choices also has a slope of $\frac{5}{2}$. There is no need to calculate the slopes; simply counting units on the graphs will suffice.	$(-\frac{2}{5}, 0), (0, 1)$ $m = \dfrac{y_2 - y_1}{x_2 - x_1}$ $= \dfrac{1 - 0}{0 - (-\frac{2}{5})} = \dfrac{1}{\frac{2}{5}} = \dfrac{5}{2}$ $m_A: \dfrac{2}{5} \rightarrow eliminate$ $m_B: \dfrac{5}{2}$
Step 3: Check that you answered the *right* question Only (B) contains a line that will not intersect the one described in the question stem. Notice you didn't have to do any additional work, such as finding *y*-intercepts. Only do as much as you need to—this saves time on Test Day.	(B)

Some questions are a little more challenging. They're usually similar in structure to the "checking account" equation described earlier, but they can involve more complicated scenarios. This next question requires you to choose the best model for a given "real-world" situation. See if you can match the graph to an appropriate model. Watch out: It's a science crossover question, so you'll need to be particularly careful to separate the question from the context.

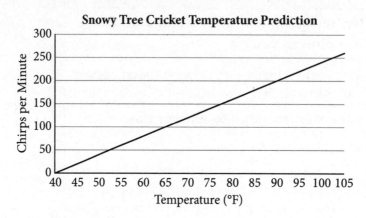

6. Snowy tree crickets have long been used to determine the ambient air temperature. The correlation between ambient air temperature and their chirp frequency is highly consistent. The graph shows the correlation between ambient air temperature, t, in degrees Fahrenheit and the number of chirps, c, per minute from a snowy tree cricket. Which of the following represents the line on the graph?

A) $c = 4t - 160$

B) $c = \dfrac{1}{4}t - 160$

C) $c = \dfrac{1}{2}t - 40$

D) $c = 4t + 40$

Although you may enjoy learning about science with your math, you don't need to waste time digesting extraneous information. The following table shows the strategic thinking that can help you solve this question.

Strategic Thinking	Math Scratchwork
Step 1: Read the question, identifying and organizing important information as you go Only the last two sentences describe the graph and your task: "The graph above shows the correlation between ambient air temperature, t, in degrees Fahrenheit and the number of chirps, c, per minute from a snowy tree cricket. Which of the following represents the line on the graph?"	

Strategic Thinking	Math Scratchwork
Step 2: Choose the best strategy to answer the question Plotting the equations in the answer choices on your calculator would be time consuming; in addition, the line's *y*-intercept is not visible, thereby introducing another hurdle. Opt for examining the answer choices closely instead. Pick a couple points on the line of best fit to determine the slope. You'll find it equals 4, so eliminate B and C.	$(40, 0)$ and $(65, 100)$ $m = \dfrac{100-0}{65-40} = \dfrac{100}{25} = 4$
Looking at the graph, you'll see that 40 cannot be the *y*-intercept because the line does not cross the *y*-axis at that point. Eliminate D.	$b \neq 40$
Step 3: Check that you answered the *right* question Choice (A) is the only option remaining. You're done! Note that you didn't have to calculate *b* to find the correct answer, so you saved some time.	

While scatterplots will be described in more detail in subsequent chapters, this next question shows that the principles covered here for graphing linear equations can be equally applied to the line of best fit on a scatterplot. See what you can conclude from the slope and *y*-intercept of the equation of the best-fit line. Note that this question is an example of a very complex word problem—don't be intimidated! If you can tackle this problem, you'll be able to handle the most difficult SAT word problems.

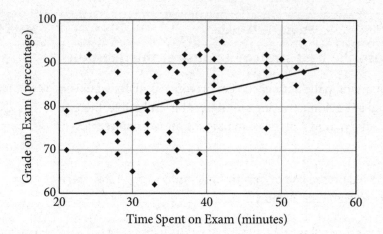

7. A physics professor presented the scatterplot above to his first-year students. What is the significance of the slope of the best-fit line?

    A) The slope represents the rate at which time spent on an exam increases based on a student's exam performance.

    B) The slope represents the average grade on the exam.

    C) The slope represents the rate at which a student's exam grade increases based on time spent on the exam.

    D) The slope has no significance.

Use the Kaplan Method for Math to make short work of this question. The following table shows the strategic thinking that can help you solve complex questions like this one.

Strategic Thinking
Step 1: Read the question, identifying and organizing important information as you go
You must determine the significance of the slope of the best-fit line on the scatterplot.
Step 2: Choose the best strategy to answer the question
Look for answer choices you can easily eliminate based on what you know about lines. A line's slope is a rate, so you can eliminate B and D. Examine A and C next. According to the graph, time spent on the exam is the independent variable, and the exam grade is the dependent variable. Pick the answer choice that reflects this.
Step 3: Check that you answered the *right* question
You've determined the significance of the slope of the line of best fit. The correct answer is (C).

Now you'll have a chance to try a few more test-like questions. Use the scaffolding as needed to guide you through the question and get the right answer.

Some guidance is provided, but you'll need to fill in the missing parts of explanations or the step-by-step math to get to the correct answer. Don't worry—after going through the examples at the beginning of this chapter, these questions should be completely doable. If you find yourself struggling, however, review the worked examples in this chapter.

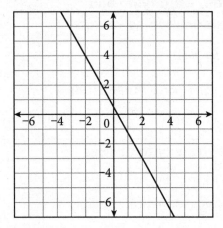

8. The line $y = -\dfrac{7x}{4} + \dfrac{1}{2}$ is shown in the graph. If the line is shifted down 2 units and then reflected over the x-axis, which of the following graphs represents the new line?

A)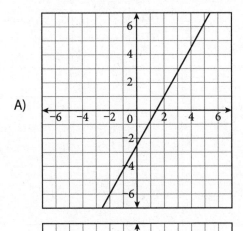

C)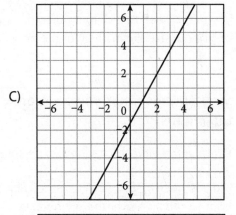

B)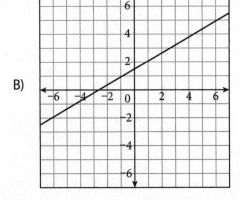

D)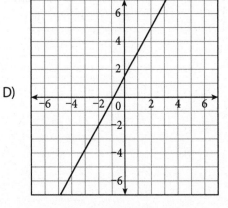

The following table can help you structure your thinking as you go about solving this problem. The Kaplan strategic thinking is provided, as are bits of structured scratchwork. If you're not sure how to approach a question like this, start at the top and work your way down.

Strategic Thinking	Math Scratchwork
Step 1: Read the question, identifying and organizing important information as you go *What are you actually solving for here?* You're asked for the graph that corresponds to the described changes made to $y = -\dfrac{7x}{4} + \dfrac{1}{2}$.	
Step 2: Choose the best strategy to answer the question *While you could apply the transformations, could picking a test point be faster?* Pick a test point on the original line. Apply the changes to it. Cross off any choices that don't pass through the new point. You might need to pick more than one point if your initial choice doesn't eliminate all of the answer choices. .	
Step 3: Check that you answered the *right* question *Which graph matches the changes described?* Did you get (D)? If so, you're correct! Beware of C; it results from a reflection over the wrong axis.	

Here's another test-like example to try with this method:

9. Three years ago, Madison High School started charging an admission fee for basketball games to raise money for new bleachers. The initial price was $2 per person; the school raised the price of admission to $2.50 this year. Assuming this trend continues, which of the following equations can be used to describe the cost of admission, c, y years after the school began charging for admission to games?

A) $c = 6y + 2$

B) $c = \dfrac{y}{6} + 2.5$

C) $c = \dfrac{y}{6} + 2$

D) $c = \dfrac{y}{2} + 2$

The following table can help you structure your thinking as you go about solving this problem. The Kaplan strategic thinking is provided, as are bits of structured scratchwork. If you're not sure how to approach a question like this, start at the top and work your way down.

Strategic Thinking	Math Scratchwork
Step 1: Read the question, identifying and organizing important information as you go *What is this question asking you to find?* You need to identify the equation that correctly relates cost to years after the admission charge implementation.	
Step 2: Choose the best strategy to answer the question *How do you start a question like this?* Look carefully; you're implicitly given two sets of coordinates. You can use these to find a key piece of a linear equation and eliminate two answer choices. *What should you do to determine which remaining choice is correct?* The school started charging admission at a certain point in time; the price at this point is your *y*-intercept. Use this to pick the correct answer.	(___, ___) (___, ___) $m = \dfrac{\rule{1cm}{0.4pt}}{\rule{1cm}{0.4pt}} = \rule{1cm}{0.4pt}$ eliminate ___ and ___ $b = $ ___

Strategic Thinking	Math Scratchwork
Step 3: Check that you answered the *right* question *Did you find the correct equation?* Did you come up with (C)? If so, great job! You're correct.	 ___

✔ **Note**

Because the question says "three years ago," it's tempting to use (–3, 2) and (0, 2.5) as your coordinates. Before you do this, think about what that means: This translates to the first admission charge being $2.50, as it's impossible to have a negative year. B is a trap waiting for students who attempt this route!

Now that you've seen the variety of ways in which the SAT can test you on linear equations, try the following questions to check your understanding. Give yourself 3.5 minutes to tackle the following three questions. Make sure you use the Kaplan Method for Math on every question. Remember, you'll need to emphasize speed and efficiency in addition to simply getting the correct answer.

10. If the line $y = -5x + 8$ is shifted down 3 units and left 2 units, what is the slope of the new line?

 A) −5

 B) 0

 C) 3

 D) 5

11. If $\frac{3}{4}y = 6 - \frac{1}{3}c$, then what is the value of $2c + \frac{9}{2}y$?

12. If m is a constant between 0 and $\frac{1}{2}$ (exclusive), which of the following could be the graph of $x - y = m(2x + y)$?

A)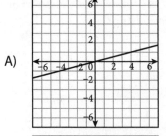

B)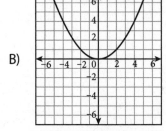

C)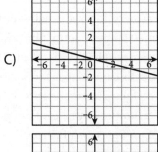

D)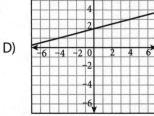

Answers and Explanations for this chapter begin on page 563.

EXTRA PRACTICE

1. Which of the following equations is linear?

   A) $y = \dfrac{3}{x}$

   B) $\sqrt{x} + y = 0$

   C) $\dfrac{1}{2}x - \dfrac{5}{8}y = 11$

   D) $y = x^2 + 2x - 4$

2. Which of the following does not represent a linear relationship?

   A) $y = \dfrac{x}{5}$

   B)

x	y
-4	12
0	2
4	-6
8	2
12	12

   C) $x = \dfrac{9}{7}y + 4$

   D) $y = 4x + 7$

3. The local Farmers' Market usually sells potatoes for $0.90 per pound. On Fridays, they sell potatoes at a 30% discount. The market also sells cantaloupes for $3.50 each. Which of the following represents the total cost, c, if a customer buys 2 cantaloupes and p pounds of potatoes on a Friday?

   A) $c = 0.63p + 7$

   B) $c = 0.9p + 7$

   C) $c = 0.3p + 3.5$

   D) $c = 0.9p + 3.5$

4. If paintbrushes cost $1.50 each and canvases cost 6 times that much, which of the following represents the cost, in dollars, of p paintbrushes and c canvases?

   A) $7.5pc$

   B) $10.5pc$

   C) $9c + 1.5p$

   D) $10.5(p + c)$

5. In states that produce natural gas, the state government typically imposes two types of taxes on producers: a local impact fee, which is a flat tax paid per well drilled, and a severance tax, which is based on the market value of the total volume of gas extracted, v. If a producer's total bill for one well is given by the equation $T = 0.004v + 50{,}000$, then the value 0.004 could represent which of the following?

   A) The local impact fee

   B) The market value of the gas extracted

   C) The total tax bill minus the local impact fee

   D) The amount of the severance tax as a percentage

Expected Property Values
2014-2028

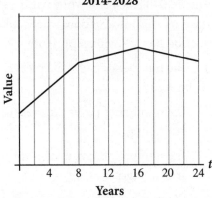

6. A realtor is studying the graph above, which shows the expected value of properties in her area over the next 24 years. If t represents the number of years after 2014, in what year should the increase in property values start to slow down?

A) 2008

B) 2018

C) 2022

D) 2030

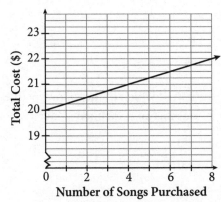

7. The graph above shows the cost of joining and buying music from a music subscription service. What does the y-intercept of the line most likely represent?

A) The cost per song

B) The cost to join the service

C) The cost of buying 20 songs

D) The cost of 20 subscriptions to the service

8. A store "breaks even" when its sales equal its expenses. Jon has just opened a new surfboard store at the beach. He buys each surfboard wholesale for $80 and has fixed monthly expenses of $3,600. He sells each surfboard for $120. How many surfboards does Jon need to sell in a month to break even?

A) 18

B) 30

C) 45

D) 90

9. Which value of x makes the equation $\frac{8}{5}\left(x+\frac{33}{12}\right)=16$ true?

A) 7.25

B) 8.75

C) 12.75

D) 13.25

$$\frac{3(n-2)+5}{4}=\frac{11-(7-n)}{6}$$

10. In the equation shown, what is the value of n?

A) $-\dfrac{1}{11}$

B) $\dfrac{5}{11}$

C) 1

D) $\dfrac{11}{7}$

Price of One Pound	Projected Number of Pounds Sold
$1.20	15,000
$1.40	12,500
$1.60	10,000
$1.80	7,500
$2.00	5,000
$2.20	2,500

11. Which of the following equations best describes the linear relationship shown in the table, where g represents the number of pounds of grain sold and d represents the price in dollars of one pound of grain?

    A) $g = 1.2d + 12,500$

    B) $g = 12,500d + 15,000$

    C) $g = -12,500d + 17,500$

    D) $g = -12,500d + 30,000$

12. Henry just set up direct deposit from his employer to his checking account. The equation $y = 360x - 126.13$ represents the balance in Henry's account if he deposits his weekly paycheck for x weeks. Based on this equation, which of the following statements is true?

    A) Henry earns $126.13 per week.

    B) Henry made an initial deposit of $126.13.

    C) Before setting up the direct deposit, Henry had overdrawn his account.

    D) When Henry set up the direct deposit, he already had $360 in his account.

13. A printing press running around the clock can print 54,000 black and white pages per day. Based on this information, what could the function $f(x) = 2,250x$ represent?

    A) The number of pages the press can print in x days

    B) The number of pages the press can print in x hours

    C) The number of days it takes the press to print x pages

    D) The number of hours it takes the press to print x pages

14. Nadim is hosting a party and is hiring a catering company to make and serve the food. The caterer charges a flat fee for serving the food plus a per person rate for the meals. If the equation used to calculate the total cost of Nadim's party is $y = 11x + 300$, then which of the following most likely represents the number of people attending the party?

    A) x

    B) y

    C) 11

    D) 300

15. The graph of which of the following linear equations has an undefined slope?

    A) $x = 3$

    B) $y = 0$

    C) $x = -y$

    D) $x - y = 0$

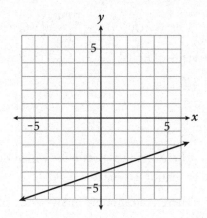

16. The graph shown represents which of the following equations?

    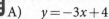

    A) $y = -3x + 4$

    B) $y = -\dfrac{1}{3}x + 4$

    C) $y = \dfrac{1}{3}x - 4$

    D) $y = 3x - 4$

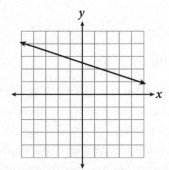

17. If the equation of the line shown in the graph above is written in the form $y = mx + b$, which of the following is true?

    A) $m < 0$ and $b < 0$

    B) $m < 0$ and $b > 0$

    C) $m > 0$ and $b < 0$

    D) $m > 0$ and $b > 0$

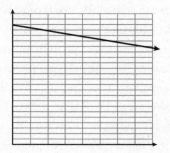

18. Which of the following scenarios could be supported by the graph shown?

    A) As the algae content in a lake increases, the number of fish decreases.

    B) As the algae content in a lake decreases, the number of fish decreases.

    C) As the algae content in a lake increases, the number of fish increases.

    D) As the algae content in a lake increases, the number of fish remains constant.

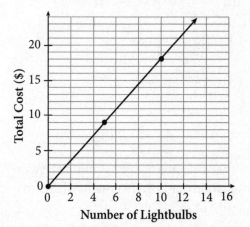

19. A hardware store sells lightbulbs in different quantities. The graph above shows the cost of various quantities. According to the graph, what is the cost of a single lightbulb?

    A) $0.56

    B) $1.80

    C) $2.50

    D) $3.60

20. A laser tag arena sells two types of memberships. One package costs $325 for one year of membership with an unlimited number of visits. The second package has a $125 enrollment fee, includes five free visits, and costs an additional $8 per visit after the first five. How many visits would a person need to use for each type of membership to cost the same amount over a one-year period?

    A) 20

    B) 25

    C) 30

    D) 40

21. Which of the following equations has no solution?

    A) $\frac{3}{8}(x-2)=\frac{8}{3}(x+2)$

    B) $-\frac{3}{2}(2x-8)=3x-12$

    C) $4\left(\frac{3}{4}x+5\right)=3x+20$

    D) $6\left(\frac{2}{3}x+5\right)=4x+5$

$$2\left(x-\frac{5}{2}\right)=c\left(\frac{4}{5}x-2\right)$$

22. If the equation above has infinitely many solutions and c is a constant, what is the value of c?

    A) -2

    B) $-\frac{4}{5}$

    C) $\frac{5}{4}$

    D) $\frac{5}{2}$

23. If $\frac{1}{4}(10h)-\frac{3}{2}(h+1)=-\frac{2}{3}\left(\frac{9}{2}h\right)+6$, what is the value of h?

    A) $\frac{9}{8}$

    B) $\frac{15}{8}$

    C) There is no value of h for which the equation is true.

    D) There are infinitely many values of h for which the equation is true.

24. A cell phone tower has a safety light to warn airplanes of its location. It blinks once every 3.5 seconds. If $f(m)$ gives the number of times the light blinks over the course of m minutes, which of the following equations defines f?

    A) $f(m)=2.5m$

    B) $f(m)=\frac{3.5m}{60}$

    C) $f(m)=\frac{60m}{3.5}$

    D) $f(m)=210m$

25. Vera is on her school's track and field team. In a practice long-jump competition against her teammates, she gets 5 points for landing over the closer line and 10 points for landing over the farther line. She gets a total of 7 jumps and lands x times over the farther line and the rest of the times over the closer line. Which of the following functions represents Vera's total score?

    A) $f(x) = 10x$

    B) $f(x) = 5x + 35$

    C) $f(x) = 10x + 5$

    D) $f(x) = 70 - 5x$

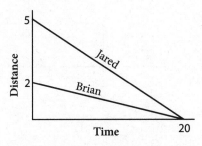

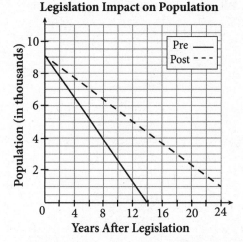

Legislation Impact on Population

26. Brian and Jared live in the same apartment complex and they both bike to and from work every day. The figure above shows a typical commute home for each of them. Based on the figure, which of the following statements is true?

A) It takes Brian longer to bike home because his work is farther away.

B) It takes Jared longer to bike home because his work is farther away.

C) Jared and Brian arrive home at the same time, so they must bike at about the same rate.

D) Jared bikes a longer distance than Brian in the same amount of time, so Jared must bike at a faster rate.

27. When graphing a linear equation that is written in the form $y = mx + b$, the variable m represents the slope of the line and b represents the y-intercept. Assuming that $b > 0$, which of the following best describes how reversing the sign of b would affect the graph?

A) The new line will shifted down b units.

B) The new line will be shifted down $b \times 2$ units.

C) The new line will be a perfect reflection across the x-axis.

D) The new line will be a perfect reflection across the y-axis.

28. The federal government in the United States has the authority to protect species whose populations have reached dangerously low levels. The graph above represents the expected population of a certain endangered species before and after a proposed law aimed at protecting the animal is passed. Based on the graph, which of the following statements is true?

A) The proposed law is expected to accelerate the decline in population.

B) The proposed law is expected to stop and reverse the decline in population.

C) The proposed law is expected to have no effect on the decline in population.

D) The proposed law is expected to slow, but not stop or reverse, the decline in population.

29. What value of n satisfies the equation $\frac{7}{8}(n-6)=\frac{21}{2}$?

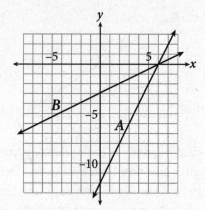

30. If the equation of line A in the graph above is given by $y = mx + b$ and the equation of line B is given by $y = k(mx + b)$, what is the value of k?

CHAPTER 2

Systems of Equations

CHAPTER OBJECTIVES

By the end of this chapter, you will be able to:

1. Distinguish between independent and dependent equations

2. Solve two-variable systems of equations

3. Determine the most efficient way to solve systems of equations

4. Translate word problems into multiple equations

SMARTPOINTS

Point Value	SmartPoint Category
40 Points	Systems of Linear Equations

SYSTEMS OF EQUATIONS

The linear equations detailed in the previous chapter are well suited for modeling a variety of scenarios and for solving for a single variable in terms of another that is clearly defined (e.g., what is the cost of a data plan if you consume 4 GB of data in a month). However, sometimes you will be given a set of multiple equations with multiple variables that are interdependent. For example, perhaps you know that a $50/month cell phone plan can be consumed by $0.05 text messages and $0.40 voice calls. Further, the plan has a cap of 1,000 combined text messages and voice calls.

This scenario can be represented by the following system of equations:

$$\$0.05t + \$0.40v = \$50$$
$$t + v = 1{,}000$$

Solving such a system would enable you to determine the maximum number of text messages and voice calls you could make under your plan, optimizing your usage. To solve systems of equations, you'll need to rely on a different set of tools that builds on the algebra you're already familiar with. The following question shows an example of such a system in the context of a test-like question.

1. If $28x - 5y = 36$ and $15x + 5y + 18 = 68$, what is the value of x?

    A) 1

    B) 2

    C) 3

    D) 4

You might be tempted to switch on math autopilot at this point and employ substitution, solving the first equation for y in terms of x:

$$y = \frac{1}{5}(-36 + 28x)$$

You could plug this back into the original question and eventually solve for x, but remember, the SAT tests your ability to solve math problems in the most efficient way. The following table contains some strategic thinking designed to help you find the most efficient way to solve this problem on Test Day, along with some suggested scratchwork.

Strategic Thinking	Math Scratchwork
Step 1: Read the question, identifying and organizing important information as you go This question is straightforward: You're being asked to solve for x.	
Step 2: Choose the best strategy to answer the question Looking at the coefficients, it's evident that combination will be much faster than substitution. Begin by combining like terms. The y term coefficients are equal in magnitude but opposite in sign, so no equation manipulation is necessary. Once the y terms are eliminated, solve for x.	$28x - 5y = 36$ $15x + 5y + 18 = 68$ $28x - 5y = 36$ $+\quad 15x + 5y = 50$ $\overline{ 43x = 86}$ $x = 2$
Step 3: Check that you answered the *right* question You've solved for x, the requested quantity. You can confidently select (B).	$x = 2$

✔ **Note**

We will not explicitly include an explanation for each simplifying step in this chapter. If you get stuck, review the information on simplifying and solving equations in chapter 1.

INDEPENDENT VERSUS DEPENDENT EQUATIONS

Generally, when you are given a situation involving *n* variables, you will need a system of *n* independent equations to arrive at fixed values for these variables. Thus, if you have a system of two variables, you'll need two independent equations to solve for each of the variables. Three variables would require three independent equations, and so on and so forth.

Systems of equations are extremely useful in modeling and simulation. Complex mathematical problems such as weather forecasting or crowd control predictions often require 10 or more equations to be simultaneously solved for multiple variables. Fortunately, you won't encounter anything this daunting on Test Day; following is an example of what you might see on the SAT.

$$y - 3x = 14$$
$$x - 5 = 6y$$

Before we outline the process for solving two-variable systems of equations, let's clarify one of the key requirements to solve these problems. We'll need two independent equations to solve for two variables. What exactly is an independent equation? Consider the equation $4x + 2y = 8$. We could use properties of equality to transform this equation in a number of different ways. For example, we could multiply both sides by 2, resulting in the equation $8x + 4y = 16$.

While it seems as though we've just created an additional equation, this is misleading, as our second equation has the same core variables and relationships as our first equation. This is termed a dependent equation, and two dependent equations cannot be used to solve for two variables. Look what happens when we try to use substitution. Let's isolate *y* in our original equation:

$$y = 4 - 2x$$

If we plug that into our second equation, notice what happens:

$$8x + 4(4 - 2x) = 16$$
$$8x + 16 - 8x = 16$$
$$16 = 16$$

While it's always good to see that $16 = 16$, this doesn't bring us any closer to solving for either of our variables. In fact, if you arrive at a result like this when you are solving a system of equations, it's a strong sign that your two equations are *dependent* on one another. In this case, we'd say that our system has infinitely many solutions because we could choose any number of possible values for *x* and *y*.

> ✔ **Note**
>
> When two equations are dependent, one equation could be obtained by algebraically manipulating the other equation. Graphically, dependent equations both describe the same line in the coordinate plane.

At other times, you'll encounter equations that are fundamentally incompatible with each other. For example, if we have the two equations $4x + 2y = 8$ and $4x + 2y = 9$, it should be obvious that there are no values for x and y that will satisfy both equations at the same time. Doing so would violate fundamental laws of math. In this case, we'd have a system of equations with no solution. These two equations define parallel lines, which by definition never intersect.

Knowing how many solutions a set has will tell you how graphing them together should look. Remember, the solution of a system of equations consists of the point or points where their graphs intersect.

If your system has . . .	. . . then it will graph as:	Reasoning
no solution	two parallel lines	Parallel lines never intersect.
one solution	two lines intersecting at a single point	Two straight lines have only one intersection.
infinitely many solutions	a single line (one line directly on top of the other)	One equation is a manipulation of the other—they graph the same line.

Because you could encounter any of these three on Test Day, ensure you are familiar with all of them.

Let's examine a sample problem that investigates the requirements for solving a system of equations:

$$5x - 3y = 10$$
$$6y = kx - 42$$

2. In the system of linear equations above, k represents a constant. If the system of equations has no solution, what is the value of $2k$?

   A) $\dfrac{5}{2}$

   B) 5

   C) 10

   D) 20

Work through the Kaplan Method for Math step-by-step to solve this question. The following table shows Kaplan's strategic thinking on the left, along with suggested math scratchwork on the right.

Strategic Thinking	Math Scratchwork
Step 1: Read the question, identifying and organizing important information as you go You are looking for the value of 2*k*. You're given a system of equations with no solution.	
Step 2: Choose the best strategy to answer the question The fact that the system of equations has no solution is key to finding the correct answer. When the two variables have identical coefficients in both equations, they should be equal to different constants. Start by manipulating the second equation into the same format as the first. After manipulating the second equation, divide it by 2 to yield a −3 coefficient for *y* to match *y*'s coefficient in the first equation. $\frac{k}{2}$ must equal 5, the coefficient of *x* in the first equation. Solve for *k*.	$5x - 3y = 10$ $6y = kx - 42$ $-kx + 6y = -42$ $kx - 6y = 42$ $\frac{k}{2}x - 3y = 21$ $\frac{k}{2} = 5$ $k = 10$
Step 3: Check that you answered the *right* question Be careful: You're asked for 2*k*, not *k*. Multiply both sides by 2 to get 2*k* = 20, which is (D).	$2k = 20$

SOLVING SYSTEMS OF EQUATIONS: COMBINATION & SUBSTITUTION

Now that you understand the requirements that must be satisfied to solve a system of equations, we can go into more depth about methods for solving these equations effectively. The two main methods of solving a system of linear equations are substitution and combination (sometimes referred to as *linear elimination*).

Substitution is the most straightforward method for solving equations, and it can be applied in every situation. Unfortunately, it is often the longest and most time-consuming route for solving systems of equations as well. To use substitution, solve the simpler of the two equations for one variable, and then substitute that result into the other equation. We could use substitution to answer the question on the next page, but you'll see that there's a quicker way: combination.

Combination involves adding the two equations together to eliminate a variable. Often, one or both of the equations are multiplied by a constant before they are added together. Combination is almost always the best technique to use to solve a system of equations when the question only asks you for the value of one of the variables, but even when a question asks you for both variables, combination is often faster than substitution.

Unfortunately, even though most students prefer substitution, problems on the SAT are often designed to be quickly solved with combination. To really boost your score on Test Day, practice combination as much as you can on Practice Tests and in homework problems so that it becomes second nature.

3. If $\frac{1}{4}x + 2y = \frac{11}{4}$ and $-6y - x = 7$, what is half of y?

Work through the Kaplan Method for Math step-by-step to solve this question. The following table shows Kaplan's strategic thinking on the left, along with suggested math scratchwork on the right.

Strategic Thinking	Math Scratchwork
Step 1: Read the question, identifying and organizing important information as you go Read carefully: You need to find *half* of y.	
Step 2: Choose the best strategy to answer the question Resist the urge to automatically use substitution. The presence of fractions in the question stem tells you that you should use combination. Multiply the first equation by 4 to clear out its fractions, and then add the equations together and solve for y.	$\frac{1}{4}x + 2y = \frac{11}{4}$ $-6y - x = 7$ $4\left(\frac{1}{4}x + 2y = \frac{11}{4}\right) \rightarrow$ $x + 8y = 11$ $\begin{array}{r} x + 8y = 11 \\ +\quad -x - 6y = 7 \\ \hline 2y = 18 \\ y = 9 \end{array}$
Step 3: Check that you answered the *right* question Don't stop yet: You need to find half of y. Grid in 9/2 or 4.5, and you're done.	$\frac{y}{2} = \frac{9}{2} = 4.5$

Combination can also be used when the testmakers ask you for a strange quantity, as in the following problem:

4. If $7c - 2b = 15$ and $3b - 6c = 2$, what is the value of $b + c$?

    A) −27

    B) −3

    C) 8

    D) 17

Work through the Kaplan Method for Math step-by-step to solve this question. The following table shows Kaplan's strategic thinking on the left, along with suggested math scratchwork on the right.

Strategic Thinking	Math Scratchwork
Step 1: Read the question, identifying and organizing important information as you go You are being asked to find the value of $b + c$. The question stem provides two equations involving b and c.	$7c - 2b = 15$ $3b - 6c = 2$
Step 2: Choose the best strategy to answer the question The fact that you're solving for $b + c$ suggests that there's a short-cut that will save time on Test Day. Add the equations together to yield $b + c$ equal to a constant.	$\begin{aligned} -2b + 7c &= 15 \\ + \quad 3b - 6c &= 2 \\ \hline b + c &= 17 \end{aligned}$
Step 3: Check that you answered the *right* question Choice (D) correctly reflects the sum of b and c.	$b + c = 17$

That was much easier and faster than substitution. With substitution, you could spend more than two minutes solving a question like this. However, a bit of analysis and combination gets the job done in much less time.

TRANSLATING WORD PROBLEMS INTO MULTIPLE EQUATIONS

While solving systems of equations can be relatively straightforward once you get the hang of it, sometimes, to complicate things, the SAT will give you a complex word problem and make you translate it into a system of equations and then solve. It sounds a lot scarier than it actually is. Remember to use the Kaplan Strategy for Translating English into Math to set up your equations, and then solve using either substitution or combination.

> ✔ **Note**
>
> The Kaplan Strategy for Translating English into Math can be found in chapter 1.

5. At a certain toy store, tiny stuffed pandas cost $3.50 and giant stuffed pandas cost $14. If the store sold 29 panda toys and made $217 in revenue in one week, how many tiny stuffed pandas and giant stuffed pandas were sold?

    A) 18 tiny stuffed pandas, 11 giant stuffed pandas

    B) 11 tiny stuffed pandas, 18 giant stuffed pandas

    C) 12 tiny stuffed pandas, 17 giant stuffed pandas

    D) 18 tiny stuffed pandas, 13 giant stuffed pandas

Work through the Kaplan Method for Math to solve this question step-by-step. The following table shows Kaplan's strategic thinking on the left, along with suggested math scratchwork on the right.

Strategic Thinking	Math Scratchwork
Step 1: Read the question, identifying and organizing important information as you go You need to find the number of tiny stuffed pandas and giant stuffed pandas sold.	tiny: $3.50 giant: $14 29 total sold $217.00 in revenue

Strategic Thinking	Math Scratchwork
Step 2: Choose the best strategy to answer the question This is a word problem, so use the Kaplan Strategy for Translating English into Math. Because both toys are pandas, *p* is likely to be a confusing choice for a variable. Instead, use *t* for tiny and *g* for giant. Break off each piece of relevant information into a separate phrase. Translating each phrase into a math expression will get you the components of a system of equations. After piecing together the system of equations, use combination to quickly eliminate *g*. Multiply the first equation by –14 before combining with the second. Solve for *t*. Choices B and C have different values for *t*, so eliminate them. Plug 18 into the first equation for *t*, and then solve for *g*.	t = tiny g = giant tiny: \$3.50 → $3.5t$ giant: \$14 → $14g$ 29 total sold → $= 29$ \$217.00 in revenue → $= 217$ $t + g = 29$ $3.5t + 14g = 217$ $-14t - 14g = -406$ $+ \quad 3.5t + 14g = 217$ ───────────── $-10.5t = -189$ $t = 18$ $t + g = 29$ $18 + g = 29$ $g = 11$
Step 3: Check that you answered the _right_ question The only answer choice that contains both quantities you found is (A).	$t = 18, g = 11$

Watch out for B, a trap answer designed to catch students who switched the variables, possibly due to choosing an ambiguous letter such as *p*. Choosing descriptive variable names might sound silly, but in the high-stakes environment of the SAT, you must do everything you can to avoid careless errors and subsequent lost points.

> ✔ **Note**
>
> Always choose variable names that make sense to you. Countless students struggle on multi-part problems due to disorganized notes. Don't let that happen to you. Move beyond *x* and *y* when selecting variable names on the SAT.

Other questions of this type will simply ask you to choose from a series of answer choices that describes the system of equations—they won't actually ask you to calculate a solution! These questions can be great time-savers. Consider the following example:

6. A state college has separate fee rates for resident students and nonresident students. Resident students are charged $421 per semester, and nonresident students are charged $879 per semester. The college's sophomore class of 1,980 students paid a total of $1,170,210 in fees for the most recent semester. Which of the following systems of equations represents the number of resident (r) and nonresident (n) sophomores and the amount of fees the two groups paid?

A) $r + n = 1{,}170{,}210;\ 421r + 879n = 1{,}980$

B) $r + n = 1{,}980;\ 879r + 421n = 1{,}170{,}210$

C) $r + n = 1{,}980;\ 421r + 879n = 1{,}170{,}210$

D) $r + n = 1{,}170{,}210;\ 879r + 421n = 1{,}980$

Work through the Kaplan Method for Math to solve this question step-by-step. The following table shows Kaplan's strategic thinking on the left, along with suggested math scratchwork on the right.

Strategic Thinking	Math Scratchwork
Step 1: Read the question, identifying and organizing important information as you go You're asked for the system of equations that represents the given situation.	
Step 2: Choose the best strategy to answer the question This question is wordy, so use the Kaplan Strategy for Translating English into Math. The first step (assigning variables) has been done for you, so you can go right to breaking up the question stem into smaller pieces. Convert these into math, and then assemble your equations.	r = resident n = nonresident r: $421 in fees n: $879 in fees 1,980 students $1,170,210 collected r: $421 → $421r$ n: $879 → $879n$ $\quad\quad\quad = 1{,}980$ $\quad\quad\quad = 1{,}170{,}210$ $\quad r + n = 1{,}980$ $421r + 879n = 1{,}170{,}210$

Strategic Thinking	Math Scratchwork
Step 3: Check that you answered the *right* question Choice (C) is the only answer choice that contains both equations you built.	

Be careful! Choice B is close but switches the fee structure, drastically overcharging the in-state students! Pay close attention to the differences between answer choices to avoid traps on Test Day.

Now you'll have a chance to try a few more test-like questions. Use the scaffolding as needed to guide you through the question and get the right answer.

Some guidance is provided, but you'll need to fill in the missing parts of explanations or the step-by-step math to get to the correct answer. Don't worry—after going through the examples at the beginning of this chapter, these questions should be completely doable. If you find yourself struggling, however, review the worked examples in this chapter and their explanations.

7. A bead shop sells wooden beads for $0.20 each and crystal beads for $0.50 each. If a jewelry artist buys 127 beads total and pays $41 for them, how much more did she spend on crystal beads than wooden beads?

A) $11

B) $15

C) $23

D) $26

The following table can help you structure your thinking as you go about solving this problem. The Kaplan strategic thinking is provided, as are bits of structured scratchwork. If you're not sure how to approach a question like this, start at the top and work your way down.

Strategic Thinking	Math Scratchwork
Step 1: Read the question, identifying and organizing important information as you go *What are you being asked to do here?* You're asked how much more the jewelry artist spent on crystal beads than on wooden beads.	

Strategic Thinking	Math Scratchwork
Step 2: Choose the best strategy to answer the question *Where should you start?* The Kaplan Strategy for Translating English into Math is a great choice. *What variables should you use?* Variables are easy to pick for this question. Think about what letters the words start with. *How do you break apart the question into smaller phrases? What can you do with them?* Separate each numerical piece into its own phrase, then convert to math.	wooden: _____ crystal: _____ _____ per wooden _____ per crystal _____ total bought _____ spent _____ per wooden → _____ _____ per crystal → _____ _____ total bought → _____ _____ spent → _____
What should you do with the phrases? Assemble a system of equations, then solve. You can use either substitution or combination to solve for the quantity of each bead type. Remember to think critically about which approach would be faster in this situation. *Am I done once I've solved the system?* Almost. Determine how much the jewelry artist spent on each type of bead, then take the difference.	_____ + _____ = _____ _____ + _____ = _____ _____ = _____ _____ = _____ $ _____ on wooden $ _____ on crystal _____ – _____ = _____
Step 3: Check that you answered the *right* question *Which answer choice matches the difference you found?* If you came up with (A), you're absolutely correct.	_____

8. If $y = -x - 15$ and $\dfrac{5y}{2} - 37 = -\dfrac{x}{2}$, what is the value of $2x + 6y$?

Larger numbers don't make this question any different; just be careful with the arithmetic. Again, the following table can help you structure your thinking as you go about solving this problem. The Kaplan strategic thinking is provided, as are bits of structured scratchwork. If you're not sure how to approach a question like this, start at the top and work your way down.

Strategic Thinking	Math Scratchwork
Step 1: Read the question, identifying and organizing important information as you go *What are you being asked to do here?* You're asked to find the value of $2x + 6y$.	
Step 2: Choose the best strategy to answer the question *The equations look complicated. Where should I start?* Start by rearranging the equations so that they're in the same general format. Because you're asked for an expression, look for a shortcut. Don't bother trying to solve for either x or y individually. *Which system of equations tactic would work best here?* A good bet: clearing the fractions from the second equation so you can use combination. Once the fractions are gone, confirm that adding the second equation to the first will yield the expression you need.	$y = -x - 15$ $\dfrac{5y}{2} - 37 = -\dfrac{x}{2}$ ____ + ____ = ____ ____ + ____ = ____ ____ (____ + ____ = ____) ____ + ____ = ____ + ____ + ____ = ____ ____ + ____ = ____
Step 3: Check that you answered the *right* question *What's the value of $2x + 6y$?* If your answer is 59, you're correct!	____

Now that you've seen the variety of ways in which the SAT can test you on systems of linear equations, try the following questions to check your understanding. Give yourself 4.5 minutes to tackle the following three questions.

$$6x + 3y = 18$$

$$qx - \frac{y}{3} = -2$$

9. In the system of linear equations above, q is a constant. If the system has infinitely many solutions, what is the value of q?

   A) –9

   B) $-\frac{2}{3}$

   C) $\frac{2}{3}$

   D) 9

10. If $12x + 15y = 249$ and $5x + 13y = 124$, then what is $\frac{y}{x}$?

11. A pizzeria's top-selling pizzas are The Works and The Hawaiian. The Works sells for $17, and The Hawaiian sells for $13. Ingredient costs for The Works are $450 per week, and ingredient costs for The Hawaiian are $310 per week. Assuming the pizzeria sells an equal number of both pizzas in one week, at what point will profits for one pizza overtake the other?

   A) After 35 pizzas each, Hawaiian profits will overtake Works profits.

   B) After 145 pizzas each, Hawaiian profits will overtake Works profits.

   C) After 35 pizzas each, Works profits will overtake Hawaiian profits.

   D) After 145 pizzas each, Works profits will overtake Hawaiian profits.

Answers and Explanations for this chapter begin on page 576.

EXTRA PRACTICE

1. If $2x - 3y = 14$ and $5x + 3y = 21$, then what is the value of x?

   A) -1

   B) 0

   C) $\dfrac{7}{3}$

   D) 5

2. A school is hosting a teacher's professional development luncheon. Attending teachers can choose one of two different meals, a veggie burger or a roast beef sandwich. The catering company charges \$4.50 per veggie burger and \$6.25 per roast beef sandwich. If 56 teachers ordered lunch and the school's total bill was \$308, which of the following systems of equations could be used to find the number of teachers who ordered a veggie burger, v, and the number who ordered a roast beef sandwich, r?

   A) $\begin{cases} v + r = 308 \\ 4.5v + 6.25r = 56 \end{cases}$

   B) $\begin{cases} v + r = 56 \\ 4.5v + 6.25r = 308 \end{cases}$

   C) $\begin{cases} v + r = 56 \\ 4.5v + 6.25r = \dfrac{308}{2} \end{cases}$

   D) $\begin{cases} 2(v + r) = 56 \\ 4.5v + 6.25r = 308 \end{cases}$

$\begin{cases} 4x + 3y = 14 - y \\ x - 5y = 2 \end{cases}$

3. If (x, y) is a solution to the system of equations above, what is $x - y$?

   A) $\dfrac{1}{4}$

   B) 1

   C) 3

   D) 18

4. Charlie starts to solve a system of linear equations graphically. He puts both equations into slope-intercept form and notices that the lines have the same slope. Based on this information only, which of the following statements is true?

   A) The system could have no solution, one solution, or infinitely many solutions.

   B) The system has no solution because two equations with the same slope never intersect.

   C) The system has either no solution or infinitely many solutions, depending on the y-intercepts.

   D) The system has infinitely many solutions because two equations with the same slope represent the same line.

$$\begin{cases} hx - 4y = -10 \\ kx + 3y = -15 \end{cases}$$

5. If the graphs of the lines in the system of equations above intersect at (−3, 1), what is the value of $\dfrac{k}{h}$?

A) $\dfrac{3}{2}$

B) 2

C) 3

D) 6

$$\begin{cases} \dfrac{1}{2}x - \dfrac{2}{3}y = 7 \\ ax - 8y = -1 \end{cases}$$

6. If the system of linear equations above has no solution, and a is a constant, what is the value of a?

A) −2

B) $-\dfrac{1}{2}$

C) 2

D) 6

7. A party store has 54 packs of plates in stock. The packs are either sets of 8 or sets of 12. If the store has 496 total plates in stock, how many plates would a customer buy if he or she buys all of the packs of 12 that the store has in stock?

A) 16

B) 38

C) 192

D) 304

$$\begin{cases} 3x - 9y = -6 \\ \dfrac{1}{2}x - \dfrac{3}{2}y = c \end{cases}$$

8. If the system of linear equations above has infinitely many solutions, and c is a constant, what is the value of c?

A) −6

B) −3

C) −2

D) −1

Equation 1		Equation 2	
x	y	x	y
−2	6	−8	−8
0	4	−4	−7
2	2	0	−6
4	0	4	−5

9. The tables above represent data points for two linear equations. If the two equations form a system, what is the x-coordinate of the solution to that system?

Problem Solving & Data Analysis

BY THE END OF THIS UNIT, YOU WILL BE ABLE TO:

1. Apply the Kaplan Method for Multi-Part Math Questions

2. Use rates, ratios, proportions, and percentages

3. Interpret and extract information from scatterplots and two-way tables

4. Analyze simple and complex data sets using descriptive statistics

CHAPTER 3

Introduction to Problem Solving

CHAPTER OBJECTIVES

By the end of this chapter, you will be able to:

1. Use the Kaplan Method for Multi-Part Math Questions to answer Problem Solving questions effectively

2. Solve multi-part problems involving rates, ratios, and proportions

3. Use appropriate formulas to find percentages and single or multiple percent changes

SMARTPOINTS

Point Value	SmartPoint Category
Point Builder	Kaplan Method for Multi-Part Math Questions
100 Points	Rates, Ratios, Proportions & Percentages

The new SAT contains multiple-choice and Grid-in questions, as well as a new type of question: the Multi-Part Math question. Multi-Part Math questions have multiple parts and require more analysis and planning than multiple-choice questions. To help you answer these questions effectively, use the Kaplan Method for Multi-Part Math Questions.

KAPLAN METHOD FOR MULTI-PART MATH QUESTIONS

Step 1: Read the first part of the question, looking for clues

Step 2: Identify and organize the information you need

Step 3: Based on what you know, plan your steps to navigate the first part

Step 4: Solve, step-by-step, checking units as you go

Step 5: Did I answer the *right* question?

Step 6: Repeat for remaining questions, incorporating results from the previous parts

The next few pages will walk you through each step in more detail.

Step 1: Read the first part of the question, looking for clues

- **Focus all your energy here** instead of diluting it over the whole question; solving a Multi-Part Math question in pieces is far simpler. Further, you may need the results from earlier parts to solve subsequent ones. Don't even consider the later parts of the question until you've solved the first part.

- **Watch for hints** about what you'll need to use or how to solve. Underlining key quantities is often helpful to separate what you need from extraneous prose.

Step 2: Identify and organize the information you need

If you think this sounds like the Kaplan Method for Math, you're absolutely correct. You'll use some of those same skills. The difference: The Multi-Part Math question is just more involved with multiple pieces.

- **What information am I given?** Jot down key notes, and group related quantities to develop your strategy.

- **What am I solving for?** This is your target. As you work your way through subsequent steps, keep your target at the front of your mind. This will help you avoid unnecessary work (and subsequent time loss). You'll sometimes need to tackle these problems from both ends, so always keep your goal in mind.

> ✔ **Expert Tip**
>
> Many students freeze when they encounter a problem with multiple steps and seemingly massive amounts of information. Don't worry! Take each piece one at a time, and you won't be intimidated.

Step 3: Based on what you know, plan your steps to navigate the first part

- **What pieces am I missing?** Many students become frustrated when faced with a roadblock such as missing information, but it's an easy fix. Sometimes you'll need to do an intermediate calculation to reveal the missing piece or pieces of the puzzle.

Step 4: Solve, step-by-step, checking units as you go

- **Work quickly but carefully**, just as you've done on other SAT math questions.

Step 5: Did I answer the *right* question?

- As is the case with the Kaplan Method for Math, **make sure your final answer is the requested answer**.
- Review the first part of the question.
- Double-check your units and your work.

Step 6: Repeat for remaining questions, incorporating results from the previous parts

- Now take your results from the first part and think critically about how they fit into the subsequent parts. Previous results won't always be applicable, but when they are, they often lead to huge time savings.

When you've finished, congratulate yourself for persevering through such a challenging task. The Multi-Part Math questions are the toughest on the SAT. If you can ace these questions, you'll be poised for a great score on Test Day. Don't worry if the Kaplan Method seems complicated; we'll walk through an example shortly.

✔ **Expert Tip**

As these questions take substantially more time, consider saving Multi-Part Math questions for last.

RATES, MEASUREMENT & UNIT CONVERSIONS

By now, you've become adept at using algebra to answer many SAT math questions, which is great, because you'll need those algebraic skills to answer questions involving rates. You're likely already familiar with many different rates—kilometers per hour, meters per second, and even miles per gallon are all considered rates.

A fundamental equation involved with rates is "Distance = Rate × Time" (a.k.a. the DIRT equation—Distance Is Rate × Time). If you have two of the three components of the equation, you can easily find the third. An upcoming Multi-Part Math example demonstrates this nicely.

You'll notice units of measurement are important for rate questions (and others that require a unit conversion) and, therefore, also an opportunity to fall for trap answers if you're not careful. How can you avoid this? Use the factor-label method. The factor-label method is a simple yet powerful way to ensure you're doing your calculations correctly and getting an answer with the requested units.

For example, suppose you're asked how many cups are in two gallons. First, identify your starting quantity's units (gallons) and then identify the end quantity's units (cups). The next step is to piece together a path of relationships that will convert gallons into cups, cancelling out units as you go. Keep in mind that you will often have multiple stepping stones between your starting and ending quantities, so don't panic if you can't get directly from gallons to cups.

The SAT won't expect you to know English measurements by heart. Instead, they'll provide conversion factors when needed. A gallon is the same as 4 quarts, every quart contains 2 pints, and a pint equals 2 cups. And there you have it! Your map from gallons to cups is complete. The last step is to put it together as a giant multiplication problem. Each relationship, called a conversion factor, is written as a fraction. The basic rules of fraction multiplication apply, so you can cancel a unit that appears in both the numerator and denominator.

> ✔ **Note**
>
> **The SAT will not require you to memorize conversions for conventional imperial units. If the test asks you to convert miles into inches, for example, you will be provided with enough conversion factors to solve the problem.**

Follow along as we convert from gallons to quarts to pints to cups:

$$2 \text{ gallons} \times \frac{4 \text{ quarts}}{1 \text{ gallon}} \times \frac{2 \text{ pints}}{1 \text{ quart}} \times \frac{2 \text{ cups}}{1 \text{ pint}} = (2 \times 4 \times 2 \times 2) \text{ cups} = 32 \text{ cups}$$

The DIRT equation is actually a variation of this process. Suppose you travel at 60 mph for 5 hours. You would calculate the distance traveled with $d = rt = \frac{60 \text{ mi}}{1 \text{ h}} \times 5 \text{ h} = 300 \text{ mi}$. The hour units cancel out, leaving you with miles, which you know is a distance. This built-in check is a great way to ensure your math is correct. If your units are off, check your steps for mistakes along the way. The SAT will never ask you for a quantity such as miles^4 or gallons^3, so if you end up with funky units like that, you've made an error somewhere in your work.

> ✔ **Note**
>
> **When using the factor-label method, don't be afraid to flip fractions and rates to make your units cancel out as needed.**

1. Quinn wants to rent a self-storage unit for her college dorm room furniture for the summer. She estimates that she will need 700 cubic feet of storage space, but the self-storage provider measures its units in cubic meters. If 1 meter is approximately 3.28 feet, about how many cubic meters of space will Quinn need?

    A) 19.84

    B) 25.93

    C) 65.07

    D) 213.41

Work through the Kaplan Method for Math to solve this question step-by-step. The following table shows Kaplan's strategic thinking on the left, along with suggested math scratchwork on the right.

Strategic Thinking	Math Scratchwork
Step 1: Read the question, identifying and organizing important information as you go You need to determine how many cubic meters of space Quinn needs for her belongings.	700 ft^3 space needed $= ? \text{ m}^3$
Step 2: Choose the best strategy to answer the question The factor-label method will be the quickest path to the correct answer. You're starting in cubic feet and need to convert to cubic meters. You know that 1 m = 3.28 ft, but be careful: 1 m³ is not the same as 3.28 ft³! Consider each feet-to-meters conversion separately.	starting qty: 700 ft^3 end qty: $? \text{ m}^3$ $\dfrac{700 \text{ ft}^3}{1} \times \dfrac{1 \text{ m}}{3.28 \text{ ft}} \times \dfrac{1 \text{ m}}{3.28 \text{ ft}} \times \dfrac{1 \text{ m}}{3.28 \text{ ft}}$ $= \dfrac{700}{(3.28)^3} \text{m} \sim 19.84 \text{ m}^3$
Step 3: Check that you answered the *right* question You've correctly converted cubic feet to cubic meters to get the correct answer, which is (A).	19.84 m^3

✔ **Note**

The conversion from feet to meters is not the same as the conversion from cubic feet to cubic meters (or square feet to square meters). Trap answers will often use incorrect conversion factors. Be particularly careful when dealing with conversions that have multiple dimensions.

Next, you'll walk through a test-like Multi-Part Math question that involves rates. Follow along with the Kaplan Method for Multi-Part Math Questions, and think about how knowledge of rates is used to get to the answer.

Remember, even though these questions have multiple parts, you'll rely on the same math skills you'd use in a simple multiple-choice question to solve each part. If you find that there are missing pieces or missing quantities, use techniques such as the factor-label method to bridge the gap.

Think of solving a Multi-Part Math question as building a three-dimensional puzzle. You collect all the relevant pieces and then arrange and assemble them to make the foundation, akin to using information from the first question to map a route to its answer. Just as the top part of a 3D puzzle is built on the foundation, the second part of a Multi-Part Math question builds on what you learned in the introduction and first question. Call on this information to help you solve the second question just as you did with the first.

Use the following information to answer questions 2 and 3:
Dismantling fraud rings, intercepting enemy communications, and protecting national infrastructure are just a few tasks for which Special Agents in the FBI's Cyber Division utilize state-of-the-art computers and other technology. The New Haven field office recently seized 2.43 terabytes (TB) of encrypted information during the raid of an infrastructure-hacking operations base, which agents believe contains information on a planned attack. One TB is equal to 10^6 megabytes (MB).

2. The cyber team's decryption software can decrypt 4.5 MB per second. How many hours will it take to decrypt the entire hard drive?

3. Newly gathered intelligence indicates a high likelihood of an infrastructure attack occurring before the hard drive is fully decrypted; consequently, the New York and Boston field offices have been asked to divert resources to the decryption task. New York's decryption software is 40% faster than New Haven's, but Boston's is 20% slower than New Haven's. By how many hours will the decryption time be reduced with the three cyber teams working in tandem? Round your answer to the nearest hour.

Work through the Kaplan Method for Multi-Part Math Questions step-by-step to solve this question. The following table shows Kaplan's strategic thinking on the left, along with suggested math scratchwork on the right.

Strategic Thinking	Math Scratchwork
Step 1: Read the first part of the question, looking for clues	
You're told the size of the seized hard drive and the speed at which it will be decrypted.	2.43 TB drive 4.5 MB/s decryption

Strategic Thinking	Math Scratchwork
Step 2: Identify and organize the information you need Part 1 asks for the time required to decrypt the hard drive. The given rate will help you determine this amount.	*hours to decrypt: ?*
Step 3: Based on what you know, plan your steps to navigate the first part The hard drive's capacity is in TB, but the rate is in MB/s (and you're asked for time in hours), so the DIRT equation requires a couple of extra calculations before you can use it. The factor-label method will be faster. Map your conversion steps.	*starting qty:* 2.43 TB *desired qty:* ? h TB → MB → s → min → h
Step 4: Solve, step-by-step, checking units as you go Plug in the appropriate conversion factors. When properly set up, all units except h will cancel, and you'll have the time needed for the decryption.	$2.43 \text{ TB} \times \dfrac{10^6 \text{ MB}}{1 \text{ TB}} \times \dfrac{1 \text{ s}}{4.5 \text{ MB}} \times \dfrac{1 \text{ min}}{60 \text{ s}}$ $\times \dfrac{1 \text{ h}}{60 \text{ min}} = 150 \text{ h}$
Step 5: Did I answer the *right* question? It will take 150 h to fully decrypt the hard drive.	

✔ **Note**

You might be given extra information on questions like these. If you don't need it to get to the answer, then don't worry about it.

Now on to Step 6: Repeat for remaining parts. Kaplan's strategic thinking is on the left, along with suggested math scratchwork on the right.

Strategic Thinking	Math Scratchwork
Step 1: Read the second part of the question, looking for clues Part 2 provides a relative description of New York and Boston's decryption software speeds.	NY: 40% faster than NH B: 20% slower than NH
Step 2: Identify and organize the information you need You need to determine the reduction in decryption time (in hours) if all three systems work in tandem.	new decryption time: ?
Step 3: Based on what you know, plan your steps to navigate the second part You must calculate the decryption speeds of the New York and Boston systems; you can't use the given percents to directly get the final answer. With the speeds in hand, you can find the total rate and the adjusted decryption time.	% → MB/s TB → MB → s → min → h
Step 4: Solve, step-by-step, checking units as you go Use the percent three-part formula to determine the speeds of the New York and Boston systems, being mindful when picking which decimal to plug in for what percent. Apply the factor-label method to calculate the required decryption time with all three systems working, and then find the difference in times.	NY: $1.4 \times 4.5 = 6.3$ MB/s B: $0.8 \times 4.5 = 3.6$ MB/s total rate $= 4.5 + 6.3 + 3.6$ $\qquad\qquad = 14.4$ MB/s $2.43\,\text{TB} \times \dfrac{10^6 \text{ MB}}{1 \text{ TB}} \times \dfrac{1 \text{ s}}{14.4 \text{ MB}} \times \dfrac{1 \text{ min}}{60 \text{ s}}$ $\times \dfrac{1 \text{ h}}{60 \text{ min}} = 46.875$ h $150 - 46.875 = 103.125$
Step 5: Did I answer the *right* question? Round properly per the question stem's instructions, and you're done.	103

As you saw, using the Kaplan Method for Multi-Part Math Questions makes an intimidating question far more straightforward. You'll have a chance to try it yourself later in this chapter.

RATIOS AND PROPORTIONS

Ratios and proportions are ubiquitous in everyday life. Whether it's making a double batch of meatballs or calculating the odds of winning the lottery, you'll find that ratios and proportions are invaluable in myriad situations.

A ratio is a way of comparing one quantity to another. When writing ratios, you can compare part of a group to another part of that group, or you can compare a part to the whole group. Suppose you have a bowl of apples and oranges. You can write ratios that compare apples to oranges (part to part), apples to total fruit (part to whole), and oranges to total fruit (part to whole).

You can also combine ratios. If you have two ratios, *a*:*b* and *b*:*c*, you can derive *a*:*c* by finding a common multiple of the *b* terms. Take a look at the following table to see this in action.

a	:	*b*	:	*c*
3	:	4		
		3	:	5
9	:	12		
		12	:	20
9	:			20

What's a common multiple of the *b* terms? The number 12 is a good choice because it's the least common multiple of 3 and 4 which will reduce the need to simplify later. Where do you go from there? Multiply each ratio by the factor (use 3 for *a*:*b* and 4 for *b*:*c*) that will get you to *b* = 12.

The ratio *a*:*c* equals 9:20. Notice we didn't merely say *a*:*c* is 3:5; this would be incorrect on Test Day (and likely a wrong-answer trap!).

Proportions are simply two ratios set equal to each other. They are an efficient way to solve certain problems, but you must exercise caution when setting them up. Watching the units of each piece of the proportion will help you with this. Sometimes the SAT will ask you to determine whether certain proportions are equivalent—check this by cross-multiplying. You'll get results that are much easier to compare.

$$\text{If } \frac{a}{b} = \frac{c}{d}, \text{ then: } ad = bc, \ \frac{a}{c} = \frac{b}{d}, \ \frac{d}{b} = \frac{c}{a}, \ \frac{b}{a} = \frac{d}{c}, \text{ BUT } \frac{a}{d} \neq \frac{c}{b}$$

Each derived ratio shown except the last one is simply a manipulation of the first, so all except the last are correct. You can verify this via cross-multiplication ($ad = bc$).

Alternatively, pick numerical values for a, b, c, and d; then simplify and confirm the two sides of the equation are equal. For example, take the two equivalent fractions $\frac{2}{3}$ and $\frac{6}{9}$ ($a = 2, b = 3, c = 6, d = 9$). Cross-multiplication gives $2 \times 9 = 3 \times 6$, which is a true statement. Dividing a and b by c and d gives $\frac{2}{6} = \frac{3}{9}$, also true, and so on. However, attempting to equate $\frac{a}{d}\left(\frac{2}{9}\right)$ and $\frac{b}{c}\left(\frac{3}{6}\right)$ will not work.

Let's take a look at a test-like question that involves ratios:

4. Neil is preparing two cans of paint for a client. The first is 25 parts red paint and 60 parts blue paint; the second is 30 parts yellow paint, 70 parts blue paint, and 15 parts white paint. The client has also asked Neil to prepare a third can containing only white and red paint per the ratios of the first two cans. What ratio of white to red paint should Neil use for the third can?

A) 35:18

B) 18:35

C) 5:3

D) 3:5

Work through the Kaplan Method for Math step-by-step to solve this question. The following table shows Kaplan's strategic thinking on the left, along with suggested math scratchwork on the right.

Strategic Thinking	Math Scratchwork
Step 1: Read the question, identifying and organizing important information as you go	
You're asked for the ratio of white to red paint in the third can. Two ratios are given.	R:B = 25:60 Y:B:W = 30:70:15

Strategic Thinking	Math Scratchwork
Step 2: Choose the best strategy to answer the question The ratio terms are rather large, so reduce the first ratio with a common factor, and then repeat with the second ratio. To combine two ratios, they must share a common term. Both ratios contain blue paint, but the blue paint terms aren't identical. Find a common multiple of 12 and 14. Once you've found one, merge the two ratios to directly compare white and red paint.	R:B = 25:60 → 5:12 Y:B:W = 30:70:15 → 6:14:3 common multiple of 12 & 14: 84 R:B = (5:12) × 7 = 35:84 Y:B:W = (6:14:3) × 6 = 36:84:18 R:B:Y:W = 35:84:36:18 R:W = 35:18
Step 3: Check that you answered the *right* question The question asks for the ratio of white paint to red paint, so flip your ratio, and you're done. Choice (B) is correct.	W:R = 18:35

✔ **Note**

Beware of trap answers that contain incorrect ratios, such as A. Always confirm that you've found the ratio requested.

PERCENTAGES

Percentages aren't just for test grades; you'll find them frequently throughout life—discount pricing in stores, income tax brackets, and stock price trackers all use percents in some form. It's critical that you know how to use them correctly, especially on Test Day.

Suppose you have a bag containing 10 blue marbles and 15 pink marbles, and you're asked what percent of the marbles are pink. You can determine this easily by using the formula $\% = \dfrac{\text{Part}}{\text{Whole}} \times 100\%$. Plug 15 in for the part and 10 + 15 (= 25) for the whole, then compute to get $\dfrac{15}{25} \times 100\% = 60\%$ pink marbles.

Another easy way to solve many percent problems is to use the following statement: (blank) percent of (blank) is (blank). Translating from English into math, you obtain (blank)% × (blank) = (blank). As you saw with the DIRT equation in the rates section, knowledge of any two quantities will unlock the third.

You might also be asked to determine the percent change in a given situation. Fortunately, you can find this easily using a variant of the percent three-part formula:

$$\text{Percent increase or decrease} = \frac{(\text{Amount of increase or decrease})}{(\text{Original amount})} \times 100\%$$

> **Note**
>
> The percent three-part formula requires the percent component to be in decimal form. Remember to move the decimal point appropriately before using this formula.

Sometimes more than one change will occur. Be especially careful here, as it can be tempting to take a "shortcut" by just adding two percent changes together (which will almost always lead to an incorrect answer). Instead you'll need to find the total amount of increase or decrease and calculate accordingly. We'll demonstrate this in an upcoming problem.

The following is a test-like question involving percentages.

5. Some individuals like to dilute 100% juice drinks with water to lessen the flavor intensity and reduce caloric intake. Kristina, a personal trainer, is preparing several blends of varying juice concentrations to see which ratio her fitness club's clients prefer. She plans to make 240 oz each of 80% juice, 60% juice, 50% juice, 40% juice, and 20% juice blends. If the 100% juice Kristina plans to buy comes in 32 oz bottles and partial bottles cannot be bought, how many bottles will Kristina need to make her blends?

    A) 8

    B) 18

    C) 19

    D) 60

Work through the Kaplan Method for Math step-by-step to solve this question. The following table shows Kaplan's strategic thinking on the left, along with suggested math scratchwork on the right.

Strategic Thinking	Math Scratchwork
Step 1: Read the question, identifying and organizing important information as you go You're asked how many bottles of 100% juice Kristina needs to buy to make her five blends. You're given the percent juice content of each.	*five blends: 80%, 60%, 50%, 40%, 20% juice*
Step 2: Choose the best strategy to answer the question Although this looks like calculator busywork, there's a faster (but less obvious) route to the answer. Notice that each percentage is a multiple of 10. Therefore, all you need to do is find 10% of 240 and multiply by the appropriate number to get the ounces of juice in each blend.	*0.1 × 240 oz = 24 oz* *× 2: 20% = 48 oz juice* *× 4: 40% = 96 oz juice* *× 5: 50% = 120 oz juice* *× 6: 60% = 144 oz juice* *× 8: 80% = 192 oz juice* *sum: 600 oz.* $\dfrac{600}{32} = 18.75 \rightarrow 19$
Step 3: Check that you answered the *right* question You've found the number of juice bottles required; the correct answer is (C).	19

Here's an example of a Multi-Part Math question that tests your percentage expertise.

Use the following information to answer questions 6 and 7.

Projected Undergraduate Costs at the University of California

2014-15	2015-16	2016-17	2017-18	2018-19	2019-20
$12,192	$12,804	$13,446	$14,118	$14,820	$15,564

Source: regents.universityofcalifornia.edu

Over the last decade, colleges have come under fire for significant tuition and fee increases. The University of California recently approved a series of tuition and fee increases over the course of five years. The table above summarizes the total cost per undergraduate per year through the 2019-20 academic year.

6. If fees account for 8.75% of one year's total expenses, what is the average fee increase per academic year? Round your answer to the nearest dollar.

7. Suppose the University of California system wants to extend these increases through the 2022-23 academic year. Assuming the average yearly increase for this extension remains the same as it was from 2014-15 through 2019-20, by what percentage will total tuition and fees have increased at the end of the 2022-23 academic year since their implementation? Round your answer to the nearest whole percent.

Work through the Kaplan Method for Multi-Part Math Questions step-by-step to solve. The following table shows Kaplan's strategic thinking on the left, along with suggested math scratchwork on the right.

Strategic Thinking	Math Scratchwork
Step 1: Read the first part of the question, looking for clues You are given a table with total costs for several academic years. Part 1 states that fees account for 8.75% of one year's expenses.	
Step 2: Identify and organize the information you need Part 1 asks for the portion of the total cost increase that is comprised of fees.	*fees (in $): ?*
Step 3: Based on what you know, plan your steps to navigate the first part You'll need the total cost increase in dollars to start, as well as the average annual increase. From there, you can determine the portion of the increase that fees make up. The percent given in part 1 indicates you should use the three-part formula.	*8.75% is fees* *(blank)% of (blank) is (blank)*

Strategic Thinking	Math Scratchwork
Step 4: Solve, step-by-step, checking units as you go Instead of finding each year-to-year increase, find the total increase from 2014-15 through 2019-20. Once there, determine the average increase for each year. Use the three-part formula to find the fee portion of the average increase.	$15,564 − $12,192 = $3,372 $avg = \dfrac{\$3372}{5}$ $= \$674.40$ $0.0875 \times \$674.40 = \$59.01$
Step 5: Did I answer the *right* question? You've found the average fee increase per year. Once you round appropriately, part 1 is complete.	59

✔ Note

By finding the total increase instead of each individual increase, you saved yourself a substantial amount of time.

Part 1 is finished! Now on to Step 6: Repeat for the other parts. Kaplan's strategic thinking is on the left, along with suggested math scratchwork on the right.

Strategic Thinking	Math Scratchwork
Step 1: Read the second part of the question, looking for clues There's a proposal to extend the tuition/fee hikes through 2022-23.	
Step 2: Identify and organize the information you need Part 2 asks for the percent increase in total tuition/fee cost between 2014-15 and 2022-23.	% increase: ?
Step 3: Based on what you know, plan your steps to navigate the second part You know the average yearly increase from the first part. Use this to determine what the cost for the 2022-23 year will be, and then calculate the total increase. Use this result to calculate the percent increase.	2014-15 thru 2019-20: $3,372 avg. yearly incr.: $674.40
Step 4: Solve, step-by-step, checking units as you go Extending the increases past 2019-20 means increases for 2020-21, 2021-22, and 2022-23 – 3 years total. Multiply the average yearly increase by 3 to determine the additional increase. Add this to the increase you found in the first part to find the total increase from 2014-15 through 2022-23. To calculate the percent change, divide the total increase by the original cost from 2014-15, and multiply the result by 100.	$674.40 \times 3 = $2,023.20$ $2,023.20 + 3,372 = $5,395.20$ $\dfrac{\$5395.20}{\$12192} \times 100 = 44.252\%$
Step 5: Did I answer the _right_ question? Round the percent change per the instructions in the question stem, and you're done.	44

Now you'll have a chance to try a few test-like problems in a scaffolded way. See if you can fill in the missing pieces and solve for the correct answer without a full explanation.

We've provided some guidance, but you'll need to fill in the missing parts of explanations or the step-by-step math to get to the correct answer. Don't worry—after going through the worked examples at the beginning of this section, these problems should be completely doable.

8. Ramp meters are often used in and around metropolitan areas to reduce freeway congestion during AM and PM rush hours. Depending on freeway volume, ramp meters in Milwaukee allow one car onto the freeway every 5-9 seconds. Assuming a constant ramp car queue, between the hours of 3:30 PM and 6:30 PM, how many more cars can move through a ramp meter with a 5-second interval than one with an 8-second interval?

    A) 270

    B) 320

    C) 810

    D) 960

The following table can help you structure your thinking as you go about solving this problem. The Kaplan strategic thinking is provided, as are bits of structured scratchwork. If you're not sure how to approach a question like this, start at the top and work your way down.

Strategic Thinking	Math Scratchwork
Step 1: Read the question, identifying and organizing important information as you go *What are you being asked to find here?* You must determine how many more cars pass through a ramp meter with a 5-second interval.	

Strategic Thinking	Math Scratchwork
Step 2: Choose the best strategy to answer the question *One car per time interval . . . does this sound familiar?* It should! One car every 5 (or 8) seconds is a rate, so turn to the DIRT equation. Be careful here; you need to manipulate the given form of the rate before you can use it. *Which variable do I need to find?* The 3:30 PM-6:30 PM window translates to 3 h, which is your time. Your rate, however, involves seconds, so you'll need to convert time to seconds. Finding *d* will give you the number of cars; do this for both intervals. Watch your units! *Are you finished?* Almost. Subtract the 8-second car count from the 5-second car count to get the difference.	5-second interval: $r_5 = 1$ car per 5 s = _____ cars/s 8-second interval: $r_8 = 1$ car per 8 s = _____ cars/s 3 h x _____ x _____ = _____ s 5 seconds $d_5 =$ _____ x _____ $d_5 =$ _____ 8 seconds $d_8 =$ _____ x _____ $d_8 =$ _____ _____ − _____ = _____
Step 3: Check that you answered the *right* question *How many more cars are allowed onto the freeway with the shorter interval?* If your answer is (C), you're correct!	_____

✔ **Expert Tip**

Sometimes your distance or time units won't look like those you're used to (e.g., miles, minutes, etc.). Don't let this deter you. If you have a rate, you can use the DIRT equation.

Here's another test-like example to try using this method:

Murray's Annual Income Tax Liability

Federal (up to $9,225)	Federal ($9,226-$37,450)	Federal ($37,451-$90,750)	State (flat rate)
10%	15%	25%	4.5%

9. Murray has an annual salary of $75,400. He contributes 20% of his pre-tax income to his 401(k), and he pays $150 per month for health insurance (pre-tax, deducted after 401(k)). The table above summarizes Murray's tax liability; all taxes are calculated based on Murray's adjusted gross income (pay remaining after 401(k) and insurance payments). He must pay 10% on the first $9,225 in income, 15% on any income between $9,226 and $37,450, 25% on income between $37,451-$90,750, and a 4.5% state-tax on all of his income. All taxes are deducted simultaneously. What is Murray's biweekly take-home pay after all deductions have been made?

    A) $1,537.98

    B) $1,586.79

    C) $1,699.78

    D) $1,748.59

The following table can help you structure your thinking as you go about solving this problem. The Kaplan strategic thinking is provided, as are bits of structured scratchwork. If you're not sure how to approach a question like this, start at the top and work your way down.

Strategic Thinking	Math Scratchwork
Step 1: Read the question, identifying and organizing important information as you go *What is the question asking? What information will help you find the answer?* You need to find Murray's income after deductions. You have information about each deduction, as well as the order in which they're taken.	start ($_____) – _____ 401(k) – _____ insurance – taxes = take-home pay

Strategic Thinking	Math Scratchwork
Step 2: Choose the best strategy to answer the question *There's a lot going on. Where should you start?* The table provides tax information for annual income, so don't convert to biweekly yet. Follow the order you extracted in Step 1 to calculate each deduction first. *How much does Murray deduct before taxes?* Use the three-part percent formula to find his 401(k) contribution, then subtract his health insurance cost. *How should taxes be approached?* The question states that all taxes are deducted simultaneously; that is, don't deduct state tax and then take federal tax on what's left and vice versa. Use the quantity left after the insurance deduction for all tax calculations, and then subtract Murray's total tax liability from the remaining quantity post-insurance. *Am I finished?* The question asks for Murray's biweekly take-home pay. Divide by the number of pay periods in one year to get the final answer.	401(k): _____ × _____ = $ _____ annually insurance: $ _____ × _____ = $ _____ annually $ _____ – $ _____ – $ _____ = $ _____ annual pre-tax taxes: state _____ × _____ = _____ M. owes $ _____ for state fed 10% bracket _____ × _____ = _____ M. owes $ _____ for 10% br. fed 15% bracket _____ × _____ = _____ M. owes $ _____ for 15% br. fed 25% bracket _____ × _____ = _____ M. owes $ _____ for 25% br. total tax: $ _____ take-home: $ _____ – $ _____ = $ _____ annually $ _____ / wks = $ _____ biweekly
Step 3: Check that you answered the *right* question *How much money does Murray get to take home?* If you chose (D), you're right.	 _____

✔ **Note**

Read carefully; it's easy to erroneously take a flat 25% of Murray's check for federal taxes instead of using the tiers (and real-life taxes would be far more painful this way).

Now try your hand at a Multi-Part Math question.

Use the following information to answer questions 10 and 11.

Shuang has a set of square ceramic plates she'd like to glaze. She wants to create evenly spaced concentric squares on the plates with gray and black glaze as shown in the diagram above. The squares' edges are each 0.5 in. apart.

10. What fraction of one plate will Shuang cover with gray glaze?

11. Shuang also plans to glaze smaller square plates with the same type of pattern as the plate in the figure. The smaller plates' squares are the same size and distance apart as those of the larger plates. If a small plate has four concentric squares, By how many times is the fraction of a small plate that Shuang will cover with black glaze greater than that of a large plate?

The following table can help you structure your thinking as you go about solving this problem. The Kaplan strategic thinking is provided, as are bits of structured scratchwork. If you're not sure how to approach a question like this, start at the top and work your way down.

Strategic Thinking	Math Scratchwork
Step 1: Read the first part of the question, looking for clues *What information do part 1 and the intro provide?* You're given a picture of one of Shuang's plates and told that she will use two colors to create the design.	
Step 2: Identify and organize the information you need *What does part 1 ask you to find?* You need to find the fraction of the plate that will be gray.	gray/total: ?
Step 3: Based on what you know, plan your steps to navigate the first part *Anything missing? How do you get around not having the plate's exact dimensions?* You might think this problem is bogus, but it asks for a relative quantity, not an absolute quantity. You'll need to pick a value for the area of one square and calculate the others based on the one you set. Label the squares to help keep your calculations clear.	

Strategic Thinking	Math Scratchwork
Step 4: Solve, step-by-step, checking units as you go *What is the side length of square 1? How do you calculate the others?* Pick a small, manageable number for this value. Remember how far apart the square edges are; this will help you find the side lengths and areas of the other squares. Also keep in mind you'll need to account for the fact that each square outside the first is not actually a full square. *What is the ratio of gray glaze to total glaze?* Divide the gray glaze area by the total glaze area.	sq. 1 = __ in.^{2} sq. 2 = __^{2} – __ = __ in.^{2} sq. 3 = __^{2} – __ = __ in.^{2} sq. 4 = __^{2} – __ = __ in.^{2} sq. 5 = __^{2} – __ = __ in.^{2} sq. 6 = __^{2} – __ = __ in.^{2} sq. 7 = __^{2} – __ = __ in.^{2} sq. 8 = __^{2} – __ = __ in.^{2} gray: __ + __ + __ + __ = __ in.^{2} black: __ + __ + __ + __ = __ in.^{2} gray/total = _____
Step 5: Did I answer the *right* question? *What fraction of each plate is gray?* If you got 7/16, great job! You're correct.	_____

Fantastic! Now repeat for the other parts. Once again, Kaplan strategic thinking is provided, as are bits of structured scratchwork. If you're not sure how to approach the second part, start at the top and work your way down.

Strategic Thinking	Math Scratchwork
Step 1: Read the second part of the question, looking for clues *What's new in part 2?* You're told a smaller plate has four concentric squares with edges 0.5 in. apart like in a larger plate.	4 squares in a small plate
Step 2: Identify and organize the information you need *What is needed to solve this part?* You'll need to find the fraction of black glaze on one small plate and one large plate.	sm. black: ? lg. black: ?
Step 3: Based on what you know, plan your steps to navigate the second part *Anything missing? How can the gray fraction from part 1 help?* You'll need to find the black fraction of the two plates. Fortunately, the black fraction for the larger plate is easy to find because you found its gray counterpart for part 1.	lg. black = 1 – ___ = ___
Step 4: Solve, step-by-step, checking units as you go *How do you find the black fraction of the small plate?* Good news: You did most of the work for this calculation in part 1. Just use the same numbers.	sq. 1 (gray) = ___ in.^{2} sq. 2 (black) = ___ in.^{2} sq. 3 (gray) = ___ in.^{2} sq. 4 (black) = ___ in.^{2} sm. gray: ___ + ___ = ___ in.^{2} sm. black: ___ + ___ = ___ in.^{2} sm. bl. vs. lg. bl.: ___ ÷ ___ = ___ × ___ = ___
Step 5: Did I answer the *right* question? *What is part 2 asking?* Did you get 10/9? If so, congrats! You're correct.	

Now that you've seen the variety of ways in which the SAT can test you on ratios, rates, and percentages, try the following questions to check your understanding. Give yourself 5 minutes to tackle the following four questions. Make sure you use the Kaplan Method for Math as often as you can (as well as the Kaplan Method for Multi-Part Math Questions when necessary). Remember, you want to emphasize speed and efficiency in addition to simply getting the correct answer.

12. Grocery stores often differ in how they price fruit; some charge by weight, and others charge per piece. FoodCo sells bananas for $0.60 a pound, Bob's charges $0.29 per banana, Acme charges $1.50 for a two-pound banana bunch, and Stu's offers a special: buying three pounds of bananas at $0.65 per pound gets you a fourth pound free. If one banana weighs $\frac{1}{3}$ lb, which of the following correctly orders the four grocers in order of decreasing cost per banana (assuming all purchases are made in 4 lb increments)?

A) Bob's, Acme, FoodCo, Stu's

B) Bob's, FoodCo, Acme, Stu's

C) Stu's, FoodCo, Acme, Bob's

D) Stu's, Acme, FoodCo, Bob's

13. The owner of an aerial adventure park wants to construct a zipline for kids who aren't tall enough to ride the regular zipline, which starts at a platform in a tree 10 m above the ground and is 26 m in length. The desired platform height for the new zipline is 3 m. If the owner wants the kids' zipline length and platform starting height to be proportional to those of the regular zipline, what will the difference in length of the two ziplines be?

Use the following information to answer questions 14 and 15.

Gas stations in the United States sell gasoline by the gallon, whereas those in Great Britain sell it by the liter. Mark is assembling a budget for a trip to Great Britain. He plans to drive from London to Edinburgh and back with various excursions along the way; he estimates his total mileage to be 960 miles. The Great Britain pound (GBP)-U.S. dollar (USD) exchange rate is currently 1:1.52, and 1 gallon (gal) is approximately 3.785 liters (L).

14. If Mark rents a car that averages 40 mpg throughout the trip and estimates an average gas cost of 1.20 GBP per liter, how much money (in USD) should Mark budget for fuel? Round your answer to the nearest dollar.

15. The rental car firm Mark is using has a special offer: for an extra 30 GBP, Mark can lock in a subsidized fuel cost of 0.75 GBP per liter for the duration of his trip. How much, in USD, would Mark save with this offer? Round your answer to the nearest dollar.

Answers and Explanations for this chapter begin on page 583.

EXTRA PRACTICE

You may use your calculator for all questions in this section.

1. An expert on car depreciation determines that a certain car that costs $35,000 new will immediately depreciate by $12,000 once it is driven off the lot. After that, for the first 50,000 miles, the car will depreciate approximately $0.15 per mile driven. For every mile after that, it will depreciate by $0.10 per mile driven until the car reaches its scrap value. How much would this car be worth after being driven 92,000 miles?

   A) $11,300

   B) $13,800

   C) $17,000

   D) $27,700

2. While reviewing for exams, a teacher knows that the number of topics he can cover is directly proportional to the length of time he has to review. If he can cover 9 topics in a single 45-minute period, how many topics can he cover in a 1-hour period?

   A) 5

   B) 7

   C) 10

   D) 12

3. Weight is dependent on the gravitational force exerted on an object. In other words, in space, you would weigh nothing because there is no gravity. Likewise, because the moon's gravitational pull is less than Earth's, objects weigh less on the moon. In general, 1 pound on Earth is equal to approximately 0.166 pounds on the moon. If a man weighs 29 pounds on the moon, about how much, in pounds, does he weigh on Earth?

   A) 21

   B) 48

   C) 175

   D) 196

4. At all trials and hearings, a court reporter types every word spoken during the proceedings so that there is a written record of what transpired. Because they must type every word, the average court reporter must be able to type at a minimum rate of 3.75 words per second in order to be certified. Suppose a trial transcript contains 25 pages with an average of 675 words per page. Assuming the court reporter typed the transcript at the minimum rate, how long was she actively typing?

   A) 1 hour, 15 minutes

   B) 1 hour, 45 minutes

   C) 2 hours, 30 minutes

   D) 3 hours

5. In 1912, the original candidates for United States President were Woodrow Wilson and William H. Taft. Because of party disagreements, former President Theodore Roosevelt also decided to run and ended up splitting the vote with his fellow Republican and incumbent, Taft. In a certain state, the ratio of the popular vote of Taft to Roosevelt to Wilson was approximately 35:41:63. If approximately 208,500 votes were cast in that state for the three candidates altogether, how many were cast for Taft?

A) 15,000

B) 45,000

C) 52,500

D) 69,500

6. When medical tests are conducted, there is always the possibility that the test will return a false positive or a false negative. A false positive means the test shows that a patient has the condition being studied, when the patient actually does not; a false negative indicates that a patient does not have the condition, when the patient actually does. Suppose a certain medical test has a false positive rate of 6 out of 3,500. How many people were tested during a period when 27 false positives came back?

A) 14,000

B) 15,750

C) 17,500

D) 21,000

7. A tutoring service offers a free one-hour tutoring session. After a client signs up, the next 10 hours of tutoring are billed at a rate of $30 per hour. For all hours after that, the client receives a discounted rate. If a client pays $664 for 25 hours of tutoring, what is the service's discounted hourly rate?

A) $24.50

B) $25.54

C) $26.00

D) $26.56

8. Political canvassers polled voters in two locations on whether they viewed a particular candidate for governor favorably. At the first location, they asked 125 people and of those, 22.4% responded favorably. At the second location, 37.5% of 272 people responded favorably. What percent of all the people surveyed responded favorably?

A) 25.7%

B) 30.0%

C) 31.5%

D) 32.7%

9. At 350°F, an oven can cook approximately 3 pounds of turkey per hour. At 450°F, it can cook approximately 4.5 pounds per hour. How many more ounces of turkey can the oven cook at 450° than at 350° in 10 minutes? (Note: 1 pound = 16 ounces)

A) 4

B) 6

C) 8

D) 12

10. In extreme climates, temperatures can vary as much as 20° Celsius in a single day. How much can these climates vary measured in degrees Fahrenheit? ($F = \frac{9}{5} C + 32$)

A) 20°F

B) 36°F

C) 62°F

D) 68°F

11. A company specializes in converting people's VHS movies and DVDs to digital formats, which, once converted, are approximately 4.5 gigabytes in size. Once converted, the company uploads the videos to a secure cloud drive, where the customers can retrieve their files. The company uploads the videos every day, from closing time at 5:00 PM until 9:00 PM. Their internet service provider has an upload speed of 12 megabytes per second. What is the maximum number of videos the company can upload each evening? (1 gigabyte = 1,024 megabytes)

A) 2

B) 37

C) 242

D) 682

12. An online movie subscription service charges *a* dollars for the first month of membership and *b* dollars per month after that. If a customer has paid $108.60 so far for the service, which of the following expressions represents the number of months he has subscribed to the service?

A) $\dfrac{108.60}{a+b}$

B) $\dfrac{108.60-a}{b}$

C) $\dfrac{108.60-a-b}{b}$

D) $\dfrac{108.60-a+b}{b}$

13. A store is running a sale, discounting merchandise by a specific percentage. Margo purchases a coffee maker with an original price of $62.00. After the sale discount, she gets an additional 10% off for using her store credit card. She ends up paying $41.85, not including tax. What was the amount of the original sale discount?

A) 15%

B) 22.5%

C) 25%

D) 75%

14. A certain real estate agent uses what he calls a *step-strategy* to sell houses. He puts a house on the market at a higher-than-expected selling price and if it hasn't sold in two weeks, he drops the price by 5%. If it still hasn't sold in another 2 weeks, he drops the price by another 5%. After that, he continues to drop the price by 3% every two weeks until it reaches a cut-off amount assigned by the homeowner, or the house sells, whichever comes first. If a house is originally listed at $200,000 and the homeowner sets a cut-off amount of $166,000, what is the final selling price given that the house sells after being on the market for 9 weeks?

    A) $162,901.25

    B) $164,737.48

    C) $166,000.00

    D) $169,832.45

15. A museum is building a scale model of Sue, the largest *Tyrannosaurus rex* skeleton ever found. Sue was 13 feet tall and 40 feet long, and her skull had a length of 5 feet. If the length of the museum's scale model skull is 3 feet, 1.5 inches, what is the difference between the scale model's length and its height?

    A) 8 feet, 1.5 inches

    B) 16 feet, 10.5 inches

    C) 25 feet

    D) 27 feet, 4 inches

16. A company reimburses employees for a portion of their gas costs for commuting to and from work based on mileage. Based on the following data, what is the rate in dollars per gallon that the company uses to reimburse employees?

    • The company has 126 employees who commute.

    • The average employee traveled 12,250 miles to and from work over the course of the year.

    • The average gas mileage reported by all employees was 22.5 miles per gallon.

    • The company paid out a total of $96,040.00 in gas reimbursements.

    A) $0.44

    B) $0.71

    C) $1.40

    D) $1.60

17. On average, Betsy reads 1 page of her book every 1.5 minutes. Her book has 116 pages. Raymond starts a 94-page book on Saturday morning at 8:30AM and reads straight through until he finishes it at 11:38AM. How many more minutes does it take Raymond to read his book than Betsy to read hers?

18. Katrina is working on a school project and determines that she needs 576 square inches of cardboard, but the craft store only sells cardboard by the square foot. How many square feet of cardboard does she need?

19. A county employee is collecting water samples from all the houses in a subdivision where trace amounts of lead were found in the water. There are 45 houses in the subdivision. If he starts the first house at 9:00 AM and starts the sixth house at 10:00 AM, how many minutes will it take the employee to collect samples from all the houses in the subdivision, assuming it takes the same amount of time at each house?

20. On a map, the scale is the ratio of the distance shown on the map to the actual distance. A geography teacher has a map on her wall with a scale of 1 inch:100 miles. She uses the school's copier to shrink the large wall map down to the size of a piece of paper to hand out to each of her students. To do this, she makes the map $\frac{1}{4}$ of its original size. Suppose on the students' maps, the distance between two cities is 2.5 inches. How many actual miles apart are those cities?

21. A bank offers a long-term savings account with a 1.0% annual interest rate. At the end of each year, the interest is rounded down to the nearest cent and added to the principal. If the initial deposit was $1,500, how much interest has the account earned at the end of 5 years?

22. A power company divides the geographic regions it serves into grids. The company is able to allocate the power it generates based on the usage and needs of a particular grid. Certain grids use more power at certain times of the day, so companies often shift power around to different grids at various times. On any given day, the company makes several changes in the power allocation to Grid 1. First, it increases the power by 20%. Then, it decreases it by 10%. Finally, it increases it by 30%. What is the net percent increase in this grid's power allocation? (Round to the nearest whole percent and ignore the percent sign when entering your answer.)

23. An emergency room doctor prescribes a certain pain medication to be delivered through an IV drip. She prescribes 800 mL of the medication to be delivered over the course of 8 hours. The IV delivers 1 mL of medication over the course of 30 drips. How many drips per minute are needed to deliver the prescribed dosage?

Questions 24 and 25 refer to the following information.

Every Saturday morning, three friends meet for breakfast at 9:00 AM. Andrea walks, Kellan bikes, and Joelle drives.

24. Last Saturday, all three friends were exactly on time. Andrea left her house at 8:30 AM and walked at a rate of 3 miles per hour. Kellan left his house at 8:15 AM and biked at a rate of 14 mph. Joelle left her house at 8:45 AM and drove an average speed of 35 mph. How many miles from the restaurant does the person who travelled the farthest live?

25. Kellan lives 12 miles away from Andrea. On a different Saturday, Kellan biked at a rate of 15 mph to Andrea's house. The two then walked to the restaurant at a rate of 2.5 mph, and they arrived five minutes early. What time did Kellan leave his house? Enter your answer as three digits and ignore the colon. For example, if your answer is 5:30 AM, enter 530.

Questions 26 and 27 refer to the following information.

Mia is planning to work as a hostess at a restaurant. Two restaurants in her area have offered her jobs, both of which utilize "tip share," which means that the hostess gets a portion of all tips left by all customers. Restaurant A has a tip share for hostesses of 7%, while Restaurant B has a tip share of only 4%.

26. Mia does some research and finds that, on average, restaurants in her area bring in approximately $1,100 in tips for the evening shift. Based on this information, how much more in dollars would Mia make in tips at Restaurant A than at Restaurant B if she worked 5 evenings a week for 4 weeks?

27. Upon further research, Mia discovers that Restaurant B is making some improvements to become a more upscale establishment, which will result in an increase in meal prices and, consequently, should also increase tips. Assuming both restaurants originally brought in the average tips given in the previous question, what percent increase would Restaurant B need to experience in tips in order for Mia to make the same amount of money in one evening at both restaurants from the hostess tip share? Assume that Restaurant B doesn't increase its tip share percentage. Enter your answer as a whole number and ignore the percent sign.

Questions 28 and 29 refer to the following information.

Bridget is starting a tutoring business to help adults get their GEDs. She already has five clients and decides they can share a single textbook, which will be kept at her office, and that she also needs one notebook and four pencils for each of them. She records her supply budget, which includes tax, in the table shown.

Supply	Total Number Needed	Cost Each
Textbook	1	$24.99
Notebooks	5	$3.78
Pencils	20	$0.55

28. The textbook makes up what percent of Bridget's total supply budget? Round to the nearest tenth of a percent and ignore the percent sign when entering your answer.

29. Bridget's business does very well, and she needs more supplies. She always orders them according to the table above, for five clients at a time. At the beginning of this year, she orders the supplies for the whole year, which cost $988.02. Halfway through the year, she decides to take inventory of the supplies. She has used $713.57 worth of the supplies. How many pencils should be left, assuming the supplies were used at the rate for which she originally planned?

CHAPTER 4

Scatterplots

CHAPTER OBJECTIVES

By the end of this chapter, you will be able to:

1. Decide whether a linear, quadratic, or exponential model describes the data presented in a scatterplot

2. Use an equation for a line of best fit to describe trends between variables in a scatterplot

SMARTPOINTS

Point Value	SmartPoint Category
30 Points	Scatterplots

SCATTERPLOT BASICS

Some students tend to associate scatterplots with nasty-looking statistical analyses and consequently become nervous when they hear they'll likely encounter a few scatterplots on Test Day. However, these seemingly difficult plots are usually straightforward—if you know what to look for. We'll go over the foundational concepts of scatterplots, growth and decay examples, and modeling with scatterplots over the next several pages.

First, let's look at the anatomy of a scatterplot.

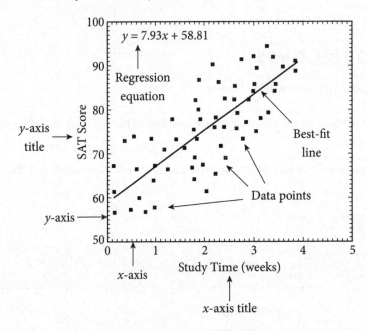

- You're already familiar with the **x- and y-axes**, but something that might be new is their **units**. Most scatterplots that use real data have units on the axes; these are important when trying to draw conclusions and inferences based on data (more on this later).

- The **best-fit line** is drawn through the **data points** to describe the relationship between the two variables as an equation. This line does not need to go through most or all data points, but it should accurately reflect the trend shown by the data with about half the points above the line and half below. As in "plain" equations, x is the independent variable, and y is the dependent variable.

- The **best-fit equation** (also called the **regression equation**) is the equation that describes the best-fit line algebraically. This equation can be linear, quadratic, exponential, or another shape, but the first three are those you'll most likely encounter on Test Day.

Below is a test-like question that involves a scatterplot.

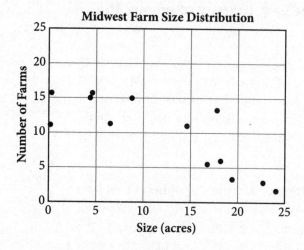

1. In 2012, the United States Department of Agriculture conducted a survey on the frequency of various farm sizes in select areas of the Midwest region of the country. Which of the following best describes the relationship between the size and number of farms?

    A) There is a strong positive correlation between farm size and farm count.

    B) There is a strong negative correlation between farm size and farm count.

    C) There is a weak positive correlation between farm size and farm count.

    D) There is no correlation between farm size and farm count.

Work through the Kaplan Method for Math step-by-step to solve this question. The following table shows Kaplan's strategic thinking on the left, along with suggested math scratchwork on the right.

Strategic Thinking	Math Scratchwork
Step 1: Read the question, identifying and organizing important information as you go You must determine the correlation, if any, between farm count and farm size.	
Step 2: Choose the best strategy to answer the question The answer choices imply that you can model the relationship between the variables with a line or curve. Draw a line of best fit to visualize this relationship. A line of best fit follows the overall trend of the data points. Draw your line accordingly, keeping in mind that it need not pass through the majority of the points. According to the scatterplot and the line of best fit, as farm size increases, the number of farms of that size decreases, which indicates a negative correlation. The majority of the data points are fairly close to the line of best fit, which means the correlation is strong.	**Midwest Farm Size Distribution**
Step 3: Check that you answered the *right* question There is a strong negative correlation between the two variables, making (B) the correct answer.	

✔ Note

Remember that the line of best fit does not necessarily pass through the greatest number of points; in fact, it does not have to pass through any.

GROWTH AND DECAY

The real world is full of examples of growth and decay, and you're bound to see some examples on Test Day. To start, let's take a look at the basic structure of linear and exponential equations. Following is the model of the linear equation:

$$y = kx + x_0$$

If this equation looks familiar, it would be for good reason: It's a linear equation in slope-intercept form with different variables standing in for the ones you've seen in the past. You should be able to match each piece to a quantity in the slope-intercept form of an equation. Take a look at the following table for a translation of the new components.

Linear Growth/ Decay Piece	What It Represents	Slope-Intercept Counterpart
x_0	y-intercept or initial quantity in a word problem	b
k	rate of change, slope	m

Recognizing that the previous equation, which might look weird at first glance, is really something you've seen before, will go a long way on Test Day.

> ✔ **Note**
>
> You might also see this expressed in function notation. We've included several homework problems in this format for you to try. For an overview of functions and function notation, see chapter 7.

A more complex equation is the exponential equation:

$$y = x_0(1 + r)^x$$

You'll notice most of the terms, such as y, x_0 (pronounced "x-naught"), and x are in both linear and exponential equations which makes exponential equations a bit easier to understand. The lone new variable, r, is the rate of change, akin to k in the linear equation. Also note that x is now an exponent.

What happens if you have a negative exponential rate of change? It's similar to k with linear decay (just like with m in regular linear equations from a few sections back).

Suppose $r = -\frac{3}{4}$ and $x_0 = 100$. This gives $y = 100(1 - \frac{3}{4})^x = 100(\frac{1}{4})^x$. Using our exponent rules to distribute the x, we get $y = 100 \times \frac{1^x}{4^x}$. Because 1^x will always be 1, we can drop it and move 100 to the numerator to give the final equation, $y = \dfrac{100}{4^x}$. This can also be written as $y = 100 \times 0.25^x$, so be ready for both fraction and decimal forms. Here's an easy way to remember whether you have exponential growth or decay: If r is positive, you're looking at growth; if r is negative, decay is occurring. An r of 0 will give you 1^x, which drops out and leaves y equal to a constant (and therefore a horizontal line instead of an exponential curve).

Another key difference to note: The rate of change in linear growth and decay is constant, but it is variable in a case of exponential growth or decay. Graphwise, linear growth/decay is a straight line, whereas exponential growth/decay has a curve. This will often help you identify which is occurring in a given situation.

Now let's look at a question that involves growth. It's up to you to figure out whether it is linear or exponential.

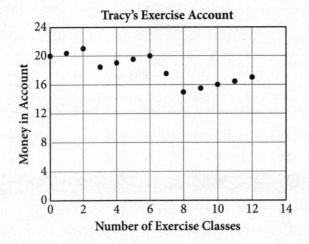

2. Tracy recently joined a workout group in which each member commits to attending three exercise classes per week. To increase accountability, each member sets aside $20 in an account. If a member misses a class, that individual will lose $2.50, which is then equally distributed among the members who attended that class. After missing three classes, Tracy vows to hold herself more accountable and not miss any more. The scatterplot above shows Tracy's account balance over time. Assuming exactly one person is absent from any given class and no one else has joined or left the group since its inception, which of the following equations could represent Tracy's account balance after she resolves not to miss any further classes?

A) $y = 20\,(1.5)^x$

B) $y = x^{1.5} + 11$

C) $y = 0.5x + 11$

D) $y = 0.5x + 20$

Work through the Kaplan Method for Math step-by-step to solve this question. The following table shows Kaplan's strategic thinking on the left, along with suggested math scratchwork on the right.

Strategic Thinking	Math Scratchwork
Step 1: Read the question, identifying and organizing important information as you go You need to determine which equation correctly represents Tracy's account balance after her second missed class, assuming she does not miss any after that. You're given some information about the account's behavior.	$20 @ start present: + x no-show: − $2.50
Step 2: Choose the best strategy to answer the question Find the relevant data points on the scatterplot. The last class Tracy missed corresponds to the third (and final) decrease on the scatterplot. You need the equation that represents Tracy's account balance after that class, so you can disregard her attendance prior to that. Because the no-show count and group size do not change, you can assume Tracy's account balance will increase at a constant rate, indicating a linear equation. You can therefore eliminate A and B. To determine which of the remaining answer choices is correct, draw a line of best fit through the appropriate points. The y-intercept is 11, meaning (C) must be correct.	*Tracy's Exercise Account* (scatterplot: Money in Account vs. Number of Exercise Classes) *Tracy's Exercise Account* (scatterplot: Money in Account vs. Number of Exercise Classes)
Step 3: Check that you answered the *right* question Only choice (C) contains a linear equation with the correct y-intercept.	$y = 0.5x + 11$

Nice job! Let's continue our exploration of scatterplots with a section on modeling.

SCATTERPLOT MODELING

As you've seen, the new SAT can ask a variety of questions pertinent to scatterplots. In addition, you might be asked to do some more advanced tasks as mentioned previously, such as drawing conclusions and making predictions. This task sounds daunting, but it's not as challenging as you might think.

Look at the following graphs for a preview of the types of models you might see.

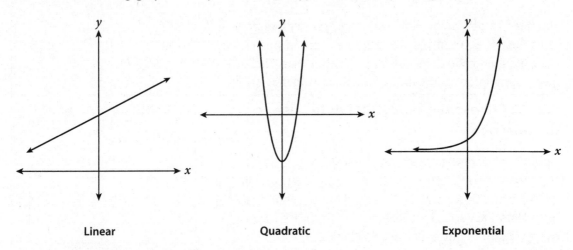

Linear   Quadratic   Exponential

A **linear** plot/graph will always increase or decrease at a constant rate, making it easy to spot. By contrast, a **quadratic** plot/graph is U-shaped, indicating a variable rate of change. Quadratics make parabola shapes and have a minimum or maximum known as a vertex (although sometimes it is not shown on the plot). Lastly, an **exponential** plot/graph typically starts with a gradual rate of change, which increases significantly over time. Unlike the quadratic, it does not have a vertex.

There are times when using a graphing calculator on Test Day is prudent; deriving an equation that fits a data set is one of them. These "best-fit" equations are called regression equations and can take several shapes depending on the data's behavior. The correlation coefficient, *r,* indicates how good a fit the regression line is; the closer to 1 it is for an increasing equation (or –1 for a decreasing equation), the better the fit. The steps for using this function on a TI-83/84 are shown here:

Step 1: Press the [**STAT**] button. Choose [**EDIT**], then enter your data for [L_1] and [L_2].

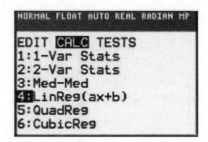

Step 2: Press the [**STAT**] button again and scroll to [**CALC**]. Select [4] for a linear regression, [5] for quadratic, or [0] for exponential and press the [**ENTER**] button. Make sure [L_1] and [L_2] are listed beside [**XList**] and [**YList**], respectively.

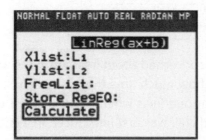 

Step 3: Scroll down to [**Calculate**], then press the [**ENTER**] button. The variable values are listed, as is the correlation coefficient. If r is not close to 1/–1, try another regression type.

Note: If r is not displayed, go to the [**CATALOG**] menu (press [**2nd**] then [0]), scroll to the Ds, then select [**DiagnosticOn**].

As mentioned, this is a useful feature, but you must exercise good judgment when deciding whether to use it for a particular question on Test Day.

✔ Note

If you have a calculator other than the TI-83/84, make sure you read its manual prior to Test Day so you're familiar with how to use this function on it.

Below is a test-like example that asks you to determine a correlation type and extrapolate data.

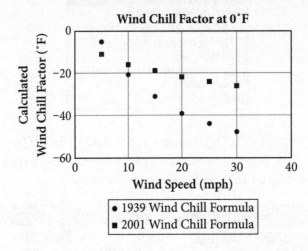

3. Inhabitants of colder climates are often concerned about frostbite in the winter months and use the wind chill factor to gauge how much time they can safely spend outside. Wind chill reflects the temperature that one feels when outside based on the actual temperature and the wind speed. Wind chill was first introduced in 1939, and the formula was revised in 2001. If the outside temperature is 0°F, what is the approximate wind chill at 40 mph based on the 2001 formula, and what wind speed would produce the same wind chill using the 1939 formula?

    A)   −30°F, 10 mph

    B)   −30°F, 15 mph

    C)   −50°F, 15 mph

    D)   −50°F, 40 mph

Work through the Kaplan Method for Math step-by-step to solve this question. The following table shows Kaplan's strategic thinking on the left, along with suggested math scratchwork on the right.

Strategic Thinking	Math Scratchwork
Step 1: Read the question, identifying and organizing important information as you go You are asked to identify a wind chill value and a wind speed. Although the question stem is lengthy, most of the information is irrelevant. Pay attention to both the title and axes labels on the scatterplot when solving; there are several parameters present, and it's easy to confuse them if you're not careful.	

Strategic Thinking	Math Scratchwork
Step 2: Choose the best strategy to answer the question Use the trend of the 2001 formula data to draw a line that extends to 40 mph. Next, draw a vertical line from 40 mph on the *x*-axis to intersect the data extension that you drew, and then draw a horizontal line from that intersection to the *y*-axis to estimate the wind chill factor, which is approximately –30°F. You can eliminate C and D based on this finding. The second part asks for the temperature that would yield the same wind chill (–30°F) using the 1939 formula. The horizontal line that you drew for the first part crosses right through a point on the 1939 curve. Draw another line down to the *x*-axis from that point to find that the wind speed is approximately 15 mph.	**Wind Chill Index at 0˚F** *1939 Wind Chill Formula* *2001 Wind Chill Formula* **Wind Chill Index at 0 ˚F** *1939 Wind Chill Formula* *2001 Wind Chill Formula*
Step 3: Check that you answered the *right* question Choice (B) is the only answer choice that contains both findings.	

✔ **Note**

Watch the axis labels. Don't assume each gridline always represents one unit of the given category.

Now you'll have a chance to try a couple test-like problems in a scaffolded way. See if you can fill in the missing pieces and solve for the correct answer without a full explanation.

We've provided some guidance, but you'll need to fill in the missing parts of explanations or the step-by-step math in order to get to the correct answer. Don't worry—after going through the worked examples at the beginning of this section, these problems should be completely doable.

4. Which of the following plots could be modeled by the equation $y = 3^x + 4$?

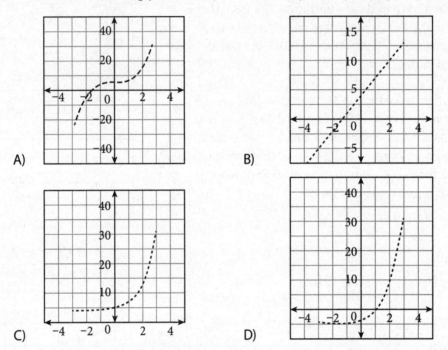

A)   B)

C)   D)

This question is different from the previous ones, but don't worry. The following table can help you structure your thinking as you go about solving this problem. The Kaplan strategic thinking is provided, as are bits of structured scratchwork. If you're not sure how to approach a question like this, start at the top and work your way down.

Strategic Thinking	Math Scratchwork
Step 1: Read the question, identifying and organizing important information as you go *What are you being asked to do?* You need to match the given equation to the correct plot.	

Strategic Thinking	Math Scratchwork
Step 2: Choose the best strategy to answer the question *What kind of graph does y = 3^x + 4 have?* The *x* in the exponent indicates that you have a certain type of graph; there are two choices you can eliminate based on this. *How do you know which of the remaining choices is correct?* Plug in a manageable value for *x*, and see what *y* is at that point. Determine which graph contains this point.	*need a(n)* _____ *graph;* *eliminate* _____ *when x =* _____, *y =* _____ _____ *matches*
Step 3: Check that you answered the *right* question *Did you match the equation to the correct graph?* If you chose (C), you'd be correct!	 _____

> ✔ **Note**
>
> Remember that 3^x is very different from 3*x* and *x*^{3}.

The following information applies to questions 5 and 6.

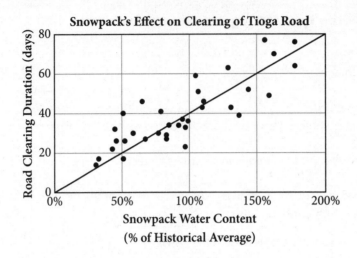

Snowpack's Effect on Clearing of Tioga Road

(data source: www.nps.gov/yose/planyourvisit/tiogaopen.htm)

Tioga (pronounced tie-OH-ga) Road is a mountain pass that crosses the Sierra Nevada through northern Yosemite National Park. Due to its high elevation and the unpredictability of Sierra weather in the winter and early spring, the road is closed from about November through late May. This time period can change depending on the quantity and nature of the season's snowfall, as well as unforeseen obstacles like fallen trees and/or rocks. The scatterplot above compares the snowpack water content on April 1 (for years 1981-2014) as a percent of the historical average to the time it takes the National Park Service to fully clear the road and open it to traffic.

5. For every 5% increase in snowpack water content, how many more days does it take the National Park Service to clear Tioga Road?

6. Assuming no unforeseen obstacles or machinery issues, if the road's snowpack water content on April 1 is 248% of the historical average, how many days will it take to fully clear Tioga Road?

The following table can help you structure your thinking as you go about solving this more involved problem. The Kaplan strategic thinking is provided, as are bits of structured scratchwork. If you're not sure how to approach a question like this, start at the top and work your way down.

Strategic Thinking	Math Scratchwork
Step 1: Read the first part of the question, looking for clues *What useful information are you given?* The infographic shows the relationship between snowpack water content and road clearing duration. A line of best fit is also drawn.	

Strategic Thinking	Math Scratchwork
Step 2: Identify and organize the information you need *What does part 1 ask you to find?* You are asked to find how much the road clearing time increases with each 5% increase in snowpack water content.	
Step 3: Based on what you know, plan your steps to navigate the first part *What missing information will help you find the answer?* You need a rate, which means you need to find the slope of the line of best fit. Pick a pair of points to use (look for places where the line passes through a gridline intersection to minimize error). Read the axes carefully when writing the coordinates!	(——, ——) (——, ——)
Step 4: Solve, step-by-step, checking units as you go *How do you find the slope of a line?* Use the slope formula to determine the change in clearing time per 1% increase in snowpack water content.	$m = \dfrac{y_2 - y_1}{x_2 - x_1} =$ ———— $=$ —— $=$ ——
Step 5: Did I answer the *right* question? *Did you find the clearing duration increase for a 5% increase in snowpack water content?* Be careful; you're not done yet! The slope represents the clearing duration increase for a 1% increase in snowpack water content. Multiply *m* by 5 to get the requested change. If you got 2, you'd be correct!	—— × —— = ——

Great job! Repeat this for the second part. Kaplan strategic thinking is on the left, and bits of scratchwork guidance are on the right.

Strategic Thinking	Math Scratchwork
Step 1: Read the second part of the question, looking for clues *Any new information presented?* Not a whole lot, just a piece of information on the snowpack water content during a particularly snowy winter.	

Strategic Thinking	Math Scratchwork
Step 2: Identify and organize the information you need *What does part 2 ask you to find? Will anything from part 1 help here?* Part 2 asks for the road clearing duration if snowpack water content is 248% of the historical average. The slope you found in part 1 could be useful here.	$m = \underline{\quad}$
Step 3: Based on what you know, plan your steps to navigate the second part *How would the slope from part 1 help you?* 248% snowpack water content is not on the graph, and you can easily make an error if you try to extend the line of best fit and estimate 248%. You can use the slope of the line to find the line's equation and extrapolate from there.	$y = mx + b$
Step 4: Solve, step-by-step, checking units as you go *What do you need in order to find the equation of the line of best fit?* Determine where the line of best fit intersects the y-axis to identify the value of b. Once there, plug 248 into the equation for the line of best fit, and then solve for y.	eqn: $= \underline{\quad} = \underline{\quad} + \underline{\quad}$ $x = 248$: $\underline{\quad} = \underline{\quad} \times \underline{\quad} + \underline{\quad}$ $\underline{\quad} = \underline{\quad} + \underline{\quad} = \underline{\quad}$
Step 5: Did I answer the *right* question? *How many days will it take to clear Tioga Road at 248% snowpack water content?* Did you get 99.2? If so, you'd be right!	$\underline{\quad}$

Well done! Fortunately, exceedingly heavy snowfall years like the one described in question 6 are relatively rare in the High Sierra of Yosemite.

Now test what you've learned by taking a brief quiz.

Now that you've seen the variety of ways in which the SAT can test you on scatterplots, try the following questions to check your understanding. Give yourself 4 minutes to tackle the following three questions. Make sure you use the Kaplan Method for Math as often as you can. Remember, you want to emphasize speed and efficiency in addition to simply getting the correct answer.

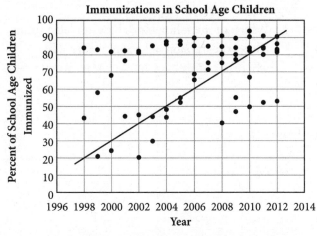

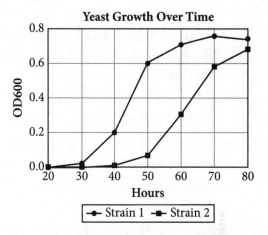

7. The graph above shows the percent of school age children in the United States who received immunizations for various illnesses between 1996 and 2012. What was the average rate of increase in the percent of children immunized over the given time period?

A) 5%

B) 10%

C) 25%

D) 70%

8. A marketing team is conducting a study on the use of smartphones. In a certain metropolitan area, there were 1.6 million smartphone users at the end of 2014. The marketing team predicts that the number of smartphone users will increase by 35% each year. If y represents the number of smartphone users in this metropolitan area after x years, then which of the following equations best models the number of smartphone users in this area over time?

A) $y = 1,600,000(1.35)^x$

B) $y = 1,600,000(35)^x$

C) $y = 35x + 1,600,000$

D) $y = 1.35x + 1,600,000$

9. A microbiologist is comparing the growth rates of two different yeast strains. She indirectly measures the number of yeast cells by recording the optical density (OD600) of each strain every ten hours. The measurements are presented in the graph above. Based on the data, which of the following is NOT a true statement?

A) Strain 1 had a higher OD600 reading than Strain 2 throughout the monitored period.

B) The growth rate of Strain 2 was less than the growth rate of Strain 1 until hour 50, at which point Strain 1's growth rate became the lesser one.

C) Between hours 50 and 70, Strain 2's OD600 reading increased by approximately 0.03 every hour.

D) The growth rate of Strain 1 was greater than the growth rate of Strain 2 throughout the monitored period.

Answers and Explanations for this chapter begin on page 598.

EXTRA PRACTICE

You may use your calculator for all questions in this section.

1. If a scatterplot shows a strong positive linear correlation, then which of the following best describes the trend of the data points?

    A) Points in a perfectly straight line that rises from left to right

    B) Points in a perfectly straight line that falls from left to right

    C) Points that fit fairly close to a straight line that rises from left to right

    D) Points that fit fairly close to a straight line that falls from left to right

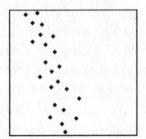

2. Which of the following is the best estimate for the slope of the line that best fits the data shown in the figure above? (Assume that the black bordered area is a square and that the scale of measurement is the same on every side.)

    A) -3

    B) $-\dfrac{1}{3}$

    C) $\dfrac{1}{3}$

    D) 3

3. Which of the following is best modeled using a linear regression equation, $y = ax + b$, where $a < 0$?

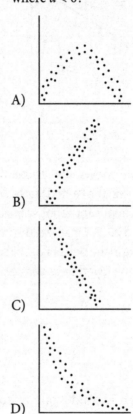

4. Adriana used the data from a scatterplot she found on the U.S. Census Bureau's website to determine a regression model showing the relationship between the population in the area where she lived and the number of years, x, after she was born. The result was an exponential growth equation of the form $y = x_0(1 + r)^x$. Which of the following does x_0 most likely represent in the equation?

A) The population in the year that she was born

B) The rate of change of the population over time

C) The maximum population reached during her lifetime

D) The number of years after her birth when the population reached its maximum

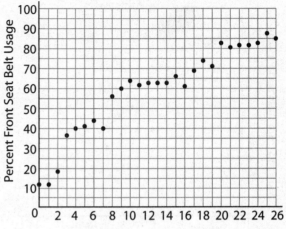

Seat Belt Use in England (1983-2009)

Years After Seat Belt Law Enacted

5. In 1983, the British Parliament enacted a mandatory seat belt law. The scatterplot above shows data collected each year after the law was enacted regarding the percent of drivers and front seat passengers who wore seat belts. Which of the following equations best represents the trend of the data shown in the figure?

A) $y = 0.4x + 25$

B) $y = 1.8x + 15$

C) $y = 2.1x + 35$

D) $y = 2.6x + 25$

Minor Muscle Strains Sustained by Athletes

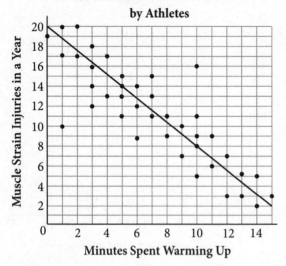

6. The scatterplot above shows the number of minor muscle strain injuries sustained in a year by athletes, plotted against their self-reported amount of time spent stretching and doing other "warm up" activities before engaging in rigorous physical activity. Which of the following best estimates the average rate of change in the number of injuries compared with the number of minutes spent warming up?

A) −1.2

B) −0.8

C) 2

D) 20

7. The Federal Reserve controls certain interest rates in the United States. Investors often try to speculate as to whether the Federal Reserve will raise or lower rates and by how much. Suppose a company conducts extensive interviews with financial analysts, and as a result, predicts that "the Fed" will increase rates by an average of 0.25 percentage points every six months for the foreseeable future. Which type of equation could be used to model the predicted interest rates over the next several years, assuming no other significant changes?

A) A linear equation

B) A quadratic equation

C) A polynomial equation

D) An exponential equation

8. Suppose a scatterplot shows a weak negative linear correlation. Which of the following statements is true?

A) The slope of the line of best fit will be a number less than −1.

B) The slope of the line of best fit will be a number between −1 and 0.

C) The data points will follow, but not closely, the line of best fit, which has a negative slope.

D) The data points will be closely gathered around the line of best fit, which has a negative slope.

Employee Sick Day Usage

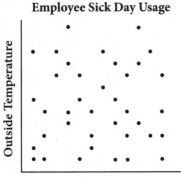

Number of Sick Days Used

9. The Human Resources department of a company tracks employee sick day usage to see if there are patterns. One of the HR representatives decides to check employee sick day usage against outside temperature. He compiles the information for the employees' sick day usage and temperature in the scatterplot above. Which of the following conclusions can he draw based on this data?

A) There is no relationship between the number of sick days used by employees in general and outside temperature.

B) There is no relationship between the number of sick days used by this company's employees and outside temperature.

C) No conclusions can be drawn about the number of sick days used by this company's employees and outside temperature.

D) There is a relationship between, but not causation by, the number of sick days used by this company's employees and outside temperature.

Regression Line Type	r^2
Linear	0.881
Polynomial	0.983
Exponential	0.623

10. Terence is trying to decide what kind of regression line is appropriate for a set of data. He calculates the r^2 value for three different regression lines, which are summarized in the table above. Given this information, which type of regression line is LEAST appropriate for Terence's data set?

A) Exponential

B) Linear

C) Polynomial

D) It cannot be determined without knowing the data points used.

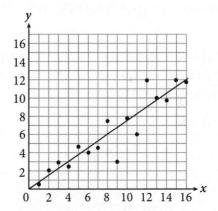

11. What is the y-value of the data point that has the highest percent error from the mean of the data shown in the scatterplot above?

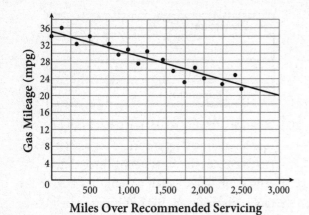

Miles Over Recommended Servicing

12. Research suggests that for any given make and model of car, the more miles the car is driven over the recommended miles between servicing, the worse gas mileage the car gets. Suppose a car dealership compiles data on a specific make and model of car and creates the scatterplot shown above. They then use the equation $y = -\dfrac{1}{200}x + 35$ to model the data.

Based on the information, how many miles per gallon could be expected if this particular car is driven 3,400 miles over the recommended miles between servicing?

Questions 13-15 refer to the following information.

Most chickens reach maturity and begin laying eggs at around 20 weeks of age. From this point forward, however, as the chicken ages, its egg production decreases. A farmer was given a flock of 100 chickens (all of which are the same age) and asked to measure daily egg output for the entire flock at random intervals starting at maturity until the chickens were 70 weeks old. The data is recorded in the scatterplot below and the line of best fit has been drawn.

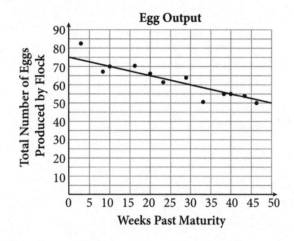

13. How many times did the farmer's data differ by at least 5 eggs from the number of eggs predicted by the line of best fit?

14. Based on the line of best fit, what is the predicted number of eggs that will be produced by the flock when it is 36 weeks past maturity?

15. A different farmer has a flock of 100 chickens that is producing 55 eggs at 20 weeks past maturity. He wants to calculate the percent error of this amount compared to that predicted by the line of best fit. What is the percent error? Round to the nearest whole percent and ignore the percent sign when entering your answer.

CHAPTER 5

Two-way Tables, Statistics, and Probability

CHAPTER OBJECTIVES

By the end of this chapter, you will be able to:

1. Use two-way tables to summarize data and calculate basic probabilities

2. Make inferences about population parameters based on sample data

3. Evaluate scenarios/reports to make inferences, justify conclusions, and determine appropriateness of data collection methods

SMARTPOINTS

Point Value	SmartPoint Category
50 Points	Statistics and Probability

TWO-WAY TABLES AND CHARTS/GRAPHS

Data can be represented in a multitude of ways. In this chapter we'll focus on a numerical approach (two-way table) and a pictorial one (chart or graph).

A two-way table is a table that contains data on two variables. This type of table can be used to make comparisons and determine whether relationships exist between the variables. You might see this data referred to as bivariate (two-variable) data.

If you're worried about having to learn a new topic, you need not be. You've likely encountered two-way tables in the past and just not known their formal name—if you've ever generated a spreadsheet, two-way tables should look familiar. Take a look at the following example that contains data on several antique book stores' sales to see what we mean.

	Bob's Books	Nalia's Novels	Tumiko's Tomes	Vladimir's Volumes	Total
Monday	14	7	15	12	48
Tuesday	8	13	15	13	49
Wednesday	10	13	12	14	49
Thursday	8	15	14	10	47
Friday	13	7	10	9	39
Total	53	55	66	58	232

Two-way tables contain a wealth of information: You can quickly determine how many books Nalia's Novels sold on Friday just by finding the appropriate cell in the table. You can also find quantities that are not explicitly written. For instance, you can determine numerous ratios: total books sold on Wednesday to total books sold on Thursday, Tumiko's Monday sales to Tumiko's total sales, and so on. You can also find percentages and probabilities.

✔ Note

Although two-way tables are generally easy to follow, they're also easy to misinterpret when you're in a rush. Take time to ensure that you've extracted the correct information for a given question.

Ratios and the like aside, you could be asked to make a prediction based on given data; that is, you'll need to extrapolate data to derive an answer. For instance, let's say the community in which these four shops are located has an annual antique appreciation week, and Nalia anticipates that her antique book sales will increase by 40% from the week for which the data is shown in the table. She sold 55 books that week, and 40% of 55 is 22. This means that if Nalia's prediction is true, she can expect to sell 55 + 22 = 77 books during antique appreciation week.

In addition to two-way tables, the SAT can also ask questions about charts and graphs, whether about the data itself or a prediction based on the data.

Take a look at the next few pages for sample questions involving two-way tables, charts, and graphs.

Use the table introduced at the beginning of this section to answer the following question.

1. Which of the four shops made the greatest fraction of its total sales on Tuesday?

   A) Bob's Books

   B) Nalia's Novels

   C) Tumiko's Tomes

   D) Vladimir's Volumes

Work through the Kaplan Method for Math step-by-step to solve this question. The following table shows Kaplan's strategic thinking on the left, along with suggested math scratchwork on the right.

Strategic Thinking	Math Scratchwork
Step 1: Read the question, identifying and organizing important information as you go Understanding what's being asked is the trickiest part of this question. You *do not* want the shop that sold the most books on Tuesday. Rather, you are solving for the shop whose Tuesday sales, as a fraction of the shop's total sales, were the greatest.	
Step 2: Choose the best strategy to answer the question Only two rows matter for this question: The Tuesday row and the Total row (*not* the Total column). Divide each shop's Tuesday sales by its total sales. The shop with the largest result is the correct answer. Because the fractions involve less manageable numbers, using a calculator to simplify the arithmetic is reasonable here. Nalia's Tuesday sales as a fraction of her total sales were highest.	need $\dfrac{Tuesday}{Total}$ B: $\dfrac{8}{53} \approx 0.1509$ N: $\dfrac{13}{55} \approx 0.2364$ T: $\dfrac{15}{66} \approx 0.2273$ V: $\dfrac{13}{58} \approx 0.2241$
Step 3: Check that you answered the *right* question You've identified the shop that had the highest fraction of its sales on Tuesday, so you're done. Choice (B) is correct.	

> **✔ Expert Tip**
>
> If you're adept at quantitative comparison of fractions, you can omit the decimal conversion calculations (and save some time).

The question below requires the table used for question 1.

2. What fraction of the books sold on Monday, Wednesday, and Friday were sold at Tumiko's Tomes and Vladimir's Volumes?

A) $\dfrac{9}{29}$

B) $\dfrac{11}{32}$

C) $\dfrac{9}{17}$

D) $\dfrac{18}{31}$

Work through the Kaplan Method for Math step-by-step to solve this question. The following table shows Kaplan's strategic thinking on the left, along with suggested math scratchwork on the right.

Strategic Thinking	Math Scratchwork
Step 1: Read the question, identifying and organizing important information as you go You need to find how many books Tumiko and Vladimir sold on Monday, Wednesday, and Friday as a fraction of the total number of books all four shops sold on those days.	
Step 2: Choose the best strategy to answer the question Use the Monday, Wednesday, and Friday rows and the Tumiko, Vladimir, and Total columns (*not* the Total row). Add the number of books Tumiko and Vladimir sold on these three days, and then repeat the process with the total number of books all four shops sold on these days. Combine these values into a fraction.	Mon + Wed + Fri for T & V: (15 + 12) + (12 + 14) + (10 + 9) = 72 Mon + Wed + Fri total: 48 + 49 + 39 = 136 $\dfrac{72}{136}$

Strategic Thinking	Math Scratchwork
Step 3: Check that you answered the _right_ question None of the answer choices match the fraction you found, but don't panic. You just need to simplify. The GCF of 72 and 136 is 8, so the most simplified form of the fraction is $\frac{9}{17}$. Select (C) and you're done.	$\frac{72}{136} = \frac{9}{17}$

Now that you've seen how to use two-way tables, keep reading for more about what you can learn from them.

STATISTICS AND PROBABILITY

While there are entire high school and college courses devoted to the study of statistics, the SAT will (fortunately) only test you on a few basic statistical concepts. If you aren't a statistics fan, now is a great time to rethink your position: Statistics is a part of almost every major in college and can be used in a variety of careers. Using an example from high school, let's take a look at the sort of concepts the SAT expects you to be familiar with.

Suppose you took five tests in a world history class and earned scores of 85, 92, 85, 80, and 96. Descriptions of six fundamental statistics figures you can find for this data set follow:

- **Mean (also called average):** The sum of the values divided by the number of values. For your history class, the mean of your test scores is $\frac{85 + 92 + 85 + 80 + 96}{5} = \frac{438}{5} = 87.6$. At most schools, that's a B or B+.

- **Median:** The value that is in the middle of the set _when the values are arranged in ascending order_. The test scores in ascending order are 80, 85, 85, 92, and 96, making the median 85. Be careful: The SAT could give you a set of numbers that is not in order. Make sure you properly arrange them before determining the median.

- **Mode:** The value that occurs most frequently. The score that appears more than any other is 85 (twice vs. once), so it is the mode. If more than one value appears the most often, that's okay: A set of data can have multiple modes.

- **Range:** The difference between the highest and lowest values. From finding the median you know the highest and lowest scores are 96 and 80, respectively; so the range is 96 − 80 = 16.

- **Standard deviation:** A measure of how far a typical data point is from the mean. A low standard deviation means most values in the set are fairly close to the mean; a high standard deviation means there is much more spread in the data set. On the SAT, **You will need to know what standard deviation is, but you won't have to calculate it.**

- **Margin of error:** A description of the maximum expected difference between a true value for a data pool (e.g., mean) and a random sampling from the data pool. A lower margin of error is achieved by increasing the size of the data pool. **As with standard deviation, you will need to know what a margin of error is on the SAT, but you won't be asked to calculate one.**

Mean, median, and mode are referred to as measures of central tendency because they can be used to represent a typical value in the data set. Range, standard deviation, and margin of error are measures of spread because they show how much the data in a set vary.

> ✔ **Note**
>
> To find the median of a data set that contains an even number of terms, arrange the terms in ascending order, then find the average of the two middle terms.

On Test Day, you might also be asked to analyze the shape of data. The shape of a data set can be either symmetric or skewed (asymmetric). Many data sets have a head, where many data points are clustered in one area, and tails, where the number of data points slowly decreases to 0. Examining the tails will help you describe the shape of a data set. A data set is skewed in the direction of its longer tail.

Symmetric

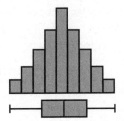

The data are evenly spread out.
mean ≈ median

Skewed to the Left

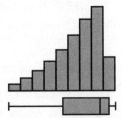

The tail is longer on the left.
mean < median

Skewed to the Right

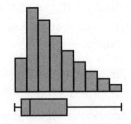

The tail is longer on the right.
mean > median

> ✔ **Expert Tip**
>
> When you have a group of evenly spaced terms (e.g., 2, 4, 6, 8, 10, 12), the mean and median will be identical. With this data set, the mean is
>
> $$\frac{2+4+6+8+10+12}{6} = \frac{42}{6} = 7,\text{ and}$$
>
> the median is $\frac{6+8}{2} = \frac{14}{2} = 7$. In addition, you can find the mean of a group of evenly spaced terms by taking the mean of the highest and lowest:
>
> $$\frac{12+2}{2} = \frac{14}{2} = 7.$$

It is possible to determine a data mean from a bar graph (also called a histogram). Suppose a teacher made a bar graph of student performance on a recent test like the one shown here.

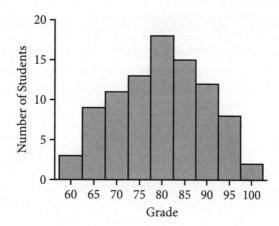

To find the mean of these data, first determine the sum of terms and number of terms and then use the average formula. We see from the graph that 3 students scored 60, 9 scored 65, 11 scored 70, and so on. Add these up to make the sum of terms; then divide by the total number of students, which is the number of terms:

$$\frac{3(60) + 9(65) + 11(70) + 13(75) + 18(80) + 15(85) + 12(90) + 8(95) + 2(100)}{3 + 9 + 11 + 13 + 18 + 15 + 12 + 8 + 2} = \frac{7265}{91} = 79.8$$

The mean score on this test was 79.8.

A concept closely linked to statistics is probability. **Probability** is a fraction or decimal comparing the number of desired outcomes to the number of total possible outcomes. For instance, if you have a full deck of playing cards and want to know the probability of drawing an ace, you would compute

$\frac{\# \text{ aces}}{\# \text{ cards}} = \frac{4}{52} = \frac{1}{13} \approx 0.077$. To find the probability that an event will *not* happen, subtract the

probability that the event will happen from 1. In the ace example, this would be

$1 - \frac{\# \text{ aces}}{\# \text{ cards}} = 1 - \frac{4}{52} = \frac{48}{52} = \frac{12}{13} \approx 0.923$.

> ✔ **Note**
>
> $$\text{Probability} = \frac{\# \text{ desired outcomes}}{\# \text{ total possible outcomes}}$$

You can also find the probability for a series of events. If you're asked for the probability of drawing an ace without replacement (the card does not go back in the deck) followed by a red nine,

multiply the probability of the first event by that of the second: $\frac{\# \text{ aces}}{\# \text{ cards}} \times \frac{\# \text{ red nines}}{\# \text{ cards} - 1} = \frac{4}{52} \times \frac{2}{51} =$

$\frac{8}{2652} \approx 0.0030$.

> **✔ Note**
>
> "With replacement" means the item chosen, in this case a card, is returned to the original group (here, the deck). The number of possible outcomes in the denominator will stay constant. "Without replacement" indicates the item is not returned; the number of possible outcomes will change to reflect the new possible outcome count.

With a two-way table, you can find the probability that a randomly selected data value (be it a person, object, etc.) will fit a certain profile. In addition, you might be asked to calculate a conditional probability. Conditional probability questions are easy to spot, as the word *given* is usually present. The following is a two-way table summarizing a survey on water preference.

	Bottled	Carbonated	Tap	Total
Female	325	267	295	887
Male	304	210	289	803
Total	629	477	584	1,690

If asked for the probability of randomly selecting a female who prefers bottled water from all the participants of the original survey for a follow-up survey, you would calculate it using the same general formula as before: $\dfrac{\text{\# female bottled}}{\text{\# total}} = \dfrac{325}{1690} = \dfrac{5}{26} \approx 0.192$.

If asked for the probability of randomly selecting a female for the follow-up survey, given that the chosen participant prefers bottled water, the setup is a little different. The clause starting with "given" indicates your number of possible outcomes is the total participants who prefer bottled water, which is 629 and not the grand total of 1,690. Your calculation is now $\dfrac{\text{\# female bottled}}{\text{\# total bottled}} = \dfrac{325}{629} \approx 0.517$.

Conversely, if you need to find the probability of selecting someone who prefers bottled water for the follow-up survey, given that the chosen participant is female, the new number of possible outcomes is the female participant total (887). The calculation becomes $\dfrac{\text{\# bottled}}{\text{\# total females}} = \dfrac{325}{887} \approx 0.366$.

Take a look at the next few pages for some test-like questions involving two-way tables and probability.

Use the following table about a survey related to favorite video game genres for a group of high school students to answer the two questions that follow. Assume that every student had a favorite video game genre and that each student could only select one favorite.

	Freshmen	Sophomores	Juniors	Seniors	Total
First-person shooters	144	122	134	115	515
Strategy games	126	140	152	148	566
Role-playing games	120	117	153	148	538
Indie games	110	114	63	98	385
Total	500	493	502	509	2004

3. The research group that conducted the survey wants to select one sophomore and one senior at random for a follow-up survey. What is the probability that both students selected will prefer a type of video game other than strategy games?

A) $\frac{140}{493}+\frac{148}{509}$

B) $\frac{140}{493}\times\frac{148}{509}$

C) $\frac{353}{493}+\frac{361}{509}$

D) $\frac{353}{493}\times\frac{361}{509}$

There's no scratchwork for this question, but Kaplan's strategic thinking follows. Follow along as we reason through the question to get the correct answer.

Strategic Thinking
Step 1: Read the question, identifying and organizing important information as you go
You need to determine the probability that a sophomore and a senior selected at random will both prefer a video game genre other than strategy games.

Strategic Thinking
Step 2: Choose the best strategy to answer the question
The answer choices are unsimplified expressions, which means that you don't need to find the actual probability—you just need to set up the correct expression.
The word "both" in the question stem signals that you need to find the probability that one event AND another will both happen. To find the probability that more than one event will occur, multiply the individual probabilities together. This means that A and C, which feature addition rather than multiplication, are incorrect.
You can determine which of the remaining answer choices is correct without any number crunching. Of the 493 sophomores, 140 prefer strategy games. Choice B contains the probability $\frac{140}{493}$, which means it's incorrect—you want the probability of picking students who *don't* prefer strategy games.
Step 3: Check that you answered the *right* question
By process of elimination, you know that (D) must be correct.

The following question pertains to the table used in question 3.

4. The research group that conducted the survey wishes to see if there is a connection between the time a student spends playing video games and that student's grade point average (GPA). The school at which the initial survey was conducted was in Dallas, Texas; and the group decides to include three additional Dallas high schools in the follow-up study. Data produced from the follow-up study showed a moderately strong negative correlation between time spent playing video games and GPA. Based on these findings, which of the following is a valid conclusion?

    A) There is an association between the amount of time a high school student in Dallas spends playing video games and his/her GPA.

    B) There is an association between the amount of time a high school student anywhere in Texas spends playing video games and his/her GPA.

    C) An increase in the amount of time a high school student in Dallas spends playing video games causes a decrease in his/her GPA.

    D) An increase in the amount of time a high school student anywhere in Texas spends playing video games causes a decrease in his/her GPA.

There's no scratchwork for this question, but Kaplan's strategic thinking follows. Follow along as we reason through the question to get the correct answer.

Strategic Thinking
Step 1: Read the question, identifying and organizing important information as you go
You're asked to identify the valid conclusion (in other words, the true statement).
Step 2: Choose the best strategy to answer the question
Carefully examine each answer choice. You're told that there is a moderately strong correlation between time spent playing video games and GPA. However, because the study utilized students in Dallas only, no conclusions about the entire Texas high school population can be drawn. Eliminate B and D.   To determine which of the two remaining answer choices is correct, carefully read each choice and compare it to the question stem. Although there is a correlation between time spent playing video games and GPA, the study did not conclude that one causes the other. Eliminate C.
Step 3: Check that you answered the *right* question
Choice (A) matches your analysis.

> ✔ **Expert Tip**
>
> Look for key details—such as the study's population, location, and any results derived—in questions like this one. These details will help you quickly solve for the correct answer.

5. A fair coin is flipped five times. What is the probability that at least four of the five flips will be heads?

   A) $\dfrac{3}{16}$

   B) $\dfrac{3}{10}$

   C) $\dfrac{7}{10}$

   D) $\dfrac{13}{16}$

Work through the Kaplan Method for Math step-by-step to solve this question. The following table shows Kaplan's strategic thinking on the left, along with suggested math scratchwork on the right.

Strategic Thinking	Math Scratchwork
Step 1: Read the question, identifying and organizing important information as you go You need to find the probability that at least four out of five coin flips will land on heads.	

Strategic Thinking	Math Scratchwork
Step 2: Choose the best strategy to answer the question	
Use the fundamental probability formula: $$\text{probability} = \frac{\text{number of desired outcomes}}{\text{number of possible outcomes}}.$$	$p = \dfrac{\textit{number desired}}{\textit{number possible}}$
There are five coin flips. Each coin flip has two possible outcomes. $2^5 = 32$ possible outcomes.	*# possible:* $2 \times 2 \times 2 \times 2 \times 2 = 2^5 = 32$
You can find the number of outcomes that have at least four heads by writing out all of the possibilities. Work systematically to ensure you don't miss anything.	*# desired:* *HHHHH* *HHHHT* *HHHTH* *HHTHH* *HTHHH* *THHHH*
There are six desired outcomes that have at least four heads.	*6 desired*
Combine these two quantities in a fraction to represent the probability that at least four of the five coin flips will land on heads.	$\dfrac{6}{32} = \dfrac{3}{16}$
Step 3: Check that you answered the *right* question	
Of the 32 possible outcomes for five coin flips, six of these contain at least 4 heads. Choice (A) is equivalent to this finding and is therefore correct.	

Following is a sample Multi-Part Math question involving the concepts you've learned in this chapter. Remember to tackle this question one step at a time, and follow the Kaplan Method for Multi-Part Math Questions.

Questions 6 and 7 refer to the following information.

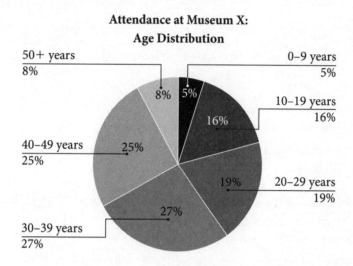

Attendance at Museum X:
Age Distribution

The pie graph above shows the age distribution of visitors to Museum X in 2014. Visitors aged 0-9 years get into Museum X for free, visitors aged 50 and older pay $5 for admission, and everyone else pays $10.

6. If 553 people aged 20 years and older visited Museum X in 2014, then approximately how many people visited Museum X in 2014?

7. Based on the pie graph and the result from the previous question, how much revenue did Museum X collect from tickets sold to people aged 40 and older in 2014?

Work through the Kaplan Method for Multi-Part Math Questions step-by-step to solve this question (for a review of this Method, see chapter 3). The following table shows Kaplan's strategic thinking on the left, along with suggested math scratchwork on the right.

Strategic Thinking	Math Scratchwork
Step 1: Read the first part of the question, looking for clues The infographic shows the age distribution of visitors to Museum X in 2014. From the accompanying text you also learn the ticket prices based on age.	0-9: free 10-49: \$10 50+: \$5
Step 2: Identify and organize the information you need You're asked to find the total number of visitors to Museum X in 2014, given that 553 of the visitors were aged 20 and up.	need total # attendees
Step 3: Based on what you know, plan your steps to navigate the first part You know the *number* of visitors aged 20 and up. If you find the accompanying percent, you can figure out the total using the three-part percent formula you learned previously.	_____ % of total is 553
Step 4: Solve, step-by-step, checking units as you go You could add the percentages for the 20-29, 30-39, 40-49, and 50+ categories, but there's a faster route. Look at the sections of the pie graph for the two groups that are *not* 20 or older: 0-9 and 10-19. Those two groups represent 5% and 16% of the total, respectively. Subtract these values from 100% to find what percent of visitors were aged 20 and up. To find the total number of visitors, plug what you know into the three-part percent formula.	% not aged 20+: 5% + 16% = 21% % aged 20+: 100% − 21% = 79% total × 0.79 = 553 total = $\dfrac{553}{0.79}$ = 700
Step 5: Did I answer the *right* question? The question asks for the total number of visitors in 2014, which is 700.	

Part 1 is complete. Now on to Step 6: Repeat for the other parts. Kaplan's strategic thinking is on the left, along with suggested math scratchwork on the right.

Strategic Thinking	Math Scratchwork
Step 1: Read the second part of the question, looking for clues From part 1, you know the total number of visitors in 2014; nothing new is given in part 2.	*700 total attendees*
Step 2: Identify and organize the information you need Part 2 asks for the revenue from tickets sold to people aged 40 and older. The total number of visitors, which you learned from part 1, will help calculate this figure.	*$ from aged 40+: ?*
Step 3: Based on what you know, plan your steps to navigate the second part Because you already know the total number of visitors, you can calculate the number of visitors aged 40-49 and 50+ using the percentages given in the pie graph.	*find # of 40-49, 50+*
Step 4: Solve, step-by-step, checking units as you go Calculate the number of attendees in the 40-49 and 50+ age groups by taking 25% of 700 and 8% of 700, respectively. The 40-49 group paid $10 per ticket, and the 50+ group paid $5 per ticket. Use these facts to determine the revenue generated from these groups.	*# aged 40-49:* $700 \times 0.25 = 175$ *# aged 50+:* $700 \times 0.08 = 56$ *175 ppl paid $10/ticket* *56 ppl paid $5/ticket* $175 \times \$10 = \$1,750$ $56 \times \$5 = \$280$ $\$1,750 + \$280 = \$2,030$
Step 5: Did I answer the *right* question? $2,030 was collected from the 40-49 and 50+ age groups; grid in 2030.	

As you saw, statistics and graphical analysis have powerful real-world applications.

✔ **Note**

It's easy to misread questions like #7 and use a part of the infographic other than the one you need. Take time to ensure that you know what you need to find.

WORD PROBLEMS

You're already well versed in deciphering SAT word problems, but word problems involving probability sometimes require you to use different skills. You'll need to use your analytical abilities to develop inferences and predictions, draw and justify logical conclusions, and evaluate the appropriateness of data collection techniques. Sometimes you'll need to consult a provided two-way table as you did for some earlier questions, and in other cases you'll just study the question stem to gather pertinent information. Perhaps the best part of these questions is the fact that they often require little or no actual mathematical calculation!

Here is a test-like sample question.

8. A local softball league has male and female members. If *m* is the average age of the males, *f* is the average age of the females, *a* is the overall average age, and 65 percent of the league's members are male, then which one of the following statements must be true about *m*, *f*, and *a*?

A) If $m < f$, then $a > \dfrac{m+f}{2}$.

B) If $m > f$, then $a < \dfrac{m+f}{2}$.

C) If $m < f$, then $a < \dfrac{m+f}{2}$.

D) $a = \dfrac{m+f}{2}$

There's no scratchwork for this question, but Kaplan's strategic thinking follows. Follow along as we reason through the question to get the correct answer.

Strategic Thinking
Step 1: Read the question, identifying and organizing important information as you go
The question asks you to identify the statement that is true. You're told that 65% of the league's members are male, and you're given the definition of three variables: *m*, *f*, and *a*.

Strategic Thinking

Step 2: Choose the best strategy to answer the question

Don't panic over the limited amount of information. Examine the answer choices to see if you can spot any useful patterns. Each answer choice makes a comparison between a (the overall average age) and $\frac{m+f}{2}$. If the male and female member counts were equal, then the overall average age would simply be the average of the male and female average ages, or $\frac{m+f}{2}$. However, because there are more males than females in the group, the overall average must be closer to the average male age than average female age. You don't know which of m or f is greater, so use a number line to visualize this information. There are two ways to do so. The first assumes that $m < f$; the second assumes that $m > f$:

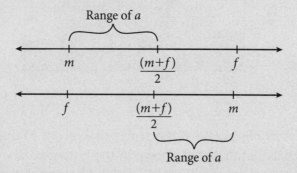

The only choice consistent with the visualization is (C): when m is less than f, the value of a is less than the average age of both groups.

Step 3: Check that you answered the *right* question

Choice (C) matches your analysis.

✔ **Note**

For questions like this, think about what information is given or not given, the conclusion(s) you can draw from either, and answers you can eliminate based on said conclusion(s).

Now you'll have a chance to try a couple test-like problems in a scaffolded way. See if you can fill in the missing pieces and solve for the correct answer without a full explanation.

We've provided some guidance, but you'll need to fill in the missing parts of explanations or the step-by-step math in order to get to the correct answer. Don't worry—after going through the worked examples at the beginning of this section, these problems should be completely doable.

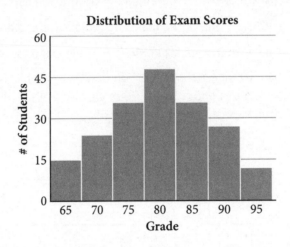

Distribution of Exam Scores

9. A history professor observes that the scores of a recent 20-question multiple choice exam are normally distributed as shown in the histogram above. However, she later discovers that 25% of the results were omitted from the distribution. Of the omitted scores, 80% are greater than what the professor thought the mean was; the rest are less. Assuming all new data points fit in the current histogram range, which of the following is most likely to occur upon adding the new scores to the data?

    A) The data will be skewed to the right.

    B) The data will be skewed to the left.

    C) The median will decrease.

    D) The range will decrease.

The following table can help you structure your thinking as you go about solving this more involved problem. The Kaplan strategic thinking is provided, as are bits of structured scratchwork. If you're not sure how to approach a question like this, start at the top and work your way down.

Strategic Thinking	Math Scratchwork
Step 1: Read the question, identifying and organizing important information as you go *What is the question asking you to do?* You need to determine the effect of adding extra data points, most of which are above the mean, to what was previously a normal (symmetric) distribution.	

Strategic Thinking	Math Scratchwork
Step 2: Choose the best strategy to answer the question *What will the distribution look like after the new data are added?* The question states that most of the new scores are above the mean. Draw a rough sketch of what the new distribution will look like. *What can you learn from the answer choices?* The choices mention skew, median, and range. Think about the effect the additions to the data set will have on each of these.	post-addition: direction of skew: _____ median shift:_____ range shift:_____
Step 3: Check that you answered the *right* question *Which answer contains an effect you found?* If you chose (B), congrats! You're correct.	_____

Now try two Multi-Part Math questions.

The following information pertains to questions 10 and 11.

	1	2	3	4	5	Total
Worker Placement	5	17	24	10	5	61
Bidding	3	12	28	8	3	54
Area Control	3	10	30	14	2	59

A small boutique sells board games online. The boutique specializes in worker placement, bidding, and area control board games. Any customer who purchases a game is invited to rate the game on a scale of 1 to 5. A rating of 1 or 2 is considered "bad," a rating of 3 is considered "average," and a rating of 4 or 5 is considered "good." The table above shows the distribution of average customer ratings of the board games sold by the boutique. For example, 24 of the worker placement games sold by the boutique have an average rating of 3.

10. According to the table, what percent of all the board games sold by the boutique received a rating of "bad"? Round your answer to the nearest tenth of a percent and ignore the percent sign.

11. The boutique decides to stop selling 50% of the board games that received a rating of "bad" to make room for promising new stock. Assuming no significant changes in ratings in the foreseeable future, what should the difference be between the percentages of board games with a rating of "bad" before and after this change? Round your answer to the nearest tenth of a percent and ignore the percent sign.

PRACTICE

The following table can help you structure your thinking as you go about solving this more involved problem. The Kaplan strategic thinking is provided, as are bits of structured scratchwork. If you're not sure how to approach a question like this, start at the top and work your way down.

Strategic Thinking	Math Scratchwork
Step 1: Read the first part of the question, looking for clues *What useful information are you given?* You're provided a chart with data on the average ratings of board games sold by a boutique.	
Step 2: Identify and organize the information you need *What does part 1 ask you to find?* You're asked to find the percent of games that received a rating of "bad", meaning a rating of 1 or 2.	find # games with "bad" rating
Step 3: Based on what you know, plan your steps to navigate the first part *How many games received a rating of 1 or 2?* Examine the chart carefully, identifying the necessary data from each type of game. *What's the next step?* Add the figures to get the total number of games that received a rating of "bad."	worker placement 1: _____ games 2: _____ games bidding 1: _____ games 2: _____ games area control 1: _____ games 2: _____ games total: _____
Step 4: Solve, step-by-step, checking units as you go *How do you find the percent of games that received a rating of "bad"?* Use the values in the table to find the total number of games in these groups. Write the "bad" *part* over the *total* game count, and then convert to a percent.	_____ × 100 = _____%

Strategic Thinking	Math Scratchwork
Step 5: Did I answer the *right* question? *What percent of the games in these groups received a rating of "bad"?* If you got 28.7, you're correct!	_____

✔ **Note**

You might see unusual jargon (such as "worker placement" and "area control" in this question) on Test Day; don't fret. This question only tests your ability to correctly interpret a two-way table and complete appropriate calculations.

Great job! Repeat for the second part. Kaplan strategic thinking is on the left, and bits of scratch-work guidance are on the right.

Strategic Thinking	Math Scratchwork
Step 1: Read the second part of the question, looking for clues *Any new information presented?* From part 1 you know the number (and percent) of games that received a rating of "bad."	# games with "bad" rating: _____; = _____%
Step 2: Identify and organize the information you need *What does this question ask you to find? Will anything from the previous question help here?* You're asked for the difference between the percentages of games that received a "bad" rating before and after 50% of such games are removed from the store's inventory. Your answer from the previous question is key to this calculation.	"bad" % pre-removal:_____% "bad" % post-removal: ?
Step 3: Based on what you know, plan your steps to navigate the second part *How do you determine the new "bad" percentage after the removal?* You know the store wants to get rid of 50% of the games that received a "bad" rating. You already know the current number with a "bad" rating, so finding the new "bad" game count is straight-forward. Once there, determine the new "bad" percentage and subtract that from the original.	_____ x old "bad" count = new "bad" count → convert to % old "bad" % − new "bad" % = answer

Strategic Thinking	Math Scratchwork
Step 4: Solve, step-by-step, checking units as you go *After the 50% reduction in "bad" games, how many games should have a "bad" rating?* Reduce the original "bad" game count by 50%. *What percent of remaining games will have a "bad" rating after the clearance?* Divide your new "bad" count by the total game count. Remember that when the number of "bad" games decreases, the total count decreases by the same amount. Write your results using a couple of decimal points to minimize rounding errors. *What's the difference between the two percents?* Subtract the new "bad" percent from the old "bad" percent.	_____ % x old "bad" count = new "bad" count _____ x _____ = _____ new "bad" %: _____ x 100 = _____ % old "bad" % – new "bad" %: _____ % – _____ % = _____ %
Step 5: Did I answer the *right* question? *How do the two percents compare?* Did you get 11.9? If so, you're absolutely correct!	% change: _____

Nice work! Now test what you've learned by taking a brief quiz.

Now that you've seen the variety of ways in which the SAT can test you on two-way tables, statistics, and probability, try the following questions to check your understanding. Give yourself 5 minutes to tackle the following 4 questions. Make sure you use the Kaplan Method for Math (and the Kaplan Method for Multi-Part Math Questions where appropriate) as often as you can. Remember, you want to emphasize speed and efficiency in addition to simply getting the correct answer.

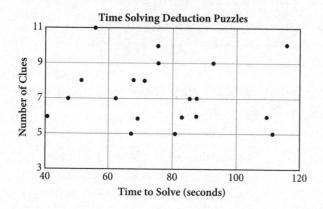

	Ceren	Han	Billy
Run 1	8.3	8.5	8.4
Run 2	7.7	8.0	8.0
Run 3	7.1	8.5	7.5
Run 4	6.6	7.8	9.0
Run 5	8.0	8.1	7.5
Run 6	6.6	7.5	7.2
Mean Score	7.38	8.07	7.93
Standard Deviation	0.73	0.39	0.67

12. Rolff recently completed a book of 20 deduction puzzles. The scatterplot above shows the time it took Rolff to solve a puzzle versus the number of clues it had. If a puzzle is selected at random from the book, what is the probability that it had fewer than six clues, took Rolff fewer than 100 seconds to solve, or both?

A) 10%

B) 15%

C) 85%

D) 90%

13. Ceren, Han, and Billy participated in a snowboarding competition. The scores for each of their six qualifying runs are in the table above. According to the data, which of the following is a valid conclusion?

A) Ceren had the smallest mean score, so her performance was the least consistent.

B) Han had the smallest standard deviation, so his performance was the most consistent.

C) Ceren had the largest standard deviation, so her performance was the most consistent.

D) Billy had the largest range in scores, so his performance was the least consistent.

Use the following information to answer questions 14 and 15.

	Scarves	Pairs of Mittens	Hats	Pairs of Socks	Total
Wilhelmina	7	2	24	19	52
Emanuel	8	2	9	14	33
Jose Raul	3	4	18	10	35
Alexandra	15	1	9	9	34
Total	33	9	60	52	154

Wilhelmina, Emanuel, Jose Raul, and Alexandra are in a knitting club. The table above shows the quantity of several different items each person has knitted over the lifetime of the club.

14. The four club members plan to knit hats to sell for Spirit Week at their college. They surveyed a group of students regarding their hat pattern preferences and found that 60% of those surveyed prefer solid-colored hats, 22% prefer stripes, and 18% prefer stars. The club anticipates that 1,800 students will each buy one hat. If the ratios in the table remain constant for Spirit Week hat production, how many solid-colored hats will Wilhelmina and Alexandra be responsible for knitting?

15. The knitting club plans to embroider a small, hidden emblem on the interior of 20% of the hats they make for Spirit Week; anyone who finds this emblem on their hat will win a free scarf. The four members will split up the making of the free scarves according to the ratios in the table. For how many winning hats and scarf prizes will Emanuel and Jose Raul be responsible?

Answers and Explanations for this chapter begin on page 606.

EXTRA PRACTICE

You may use your calculator for all questions in this section.

Questions 1 and 2 refer to the following information.

Numerous health studies have found that people who eat breakfast are generally healthier and weigh less than people who skip it. Although scientists are not certain as to the reason, it is generally believed that breakfast jumpstarts the metabolism and encourages a more regular consumption of calories throughout the day, instead of the calories being consumed in two big meals at lunch and dinner. The following table shows the results of a study related to this topic.

Breakfast Study Results

	Breakfast ≤1 time per week	Breakfast 2-4 times per week	Breakfast 5-7 times per week	Total
Within Healthy Weight Range	6	15	36	57
Outside Healthy Weight Range	38	27	9	74
Total	44	42	45	131

1. What percent of the participants who were outside a healthy weight range ate breakfast one or fewer times per week?

    A) 29.00%

    B) 51.35%

    C) 56.49%

    D) 86.36%

2. A large company that provides breakfast for all its employees wants to determine how many of them are likely to be within a healthy weight range, given that all the employees take advantage of the free breakfast all 5 weekdays. If the company has 3,000 employees, and assuming the participants in the study were a good representative sample, about how many of the employees are likely to be within a healthy weight range?

    A) 825

    B) 1,030

    C) 1,900

    D) 2,400

3. A shoe manufacturing company is thinking about introducing a new product designed to help athletes jump higher. The company conducts a marketing study by asking people outside community gymnasiums and sporting goods stores whether they would purchase such a product. Approximately 40% of 3,000 respondents said they would purchase these shoes over regular tennis shoes. Based on the study, the company concludes that 40% of shoe store customers shopping for tennis shoes would purchase their new product. Why is this not a valid conclusion?

A) The study was too small to draw any conclusions about the larger population.

B) The data from the survey does not represent the whole population because it was not conducted across the whole country.

C) The data from the survey likely underestimates the number of people interested in the new product because it only compared the new product to tennis shoes, not all types of shoes.

D) The data from the survey likely overestimates the number of people interested in the new product because the survey targeted respondents already interested in athletics.

Questions 4 and 5 refer to the following information.

At most colleges, students receive letter grades, which correspond to a GPA score, rather than a numerical grade, such as 92. The figure below shows the distribution of grades and corresponding GPA scores among students in a history class.

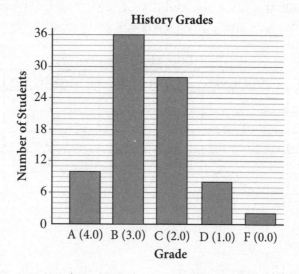

4. What is the mean history GPA for this class of students?

   A) 2.0

   B) 2.5

   C) 2.6

   D) 3.0

5. College professors sometimes use statistics to summarize class performance so that students will have an idea of how they are doing relative to the rest of the class. If this professor wants to report that at least half of the grades were a 3.0 or above, which measure of center should she use to describe the results?

   A) Mean

   B) Mode

   C) Mode or median

   D) Standard deviation

Questions 6 and 7 refer to the following information.

The amount of glucose, or sugar, in a person's blood is the primary indicator of diabetes. When a person fasts (doesn't eat) for eight hours prior to taking a blood sugar test, his/her glucose level should be below 100 mg/dL. A person is considered at risk for diabetes, but is not diagnosed as diabetic, when fasting glucose levels are between 100 and 125. If the level is above 125, the person is considered to have diabetes. The following table shows the ages and glucose levels of a group of diabetes study participants.

Diabetes Study Results

Age Group	<100 mg/dL	100-125 mg/dL	>125	Total
18-25	9	22	17	48
26-35	16	48	34	98
36-45	19	35	40	94
Older than 45	12	27	21	60
Total	56	132	112	300

6. According to the data, which age group had the smallest percentage of people with a healthy blood sugar level?

   A) 18-25

   B) 26-35

   C) 36-45

   D) Older than 45

7. Based on the table, if a single participant is selected at random from all the participants, what is the probability that he or she will be at risk for diabetes and be at least 36 years old?

   A) $\dfrac{7}{60}$

   B) $\dfrac{11}{25}$

   C) $\dfrac{31}{77}$

   D) $\dfrac{31}{150}$

8. On a used vehicle lot, 50% of the vehicles are cars, $\frac{3}{4}$ of which have automatic transmissions. Of the cars with automatic transmissions, $\frac{1}{3}$ have leather interiors. If a vehicle is chosen from the lot at random, what is the probability that it will be a car with an automatic transmission and a leather interior?

A) $\frac{1}{8}$

B) $\frac{1}{6}$

C) $\frac{1}{4}$

D) $\frac{1}{3}$

9. A United States senator is running for reelection and wants to know what the most important issue to the greatest number of people who might vote for him is. If his campaign hires a company to collect data by conducting a survey, which of the following samples should the company use?

A) United States voters

B) United States citizens

C) Voters in the senator's district

D) Citizens in the senator's district

10. An electronics manufacturer wants to know if customers would be interested in a detachable keyboard for their tablets and if so, what the most important features would be. The manufacturer partners with an electronics store to include copies of the survey with every purchase at that store for one week. Which of the following best explains why this random sample is unlikely to be a good representative sample of tablet owners' preferences for a detachable keyboard?

A) One week is likely not enough time to get a large enough sample.

B) Most people won't bother to send in the survey, which is likely to skew the results.

C) There is no way to verify whether the responders to the survey actually own a tablet.

D) The survey is biased because it was conducted through an electronics store, not the general population.

Reduction of Debt Schedule

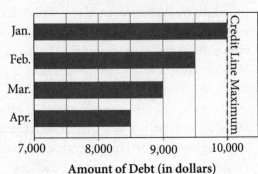

Amount of Debt (in dollars)

Final Trivia Round

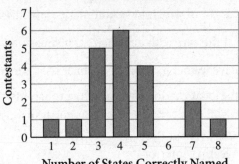

Number of States Correctly Named

11. A credit score is a number used by financial institutions to determine a person's financial health. One of the factors that affects a person's credit score is the percentage of credit available that he or she is currently utilizing. For example, a person with a credit line of $1,000 who has debt of $900 is utilizing 90% of his or her available credit. Ideally, a person should use no more than 25% of available credit. Charlie has been trying to pay down his debt to increase his credit score. Suppose Charlie has a credit line of $10,000. The graph above shows the amount of debt he is currently carrying on that credit line each month. If he continues to pay down this debt at the same rate, how many months from when Charlie reached his credit line maximum will it take him to reach 25% utilization?

A) 8

B) 15

C) 20

D) 24

12. In the final round of a trivia competition, contestants were asked to name as many states that begin with the letter M as they could in 15 seconds. The bar graph shows the number of states the contestants were able to name. How many contestants participated in the final round of this competition?

A) 6

B) 8

C) 14

D) 20

Appliance Sales

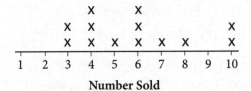

Number Sold

13. An appliance salesman sets a goal to sell an average of 6 appliances per day for the first two weeks of his new job. The dot plot shows the number he sold each day during the first 13 days. What is the minimum number of appliances he must sell on the 14th day in order to reach his goal?

A) 5

B) 6

C) 7

D) 8

14. Muscles, a membership-only gym, is hoping to open a new branch in a small city in Pennsylvania that currently has no fitness centers. According to their research, approximately 12,600 residents live within driving distance of the gym. Muscles sends out surveys to a sample of 300 randomly selected residents in this area (all of whom respond) and finds that 40 residents say they would visit a gym if one was located in their area. Based on past survey research, Muscles estimates that approximately 30% of these respondents would actually join the gym if they opened one in the area. Based on this information and the results of the sample survey, about how many residents should Muscles expect to join its new branch?

A) 134

B) 504

C) 1,680

D) 3,780

Quarterly Profits

	Branch A	Branch B	Branch C	Branch D
Q1	4.1	7.4	8.0	5.4
Q2	3.6	5.2	3.7	6.2
Q3	5.0	4.5	4.9	4.8
Q4	4.9	6.3	5.9	5.6
$\bar{x}$	4.4	5.85	5.625	5.5
s	0.67	1.27	1.82	0.58

15. A company affected by a downturn in the economy decides to close one of its four branches. The table shows each branch's quarterly profits in millions of dollars for 2014, along with the mean ($\bar{x}$) and the standard deviation (s) of the data. The accounting department recommends that the company's Board of Directors close either the store with the lowest average quarterly profits or the store that performs the least consistently. According to the data in the table, which branches will the accounting department recommend for closure to the board?

A) Branches A or C

B) Branches A or D

C) Branches B or C

D) Branches B or D

Country Music Festival Attendees

	Attendees
Entertainer A (Day 1)	1,280
Entertainer B (Day 2)	1,120
Entertainer C (Day 3)	1,600

16. Three well-known entertainers performed at a country music festival, one on each day. Tickets sold were valid for the full three-day period, and ticket holders were permitted to enter and leave as desired. The table above shows the number of people who attended each day of the festival. The host of the festival wants to know which performer was the most popular. If the host defines a performer's popularity rating as the ratio of the number of attendees on that performer's day to the combined number of attendees across all three days, then what was the most popular performer's popularity rating?

Questions 17 and 18 refer to the following information.

When people sleep, they experience various types of brain activity. Scientists have classified these types of activity into four sleep stages: 1, 2, 3, and 4 (also known as REM). Stage 3 is the only stage considered to be deep sleep. A person goes to a sleep clinic to have his/her sleeping brainwaves analyzed. A technician monitored the person's brainwaves in 15-minute intervals, for 8 continuous hours, and categorized them into one of the four stages. The bar graph below shows the results of the one-night study.

8-Hour Sleep Study Results

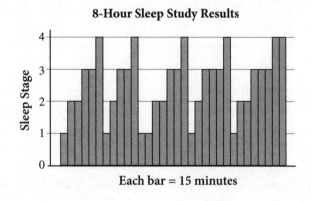

Each bar = 15 minutes

17. Based on the graph, how many minutes did the patient spend in non-deep sleep over the course of the entire night?

18. If one 15-minute time period is chosen at random, what is the probability that the patient was in deep sleep during that time?

Questions 19 and 20 refer to the following information.
The following table shows the number of houses in a development. The table categorizes the houses by type (single-family or townhouse) and by the number of bedrooms.

Development Houses

	2 Br	3 Br	4 Br	Total
Single-Family	5	19	34	58
Townhouse	24	42	30	96
Total	29	61	64	154

19. The homeowner's association partners with a local daycare center. The HOA has agreed to allow the daycare center to advertise in the development using flyers. In general, families with children typically reside in single-family homes or townhouses. These dwellings usually have 3 or more bedrooms. The daycare center has a limited budget and plans to concentrate its marketing efforts on only those homes and townhouses that have 3 or more bedrooms. What percent of the houses in the development should receive the flyer? Round to the nearest whole percent and ignore the percent sign when entering your answer.

20. In addition to sending out flyers, the daycare center decides to send out invitations for a free day of daycare, but determines that it would be too expensive to do this for all of the family residences in the development. Instead, it decides to market this benefit only to the two categories in the table with the most houses. If a house that already received a flyer is chosen at random to receive the second stage of the marketing, what is the probability that the house belongs to one of these two groups? Enter your answer as a decimal.

Questions 21 and 22 refer to the following information.

As part of its market research, a company sent out a survey to see how much consumers would be willing to pay for a certain product. The survey distinguished between a store brand version of the product and a brand name version, and people participating in the survey only received questions about one of the versions. A summary of the survey results is shown in the following bar graph.

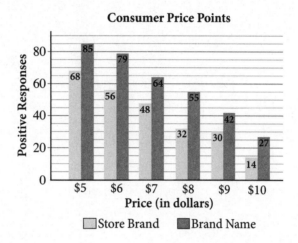

21. On average, how many more cents are consumers willing to pay for the brand name version of the product than the store brand version? Round your answer to the nearest cent.

22. If a consumer is chosen at random from all of the respondents, what is the probability that the consumer is willing to pay at least $8 for the product?

UNIT THREE

Passport to Advanced Math

BY THE END OF THIS UNIT, YOU WILL BE ABLE TO:

1. Simplify, solve, and rewrite equations involving polynomials, radicals, and exponents

2. Solve functions questions graphically and algebraically

3. Combine multiple functions

4. Solve quadratic equations with and without a calculator

5. Connect quadratic equations to features of a parabola

CHAPTER 6

Exponents, Radicals, Polynomials, and Rational Expressions

CHAPTER OBJECTIVES

By the end of this chapter, you will be able to:

1. Simplify, rewrite, and solve equations involving radicals and/or exponents

2. Perform arithmetic operations on polynomials

3. Simplify polynomial expressions

SMARTPOINTS

Point Value	SmartPoint Category
70 Points	Exponents

INTRODUCTION TO EXPONENTS AND RADICALS

We often turn to our calculators to solve difficult radical and exponent problems, especially in math-intensive classes. However, being too calculator dependent can cost you time and points on the SAT. Further, on the SAT, many radical and exponent problems are structured in such a way that your calculator can't help you, even if it is allowed.

This chapter will review many algebraic and arithmetic rules that you may have learned at some point but likely haven't used in a while. This chapter will reacquaint you with the formulas and procedures you'll need to simplify even the toughest expressions and equations on the SAT. We'll start with exponents.

Questions involving exponents often look intimidating, but when you know the rules governing them, you'll see that there are plenty of shortcuts. First, it's important to understand the anatomy of a term with an exponent. This term is comprised of two pieces: a base and an exponent (also called a power). The base is the number in larger type and is the value being multiplied by itself. The exponent, written in superscript, shows you how many times to multiply the base by itself.

$$Base \Rightarrow 3^4 \Leftarrow Exponent \text{ is the same as } 3 \times 3 \times 3 \times 3$$

The following table lists the rules you'll need to master to handle any exponent question you'll see on the SAT.

Rule	Example
When multiplying two terms with the same base, add the exponents.	$a^b \times a^c = a^{(b+c)} \rightarrow 4^2 \times 4^3 = 4^{2+3} = 4^5$
When dividing two terms with the same base, subtract the exponents.	$\dfrac{a^b}{a^c} = a^{(b-c)} \rightarrow \dfrac{4^3}{4^2} = 4^{3-2} = 4^1$
When raising a power to another power, multiply the exponents.	$(a^b)^c = a^{(bc)} \rightarrow (4^3)^2 = 4^{3 \times 2} = 4^6$; $(2x^2)^3 = 2^{1 \times 3} x^{2 \times 3} = 8x^6$
When raising a product to a power, apply the power to all factors in the product.	$(ab)^c = a^c \times b^c \rightarrow (2m)^3 = 2^3 \times m^3 = 8m^3$
Any term raised to the zero power equals 1.	$a^0 = 1 \rightarrow 4^0 = 1$
A base raised to a negative exponent can be rewritten as the reciprocal raised to the positive of the original exponent.	$a^{-b} = \dfrac{1}{a^b}$; $\dfrac{1}{a^{-b}} = a^b \rightarrow 4^{-2} = \dfrac{1}{4^2}$; $\dfrac{1}{4^{-2}} = 4^2$

Different things happen to different kinds of numbers when they are raised to powers greater than 1. Take a look at the following number line and table for a summary.

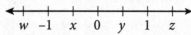

Quantity	Even Exponent Result	Odd Exponent Result	Example
w	positive, absolute value increases	negative, absolute value increases	$(-5)^2 = 25; (-5)^3 = -125$
-1	always 1	always -1	n/a
x	positive, absolute value decreases	negative, absolute value decreases	$\left(-\dfrac{1}{2}\right)^2 = \dfrac{1}{4}$; $\left(-\dfrac{1}{2}\right)^3 = -\dfrac{1}{8}$
0	always 0	always 0	n/a
y	positive, absolute value decreases	positive, absolute value decreases	$\left(\dfrac{1}{4}\right)^2 = \dfrac{1}{16}$; $\left(\dfrac{1}{4}\right)^3 = \dfrac{1}{64}$
1	always 1	always 1	n/a
z	positive, absolute value increases	positive, absolute value increases	$3^2 = 9; 3^3 = 27$

1. Which of the following expressions is equal to $\dfrac{z^{570} - z^{480}}{2z^{30}}$?

   A) $\dfrac{z^{540} - z^{450}}{2}$

   B) $\dfrac{z^{60}}{2}$

   C) z^{30}

   D) $\dfrac{z^{19} - z^{16}}{2}$

You might be tempted to try Picking Numbers to handle this question. However, if you try to plug in a number such as 2 for z, you'll quickly run into a problem, as most graphing calculators cannot handle numbers that large (2^{570} is over 150 places long and would not fit on a TI-84 calculator screen).

Instead, work through the Kaplan Method for Math and your knowledge of exponent rules to solve this question step-by-step. The following table shows Kaplan's strategic thinking on the left, along with suggested math scratchwork on the right.

Strategic Thinking	Math Scratchwork
Step 1: Read the question, identifying and organizing important information as you go *What do you need to find?* You need the simplified form of the expression.	
Step 2: Choose the best strategy to answer the question Exponent rules will help you. Be mindful that because the two z terms in the numerator have different exponents and are being subtracted, you cannot combine them into one term. Break the fraction into two pieces before applying exponent rules. Because your initial answer doesn't match any of the answer choices, you'll need to combine the two fractions back into one to reveal the correct answer.	$$\frac{z^{570} - z^{480}}{2z^{30}} = \frac{z^{570}}{2z^{30}} - \frac{z^{480}}{2z^{30}}$$ $$\frac{z^{570}}{2z^{30}} - \frac{z^{480}}{2z^{30}} = \frac{z^{570-30}}{2} - \frac{z^{480-30}}{2}$$ $$\frac{z^{540}}{2} - \frac{z^{450}}{2} = \frac{z^{540} - z^{450}}{2}$$
Step 3: Check that you answered the *right* question You've simplified as much as possible, so you're done. The correct choice is (A).	

2. Simplify the expression $2(-4j^3k^{-4})^{-3}$.

   A) $-\dfrac{k^{12}}{512j^9}$

   B) $-\dfrac{k^{12}}{32j^9}$

   C) $-\dfrac{j^9}{32k^{12}}$

   D) $-\dfrac{k^{12}}{128j^9}$

Use the Kaplan Method for Math to solve this question, working through it step-by-step. The following table shows Kaplan's strategic thinking on the left, along with suggested math scratchwork on the right.

Strategic Thinking	Math Scratchwork
Step 1: Read the question, identifying and organizing important information as you go You're asked to simplify the given expression.	
Step 2: Choose the best strategy to answer the question Use your exponent rules to quickly find the answer. Move the expression in parentheses to the denominator to make the exponent outside the parentheses positive. Once you've moved the parenthetical expression, distribute the exponent to each term it contains. You're not done yet. Look for terms you can cancel, and eliminate any remaining negative exponents by appropriately moving their respective terms.	$2(-4j^3k^{-4})^{-3}$ $\dfrac{2}{(-4j^3k^{-4})^3}$ $-\dfrac{2}{64j^9k^{-12}}$ $-\dfrac{k^{12}}{32j^9}$
Step 3: Check that you answered the *right* question Choice (B) matches your simplified expression.	

3. What is the value of $\dfrac{3^5 \times 27^3}{81^3}$?

Work through the Kaplan Method for Math step-by-step to solve this question. The following table shows Kaplan's strategic thinking on the left, along with suggested math scratchwork on the right.

Strategic Thinking	Math Scratchwork
Step 1: Read the question, identifying and organizing important information as you go You're asked to find the value of the expression presented, which means you'll need to simplify it.	
Step 2: Choose the best strategy to answer the question Simplify the expression using exponent rules. You can't combine the bases or the exponents of the expression as written. However, $27 = 3^3$ and $81 = 3^4$, so rewrite the numerator and denominator to reflect these relationships. Add the exponents of the numbers in the numerator. Once finished, subtract the exponent of the number in the denominator.	$\dfrac{3^5 \times 27^3}{81^3}$ $\dfrac{3^5 \times (3^3)^3}{(3^4)^3} = \dfrac{3^5 \times 3^9}{3^{12}} = \dfrac{3^{14}}{3^{12}} = 3^2$
Step 3: Check that you answered the *right* question After simplification is complete, you'll get 9 as the correct answer.	9

✔ Note

A calculator could probably handle numbers the size of those in the previous question, but what if the question is in the non-calculator section? Knowing the exponent rules for Test Day is critical.

RADICALS

A radical is essentially a fractional exponent. You can think of addition and subtraction (and likewise multiplication and division) as opposites, and an exponent and radical are another opposite pair. Whenever you raise a term to the nth power, taking the nth root will return the original term. For instance, three to the fourth power is $3^4 = 3 \times 3 \times 3 \times 3 = 81$; take the fourth root of 81 (that is, determine the number that can be multiplied by itself four times to get 81) to get the original term: $\sqrt[4]{81} = \sqrt[4]{3 \times 3 \times 3 \times 3} = 3$.

Radicals can also be intimidating at first, but remembering the basic rules for radicals can make them much easier to tackle. The following table contains all the formulas you'll need to know to achieve "radical" success on the SAT!

Rule	Example
When a fraction is under a radical, you can rewrite it with two radicals: one containing the numerator and the other containing the denominator.	$\sqrt{\dfrac{a}{b}} = \dfrac{\sqrt{a}}{\sqrt{b}} \rightarrow \sqrt{\dfrac{4}{9}} = \dfrac{\sqrt{4}}{\sqrt{9}} = \dfrac{2}{3}$
Two factors under a single radical can be rewritten as separate radicals multiplied together.	$\sqrt{ab} = \sqrt{a} \times \sqrt{b} \rightarrow \sqrt{75} = \sqrt{25} \times \sqrt{3} = 5\sqrt{3}$
A radical can be rewritten using a fractional exponent.	$\sqrt{a} = a^{\frac{1}{2}}, \sqrt[3]{a} = a^{\frac{1}{3}} \rightarrow \sqrt{289} = 289^{\frac{1}{2}}$
When you have a fractional exponent, the numerator is the power to which the base is raised, and the denominator is the root to be taken.	$a^{\frac{b}{c}} = \sqrt[c]{a^b} \rightarrow 5^{\frac{2}{3}} = \sqrt[3]{5^2}$
When a number is squared, the original number can be positive or negative, but the square root of a number can only be positive.	If $a^2 = 81$, then $a = \pm 9$, BUT $\sqrt{81} = 9$ *only*

✔ Note

Note the difference between the printed square root sign and taking the square root yourself as you solve an equation. By definition, when printed, the square root of a number must be positive, but when you take the square root to solve for a variable, you will have two solutions: one positive, and one negative. For instance, by definition $\sqrt{4} = 2$. However, if you are solving $x^2 = 4$, x will have two solutions, so $x = \pm 2$.

Fractions in simplest form will never contain radicals in their denominators, but it's sometimes better to keep them through intermediate steps to make your math easier (and sometimes the radical is eliminated along the way). Once all manipulations are complete, the fraction can be rationalized to remove a remaining radical from the denominator by multiplying both the numerator and denominator by that same radical.

1. Original Fraction	2. Rationalization	3. Intermediate Math	4. Resulting Fraction
$\dfrac{x}{\sqrt{5}}$	$\dfrac{x}{\sqrt{5}} \times \dfrac{\sqrt{5}}{\sqrt{5}}$	$\dfrac{x\sqrt{5}}{\sqrt{5 \times 5}} = \dfrac{x\sqrt{5}}{\sqrt{25}} = \dfrac{x\sqrt{5}}{5}$	$\dfrac{x\sqrt{5}}{5}$
$\dfrac{14}{\sqrt{x^2 + 2}}$	$\dfrac{14}{\sqrt{x^2 + 2}} \times \dfrac{\sqrt{x^2 + 2}}{\sqrt{x^2 + 2}}$	$\dfrac{14\sqrt{x^2 + 2}}{\sqrt{(x^2 + 2)(x^2 + 2)}}$ $= \dfrac{14\sqrt{x^2 + 2}}{\sqrt{(x^2 + 2)^2}}$	$\dfrac{14\sqrt{x^2 + 2}}{x^2 + 2}$

Sometimes you'll have an expression such as $2 + \sqrt{5}$ as a denominator. To rationalize this, multiply by its conjugate (found by negating the second term; in this case, the conjugate is $2 - \sqrt{5}$).

As a rule of thumb, you likely won't see a radical in the denominator of an SAT question's answer choice, so you'll need to be comfortable with rationalizing and either eliminating them or moving them to the numerator.

✔ Note

When you rationalize a denominator, you are not changing the value of the expression; you're only changing the expression's appearance. Notice that in each case, you're multiplying by 1 (the multiplicative identity), because the numerator and the denominator of the fraction are the same.

Ready to take on a test-like question that involves radicals? Take a look at the following:

4. If $-1 < x < 0$ and a is a negative integer, then which of the following must be false?

   A) $\sqrt{ax} = ax$

   B) $\sqrt{ax} < ax$

   C) $\left|x^3\right| > |x|$

   D) x^2 and x have opposite signs

There's no scratchwork for this question, but Kaplan's strategic thinking follows. Follow along as we reason through the question to get the correct answer.

Strategic Thinking
Step 1: Read the question, identifying and organizing important information as you go
You need to identify the statement that is always false.
Step 2: Choose the best strategy to answer the question
Because you're looking for the statement that is false for all values of a and x, all you need is one example of a statement being true to eliminate an answer choice. Start with the statements that appear easiest to verify first; D and C look pretty manageable. The square of a negative fraction is always positive, so D is always true; eliminate it. As you raise a negative fraction to higher powers, the absolute value of the result will decrease. This contradicts C regardless of the negative fraction you pick, so it is always false.
Step 3: Check that you answered the *right* question
Choice (C) is the only statement that is always false and is, therefore, correct.

✔ Note

Look at the Answers & Explanations for this chapter to see examples that confirm A and B are incorrect. Remember, you don't have to verify every answer choice unless you're unsure of the one you selected.

5. Which of the following represents $\dfrac{\sqrt[6]{x^{10}y^{12}}}{\sqrt[3]{x^5 y^6}}$ written in simplest form?

    A) 1

    B) 2

    C) $x^2 y^3 \sqrt{x}$

    D) $xy^2 \sqrt[3]{x^2}$

Work through the Kaplan Method for Math step-by-step to solve this question. The following table shows Kaplan's strategic thinking on the left, along with suggested math scratchwork on the right.

Strategic Thinking	Math Scratchwork
Step 1: Read the question, identifying and organizing important information as you go You must simplify the given expression.	
Step 2: Choose the best strategy to answer the question Attempting to combine the radicals as written is incorrect and will lead you to a trap answer. Rewrite each variable with a fractional exponent instead. When simplifying fractional exponents, remember "power over root." Once you have simplified, subtract the exponents for the x terms, and then repeat for the y terms.	$\dfrac{\sqrt[6]{x^{10}y^{12}}}{\sqrt[3]{x^5 y^6}} = \dfrac{x^{\frac{10}{6}} y^{\frac{12}{6}}}{x^{\frac{5}{3}} y^{\frac{6}{3}}}$ $x^{\frac{10}{6}-\frac{5}{3}} y^{\frac{12}{6}-\frac{6}{3}} = x^{\frac{10}{6}-\frac{10}{6}} y^{\frac{12}{6}-\frac{12}{6}}$ $x^0 y^0$
Step 3: Check that you answered the *right* question Any quantity raised to the zero power is equal to 1, which means (A) is correct.	$x^0 y^0 = 1$

POLYNOMIALS

By now you're used to seeing equations, exponents, and variables; another important topic you are sure to see on the SAT is polynomials. A polynomial is an expression comprised of variables, exponents, and coefficients, and the only operations involved are addition, subtraction, multiplication, division (by constant(s) *only*), and non-negative integer exponents. A polynomial can have one or multiple terms. The following table contains examples of polynomial expressions and non-polynomial expressions.

Polynomial	$23x^2$	$\dfrac{x}{5} - 6$	$y^{11} - 2y^6 + \dfrac{2}{3}xy^3 - 4x^2$	47
Not a Polynomial	$\dfrac{10}{z} + 13$	x^3y^{-6}	$x^{\frac{1}{2}}$	$\dfrac{4}{y - 3}$

✔ **Note**

Remember that constants such as 47 are considered polynomials; this is the same as $47x^0$. Also, keep in mind that division by a constant is allowed, but division by a variable is not.

Identifying like terms is an important skill that will serve you well on Test Day. You can combine like terms as you did with linear expressions and equations (x terms with x terms, constants with constants) to simplify. To have like terms, the types of variables present and their exponents must match. For example, $2xy$ and $-4xy$ are like terms; x and y are present in both, and their corresponding exponents are identical. However, $2x^2y$ and $3xy$ are not like terms because the exponents on x do not match. When combining like terms, follow the order of operations as always, being particularly careful when distributing negative signs.

Like terms	$7x, 3x, 5x$	$3, 15, 900$	$xy^2, 7xy^2, -2xy^2$
Not like terms	$3, x, x^2$	$4x, 4y, 4z$	$xy^2, x^{2y}, 2xy$

A polynomial can be named based on its **degree**. For a single-variable polynomial, the degree is the highest power on the variable. For example, the degree of $3x^4 - 2x^3 + x^2 - 5x + 2$ is 4 because the highest power of x is 4. For a multi-variable polynomial, the degree is the highest sum of the exponents on any one term. For example, the degree of $3x^2y^2 - 5x^2y + x^3$ is 4 because the sum of the exponents in the term $3x^2y^2$ equals 4.

On Test Day you might be asked about the nature of the **zeros** or **roots** of a polynomial. Simply put, zeros are the x-intercepts of a polynomial's graph, which can be found by setting each factor of the polynomial equal to 0. For example, in the polynomial equation $y = (x + 6)(x - 2)^2$, you would have three equations: $x + 6 = 0$, $x - 2 = 0$, and $x - 2 = 0$ (because $x - 2$ is squared, that binomial appears twice in the equation). Solving for x in each yields -6, 2, and 2; we say that the equation has two zeros: -6 and 2. Zeros can have varying levels of **multiplicity**, which is the number of times that a factor appears in the polynomial equation. In the example above, $x + 6$ appears once in the equation, so its corresponding zero (-6) is called a **simple zero**. Because $x - 2$ appears twice in the equation, its corresponding zero (2) is called a **double zero**.

You can recognize the multiplicity of a zero from the polynomial's graph as well. Below is the graph of $y = (x + 6)(x - 2)^2$.

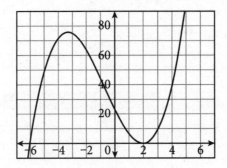

When a polynomial has a simple zero (multiplicity 1) or any zero with an odd multiplicity, its graph will cross the x-axis (as it does at $x = -6$ in the graph above). When a polynomial has a double zero (multiplicity 2) or any zero with an even multiplicity, it just touches the x-axis (as it does at $x = 2$ in the graph above).

Use your knowledge of like terms to solve the following test-like example.

6. If y is a polynomial equation that has a simple zero at $x = 4$ and a triple zero at $x = -4$, which of the following could be the factored form of y?

A) $y = (x + 4)(2x - 8)^3$

B) $y = (x - 4)(3x + 12)$

C) $y = 3(x + 4)(2x - 8)$

D) $y = (2x + 8)^3(x - 4)$

There's no scratchwork for this question, but Kaplan's strategic thinking follows. Follow along as we reason through the question to get the correct answer.

Strategic Thinking
Step 1: Read the question, identifying and organizing important information as you go
You need to determine which equation could be the factored form of the equation that contains the zeros described.
Step 2: Choose the best strategy to answer the question
Adjectives such as "simple" and "triple" indicate how many times a zero's corresponding binomial is repeated in its polynomial equation. This means that you need one binomial raised to the first power and one raised to the third. You can eliminate B and C, both of which lack the third power exponent. The remaining answer choices each contain two binomial expressions: one with an exponent of 1 (remember, if no exponent is written, it is assumed to be 1) and one with an exponent of 3. Quick mental math reveals that both have 4 and −4 as zeros. You need the equation that has the 3 exponent on the binomial that gives $x = -4$ and the 1 exponent on the binomial that gives $x = 4$. Only (D) meets this requirement.
Step 3: Check that you answered the *right* question
Choice (D) is the only answer choice that satisfies the criteria in the question.

Adding and subtracting polynomials are straightforward operations, but what about multiplying and dividing them? These operations are a little tougher but (fortunately) are far from impossible.

Multiplying polynomials is just like multiplying ordinary numbers except you want to pay special attention to distribution and combining like terms. Take the expression $(3x^3 + 5x)(2x^2 + x - 17)$ as an example. All you need to do is distribute both terms in the first set of parentheses to each term in the second set. Distribute the $3x^3$ first, then repeat with $5x$:

The following table shows the product of each step.

1	2	3
$3x^3 \cdot 2x^2 = 6x^5$	$3x^3 \cdot x = 3x^4$	$3x^3 \cdot -17 = -51x^3$
4	**5**	**6**
$5x \cdot 2x^2 = 10x^3$	$5x \cdot x = 5x^2$	$5x \cdot -17 = -85x$

All that's left to do now is write out the expression and combine any like terms.

$$6x^5 + 3x^4 - \mathbf{51x^3} + \mathbf{10x^3} + 5x^2 - 85x$$

$$6x^5 + 3x^4 - 41x^3 + 5x^2 - 85x$$

RATIONAL EXPRESSIONS

A rational expression is simply a ratio (or fraction) of polynomials. In other words, it is a fraction with a polynomial as the numerator and another polynomial as the denominator. The rules that govern fractions and polynomials also govern rational expressions, so if you know these well, you'll be in good shape when you encounter one on Test Day.

There are a few important tidbits to remember about rational expressions; these are summarized here. They are also true for rational equations.

- For an expression to be rational, the numerator and denominator must both be polynomials.

- Like polynomials, rational expressions are also designated certain degrees based on the term with the highest variable exponent sum. For instance, the expression $\dfrac{1-2x}{3x^2+3}$ has a first-degree numerator and a second-degree denominator.

- Because rational expressions by definition can have polynomial denominators, they will often be undefined for certain values. For example, the expression $\dfrac{x-4}{x+2}$ is defined for all values of x except –2. This is because when $x = -2$, the denominator of the expression is 0, which would make the expression undefined.

- Factors in a rational expression can be cancelled when simplifying, but under no circumstances can you do the same with individual terms. Consider, for instance, the expression $\dfrac{x^2-x-6}{x^2+5x+6}$.

  Many students will attempt to cancel the x^2, x, and 6 terms to give $\dfrac{1-1-1}{1+5+1} = \dfrac{-1}{7}$, which is *never* correct. Don't even think about trying this on Test Day.

- Like fractions, rational expressions can be proper or improper. A proper rational expression has a lower-degree numerator than denominator e.g., $\left(\dfrac{1-x}{x^2+3}\right)$, and an improper one has a higher-degree numerator than denominator $\left(\text{e.g., } \dfrac{x^2+3}{1-x}\right)$. The latter can be simplified using polynomial long division.

✔ Note

For those who are curious, the correct way to simplify $\dfrac{x^2-x-6}{x^2+5x+6}$ is to factor, which you'll learn about in chapter 8. For now, know that this equals $\dfrac{(x+2)(x-3)}{(x+2)(x+3)}$. Cancel the $x+2$ factors to get $\dfrac{(x-3)}{(x+3)}$.

---

7. Which of the following is equal to the expression $\dfrac{27m^4n^3+6mn^2}{18m^2n+81m^5n^2}$, given $m \neq 0$ and $n \neq 0$?

A) $\dfrac{n^2}{3m^2}$

B) $\dfrac{3}{2}m^2n^2+\dfrac{2}{27m^4}$

C) $\dfrac{n}{3m}$

D) $\dfrac{m}{3n}$

Work through the Kaplan Method for Math step-by-step to solve this question. The following table shows Kaplan's strategic thinking on the left, along with suggested math scratchwork on the right.

Strategic Thinking	Math Scratchwork
Step 1: Read the question, identifying and organizing important information as you go You're asked to identify the expression that equals the one given in the question.	
Step 2: Choose the best strategy to answer the question Start by looking for ways to simplify the expression; factoring should come to mind. You can factor a number and at least one m and one n out of both the numerator and denominator. Several terms cancel each other at this point. Note that the expressions in parentheses are identical by the commutative property of addition, so they can be cancelled. The GCF of the numerator and denominator is $3mn$; factor it out and cancel it to get your final expression.	$\dfrac{27m^4n^3+6mn^2}{18m^2n+81m^5n^2} \rightarrow \dfrac{3mn^2(9m^3n+2)}{9m^2n(2+9m^3n)}$ $\dfrac{3mn^2}{9m^2n} \rightarrow \dfrac{3mn(n)}{3mn(3m)}$ $\dfrac{n}{3m}$
Step 3: Check that you answered the _right_ question You've properly simplified the expression, so your work for this question is complete. Choice (C) is correct.	$\dfrac{n}{3m}$

You'll notice that the question indicated $m \neq 0$ and $n \neq 0$. This is because either of these values will create a denominator of 0, which makes the entire expression undefined. This becomes particularly important when dealing with rational equations, as they can have what are called **extraneous solutions**. Extraneous solutions are numbers that are found algebraically but do not solve the

original equation (such as when they generate 0 in a denominator). Plug the solutions that you find back into the original equation to make sure that the denominator does not become 0.

> **✔ Note**
>
> Extraneous solutions are solutions that cause the entire expression to become undefined. Look out for zeros in denominators and negatives under square roots.

MODELING REAL-WORLD APPLICATIONS USING POLYNOMIAL, RADICAL, AND RATIONAL EQUATIONS

Sometimes the test writers want to test your simplifying prowess by converting an expression into a "useful" form, as standard form is not always the most practical for use.

Let's say you and your friends want to enjoy a brisk fall day by going apple picking. To go apple picking, you must rent a basket for $20, and you'll be charged an additional $0.35 for each apple you pick. On top of that, a 9% sales tax will be added to your final bill. We could represent this scenario with the following equation:

$$c = 1.09 \times (0.35a + 20)$$

In this situation, c is the cost of your apple-picking experience and a is the number of apples you pick. You'll notice the 1.09 out in front of the parentheses ensures that sales tax is applied to your entire purchase, not just the apples or the rental. Now suppose you're asked to determine the true price of each additional apple; that is, how much more money will one extra apple cost you? We can't get that by just glancing at the equation, but distributing the 1.09 will help. When we do this, we arrive at a different equation for the same apple-picking experience:

$$c = 0.3815a + 21.8$$

Although this equation isn't as elegant or intuitive as our initial equation, it is much more useful for answering the question at hand. Now we can see how sales tax affects our fixed costs (basket rental) and our variable costs (each additional apple). The only term that matters here is the one that depends on the number of apples: Each additional apple will cost about $0.38 when tax is included.

Try the more challenging example that follows.

8. Laura and Donnie are researching mortgage options for a home purchase. They plan to apply for a 30-year $300,000 loan with a 3.375% annual interest rate, which they will pay off in monthly installments. They can calculate their monthly payment (m) using the formula $m = \dfrac{Pr}{1-(1+r)^{-N}}$, where P is the initial principal balance, r is the monthly interest rate expressed as a decimal, and N is the number of monthly payments that will be made over the life of the mortgage. How much will Laura and Donnie pay in mortgage payments over a six-month period? Round your answer to the nearest dollar.

Use the Kaplan Method for Math to solve this question, working through it step-by-step. The table below shows Kaplan's strategic thinking on the left, along with suggested math scratchwork on the right.

Strategic Thinking	Math Scratchwork
Step 1: Read the question, identifying and organizing important information as you go *What are you being asked to do here?* You're asked to find the amount of money Laura and Donnie will pay over six months for their mortgage.	
Step 2: Choose the best strategy to answer the question *This is a wordy question. How can you break it apart?* Use the Kaplan Strategy for Translating English into Math to wade through the words. *What should be done first?* The variables are already defined, and you're given an equation that relates them. Identify the values of the variables, and then calculate the monthly payment at 3.375% annual interest. Decimals are truncated in the scratchwork column for brevity, but don't round until you arrive at your final answer. Make sure you divide 0.03375 by 12 to convert it to the monthly interest rate. *Are you finished?* Not yet; the question asks for the amount paid over six months, not one month. Multiply m by 6 to get your final answer.	initial annual rate: 0.03375 $P = 300{,}000$ $r = \dfrac{0.03375}{12} = 0.0028125$ $N = 12 \times 30 = 360$ $m = \dfrac{Pr}{1-(1+r)^{-N}}$ $m = \dfrac{300000 \times 0.0028125}{1-(1+0.0028125)^{-360}}$ $m = \dfrac{843.75}{1-(1.0028125)^{-360}}$ $m = \dfrac{843.75}{0.6362}$ $m = 1{,}326.29$ $1{,}326.2886 \times 6 = 7{,}957.7318$
Step 3: Check that you answered the *right* question *How much will have been paid in mortgage costs after six months?* Round to get 7958.	7958

✔ **Note**

Be particularly careful when calculating the monthly payments here; you're given an annual interest rate, but r is a monthly rate. Manipulate the annual rate accordingly.

Way to go! You just answered a question involving a real-life example of an exponential equation..

SOLVING A FORMULA OR EQUATION FOR A GIVEN VARIABLE

If you've ever taken a chemistry or physics course, you probably noticed that many real-world situations can't be represented by beautiful linear equations. There are frequently radicals, exponents, and fractions galore. Furthermore, these equations can seem to lack a logical arrangement. For example, the root-mean-square velocity for particles in a gas can be described by the following equation:

$$v = \sqrt{\frac{3kT}{m}}$$

In this equation, v represents the root-mean-square velocity, k is the Boltzmann constant, T is the temperature in degrees Kelvin, and m is the mass of one molecule of the gas. It's a great equation if you have k, T, and m and are looking for v. However, if you're looking for a different quantity, having that unknown buried among others (and under a radical to boot) can be unnerving, but unearthing it is easier than it appears. Let's say we're given v, k, and m but need to find T. First, square both sides to eliminate the radical to yield $v^2 = \frac{3kT}{m}$. Next, isolate T by multiplying both sides by m and dividing by $3k$: $\frac{mv^2}{3k} = T$.

At this point, you can plug in the values of m, v, and k to solve for T. Sometimes the SAT will have you do just that: Solve for the numerical value of a variable of interest. In other situations, you'll need to rearrange an equation so that a different variable is isolated. The same rules of algebra you've used all along apply. The difference: You're manipulating solely variables.

Now you'll have a chance to try a few more test-like questions. Some guidance is provided, but you'll need to fill in the missing parts of explanations or the step-by-step math to get to the correct answer. Don't worry—after going through the examples at the beginning of this chapter, these questions should be completely doable. If you're still struggling, review the worked examples in this chapter.

9. Special relativity is a branch of physics that deals with the relationship between space and time. The Lorentz term, a term that relates the change in time, length, and relativistic mass of a moving object, is given by the following formula:

$$\gamma = \frac{1}{\sqrt{1 - \dfrac{v^2}{c^2}}}$$

where v is the relative velocity of the object and c is the speed of light in a vacuum. Which of the following equations correctly represents the relative velocity in terms of the other variables?

A) $v = c\sqrt{\dfrac{1}{\gamma^2} - 1}$

B) $v = c\sqrt{1 - \gamma^2}$

C) $v = c\left(1 - \dfrac{1}{\gamma^2}\right)$

D) $v = c\sqrt{1 - \dfrac{1}{\gamma^2}}$

Use the scaffolding below as your map through the question. Strategic thinking is on the left, and bits of scratchwork are on the right. If you aren't sure where to start, answer the questions in italics, and fill in the blanks in the table as you work from top to bottom.

Strategic Thinking	Math Scratchwork
Step 1: Read the question, identifying and organizing important information as you go *What are you being asked to do here?* You need to identify the expression that equals relative velocity. Translation: solve the given equation for v.	

Strategic Thinking	Math Scratchwork
Step 2: Choose the best strategy to answer the question *There are several variables and weird symbols. How should this be solved?* Don't let the multiple variables intimidate you; just treat them as you would when manipulating a "friendlier" equation. Start by undoing the radical so you can get to what's underneath, and then isolate the correct variable.	$$\gamma = \dfrac{1}{\sqrt{1 - \dfrac{v^2}{c^2}}}$$ _____ = _____ _____ = _____ _____ = _____ _____ = _____ _____ = _____ _____ = _____
Step 3: Check that you answered the *right* question *Did you solve for the right term?* Did you get (D)? If so, you're absolutely correct!	_____

✔ **Note**

Don't panic over the unfamiliarity of the physics terms; just identify what you need to do (in this case, isolate *v* on one side of the equation).

10. Given that g and h are both positive, which of the following is equivalent to the expression $\sqrt[3]{g^6 h^3 - 27 g^4 h^3}$?

    A) $\dfrac{1}{3} gh \sqrt[3]{g^2 - 27}$

    B) $gh \sqrt[3]{g^3 - 27g}$

    C) $g^2 h - 3gh \sqrt[3]{g}$

    D) $g^2 h - 3 \sqrt[3]{g}$

Use the scaffolding that follows as your map through the question. Strategic thinking is on the left, and bits of scratchwork are on the right. If you aren't sure where to start, answer the questions in italics and fill in the blanks in the table as you work from top to bottom.

Strategic Thinking	Math Scratchwork
Step 1: Read the question, identifying and organizing important information as you go *What are you being asked to do here?* You need to simplify the given expression.	
Step 2: Choose the best strategy to answer the question *Can anything be factored out of the radicand?* Identifying the GCF should be your first step. Once this is complete, check to see whether any part of it can be "cube rooted" and placed outside the radical. *Is there any other factoring/simplification that can be done?* Double check to make sure no factoring was missed, and then look for a match in the answer choices. If you can't find one, try rewriting the expression.	GCF: _____ $\sqrt[3]{\underline{\quad}(\underline{\quad}-\underline{\quad})}$ $\underline{\quad}\sqrt[3]{\underline{\quad}(\underline{\quad}-\underline{\quad})}$ $\underline{\quad}\sqrt[3]{\underline{\quad}}-\underline{\quad}$
Step 3: Check that you answered the *right* question *Which choice matches your simplified expression?* If your answer is (B), congrats! You're correct.	_____

11. Human blood contains three primary cell types: red blood cells (RBC), white blood cells (WBC), and platelets. In an adult male, a single microliter (1×10^{-3} milliliters) of blood contains approximately 5.4×10^6 RBC, 7.5×10^3 WBC, and 3.5×10^5 platelets on average. What percentage of an adult male's total blood cell count is comprised of red blood cells?

    A) 1.30%

    B) 6.21%

    C) 60.79%

    D) 93.79%

Use the scaffolding that follows as your map through the question. Strategic thinking is on the left, and bits of scratchwork are on the right. If you aren't sure where to start, answer the questions in italics and fill in the blanks in the table as you work from top to bottom.

Strategic Thinking	Math Scratchwork
Step 1: Read the question, identifying and organizing important information as you go *What is the question asking?* You need to calculate the percent of an adult male's blood that is comprised of red blood cells.	
Step 2: Choose the best strategy to answer the question *Can you set up an equation?* Remember that a percentage is derived from a ratio that compares a partial quantity to a total quantity. Write an equation that compares the RBC count to the total blood cell count and solve. You can save time by using exponent rules instead of punching everything into your calculator. Note that the answer choices are fairly far apart. Compare the numerator and denominator of your simplified expression; you can estimate the resulting quantity and eliminate incorrect answers accordingly. *Am I finished?* Multiply the RBC fraction you found by 100 to convert it to a percent.	RBC % = _____ __+____+__ = _____ = _____ = _____ _____ × 100 = _____ %
Step 3: Check that you answered the *right* question *What percent of an adult male's blood is comprised of red blood cells?* Did you get (D)? If so, you're absolutely correct!	____

✔ Expert Tip

You can do this question almost entirely without a calculator. Just use your exponent and scientific notation expertise.

Now that you've seen the variety of ways in which the SAT can test you on the topics in this chapter, try the following questions to check your understanding. Give yourself 3.5 minutes to tackle the following three questions. Make sure you use the Kaplan Method for Math as often as you can. Remember, you want to emphasize speed and efficiency in addition to simply getting the correct answer.

12. An object launched straight up into the air is said to have parabolic motion (because it goes up, reaches a maximum height, and then comes back down). The height (h) of a projectile at time t is given by the equation $h = \frac{1}{2}at^2 + v_0 t + h_0$, where a is the acceleration due to gravity and v_0 and h_0 are the object's initial velocity and initial height, respectively. Which of the following equations correctly represents the object's acceleration due to gravity in terms of the other variables?

A) $a = \dfrac{h - v_0 t - h_0}{t}$

B) $a = \dfrac{h - v_0 t - h_0}{2t^2}$

C) $a = \dfrac{2(h - v_0 t - h_0)}{t^2}$

D) $a = t\sqrt{2(h - v_0 t - h_0)}$

13. Which of the following expressions is equal to $\dfrac{3 + \sqrt{72}}{3 - \sqrt{72}}$?

A) $\dfrac{9 + 4\sqrt{2}}{-7}$

B) $\dfrac{9 + 2\sqrt{2}}{-7}$

C) $\dfrac{9}{-7}$

D) $1 + \dfrac{4\sqrt{2}}{9}$

14. Car dealerships often require car buyers to provide a down payment (money paid up front), which is a percent of a car's price. The down payment is deducted from the purchase price, and the buyer usually takes out a loan to pay for what is left. Teri is buying a car that costs $19,560. Her monthly car payment is given by $m = \dfrac{Pr}{1 - (1 + r)^{-N}}$, where P is the initial loan balance, r is the monthly interest rate expressed as a decimal, and N is the number of payments to be made over the duration of the loan. If Teri wants to fully pay off the loan in five years at 1.5% annual interest and wishes to have a monthly payment of $200, what percent of the purchase price will she need for her down payment? Round your answer to the nearest whole percent.

Answers and Explanations for this chapter begin on page 616.

EXTRA PRACTICE

1. Which of the following expressions is equivalent to $-x^{\frac{1}{4}}$?

   A) $-\dfrac{1}{4x}$

   B) $-\dfrac{1}{x^4}$

   C) $-\sqrt[4]{x}$

   D) $\dfrac{1}{\sqrt[4]{-x}}$

2. If $\dfrac{7\sqrt{x}}{2} = 14$, what is the value of x?

   A) 2

   B) 4

   C) 16

   D) 49

$$\frac{4x+8y}{24x-12}$$

3. Which of the following is the simplified form of the rational expression above?

   A) $\dfrac{1}{6} - \dfrac{2y}{3}$

   B) $\dfrac{x+2y}{6x-3}$

   C) $\dfrac{x+2y}{2x-1}$

   D) $\dfrac{x+8y}{6x-12}$

4. What is the resulting coefficient of x when $-x + 6$ is multiplied by $2x - 3$?

   A) -15

   B) -2

   C) 9

   D) 15

5. What is the difference when $\dfrac{3x+7}{x-1}$ is subtracted from $\dfrac{8x-5}{x-1}$?

   A) $\dfrac{5x+2}{x-1}$

   B) $\dfrac{5x+2}{2x-1}$

   C) $\dfrac{5x-12}{x-1}$

   D) $\dfrac{-5x+12}{x-1}$

6. If $p(x)$ is a polynomial that has a simple zero at $x = -3$ and a double zero at $x = \dfrac{5}{4}$, which of the following could be the factored form of $p(x)$?

   A) $p(x) = 2(x + 3)(5x - 4)$

   B) $p(x) = (x + 3)(5x - 4)^2$

   C) $p(x) = 2(x + 3)(4x - 5)$

   D) $p(x) = (x + 3)(4x - 5)^2$

$$v = \frac{2\pi r}{T}$$

7. Uniform circular motion is used in physics to describe the motion of an object traveling at a constant speed in a circle. The speed of the object is called tangential velocity, and it can be calculated using the formula above, where r is the radius of the circle and T is the time is takes for the object to make one complete circle, called a period. Which of the following formulas could be used to find the length of one period if you know the tangential velocity and the radius of the circle?

    A) $T = \dfrac{v}{2\pi r}$

    B) $T = \dfrac{2\pi r}{v}$

    C) $T = 2\pi rv$

    D) $T = \dfrac{1}{2\pi rv}$

$$\sqrt{0.75} \times \sqrt{0.8}$$

8. Which of the following has the same value as the expression above?

    A) $\dfrac{3}{5}$

    B) $\dfrac{\sqrt{15}}{5}$

    C) $\sqrt[4]{0.6}$

    D) $\sqrt{1.55}$

9. Which of the following expressions is equivalent to $(27x^6 y^{12})^{\frac{1}{3}}$?

    A) $3x^2 y^4$

    B) $9x^2 y^4$

    C) $\dfrac{27x^6 y^{12}}{3}$

    D) $(27x^6 y^{12})^{-3}$

$$8 + \frac{\sqrt{2x+29}}{3} = 9$$

10. 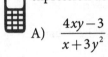 For what value of x is the equation above true?

    A) -10

    B) -2

    C) 19

    D) No solution

$$\frac{12x^3 y^2 - 9x^2 y}{6x^4 y + 18x^3 y^3}$$

11. Which of the following is equivalent to the expression above?

    A) $\dfrac{4xy - 3}{x + 3y^2}$

    B) $\dfrac{3x^2 y - 3xy}{x + 3y^2}$

    C) $\dfrac{4xy - 3}{2x^2 + 6xy^2}$

    D) $\dfrac{4xy - 9}{2x^2 + 18xy^3}$

12. If $30x^3 + 45x^2 - 10x$ is divided by $5x$, what is the resulting coefficient of x?

    A) 6

    B) 9

    C) 25

    D) 40

$$\sqrt{9m^5 n^2 - m^4 n^2}$$

13. Which of the following expressions is equivalent to the expression above, given that m and n are positive?

    A) $3\sqrt{m}$

    B) $3mn$

    C) $3n\sqrt{m}$

    D) $m^2 n\sqrt{9m - 1}$

$$T = 2\pi\sqrt{\dfrac{L}{g}}$$

14. The formula above was created by Italian scientist Galileo Galilei in the early 1600s to demonstrate that the time it takes for a pendulum to complete a swing, called its period (T), can be found using only the length of the pendulum, L, and the force of gravity, g. He proved that the mass of the pendulum did not affect its period. Based on the equation above, which of the following equations could be used to find the length of the pendulum given its period?

A) $L = \dfrac{gT}{2\pi}$

B) $L = \dfrac{gT^2}{4\pi^2}$

C) $L = \dfrac{T^2}{4\pi^2 g}$

D) $L = \dfrac{g}{4\pi^2 T^2}$

15. If $A = 4x^2 + 7x - 1$ and $B = -x^2 - 5x + 3$, then what is $\dfrac{3}{2}A - 2B$?

A) $4x^2 + \dfrac{31}{2}x - \dfrac{9}{2}$

B) $4x^2 + \dfrac{41}{2}x - \dfrac{15}{2}$

C) $8x^2 + \dfrac{31}{2}x - \dfrac{9}{2}$

D) $8x^2 + \dfrac{41}{2}x - \dfrac{15}{2}$

$$\sqrt{2} \times \sqrt[4]{2}$$

16. Which of the following is equivalent to the product given above?

A) $\sqrt[4]{8}$

B) $\sqrt[6]{2}$

C) $\sqrt[8]{2}$

D) $\sqrt[8]{4}$

$$\dfrac{\sqrt[3]{x} \cdot x^{\frac{5}{2}} \cdot x}{\sqrt{x}}$$

17. If x^n is the simplified form of the expression above, what is the value of n?

18. If $12 + \dfrac{3\sqrt{x-5}}{2} = 18$, what is the value of x?

CHAPTER 7

Functions & Function Notation

CHAPTER OBJECTIVES

By the end of this chapter, you will be able to:

1. Use function notation to answer questions containing equations, tables, and/or graphs

2. Interpret functions and functional statements that represent real-world scenarios

3. Combine functions properly using basic operations and compute compositions of functions correctly

4. Determine if a function is increasing, decreasing, or constant and correctly apply transformations to a given function or functions

SMARTPOINTS

Point Value	SmartPoint Category
70 points	Functions

FUNCTIONS & FUNCTION NOTATION

Functions act as rules that transform inputs into outputs, and they differ from equations in that each input must have only one corresponding output. For example, imagine a robot: Every time you give it an apple, it promptly cuts that apple into three slices. The following table summarizes the first few inputs and their corresponding outputs.

Domain x: # apples given to robot	Range $f(x)$: # slices returned by robot
0	0
1	3
2	6
3	9

From the table you see that the output will always be triple the input, and you can express that relationship as the function $f(x) = 3x$ (read "f of x equals three x").

SAT questions, especially those involving real-world situations, might ask you to derive the equation of a function, so you'll need to be familiar with the standard forms. Following, for instance, is the standard form of a linear function:

$$f(x) = kx + f(0)$$

The input, or **domain**, is the value represented by x. Sometimes the domain will be constrained by the question (e.g., x must be an integer). Other times, the domain could be defined by real-world conditions. For example, if x represents the time elapsed since the start of a race, the domain would need to exclude negative numbers. The output, or **range**, is the result of what you plug into the function and is represented by $f(x)$. The initial condition or **y-intercept** is represented by $f(0)$—the value of the function at the very beginning. If you think this looks familiar, you're absolutely right! It's just a dressed-up version of the standard $y = mx + b$ equation you've already seen. Take a look at the following table for a translation:

Linear Function Piece	What It Represents	Slope-Intercept Counterpart
$f(x)$	dependent variable or output	y
k	rate of change, slope	m
$f(0)$	y-intercept or initial quantity in a word problem	b

As you might have guessed, an exponential equation has a standard function notation as well. Here we've used g in place of f for visual clarity. Know that the letter used to represent a function (f, g, h, etc.) is sometimes arbitrarily chosen.

$$g(x) = g(0)(1+r)^x$$

Analogous to the linear standard function form, $g(x)$ has replaced y, and $g(0)$ has replaced $f(0)$. Recognizing that function notation is a variation of something you already know will go a long way toward reducing nerves on Test Day. You should also note that graphing functions is a straight-forward process: In the examples above, just set the side on the right equal to y and enter into your graphing calculator.

> ✔ **Note**
>
> A quick way to determine whether an equation is a function is to conduct the vertical line test: If a vertical line passes through the graph of the equation more than once at any time, the equation is not a function.

Below is an example of a test-like functions question.

1. The cube of x subtracted from the fourth root of the sum of three and the square of the product of two and x is less than $f(x)$. Which of the following correctly depicts the function described?

   A) $f(x) < \sqrt[4]{3+4x^2} - x^3$

   B) $f(x) > x^3 - \sqrt[4]{3+4x^2}$

   C) $f(x) > \sqrt[4]{3+4x^2} - x^3$

   D) $f(x) > \sqrt[4]{3+2x^2} - x^3$

Because there isn't any scratchwork required for a question like this, only the column containing Kaplan's strategic thinking is included. Follow along as we reason our way through this question.

Strategic Thinking
Step 1: Read the question, identifying and organizing important information as you go
The question asks for the function that correctly describes the situation presented.

Strategic Thinking
Step 2: Choose the best strategy to answer the question
This is an exercise in translating English into math, so utilize tactics from that Kaplan Strategy. Take each piece one at a time. "The cube of *x*" becomes x^3. "The fourth root of the sum of three and the square of the product of two and *x*" becomes $\sqrt[4]{3+(2x)^2}$; don't forget the parentheses around 2*x*!
Read carefully when deciding how to combine these two pieces. "The cube of *x*" is being subtracted from "the fourth root . . . ," so the expression should now read $\sqrt[4]{3+(2x)^2} - x^3$. According to the question, this entire quantity is less than *f(x)* (in other words, *f(x)* is greater than . . .). The inequality should read $f(x) > \sqrt[4]{3+(2x)^2} - x^3$.
Your inequality isn't among the answer choices, but don't worry. The $(2x)^2$ can be simplified to $4x^2$; once you make the switch, you'll see a match.
Step 3: Check that you answered the *right* question
Choice (C) is the correct answer.

Once broken into simpler pieces, this function question became much easier. Read on for more information about other ways the SAT can test your knowledge of functions.

GRAPHICAL & TABULAR FUNCTION INTERPRETATION

The ability to interpret the graphs of functions will serve you well on Test Day (as well as in real life . . . even outside of math class!). Better yet, to interpret graphs of functions, you'll need to utilize the same skills you use to interpret "regular" equations on the coordinate plane, so this material shouldn't be completely foreign.

You know from the first part of this chapter that a function is merely a dressed-up equation, so translating from function to "regular" notation or vice versa is a straightforward process. Consider the following brief example.

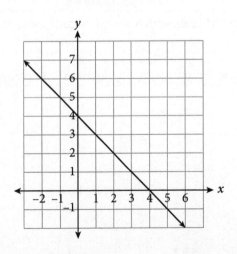

Suppose you're asked to find the value of x for which $f(x) = 6$. Because $f(x)$ represents the output value, or range, translate this as "When does the y value equal 6?" To answer the question, find 6 on the y-axis, then trace over to the function (the line). Read the corresponding x value: It's –2, so when $f(x) = 6$, x must be –2.

The SAT might also present functions in the form of tables. These may or may not have an equation associated with them, but regardless, you'll need to be adept at extracting the information necessary to answer questions. Most of the time the table will have just two columns, one for the domain and another for the range.

✔ **Note**

Remember: A value of $f(x)$ corresponds to a location on the y-axis. A value of x corresponds to a location on the x-axis.

Now try a test-like example.

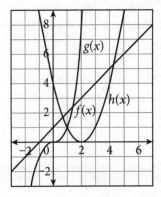

2. In the figure above, what is the value of $h(0) - 3(g(2) - f(2))$?

A) -23

B) -11

C) $-\dfrac{11}{2}$

D) $-\dfrac{3}{2}$

Work through the Kaplan Method for Math step-by-step to solve this question. The following table shows Kaplan's strategic thinking on the left, along with suggested math scratchwork on the right.

Strategic Thinking	Math Scratchwork
Step 1: Read the question, identifying and organizing important information as you go You're asked to determine the value of $h(0) - 3(g(2) - f(2))$. In other words, you need to find the y-value of function h when $x = 0$, the y-value of function g when $x = 2$, and the y-value of function f when $x = 2$. You then need to manipulate them as dictated in the given expression.	

Strategic Thinking	Math Scratchwork
Step 2: Choose the best strategy to answer the question Consider each value in the expression one at a time. Study the graph to determine the value of each function at the specified *x*-values. Plug each value into the original expression, and then follow the order of operations to simplify. Be careful as you do this, as it's easy to make careless mistakes, especially with negative signs.	 $h(O) - 3(g(2) - f(2))$ $4 - 3(8 - 3) = 4 - 3(5) = -11$
Step 3: Check that you answered the *right* question You found that the expression equals −11, which is (B).	

✔ Note

Watch your axis scales; like scatterplot questions, questions involving graphs of functions often contain trap answers for students who misread the axes.

Although this question would have been much simpler if the graph had labeled the points or given you an equation to plug values into, it wouldn't be testing your knowledge of functions if it did. Your ability to figure out what functions questions are actually asking you for is key to solving them correctly on Test Day.

Try out a tabular function interpretation question.

Day	Vote Count
3	21
4	35
5	53
6	75
7	101

3. Clara is one of five contest finalists in the running for a year's worth of college book expenses. The winner is the finalist with the highest number of votes on the contest host's website. Clara recorded her vote total each day of the contest; data for five days are in the table above. Which of the following represents Clara's vote count, v, as a function of time, t, in days?

A) $v(t) = 2t^2 + 3$

B) $v(t) = \dfrac{t^2}{2} + 3$

C) $v(t) = 2t^2 + 21$

D) $v(t) = \dfrac{t^2}{2} + 21$

Work through the Kaplan Method for Math step-by-step to solve this question. The following table shows Kaplan's strategic thinking on the left, along with suggested math scratchwork on the right.

Strategic Thinking	Math Scratchwork
Step 1: Read the question, identifying and organizing important information as you go The question is asking which function accurately depicts the relationship between time (t) and Clara's vote count (v). A table with data for selected days is given.	

Strategic Thinking	Math Scratchwork
Step 2: Choose the best strategy to answer the question Look for answer choices you can easily eliminate. From the table, you can tell that the rate of change of $v(t)$ is not constant and therefore not linear, but none of the choices are linear. However, the first table entry indicates Clara has 21 votes on day 3, and two choices have 21 as a y-intercept. The y-intercept is where $t = 0$; according to the table, $v(t) = 21$ at $t = 3$, not 0. Therefore, you can eliminate C and D. To evaluate the remaining choices, try plugging a pair of data points into the remaining choices. The point (4, 35) validates (A). To ensure (A) is the correct answer, you can repeat this process with B.	$v(3) = 21, v(0) \neq 21$ use $(4, 35)$ A: $35 = 2 \times 4^2 + 3$ $35 = 2 \times 16 + 3$ $35 = 32 + 3$ $35 = 35$ B: $35 = \dfrac{1}{2} \times 4^2 + 3$ $35 = \dfrac{1}{2} \times 16 + 3$ $35 = 8 + 3$ $35 \neq 11$
Step 3: Check that you answered the *right* question The only function that fits the data is (A).	

As you saw, you won't always have to plug points into each answer choice; you can often reduce your work by eliminating blatantly incorrect answers first. This is crucial for saving time on the SAT and quickly getting to the correct answer.

✔ **Note**

When you have only one answer choice remaining, it isn't necessary to evaluate it. If you've done your math correctly up until that point, you know the remaining answer choice *has* to be correct. However, if you're at all worried that you made a mistake earlier, check the remaining answer choice to validate your math.

REAL-WORLD APPLICATION OF FUNCTIONS

Because functions are equations, you have a great deal of flexibility in working with them. For example, order of operations (PEMDAS) and the basic rules of algebra apply to functions just as they do to equations. You learned in unit 1 that equations can represent real-world situations in convenient ways, and the same is true for functions.

For example, suppose a homeowner wants to determine the cost of installing a certain amount of carpet in her living room. In prose, this would quickly become awkward to handle, as a description would need to account for the cost per square foot, fixed installation fee, and sales tax to get the final cost. However, you can easily express this as a function.

Suppose that, in the homeowner example, carpet costs \$0.86 per square foot, the installer charges a \$29 installation fee, and sales tax on the total cost is 7%. Using your algebra and function knowledge, you can describe this situation in which the cost, c, is a function of square footage, f: $c = 1.07(0.86f + 29)$. In function notation, this becomes $c(f) = 1.07(0.86f + 29)$, where $c(f)$ is shorthand for "cost as a function of square footage." The following table summarizes the origin of each piece of the function.

English	Overall cost	Square footage	Material cost	Installation fee	Sales tax
Math	c	f	$0.86f$	29	1.07

✔ Note

Why does a 7% tax translate to 1.07? Using 0.07 would only provide the sales tax due. Because the function is meant to express the total cost, 1.07 is used to retain the carpet cost and installation fee while introducing the sales tax. Think of it as 100% (the original price) + the 7% sales tax on top. In decimal form, $1 + 0.07 = 1.07$.

This test-like question will test your ability to write a function.

4. Each calendar year, a certain credit card gives cardholders 5% cash back on gasoline purchases up to $1,500 and 2% cash back on any amount spent on gasoline thereafter. If $g(x)$ and $e(x)$ represent cash back earned on gasoline purchases up to $1,500 and in excess of $1,500, respectively, which of the following sets of functions could be used to determine the amount of cash back earned at each tier?

A) $g(x) = 0.05x$, $0 \leq x < 1,500$; $e(x) = 0.02(x - 1,500)$, $x \geq 1,500$

B) $g(x) = 0.05x$, $0 < x \leq 1,500$; $e(x) = 0.02x$, $x > 1,500$

C) $g(x) = 0.05x$, $0 \leq x \leq 1,500$; $e(x) = 0.02(x - 1,500)$, $x > 1,500$

D) $g(x) = 0.05x$, $0 \leq x \leq 1,500$; $e(x) = 0.02(1,500 - x)$, $x > 1,500$

A word problem like this is a great time to reach for the Kaplan Strategy for Translating English into Math. The following table shows Kaplan's strategic thinking on the left, along with suggested math scratchwork on the right.

Strategic Thinking	Math Scratchwork
Step 1: Read the question, identifying and organizing important information as you go You're asked to find the functions that describe the situation given.	

Strategic Thinking	Math Scratchwork
Step 2: Choose the best strategy to answer the question Use the Kaplan Strategy for Translating English into Math to extract what you need. The question has already defined the variables for you. The function $g(x)$ represents cash back on gasoline purchases up to $1,500, which the question states is 5%. Therefore, a cardholder earns $0.05x$ on this portion of gasoline purchases. Because this rate applies only to the first $1,500, there is a restriction on the function domain: $0 \leq x \leq 1,500$. Eliminate A and B. The function $e(x)$ is used for cash back on gasoline purchases over $1,500. To account for this $1,500, you must subtract it from x. The difference is then multiplied by 0.02 to calculate the additional cash back for gasoline purchases beyond $1,500. Like $g(x)$, $e(x)$ has a domain restriction.	$g(x) = 5\%$ *on gas up to* $1,500$ $g(x) = 0.05x, 0 \leq x \leq 1,500$ $e(x) = 2\%$ *above* $1,500$ $e(x) = 0.02(x - 1,500), x > 1,500$
Step 3: Check that you answered the *right* question Choice (C) is the only choice with both of the functions you built. Watch out for choice A, which lacks the correct inequality symbols in the domain restrictions.	

Notice that even with a more difficult word problem, the Kaplan Strategy for Translating English into Math gets the job done.

MULTIPLE FUNCTIONS

There are several ways in which the SAT might ask you to juggle multiple functions simultaneously. Fortunately, the rules governing what to do are easy to understand. To start, we'll look at how to combine functions. This technique simply involves adding, subtracting, multiplying, and/or dividing the functions in play. Check out the following table for a synopsis of how to combine functions with the four basic operations (and make them look less intimidating).

When you see . . .	. . . convert it to:
$(f + g)(x)$	$f(x) + g(x)$
$(f - g)(x)$	$f(x) - g(x)$
$(fg)(x)$	$f(x) \times g(x)$
$\left(\dfrac{f}{g}\right)(x)$	$\dfrac{f(x)}{g(x)}$

You'll have a chance to solve a problem involving combined functions shortly.

A more challenging type of function combination you're apt to see is a **composition of functions** or **nested functions**. Questions involving a composition of functions require you to find the range of a function at a given value and plug that range into the domain of another function to get the final solution. A composition of functions would be written as $f(g(x))$, (f of g of x), or $(f \circ g)(x)$ (f follows g(x)). Remember PEMDAS. To tackle these questions, start with the innermost parentheses and work your way out. A hypothetical situation follows.

> ✔ Note
>
> You might see a composition of functions written as $(f \circ g)(x)$. Just remember that it's the same as $(f(g(x))$, and solve as you would normally, working from the inside outward.

If $f(x) = 8x$ and $g(x) = x + 3$, find the value of $f(g(1))$. Your steps are as follows:

1. Determine $g(1)$, the innermost function when $x = 1$.

2. By substituting 1 for x in $g(x)$, you can quickly see that $g(1) = 4$. Now use substitution. If $g(1) = 4$, then you can plug in a 4 every time you see a $g(1)$. Rewrite $f(g(1))$ as $f(4)$.

3. Find $f(4)$, the outer function when $x = 4$. Substituting 4 for x in function f, we quickly realize that our final answer must be 32.

> ✔ **Note**
>
> Note that $f(g(x))$ does *not* equal $g(f(x))$! Not only is interchanging these incorrect, but this practice might also lead you to a trap answer on Test Day.

On Test Day, you might see **piecewise functions**. A piecewise function is a function that is, literally, multiple pieces. What breaks a function into pieces are different rules that govern different parts of a function's domain. Following is an example of this.

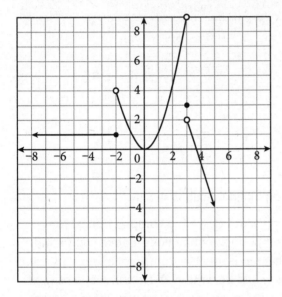

$$f(x) = \begin{cases} 1 & \text{if } x \leq -2 \\ x^2 & \text{if } -2 < x < 3 \\ 3 & \text{if } x = 3 \\ -3x + 11 & \text{if } x > 3 \end{cases}$$

In the function shown, the function behavior depends on the domain. Linear, quadratic, and even single point intervals are possible. We write each "rule" inside an open bracket; to the right is the domain interval for which the "rule" applies. An open dot indicates that a point is not included in that interval; a closed dot indicates one that is. Note the different inequality signs used depending on whether a dot is open or closed. For a single-point interval, an equal sign is used.

5. If $p(x) = x^2 - 4x + 8$ and $q(x) = x - 3$, what is the value of $\dfrac{q(p(5))}{p(q(5))}$?

   A) 0

   B) 0.4

   C) 1

   D) 2.5

Appearances can be deceiving. At first glance, this question looks tough, but the following table will clarify anything confusing. Kaplan's strategic thinking is on the left, along with suggested math scratchwork on the right.

Strategic Thinking	Math Scratchwork
Step 1: Read the question, identifying and organizing important information as you go You're asked for the value of $\dfrac{q(p(5))}{p(q(5))}$.	
Step 2: Choose the best strategy to answer the question The numerator and denominator look quite similar, so keep track of your calculations. Start with the numerator: Compute the innermost set of parentheses first, and then work your way outward. Repeat this process with the denominator. Once finished, combine the final values in the original expression.	$p(5) = 5^2 - 4 \times 5 + 8 = 13$ $q(13) = 13 - 3 = 10$ $q(p(5)) = 10$ $q(5) = 5 - 3 = 2$ $p(2) = 2^2 - 4 \times 2 + 8 = 4$ $p(q(5)) = 4$ $\dfrac{q(p(5))}{p(q(5))} = \dfrac{10}{4} = 2.5$
Step 3: Check that you answered the *right* question You've correctly calculated the expression. The correct answer is (D).	

Below is another example of a real-world scenario involving functions. Recall that the notation $(f \circ g)(x)$ means that f and g are functions of x such that $f(x)$ is computed based on $g(x)$.

6. Everett works at an electronics store. His base salary is $1,000 per week, and he earns a 10% commission on any sales over his $4,000 per week goal. If Everett's commission (c) and sales in excess of $4,000 ($e$) are both functions of his overall sales (s), which of the following correctly describes Everett's total weekly pre-tax pay?

    A) $(c \circ e)(s + 1,000)$

    B) $(e \circ c)(s + 1,000)$

    C) $(e \circ c)(s) + 1,000$

    D) $(c \circ e)(s) + 1,000$

Because there isn't any scratchwork required for a question like this, only the column containing Kaplan's strategic thinking is included. Follow along as we reason our way through this question.

Strategic Thinking
Step 1: Read the question, identifying and organizing important information as you go
You need to identify the expression that correctly depicts Everett's total weekly pay.
Step 2: Choose the best strategy to answer the question
Consider each part of Everett's pay separately. To find Everett's commission, you must first determine the portion of his sales to use for the commission calculation. In other words, commission (c) depends on sales in excess of $4,000 ($e$). This means you'll have a composition of functions with c computed based on e, which translates to $(c \circ e)(s)$. Everett earns $1,000 regardless of sales, so this figure is independent of functions c and e. It should be added on outside the functions. You can eliminate incorrect answer choices based on this information and the information above.
Step 3: Check that you answered the *right* question
The only match for your function is (D).

Handling multiple functions in the same question or equation is only slightly more involved than manipulating a single function. Be sure to read particularly carefully when the question is embedded in a real-world scenario.

RELATIONSHIPS BETWEEN FUNCTION VARIABLES AND FUNCTION TRANSFORMATIONS

When describing a graph of a function or an interval (a specific segment) of a function, the trend of the relationship between the *x* and *y* values while reading the graph from left to right is often important. Three terms you are sure to see in more difficult function questions are **increasing**, **decreasing**, and **constant**. Let's look carefully at what these terms mean and how they apply to SAT questions.

- **Increasing** functions have *y* values that *increase* as the corresponding *x* values increase.

- **Decreasing** functions have *y* values that *decrease* as the corresponding *x* values increase.

- **Constant** functions have *y* values that *stay the same* as the *x* values increase.

The SAT can ask about function trends in a variety of ways. The most basic would be to examine a function's interval and determine if the function is increasing, decreasing, or constant. Tougher questions might ask you to identify the trend and then explain what it means in the context of a real-life situation presented in the question, or to identify the effect a transformation would have on the trend of a function.

A function transformation occurs when a change is made to the function's equation or graph. Transformations include translations (moving a graph up/down, left/right), reflections (flips about an axis or other line), and expansions/compressions (stretching or squashing horizontally or vertically). How do you know which is occurring? The following table provides some rules for guidance when altering a hypothetical function *f(x)*.

Algebraic Change	Corresponding Graphical Change	Graph	Algebraic Change	Corresponding Graphical Change	Graph
f(x)	N/A—original function		*f(x + a)*	*f(x)* moves left *a* units	
f(x) + a	*f(x)* moves up *a* units		*f(x − a)*	*f(x)* moves right *a* units	

Algebraic Change	Corresponding Graphical Change	Graph	Algebraic Change	Corresponding Graphical Change	Graph
$f(x) - a$	$f(x)$ moves down a units		$-f(x)$	$f(x)$ reflected over the x-axis (top-to-bottom)	
$f(-x)$	$f(x)$ reflected over the y-axis (left-to-right)		$af(x)$ $(0 < a < 1)$	$f(x)$ undergoes vertical compression	
$f(ax)$ $(0 < a < 1)$	$f(x)$ undergoes horizontal expansion		$af(x)$ $(a > 1)$	$f(x)$ undergoes vertical expansion	
$f(ax)$ $(a > 1)$	$f(x)$ undergoes horizontal compression				

If you forget what a particular transformation looks like, you can always plug in a few values for x and plot the points to determine the effect on the function's graph.

✔ **Expert Tip**

Adding or subtracting inside the parentheses of a function will always effect a horizontal change (e.g., shift left/right, horizontal reflection); if the alteration is outside, you're looking at a vertical change.

A function transformation question for you to try follows.

7. Given function $j(x)$, which of the following choices corresponds to a horizontal compression, reflection about the x-axis, and an upward shift?

A) $-j(2x) + 2$

B) $-j(2x + 2)$

C) $j(-2x) + 2$

D) $-j(\frac{1}{2}x) + 2$

Because there isn't any scratchwork required for a question like this, only the column containing Kaplan's strategic thinking is included. Follow along as we reason our way through this question.

Strategic Thinking
Step 1: Read the question, identifying and organizing important information as you go
You must determine which function shows the transformations specified in the question stem.
Step 2: Choose the best strategy to answer the question
Remember your transformation rules. A horizontal compression requires a variable coefficient greater than 1 (for example, $f(3x)$); D doesn't contain this, so eliminate it. A reflection about the x-axis (vertical) requires a negative sign before j. Eliminate C. An upward shift (also vertical) means the constant quantifying the shift must be outside the function argument parentheses. Of the remaining choices, (A) is the only function that satisfies the conditions in the question stem.
Step 3: Check that you answered the *right* question
The only matching function is (A).

Now you'll have a chance to try a few test-like problems in a scaffolded way. See if you can fill in the missing pieces and solve for the correct answer without a full explanation.

8. Joan is an entomologist (a scientist who studies insects) researching possible causes of honeybee disappearance. At the start of a recent study, she estimated the number of honeybees in a 50 mi^2 area to be $4.23×10^8$ distributed among 7,050 hives. Joan discovered that the honeybee population in this area decreases by 35% every month. Assuming the rate of disappearance remains 35% every month, approximately how many honeybees will remain after one year?

A) 340

B) 1,430

C) 2,406,000

D) 116,166,000

The following table can help you structure your thinking as you go about solving this question. The Kaplan strategic thinking is provided, as are bits of structured scratchwork. If you're not sure how to approach a question like this, start at the top and work your way down.

Strategic Thinking	Math Scratchwork
Step 1: Read the question, identifying and organizing important information as you go *What are you being asked to find?* You need to determine the approximate number of honeybees remaining in Joan's study area after one year.	

Strategic Thinking	Math Scratchwork
Step 2: Choose the best strategy to answer the question *How can you find the requested information? Is there an equation you can use?* You bet! You're asked about the honeybee population, so zero in on information on the honeybee count and any rates of change, and ignore the rest. *What kind of change is this? What should the function look like?* A reduction of 35% each month means the exact number of honeybees lost will change over time, so you're looking at exponential decay. Add the values you know to create your function. *Am I done?* The question wants a value, so plug in the correct duration into your function to find the number of remaining honeybees. Watch your time units!	exponential change: $y = x_O(1 + r)^x$ $p(t)$ = honeybee pop. t = time in _____ $p(t) = ($_____$)(1 +$_____$)^t$ $p($__$) = ($_____$)($_____$)$—— = _____
Step 3: Check that you answered the *right* question *How many honeybees are left after one year?* If you picked (C), you'd be correct.	_____

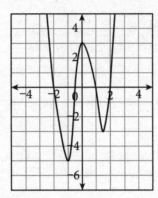

9. The graph of the function $a(x)$ is shown above. If $b(x) = \dfrac{1}{x}$, which of the following is a true statement about $(b \circ a)(x)$?

A) $(b \circ a)(x)$ is defined for all real numbers.

B) $(b \circ a)(x)$ is undefined for three real values of x.

C) $(b \circ a)(x)$ is undefined for four real values of x.

D) $(b \circ a)(x)$ is undefined for all real numbers.

The following table can help you structure your thinking as you go about solving this problem. The Kaplan strategic thinking is provided, as are bits of structured scratchwork. If you're not sure how to approach a question like this, start at the top and work your way down.

Strategic Thinking	Math Scratchwork
Step 1: Read the question, identifying and organizing important information as you go *What do you ultimately need to find?* You need to figure out when the composition of functions is undefined.	

Strategic Thinking	Math Scratchwork
Step 2: Choose the best strategy to answer the question *What does the composition notation indicate? What is function b doing to function a?* The range of one function is the domain of the other. *What value of a(x) would cause b(x) to be undefined? What should you look for on the graph to indicate this?* You'll notice there's an x in the denominator of b(x); think about what restriction this places on b(x) and when this would make (b∘a)(x) undefined. *How many times does that value occur?* Examine the graph of a(x) to determine this.	 $(b \circ a)(x) \rightarrow b(a(x))$ range of ____ = domain of ____ if $b(x) = \dfrac{1}{x}$, then $x \neq$ ____ $\rightarrow a(x) \neq$ ____ in $(b \circ a)(x)$ $a(x) =$ ____ at ____ places
Step 3: Check that you answered the *right* question *When is (b∘a)(x) undefined?* If you got (C), you're absolutely correct!	 _____

Now that you've seen the variety of ways in which the SAT can test you on functions, try the following questions to check your understanding. Give yourself 4.5 minutes to tackle the following three questions. Make sure you use the Kaplan Method for Math as often as you can. Remember, you want to emphasize speed and efficiency in addition to simply getting the correct answer.

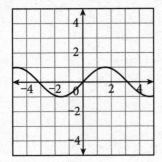

10. The graph of $h(x) = \sin x$ is shown above. Which of the following correctly depicts the transformations effected in $\dfrac{h(2x)}{3} - 4$?

A)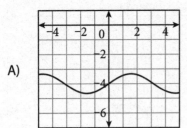

B)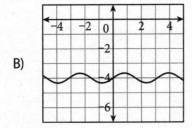

C)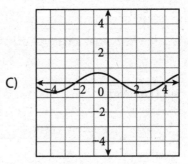

D)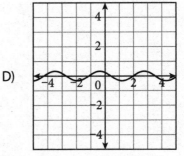

11. Briana is writing a 60-page paper for a law school class; she has a full outline of the paper and needs to convert it to prose. She estimates that she will average 45 words per minute while typing. If one page of prose contains approximately 500 words, which of the following correctly estimates the number of prose pages, p, remaining as a function of the number of minutes, m, that Briana types?

A) $p(m) = 60 - \dfrac{9m}{100}$

B) $p(m) = \dfrac{60 - 100}{9m}$

C) $p(m) = 60 - \dfrac{100}{9m}$

D) $p(m) = \dfrac{60 - 9m}{100}$

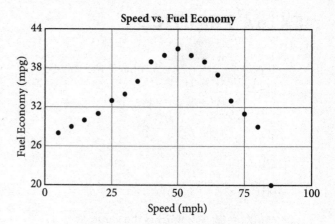

Speed vs. Fuel Economy

12. The graph above shows a compact car's fuel economy as a function of speed. Which of the following is true?

A) The rate of increase in fuel economy below 50 mph is greater than the rate of decrease in fuel economy above 50 mph.

B) The rate of increase in fuel economy below 50 mph is equal to the rate of decrease in fuel economy above 50 mph.

C) Fuel economy peaks at 50 mph, but nothing can be said about the rates of change in fuel economy above and below 50 mph.

D) The rate of increase in fuel economy below 50 mph is less than the rate of decrease in fuel economy above 50 mph.

Answers and Explanations for this chapter begin on page 627.

EXTRA PRACTICE

1. If $g(x) = -2x^2 + 7x - 3$, what is the value of $g(-2)$?

    A) −25

    B) −9

    C) −1

    D) 3

2. If $k(x) = 5x + 2$, what is the value of $k(4) - k(1)$?

    A) 15

    B) 17

    C) 19

    D) 21

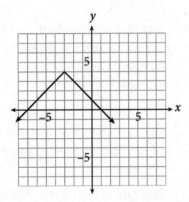

3. The graph of $f(x)$ is shown above. Which of the following represents the domain and range of the function?

    A) Domain: $f(x) \geq 4$; Range: all real numbers

    B) Domain: $f(x) \leq 4$; Range: all real numbers

    C) Domain: all real numbers; Range: $f(x) \geq 4$

    D) Domain: all real numbers; Range: $f(x) \leq 4$

4. If $g(x) = (x - 2)^2 - 5$, which of the following statements is true?

    A) The function $g(x)$ is increasing over the entire domain.

    B) The function $g(x)$ is decreasing over the entire domain.

    C) The function $g(x)$ is increasing for $x < 2$ and decreasing for $x > 2$.

    D) The function $g(x)$ is decreasing for $x < 2$ and increasing for $x > 2$.

5. A function is defined by the equation $f(x) = \dfrac{x^2}{4} - 11$. For this function, which of the following domain values corresponds to a range value of 14?

    A) −4

    B) 10

    C) 38

    D) 100

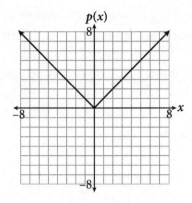

6. The figure shows the function $p(x) = |x|$. Which statement about the function is not true?

A) $p(0) = 0$

B) $p(-4) = 4$

C) $p(4) = -4$

D) The domain of $p(x)$ is all real numbers.

$$f(x) = \begin{cases} x^2 + 1, & \text{if } x \leq 0 \\ \dfrac{2x}{3} - 1, & \text{if } 0 < x \leq 3 \\ 4 - x, & \text{if } x > 3 \end{cases}$$

7. For the piecewise function $f(x)$ defined above, what is the value of $f(-3)$?

A) -3

B) 7

C) 10

D) $-3, 7,$ and 10

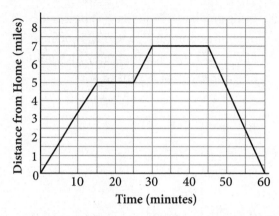

8. The graph above shows Carmel's distance from home over a one-hour period, during which time he first went to the library, then went to the grocery store, and then returned home. Which of the following statements could be true?

A) The grocery store is about 5 miles from Carmel's house.

B) Carmel traveled a total of 7 miles from the time he left home until he returned.

C) The grocery store is 7 miles farther from Carmel's house than the library is.

D) Carmel spent 10 minutes at the library and 15 minutes at the grocery store.

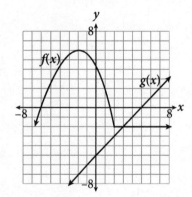

9. Based on the figure above, what is the value of $f(-2) + g(2)$?

A) -3

B) 0

C) 3

D) 6

10. If the graph of a function $g(x)$ passes through the point (5, 3), and $h(x)$ is defined as $h(x) = -g(x - 2) + 8$, through which point does the graph of $h(x)$ pass?

A) (–3, 11)

B) (3, 5)

C) (7, 5)

D) (7, 11)

11. If $f(x) = x^2 + \dfrac{5}{2}$ and $g(x) = \dfrac{x}{4} - 1$, what is the value of $(f \circ g)(6)$?

A) 2.75

B) 3

C) 3.5

D) 8.625

12. If p is a function defined over the set of all real numbers and $p(x + 2) = 3x^2 + 4x + 1$, then which of the following defines $p(x)$?

A) $p(x) = 3x^2 - 7x + 3$

B) $p(x) = 3x^2 - 8x + 5$

C) $p(x) = 3x^2 + 16x + 9$

D) $p(x) = 3x^2 + 16x + 21$

13. A company uses the function $P(x) = 150x - x^2$ to determine how much profit the company will make when it sells 150 units of a certain product that sells for x dollars per unit. How much more profit per unit will the company make if it charges $25 for the product than if it charges $20?

14. The customer service department of a wireless cellular provider has found that on Wednesdays, the polynomial function $C(t) = -0.0815t^4 + t^3 + 12t$ approximates the number of calls received by any given time, where t represents the number of hours that have passed since the department opened at 7 AM. Based on this function, how many calls can be expected by 5 PM?

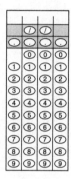

CHAPTER 8

Quadratic Equations

CHAPTER OBJECTIVES

By the end of this chapter, you will be able to:

1. Solve quadratic equations via algebra, graphing, or the quadratic formula

2. Sketch the graph of a given quadratic equation

3. Identify how various components of a quadratic equation are significant to its graph or a real-world scenario

SMARTPOINTS

Point Value	SmartPoint Category
50 Points	Quadratics

INTRODUCTION TO QUADRATIC EQUATIONS

A quadratic equation or expression is simply one that contains a squared variable (x^2) as the highest-order term (also called highest-powered term). In standard form, a quadratic equation is written as $ax^2 + bx + c = 0$, where a, b, and c are constants. However, quadratics can be written in a variety of other forms as well, such as these:

$$x^2 - 9 = 0 \qquad\qquad 2r^2 - 8r + 10 = 4 \qquad\qquad 2(x - 3)^2 = 8 \qquad\qquad (x - 2)(x + 3) = 6$$

 Note

At first glance, the last equation might not look quadratic, but it is; it's merely masquerading as a product of binomials. You'll learn a strategy for unveiling its x^2 term shortly.

All quadratic equations will have 0, 1, or 2 real solutions. When you are asked to find the solutions of a quadratic, all you need to do is equate the variable to a constant. Solutions might also be called roots, x-intercepts, or zeros.

Before you can solve, however, there is a step you must always complete: **Set the equation equal to 0**. In other words, move everything to one side of the equation so that 0 is the only thing left on the other side. Once your quadratic equation is equal to 0, you can take one of three routes to determine how many solutions it has: **algebra**, **graphing**, or the **quadratic formula**. Read on for more information about these three techniques.

SOLVING QUADRATICS ALGEBRAICALLY

Algebra is often the most efficient way to work through quadratics, so getting comfortable with it is critical. We'll start with a technique that is highly useful for manipulating quadratics: FOIL. **FOIL is essential for putting a quadratic into standard form.**

✔ **Expert Tip**

If you're really stuck on the algebra in a quadratics question, Picking Numbers can often help. Just remember that it might take more time than the algebra route, so use good judgment if you're in a bind—and remember that you can always skip the question and revisit it later.

FOIL

Whenever you see a pair of binomials on the SAT, your default algebra strategy should be FOIL, which stands for First, Outer, Inner, Last. This acronym helps ensure that you don't forget any terms when distributing. You multiply the first terms in each binomial together, then repeat with the outer, inner, and last terms. Then you add the four products together, combining like terms as needed. Here is a generic scheme for the FOIL procedure:

$$(a + b)(c + d) = ac + ad + bc + bd$$

(Binomial 1)(Binomial 2) = First + Outer + Inner + Last

It is often tempting to FOIL in your head, but this is risky: It is very easy to lose a negative sign or switch a pair of coefficients (and arrive at a trap answer). Show *all* of your work when using FOIL.

Factoring

Factoring, also known as reverse-FOIL, allows you to go from a quadratic to a product of two binomials. This is a very powerful tool; once you have a binomial pair, you're a few short algebraic steps away from the solution(s). The factoring process is demonstrated in the following table:

Step	Scratchwork
Starting point. Notice a, the coefficient in front of x^2, is equal to 1, a great condition for factoring!	$x^2 + 5x + 6 = 0 \rightarrow (x \pm ?)(x \pm ?) = 0$
1. What are the factors of c? Remember to include negatives.	factors of 6: 1 & 6, -1 & -6, 2 & 3, -2 & -3
2. Which factor pair, when added, equals b, the coefficient in front of x?	$2 + 3 = 5$
3. Write as a product of binomials.	$(x + 2)(x + 3) = 0$
4. Split the product of binomials into two equations set equal to 0.	$x + 2 = 0$, $x + 3 = 0$
5. Solve each equation.	$x = -2$, $x = -3$

Factoring is easiest when a is 1, so whenever possible, try to simplify your expression so that is the case. In addition, if you see nice-looking numbers (integers, simple fractions) in your answer choices, this is a clue that factoring is possible. If you're ever not sure that you've done your factoring correctly, go ahead and FOIL to check your work. You should get the expression you started with.

✔ **Note**

Sometimes the two factors you choose for your binomials will be identical. In this case, the quadratic will have only one real solution (because the two solutions are identical).

Completing the Square

For more difficult quadratics, you'll need to turn to a more advanced strategy: completing the square. In this process you'll create a perfect square trinomial, which has the form $(x + h)^2 = k$, where h

and k are constants. This route takes some practice to master but will pay dividends when you sail through the most challenging quadratics questions on Test Day. The following table illustrates the procedure along with a corresponding example.

Step	Scratchwork
Starting point.	$x^2 + 6x - 7 = 0$
1. Move the constant to the opposite side.	$x^2 + 6x = 7$
2. Divide b by 2, then square the quotient.	$b = 6; \left(\dfrac{b}{2}\right)^2 = \left(\dfrac{6}{2}\right)^2 = (3)^2 = 9$
3. Add the number from the previous step to both sides of the equation, then factor.	$x^2 + 6x + 9 = 7 + 9 \rightarrow (x+3)(x+3) = 16 \rightarrow$ $(x+3)^2 = 16$
4. Take the square root of both sides.	$\sqrt{(x+3)^2} = \pm\sqrt{16} \rightarrow x + 3 = \pm 4$
5. Split the equation in two and solve.	$x + 3 = 4, \ x + 3 = -4 \rightarrow x = 1, \ x = -7$

A note about completing the square: a needs to be 1 to use this process. You can divide the first term by a to convert the coefficient to 1, but if you start getting strange-looking fractions, it may be easier to use the quadratic formula instead.

Grouping

Although less commonly seen than other strategies, grouping is useful with the more challenging quadratics, especially those with a values greater than 1. You'll need two x terms to use this route. The goal of grouping is to identify the greatest common factor (GCF) of the first two terms, repeat for the second two terms, then finally combine the two GCFs into a separate binomial. Check out the following example if this seems murky.

Step	Scratchwork
Starting point.	$2x^2 - 7x - 15 = 0$
1. You need to split the x term in two; the sum of the new terms' coefficients must equal b, and their product must equal ac.	$a \times c = 2 \times -15 = -30, b = -7$ new x-term coefficients : 3 and -10 $2x^2 - 10x + 3x - 15 = 0$
2. What's the GCF of the first pair of terms?	GCF of $2x^2$ and $-10x$: $2x$
3. Factor out the GCFs.	$2x^2 - 10x + 3x - 15 = 0 \rightarrow$ $2x(x-5) + 3(x-5) = 0$

4. Factor out the newly formed binomial and combine the GCFs into another.	$2x(x-5)+3(x-5)=0 \rightarrow (2x+3)(x-5)=0$
5. Split into two equations and solve as usual.	$2x+3=0,\ x-5=0 \rightarrow x=-\dfrac{3}{2},\ x=5$

Straightforward Math

Sometimes you can get away with not having to FOIL or factor extensively, but you need to be able to spot patterns or trends. When you're missing an x term or constant, that's a good clue that straightforward math will work. Don't resort to complex techniques when some easy simplification will get the job done. Equations similar to the following examples are highly likely to appear on the SAT.

No Middle Term	No Last Term	Squared Binomial
$x^2 - 9 = 0$	$x^2 - 9x = 0$	$(x-3)^2 = 9$
$x^2 = 9$	$x(x-9) = 0$	$(x-3) = \pm\sqrt{9}$
$x = \pm 3$	$x = 0, 9$	$(x-3) = \pm 3$
		$x - 3 = 3 \qquad x - 3 = -3$ $x = 6 \qquad\qquad x = 0$

> ✔ **Expert Tip**
>
> You can also factor $x^2 - 9$ to get $(x + 3)(x - 3)$; this is called a difference of squares. Note that this only works when the terms are being subtracted.

Quadratic Formula

The quadratic formula can be used to solve any quadratic equation. However, because the math can often get complicated, use this as a last resort or when you need to find exact (e.g., not rounded; fractions and/or radicals intact) solutions.

The quadratic formula that follows outputs solutions to a quadratic equation, given values of a, b, and c from the equation of a parabola in standard form.

$$x = \frac{-b \pm \sqrt{b^2 - 4ac}}{2a}$$

The ± operator indicates you will use two equations to solve to get all potential solutions, so remember to compute both.

The expression under the radical ($b^2 - 4ac$) is called the discriminant, and its sign determines the number of real solutions. If this quantity is positive, there are two distinct real solutions; if it is equal to zero, there is just one distinct real solution; and if it's negative, then there are no real solutions.

✔ Note

Being flexible and familiar with your strengths on Test Day is essential. By doing so, you can identify the path to the answer to a quadratics question that is the most efficient for you.

On the next few pages, you'll get to try applying some of these strategies to test-like SAT problems.

1. Which of the following is an equivalent form of the expression $(6 - 5x)(15x - 11)$?

    A) $-75x^2 + 35x - 66$

    B) $-75x^2 + 145x - 66$

    C) $90x^2 - 141x + 55$

    D) $90x^2 + 9x + 55$

Work through the Kaplan Method for Math step-by-step to solve this question. The following table shows Kaplan's strategic thinking on the left, along with suggested math scratchwork on the right.

Strategic Thinking	Math Scratchwork
Step 1: Read the question, identifying and organizing important information as you go You're asked to identify the quadratic expression equivalent to $(6 - 5x)(15x - 11)$.	
Step 2: Choose the best strategy to answer the question You have binomials in the question stem and standard form quadratics in the answer choices, so FOIL is the quickest route. Follow the standard FOIL procedure, and then simplify.	$(6 - 5x)(15x - 11)$ $(6)(15x) + (6)(-11) + (-5x)(15x) + (-5x)(-11)$ First + Outer + Inner + Last $90x - 66 - 75x^2 + 55x$ $-75x^2 + 145x - 66$

Strategic Thinking	Math Scratchwork
Step 3: Check that you answered the *right* question You correctly expanded the quadratic using FOIL and got an exact match for (B), the correct answer.	$-75x^2 + 145x - 66$

✔ **Expert Tip**

Although you could Pick Numbers here, remember you have only a few seconds to solve questions like this on Test Day. FOIL is much faster and should be your preferred method.

Although it's technically not a quadratic expression, the expression in the following question provides a chance to practice the strategies you've learned in this section.

2. Which of the following is equivalent to $\dfrac{x^2-10x+25}{3x^2-75}$?

    A) $\dfrac{3(x-5)}{(x+5)}$

    B) $\dfrac{3(x+5)}{(x-5)}$

    C) $\dfrac{(x-5)}{3(x+5)}$

    D) $\dfrac{(x+5)}{3(x-5)}$

Work through the Kaplan Method for Math step-by-step to solve this question. The following table shows Kaplan's strategic thinking on the left, along with suggested math scratchwork on the right.

Strategic Thinking	Math Scratchwork
Step 1: Read the question, identifying and organizing important information as you go You need to identify which answer choice contains an expression equivalent to the one in the question stem.	

Strategic Thinking	Math Scratchwork
Step 2: Choose the best strategy to answer the question There are a few x^2 terms, so you should be thinking about quadratics and factoring. Also, whenever you're given a fraction, think about ways to cancel terms. Examine the numerator first: You can use the quadratic short-cut $a^2 - 2ab + b^2 = (a - b)^2$ to rewrite it. The denominator is more involved. Factor out a 3 first, and then factor the quadratic, which is a difference of squares. Lastly, cancel any factors that the numerator and denominator share.	$\dfrac{x^2-10x+25}{3x^2-75}$ $\dfrac{(x-5)(x-5)}{3(x^2-25)}$ $\dfrac{(x-5)\cancel{(x-5)}}{3(x+5)\cancel{(x-5)}}$
Step 3: Check that you answered the _right_ question The expression is now in simplest form, so you're done. Choice (C) is correct.	$\dfrac{(x-5)}{3(x+5)}$

✔ Expert Tip

Utilize the special quadratics, such as difference of squares, to eliminate factoring tasks and save time on Test Day.

---

3. Which of the following is a value of x that satisfies the equation $x^2 + 2x - 5 = 0$?

    A) -1

    B) $1-\sqrt{6}$

    C) $1+\sqrt{6}$

    D) $-1-\sqrt{6}$

This question is full of radicals, but don't panic. You can use the Kaplan Method for Math to efficiently tackle this kind of question on Test Day. The following table shows Kaplan's strategic thinking on the left, along with suggested math scratchwork on the right.

Strategic Thinking	Math Scratchwork
Step 1: Read the question, identifying and organizing important information as you go The question asks for a solution to the given equation.	

Strategic Thinking	Math Scratchwork
Step 2: Choose the best strategy to answer the question The equation is a quadratic, so you have a few potential options. Because –5 does not have factors that add up to 2, you cannot factor or group. However, because the coefficient of x^2 is 1, completing the square is doable. We'll use that method here, but you can use the quadratic formula if you prefer.	$x^2 + 2x - 5 = 0$ $x^2 + 2x = 5$ $\left(\dfrac{b}{2}\right)^2 = \left(\dfrac{2}{2}\right)^2 = 1^2 = 1$ $x^2 + 2x + 1 = 5 + 1$ $(x + 1)^2 = 6$ $(x+1) = \sqrt{6}$ and $(x+1) = -\sqrt{6}$ $x = -1 \pm \sqrt{6}$
Step 3: Check that you answered the *right* question The question asks for one possible value of *x*, so you should expect to see one (but not both) of the possible values in the choices. Choice (D) contains one of these values.	$x = -1 + \sqrt{6}$ or $x = -1 - \sqrt{6}$

CONNECTIONS BETWEEN QUADRATICS AND PARABOLAS

A quadratic function is simply a quadratic equation set equal to *y* or *f*(*x*) instead of 0. To solve one of these, you would follow the same procedure as before: Substitute 0 for *y* or *f*(*x*), then solve using one of the three methods demonstrated (algebra, graphing, quadratic formula). Consider the graphical connection: When you set *y* equal to 0, you're really solving for *x*-intercepts.

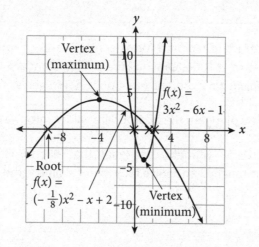

All quadratic functions will graph as parabolas (U-shaped), opening up or down. To determine whether a parabola will open up or down, examine the *a* value in your function's equation. If *a* is

positive, the parabola will open upward; if *a* is negative, it will open downward. Take a look at the examples below to see this graphically.

Like quadratic equations, quadratic functions will have zero, one, or two real solutions, corresponding to the number of times a parabola crosses the *x*-axis. As you saw with previous examples, graphing is a powerful way to determine the number of solutions a quadratic function has.

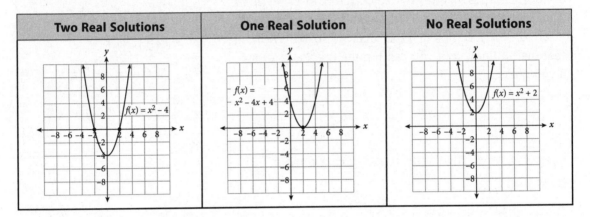

Two Real Solutions	One Real Solution	No Real Solutions
$f(x) = x^2 - 4$	$f(x) = x^2 - 4x + 4$	$f(x) = x^2 + 2$

There are three forms that a quadratic function can take: standard, factored, and vertex. Each is provided in the following table along with some helpful properties of each form.

Standard	Factored	Vertex
$y = ax^2 + bx + c$	$y = a(x - m)(x - n)$	$y = a(x - h)^2 + k$
y-intercept: *c*	Solutions are *m* and *n*	Vertex is (*h*, *k*)
In real-world contexts, starting quantity is *c*		Min/max function value (vertex) is *k*
Format used to solve via quadratic formula		

You've already seen standard and factored forms earlier in this chapter, but vertex form might be new to you. In vertex form, *a* is the same as the *a* from standard form, and *h* and *k* are the coordinates of the vertex (*h*, *k*). If a quadratic function is not in vertex form, you can still find the

x-coordinate of the vertex by plugging the appropriate values into the equation $h = \frac{-b}{2a}$, which is

also the equation for the axis of symmetry (see graph that follows). Once you determine *h*, plug this value into the quadratic function and solve for *y* to determine *k*, the *y*-coordinate of the vertex.

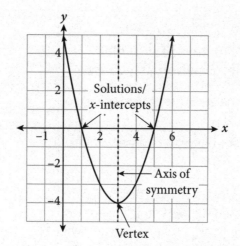

In addition to familiarity with the various forms a quadratic equation/function can take, you should have a foundational knowledge of the structure of a parabola. Some of the basic pieces you could be asked about on Test Day are shown here. You already know how to determine the solutions and vertex, and the axis of symmetry is straightforward. **The equation of the axis of symmetry of a parabola is $x = h$, where h is the x-coordinate of the vertex.**

> ✔ **Note**
>
> The formula for a parabola's axis of symmetry is easy to remember: It's the quadratic formula without the radical component. If the x-intercepts are rational numbers, you can also determine the axis of symmetry by finding the midpoint, the point exactly halfway between.

Take some time to explore the questions on the next several pages to test your new wealth of quadratic knowledge.

A question like this next one could arise in either the calculator or the non-calculator section. Think critically about how you'd solve it in either case.

4. What are the x-intercepts of the parabolic function $f(x) = 3x^2 - 2x - 8 = 0$?

    A) $\dfrac{1}{3}$ and -25

    B) $\dfrac{4}{3}$ and -2

    C) $-\dfrac{4}{3}$ and 2

    D) $-\dfrac{4}{3}$ and -2

Work through the Kaplan Method for Math step-by-step to solve this question. The following table shows Kaplan's strategic thinking on the left, along with suggested math scratchwork on the right.

Strategic Thinking	Math Scratchwork
Step 1: Read the question, identifying and organizing important information as you go You're given a quadratic in standard form and asked to find its x-intercepts.	
Step 2: Choose the best strategy to answer the question Because the coefficient of x^2 isn't 1, you can't easily factor. However, the grouping method will work. You'll need two numbers whose product is ac (−24) and whose sum is b (−2); the two magic numbers are −6 and 4. Rewrite the middle term using these numbers before you group, factor, and solve for x.	$f(x) = 3x^2 - 2x - 8 = 0$ $ac = 3 \times -8 = -24$ $b = -2$ $3x^2 - 6x + 4x - 8 = 0$ $3x(x - 2) + 4(x - 2) = 0$ $(3x + 4)(x - 2) = 0$ $(3x + 4) = 0 \text{ or } (x - 2) = 0$
Step 3: Check that you answered the *right* question The question asks for the x-intercepts of the equation, which is what you calculated. Select (C) and move on.	$x = -\dfrac{4}{3} \text{ or } x = 2$

✔ **Note**

If a question like this were in the calculator section, you could also solve it by graphing.

In one final type of quadratic-related problem, you may be asked to match a function to a graph or vice-versa. An example of this appears below; unfortunately, it is not likely to appear in the calculator section of the test.

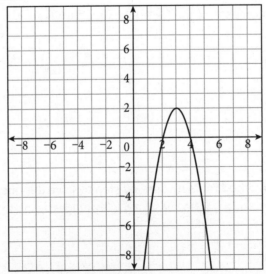

5. The previous function is represented by the equation $f(x) = a(x - h)^2 + k$. Which of the following statements is NOT true?

A) The value of a is negative.

B) $f(x)$ is symmetrical across the line $y = 3$.

C) The function $g(x) = \dfrac{2x}{3}$ intersects $f(x)$ at its vertex.

D) The value of h is positive.

Because there isn't any scratchwork required for a question like this, only the column containing Kaplan's strategic thinking is included. Try to ask yourself similar questions as you work through questions like this on Test Day.

Strategic Thinking
Step 1: Read the question, identifying and organizing important information as you go
The equation given is in vertex form. You must pick the answer choice that is *not* true.
Step 2: Choose the best strategy to answer the question
Take control of this question—tackle everything in a strategic order. Choices A and D contain the simplest statements, so check them first. Choice A says that a is negative. For parabolas that open downward, a will always be negative, so this statement is true. Eliminate it.
Choice D says that h is positive. Recall that when a parabola is written in vertex form, h represents the x-coordinate of the vertex. Because the vertex is (3, 2), h must indeed be positive. Choice D is therefore true, so eliminate it.
Of the remaining answer choices, B is simpler: It involves the parabola's axis of symmetry, which you can quickly find. Because the x-coordinate of the vertex is 3, the axis of symmetry is the line $x = 3$. Choice B says that the axis of symmetry is $y = 3$ and is therefore false.
Step 3: Check that you answered the *right* question
Remember that you're looking for a false statement, not a true statement. Choice (B) is false, so you can select it confidently without even bothering to evaluate C.

✔ **Note**

Stay on the lookout for words such as "not" that are easily missed if you don't read the question stem carefully. This is especially true of questions testing more involved topics.

GRAPHING QUADRATICS ON A CALCULATOR

At this point, you've become quite an expert at working with quadratics on paper. In this part, we'll explore how you can use your calculator to efficiently graph quadratics. Calculators can be great time-savers *when you're allowed to use them.*

Graphing

All quadratics can be solved by graphing. That said, you might ask why you should bother learning all the aforementioned algebra gymnastics. There are a few reasons why graphing shouldn't be the first option you turn to:

- Remember, there's a non-calculator section on the SAT; graphing isn't an option here.

- Graphing is often slower because entering complex equations and then zooming to trace the graph(s) can be tedious.

- It is easy to accidentally mistype when you're being timed—a misplaced parenthesis or negative sign will likely lead to a trap answer choice.

However, if you have complicated algebra ahead (e.g., fractional coefficients), decimals in the answer choices, or time-consuming obstacles to overcome, graphing can be a viable alternative to solving quadratics algebraically. A set of straightforward steps for graphing on a calculator follows:

1. Manipulate your equation so that it equals 0.

2. Substitute $y =$ or $f(x) =$ for the 0.

3. Enter the function into your calculator.

4. Trace the graph to approximate the x-intercepts (usually the answer choices will be sufficiently different to warrant approximation over an exact value) or use your calculator's built-in capability to find the x-intercepts exactly.

Graphing on the TI-83/84

While on the home screen, press [Y=]. Then enter your function to be graphed. Press [GRAPH] and allow the function to plot. If you can't see everything or want to ensure there isn't something hiding, consider pressing [WINDOW] to set your own manual parameters or hitting [ZOOM] to quickly zoom in and out, among other quick options. If you want to simply investigate your graph, press [TRACE] and use the right and left arrow keys to move around on the graph. If you type in any x-value and press [ENTER], the y-value will be returned on screen.

Determining Solutions on the TI-83/84

Once you have your graph on screen, you're ready to find solutions. Press [2ND] [TRACE] to pull up the CALC menu, which has options for finding points of interest. Select option 2: ZERO by highlighting and pressing [ENTER]. You will be taken back to the graph. Use the arrow keys to move to the left of the x-intercept (zero) that you want to calculate. Once you are just to the left of only the zero you are interested in, press [ENTER]—this is called the Left Bound. Next, move to the right of that zero only, careful not to go past any others, and press [ENTER]—this is called the Right Bound. Finally, the calculator will ask you to "Guess," so move left or right to approximate this zero, and press [ENTER].

Because you've already set your quadratic equation equal to zero, you know the zeros that your calculator returns will be the solutions to the overall equation.

✔ **Note**

Take the time to get comfortable with your calculator functions regardless of what calculator you have. You can find great instructions and even video demonstrations on the Internet.

Next, you'll get to try a sample test-like problem that could be solved via graphing or the quadratic formula. Choose wisely. In almost every case, graphing will be faster, but familiarize yourself with the quadratic formula approach in case you encounter a problem like this in the non-calculator section.

6. Which are the real values of x that satisfy the equation $2x^2 - 5x - 2 = 0$?

    A) 1 and 4

    B) $-\dfrac{5}{4} + \dfrac{\sqrt{41}}{4}$ and $-\dfrac{5}{4} - \dfrac{\sqrt{41}}{4}$

    C) $\dfrac{5}{4} + \dfrac{\sqrt{41}}{4}$ and $\dfrac{5}{4} - \dfrac{\sqrt{41}}{4}$

    D) No real solutions

Work through the Kaplan Method for Math step-by-step to solve this question. The following table shows Kaplan's strategic thinking on the left, along with suggested math scratchwork on the right.

Strategic Thinking	Math Scratchwork
Step 1: Read the question, identifying and organizing important information as you go You need to identify the values of x that satisfy the given equation.	

Strategic Thinking	Math Scratchwork
Step 2: Choose the best strategy to answer the question When solving quadratics, you have three options: factor, graph, or use the quadratic formula. Attempting to factor is not wise, as the coefficients aren't factoring-friendly. Using a calculator would work, but it's likely to be messy: Two answer choices contain radicals, so you'd have to plug both solutions into the calculator and use the [TRACE] feature to see which ones approximately match the values you find. The quadratic formula, although a longer route, is actually the most efficient option for this question. Plug in your coefficients and constants appropriately. Labeling the equation will help keep the values of a, b, and c straight.	$2x^2 - 5x - 2 = 0$ $\quad a \quad\quad b \quad\quad c$ $x = \dfrac{-b \pm \sqrt{b^2 - 4ac}}{2a}$ $x = \dfrac{-(-5) \pm \sqrt{(-5)^2 - 4(2)(-2)}}{2(2)}$ $x = \dfrac{5 \pm \sqrt{25 - (-16)}}{4}$ $x = \dfrac{5 \pm \sqrt{41}}{4}$ $x = \dfrac{5}{4} + \dfrac{\sqrt{41}}{4}$ or $x = \dfrac{5}{4} - \dfrac{\sqrt{41}}{4}$
Step 3: Check that you answered the *right* question The question asks for the solutions to the equation, so you're finished. Your match is (C).	$x = \dfrac{5}{4} \pm \dfrac{\sqrt{41}}{4}$

✔ **Note**

Note that in this question, the quadratic formula was the most efficient way to solve the question. Be prepared to use any of the quadratics tools at your disposal on Test Day.

Nicely done! Take a look at another example.

7. The equation $\dfrac{1}{4}(4x^2 - 8x - k) = 30$ is satisfied when $x = -5$ and when $x = 7$. What is the value of $2k$?

A) 40

B) 20

C) 0

D) −20

Although this question seems more complicated than others you've seen in this chapter, if you use the Kaplan Method for Math, you'll find the correct answer. The following table shows Kaplan's strategic thinking on the left, along with suggested math scratchwork on the right.

Strategic Thinking	Math Scratchwork
Step 1: Read the question, identifying and organizing important information as you go You're asked to find the value of $2k$.	
Step 2: Choose the best strategy to answer the question Notice that the equation in the question stem is not in standard form. Distributing the $\frac{1}{4}$ won't result in unmanageable fractions, so doing so won't cost you a lot of time. After distributing, set the equation equal to 0. The "normal" routes to the solutions (factoring, etc.) would be difficult to take here because of the presence of k. Instead, use the solutions to construct and FOIL two binomials. The quadratic expressions must be equal because they share the same solutions. Set them equal to each other, and then use algebra to solve for k.	$\frac{1}{4}(4x^2-8x-k)=30$ $x^2-2x-\frac{k}{4}=30$ $x^2-2x-\frac{k}{4}-30=0$ $(x-7)(x+5)=0$ $x^2-2x-35=0$ $x^2-2x-\frac{k}{4}-30=x^2-2x-35$ $-\frac{k}{4}=-5$ $-k=-20$ $k=20$
Step 3: Check that you answered the *right* question Be careful! Many students will select B, but you're asked for $2k$. Multiply the value of k by 2, and select (A).	$k=20$ $2k=40$

As demonstrated, even the most daunting quadratics questions are made more straightforward by using the Kaplan Method for Math.

Now you'll have a chance to try a few more test-like questions. Use the scaffolding as needed as a guide through the question and to the right answer.

Some guidance is provided, but you'll need to fill in the missing parts of explanations or the step-by-step math in order to get to the correct answer. Don't worry—after going through the examples at the beginning of this chapter, these questions should be completely doable. If you're still struggling, review the worked examples in this chapter.

8. The height of a potato launched from a potato gun can be described as a function of elapsed time according to the following quadratic equation: $y(t) = -16t^2 + 224t + 240$. What is the sum of the potato's maximum height and the time it takes the potato to reach the ground?

   A) 15

   B) 240

   C) 1,024

   D) 1,039

Use the following scaffolding as your map through the question. If you aren't sure where to start, answer the questions in italics and fill in the blanks in the table as you work from top to bottom.

Strategic Thinking	Math Scratchwork
Step 1: Read the question, identifying and organizing important information as you go *What are you being asked to do here?* You're asked to find the sum of the maximum height and the time it takes the potato to hit the ground. The t^2 indicates a quadratic (and therefore a parabolic trajectory).	

Strategic Thinking	Math Scratchwork
Step 2: Choose the best strategy to answer the question	$h = \dfrac{-b}{2a} = \underline{\qquad}$
How can you tackle this systematically? What component of the parabola would correspond to the maximum height?	$k = y(h)$
Because *a* (the t^2 coefficient) is negative, this parabola opens down, which means the maximum height would be at the vertex.	$k = -16(\underline{\ })^2 + 224x\underline{\ } + 240$
	$k = \underline{\hspace{3cm}}$
The vertex form of a parabola is f(x) = a(x − h)² + k. *Which variable represents the height? What is the max height the potato will reach?*	$O = \underline{\hspace{3cm}}$
	$O = (\underline{\hspace{1.5cm}})(\underline{\hspace{1.5cm}})$
Find *h*, then use it to find the maximum height.	$t = \underline{\hspace{3cm}}$
What is the height of the potato when it hits the ground?	$t = \underline{\hspace{3cm}}$
	sum = \underline{\hspace{1.5cm}} + \underline{\hspace{1.5cm}}
When the potato hits the ground, its height will be zero. Translation: factor!	
What are the possible solutions for t? *Which of these solutions doesn't make sense in the context of the question? Is there anything left to do?*	
Remember, the question asks you for the sum of the potato's maximum height and the time it takes the potato to hit the ground.	
Step 3: Check that you answered the *right* question	
Did you calculate the sum of the maximum height and the time the potato spent in the air?	
If you came up with (D), you're absolutely correct.	\underline{\hspace{2cm}}

9. If $ab > 0$, $b^2ac < 0$, *a* is a constant, and *b* and *c* are distinct *x*-intercepts of the function $f(x)$, then $f(x)$ could equal which of the following?

   A) $5x^2 + 1$

   B) $(x - \sqrt{17})(x + \sqrt{24})$

   C) $(x - \sqrt{17})(x - \sqrt{24})$

   D) $(x + \sqrt{17})(x + \sqrt{24})$

Use the scaffolding that follows as your map through the question. If you aren't sure where to start, answer the questions in italics and fill in the blanks in the table as you work from top to bottom.

Strategic Thinking	Math Scratchwork
Step 1: Read the question, identifying and organizing important information as you go *What do you need to find?* You need to select the equation that satisfies the given properties of $f(x)$.	
Step 2: Choose the best strategy to answer the question *What can you deduce about a and b?* If $ab > 0$, then a and b are either both positive or both negative. *What can you deduce about c?* In the inequality $b^2ac < 0$, b^2 will be positive regardless of the sign of b. Therefore, either a or c is positive, and the other must be negative. *What must be true about the x-intercepts of f(x)?* The *x*-intercepts are b and c. Since b has the same sign as a, while c has the opposite sign as a, it follows that b and c also have opposite signs. *What does that imply?* The correct answer must be a function with one negative root and one positive root. Scan the functions to find the correct one. Ignore the complicated-looking numbers; all that matters are the signs!	$ab > 0$ a and b have _____ sign $b^2ac < 0$ a and c have _____ signs b and c are roots of $f(x)$ $f(x)$ has one _____ root and one _____ root A's roots are _____ B's roots are _____ C's roots are _____ D's roots are _____
Step 3: Check that you answered the *right* question *Do you need to go any further?* If you picked (B), then you got it!	_____

Now that you've seen the variety of ways in which the SAT can test you on quadratics, try the following questions to check your understanding. Give yourself 5 minutes to tackle the following four questions. Make sure you use the Kaplan Method for Math as often as you can. Remember, you want to emphasize speed and efficiency in addition to simply getting the correct answer.

10. If $4x - 12\sqrt{x} + 9 = 16$, then $10\sqrt{x} - 15 =$

   A) 20

   B) 25

   C) 30

   D) 35

11. How many times do the parabolas $f(x) = 3(x - 4)^2 + 4$ and $g(x) = (x + 5)^2 + 2x - 135$ intersect?

   A) Never

   B) Once

   C) Twice

   D) More than twice

12. What is positive difference between the x-intercepts of the parabola $g(x) = -2.5x^2 + 10x - 7.5$?

13. What is the axis of symmetry of the function $f(x) = -\dfrac{11}{3}x^2 + 17x - \dfrac{43}{13}$?

   A) $x = -\dfrac{102}{11}$

   B) $x = -\dfrac{51}{22}$

   C) $x = \dfrac{51}{22}$

   D) $x = \dfrac{102}{11}$

Answers and Explanations for this chapter begin on page 635.

EXTRA PRACTICE

1. Which of the following is equivalent to $(2a + 5b)(a - 3b)$?

   A) $2a^2 - 2ab - 15b^2$

   B) $2a^2 - ab - 15b^2$

   C) $2a^2 + 2ab - 15b^2$

   D) $2a^2 + 11ab - 15b^2$

2. Which of the following are roots of the quadratic equation $(x + 3)^2 = 49$?

   A) $x = -10, x = 4$

   B) $x = -10, x = 10$

   C) $x = -4, x = 10$

   D) $x = 3 \pm 2\sqrt{13}$

3. The factored form of a quadratic equation is $y = (2x + 1)(x - 5)$, and the standard form is $y = x^2 - 3x - 5$. Which of the following statements accurately describes the graph of y?

   A) The x-intercepts are –1 and 5, and the y-intercept is –5.

   B) The x-intercepts are $-\frac{1}{2}$ and 5, and the y-intercept is –5.

   C) The x-intercepts are $-\frac{1}{2}$ and 5, and the y-intercept is 5.

   D) The x-intercepts are 1 and –5, and the y-intercept is –5.

4. What information does the value of c reveal when a quadratic equation is written in the form $y = ax^2 + bx + c$, assuming $a \neq 0$, $b \neq 0$, and $c \neq 0$?

   A) The solution (zero) of the equation

   B) The location of the graph's axis of symmetry

   C) The y-intercept of the graph of the equation

   D) The maximum or minimum value of the equation

5. Taylor fires a toy rocket from ground level. The height of the rocket with respect to time can be represented by a quadratic function. If the toy rocket reaches a maximum height of 34 feet, 3 seconds after it was fired, which of the following functions could represent the height, h, of the rocket t seconds after it was fired?

   A) $h(t) = -16(t - 3)^2 + 34$

   B) $h(t) = -16(t + 3)^2 + 34$

   C) $h(t) = 16(t - 3)^2 + 34$

   D) $h(t) = 16(t + 3)^2 + 34$

6. Which of the following could be the graph of the equation $y = x^2 + 2x - 8$?

A)
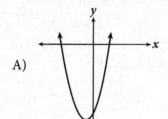

B)
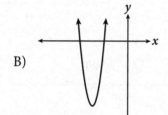

C)
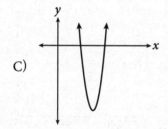

D)
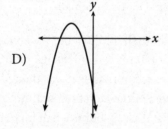

7. If $x^2 - 7x = 30$ and $x > 0$, what is the value of $x - 5$?

A) 5

B) 6

C) 10

D) 25

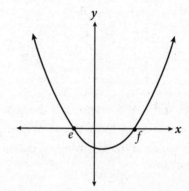

8. If e is half as far from the origin as f in the figure above, which of the following could be the factored form of the graph's equation?

A) $y = (x - \frac{1}{2})(x + 1)$

B) $y = (x - 1)(x + 2)$

C) $y = (x - 1)(2x + 1)$

D) $y = (x + \frac{1}{2})(2x + 1)$

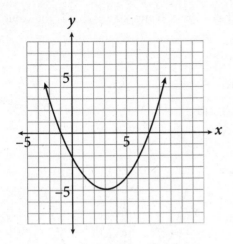

$$\begin{cases} y = 2x \\ 2x^2 + 2y^2 = 240 \end{cases}$$

12. If (x, y) is a solution to the system of equations above, what is the value of x^2?

    A) 24

    B) 40

    C) 120

    D) 576

9. If $f(x) = ax^2 + bx + c$ represents the quadratic function whose graph is shown in the figure above, which of the following statements is NOT true?

    A) $a > 0$

    B) $b > 0$

    C) $c < 0$

    D) All of the statements are true.

10. Which of the following equations has the same solutions as the equation $40 - 6x = x^2$?

    A) $y = (x - 6)^2 - 40$

    B) $y = (x - 6)^2 + 40$

    C) $y = (x + 3)^2 - 49$

    D) $y = (x + 3)^2 + 49$

11. Which of the following equations could represent a parabola that has a minimum value of 5 and whose axis of symmetry is the line $x = -3$?

    A) $y = (x - 3)^2 + 5$

    B) $y = (x + 3)^2 + 5$

    C) $y = (x - 5)^2 + 3$

    D) $y = (x + 5)^2 - 3$

Tyree's Punt

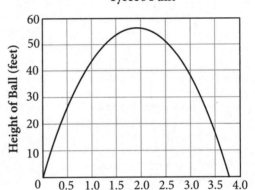

13. Tyree punts a football into the air. The equation $h = -16t^2 + 60t$ represents the height of the ball in feet, t seconds after it was punted. The graph of part of the equation is shown in the figure above. If Craig punts a ball higher than Tyree did, which of the following equations could be use to find the height of Craig's punt?

    A) $h = -16(t^2 - 3t)$

    B) $h = -8t(2t - 9)$

    C) $h = -4(2t - 5)^2 + 48$

    D) $h = -4(2t - 6)^2 + 52$

14. What is the positive difference between the roots of the equation $y = \frac{1}{3}x^2 - 2x + 3$?

16. If the graph of $y = ax^2 + bx + c$ passes through the points $(-2, -10)$, $(0, 2)$, and $(4, 14)$, what is the value of $a + b + c$?

15. If $x = -5$ when $x^2 + 2xk + k^2 = 0$, what is the value of k?

Additional Topics in Math

BY THE END OF THIS UNIT, YOU WILL BE ABLE TO:

1. Solve geometry questions with lines, angles, and triangles

2. Use special right triangles and Pythagorean triplets to save time on Test Day

CHAPTER 9

Lines, Angles, and Triangles

CHAPTER OBJECTIVES

By the end of this chapter, you will be able to:

1. Apply the properties of lines and angles to solve geometry questions

2. Use the Pythagorean theorem, Pythagorean triplets, and special right triangles to answer questions involving triangles

3. Identify simple shapes within complex figures and use them to solve questions

SMARTPOINTS

Point Value	SmartPoint Category
30 Points	Geometry

LINES AND ANGLES

Lines and angles are the foundation of SAT geometry. Therefore, mastering their basic rules will make solving these questions, as well as related geometry questions, easier. With the knowledge you'll gain from this chapter, you can quickly identify geometric relationships, build upon the information given in the question, and often bypass complex algebra.

Familiarity with angle types will often unlock information that is not explicitly given in a question. This makes getting to the answer much easier on even the toughest geometry questions. First, let's take a look at the types of angles you should be able to recognize.

Angle Type	Angle Measurement	Example
Acute	Less than 90°	
Right	90°	
Obtuse	Between 90° and 180°	
Straight	180°	

More often than not, you'll work with multiple angles in a single question. Therefore, it's worth noting two likely familiar terms that involve working with two or more angles: complementary and supplementary angles. Two angles are **complementary** if their measures add up to 90°; if two angles' measures add up to 180°, the angles are **supplementary**.

> ✔ Note
>
> Two angles need *not* be adjacent to be complementary or supplementary.

Intersecting lines create angles with special relationships you'll need to know as well. When two lines intersect, adjacent angles are supplementary, and **vertical** angles (two angles opposite a vertex) are equal, or **congruent**. Take a look at the following figure for an example.

The angles marked $a°$ and $b°$ are supplementary; therefore, $a + b = 180$. The angle marked $a°$ is vertical (and thus equal) to the one marked 60°, so $a = 60$. With this new information, you can find b: $a + b = 60 + b = 180$, so $b = 120$.

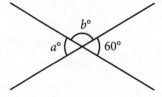

When two parallel lines are intersected by another line (called a **transversal**), all acute angles are equal, and all obtuse angles are equal. Additionally, **corresponding angles** are angles that are in the same position but on different parallel lines/transversal intersections; they are also equal. Furthermore, **alternate interior angles** and **alternate exterior angles** are equal. Alternate interior angles are angles that are positioned between the two parallel lines on opposite sides of the transversal, whereas alternate exterior angles are positioned on the outside of the parallel lines on opposite sides of the transversal. Consider the following figure:

- Line 1 and Line 2 are parallel and cut by transversal ℓ.

- Angles a, d, e, and h are obtuse and equal.

- Angles b, c, f, and g are acute and equal.

- Angle pairs (b and f), (c and g), (a and e), and (d and h) are corresponding angles.

- Angle pairs (a and h) and (b and g) are alternate exterior angles.

- Angle pairs (d and e) and (c and f) are alternate interior angles.

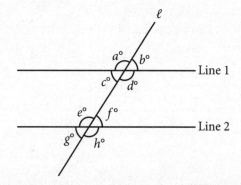

Now use your knowledge of lines and angles to tackle a test-like question.

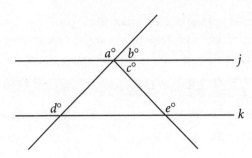

Note: Figure not drawn to scale.

1. In the figure above, if lines *j* and *k* are parallel, which of the following statements must be true?

    A) $a = e$

    B) $b = c$

    C) $d = 180 - c$

    D) $b + d - c = e$

 Note

"Figure not drawn to scale" means that you can't eyeball angles, line measurements, or relationships.

Work through the Kaplan Method for Math step-by-step to solve this question. The following table shows Kaplan's strategic thinking on the left, along with suggested math scratchwork on the right.

Strategic Thinking	Math Scratchwork
Step 1: Read the question, identifying and organizing important information as you go You're asked to find which answer choice contains a true statement. You're told that lines *j* and *k* are parallel. Two transversals are also drawn.	

Strategic Thinking	Math Scratchwork
Step 2: Choose the best strategy to answer the question Two parallel lines cut by a transversal yield four equal obtuse angles and four equal acute angles. In this figure, however, there are two transversals, so you must take care not to draw erroneous conclusions about two angles formed by different transversals. Angles from different transversals have nothing to do with each other. Identify relationships among the angles. Angles a and d are corresponding angles and are therefore equal. Angles a and b are supplementary, as are angles c and e. By extension, angles d and b are supplementary as well. However, note that angles a, b, and d have no relation to angles c and e, as the two groups are formed by different transversals. Now look for answers you can eliminate based on what you know. Choice A claims a relationship between a and e, which are formed by different transversals, so eliminate it. Similarly, because b and c are formed by different transversals, b is incorrect. Choice C is incorrect for the same reason: d and c are formed by different transversals.	$a = d$ $d + b = 180$ $c + e = 180$ $a + b = 180$ No relationships between $\{a, b, d\}$ and $\{c, e\}$
Step 3: Check that you answered the *right* question Choice (D) must be correct by process of elimination.	

> **✔ Note**
>
> Choice (D) is correct because $b + d - c = e$ is equivalent to $b + d = e + c$. This is a true statement because b is supplementary to d and e is supplementary to c, making the two sums both equal to 180 and therefore each other as well.

TRIANGLES

Lines and angles form the basis of triangles—some of the most commonly occurring shapes on the SAT. Luckily, triangle questions usually don't involve a lot of complex algebra and are a great way to earn a few quick points on Test Day. A strong command of triangle properties will help you recognize and solve these questions quickly. Many seemingly difficult questions will become easier once you can confidently speak the language of triangles.

All triangles follow the rules listed here, regardless of the type of triangle, so take the time now to get comfortable with them. We've provided a sample figure to help you visualize the rules.

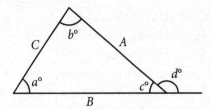

- The sum of the interior angles add up to 180°. In the triangle shown, $a + b + c = 180$.

- The exterior angle of a triangle is equal to the sum of the two opposite interior angles. In this example, $d = a + b = 180 - c$.

- A side opposite a greater angle is longer than a side opposite a smaller angle. For instance, if $a = 50$, $b = 60$, and $c = 70$, then $A < B < C$.

- Triangle Inequality theorem: The sum of two side lengths must be greater than the third side length, and the positive difference of two side lengths must be less than the third side length. For example, $A + B > C$ and $A - B < C$.

Up next is a sample question that tests your knowledge of these rules. Don't forget about the angle properties, either.

2. During a camping trip, Aundria and Annette decide to climb a mountain using two different routes to the top. Aundria takes the hiking route that travels 5 mi south, 6 mi east, 7 mi south, and 2 mi west to the summit; Annette uses the climbing route that starts at the same point as the hiking route but goes directly from there to the summit. Assuming vertical travel distance is not considered, about how many miles in all will the two travel?

A) 32.65

B) 33.42

C) 34.00

D) 34.42

Work through the Kaplan Method for Math step-by-step to solve this question. The following table shows Kaplan's strategic thinking on the left, along with suggested math scratchwork on the right.

Strategic Thinking	Math Scratchwork
Step 1: Read the question, identifying and organizing important information as you go You need to determine the total distance Aundria and Annette traveled.	
Step 2: Choose the best strategy to answer the question Draw a diagram to visualize the situation, and label it with what you know. Next, draw additional lines to reveal hidden shapes, such as right triangles. When you draw the right triangle, you'll also create a rectangle. Opposite sides of a rectangle are congruent, so you can transfer this information to the unknown pieces you drew.	

Strategic Thinking	Math Scratchwork
Annette's route is the hypotenuse of the triangle. You know the lengths of the legs, so you can find the hypotenuse using the Pythagorean theorem. Read carefully! You need the sum of the two distances traveled. Add all the segments of Aundria's route together, and then add that number to Annette's total distance traveled.	Start 5 mi 6 mi 7 mi 7 mi 4 mi 2 mi Annette $$(5+7)^2 + 4^2 = c^2$$ $$c^2 = 144 + 16 = 160$$ $$c = \sqrt{160} = 4\sqrt{10}$$ Aundria $$5 + 6 + 7 + 2 = 20$$ total: $20 + 4\sqrt{10}$
Step 3: Check that you answered the *right* question	
The answer choices are in decimal form, so round your radical figure, add it to 20, and you're finished. The result matches (A).	32.65

> ✔ **Note**
>
> Stay focused on what the question asks. Don't stop until you're sure you've found what you need.

THE PYTHAGOREAN THEOREM, PYTHAGOREAN TRIPLETS & SPECIAL RIGHT TRIANGLES

The Pythagorean theorem is one of the most fundamental equations in geometry, and it will be of great use to you on the SAT. Common Pythagorean triplets and special right triangle ratios that originate from this formula will also serve you well on Test Day.

The **Pythagorean theorem** is an important triangle topic that you are probably familiar with already. If you know any two lengths of a right triangle, you can use the Pythagorean theorem equation to find the missing side. It is expressed as $a^2 + b^2 = c^2$, where a and b are the shorter sides of the triangle (called legs) and c is the hypotenuse, which is always across from the right angle of the triangle.

> ✔ **Note**
>
> The Pythagorean theorem can only be applied to right triangles.

Consider an example: A right triangle has a leg measuring 9 and a hypotenuse measuring 14. To find the missing leg, plug the known values into the Pythagorean theorem: $9^2 + b^2 = 14^2$. This simplifies to $81 + b^2 = 196$, which becomes $b^2 = 115$. Take the square root of both sides to get $b = \sqrt{115}$. Because no factors of 115 are perfect squares, $b = \sqrt{115}$ is the answer.

> ✔ **Note**
>
> Wait to simplify radicals until you have your final answer. Leave answers in radical form unless a question says otherwise or the answer choices are written as decimals.

Because time is such a premium on the SAT, time-saving strategies are invaluable, and there are two that will come in handy on triangle questions. The first is knowing common **Pythagorean triplets**, which are right triangles that happen to have integer sides. These triangles show up *very* frequently on the SAT. The two most common are 3-4-5 and 5-12-13. Multiples of these (e.g., 6-8-10, 10-24-26) can also pop up, so watch out for them, as well. The beauty of these triplets is that if you see any two sides, you can automatically fill in the third without having to resort to the time-consuming Pythagorean theorem.

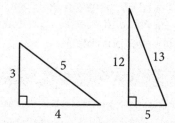

The second time-saving strategy involves recognizing **special right triangles**. Like Pythagorean triplets, special right triangles involve a ratio comparing a right triangle's legs and hypotenuse, but with these triangles, you only need to know one side in order to calculate the other two. These triangles are defined by their angles.

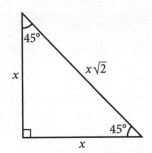

The ratio of the sides in a **45-45-90** triangle is $x : x : x\sqrt{2}$, where x is the length of each leg and $x\sqrt{2}$ is the length of the hypotenuse.

The ratio of the sides in a **30-60-90** triangle is $x : x\sqrt{3} : 2x$, where x is the shorter leg, $x\sqrt{3}$ is the longer leg, and $2x$ is the hypotenuse.

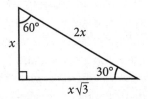

While the Pythagorean theorem can always be used to solve right triangle questions, it is not always the most efficient way to proceed. Further, many students make errors when simplifying radicals and exponents. The Pythagorean triplets and special right triangles allow you to save time and avoid those mistakes. Use them whenever possible!

> ✔ **Note**
>
> **Although you will be given the special right triangle ratios on Test Day, you can save yourself time by memorizing them. That way you won't have to keeping flipping back to the formula page!**

On Test Day you might also be asked to determine the area of a triangle. The area of a triangle can be determined using $A = \frac{1}{2}bh$, where b is the triangle base and h is the triangle height.

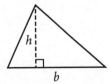

When you have a right triangle, you can use the legs as the base and the height. If the triangle isn't a right triangle, you'll need to draw the height in, as demonstrated in the figure shown. Remember that the height *must* be perpendicular to the base.

Similar triangles have the same angle measurements and proportional sides. In the figure below, ∆ABC and ∆DEF have the same angle measurements, so the side lengths can be set up as

the following proportion: $\dfrac{A}{D} = \dfrac{B}{E} = \dfrac{C}{F}$.

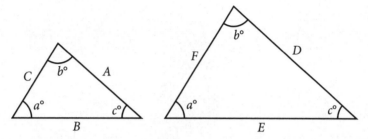

Drawing multiple heights in one triangle creates similar triangles, as shown in the diagram below. When you encounter a question like this, redrawing the similar triangles with their angles and sides in the same positions will help keep information in order.

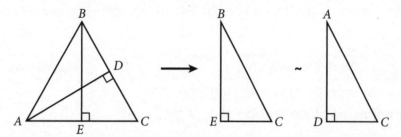

Complex figures are also a recurring SAT geometry topic. A complex figure is not a shape such as a dodecahedron: Instead, a complex figure is usually a larger shape that is composed of multiple (familiar) shapes; these can be obvious or cleverly hidden. These figures can always be broken down into squares, rectangles, triangles, and/or circles. Although this chapter emphasizes triangles, you'll get plenty of practice with other figures over the next few questions. No matter how convoluted the figure, following the guidelines here will lead you to the correct answer on Test Day.

- Transfer information from the question stem to the figure. If a figure isn't provided, draw one!

- Break the figure into familiar shapes.

- Determine how one line segment can play multiple roles in a figure. For example, if a circle and triangle overlap correctly, the circle's radius might be the triangle's hypotenuse.

- Work from the shape with the most information to the shape with the least information.

A final note about triangles: You are likely to see triangle questions involving real-world situations. But don't fret: All you need to do is follow the Kaplan Strategy for Translating English into Math. Extract the geometry information you need, then solve!

Take a look at the next few pages for more test-like triangle questions.

3. Uwe has a rectangular field that he would like to split into two triangular fields—one for planting grain and one for planting vegetables—by building a fence from one corner of the field to the opposite corner. If the area of the field is 540 m² and the length of the field is 36 m, how many meters of fence will Uwe need?

Work through the Kaplan Method for Math step-by-step to solve this question. The following table shows Kaplan's strategic thinking on the left, along with suggested math scratchwork on the right.

Strategic Thinking	Math Scratchwork
Step 1: Read the question, identifying and organizing important information as you go You need to find the length of the fence (the diagonal of the rectangular field).	
Step 2: Choose the best strategy to answer the question Draw a figure to visualize the situation. Sketch the rectangle and label what you know. The area of a rectangle is the product of its length and width. Because you know the length and the area, you can find the width.	36 $A = 540 = 36 \times h$ $h = 540 \div 36 = 15$

Strategic Thinking	Math Scratchwork
The diagonal of the rectangle is also the hypotenuse of a right triangle with legs of lengths 15 and 36. This is a multiple of the 5-12-13 Pythagorean triplet. Multiply 3 by 13 to find the length of the hypotenuse (and that of the diagonal of the rectangle).	 $15 = 5 \times 3$ $36 = 12 \times 3$ diagonal $= 13 \times 3 = 39$
Step 3: Check that you answered the *right* question The question asks for the length of the fence, which is represented by the diagonal, so you're done. Grid in 39 and move on.	39

✔ **Note**

If you didn't recognize the multiple of the Pythagorean triplet, you could have used the Pythagorean theorem to find the length of the diagonal.

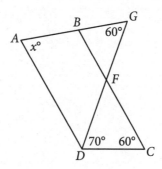

4. In the figure above, $\overline{AD}$ and $\overline{BC}$ are parallel. What is the value of x?

A) 60

B) 70

C) 80

D) 110

Work through the Kaplan Method for Math step-by-step to solve this question. The following table shows Kaplan's strategic thinking on the left, along with suggested math scratchwork on the right.

Strategic Thinking	Math Scratchwork
Step 1: Read the question, identifying and organizing important information as you go You're asked for the value of x.	
Step 2: Choose the best strategy to answer the question Look for familiar shapes within the given figure. There are three triangles present. Because $\overline{AD}$ and $\overline{BC}$ are parallel, $BFDA$ is a trapezoid. Although x might seem far removed from the known angles, you can find it. It will just take more than one step. In $\triangle FDC$, only one angle is missing, so you can solve for it and fill it in easily. Note that $\angle DFC$ and $\angle BFG$ are vertical angles, so $\angle BFG$ is also 50°. At this point, you have two of the three angles in $\triangle BFG$, so you can solve for the third. $\angle FBG$ and $\angle BAD$ are corresponding angles (and are therefore congruent). You can now conclude that $x = 70$.	$m\angle DFC = 180° - 70° - 60°$ $\qquad = 50°$ $m\angle BFG = m\angle DFC = 50°$ $m\angle FBG = 180° - 50° - 60°$ $\qquad = 70°$ $m\angle BAD = x = m\angle FBG = 70°$ *(figure: triangles with labeled angles; points A, B, G, F, D, C; angles $x°$ at A, 70° and 60° at B/G, 50° at F, 50° at F, 70° and 60° at D/C)*
Step 3: Check that you answered the *right* question You're asked for x, so select (B), and you're done.	$x = 70$

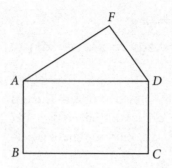

5. In the figure above, *ABCD* is a rectangle and ∠*F* is a right angle. If $\overline{FD} = \overline{DC}$, $\overline{AB} = 6$, and the perimeter of rectangle *ABCD* is 30, then what is the length of $\overline{FA}$?

    A) 6

    B) $3\sqrt{5}$

    C) 8

    D) $5\sqrt{3}$

Work through the Kaplan Method for Math step-by-step to solve this question. The following table shows Kaplan's strategic thinking on the left, along with suggested math scratchwork on the right.

Strategic Thinking	Math Scratchwork
Step 1: Read the question, identifying and organizing important information as you go You need to find the length of $\overline{FA}$.	

Strategic Thinking	Math Scratchwork
Step 2: Choose the best strategy to answer the question Look for familiar shapes within the provided figure: There is a rectangle and a right triangle. You're told that $\overline{AB} = 6$ and $\overline{FD} = \overline{DC}$. Because $ABCD$ is a rectangle, $\overline{AB}$ must equal $\overline{DC}$, so $\overline{AB} = \overline{DC} = \overline{FD} = 6$. You're also told that the perimeter of rectangle $ABCD$ is 30. Because you know the length of two sides of the rectangle, you can find the other two. Unfortunately, with a hypotenuse of 9 and a leg of 6, $\triangle FAD$ isn't a Pythagorean triplet or special right triangle. Use the Pythagorean theorem to find the missing side. Although $\sqrt{45}$ isn't an answer choice, it doesn't mean you made an error. When your answer is a radical and you don't see it among the choices, that means you need to simplify the radical.	$\overline{AB} = 6$, $\overline{FD} = \overline{DC}$ $\overline{AB} = \overline{FD} = \overline{DC} = 6$ $30 = 6 + 6 + \overline{AD} + \overline{BC}$ $\overline{AD} + \overline{BC} = 18$ $\overline{AD} = \overline{BC} = 9$ $6^2 + FA^2 = 9^2$ $FA^2 = 81 - 36 = 45$ $FA = \sqrt{45}$ $\sqrt{45} = \sqrt{9} \times \sqrt{5} = 3\sqrt{5}$
Step 3: Check that you answered the *right* question You've provided what the question asks for, so (B) is correct.	

Now you'll have a chance to try a few more test-like questions. Use the scaffolding as needed as a guide through the question and to the right answer.

Some guidance is provided, but you'll need to fill in the missing parts of explanations or the step-by-step math in order to get to the correct answer. Don't worry—after going through the examples at the beginning of this chapter, these questions should be completely doable. If you're still struggling, review the worked examples in this chapter.

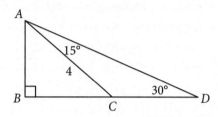

6. Given $\triangle ABC$ and $\triangle ABD$ above, what is the perimeter of $\triangle ACD$?

A) $2\sqrt{6} - 2\sqrt{2}$

B) $4\sqrt{3}$

C) $4 + 2\sqrt{6} + 2\sqrt{2}$

D) $2\sqrt{6} + 6\sqrt{2}$

Use the following scaffolding as your map through the question. If you aren't sure where to start, answer the questions in italics and fill in the blanks in the table as you work from top to bottom.

Strategic Thinking	Math Scratchwork
Step 1: Read the question, identifying and organizing important information as you go *What are you being asked to find here?* You need to find the perimeter of $\triangle ACD$.	

Strategic Thinking	Math Scratchwork
Step 2: Choose the best strategy to answer the question *How can you use the figure to get to the answer?* Look for unknown values that you can derive from the information in the question stem. For instance, you can find ∠ACD from the two given angles. From there you can easily determine the measures of the angles in △ABC. Fill in the blanks on the right as you go. *What do you notice about the two triangles?* Both △ABC and △ABD have special characteristics. Use these to determine the length of each missing side. Once again, update the figure on the right as you work. △ACD *isn't a special right triangle. How can you find* $\overline{CD}$*?* $\overline{BD}$ is the sum of $\overline{BC}$ and $\overline{CD}$. Subtract $\overline{BC}$ from $\overline{BD}$ to find $\overline{CD}$. Once you find all three sides of △ACD, add them together to find its perimeter.	$m \angle ACD = \underline{\quad}° - \underline{\quad}° - \underline{\quad}°$ $= \underline{\quad}°$ *(figure: triangle with vertices A, B, C, D; right angle at B; angle 15° at A; segment labeled 4; angle 30° at D)* △ABC: $\underline{\quad} - \underline{\quad} - \underline{\quad}$ △ABD: $\underline{\quad} - \underline{\quad} - \underline{\quad}$ $\overline{CD} = \underline{\quad} - \underline{\quad} = \underline{\qquad}$ $P_{\triangle ACD} = \underline{\quad} + (\underline{\qquad}) + \underline{\quad}$ $= \underline{\qquad}$
Step 3: Check that you answered the *right* question *What is the perimeter of* △ACD*?* If you got (C), you are correct!	$\underline{\qquad}$

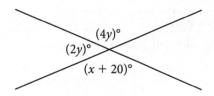

7. In the figure above, what is the value of x?

Use the following scaffolding as your map through the question. If you aren't sure where to start, answer the questions in italics and fill in the blanks in the table as you work from top to bottom.

Strategic Thinking	Math Scratchwork
Step 1: Read the question, identifying and organizing important information as you go *What are you being asked to find?* You need to find the value of x.	
Step 2: Choose the best strategy to answer the question *How can you use the figure to get to the answer?* A quick option is to solve for y using the fact that supplementary angles add up to 180°. You can then solve for x using the fact that vertical angles are equal.	supp. ____ + ____ = 180 ____ = 180 y = ____ , $4y$ = ____ vertical ____ = ____ x = ____

Strategic Thinking	Math Scratchwork
Step 3: Check that you answered the *right* question *What is the value of x?* Make sure you grid in the value of *x*, not *y*. You're correct if you got 100!	____

Below is a real-world rectangle question for you to try. Don't worry if you have no picture framing experience.

8. The size of a TV is dictated by the length of its diagonal. Whitney would like to purchase a new TV but must first determine the maximum size TV she can mount on her living room wall. She would like a 3-inch space on each side of the TV, effectively creating a frame of empty space around the TV that is 3 inches wide on each side. If the rectangular wall space Whitney plans to use for her TV is 28.25 inches by 53 inches, what is the largest size TV (in inches) that she can fit on the wall? Round your answer to the nearest inch.

Use the following scaffolding as your map through the question. If you aren't sure where to start, answer the questions in italics and fill in the blanks in the table as you work from top to bottom.

Strategic Thinking	Math Scratchwork
Step 1: Read the question, identifying and organizing important information as you go *What do you ultimately need to find?* You're asked for the largest size TV Whitney can mount on her wall; in other words, you need to calculate the length of its diagonal.	

Strategic Thinking	Math Scratchwork
Step 2: Choose the best strategy to answer the question *This is a geometry question presented in word form. What's a good route to consider?* Draw a figure! First, draw a rectangle to represent the wall space. Next, draw another rectangle inside the first to represent the TV. Label the diagram with the information the question provides. *How do you find the dimensions of the TV?* Subtract the width of the empty wall space from the given dimensions. Once there, use the Pythagorean theorem to find the diagonal of the TV area, and then subtract the area of the picture from it.	 3 3 3 22.25 ? 47 3 wall space: _____ x _____ TV space: _____ x _____ _____^{2} x _____^{2} = _____^{2} _____ + _____ = _____
Step 3: Check that you answered the *right* question *What's the largest diagonal Whitney's TV can have?* If you got 52, you'd be correct!	 _____

Chapter 9: Lines, Angles, and Triangles   257

Now that you've seen the variety of ways in which the SAT can test you on triangles, try the following questions to check your understanding. Give yourself 5 minutes to tackle the following four questions. Make sure you use the Kaplan Method for Math as often as you can. Remember, you want to emphasize speed and efficiency in addition to simply getting the correct answer.

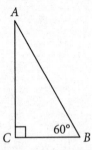

Note: Figure not drawn to scale.

9. If the area of $\triangle ABC$ is $8\sqrt{3}$, what is the length of $\overline{AB}$?

A) 4
B) 6
C) 7
D) 8

Note: Figure not drawn to scale.

10. Four squares are inscribed inside each other as shown in the figure above. Each progressively larger square has a perimeter that is 4 cm greater than that of the previous square. If the innermost square has a perimeter of 4 cm, what is the probability of randomly selecting a point within one of the white regions?

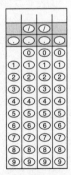

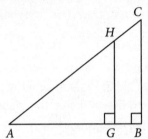

Note: Figure not drawn to scale.

11. $\triangle ABC$ above has an area of 150 square units. If $\overline{AB} = \overline{AH} = 20$, then what is the length of $\overline{HG}$?

A) 5
B) 12
C) 16
D) 20

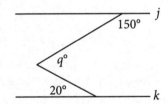

Note: Figure not drawn to scale.

12. In the figure above, lines j and k are parallel. What is the value of $\angle q$?

A) 50
B) 55
C) 75
D) 130

Answers and Explanations for this chapter begin on page 645.

EXTRA PRACTICE

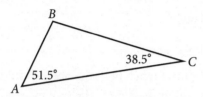

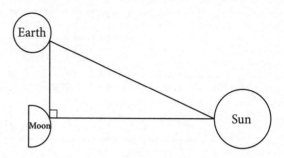

1. If the length of $\overline{AB}$ in the triangle above is 28 cm and the length of $\overline{BC}$ is 45 cm, what is the length in centimeters of $\overline{AC}$?

    A) 35

    B) 45

    C) 53

    D) 64

3. The moon goes through several phases, such as new, crescent, quarter, and full. During the quarter phase, we see half the moon. During this phase, the sun (relative to Earth) forms a right angle with the moon as shown in the figure above. If the distance from Earth to the moon is approximately 240,000 miles, and the distance from the moon to the sun is approximately 91,674,000 miles, how many miles are between Earth and the sun?

    A) 84,042,000

    B) 88,434,000

    C) 91,674,000

    D) 8,404,180,000

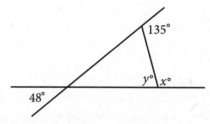

2. The sides of the triangle above have been extended as shown. What is the value in degrees of $\angle x - \angle y$?

    A) 3

    B) 6

    C) 87

    D) 180

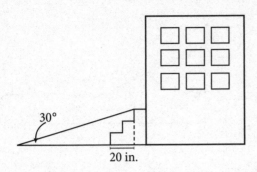

20 in.

Note: Figure not drawn to scale.

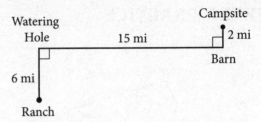

4. A company designs removable handicap access ramps as temporary measures for buildings to become compliant with the Americans with Disabilities Act (ADA). The particular ramp shown in the figure must be placed at a 30° angle, eight feet from the bottom step. About how long, in inches, is the ramp?

A) 67

B) 116

C) 128

D) 134

5. The longer leg of a right triangle is three times the length of the shorter leg. Given that the length of each leg is a whole number, which of the following could be the length of the hypotenuse?

A) $\sqrt{40}$

B) $\sqrt{47}$

C) $\sqrt{55}$

D) $\sqrt{63}$

6. A tourist ranch built the horse-riding trail shown in the figure. The trail takes a rider from the ranch to an old watering hole, then to a historic barn, and finally to a campsite where riders can spend the night. If a rider takes a horse on a direct path from the ranch to the campsite, how much shorter, in miles, would the trip be?

A) 6

B) 8

C) 17

D) 23

7. A geometry teacher drew a right triangle on the board and measured the lengths of the sides. Which of the following could NOT have been the lengths of the sides of the triangle she drew?

A) 5 inches, 12 inches, 13 inches

B) $\frac{1}{3}$ of a foot, $\frac{1}{4}$ of a foot, $\frac{1}{5}$ of a foot

C) 9 cm, 40 cm, 41 cm

D) $\frac{3}{4}$ of a foot, 1 foot, 15 inches

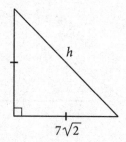

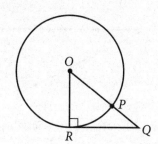

8. What is the value of *h* in the figure above?

    A) 3.5

    B) 7

    C) 12.5

    D) 14

10. The radius of circle *O* shown in the figure is
    1.5. If $\overline{RQ}$ = 2, what is the length of $\overline{PQ}$?

    A) 0.5

    B) 1

    C) 2.5

    D) 4

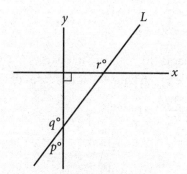

9. In the figure above, if ∠*q* = 140, what is the
    value of ∠*r* − ∠*p*?

    A) 0

    B) 10

    C) 90

    D) 130

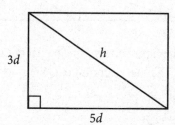

11. In the figure above, the diagonal of the rec-
    tangle has length *h*. What is the value of *h* in
    terms of *d*?

    A) *d*

    B) 4*d*

    C) $\sqrt{34}d$

    D) $d\sqrt{34}$

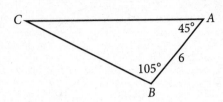

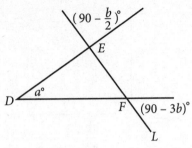

12. What is the area of the triangle shown in the figure?

    A) $18\sqrt{3}$

    B) $9+9\sqrt{3}$

    C) $9+18\sqrt{3}$

    D) $18+18\sqrt{3}$

15. In the figure above, $\overline{EF}$ of $\triangle DEF$ is on line L. What is a in terms of b?

    A) $3b$

    B) $\dfrac{3b}{2}$

    C) $\dfrac{7b}{2}$

    D) $180 - b$

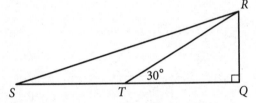

13. In the figure above, the length of $\overline{QR}$ is 4, and T is the midpoint of $\overline{QS}$. What is the length of $\overline{RS}$?

    A) 4

    B) $2\sqrt{3}$

    C) $2\sqrt{13}$

    D) $4\sqrt{13}$

16. What is the measure in degrees of the smallest angle of a triangle that has sides of length 1.5, $\dfrac{3\sqrt{3}}{2}$, and 3?

14. The area of a right triangle is 35 square inches. If the longer leg is 3 inches longer than the shorter leg, what is the length of the hypotenuse in inches?

    A) 10

    B) $\dfrac{\sqrt{35}}{2}$

    C) $7\sqrt{10}$

    D) $\sqrt{149}$

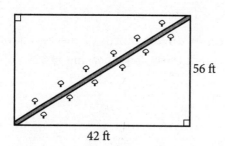

56 ft

42 ft

Note: Figure not drawn to scale.

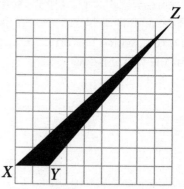

17. A college has a sidewalk that cuts through a
    block of greenspace on the campus. To ensure
    student safety, the college decides to put lights
    along both sides of the sidewalk. If the lights
    should be placed 5 feet apart as shown in the
    figure, how many lights does the college need?

18. The figure above consists of 81 small squares,
    each with a side length of $\frac{1}{2}$ centimeter. What is
    the area in square centimeters of $\triangle XYZ$?

Questions 19 and 20 refer to the following information.

The capital of North Dakota is Bismarck, which is almost directly north of the capital of South Dakota, which is Pierre. An airplane leaving from Bismarck travels on a bearing of 120°, as shown in the figure below.

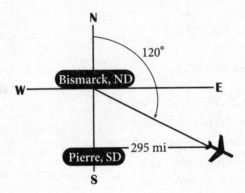

19. If the plane is 295 miles directly east of Pierre, how far apart are Bismarck and Pierre? Round your answer to the nearest mile.

20. If the plane flew at an average rate of 400 miles per hour, how many minutes had it been in the air when it was 295 miles from Pierre? Round your answer to the nearest whole minute.

PART TWO

Evidence-Based Reading and Writing

UNIT FIVE

Reading

BY THE END OF THIS UNIT, YOU WILL BE ABLE TO:

1. Apply the Kaplan Method for Reading Comprehension

2. Identify many kinds of Reading Test questions and apply the appropriate strategies to correctly answer them

CHAPTER 10

The Kaplan Method for Reading Comprehension

 ## CHAPTER OBJECTIVES

By the end of this chapter, you will be able to:

1. Read actively using the Kaplan Method for Reading Comprehension

2. Take efficient and organized notes on a passage

3. Answer questions using a Passage Map

SMARTPOINTS

Point Value	SmartPoint Category
Point Builder	The Kaplan Method for Reading Comprehension
Point Builder	Passage Mapping

THE KAPLAN METHOD FOR READING COMPREHENSION

Use the Kaplan Method for Reading Comprehension to analyze every SAT Reading passage and question you encounter, whether practicing, completing your homework, working on a Practice Test, or taking the actual exam on Test Day.

The Kaplan Method for Reading Comprehension consists of three steps:

> Step 1: Read actively
>
> Step 2: Examine the question stem
>
> Step 3: Predict and answer

Let's take a closer look at each step.

✔ Remember

There are three Reading Test passage types: U.S. and World Literature, History/Social Studies, and Science.

Step 1: Read actively

Active reading means:

- Ask questions and take notes *as* you read the passage. Asking questions about the passage and taking notes is an integral part of your approach to acing the SAT Reading Test.

Some of the questions you might want to ask are:

- Why did the author write this word/detail/sentence/paragraph?
- Is the author taking a side? If so, what side is he or she taking?
- What are the tone and purpose of the passage?

Make sure you remember to:

- Identify the passage type.
- Take notes, circle keywords, and underline key phrases.

✔ Expert Tip

Questions will range from general to specific. By using clues in the question stem to identify what the questions looking for, you will be better able to complete Step 3 of the Kaplan Method for Reading Comprehension.

Step 2: Examine the question stem

This means you should:

- Identify keywords and line references in the question stem.

- Apply question type strategies as necessary.

Step 3: Predict and answer

This means you should:

- Predict an answer before looking at the answer choices, also known as "predict before you peek."

- Select the best match.

Predicting before you peek helps you:

- Eliminate the possibility of falling into wrong answer traps.

PASSAGE MAPPING

Step 1 of the Kaplan Method for Reading Comprehension dictates that you must take notes as you read the passage. We call these notes a Passage Map because they guide you through the passage and will lead you to the correct answers.

> ✔ **On Test Day**
>
> A Passage Map should not replace the occasional underline or circle—it is important that you underline, circle, *and* take notes to create the most effective Passage Map.

Make sure you pay attention and take note of the following when you map the passage:

- The "why" or the central idea of the passage—in other words, the thesis statement

- Transitions or changes in direction in a passage's logic

- The author's opinions and other opinions the author cites

- The author's tone and purpose

While Passage Mapping may seem time-consuming at first, with practice it will become second nature by Test Day, and your overall Reading Test timing will greatly improve because you'll be spending less time searching the passage for answers to the questions.

SAT experts always map Reading Test passages. Look at the test-like excerpt and question on the next page. Make sure you spend some time looking over the sample Passage Map—these are the types of notes you should practice taking as you read Reading Test passages. Also, look at the questions an SAT expert would ask himself or herself and what kind of prediction he or she would make on Test Day when presented with a Reading Test question.

> ✔ **Remember**
>
> The SAT Reading Test is an open-book test! The answer is always in the passage.

Strategic Thinking

Step 1: Read actively

Read the passage and the notes provided. Remember, a well-crafted Passage Map should summarize the central idea of each paragraph, as well as important topics or themes. Use your Passage Map to help you answer each question.

Question 1 is based on the following passage.

The following passage discusses how the evolution of ancient Greek society affected early Greek poetry.

Early Greek poetry

The poems of the earliest Greeks, like those of other ancient societies, consisted of magical charms, mysterious predictions, prayers, and

Line traditional songs of work and war. These poems
5 were intended to be sung or recited, not written down, because they were created before the Greeks began to use writing for literary purposes. All that remains of these poems are fragments mentioned by later Greek writers. Homer, for example, quoted
10 an ancient work song for harvesters, and Simonides adapted the ancient poetry of ritual lamentation, songs of mourning for the dead, in his writing.

Not written, H quoted

The different forms of early Greek poetry all had something in common: they described the
15 way of life of a whole people. Poetry expressed ideas and feelings that were shared by everyone in a community—their folktales, their memories of historical events, and their religious speculation. The poems were wholly impersonal, with little
20 emphasis on individual achievement. It never occurred to the earliest Greek poets to tell us their names or to try to create anything completely new.

Poems re: entire society

In the "age of heroes," however, the content and purpose of Greek poetry changed. By this later
25 period, Greek communities had become separated into classes of rulers and ruled. People living in the same community, therefore, had different, even opposing, interests; they shared fewer ideas and emotions. The particular outlook of the warlike
30 upper class gave poetry a new content, one that

AoH / later poetry

focused on the lives of individuals. Poets were assigned a new task: to celebrate the accomplishments of outstanding characters, whether they were real or imaginary, rather than the activity and history of
35 the community.

Focused on indiv.

Poet's role changed

In the heroic age, poets became singers of tales and performed long poems about the fates of warriors and kings. One need study only Homer's *The Iliad* and *The Odyssey*, which are recorded examples
40 of the epic poetry that was sung in the heroic age, to understand the influence that the upper class had on the poet's subject matter. Thus, the poetry of the heroic age replaced the folk poetry that had preceded it. In this era of heroic poetry, poets no longer
45 remained anonymous, and the poems themselves were decidedly less religious in character compared to earlier works.

Upper class: H's epics

Question	Strategic Thinking
1. The main purpose of the passage is to A) argue that earlier forms of Greek poetry were artistic and later forms were political. B) discuss how changes in ancient Greek society brought about changes in ancient Greek poetry. C) provide an example of how an ancient society's shift from an oral to a written tradition had positive and negative effects. D) show that artistic expression can be used either to build people into communities or separate people into classes.	**Step 2: Examine the question stem** Identify the key words and phrases in the question stem. The words "main purpose" indicate that you're looking for the central idea of the passage. Review the Passage Map to identify the central idea or main purpose of the passage. You can use the entire map to get a sense of the central idea of the passage. The notes are about Greek poetry and how it changed over time. **Step 3: Predict and answer** This passage begins by discussing early Greek poetry, then summarizes how and why it changed over time. Choice (B) matches this prediction.

✔ **Note**

Resist the temptation to reread large portions of the passage. Your Passage Map can help you predict and answer questions correctly without having to dive back into the text. Doing so will save you time on Test Day!

You have seen the kinds of notes SAT experts take and the critical thinking questions they ask themselves when they encounter Reading Test passages and questions.

Look at the Reading Test passage excerpt that follows. There are two questions associated with it. Since part of the passage has been mapped for you, your first step is to complete the Passage Map. Then, use the Kaplan Method for Reading Comprehension to answer the questions. Remember to look at the strategic thinking questions that have been laid out for you—some of the answers have been filled in, but you will have to fill in the answers to others.

Use your answers to the strategic thinking questions to select the correct answer, just as you will on Test Day.

Strategic Thinking

Step 1: Read actively

The passage below is partially mapped. Read the passage and the first part of the Passage Map. Then, complete the Passage Map on your own. Remember to focus on the central ideas of each paragraph as well as the central idea of the overall passage. Use your Passage Map as a reference when you're answering questions.

Questions 2-3 are based on the following passage.

The following passage discusses facts and speculation about a spy during the American Revolution.

Although he may not have been the first American spy, when Captain Nathan Hale uttered his famous final words, "I only regret that I have but
Line one life to lose for my country," he likely that

NH = Am. spy during Rev. War

5 he would long be remembered as the first patriotic martyr of the American Revolution. Even today, Hale's story serves as an inspiration for others who have chosen to enter the often deadly and thankless profession of covert intelligence gathering. Yet, as

mission details unknown

10 it seems clear that the sacrifice Hale made in the autumn of 1776 will long be valued, relatively little is actually known about his fateful mission.

bkgd & educ

Born in Connecticut in 1755 as the sixth child of Richard Hale, a prosperous farmer, Nathan's
15 childhood and education were rather accelerated. Nathan was only 14 years old when he entered Yale University as a freshman, just 18 when he graduated as one of the top students in his class, and not yet 20 when he enlisted in the militia in 1774. With
20 the whole country abuzz from military movements and with many joining the separatist cause, Nathan

military bkgd: CT Reg

quickly became involved in the military organization of his hometown. Historical records indicate that, by the time news of the first battles of the war reached
25 Connecticut in 1775, Hale had already become an outspoken leader of the independence movement.

His subsequent commissioning as an officer in the Connecticut regiment is also well documented, but it is the events of 1776, when Hale began his secret
30 mission, that are largely unknown.

It is known that Hale was indeed a spy and that he had been a member of the Knowlton Rangers, a small group of elite soldiers operating under what was called a "detached command," taking orders
35 directly from General George Washington. Historians also believe that it was Hale who accompanied a young sergeant named Stephen Hempstead on a mission involving Washington's Long Island forces. But, perhaps due to chaos in New York City created
40 by the great fires that had been set in September of 1776, the precise details of Hale's mission and capture are unclear. Historical accounts pick up the story when he was taken before the commanding British General and, after honestly providing his
45 rank and name, was immediately condemned to death by hanging. There was no formal trial, but, according to the British, the papers Hale had on his person were damning enough, and the next morning he was hanged in an apple orchard in the middle
50 of Manhattan. Yet, despite the uncertainty surrounding Hale's story of espionage, a clear and undisputed written record verifies the young martyr's final words, for which he will likely be forever remembered and admired.

Don't get distracted by less important details. While there is a lot going on in this passage, your additions to the Passage Map should note Nathan Hale's role in the Revolutionary War and his ultimate fate. If you're stuck, review the example Passage Map in the Answers & Explanations for this chapter on page 657.

Questions	Strategic Thinking
2. According to the passage, Hale received a commission in A) the independence movement. B) the Knowlton Rangers. C) the Long Island forces. D) the Connecticut regiment.	**Step 2: Examine the question stem** *What are the key words and phrases in the question stem?* "According to the passage," and "commission." "According to the passage" implies that the answer can be directly found in the passage. *What parts of your Passage Map are relevant?* Paragraph 2 discusses Hale's military background. Look at your Passage Map, particularly the notes for paragraph 2, to find information about Hale's "commission." **Step 3: Predict and answer** *What does the author say Hale received a commission in?* _____ _____ _____ *What answer choice matches this prediction?* _____

Questions	Strategic Thinking
3. The main purpose of the passage is to A) provide background information on Hale's secret mission to New York. B) discuss the history and development of covert operations during the War of Independence. C) suggest that Hale deserves the respect and admiration that he receives. D) challenge the relevance of Hale's quotation in light of the questions about his mission.	**Step 2: Examine the question stem** *What are the key words and phrases in the question stem?* _____ _____ _____ _____ *What parts of your Passage Map are relevant?* _____ _____ _____ _____ **Step 3: Predict and answer** *What is the author's purpose?* _____ _____ _____ _____ *Which answer choice matches this prediction?* _____

Now, try a test-like Reading Test passage on your own. Give yourself 5 minutes to read and map the passage and answer the questions.

Questions 4-5 are based on the following passage.

This passage discusses the cane toad's introduction to and effect on the Australian environment.

The cane toad, a large, brightly colored amphibian that can weigh more than a pound, was first introduced to the Australian continent by the sugarcane industry. The cane toad was a known predator of the cane beetle, which had been devouring the sugarcane crops since the early 1900s. Australian farmers thought that by importing these toads from their native habitats in the Americas, they could effectively use the toads to feast on pests like the cane beetle and eradicate the growing insect threat. So, in 1935, roughly 100 cane toads were carefully packed into crates and shipped to Australia. Upon their toads' arrival, the cane farmers eagerly brought them to a pond in the northeast province of Queensland.

Before long, the female cane toads had laid hundreds of thousands of eggs in elongated, gelatinous strings, and the farmers waited for their new predators to be born. As the eggs hatched, the pond became filled with great clouds of squirming, wriggling tadpoles that, upon reaching maturity, were taken to the sugarcane fields and turned loose. The situation that resulted from this fateful release, however, did not coincide with the farmers' plan. In fact, the introduction of cane toads into the wild in Australia has since been deemed nothing short of an ecological disaster.

Easily numbering well into the millions—an exact figure has been impossible to calculate— the cane toads soon dominated the landscape in Queensland. Following their release, some of the toads descended as planned on the sugarcane crops and began to eat the beetles. However, they soon lost interest in their new habitat. For one thing, the mature cane beetles could fly away from their predators, forcing these slow, fat toads to work very hard for their food. In addition, the fields were hot and dry and provided little sleeping shelter for the newcomers, who generally prefer wet shade. These adverse conditions were not severe enough to kill off the toads, but instead the toads began to look elsewhere for food and shelter. Nearby towns, full of lush gardens and well-watered lawns, were extremely inviting, and soon the toads had overrun entire residential areas. They covered the lawns, filled the gardens, found shelter under flowerpots or on porches, and even began to eat bowls of food left outside for pets like cats and dogs.

Today, the people of Queensland hunt cane toads as if they were mosquitoes. But the toads continue to spread south and west through Australia in staggering numbers. As for the sugarcane industry, just five years after the release of the toads, an effective insecticide spray became available, and the cane beetles were easily exterminated. Scientists as well as the Australian government, however, continue to grapple with the cane toad problem.

4. All of the following are true EXCEPT

A) the cane toad was introduced to Australia to control the cane beetle.

B) the cane toad bred readily in Australia.

C) the introduction of the cane toad to Australia is considered an ecological disaster.

D) the cane toad quickly adapted to the conditions in the sugarcane fields.

5. The author would most likely agree with which of the following statements?

    A) Human intervention in a natural ecosystem always results in disaster.

    B) The introduction of a non-native species can have unfortunate effects on the local environment.

    C) The sugarcane farmers should have considered the potential risks before initiating their plan.

    D) A possible solution to this problem is the introduction of a natural predator of the cane toad.

Answers & Explanations for this chapter begin on page 657.

EXTRA PRACTICE

Questions 1-11 are based on the following passage and supplementary materials.

The following passage describes the discovery of gold in California and the effects of that discovery on the United States.

People around the world unanimously agree that gold is a valuable mineral. Gold has been seen as a precious commodity by many cultures throughout
Line time, and Americans of the 1840s were no different.
5 When James W. Marshall, a carpenter and sawmill owner, discovered a gold nugget in the American River, California was forever changed. News of his discovery attracted thousands of immigrants from other parts of California, as well as other places around the United
10 States and the world.

In the Sierra Nevada, a mountain range that runs 400 miles through California, years of erosion caused by rainfall and the downhill flow of mountain streams loosened pieces of gold that had been embedded in
15 the solid rock formed over 100 million years ago. California is largely made of quartz previously found at the bottom of the Pacific Ocean. Underwater volcanoes melted the quartz into magma and pushed it up towards the surface, sometimes forming islands. Due to the
20 movements of the Earth's tectonic plates, these islands were pushed together and against the West Coast. This movement and accumulation of land over millions of years formed the area known as California. The gold that was dispersed across the sea floor became
25 concentrated and redistributed throughout the veins of quartz in the Sierra Nevada Mountains.

Marshall's discovery was quickly verified and publicized by the New York Herald in August of 1848. Current California residents of the time were able to
30 get to the gold fields first. Soon after, President James Polk confirmed the discovery in an address to Congress. His address prompted many Americans to move west, as well as other fortune-seekers from around the world to immigrate to the United States. This influx of people
35 caused California's population to increase, as well as experience a change in demographics. The particular geologic makeup made California the prime location

for mining gold. The Northern California city of San Francisco grew from 1,000 people in 1848 to more than
40 20,000 people in just two years. Because of the rapid population increase, the United States government incorporated the territory into the Union. California became the Union's 31st state in 1850, though it had only been acquired from Mexico two short years before. This
45 was the fastest any new territory has ever been given statehood in the history of the United States.

Americans from places east of California migrated via two very long and often dangerous paths. Some endured a six-month boat voyage, which departed from
50 New York City and sailed south as far as the tip of South America before heading north to California. The trip was so perilous that most Americans relocating to California opted to travel the famous Oregon Trail. Riding in covered wagons through dangerous conditions, trav-
55 elers who opted to move by land also had a six-month trip to endure. By 1850, the sheer number of people attempting the voyage inspired the creation of the Panama Railway. Built specifically to reduce travel time to California, the first transcontinental railroad decreased
60 the length of the trip by several months.

Forty-Niners came to California from many different countries around the globe, including China, Germany, Mexico, Turkey, France, and Ireland. The largest group of people to successfully
65 immigrate to California from abroad was the Chinese. Many did not intend to settle in the United States, but instead planned to return home with their fortunes. While many did so, when gold grew scarce and the Chinese Exclusion Act was
70 passed in 1882, prohibiting Chinese immigration for 10 years, many immigrants instead put down roots in California. The result was the most ethnically diverse state in the Union by the middle of the 19th century.
75 Though the gold in California didn't last long after its discovery, the effects that it had on the population, including the number of people in the state, their ethnicities, and the way they travelled, have lasted to the modern day.

Percent Population Change, 1850–1860

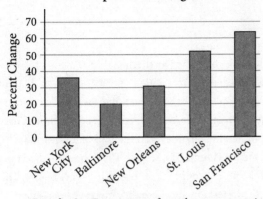

*Data for San Francisco are from the state census in 1852. The 1850 census data were destroyed in a fire.

Data from the *United States Bureau of the Census.*

1. The author includes the second paragraph primarily to

    A) illustrate why gold is such a valuable metal.

    B) show why California was a prime location for gold mining.

    C) explain why California became a state so rapidly.

    D) give scientific information about how gold is formed over time.

2. According to the passage, which of the following was a main cause of westward migration?

    A) President Polk's speech about the gold rush

    B) California's acceptance into the union as a state

    C) The development of new gold extraction techniques

    D) New immigration restrictions passed by the federal government

3. As used in line 34, "influx" most nearly means

    A) assault.

    B) movement.

    C) news.

    D) rush.

4. The passage suggests that which of the following was unusual about California's entry into the Union, as compared to the other new states?

    A) It had more natural resources.

    B) It had a smaller population.

    C) It had less wealth.

    D) It had spent less time as a territory.

5. Which choice provides the best evidence for the answer to the previous question?

    A) Lines 27-28 ("Marshall's discovery … August 1848")

    B) Lines 32-34 ("His address … United States")

    C) Lines 44-46 ("This was … United States")

    D) Lines 68-72 ("While many … in California")

6. According to the passage, what was one result of the presence of many dangers on the journey to California?

    A) Expansion of the population across the entire country

    B) Increased wealth for those living along the Oregon Trail

    C) Decreased immigration to other parts of the country

    D) Improved transportation options between the East Coast and California

7. What can be inferred about immigrants who came to California?

   A) They were forbidden from returning home once California became a state.

   B) Migrating to California was more attractive for them than for other Americans.

   C) They came from more nations than did immigrants to other states.

   D) Most were escaping difficult political conditions at home rather than seeking fortune.

8. Which choice provides the best evidence for the answer to the previous question?

   A) Lines 61-64 ("Forty-Niners … and Ireland")

   B) Lines 64-66 ("The largest … the Chinese")

   C) Lines 68-72 ("While many … in California")

   D) Lines 72-74 ("The result … the 19th century")

9. As used in line 52, "perilous" most nearly means

   A) boring.

   B) exotic.

   C) dangerous.

   D) expensive.

10. The overall structure of the passage can be described as

    A) a history of gold in California, followed by a discussion of why gold is valuable.

    B) an analysis of why gold is important, followed by criticism of the politics surrounding gold.

    C) a list of the causes of a gold rush, followed by an analysis of the effects of gold on a region.

    D) a discussion of the benefits of the gold rush in California, followed by a list of consequences.

11. Based on the chart, which conclusion is best supported?

    A) The United States grew greatly from 1850 to 1860.

    B) San Francisco was the largest city in the United States in 1860.

    C) From 1850 to 1860, cities in the East lost population, while San Francisco gained population.

    D) Of all five cities, San Francisco gained the largest total number of people from 1850 to 1860.

CHAPTER 11

Citing Textual Evidence and Determining Central Ideas & Themes

 ## CHAPTER OBJECTIVES

By the end of this chapter, you will be able to:

1. Locate appropriate textual evidence to support the answer to a previous question

2. Summarize the passage or key information and ideas within the passage

3. Identify central ideas and themes of a passage to answer questions about central ideas and themes

SMARTPOINTS

Point Value	SmartPoint Category
20 Points	Global
70 Points	Command of Evidence

GLOBAL QUESTIONS

Global questions require you to both identify explicit and determine implicit central ideas or themes in a text. If you pay attention to the big picture—the author's central idea and purpose—while reading SAT Reading passages, you will be able to answer Global questions with little to no rereading of the passage. To fully understand the central ideas and themes of a passage, you must synthesize the different points the author makes with his or her thesis statement, which you should underline when Passage Mapping.

Global questions may also ask you to choose a correct summary of the passage as a whole or key information and ideas within the passage. When presented with this type of Global question, you can use your Passage Map, which is essentially a brief summary of what you have read.

> ✔ **On Test Day**
>
> The italicized portion at the beginning of an SAT Reading passage can be very helpful in determining the author's central ideas and themes. Make sure you take the time on Test Day to read this information—it orients you to the passage.

You can recognize Global questions because they typically do not reference line numbers or even individual paragraphs. To confidently answer Global questions, you need to not only identify the central idea or theme of the passage but also avoid choosing answers that summarize secondary or supplementary points.

Do note there is a slight difference between nonfiction and fiction passages. Science and History/Social Studies passages are nonfiction and will have a definite central idea and thesis statement; U.S. and World Literature passages are fiction and will have a central theme but no thesis statement.

> ✔ **Remember**
>
> History/Social Studies and Science passages on the SAT Reading Test are just well-written essays or article excerpts. You can normally find the thesis statement of a well-written piece at the end of the introductory paragraph.

COMMAND OF EVIDENCE QUESTIONS

A Command of Evidence question relies on your answer to the question that precedes it. These questions require you to identify the portion of the text that provides the best evidence for the conclusion you reached when selecting your answer to the previous question.

Kaplan's Strategy for Command of Evidence questions involves retracing your steps; that is, you must return to the previous question to ensure you answer the Command of Evidence question correctly. The question preceding a Command of Evidence question can be any other question type.

To answer Command of Evidence questions efficiently and correctly, employ the following Kaplan Strategy:

- When you see a question asking you to choose the best evidence to support your answer to the previous question, review how you selected that answer

- Avoid answers that provide evidence for incorrect answers to the previous question

- The correct answer will support why the previous question's answer is correct

✔ **Expert Tip**

You can recognize Command of Evidence questions easily. The question stem usually reads, "Which choice provides the best evidence for the answer to the previous question?" Furthermore, the answer choices are always line numbers with parentheses containing the first and last word of the intended selection. Answer choices are listed in the order they appear in the passage.

Command of Evidence questions ask that you cite the textual evidence that best supports a given claim or point. The given claim or point will be the correct answer choice to the previous question. Then, you will choose one of the four excerpts from the passage as the best evidence or support for that answer.

The first step to approaching a Command of Evidence question is to make sure you answered the previous question—no matter its type—correctly. If you answer the question preceding a Command of Evidence question incorrectly, you have a smaller chance of selecting the correct answer.

✔ **Remember**

There is no wrong answer penalty on the SAT, so even if you have no idea of how to approach a question, take your best guess and move on.

Let's look at the following example of a test-like U.S. and World Literature passage and question set. After the mapped passage, the left column contains questions similar to those you'll see on the Reading Test on Test Day. The column on the right features the strategic thinking a test expert employs when approaching the passage and questions presented. Pay attention to how a test expert varies his or her approach to the different question types.

Strategic Thinking
Step 1: Read actively Read the passage and the notes provided. Remember, a well-crafted Passage Map should summarize the central idea of each paragraph as well as important topics or themes. Use your Passage Map to help you answer each question.

Questions 1-3 are based on the following passage.

The following is excerpted from Frederick Douglass's autobiographical Narrative of the Life of Frederick Douglass, An American Slave.

Mrs. helped FD read

 His mistress had been severely reprimanded by her husband for helping Frederick Douglass learn to read. After all, the husband admonished, giving a
Line *slave the knowledge to read was like giving the slave*
5 *access to thinking he or she was human. If you give the slaves an inch, they will take the ell.*

Mr. = "slaves not human"

 My mistress was, as I have said, a kind and tender-hearted woman; and in the simplicity of her soul she commenced, when I first went to live with

Mrs. = kind at first

10 her, to treat me as she supposed one human being ought to treat another. In entertaining upon the duties of a slaveholder, she did not seem to perceive that I sustained to her the relation of a mere chattel, and that for her to treat me as a human being

15 was not only wrong, but dangerously so. Slavery proved as injurious to her as it did to me. When

BUT slavery hurt Mrs.

I went there, she was a pious, warm, and tender-hearted woman. There was no sorrow or suffering for which she had not a tear. She had bread for

20 the hungry, clothes for the naked, and comfort for every mourner that came within her reach. Slavery soon proved its ability to divest her of these heavenly qualities. Under its influence, the tender heart

Mrs. became hard and mean

became stone, and the lamblike disposition gave

25 way to one of tiger-like fierceness. The first step in her downward course was in her ceasing to instruct me. She now commenced to practice her husband's precepts. She finally became even more violent in her opposition [to my learning to read] than her

30 husband himself. She was not satisfied with simply doing as well as he had commanded; she seemed anxious to do better. Nothing seemed to make her

more angry than to see me with a newspaper. She seemed to think that here lay the danger. I have had
35 her rush at me with a face made all up of fury, and snatch from me a newspaper, in a manner that fully revealed her apprehension. She was an apt woman; and a little experience soon demonstrated, to her satisfaction, that education and slavery were incom-
40 patible with each other.

Mrs. became as bad as Mr.

 From this time I was most narrowly watched. If I was in a separate room any considerable length of time, I was sure to be suspected of having a book, and was at once called to give an account of myself.
45 All this, however, was too late. The first step had been taken. Mistress, in teaching me the alphabet, had given me the inch, and no precaution could prevent me from taking the *ell.*

 The plan which I adopted, and the one by which
50 I was most successful, was that of making friends of all the white children whom I met in the street. As many of these as I could, I converted into teachers. With their kindly aid, obtained at different times and in different places, I finally succeeded
55 in learning to read. When I was sent on errands, I always took my book with me, and by going one part of my errand quickly, I found time to get a lesson before my return. I used also to carry bread with me, enough of which was always in the house,
60 and to which I was always welcome, for I was much better off in this regard than many of the poor white children in our neighborhood. This bread I used to bestow upon the hungry little urchins, who, in return, would give me that more valuable bread
65 of knowledge. I am strongly tempted to give the names of two or three of those children, as a testimonial of the gratitude and affection I bear

friends → teachers → full literacy

gave bread in exchg. for learning

them; but prudence forbids;—not that it would injure me, but it might embarrass them; for it is al-
70 most a unpardonable offence to teach slaves to read in this Christian country. I used to talk this matter of slavery over with them. I would sometimes say to them, I wished I could be as free as they would be when they got to be men. This used to trouble
75 them; they would express for me the liveliest sympathy, and console me with the hope that something would occur by which I might be free.

antislavery sentiment

Questions	Strategic Thinking
1. The main purpose of the passage is to A) emphasize the cruelty of slavery. B) refute the idea that education and slavery are incompatible. C) offer historical background to provide context for positions Douglass later espoused. D) describe the risks Douglass willingly took to learn to read.	**Step 2: Examine the question stem** Identify the keywords in the question stem. The words "main purpose" indicate that you will find the answer by using the entire Passage Map to summarize the central idea and purpose of the passage. **Step 3: Predict and answer** While the beginning of the passage discusses Douglass's relationship with his mistress, it is primarily about how Douglass learned to read despite his slave status. Choice (D) matches this prediction.
2. The statement in lines 15-16 ("Slavery proved … to me") suggests that A) the mistress and Douglass suffered equally from the institution of slavery. B) owning slaves destroyed the mistress's admirable human qualities. C) the mistress regretted the actions she was forced to take as a slave owner. D) Douglass pitied the mistress for the sacrifices she made.	**Step 2: Examine the question stem** Identify the keywords in the question stem: The line references and parenthetical quotation, as well as the phrase "suggests that." You can find your answer by using your Passage Map notes near lines 15-16, particularly those about the mistress, to answer the question. **Step 3: Predict and answer** In this section, the Passage Map notes about the mistress say that she was kind at first but slavery eventually was harmful to her as well because she became hard and mean. Choice (B) matches this prediction.

Questions	Strategic Thinking
3. Which choice provides the best evidence for the answer to the previous question? A) Lines 11-15 ("In entertaining … dangerously so") B) Lines 23-25 ("Under its … fierceness") C) Lines 41-44 ("If I … of myself") D) Lines 53-55 ("With their … to read")	**Step 2: Examine the question stem** This question stem indicates that you will need to choose the answer choice featuring the lines from the passage that best support your answer to the previous question. Use the Kaplan Strategy for Command of Evidence questions when you encounter this question stem. **Step 3: Predict and answer** You found the answer to the previous question—that owning slaves destroyed the mistress's admirable human qualities—by using the Passage Map notes surrounding the cited sentence in lines 15-16. The Passage Map says that the mistress became hard and mean. This is supported from line 21 through the end of the paragraph (line 40). Choice (B) is the only answer choice that falls within these lines and is therefore correct.

✔ **Note**

Remember the Kaplan Strategy for Command of Evidence questions: Review how you selected the answer to the previous question and avoid answer choices that provide evidence for incorrect answer choices to it. The correct answer will support why the previous question's answer is correct.

You have now seen how to answer both Global and Command of Evidence questions.

Look at the test-like Science passage that follows. There are three questions associated with it. Part of the passage has been mapped already. Your first step is to complete the Passage Map. Then, use the Kaplan Method for Reading Comprehension and the strategies discussed in this chapter to answer the questions. Strategic thinking questions have been included to guide you—some of the answers have been filled in, but you will have to fill in the answers to others.

Use your answers to the strategic thinking questions to select the correct answer, just as you will on Test Day.

Strategic Thinking
Step 1: Read actively
The passage below is partially mapped. Read the passage and the first part of the Passage Map. Then, complete the Passage Map on your own. Remember to focus on the central ideas of each paragraph as well as the central idea of the overall passage. Use your Passage Map as a reference when you're answering questions.

Questions 4-6 are based on the following passage.

The following passage explains the challenges facing a population of trees and possible solutions.

Today, oaks are plagued with problems. There is lack of regeneration in populations of certain species. Pests such as the acorn weevil and the filbert
Line worm eat away at acorns and prevent germination.
5 By undermining the root systems of seedlings and saplings, ground squirrels, gophers, and other small mammals often prevent these young plants from reaching tree size. Severe diseases, such as sudden oak death, kill many adult oaks. Many mature oaks
10 are having a tough time with fire suppression. In the past, with light surface fires, the oaks had been able to maintain a stronghold where other plants were not able to compete and died out. Now oaks are being toppled by trees that have a higher toler-
15 ance for shade and are not fire-resistant; earlier such trees would have been killed when Native Americans set fires.

Given all of these challenges, the "old-growth" oaks—the large old valley oaks, Garry oaks, coast
20 live oaks, and canyon live oaks that have huge girth and large canopies—may become a thing of the past. These oaks in particular are important because there are often more terrestrial vertebrates living in mature oak stands than in seedling and sapling
25 areas. This prevalence of animals occurs because the large crowns of such oaks provide cover and feeding sites for a large variety of wildlife.

The University of California has embarked on an ambitious and necessary research program called
30 the Integrated Hardwood Range Management Program to explore the significant causes of oak decline and offer varied solutions. These include

investigating the use of grassing regimes that are compatible with oak seedling establishment, reveg-
35 etating sites with native grasses to facilitate better germination of oak seedlings, documenting insects and pathogens that attack oaks, and exploring the ways that native people managed oaks in the past. Scientists at the Pacific Northwest Research Station
40 in Olympia, Washington, and at Redwood National Park in northern California are reintroducing the burning practices of Native Americans. When used in Garry oak ecosystems, fires keep Douglas firs from encroaching on the oaks and promote
45 the growth of wildflowers that are important food plants. Further investigations about these fire practices may be essential in figuring out how to maintain oaks in the western landscape today, given that the fires address many of the factors that are
50 now causing oak decline—from how to eliminate insect pests of acorns to how to maintain an open structure in oak groves.

Ecological restoration, the traditional approach to woodland maintenance, refers to humans
55 intervening on a very limited time scale to bring back plants and animals known to have historically existed in an area. The decline of oaks, one of the most significant plants to Native Americans, shows us that humans may play an integral part in the
60 restoration of oak areas. While animals such as jays have been recognized as crucial partners in oak well-being, human actions through the eons may also have been key to the oaks' flourishing.

Sudden oak death, for example, although of
65 exotic origin, may be curtailed locally by thinning around coastal oaks and tan oaks and setting light surface fires, simulating ancient fire management

Margin notes:

oak problems: pests & disease, other trees

oaks may die out

research into problems & solutions

Nat. Am. approach

practices of Native Americans. Indigenous shrubs and trees that grow in association with oaks
70 are hosts to the sudden oak death pathogen. By limiting the growth of these shrubs, burning that mimics earlier Native American ways may reduce opportunities for disease agents to jump from other plants to oak trees. With a more open envi-
75 ronment, it may be harder for sudden oak death to spread.

The oak landscapes that we inherited, which still bear the marks of former Native American interactions, demand a new kind of restoration that
80 complements other forms of ecological restoration. This new kind of restoration could be called ethnobotanical restoration, defined as reestablishing the historic plant communities of a given area and restoring indigenous harvesting, vegetation

85 management, and cultivation practices (seedbearing, burning, pruning, sowing, tilling, and weeding) necessary to maintain these communities in the long term.

Thus, this kind of restoration is not only about
90 restoring plants but also about restoring the human place within nature. Ethnobotanical restoration is viewed not as a process that can be completed but rather as a continuous interaction between people and plants, as both of their fates are intertwined in
95 a region. Using oaks (through harvesting acorns and making products from all parts of the tree) and human intervention (by thinning tree populations and lighting light fires) may offer us ways to beneficially coexist while improving the long-term health
100 and well-being of the remarkable oak.

Don't get distracted by less important details. While there is a lot going on in this passage, your additions to the Passage Map should note the views regarding human involvement in ecological restoration as well as the definitions of unfamiliar terms like "ecological restoration" and "ethnobotanical restoration." If you're stuck, review the example Passage Map in the Answers & Explanations for this chapter on page 663.

Questions	Strategic Thinking
4. Throughout the passage, the author emphasizes that a key element in the restoration of the oak tree is A) protecting the wildlife diversity found in the oaks' large crowns. B) preventing Douglas firs from encroaching on oak tree habitats. C) utilizing a continuous restoration process focused on human and oak interactions. D) curtailing sudden oak death by eliminating exotic pathogens.	**Step 2: Examine the question stem** *What are the key words and phrases in the question stem?* The key phrases in this question stem are "throughout the passage" and "a key element in the restoration of the oak tree." *What parts of your Passage Map are relevant?* The author begins to focus on the restoration of the oak tree in line 53. Look at your Passage Map notes from this point through the end of the passage to determine what the "key element" is. **Step 3: Predict and answer** *What can you predict?* The Passage Map notes from this point on focus on how humans can affect ecological restoration. *Which answer choice matches this prediction?* _____

Questions	Strategic Thinking
5. According to the passage, an important distinction between "ecological restoration" in line 53 and "ethnobotanical restoration" in lines 81-82 is that the latter A) recreates ecosystems that accurately reflect historical uses of an area. B) aspires to reintegrate humans into the continuous maintenance of plant communities. C) intervenes for a limited time to restore an area to an earlier condition. D) uses fire suppression more effectively to reduce risks from a variety of factors.	**Step 2: Examine the question stem** *What are the key words and phrases in the question stem?* The keywords in this question stem are "according to the passage," which implies the answer will be directly stated in the text, as well as the two quoted phrases and the lines in which they appear. *What parts of your Passage Map are relevant?* Use your Passage Map near these lines to compare the two types of restoration. **Step 3: Predict and answer** *What is the primary difference between ecological restoration and ethnobotanical restoration?* _____ _____ _____ _____ *Which answer choice matches this prediction?* _____

Questions	Strategic Thinking
6. Which choice provides the best evidence for the answer to the previous question? A) Lines 10-13 ("In the … died out") B) Lines 42-46 ("When used … plants") C) Lines 70-74 ("By limiting … trees") D) Lines 89-91 ("Thus, this … nature")	**Step 2: Examine the question stem** *What are the key words and phrases in the question stem?* _____ _____ _____ _____ _____ *What parts of your Passage Map are relevant?* _____ _____ _____ _____ **Step 3: Predict and answer** *What part of the passage supports your answer to the previous question?* _____ _____ _____ *Which answer choice matches this prediction?* _____

Now, use the strategies you learned about in this chapter to answer questions for a Science passage. Give yourself 8 minutes to read and map the passage and answer the questions.

Questions 7-11 are based on the following passage.

The following passage details findings from different eras of prenatal screening and the methods and experiments those findings prompted.

Screening newborns for rare genetic diseases is a relatively new practice that began approximately forty years ago. Prior to the advent of screening,
Line biomedical researchers and health professionals
5 were preoccupied with the most prominent causes of newborn mortality, such as diarrheal diseases, influenza, and other infectious diseases. By 1960, however, the infant mortality rate had dropped to less than three percent of live births from over
10 ten percent fifty years earlier. The declining rate was due, in part, to the widespread use of antibiotics; the development of vaccines, particularly the Salk and Sabin polio vaccines; improved nutrition; better education; and generally im-
15 proved sanitary practices. As infant mortality rates dropped, attention shifted to the etiology of rare diseases. The first major milestone in this focus shift occurred in 1962, when President Kennedy announced that the federal government would
20 begin exploring the problem of mental disability—until then, a largely ignored issue. He created the President's Panel on Mental Retardation to lead this exploration.

During roughly the same time period, a major
25 scientific breakthrough in the study of phenylke-tonuria, or PKU, was underway. In 1934, Dr. Asbjorn Folling of Norway first described the condition when he observed that some of his mentally disabled patients had phenylpyruvic acid
30 in their urine, a finding indicative of a deficiency in the enzyme that converts phenylalanine to tyrosine, a necessary component for protein synthesis. When this transformation does not occur, phenylalanine accumulates in the blood. High levels of phenylala-
35 nine are toxic to the developing brain of an infant

and cause mental retardation. At the time, the preventive strategy was to reduce phenylalanine levels in the patient's diet. This approach had one serious drawback, though. Phenylalanine is an essential
40 amino acid necessary for proper growth, so deficiencies in it may also lead to mental retardation.

Despite this risk, the younger siblings of children with PKU were given diets low in phenylalanine from a very early age. The results were somewhat
45 encouraging and, in light of the beneficial evidence from this special diet, two therapeutically promising research initiatives were launched. One was to devise a source of protein free of phenylalanine. The outcome was the infant formula Lofenalac, which is
50 still in use today. The other initiative was aimed at developing a method for detecting high phenylalanine levels before damage to the developing brain could occur.

Dr. Robert Guthrie led the second initiative,
55 which yielded a breakthrough in the early 1960s. He developed a test to detect PKU before it became clinically symptomatic. The test consisted of a culture of *Bacillus subtilis* and B-2-thienylalanine, which inhibits the growth of the bacteria. Once
60 a blood sample from the newborn was added to this culture, the bacteria would leach the phenylalanine from the blood spot, overcome the inhibition caused by the B-2-thienylalanine, and grow. Bacterial growth beyond a normal range indicated
65 elevated levels of phenylalanine and thus the presence of PKU in the newborn.

The test was not perfect. Over the next few years, it produced quite a few false positives, and some children unnecessarily received low phenylala-
70 nine diets. To compound the problem, there was uncertainty about the amount of phenylalanine to cut from the diet; as a result, some healthy children developed mental disabilities because of the treatment. Nevertheless, PKU screening was generally

75 considered a success, and spurred questions about whether other diseases might be prevented through early detection. After further study it became clear that they could. By the late 1960s, newborn screening for rare genetic diseases had become a perma-
80 nent part of infant health care in the United States.

7. The passage most strongly suggests that prior to the research initiatives described in lines 42-53,

   A) little research had been conducted on the causes of newborn mortality.

   B) influenza research had yielded the most effective treatments.

   C) a treatment for PKU was implemented, despite its inherent risks.

   D) screening newborns for genetic diseases was a well-established practice.

8. Which choice provides the best evidence for the answer to the previous question?

   A) Lines 1-3 ("Screening newborns … years ago")

   B) Lines 6-7 ("such as … diseases")

   C) Lines 32-34 ("When this … blood")

   D) Lines 39-41 ("Phenylalanine … retardation")

9. This passage can best be described as

   A) a brief history of biomedical research in the 20th century.

   B) a description of how an important diagnostic tool grew out of an attempt to treat a specific disease.

   C) an argument in support of genetic screening for rare diseases.

   D) an essay questioning the ethical nature of using untested medical treatments.

10. According to the passage, which of the following contributed to the practice of screening newborns for rare genetic diseases?

    A) Increased use of antibiotics

    B) The development of Lofenalac

    C) The false positives produced by Dr. Guthrie's test

    D) The success of PKU screening

11. Which choice provides the best evidence for the answer to the previous question?

    A) Lines 10-15 ("The declining … practices")

    B) Lines 48-50 ("The outcome … today")

    C) Lines 67-70 ("Over the … diets")

    D) Lines 74-77 ("Nevertheless, PKU … detection")

Answers & Explanations for this chapter begin on page 663.

EXTRA PRACTICE

Questions 1-11 are based on the following passage and supplementary material.

This passage describes how tree farms, widely thought to offer little support to wildlife, became home to a rare species of birds.

As our environment changes over time, certain species thrive while others become rarer. One such species is the small, difficult-to-find Swainson's
Line warbler. Scientists struggle to estimate the popula-
5 tion of this songbird because it is challenging to track. America's foremost wildlife artist, John James Audubon, attempted to describe the bird in the 1830s. Even then, it was considered uncommon. Some of the other birds studied by Audubon have
10 already become extinct, including the ivory-billed woodpecker. Others, such as the Allen's hum- mingbird, the spotted owl, and the osprey, are at increased risk of extinction due to their habitats disappearing. Against all odds, the Swainson's
15 warbler has held on by changing where it spends its summer seasons.

The Swainson's warbler has been at risk for extinction due to the specificity of its needs. Dur- ing breeding season, summer, the bird tradition-
20 ally spends time in the southeastern United States forests and lowlands. It then migrates to subtropical locations in the winter, seeking the dry forests of Jamaica or other evergreen forests in Mexico and Cuba. The low population has been attributed to
25 the loss of these habitats due to the gradual conversion of hardwood forests into farmland, reservoirs, and urban or suburban areas. With num- bers as low as 90,000 worldwide, the prognosis for the continued survival of the bird has been bleak.
30 Scientists have been studying the birds across the southern United States for more than two decades, but attempts to conserve the species have fallen short due to a lack of understanding of their true habitat needs. Scientists tried to shift the Swainson's
35 warbler to national forests, public refuges, and pri- vate sanctuaries, but success was limited. Recently, though, researchers found that the population is

increasing. Since the 1990s, Swainson's warblers have been doing what scientists attempted to do for
40 them: the birds have created new breeding grounds for themselves by moving into industrial pine plan- tations that have been planted in ten different states.

Millions of acres of industrial pine forests have been planted since the 1920s. Some of these planta-
45 tions are even located in the same areas that Swain- son's warblers used to use for breeding grounds before the area's natural forests disappeared. With trees cut every 25 to 35 years, these plantations sup- port a $200 billion industry that produces wood-
50 based goods from housing lumber to notebook paper. The pine plantations were once thought by scientists to offer little support to any wildlife. They do not make ideal habitats due to the even spac- ing of planted rows and the lack of diversity in tree
55 species. These plantations, though, happen to offer the Swainson's warbler two of the things they most require from their habitats.

When the pines at these tree farms reach about twenty feet high, they hit the one specific stage of
60 growth that appeals to the birds. This height creates high-density undergrowth that the birds rely on for protection during their breeding season. This point of the pine development best mimics the bird's traditional habitat. Before deforestation occurred in
65 the Southeastern United States, Swainson's warblers lived in thickets of cane or areas with dense vines and tangled undergrowth. At the pine plantations, the habitat lasts for about seven to eight years be- fore the trees grow too tall to provide the birds the
70 coverage that they seek. The birds move on once the tangled undergrowth they prefer disappears.

The Swainson's warbler's secondary requirement that pine plantations can easily provide is space. A single breeding pair of the species requires between
75 10 and 20 acres of land. This large amount of space is one of the reasons why the species was so vulner- able to deforestation.

Today, pine plantations occupy some 40 mil- lion acres in the southern United States. Not all of

80 these acres are usable to the birds, though. When the cutting cycles and the amount of time the trees offer the type of undergrowth desirable to the Swainson's warblers are considered, it is estimated that approximately 10 million acres of pine plantations
85 are available to the birds at one time.

These numbers suggest that pine plantations will become the Swainson's warbler's primary habitat over time. The species owes its continued existence to its ability to adapt. While other species of warbler have dis-
90 appeared entirely due to the clearing of natural forests, the Swainson's warbler has remained flexible, shifting its behavior to ensure its own preservation.

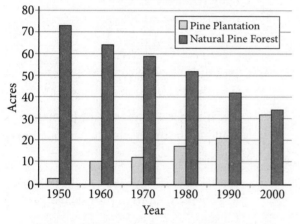

Planted vs. Natural Pine Forests in the Southern U.S.

Adapted from *United States Geological Survey, Land Cover Trends Project.*

1. The central idea of the passage is primarily concerned with

   A) the impact of deforestation on endangered birds throughout North America and the Caribbean.

   B) how industrial pine plantations have affected the manufacturing of wood-based commercial goods.

   C) how the population of the Swainson's warbler is recovering despite the destruction of the bird's natural habitat.

   D) the ways in which scientists have struggled to increase populations of the Swainson's warbler.

2. The author refers to the Allen's hummingbird, spotted owl, and osprey in lines 11-12 to

   A) contrast the habitat needs of the Swainson's warbler with that of other bird species.

   B) illustrate the difficulties faced by conservationists attempting to protect threatened birds.

   C) provide examples of other birds threatened by the disappearance of their habitats.

   D) imply that more species of birds will find alternative habitats as deforestation continues.

3. Based on the information in the passage, conservation efforts to protect the Swainson's warbler have been unsuccessful because scientists have

   A) been unable to track the Swainson's warbler population.

   B) not had the resources to move the birds to new habitats.

   C) not understood the bird's habitat needs.

   D) been unable to get the birds to breed in captivity.

4. Which choice provides the best evidence for the answer to the previous question?

   A) Lines 4-6 ("Scientists struggle ... track")

   B) Lines 18-21 ("During breeding ... lowlands")

   C) Lines 30-34 ("Scientists have been ... habitat needs")

   D) Lines 58-60 ("When the pines ... birds")

5. As used in line 26, "conversion" most nearly means

    A) translation.

    B) destruction.

    C) variation.

    D) transformation.

6. Based on the information in the passage, the reader can infer that

    A) bird populations will continue to decrease if their natural habitats are destroyed.

    B) the Swainson's warbler's population will decrease again if more pine forests are not planted.

    C) the profitability of the pine forests is increased by the presence of the Swainson's warbler.

    D) populations of other endangered birds would increase if they moved to private sanctuaries.

7. Which choice provides the best evidence for the answer to the previous question?

    A) Lines 1-4 ("As our environment …warbler")

    B) Lines 11-14 ("Others, such as … disappearing")

    C) Lines 43-44 ("Millions of acres … 1920s")

    D) Lines 51-52 ("The pine plantations … wildlife")

8. The primary purpose of this passage is to

    A) argue that more must be done to protect endangered bird species.

    B) persuade readers to learn more about how they can help protect birds.

    C) summarize the ways that conservation groups have failed to protect endangered birds.

    D) explain how one threatened species of bird has adapted to its disappearing habitat.

9. The migration of the Swainson's warbler to industrial pine forests is most similar to which of the following?

    A) Beavers building dams using sticks and logs

    B) Spiders creating cobwebs in bushes and trees

    C) Aquatic animals creating artificial reefs from shipwrecks

    D) Raccoons foraging for food in garbage bins

10. As used in line 62, "point" most nearly means

    A) stage.

    B) purpose.

    C) detail.

    D) level.

11. Which of the following conclusions is supported by the information in the graph?

    A) The number of acres of pine plantation could soon surpass that of natural pine forests.

    B) Natural pine forests have been converted to pine plantations to provide habitats for birds.

    C) Natural pine forests will be completely replaced by pine plantations by the year 2050.

    D) Pine plantations produce more useable lumber per acre than natural pine forests.

CHAPTER 12

Inferring Relationships and Vocab-in-Context Questions

 ## CHAPTER OBJECTIVES

By the end of this chapter, you will be able to:

1. Identify explicitly stated cause-and-effect, compare-and-contrast, and sequenced relationships in a passage

2. Determine implicit cause-and-effect, compare-and-contrast, and sequenced relationships in a passage

3. Interpret words and phrases in context to answer test-like questions

SMARTPOINTS

Point Value	SmartPoint Category
40 Points	Inference
55 Points	Vocab-in-Context

INFERENCE QUESTIONS: EXPLICIT RELATIONSHIPS

Before we jump into the specifics about inferring relationships—explicit and implicit—let's look at different kinds of relationships that can exist in an SAT Reading passage.

Relationship questions ask about how two events, characters, or ideas are connected. The three most common relationship types are:

1. **Cause-and-Effect** relationships require you to identify an action or condition that brings about a predictable result. You can identify cause-and-effect relationships by the keywords *caused by*, *results in*, *because*, and *therefore*.

2. **Compare-and-Contrast** relationships highlight the similarities or differences between two items. Common compare-and-contrast keywords are *similar*, *different*, *despite*, and *like*.

3. **Sequential** relationships describe the chronology, or order, in which the items are arranged or occur. Keywords include *first*, *second*, *following*, and *after*.

Some Inference questions about relationships will ask about explicit relationships. Questions about explicit relationships will provide one part of the relationship and ask you to find the other part. In an Explicit Relationship question, the wording of the correct answer will be very similar to the wording of the passage.

> **✔ Remember**
>
> Don't forget Step 2 of the Kaplan Method for Reading Comprehension: Examine the question stem.

INFERENCE QUESTIONS: IMPLICIT RELATIONSHIPS

Questions about implicit relationships, like those about explicit relationships, ask you to identify how items are connected. However, unlike explicit relationship questions, an Implicit Relationship question requires you to find a connection that may not be directly stated in the passage.

When answering Implicit Relationship questions, describe the relationship being tested in your own words by using keywords like *because*, *although*, and *in order to*.

> **✔ Expert Tip**
>
> Eliminating answer choices that are clearly wrong will help you answer even the toughest Implicit Relationship questions correctly.

VOCAB-IN-CONTEXT QUESTIONS

Vocab-in-Context questions require you to deduce the meaning of a word or phrase by using the context in which the word or phrase appears. You can recognize Vocab-in-Context questions because the wording of the question stem is often like this: "As used in line 7, 'clairvoyant' most nearly means…"

Kaplan's Strategy for Vocab-in-Context questions relies heavily on Step 3 of the Kaplan Method for Reading Comprehension: Predict and answer. If you need to review the Kaplan Method for Reading Comprehension, please turn to chapter 10.

To answer Vocab-in-Context questions efficiently and correctly, employ the following Kaplan Strategy:

- Pretend the word is a blank in the sentence
- Predict what word could be substituted for the blank
- Select the answer choice that best matches your prediction

Let's look at the following example of a test-like, primary source History/Social Studies passage and question set. After the mapped passage, the left column contains questions similar to those you'll see on the Reading Test on Test Day. The column on the right features the strategic thinking a test expert employs when approaching the passage and questions presented. Pay attention to how a test expert varies his or her approach to the different question types.

Strategic Thinking

Step 1: Read actively

Read the passage and the notes provided. Remember, a well-crafted Passage Map should summarize the central idea of each paragraph, as well as important topics or themes. Use your Passage Map to help you answer each question.

Questions 1-3 are based on the following passage.

The following passage is adapted from President Abraham Lincoln's Second Inaugural Address, delivered on March 4, 1865.

1st vs 2nd AL inaug. add.

At this second appearing to take the oath of the Presidential office there is <u>less occasion for an extended address</u> than there was at the first. Then,
Line a statement somewhat in detail of a course to be
5 pursued seemed fitting and proper. (Now,) at the expiration of four years, during which public declarations have been constantly called forth on every point and phase of the great contest which still absorbs the attention and engrosses the energies
10 of the nation, <u>little that is new would be presented</u>.

public knows too

The progress of our arms, upon which all else chiefly depends, is as <u>well known to the public as to myself</u>, and it is, I trust, reasonably satisfactory and encouraging to all. With high hope for the future,
15 no prediction in regard to it is ventured.

war about to happen but no one wanted it

On the occasion corresponding to this four years ago <u>all</u> thoughts were anxiously directed to an impending civil war. <u>All</u> dreaded it, <u>all</u> sought to avert it. (While) the inaugural address was being delivered
20 from this place, devoted altogether to *saving* the Union without war, urgent agents were in the city

bad guys made war to destroy Union; good guys accepted to save it

seeking to *destroy* it without war—seeking to dissolve the Union and divide effects by negotiation. Both parties deprecated war, (but) one of them would
25 *make* war rather than let the nation survive, and the other would *accept* war rather than let it perish, and the war came.

most slaves in South

One-eighth of the whole population were black slaves, not distributed generally over the Union,
30 but localized in the southern part of it. These slaves

slavery = cause of war

constituted a peculiar and powerful interest. All knew that this interest was somehow the cause of

the war. <u>To strengthen, perpetuate, and extend this interest was the object for which the insurgents</u>
35 <u>would rend the Union, even by war</u>; while the (Government) claimed no right to do more than to restrict the territorial enlargement of it. <u>Neither party expected</u> for the war the magnitude or the duration which it has already attained. <u>Neither an-</u>
40 <u>ticipated</u> that the cause of the conflict might cease with or even before the conflict itself should cease. Each looked for an easier triumph, and a result less fundamental and astounding.

goals of both sides

no one knew how big or how long war would be

Questions	Strategic Thinking
1. Which choice best describes the differing attitudes of the insurgents and the government toward slavery? A) The insurgents wanted to preserve slavery's reach, while the government wanted to reduce it. B) The insurgents wanted to extend slavery's reach, while the government wanted to abolish the institution. C) The insurgents wanted to extend slavery's reach, while the government wanted to limit the expansion of slavery. D) The insurgents wanted to reduce slavery's reach, while the government wanted to preserve it.	**Step 2: Examine the question stem** Identify the key words and phrases in the question stem: "differing attitudes of the insurgents and the government toward slavery." The Passage Map note "goals of both sides" indicates that the answer will be found in the third paragraph. **Step 3: Predict and answer** According to the third paragraph, the insurgents wanted to "strengthen, perpetuate, and extend" slavery (line 33) and the government wanted to "restrict the territorial enlargement" of slavery (line 37). Choice (C) matches this prediction.
2. As used in line 34, "interest" most nearly means A) involvement. B) attention. C) claim. D) return.	**Step 2: Examine the question stem** The key words and phrases in this question stem are the cited word and "most nearly means." Use the Kaplan Strategy for Vocab-in-Context questions to answer question stems with this phrasing. **Step 3: Predict and answer** "Interest" is used three times in lines 31-34, but this question is asking about its third appearance. The context of "interest" in this sentence is related to the goals of the insurgents, who wanted to extend slavery. "Interest" could be replaced by "ownership" or "privilege." Choice (C) matches this prediction.

Questions	Strategic Thinking
3. The result referred to in lines 42-43 ("a result … astounding") was most likely caused by the A) magnitude of the war. B) limitation of slavery. C) duration of the war. D) dissolution of the Union.	**Step 2: Examine the question stem** The key words and phrases in the question stem are the cited phrase and "most likely caused by." The Passage Map notes surrounding the cited lines will point toward the correct answer. **Step 3: Predict and answer** The Passage Map notes earlier in this paragraph cite that slavery was the cause of the war. Choice (B) matches this prediction.

You have now seen how to approach these question types on Test Day.

Look at the test-like U.S. and World Literature passage that follows. There are three questions associated with it—one of each kind reviewed in this chapter. Part of the passage has been mapped already. Your first step is to complete the Passage Map. Then, use the Kaplan Method for Reading Comprehension and the strategies discussed in this chapter to answer the questions. Strategic thinking questions have been included to guide you—some of the answers have been filled in, but you will have to fill in the answers to others.

Use your answers to the strategic thinking questions to select the correct answer, just as you will on Test Day.

Strategic Thinking
Step 1: Read actively The passage below is partially mapped. Read the passage and the first part of the Passage Map. Then, complete the Passage Map on your own. Remember to focus on the central ideas of each paragraph as well as the central idea of the overall passage. Use your Passage Map as a reference when you're answering questions.

Questions 4-6 are based on the following passage.

The following passage is an excerpt from the preface of Moll Flanders *(1722) by Daniel Defoe.*

auth. to reader: story might not seem true

The world is so taken up of late with novels and romances, that it will be hard for a private history to be taken for genuine, where the names and other
Line circumstances of the person are concealed, and on
5 this account we must be content to leave the reader to pass his own opinion upon the ensuing sheet, and take it just as he pleases.

MF = autobio but not real ID

The author is here supposed to be writing her own history, and in the very beginning of her
10 account she gives the reasons why she thinks fit to conceal her true name, after which there is no occasion to say any more about that.

writing style altered to be tamer

It is true that the original of this story is put into new words, and the style of the famous lady we here
15 speak of is a little altered; particularly she is made to tell her own tale in modester words than she told it at first, the copy which came first to hand having been written in language more like one still in Newgate than one grown penitent and humble, as
20 she afterwards pretends to be.

The pen employed in finishing her story, and making it what you now see it to be, has had no little difficulty to put it into a dress fit to be seen, and to make it speak language fit to be read. When
25 a woman debauched from her youth, nay, even being the offspring of debauchery and vice, comes to give an account of all her vicious practices, and even to descend to the particular occasions and circumstances by which she ran through in threescore
30 years, an author must be hard put to wrap it up so clean as not to give room, especially for vicious readers, to turn it to his disadvantage.

MF story = dark

All possible care, however, has been taken to give no lewd ideas, no immodest turns in the new
35 dressing up of this story; no, not to the worst parts of her expressions. To this purpose some of the vicious part of her life, which could not be modestly told, is quite left out, and several other parts are very much shortened. What is left 'tis hoped will
40 not offend the chastest reader or the modest hearer; and as the best use is made even of the worst story, the moral 'tis hoped will keep the reader serious, even where the story might incline him to be otherwise. To give the history of a wicked life repented
45 of, necessarily requires that the wicked part should be make as wicked as the real history of it will bear,

to illustrate and give a beauty to the penitent part, which is certainly the best and brightest, if related with equal spirit and life.

50 But as this work is chiefly recommended to those who know how to read it, and how to make the good uses of it which the story all along recommends to them, so it is to be hoped that such readers will be more pleased with the moral than the

55 fable, with the application than with the relation, and with the end of the writer than with the life of the person written of.

There is in this story abundance of delightful incidents, and all of them usefully applied. There is

60 an agreeable turn artfully given them in the relating, that naturally instructs the reader, either one

way or other. The first part of her lewd life with the young gentleman at Colchester has so many happy turns given it to expose the crime, and warn all

65 whose circumstances are adapted to it, of the ruinous end of such things, and the foolish, thoughtless, and abhorred conduct of both the parties, that it abundantly atones for all the lively description she gives of her folly and wickedness.

70 Upon this foundation this book is recommended to the reader as a work from every part of which something may be learned, and some just and religious inference is drawn, by which the reader will have something of instruction, if he pleases to

75 make use of it.

Don't get distracted by less important details. While there is a lot going on in this passage, your additions to the Passage Map should show that Moll Flanders did eventually change and how the author thinks the reader should respond to the story. If you're stuck, review the example Passage Map in the Answers & Explanations for this chapter on page 672.

Questions	Strategic Thinking
4. According to the passage, the narrator is concerned that readers may not believe the story because A) each reader is entitled to form his or her own opinion about the story. B) some parts of the story have been omitted. C) different readers will interpret the story in different ways. D) readers will assume that the story is a novel.	**Step 2: Examine the question stem** *What are the key words and phrases in this question stem?* The key phrases in the question stem are "According to the passage" and "readers may not believe the story." The answer will be found in the passage. *What parts of your Passage Map are relevant?* The Passage Map notes for the first paragraph say that the story might not seem true, which corresponds to the question stem. The answer will be in the first paragraph. **Step 3: Predict and answer** *What can you predict?* The author is concerned that the readers might not believe the story because "the world is so taken up of late with novels and romances," which may cause many readers to believe that the story is fictional (lines 1-2). *Which answer choice matches this prediction?* _____

Questions	Strategic Thinking
5. Based on the passage, the narrator hopes that readers of the story will A) understand the reasons for omitting certain parts of the story. B) recognize the harm that a misguided reading might cause. C) use the moral of the story to improve their own lives. D) enjoy the story for the vividness of the characterizations.	**Step 2: Examine the question stem** *What are the key words and phrases in this question stem?* The key words in this question stem are the phrase "Based on the passage," which implies that the correct answer is not explicitly stated, and "narrator hopes." *What parts of the passage are relevant?* The narrator discusses his hopes for the reader in the final paragraph, which is where you will find the answer. **Step 3: Predict and answer** *What does the narrator specifically want the reader to take away from the story?* _____ _____ _____ _____ *Which answer choice matches this prediction?* _____

Questions	Strategic Thinking
6. As used in line 59, "usefully applied" most nearly means A) well written. B) consistent with the author's purpose. C) useful in the proper context. D) humorously recounted.	**Step 2: Examine the question stem** *What are the key words and phrases in this question stem?* _____ _____ _____ _____ *How can you find the answer?* _____ _____ _____ _____ **Step 3: Predict and answer** *What word or phrase can you substitute for the phrase in question?* _____ _____ _____ *Which answer choice matches this prediction?* _____

Now, use the strategies you learned in this chapter to answer questions about a Science passage. Give yourself 6 minutes to read and map the passage and answer the questions.

Questions 7-10 are based on the following passage.

The following passage is about the role chemistry plays in archeology.

Demonstrating that chemistry sometimes can inform history, researchers from the National Institute of Standards and Technology (NIST), Colorado
Line College and Mount Saint Mary's University in
5 Emmitsburg, Maryland, have shown that sensitive nondestructive evaluation (NDE) techniques can be used to determine the elemental composition of ancient coins, even coins that generally have been considered too corroded for such methods. Along
10 the way, the researchers' analysis of coins minted in ancient Judea has both raised new questions about who ruled the area and given insight into trading patterns and industry in the region.

Elemental and isotope analysis of the metals in
15 ancient artifacts sometimes can pinpoint the places where the metal was mined, because ores in a given region often have a unique composition. This can be combined with historical records of when mines in the area were operating to determine when the
20 coin was likely struck. The results not only help date the coin, but also offer insight into trade and power relationships in the region.

To compare the effectiveness of various nondestructive analytical methods with destructive
25 methods often used to determine the age and origin of ancient coins, the group studied coins minted by Kings Herod Agrippa I and Herod Agrippa II in what is modern day Palestine and Israel, during a biblically and historically significant period.

30 The vast numbers of a particular coin, a prutah, found in the archaeological record has led scholars to disagree about when they were struck and by whom. The provenance of the coin is important because it is used to establish dates for places and
35 events in the early years of Christianity and the onset of the Jewish War (66-70 CE) against the Romans and the Diaspora that followed.

To better establish whether the coins were minted by Agrippa I (41-45 CE) or Agrippa II
40 (after 61 CE), the team performed X-ray fluorescence and lead isotope analysis to fingerprint the ores used in the production of the coins. These NDE methods are not commonly used on corroded coins because the corrosion can affect the
45 results—in some cases making it difficult to get a result at all. The team showed that these problems could be overcome using polarizing optics and powerful new software for X-ray fluorescence analysis, combined with careful calibration of
50 the mass spectrometer using Standard Reference Materials from NIST.

The lead isotope analysis, performed at NIST, showed that the coins that had been attributed to Agrippa I were indeed from that era. More interest-
55 ingly, however, the group found that the copper from which the coins were made most likely came from mines that scholars thought hadn't been opened until a century later.

"All the archaeological evidence has thus far
60 suggested that the Romans had moved into Arabia in the second century CE," says Nathan Bower of Colorado College. "What this analysis shows is that the Romans may have reached the region earlier or found that these mines had already been
65 opened. Either way, our findings suggest that the Romans had a much closer relationship with this particular region than scholars had previously thought."

To follow up on their research, the group is
70 planning to perform more tests to determine if the mines in question may have been operating even earlier than their recent findings suggest.

7. As used in line 32, "struck" most nearly means

   A) made.

   B) hit.

   C) ignited.

   D) discovered.

8. The passage strongly suggests that the results of the lead isotope analysis on the ancient coins

   A) proved the value of an experimental method of analysis.

   B) were enhanced by the corrosion of the coins.

   C) established that the coins were minted by Agrippa II (after 61 CE).

   D) answered old questions and raised new ones.

9. According to the passage, the researchers chose to analyze a particular coin because

   A) it was less corroded than other coins of the same era.

   B) historians knew very little about the era during which it was minted.

   C) the metal used to mint the coin came from mines in Arabia.

   D) scholars disagreed about the origin of the coin.

10. As used in line 38, "establish" most nearly means

    A) ascertain.

    B) install.

    C) build.

    D) begin.

Answers & Explanations for this chapter appear on page 672.

EXTRA PRACTICE

Questions 1-10 are based on the following passage.

The following passage is adapted from Around the World in Eighty Days *by Jules Verne.*

Phileas Fogg, having shut the door of his house at half-past eleven, and having put his right foot before his left five hundred and seventy-five times,
Line and his left foot before his right five hundred and
5 seventy-six times, reached the Reform Club. He repaired at once to the dining-room and took his place at the habitual table, the cover of which had already been laid for him. A flunkey handed him an uncut Times, which he proceeded to cut with a
10 skill which betrayed familiarity with this delicate operation. The perusal of this paper absorbed Phileas Fogg until a quarter before four, whilst the Standard, his next task, occupied him till the dinner hour. Dinner passed as breakfast had done,
15 and Mr. Fogg re-appeared in the reading-room and sat down to the Pall Mall[1] at twenty minutes before six. Half an hour later several members of the Reform came in and drew up to the fireplace. They were Mr. Fogg's usual partners at whist:[2]
20 Andrew Stuart, an engineer; John Sullivan and Samuel Fallentin, bankers; Thomas Flanagan, a brewer; and Gauthier Ralph, one of the Directors of the Bank of England.

"Well, Ralph," said Thomas Flanagan, "what
25 about that robbery?"

"Oh," replied Stuart, "the Bank will lose the money."

"On the contrary," broke in Ralph, "I hope we may put our hands on the robber. Skillful detectives
30 have been sent to all the principal ports of America and the Continent, and he'll be a clever fellow if he slips through their fingers."

"But have you got the robber's description?" asked Stuart.

35 "In the first place, he is no robber at all," returned Ralph, positively.

"What! a fellow who makes off with fifty-five thousand pounds, no robber?"

"No."

40 "Perhaps he's a manufacturer, then."

"The Daily Telegraph says that he is a gentleman."

It was Phileas Fogg, whose head now emerged from behind his newspapers, who made this
45 remark. A package of banknotes, to the value of fifty-five thousand pounds, had been taken from the principal cashier's table, that functionary being at the moment engaged in registering the receipt of three shillings and sixpence. Let it be observed that
50 the Bank of England reposes a touching confidence in the honesty of the public. There are neither guards nor gratings to protect its treasures; gold, silver, banknotes are freely exposed, at the mercy of the first comer. A keen observer of English customs
55 relates that, being in one of the rooms of the Bank one day, he had the curiosity to examine a gold ingot weighing some seven or eight pounds. He took it up, scrutinised it, passed it to his neighbour, he to the next man, and so on until the ingot, going from
60 hand to hand, was transferred to the end of a dark entry; nor did it return to its place for half an hour. Meanwhile, the cashier had not so much as raised his head. But in the present instance things had not gone so smoothly. The package of notes not being
65 found when five o'clock sounded from the ponderous clock in the "drawing office," the amount was passed to the account of profit and loss.

There were real grounds for supposing, as the Daily Telegraph said, that the thief did not belong
70 to a professional band. On the day of the robbery a well-dressed gentleman of polished manners, and with a well-to-do air, had been observed going to and fro in the paying room where the crime was committed. A description of him was easily pro-
75 cured and sent to the detectives; and some hopeful spirits, of whom Ralph was one, did not despair of his apprehension. The papers and clubs were full of the affair, and everywhere people were discussing the probabilities of a successful pursuit; and the

80 Reform Club was especially agitated, several of its members being Bank officials.

Ralph would not concede that the work of the detectives was likely to be in vain, for he thought that the prize offered would greatly stimulate their

85 zeal and activity. But Stuart was far from sharing this confidence; and, as they placed themselves at the whist-table, they continued to argue the matter.

"I maintain," said Stuart, "that the chances are in favour of the thief, who must be a shrewd fellow."

90 "Well, but where can he fly to?" asked Ralph. "No country is safe for him."

"Pshaw!"

"Where could he go, then?"

"Oh, I don't know that. The world is big enough."

95 "It was once," said Phileas Fogg, in a low tone.

[1] Pall Mall: a street in the city of Westminster, London
[2] Whist: a trick-taking card game. Modern derivatives include Hearts and Spades.

1. As used in line 6, "repaired" most nearly means

   A) fixed.

   B) returned.

   C) stormed.

   D) proceeded.

2. The passage suggests that Phileas Fogg is a man who

   A) focuses on cultural activites.

   B) lives beyond his means.

   C) enjoys routine.

   D) keeps to himself.

3. Which choice provides the best evidence for the answer to the previous question?

   A) Lines 5-8 ("He repaired … for him")

   B) Lines 8-11 ("A flunkey … delicate operation")

   C) Lines 14-17 ("Dinner passed … before six")

   D) Lines 29-32 ("Skillful detectives … their fingers")

4. The passage suggests that Fogg

   A) keeps abreast of current events.

   B) is a political reformer.

   C) has strong opinions about crime.

   D) makes his living as a banker.

5. Which choice provides the best evidence for the answer to the previous question?

   A) Lines 8-11 ("A flunkey … delicate operation")

   B) Lines 17-18 ("Half an hour … the fireplace")

   C) Lines 29-32 ("Skillful detectives … their fingers")

   D) Lines 43-45 ("It was … this remark")

6. According to the passage, which statement about the Bank of England is true?

   A) The public has faith in the integrity of the Bank.

   B) The Bank has taken few precautions to guard against theft.

   C) The Bank has a history of money being stolen.

   D) The Bank has carefully managed public relations.

7. As used in line 47, "functionary" most nearly means

   A) official.

   B) money.

   C) servant.

   D) criminal.

8. The passage suggests that the thief was not part of a professional crime ring because

    A)   the suspect acted alone.

    B)   the Bank had never been burglarized before.

    C)   the suspect was described as a gentleman.

    D)   the Bank carefully screened the customers.

9. The purpose of line 95 ("'It was once,' ... a low tone") is to

    A)   create an ominous atmosphere at the table.

    B)   foreshadow Fogg's ideas about the world.

    C)   illustrate Fogg's proper demeanor and social skills.

    D)   introduce the conflict of the plot.

10. What is the primary purpose of the passage?

    A)   To illustrate the problems with theft at the Bank of England

    B)   To examine the lives of wealthy men in England

    C)   To introduce Phileas Fogg and his social circle at the Reform Club

    D)   To parody the social customs of the upper class

CHAPTER 13

Rhetoric I

CHAPTER OBJECTIVES

By the end of this chapter, you will be able to:

1. Determine the author's purpose in a given passage

2. Determine the author's point of view in a given passage

3. Determine why the author used a certain word or phrase in a given passage

SMARTPOINTS

Point Value	SmartPoint Category
70 Points	Rhetoric

RHETORIC QUESTIONS: ANALYZING PURPOSE

Some Analyzing Purpose questions ask about the purpose of the passage as a whole. Every author has a reason for writing. To identify that reason—or purpose—ask these two questions:

- Why did the author write this passage?

- What does the author want the reader to think about this topic?

Other Analyzing Purpose questions will ask you to identify the purpose of part of a passage, usually one or more paragraphs. To answer this type of question, read around the cited portion, review your Passage Map, and ask these two questions:

- What is the function of this section?

- How does this section help achieve the author's purpose?

> ✔ **Remember**
>
> **Everything an author includes in a passage is there to help achieve his or her purpose in writing.**

RHETORIC QUESTIONS: ANALYZING POINT OF VIEW

Rhetoric questions that ask you to analyze point of view require you to establish the author's perspective and how that perspective affects the content and the style of the passage. That is, you need to figure out not only what the author says but also how the author says it. Your Passage Map will help you determine the author's point of view.

When answering these types of questions, ask:

- Is the author's tone positive, negative, or neutral?

- Does the author want things to change or stay the same?

- Is the author addressing supporters or opponents?

> ✔ **Expert Tip**
>
> **As you study, practice asking these questions as you read every passage you encounter. The author is always trying to tell you something, so the more accustomed you are to asking these questions, the easier it will be for you to determine the author's point of view.**

RHETORIC QUESTIONS: ANALYZING WORD CHOICE

Rhetoric questions about word choice ask about how a particular word or phrase affects your understanding of the author's purpose and point of view.

While these questions do focus on a word or phrase, do not confuse them with Vocab-in-Context questions. Vocab-in-Context questions ask about the meaning of a word or phrase; Analyzing Word Choice questions ask about the function of a word or phrase within the passage. That is, why did the author use this word or phrase?

If you want to review Vocab-in-Context questions, turn to chapter 12.

To answer Analyzing Word Choice questions, ask what the function of the cited word or phrase is. Common functions of words or phrases include:

- Setting a mood
- Conveying an emotion
- Building to a conclusion
- Calling to action
- Stating an opinion

✔ **Remember**

Correct answers to Analyzing Word Choice questions will always be in line with the author's overall purpose.

Let's look at the following example of a test-like Science passage and question set. After the mapped passage, the left column contains questions similar to those you'll see on the Reading Test on Test Day. The column on the right features the strategic thinking a test expert employs when approaching the passage and questions presented. Pay attention to how a test expert varies his or her approach to the different question types.

Strategic Thinking
Step 1: Read actively
Read the passage and the notes provided. Remember, a well-crafted Passage Map should summarize the central idea of each paragraph as well as important topics or themes. Use your Passage Map to help you answer each question.

Questions 1-3 are based on the following passage.

This passage details the varying and changing scientific theories surrounding sunspots.

Astronomers noted more than 150 years ago that sunspots wax and wane in number in an 11-year cycle. Ever since, people have speculated
Line that the solar cycle might exert some influence on
5 the Earth's weather. In this century, for example, scientists have linked the solar cycle to droughts in the American Midwest. Until recently, however, none of these correlations has held up under close scrutiny.

10 One problem is that sunspots themselves are so poorly understood. Observations have revealed that the swirly smudges represent areas of intense magnetic activity where the sun's radiative energy has been blocked and that they are considerably cooler
15 than bright regions of the sun. Scientists have not been able, however, to determine just how sunspots are created or what effect they have on the solar constant (a misnomer that refers to the sun's total radiance at any instant).

20 The latter question, at least, now seems to have been resolved by data from the *Solar Maximum Mission* satellite, which has monitored the solar constant since 1980, the peak of the last solar cycle. As the number of sunspots decreased through 1986,
25 the satellite recorded a gradual dimming of the sun. Over the past year, as sunspots have proliferated, the sun has brightened. The data suggest that the sun is 0.1 percent more luminous at the peak of the solar cycle, when the number of sunspots is greatest,
30 than at its nadir, according to Richard C. Willson of the Jet Propulsion Laboratory and Hugh S. Hudson of the University of California at San Diego.

The data show that sunspots do not themselves make the sun shine brighter. Quite the contrary.
35 When a sunspot appears, it initially causes the sun to dim slightly, but then after a period of weeks or months islands of brilliance called faculas usually emerge near the sunspot and more than compensate for its dimming effect. Willson says faculas may rep-
40 resent regions where energy that initially was blocked beneath a sunspot has finally breached the surface.

Does the subtle fluctuation in the solar constant manifest itself in the Earth's weather? Some recent reports offer statistical evidence that it does, albeit
45 rather indirectly. The link seems to be mediated by a phenomenon known as the quasi-biennial oscillation (QBO), a 180-degree shift in the direction of stratospheric winds above the Tropics that occurs about every two years.

50 Karin Labitzke of the Free University of Berlin and Harry van Loon of the National Center for Atmospheric Research in Boulder, Colorado, were the first to uncover the QBO link. They gathered temperature and air-pressure readings from vari-
55 ous latitudes and altitudes over the past three solar cycles. They found no correlation between the solar cycle and their data until they sorted the data into two categories: those gathered during the QBO's west phase (when the stratospheric winds blow
60 west) and those gathered during its east phase. A remarkable correlation appeared: temperatures and pressures coincident with the QBO's west phase rose and fell in accordance with the solar cycle.

Building on this finding, Brian A. Tinsley of the
65 National Science Foundation discovered a statistical correlation between the solar cycle and the posi-

Margin notes:

sunspot cycle & weather

sunspots = poorly understood

SMM = effects of spots on solar constant

initially, spots dim

eventually become much brighter

spots indirectly affect weather (QBO)

KL & HvL studied

QBO west phase = link to temp & pressure

BT → found link btwn. solar cycle & storms

findings mysterious → why west phase?

tion of storms in the North Atlantic. The latitude of storms during the west phase of the QBO, Tinsley
70 found, varied with the solar cycle: storms occurring toward the peak of a solar cycle traveled at latitudes about six degrees nearer the Equator than storms during the cycle's nadir.

Labitzke, van Loon, and Tinsley acknowledge that their findings are still rather mysterious. Why
75 does the solar cycle seem to exert more of an influence during the west phase of the QBO than it does during the east phase? How does the 0.1 percent variance in solar radiation trigger the much

larger changes—up to six degrees Celsius in polar
80 regions—observed by Labitzke and van Loon? Van Loon says simply, "We can't explain it."

John A. Eddy of the National Center for Atmospheric Research, nonetheless, thinks these QBO findings as well as the *Solar Maximum Mission* data
85 "look like breakthroughs" in the search for a link between the solar cycle and weather. With further research, for example, into how the oceans damp the effects of solar flux, these findings may lead to models that have some predictive value. The next
90 few years may be particularly rich in solar flux.

breakthroughs, but more research to be done

Questions	Strategic Thinking
1. The author's point of view can best be described as that of A) a meteorologist voicing optimism that the findings of recent solar research will improve weather forecasting. B) an astronomer presenting a digest of current findings to a review board of other astronomers. C) a science writer explaining the possible influence of a solar phenomenon on terrestrial weather patterns. D) a historian detailing the contributions to climate science made by the *Solar Maximum Mission*.	**Step 2: Examine the question stem** Identify the key words and phrases in the question stem: "The author's point of view." Any Passage Map notes about the author's viewpoint will help answer this question. However, the Passage Map doesn't note any specific view or opinion the author offers. **Step 3: Predict and answer** Because the author doesn't express his or her own opinions regarding the topic, the correct answer will accurately reflect the informative style and neutral tone of the passage as well as the passage's central idea. Choice (C) matches this prediction.

Questions	Strategic Thinking
2. The main purpose of the questions in paragraph 8 (lines 73-81) is to A) emphasize how little scientists know about the solar constant. B) explain more fully the mysterious nature of the scientists' findings. C) question the basis upon which these scientists built their hypotheses. D) express doubts about the scientists' interpretations of their findings.	**Step 2: Examine the question stem** Identify the key words and phrases in the question stem: "Main purpose of the questions" and "paragraph 8." Look at the Passage Map notes for paragraph 8 to answer this question. **Step 3: Predict and answer** The notes next to paragraph 8 say, "Findings mysterious → why west phase?" The correct answer will allude to the uncertainty that surrounds Labitzke, van Loon, and Tinsley's findings. Choice (B) matches this prediction.
3. The use of the quoted phrase "look like breakthroughs" in line 85 is primarily meant to convey the idea that A) new research into the solar cycle has allowed scientists to build models that predict changes in Earth's complex climate system. B) recent advances in scientific understanding of the link between the solar cycle and Earth's weather may yield useful models. C) despite the associated costs, space missions can make important discoveries that are worth the expense. D) although the QBO findings may seem conclusive, it is important to keep an open mind about alternative interpretations of the data.	**Step 2: Examine the question stem** Identify the key words and phrases in the question stem. The key words include not only the cited phrase and its line number but also "primarily meant to convey the idea." The correct answer will not restate the meaning of the cited phrase but its purpose within the passage. Look at the Passage Map notes surrounding "look like breakthroughs" in line 85. **Step 3: Predict and answer** The cited phrase is a quotation from an official at the National Center for Atmospheric Research. The note next to this part of the passage says that more research is required to fully comprehend any possible link between the solar cycle and weather. Choice (B) matches this prediction.

You have now seen how to approach these question types on Test Day.

Look at the test-like U.S. and World Literature passage that follows. Part of the passage has been mapped already. Your first step is to complete the Passage Map. Then, use the Kaplan Method for Reading Comprehension and the strategies discussed in this chapter to answer the questions. Strategic thinking questions have been included to guide you—some of the answers have been filled in, but you will have to fill in the answers to others.

Use your answers to the strategic thinking questions to select the correct answer, just as you will on Test Day.

Strategic Thinking
Step 1: Read actively
The passage below is partially mapped. Read the passage and the first part of the Passage Map. Then, complete the Passage Map on your own. Remember to focus on the central ideas of each paragraph as well as the central idea of the overall passage. Use your Passage Map as a reference when you're answering questions.

Questions 4-6 are based on the following passage.

The following is an excerpt from The Woman in White, *a novel by Wilkie Collins published in 1859 and considered to be one of the first novels of the mystery genre.*

*P's face →
smthg
happened*

(Pesca's) face and manner, on the evening when we confronted each other at my mother's gate, were more than sufficient to inform me that <u>something</u>
Line <u>extraordinary had happened</u>. It was quite useless,
5 however, to ask him for an immediate explanation. I could only conjecture, while he was dragging me in by both hands, that, knowing my habits, he had come to the cottage to make sure of meeting me that night and that <u>he had some news to tell of an</u>
10 <u>unusually agreeable kind.</u>

*Mom accepts
's oddities*

We both bounced into the parlor in a highly abrupt and undignified manner. My mother sat by the open window laughing and fanning herself. Pesca was one of her especial favorites, and his
15 wildest eccentricities were always pardonable in her eyes. From the first moment she found out that the little Professor was deeply and gratefully attached to her son, she opened her heart to him unreservedly and took <u>all his puzzling foreign peculiarities for</u>

P = prof?

20 granted, without so much as attempting to understand any one of them.

My sister Sarah, with all the advantages of youth, was, strangely enough, less pliable. She did full justice to Pesca's excellent qualities of heart, but
25 she could not accept him implicitly, as my mother accepted him, for my sake. Her insular notions of propriety rose in perpetual revolt against Pesca's constitutional contempt for appearances, and she was always more or less undisguisedly astonished
30 at her mother's familiarity with the eccentric little foreigner. I have observed, not only in my sister's case, but in the instances of others, that <u>we of the</u>
<u>young generation are nowhere near as hearty and</u>
<u>impulsive as some of our elders.</u> I constantly see
35 old people flushed and excited by the prospect of some anticipated pleasure which altogether fails to ruffle the tranquility of their serene grandchildren. Are we, I wonder, quite such genuine boys and girls now as our seniors were in their time? Has the great
40 advance in education taken rather too long a stride, and are we in these modern days just the least trifle in the world too well brought up?

*S does not
accept
P bc of
propriety*

*elders = more
excited by
new things;
youth = unaf-
fected*

*kids = too
well raised?*

Without attempting to answer those questions decisively, I may at least record that I never saw my
45 mother and my sister together in Pesca's society without finding my mother much the younger woman of the two. On this occasion, for example, while the old lady was laughing heartily over the boyish manner in which we tumbled into the par-
50 lor, Sarah was perturbedly picking up the broken pieces of a teacup, which the Professor had knocked off the table in his precipitate advance to meet me at the door.

"I don't know what would have happened,
55 Walter," said my mother, "if you had delayed much longer. Pesca has been half mad with impatience, and I have been half mad with curiosity. The Professor has brought some wonderful news with him, in which he says you are concerned, and he has
60 cruelly refused to give us the smallest hint of it till his friend Walter appeared."

"Very provoking: it spoils the set," murmured Sarah to herself, mournfully absorbed over the ruins of the broken cup.

65 While these words were being spoken, Pesca, happily and fussily unconscious of the irreparable wrong which the crockery had suffered at his hands, was dragging a large arm-chair to the opposite end of the room, so as to command us all
70 three, in the character of a public speaker addressing an audience. Having turned the chair with its back towards us, he jumped into it on his knees and excitedly addressed his small congregation of three from an impromptu pulpit.

75 "Now, my good dears," began Pesca, "listen to me. The time has come—I recite my good news—I speak at last."

"Hear, hear," said my mother, humoring the joke.

"The next thing he will break, Mamma," whis-
80 pered Sarah, "will be the back of the best arm-chair."

"Among the fine London Houses where I teach the language of my native country," said Pesca, "is one, mighty fine, in the big place called Portland. The golden Papa there, the mighty merchant, says 'I
85 have got a letter from my friend, the Mister, and he wants a recommend from me, of a drawing-master, to go down to his house in the country. Perhaps you know of a drawing master that I can recommend?'

"I address myself to the mighty merchant, and
90 I say, 'Dear sir, I have the man! The first and foremost drawing-master of the world!'"

Don't get distracted by less important details. While there is a lot going on in this passage, your additions to the Passage Map should note how the different characters interact with and regard each other. If you're stuck, review the example Passage Map in the Answers & Explanations for this chapter on page 679.

Questions	Strategic Thinking
4. The central purpose of the first paragraph is to A) provide insight into the narrator's habits. B) demonstrate Pesca's disregard for the narrator's feelings. C) introduce the tone and setting of the passage. D) build suspense regarding the nature of the news Pesca has brought.	**Step 2: Examine the question stem** *What are the key words and phrases in this question stem?* The key words in this question stem are "central purpose" and "first paragraph." *What parts of your Passage Map are relevant?* The Passage Map notes for the first paragraph ("P's face → something happened"). Considering this information in the context of the entire passage will help answer this question. **Step 3: Predict and answer** *What can you predict?* The Passage Map note for the first paragraph highlights that Pesca is about to reveal something that has happened. The remainder of the passage describes how Pesca stalls and eventually relates the information to the other characters. *Which answer choice matches this prediction?* _____

Questions	Strategic Thinking
5. The description of Pesca and the narrator in lines 11-12 ("highly abrupt…manner") is primarily meant to A) illustrate the personalities of the narrator and Pesca. B) suggest that their behavior was inappropriate for the situation. C) portray Pesca as a bad influence on the narrator. D) provide a humorous contrast to the seriousness of the narrator's mother.	**Step 2: Examine the question stem** *What are the key words and phrases in this question stem?* The keywords in this question stem include the cited description of Pesca and the narrator as well as the phrase "primarily meant to." *What parts of your Passage Map are relevant?* The Passage Map notes surrounding these lines will help determine the purpose of the description. The Passage Map note in the previous paragraph says that you could tell from Pesca's face that something had happened. Shortly after these lines, the Passage Map note says that the narrator's mother accepted Pesca's oddities. **Step 3: Predict and answer** *What does the cited phrase accomplish when viewed in the context of the entire passage?* _____ _____ _____ _____ *Which answer choice matches this prediction?* _____

Questions	Strategic Thinking
6. The narrator's stance is best described as that of A) an artist learning about a possible teaching job. B) a social historian chronicling generational changes produced by evolving social conventions. C) a young man eager to set out on his own, free of the strictures of his family. D) a careful observer describing the natures of two characters he knows well.	**Step 2: Examine the question stem** *What are the key words and phrases in the question stem?* _____ _____ _____ _____ _____ *What parts of your Passage Map are relevant?* _____ _____ _____ _____ **Step 3: Predict and answer** *What is the narrator's overall tone and attitude?* _____ _____ _____ _____ *Which answer choice matches this prediction?* _____

Now, use the strategies you learned about in this chapter to answer questions about a History/Social Studies passage. Give yourself 6 minutes to read and map the passage and answer the questions.

Questions 7-9 are based on the following passage.

The following is adapted from Helen Keller's address to the American Association to Promote the Teaching of Speech to the Deaf at Mt. Airy, Philadelphia, Pennsylvania (July 8, 1896).

If you knew all the joy I feel in being able to speak to you today, I think you would have some idea of the value of speech to the deaf, and you
Line would understand why I want every little deaf
5 child in all this great world to have an opportunity to learn to speak. I know that much has been said and written on this subject, and that there is a wide difference of opinion among teachers of the deaf in regard to oral instruction. It seems very strange to
10 me that there should be this difference of opinion; I cannot understand how any one interested in our education can fail to appreciate the satisfaction we feel in being able to express our thoughts in living words. Why I use speech constantly, and I cannot
15 begin to tell you how much pleasure it gives me to do so. Of course I know that it is not always easy for strangers to understand me, but it will be by and by; and in the meantime I have the unspeakable happiness of knowing that my family and friends
20 rejoice in my ability to speak. My little sister and baby brother love to have me tell them stories in the long summer evenings when I am at home; and my mother and teacher often ask me to read to them from my favourite books. I also discuss the politi-
25 cal situation with my dear father, and we decide the most perplexing questions quite as satisfactorily to ourselves as if I could see and hear. So you see what a blessing speech is to me. It brings me into closer and tenderer relationship with those I love, and
30 makes it possible for me to enjoy the sweet companionship of a great many persons from whom I should be entirely cut off if I could not talk.

I can remember the time before I learned to speak, and how I used to struggle to express my
35 thoughts by means of the manual alphabet—how my thoughts used to beat against my fingertips like little birds striving to gain their freedom, until one day Miss Fuller opened wide the prison-door and let them escape. I wonder if she remembers how
40 eagerly and gladly they spread their wings and flew away. Of course, it was not easy at first to fly. The speech-wings were weak and broken, and had lost all the grace and beauty that had once been theirs; indeed, nothing was left save the impulse to fly,
45 but that was something. One can never consent to creep when one feels an impulse to soar. But, nevertheless, it seemed to me sometimes that I could never use my speech wings as God intended I should use them; there were so many difficulties
50 in the way, so many discouragements; but I kept on trying, knowing that patience and perseverance would win in the end. And while I worked, I built the most beautiful air-castles, and dreamed dreams, the pleasantest of which was of the time when I
55 should talk like other people; and the thought of the pleasure it would give my mother to hear my voice once more, sweetened every effort and made every failure an incentive to try harder the next time. So I want to say to those who are trying to
60 learn to speak and those who are teaching them: Be of good cheer. Do not think of today's failures, but of the success that may come tomorrow. You have set yourselves a difficult task, but you will succeed if you persevere; and you will find a joy in over-
65 coming obstacles—a delight in climbing rugged paths, which you would perhaps never know if you did not sometime slip backward—if the road was always smooth and pleasant. Remember, no effort that we make to attain something beautiful is ever
70 lost. Sometime, somewhere, somehow we shall find that which we seek. We shall speak, yes, and sing, too, as God intended we should speak and sing.

7. The author's use of the phrase in lines 35-37 ("how my ... freedom") is primarily meant to convey

    A) the frustration the author experienced before she could speak.

    B) that the author was unable to organize her ideas effectively when using the manual alphabet.

    C) the importance of patience when faced with difficult obstacles.

    D) the differences between written and oral communication.

8. The author's point of view can best be described as that of

    A) an adviser detailing the positive and negative aspects of a course of action.

    B) an educator outlining a new approach to teaching speech.

    C) a reformer using personal experience to persuade an audience.

    D) a student promoting the benefits of an experimental learning method.

9. The main purpose of the first paragraph is to

    A) encourage members of the audience to communicate with their friends and families.

    B) provide specific examples of ways in which the course of action the author advocates improved her quality of life.

    C) help the audience understand her experiences by using personal anecdotes.

    D) inspire other deaf students to persevere through the hardships they will encounter on their own journeys.

Answers & Explanations for this chapter begin on page 679.

EXTRA PRACTICE

Questions 1-11 are based on the following passage.

The following passage explores the history and impact of public higher education in the United States.

Every year, hundreds of thousands of students graduate from U.S. public universities. Many of the largest and most elite schools in the nation fall into
Line the category of public, or state, institutions. Unlike
5 private universities, which generally operate independently from any government influence, public higher education was established through government legislation and is sustained through state or federal involvement in various ways. A look into
10 the history of U.S. public higher education can shed light on the changing ideals of the American story over the past century and a half.

America's earliest higher-education institutions, like Harvard, were initially developed by and for
15 clergy, or church workers. For 17th-century Puritans in America, church leadership was of utmost importance. At that time, clergy was the main profession for which college degrees were offered. But during the 18th and 19th centuries, paralleling
20 the onset of secular (and increasingly scientifically inclined) modern thought, the nation and government acknowledged the need for broader higher education opportunities. Philosophers and politicians alike were aware that well-educated citizens
25 were a vital element of a functional democracy. A better-informed voting population could secure a better political future. Moreover, with aims to advance the fields of technology and agriculture through higher education, legislators anticipated
30 potential economic improvements nationwide as well. It was in the nation's best interest to make college more accessible.

In 1862, President Lincoln signed the Morill Land-Grant Act. This was, in many ways, the force
35 behind the public university system. The Morill Act ensured that public land would be set aside for the establishment of universities across the country.

The coming decades saw a massive increase in the opening of universities in the nation. Hundreds
40 of U.S. public universities began to operate. These schools received federal and state support, offered practical, accessible education, and sought, originally, to advance the fields of agriculture and mechanics. Soon these schools offered wide variet-
45 ies of subjects and specialties. These universities would be operated by their respective states, but all would adhere to certain broad federal regulations.

At the time, the government was seeking to mend racial injustices through legislation. To this
50 effect, a second Land Act was passed in 1890 in hopes of inhibiting discrimination in public universities. While at the time this did not accomplish the intended openness and diversity, it paved the way for the culture of diversity the
55 American university system enjoys today. Many public universities are now richly diverse, with regulations in place to accept students of any race, ethnicity, or socioeconomic status. In a similar vein, women—once a minority in colleges—increasingly
60 gained a strong presence in U.S. universities over the past 150 years. Women actually surpassed men in overall U.S. college attendance around the turn of the 21st century.

Since the legislation of the 19th-century, public
65 universities have undergone momentous growth. The system has evolved to address and accommodate the nuances of 20th- and 21st-century American culture and development. Offering to in-state students some of the most affordable degree
70 programs in higher education, these schools have now graduated millions of undergraduate and graduate students. Public universities also manage the majority of the nation's government-funded academic research initiatives. Featuring some of the
75 most competitive athletic programs in the world, as well as elite scholarship and arts programs, the U.S. public universities' accomplishments seem boundless. With schools in Alaska, Hawaii, and even

U.S. territories like Puerto Rico and Guam, public
80 university impact reaches the farthest corners and
populations of the nation. The state school system
has been formative for American culture, philoso-
phy, economics, medicine, politics, and much more.

The eminence of the U.S. public university net-
85 work stretches beyond the United States. Students
travel from across the globe to study at the top programs. Cutting-edge schools like the University of
Virginia (UVA) and University of California at Los
Angeles (UCLA) receive continual international
90 attention for their accomplishments in scholarship
and research. Programs, faculty, and students from
these schools participate in the global conversation
in significant ways, working toward a better future
for the planet.

95 Given those early visions for a more robustly
educated voting population, the enormity of the
system that the Morill Act launched is
remarkable. U.S. public universities have both
shaped and employed many of America's greatest
100 thinkers. Considering their timeline and their
accomplishments, these schools seem to reflect
the post–Civil War history of diversity, liberty,
creativity, and equal opportunity that in many ways
distinguishes the American cultural identity.

1. In the second paragraph, the author uses the
idea that educated citizens are necessary for a
functioning democracy to

A) show why an educated work force
increased agricultural production.

B) demonstrate the continued role of the
clergy in American public life.

C) explain why the government was playing
a larger role in public education.

D) emphasize the importance of
technological innovation for the
economy.

2. Which choice provides the best evidence for
the answer to the previous question?

A) Lines 17-18 ("At that time … were
offered")

B) Lines 19-23 ("But during …
opportunities")

C) Lines 25-27 ("A better-informed …
political future")

D) Lines 27-31 ("Moreover, with aims …
nationwide as well")

3. The purpose of the third paragraph is to

A) highlight an example of the government
increasing access to public education.

B) discuss initial technological advances in
agriculture and mechanics.

C) outline the effects of the Morill Land-
Grant Act on the U.S. economy.

D) explain the relationship between federal
and state control of public universities.

4. In line 42, the author's use of the word
"accessible" implies that

A) public universities would expand course
offerings to encompass a range of
subjects.

B) the likelihood that people with limited
means could attend a university was
increasing.

C) agriculture and mechanics would receive
the most federal and state support.

D) President Lincoln supported passage of
the Morill Land-Grant Act to expand
education.

5. As used in line 47, "adhere" most nearly means

    A) resist.

    B) notice.

    C) acquiesce.

    D) comply.

6. Which of the following pieces of evidence would most strengthen the author's line of reasoning throughout the passage?

    A) Information about the ways in which private and public universities differ in paragraph 1

    B) An example of how the 17th-century clergy benefited from higher education in paragraph 2

    C) Statistics showing increased enrollment numbers of minority students in paragraph 4

    D) An example of a competitive public university athletic program in paragraph 5

7. In the fourth paragraph, the author uses the fact that more women than men now attend college to

    A) contrast the advances of women's rights with racial injustice in public universities.

    B) provide an example of how the land acts initially failed to stop discrimination.

    C) show that public universities have grown increasingly diverse over time.

    D) illustrate the challenges many people still face to attend public universities.

8. Which choice provides the best evidence for the answer to the previous question?

    A) Lines 49-52 ("To this effect ... public universities")

    B) Lines 52-55 ("While at the time ... enjoys today")

    C) Lines 55-58 ("Many public universities ... status")

    D) Lines 58-61 ("In a similar vein ... 150 years")

9. As used in line 67, "nuances" most nearly means

    A) eras.

    B) categories.

    C) circumstances.

    D) variations.

10. The passage's primary purpose is to

    A) summarize the accomplishments of U.S. public universities since the 19th century.

    B) explain the historical influence of religion on the development of the university system.

    C) discuss the relationship between U.S. higher education and the cultural values of the nation.

    D) summarize the historical effect of the Morill Land-Grant Act on U.S. public universities.

11. The fifth paragraph supports the central idea of the passage by

    A) discussing how public university athletic programs have grown increasingly competitive.

    B) providing evidence of the success of federal legislation meant to invest in public universities.

    C) explaining that in-state tuition rates have increased enrollment in United States public universities.

    D) noting that the U.S. public university system has expanded into U.S. territories.

CHAPTER 14

Rhetoric II

CHAPTER OBJECTIVES

By the end of this chapter, you will be able to:

1. Evaluate both the overall and part-to-whole text structure of a given test-like passage

2. Distinguish between claims and counterclaims and evaluate the author's use of evidence to support either

3. Assess the soundness of the author's reasoning

SMARTPOINTS

Point Value	SmartPoint Category
70 Points	Rhetoric

RHETORIC QUESTIONS: ANALYZING TEXT STRUCTURE

Some Rhetoric questions on the SAT Reading Test will require you to analyze the structure of the passage. These questions tend to focus on the passage's form rather than its content.

> ✔ **Definition**
>
> *Form* refers to a passage's style and rhetorical techniques. *Content* is what the work is telling you about. Analyzing Text Structure questions generally rely on your understanding of a passage's form.

The SAT Reading Test will ask about two kinds of text structures:

1. **Overall text structure** refers to how the information within a passage is organized. Some common text structures are cause-and-effect, compare-and-contrast, sequence, problem-and-solution, and description.

2. **Part-whole relationships** describe how a particular part of the passage (e.g., a sentence, quotation, or paragraph) relates to the overall text. When asked about a part-whole relationship, make sure you determine what function the part plays in the passage.

> ✔ **Expert Tip**
>
> Include how a passage is structured in your Passage Map. Identifying the structure of the text will make it easier to understand and analyze its content.

RHETORIC QUESTIONS: ANALYZING ARGUMENTS

Other Rhetoric questions on the SAT Reading Test will ask you to analyze arguments within the text for both their form and content.

Questions that ask you to analyze a text's arguments vary in scope. There are three types of Analyzing Arguments questions. You may be asked to:

1. **Analyze claims and counterclaims.** A claim is not an opinion but rather the main point or thesis of a passage the author promotes. A counterclaim is the opposite of a claim—it will negate or disagree with the thesis or central idea of the passage.

2. **Assess reasoning.** The reasoning of a passage is composed of the statements offering support for claims and counterclaims. On the SAT, you may be asked whether an author's or character's reasoning is *sound*—that is, whether the argument is valid and the reasoning for the argument is true.

3. **Analyze evidence.** Evidence can be facts, reasons, statistics, and other information the author employs to *support* a claim or counterclaim. You will have to assess how this evidence is used and whether it is used successfully by recognizing logical traps and fallacies.

Let's look at the following example of a test-like U.S. and World Literature passage and question set. After the mapped passage, the left column contains questions similar to those you'll see on the Reading Test on Test Day. The column on the right features the strategic thinking a test expert employs when approaching the passage and questions presented. Pay attention to how a test expert varies his or her approach to the different question types.

Strategic Thinking

Step 1: Read actively

Read the passage and the notes provided. Remember, a well-crafted Passage Map should summarize the central idea of each paragraph as well as important topics or themes. Use your Passage Map to help you answer each question.

Questions 1-2 are based on the following passage.

The following is an adapted excerpt from Samuel Richardson's 1740 novel Pamela.

And one day he came to me, as I was in the summer-house in the little garden, at work with my needle, and Mrs. Jervis was just gone from me; and I would have gone out; but he said, "Don't go, Pamela: I have something to say to you; and you always fly me, when I come near you, as if you were afraid of me."

I was much out of countenance you may well think; and began to tremble, and the more when he took me by the hand; for no soul was near us.

"Lady Davers," said he, (and seemed, I thought, to be as much at a loss for words as I) "would have had you live with her; but she would not do for you what I am resolved to do, if you continue faithful and obliging. What say you, my girl?" said he, with some eagerness; "had you not rather stay with me than go to Lady Davers?" He looked so, as filled me with fear; I don't know how; wildly, I thought.

I said, when I could speak, "Your Honour will forgive me; but as you have no lady for me to wait upon, and my good lady has been now dead this twelvemonth, I had rather, if it would not displease you, wait upon Lady Davers, because—"

I was proceeding, and he said a little hastily, "Because you are a little fool, and know not what's good for yourself. I tell you, I will make a gentlewoman of you, if you are obliging, and don't stand in your own light." And so saying, he put his arm about me, and kissed me.

Now, you will say, all his wickedness appeared plainly. I struggled, and trembled, and was so benumbed with terror, that I sunk down, not in a fit, and yet not myself; and I found myself in his arms, quite void of strength; and he kissed me two or three times, with frightful eagerness. At last I burst from him, and was getting out of the summer-house; but he held me back, and shut the door.

I would have given my life for a farthing.* And he said, "I'll do you no harm, Pamela; don't be afraid of me."

I said, "I won't stay."

"You won't! Do you know who you speak to?"

I lost all fear, and all respect, and said, "Yes, I do, sir, too well! Well may I forget that I am your servant, when you forget what belongs to a master." I sobbed and cried most sadly. Said he: "Have I done you any harm?" "Yes, sir" said I, "the greatest harm in the world: You have taught me to forget myself, and what belongs to me; and have lessened the distance that fortune has made between us, by demeaning yourself, to be so free to a poor servant. Yet, sir, I will be bold to say, I am honest, though poor: And if you were a prince, I would not be otherwise than honest."

*farthing former British coin equaling ¼ of a penny

Notes: man accuses P of fear; wants to talk. live with him or Lady D? P prefers Lady D bc she's a woman. man says he'll make P into woman → kisses her. P = does not like kiss; runs. P wants to leave; man insults P. man = P's master; he insults her & pulls rank. P tells master that he took away her sense of self.

Questions	Strategic Thinking
1. Over the course of the passage, the main focus of the narrative shifts from Pamela's A) curiosity about her master's motives to a fuller understanding of his purpose. B) fear in the presence of her master to disrespect for his actions. C) hopes for her future to her disappointment when she realizes the gravity of her situation. D) obligation to her master for providing her with a livelihood to the forgiveness she receives from him for fulfilling her duties.	**Step 2: Examine the question stem** Identify the key words and phrases in the question stem: "main focus of the narrative shifts." Looking at how the Passage Map notes change as the passage progresses will help you find the answer. **Step 3: Predict and answer** The first Passage Map note about Pamela says that she's afraid of her master. The note next to lines 48-51 highlights what Pamela says to her master when she stands up for herself. Choice (B) matches this prediction.

Questions	Strategic Thinking
2. The passage most strongly suggests that Pamela believes which of the following? A) Servants and masters differ only in their economic status, not in their basic human rights. B) Servants and masters may develop more equal relationships only if each retains an understanding of the distance between them. C) Masters are obligated to respect their servants despite the differences in social status. D) Servants are appropriately subordinate to their masters, who have the right to command them.	**Step 2: Examine the question stem** Identify the key words and phrases in the question stem: "most strongly suggests" and "Pamela believes." The Passage Map notes detailing Pamela's thoughts and reactions will lead you to the correct answer. **Step 3: Predict and answer** In the final paragraph (lines 42–53), Pamela stands up to her master's mistreatment of her. She admits that she is a "poor servant" (line 50), but defends herself, asserting that she is her own owner. Choice (A) matches this prediction.

You have now seen how to approach two kinds of Rhetoric questions: Analyzing Text Structure and Analyzing Arguments.

Look at the test-like History/Social Studies passage that follows. There are four questions associated with it. Part of the passage has been mapped already. Your first step is to complete the Passage Map. Then, use the Kaplan Method for Reading Comprehension and the strategies discussed in this chapter to answer the questions. Strategic thinking questions have been included to guide you—some of the answers have been filled in, but you will have to fill in the answers to others.

Use your answers to the strategic thinking questions to select the correct answer, just as you will on Test Day.

Strategic Thinking
Step 1: Read actively
The passage below is partially mapped. Read the passage and the first part of the Passage Map. Then, complete the Passage Map on your own. Remember to focus on the central ideas of each paragraph as well as the central idea of the overall passage. Use your Passage Map as a reference when you're answering questions.

Questions 3-6 are based on the following passage.

The following passage was written (on the last night of 1849) by Florence Nightingale. She was not only a pioneer in the profession of nursing but also one of the first European women to travel to Egypt (1849-1850) and keep a detailed journal of her letters and reflections of her journey.

My Dear People,

Yes, I think your imagination has hardly followed me through the place where I have been
Line spending the last night of the old year. Did you
5   listen to it passing away and think of me? Where
do you think I heard it sigh out its soul? In the dim
unearthly colonnades of Karnak, which stood and
watched it, motionless, silent, and awful, as they had
done for thousands of years, to whom, no doubt,
10 thousands of years seem but as a day. Would that
I could call up Karnak before your eyes for one
moment, but it "is beyond expression."
    No one could trust themselves with their
imagination alone there. Gigantic shadows spring
15 upon every side; "the dead are stirred up for thee to
meet thee at thy coming, even the chief ones of the
earth," and they look out from among the columns,
and you feel as terror-stricken to be there, miserable

intruder, among these mighty dead, as if you had
20 awakened the angel of the Last Day. Imagine six
columns on either side, of which the last is almost
out of sight, though they stand very near each other,
while you look up to the stars from between them,
as you would from a deep narrow gorge in the Alps,
25 and then, passing through 160 of these, ranged in
eight aisles on either side, the end choked up with
heaps of rubbish, this rubbish consisting of stones
twenty and thirty feet long, so that it looks like a
mountain fallen to ruin, not a temple. How art thou
30 fallen from heaven, oh Lucifer, son of the morning!
He did exalt his throne above the stars of God; for
I looked through a colonnade, and under the roof
saw the deep blue sky and star shining brightly; and
as you look upon these mighty ruins, a voice seems
35 continually saying to you, And seekest thou good
things for thyself? Seek them not, for is there ought
like this ruin? One wonders that people come back
from Egypt and live lives as they did before.
    Yet Karnak by starlight is not to me painful: we
40 had seen Luxor in the sunshine. I had expected
the temples of Thebes to be solemn, but Luxor was
fearful. Rows of painted columns, propylae, colossi,

Notes (margin):
imagination near Karnak?
K = impossible to describe
imagination runs wild → fear
details of Karnak = temple

and—built up in the Holy Place—mud [not even huts, but] unroofed enclosures chalked out, or
45 rather mudded out, for families, with their one oven and broken earthen vessel; and, squatting on the ground among the painted hieroglyphs, creatures with large nose-rings, the children's eyes streaming with matter, on which the mothers let the flies rest,
50 because "it is good for them," without an attempt to drive them off; tattooed men on the ground, with camels feeding out of their laps, and nothing but a few doura stalks strewed for their beds;—I cannot describe the impression it makes: it is as if one
55 were steering towards the sun, the glorious Eastern sun, arrayed in its golden clouds, and were to find, on nearing it, that it were full—instead of glorified beings as one expected—of a race of dwarf cannibals, stained with blood and dressed in bones. The
60 contrast could not be more terrible than the savages of the Present in the temples of the Past at Luxor.

But Karnak by starlight is peace; not peace and joy, but peace—solemn peace. You feel like spirits revisiting your former world, strange and fallen to
65 ruins; but it has done its work, and there is nothing agonizing about it. Egypt should have no sun and no day, no human beings. It should always be seen in solitude and by night; one eternal night it should have, like Job's, and let the stars of the twilight be its
70 lamps; neither let it see the dawning of the day.

Don't get distracted by less important details. While there is a lot going on in this passage, your additions to the Passage Map should continue to note how the author perceives and describes what she experienced on her trip to Egypt. If you're stuck, review the example Passage Map in the Answers & Explanations for this chapter on page 687.

Questions	Strategic Thinking
3. The statement in lines 37-38 ("One wonders ... before") is primarily included to A) suggest that many people who visit Egypt overlook many of its important temples. B) express how profoundly Egypt has affected the author. C) emphasize how difficult it can be to understand someone else's experience. D) criticize travelers who do not experience Egypt in the same way the author did.	**Step 2: Examine the question stem** *What are the key words and phrases in this question stem?* The key words in this question stem are the cited statement and "primarily included to." *What parts of your Passage Map are relevant?* Looking at how the Passage Map notes surrounding the cited lines serve the passage as a whole will help you find the answer. **Step 3: Predict and answer** *What can you predict?* The Passage Map note next to the cited phrase should reveal that the author believes traveling to Egypt is a life-changing experience. *Which answer choice matches this prediction?* ————————

Questions	Strategic Thinking
4. What is the most likely reason the author draws a distinction between the two cities in lines 39-40 ("Yet Karnak … sunshine")? A) To show that some ancient ruins have retained special relevance while others have reverted to everyday use B) To argue that Egyptian authorities should do more to protect Luxor C) To communicate how dreadful it was to find mundane activities in a place meant to hold great spiritual significance D) To demonstrate how much more difficult it is to describe Karnak than it is to describe Luxor	**Step 2: Examine the question stem** *What are the key words and phrases in this question stem?* The key words in this question stem are "the most likely reason," "distinction between the two cities," and the cited lines. **Step 3: Predict and answer** *What parts of your Passage Map are relevant?* Look at your Passage Map for notes about the author's contrast of the two cities. The author has a generally positive toward Karnak and a generally negative attitude toward Luxor. *What purpose does providing this contrast serve in the passage as a whole?* _____ _____ _____ _____ _____ _____ *Which answer choice matches this prediction?* _____

Questions	Strategic Thinking
5. Throughout the passage, the author employs which of the following techniques to convey her meaning? A) Physical descriptions interspersed with lyrical portrayals B) A series of analogies emphasizing the difference between past and present C) An extended metaphor evoking eternal truths D) Expository prose describing a journey to Egypt	**Step 2: Examine the question stem** *What are the key words and phrases in this question stem?* The key words in the question stem are "throughout the passage" and "techniques." The answer to the question will be found by analyzing how the author conveys her meaning rather than what that meaning is. *What parts of your Passage Map are relevant?* Your Passage Map probably will not contain the answer, but it can guide you to the more important parts of the passage. **Step 3: Predict and answer** *What are the consistencies in the author's style and tone throughout the passage?* _____ _____ _____ _____ _____ *Which answer choice matches this prediction?* _____

Questions	Strategic Thinking
6. Does the author successfully support the claim that "Luxor was fearful" in lines 41-42? A) Yes, because seeing things in the sunshine can reveal more detail than seeing things by starlight. B) Yes, because the graphic descriptions of conditions in Luxor effectively convey the author's alarm. C) No, because without taking more time to learn about the inhabitants, the author may be misinterpreting the facts. D) No, because the evidence used to support the claim suggests that the inhabitants of Luxor were unfortunate, not frightening.	**Step 2: Examine the question stem** *What are the key words and phrases in the question stem?* _____ _____ _____ _____ *What parts of your Passage Map are relevant?* _____ _____ _____ _____ **Step 3: Predict and answer** *Does the author successfully support the claim in the cited line?* _____ *How does the author support, or not support, the claim?* _____ _____ _____ _____ *Which answer choice matches this prediction?* _____

Now, use the strategies you learned about in this chapter to answer questions for a Science passage. Give yourself 6 minutes to read and map the passage and answer the questions.

Questions 7-10 are based on the following passage.

This passage explores the differences in perception between humans and owls.

It's not difficult to believe that humans and animals perceive the world in different ways. As humans, sight is the sense with which we primarily interpret the
Line information around us, and other senses are gener-
5 ally subordinate. Our sense of survival is fortunately not dependent on our acute senses, or we would surely starve to death or be hunted into extinction. Owls, however, are masters of their senses, making such optimal use of their biological strengths that
10 we, by comparison, can best be described as wearing blindfolds and earplugs. Were an owl to attempt to hunt with our limited senses, it would most likely call us the lesser species, and possibly initiate attempts to label us as endangered.

15 As evidenced by our expression "owl-eyed," owls are known for their acute vision and all-seeing nature. Surprisingly, however, owls have a more limited range of view than humans. Whereas a human can see 180 degrees without turning his or
20 her head, an owl can only see 110 degrees under the same conditions. Owls have extremely well-developed eyes, but their structure is such that they are fixed in one position: an owl can look nowhere but straight ahead. They are farsighted, prevented
25 from seeing clearly anything within a few inches of their eyes; the popular image of a cartoon owl with reading glasses is not far removed from truth. Despite these limitations, however, owls maximize their advantages. Their sensitive eyes are very
30 effective at collecting and processing light, mak-ing them efficient night hunters. They can turn their heads almost completely around and nearly upside down, capitalizing on this range of move-ment to see over their own shoulders and directly
35 beneath themselves. They optimize their farsight-edness to spot the minute movements of prey at great distances. With regard to auditory efficiency,

owls, like humans, hear a limited range of audible sounds. Within that range, however, they have
40 acute hearing at certain frequencies, helping them detect diminutive movements in the undergrowth. Some nocturnal species, such as the barn owl, have asymmetrical ear openings and disc-like facial feathers to facilitate the channeling and interpreta-
45 tion of sounds. They aggregate sensory information instantaneously to produce a mental map of their surroundings and location of possible prey.

Like owls, we use our senses to map the world around us, but there the similarities end. We cannot
50 understand the complex means by which the owl's hearing and sight work conjunctively to detect the subtle shifting of snow or leaves that signals food. The comparison itself is ludicrous, in fact, because our means for survival are so different: humans do
55 not live solitary lives, constantly alert to the move-ment of prey that determines whether we live or die. We do not think in the same way, if thought is even the right concept: we interpret information using extremely different cerebral processes, and we
60 can't know whether owls are even consciously aware of the complex workings of their brains. When I sit in the forest and study my environment, my world is interpreted with language. The owl's world is—well, it's impossible to tell, isn't it?

65 The owl may see the same forest we see, but he is aware of it in a completely different way. I admire the foliage and the rustling leaves, and listen to birdsong. He hears the soft rustle of a leaf and knows that a chipmunk moves thirty feet off to our
70 right, directly underneath the poplar tree. I can say that the owl thinks about the chipmunk, but not how, for I don't have the correct mental processes to describe the complex interpretations of sensory detail into impulse and action; I am governed by
75 words instead of instinct.

7. Which of the following statements supports the author's central argument?

   A) Owls are better adapted to survive than humans because owls are masters of their senses.

   B) Owls, as opposed to humans, overcome limitations by maximizing their advantages.

   C) Humans and owls evolved in differing environments, resulting in a variety of adaptations.

   D) Human brains and owl brains share few, if any, similarities in how sensory input is interpreted.

8. The author provides support for which of the following claims about owls?

   A) Their survival is not dependent on their acute senses.

   B) They do not live solitary lives.

   C) They maximize their advantages.

   D) They have a greater range of view than humans.

9. In line 42, the author refers to the barn owl in order to

   A) contrast the barn owl's hearing to human hearing.

   B) illustrate the range of evolutionary adaptations displayed by various species.

   C) imply that feathers are uniquely suited to channeling sound.

   D) provide an example of adaptation that improves the owl's ability to locate prey.

10. The structure of the passage can best be described as a

    A) comparison between humans and other animals using specific examples to illustrate similarities and differences.

    B) discussion of the evolutionary advantages afforded by differing adaptations to various environmental stimuli.

    C) philosophical discourse on the role of language and its limitations when discussing the acquisition of knowledge.

    D) hypothetical situation presented in the context of adaptive strategies employed by various species in response to environmental stress.

Answers & Explanations for this chapter begin on page 687.

EXTRA PRACTICE

Questions 1-11 are based on the following passage.

This passage is adapted from Carrie Chapman Catt's 1917 "Address to the United States Congress." Catt served as president of the National American Woman Suffrage Association; the closing arguments of her speech are excerpted below.

Your party platforms have pledged woman suffrage. Then why not be honest, frank friends of our cause, adopt it in reality as your own,
Line make it a party program and "fight with us"? As
5 a party measure—a measure of all parties—why not put the amendment through Congress and the Legislatures? We shall all be better friends, we shall have a happier nation, we women will be free to support loyally the party of our choice, and we shall
10 be far prouder of our history.

"There is one thing mightier than kings and armies"—aye, than Congresses and political parties—"the power of an idea when its time has come to move." The time for woman suffrage has come.
15 The woman's hour has struck. If parties prefer to postpone action longer and thus do battle with this idea, they challenge the inevitable. The idea will not perish; the party which opposes it may. Every delay, every trick, every political dishonesty from now
20 on will antagonize the women of the land more and more, and when the party or parties which have so delayed woman suffrage finally let it come, their sincerity will be doubted and their appeal to the new voters will be met with suspicion. This is
25 the psychology of the situation. Can you afford the risk? Think it over.

We know you will meet opposition. There are a few "woman haters" left, a few "old males of the tribe," as Vance Thompson calls them, whose duty
30 they believe it to be to keep women in the places they have carefully picked out for them. Treitschke, made world famous by war literature, said some years ago: "Germany, which knows all about Germany and France, knows far better what is good

35 for Alsace-Lorraine than that miserable people can possibly know." A few American Treitschkes we have who know better than women what is good for them. There are women, too ... But the world does not wait for such as these, nor does Liberty pause to
40 heed the plaint of men and women with a grouch. She does not wait for those who have a special interest to serve, nor a selfish reason for depriving other people of freedom. Holding her torch aloft, Liberty is pointing the way onward and upward and
45 saying to America, "Come."

To you the supporters of our cause, in Senate and House, and the number is large, the suffragists of the nation express their grateful thanks. This address is not meant for you. We are more truly
50 appreciative of all you have done than any words can express. We ask you to make a last, hard fight for the amendment during the present session. Since last we asked a vote on this amendment your position has been fortified by the addition
55 to suffrage territory of Great Britain, Canada, and New York.

Some of you have been too indifferent to give more than casual attention to this question. It is worthy of your immediate consideration—a ques-
60 tion big enough to engage the attention of our Allies in war time, is too big a question for you to neglect. . .

Gentlemen, we hereby petition you, our only designated representatives, to redress our griev-
65 ances by the immediate passage of the influence to secure its ratification in your own state, in order that the women of our nation may be endowed with political freedom that our nation may resume its world leadership in democracy.

70 Woman suffrage is coming—you know it. Will you, Honorable Senators and Members of the House of Representatives, help or hinder it?

1. What is Carrie Chapman Catt's purpose in giving this speech?

   A) To assert that women will vote for the party that supports their cause

   B) To demand more women candidates on political party tickets

   C) To persuade lawmakers to pass a law for women's right to vote

   D) To rally support for women's equal representation in Congress

2. What is the explicit meaning of the phrase in line 70 ("Woman suffrage … know it")?

   A) All women support woman suffrage.

   B) States have already approved woman suffrage.

   C) Women have always had the right to vote.

   D) Women will eventually gain the right to vote.

3. The phrase in lines 21-24 ("when the party … with suspicion") most nearly implies that

   A) women voters will not support lawmakers who do not support suffrage.

   B) women will not run for office because they do not trust politicians.

   C) women will vote more women into political office.

   D) women's influence on Congress will be minimal and is not a threat.

4. As used in line 64, "redress" most nearly means

   A) appeal.

   B) communicate.

   C) implement.

   D) remedy.

5. Catt most likely concludes her speech with a question in order to

   A) challenge lawmakers to investigate her claims.

   B) make clear that she is fair-minded and open to reason.

   C) open the matter of suffrage to debate.

   D) put responsibility for the choice on each lawmaker.

6. As used in line 20, "antagonize" most nearly means

   A) dishearten.

   B) embitter.

   C) humiliate.

   D) inhibit.

7. What counterclaim does Catt offer to the argument that some men and women still oppose suffrage?

   A) They are not voicing their opinions in Congress.

   B) They cannot stop the inevitable.

   C) They do have just cause for opposition.

   D) They have no legal basis for their claims.

8. Which choice provides the best evidence for the answer to the previous question?

   A) Lines 7-10 ("We shall all … our history")

   B) Lines 46-48 ("To you … grateful thanks")

   C) Lines 53-56 ("Since last … New York")

   D) Lines 58-62 ("It is worthy … to neglect")

9. Which choice most clearly reflects the inference expressed in lines 66-69 ("in order that ... in democracy")?

   A) No citizen in our democracy is free as long as women cannot vote.

   B) Other nations have demanded that our government grant woman suffrage.

   C) A nation needs more women in positions of leadership.

   D) Woman suffrage is essential to true democracy.

10. The stance that Catt takes is best described as that of

   A) a historian reflecting on historical events.

   B) an official campaigning for political office.

   C) an activist advocating for legislative reform.

   D) a reporter investigating a current controversy.

11. Which choice provides the best evidence for the answer to the previous question?

   A) Lines 11-14 ("There is one thing ... to move")

   B) Lines 27-29 ("There are a few ... calls them")

   C) Lines 53-56 ("Since last we ... New York")

   D) Lines 63-66 ("Gentlemen, we hereby ... own state")

CHAPTER 15

Synthesis

CHAPTER OBJECTIVES

By the end of this chapter, you will be able to:

1. Apply the Kaplan Strategy for Paired Passages to History/Social Studies and Science paired passages and question sets

2. Synthesize, compare, and contrast information from two different but related passages

3. Analyze quantitative information and infographics and combine information from infographics and text

4. Use the Kaplan Method for Infographics to answer questions about charts and graphs

SMARTPOINTS

Point Value	SmartPoint Category
Point Builder	The Kaplan Method for Infographics
50 Points	Synthesis

PAIRED PASSAGES

There will be exactly one set of Paired Passages on the SAT Reading Test. These passages will be either History/Social Studies passages or Science passages.

The Kaplan Strategy for Paired Passages helps you attack each pair you face by dividing and conquering, rather than simultaneously processing two different passages with 10–11 questions:

- Read Passage 1, then answer its questions
- Read Passage 2, then answer its questions
- Answer questions about both passages

By reading Passage 1 and answering its questions before moving on to Passage 2, you avoid falling into wrong answer traps that reference the text of Passage 2. Furthermore, by addressing each passage individually, you will have a better sense of the central idea and purpose of both passages, and this will help you answer questions that ask you to synthesize information.

> ✔ **Remember**
>
> **Even though the individual passages are shorter in a Paired Passage set, you should still Passage Map both of them.**

Questions in a Paired Passage set that ask about only one of the passages will be no different from questions you've seen and answered about single passages. Use the same methods and strategies you've been using to answer these questions.

Other questions in a Paired Passage set will ask you questions about both passages. You may be asked to identify similarities or differences between the passages or how the author of one passage may respond to a point made by the author of the other passage.

THE KAPLAN METHOD FOR INFOGRAPHICS

The SAT Reading Test will contain one or more passages and/or questions that include one or more infographics. Each infographic will convey or expand on information from or related to the passage.

The Kaplan Method for Infographics consists of three steps:

Step 1: Read the question

Step 2: Examine the infographic

Step 3: Predict and answer

Let's take a closer look at each step.

Step 1: Read the question

Assess the question stem for information that will help you zero in on the specific parts of the infographic that apply to the question.

Step 2: Examine the infographic

Make sure to:

- Circle parts of the infographic that relate directly to the question
- Identify units of measurement, labels, and titles

✔ **Expert Tip**

For more data-heavy infographics, you should also make note of any present variables or categories, trends in the data, or relationships between variables.

Step 3: Predict and answer

Just as in Step 3 of the Kaplan Method for Reading Comprehension, do not look at the answer choices until you've used the infographic to make a prediction.

Let's look at the following example of an abbreviated History/Social Studies Paired Passage set. After the mapped passage, the left column contains questions similar to those you'll see on the Reading Test on Test Day. The column on the right features the strategic thinking a test expert employs when approaching the passage and questions presented.

Strategic Thinking

Step 1: Read actively

Read the paired passages and the notes provided. Remember, a well-crafted Passage Map should summarize the central idea of each paragraph as well as important topics or themes. Use your Passage Map to help you answer each question.

Questions 1-3 are based on the following passages and supplementary material.

Passage 1 warns against society becoming preoccupied with the rehabilitation of criminals. Passage 2 discusses the merits of said rehabilitation.

Passage 1

Nowadays, you hear quite a bit of mealy-mouthed hogwash about diversion and rehabilitation of criminals. If we were to listen to
Line the so-called experts, we would conclude as a soci-
5 ety that criminals are simply misunderstood, and that the only thing that separates good, law-abiding citizens from the worst scofflaws is an accident of birth. These pundits can quote all sorts of statistics and studies, but they seem to do so at the expense
10 of one simple fact: as a society, we must uphold the standards of right and wrong. If we lose track of this obligation to reward the just and punish the guilty, then it is not just the criminals who have lost their moral compass, but society itself.

criminal rehab = good?

can lose sight of punishing & moral standards

Passage 2

15   When a crime is committed in our society, we are always quick to cast blame. The politicians and pundits who profit from fear and anger will be quick to promote newer and harsher penalties nearly every time that a violent crime appears in
20 the national news, locking up the criminals for longer at greater expense to the taxpayers and society itself, and yet nothing changes. The root cause of the crime has not been addressed, and

rehab = less $$ and time alternative

in the rush to blame, nothing has been done to
25 prevent the next violent crime from occurring. For only a fraction of the money it takes to lock up an offender, we could intercede earlier on, mentoring at-risk kids and making sure that they have the educational opportunities that will
30 steer them away from crime. Instead of locking up criminals forever, we can give them the counseling and job training they need to become productive members of society. It is easy to blame, but changing things for the better requires
35 more.

focus on prevention

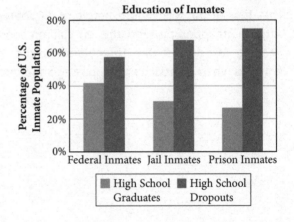

Questions	Strategic Thinking
1. The authors of both passages agree that A) the root causes of crime need to be addressed. B) society must uphold standards of right and wrong. C) it is important for society to confront the problem of crime. D) diversion and rehabilitation can help criminals become productive members of society.	**Step 2: Examine the question stem** Identify the key words and phrases in the question stem: "authors of both passages agree." The correct answer will describe a point on which the authors of both passages agree. Look at the passages for similarities. **Step 3: Predict and answer** Both authors believe that the issue of crime needs to be addressed. Choice (C) matches this prediction.
2. One difference between the conclusions reached in the two passages is that unlike the author of Passage 1, the author of Passage 2 A) recommends lighter sentences for violent criminals. B) argues that increasing educational opportunities can help reduce crime. C) blames politicians instead of pundits for the increase in criminal behavior. D) believes that individuals must be held accountable for their actions.	**Step 2: Examine the question stem** The key words and phrases in this question stem are "one difference between the conclusions" and "unlike the author of Passage 1, the author of Passage 2." The correct answer will focus on how the conclusion of Passage 2 differs from that of Passage 1. **Step 3: Predict and answer** The author of Passage 1 concludes, "we must uphold the standards of right and wrong" (lines 10-11). The author of Passage 2 concludes that we should make sure there are more "educational opportunities that will steer [at-risk kids] away from crime" (lines 29-30). Choice (B) matches this prediction.

Questions	Strategic Thinking
3. Based on the graph, if society adapted the practices outlined in Passage 2, the percentage of high school dropouts in inmate populations would most likely A) decrease. B) increase. C) remain the same. D) fall below that of high school graduates.	**Step 1: Read the question** Assess the question for information on what part of the infographic to focus on: the bars that represent the percentage of high school dropouts in inmate populations. The bars that represent the percentage of high school graduates can be ignored for the sake of this question. **Step 2: Examine the infographic** The unit of measurement on the *y*-axis is the percentage of the inmate population. The labels on the *x*-axis are different kinds of inmates: federal, jail, and prison. The key also provides labels for the two different categories: high school graduates and high school dropouts. The title of the graph is "Education of Inmates." **Step 3: Predict and answer** If the practices in Passage 2 were adopted, the percentage of high school dropouts in inmate populations would decrease. Choice (A) matches this prediction.

Strategic Thinking
Step 1: Read actively
The paired passage set below is partially mapped. Read the first passage and its Passage Map. Then, complete the Passage Map for the second passage on your own. Remember to focus on the central ideas of each paragraph as well as the central idea of the overall passage. Use your Passage Map as a reference when you're answering questions.

Questions 4-6 are based on the following passages and supplementary material.

Passage 1 describes how scientists study stem cells and possible uses. Passage 2 discusses the potential risks of stem cell research.

Passage 1

how SCs work, why powerful

Stem cells truly are science's miracle cure. These underdifferentiated cells have not yet chosen what type of cell to become, and can be nudged into becom-
Line ing whatever type of cell is needed to help a sick
5 patient. Stem cells can be used to replace damaged cells in a person who has a degenerative disease or a serious injury.

embryonic > adult SCs

Scientists obtain stem cells primarily from discarded embryos. True, they can also be obtained
10 from the blood or organs from healthy adults, but these stem cells, while showing some usefulness, are not as adaptable as embryonic stem cells. Embry-onic stem cells are incredibly helpful and can mean a revolutionary change in quality of life for patients

w/o emb. SCs, research = slower

15 suffering from debilitating diseases such as Par-kinson's or Alzheimer's. Someday stem cells could even eliminate the need for human test subjects in drug tests. Without the use of embryonic stem cells, though, that could take an immeasurably longer
20 amount of time to become a reality.

SC research should continue

With stem cell research, the benefits for living, breathing, sentient people outweigh any debate regarding the origins of the cells themselves. In this age of scientific enlightenment, we must always ask
25 ourselves: What action can best benefit humanity? By answering, we see clearly that stem cell research must continue.

Passage 2

We stand at an important crossroads in scientific progress. We have the capability now to improve
30 humanity in ways never thought possible, but at what cost? At what point must progress bow before conscience? Just because we can, is it true that we should?

Stem cell research has the potential to be an
35 enormous boon to the medical industry. The advance of diseases can be assuaged or halted completely through this remarkable new medicine. But scientists assault the dignity of life when they use embryonic stem cells for their work. By taking
40 cells from discarded embryos, we begin treading on a slippery slope. It is all too easy to transition from using discarded embryos to creating embryos solely for the purpose of stem cell medicine.

Since stem cells can be obtained from healthy
45 adults with no cost to life, this is the path on which we should be progressing. These stem cells, safely obtained, can have a significant positive impact on the lives of patients.

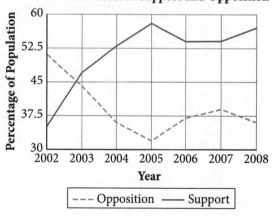

Stem Cell Research Support and Opposition

- - - Opposition ——— Support

Don't get distracted by less important details. Your Passage Map for Passage 2 should note the author's views on the ethics surrounding embryonic stem cell research. If you're stuck, review the example Passage Map in the Answers & Explanations for this chapter on page 696.

Questions	Strategic Thinking
4. Which assumption do the authors of both passages share? A) Embryonic stem cells have greater potential than adult stem cells. B) The medical benefits of stem cell research outweigh any ethical concerns. C) Stem cell research could provide enormous benefits to humanity. D) The medical benefits of stem cell research must be weighed against ethical concerns.	**Step 2: Examine the question stem** *What are the key words and phrases in this question stem?* The key words and phrases in this question stem are "assumption" and "both passages share." The correct answer will describe an assumption both authors make. **Step 3: Predict and answer** *What can you predict?* The authors of both passages claim that stem cell research is potentially beneficial. *Which answer choice matches this prediction?* _____
5. The authors of the passages disagree most strongly on which issue? A) The sources of stem cells available to researchers B) The value of stem cell research to medical science C) The adaptability of adult stem cells D) The ethics of using embryonic stem cells	**Step 2: Examine the question stem** *What are the key words and phrases in this question stem?* The key words and phrases in this question stem are "disagree most strongly." You will find the correct answer by finding the biggest difference between the two different opinions. **Step 3: Predict and answer** *What is the central idea of Passage 1?* _____ _____ *What is the central idea of Passage 2?* _____ _____ *What is the biggest difference between these central ideas?* _____ _____ *Which answer choice matches this prediction?* _____

Questions	Strategic Thinking
6. What claim about stem cell research is supported by the graph? A) Between 2003 and 2005, support for stem cell research increased more than opposition to stem cell research decreased. B) Between 2004 and 2006, support for stem cell research decreased and then increased. C) Between 2005 and 2007, opposition to stem cell research increased more than support for stem cell research decreased. D) Between 2006 and 2008, opposition to stem cell research decreased and then increased.	**Step 1: Read the question** *What are the key words and phrases in this question stem?* The question stem does not offer any information about what part of the infographic will provide the answer. **Step 2: Examine the infographic** *What are the units of measurement, labels, or titles of the infographic?* _____ _____ _____ _____ _____ _____ **Step 3: Predict and answer** *What can you predict?* Because this question stem is general and does not provide information on what part of the graph to look at, it is difficult to make a prediction. Evaluate each answer choice. *Look at A. Did support for stem cell research increase more than opposition to stem cell research decreased between 2003 and 2005? How do you know?* No, because the increase of support and the decrease of opposition are equal, according to the graph. (You can determine they're equal by counting the number of boxes each line spans.) *Look at B. Did support for stem cell research decrease and then increase between 2004 and 2006? How do you know?* _____ _____ _____ _____ _____ _____

Questions	Strategic Thinking
	Look at C. Did opposition to stem cell research increase more than support for stem cell research decreased between 2005 and 2007? How do you know? _____ _____ _____ _____ _____ _____ *Look at D. Did opposition to stem cell research decrease and then increase between 2006 and 2008? How do you know?* _____ _____ _____ _____ _____ _____ *What is the correct answer?* _____

Now, use the strategies you learned about in this chapter to answer questions for a History/Social Studies Paired Passage set. Give yourself 8 minutes to read and map the passages and answer the questions.

Questions 7-9 are based on the following passages and supplementary material.

The following passages reflect on the Machnovschina, an anarchist peasant uprising in the Ukraine active from approximately 1917 to 1922 under the leadership of Nestor Makhno. During their brief and turbulent history, the Makhnovshchina (also known as Makhnovists) fought against the Central Powers, the White Army, and the Red Army, their sometimes ally that eventually turned on them and defeated them. The first passage discusses the relationship between the Makhnovists and their supporters, while the second discusses the differences between the Makhnovists on the outskirts of the emerging Soviet Union and the Bolsheviks who controlled it.

Passage 1

Even had the Ukrainian civilians wanted to ignore the sectarianism of their time and remain neutral, they did not have that luxury—the turmoil
Line was too absolute, the excitement and terror of
5 revolutionary upheaval too absolutely compelling. Even for the most isolated of peasants, political impartiality was impossible. From the beginning, there was a bond among revolutionary intellectuals, civilians, and military leaders.

10 The causes of civil unrest compounded. Adding to the burden of uncounted years of economic and political subjugation under a quasi-feudal system[1] was the added pressure of an invading Austro-Hungarian army. Meanwhile, Russia was in a state
15 of chaos, and the Bolsheviks[2] were rapidly consolidating power in a system that promised equality and the rule of the proletariat. There was no central authority to organize them (Russia had all but given up the Ukraine to the invading Central Powers[3]),
20 and the traditional power of the rich landlords had collapsed with the Czarist government. There was no status quo and no safe choice.

Faced with this state of affairs, many Ukrainian peasants chose to organize themselves within
25 the Makhnovshchina. Educated in the field and trained behind the plow, they were now charged with the task of organizing and defending a new

society under conditions of tremendous adversity. Although the Makhnovshchina was an anarchist,
30 revolutionary movement, it was one that emerged out of necessity. It was a way for peasants to join together for mutual aid, revolutionary intellectuals to explore the possibility of a society without central authority, and generals to attempt to secure the rights
35 of the Ukrainian people to self-determination.

Passage 2

The revolutionary period in Russian history is a classic example of the conflicts between the programs of dogmatic, rigid leaders and the desires and needs of ordinary people. One of the best
40 examples of this is the struggle between the Bolsheviks and the Makhnovshchina. Not only did the word "revolution" mean very different things to the Kremlin[4] bureaucrats and the Ukrainian partisans, but the reality of the revolution was very different
45 as well. This fact was noted by one anonymous soldier who, beginning his career as a Kremlin guard, eventually became a member of the Makhnovist army. He noted that "conditions could not have been more different between the two camps.
50 In the one, decisions were based on the political theories of Marx[5] and Lenin,[6] theories which were never doubted or questioned in the least. In the other, theories were even more important—debated vigorously and openly—but only after the day's
55 work had been done and the important decisions had been made based on the needs of the community for food, freedom, and self-defense."

Although the Kremlin's approach might seem like harmless intellectualism, it had disastrous con-
60 sequences that the anonymous soldier couldn't have forseen. As the Bolshevik Party gained increasing power, it began to control the official view of events with a systematic paranoia unprecedented in history. If the events differed from the official view, the

65　events themselves (and those who participated in them) were deemed the enemy.

The wartime writings of Leon Trotsky[7] are the best indication of this trend. He alternately characterized the Makhnovists as heroes and traitors depending
70　on the current needs of the Bolsheviks. When he required Makhnovists to fight alongside the Red Army,[8] he portrayed them as courageous heroes and valiant fighters, but when he did not, they suddenly became traitors and enemies of the revolu-
75　tion. In 1920, as the Makhnovshchina and the Red Army united to fight against a powerful White Army[9] campaign, Trotsky wrote:

"The working class of the Ukraine can never, and especially not in conditions of tremendous military
80　danger, allow particular units sometimes to fight in our ranks and sometimes to stab us in the back.[+] Waging war against the world's exploiters, the workers' and peasants' Red Army says: 'Who is not with me is against me, and whoever is with me is to
85　remain in my ranks and not leave them till the end.'"

The Ukranian partisans, even as peasants and workmen, were painted as the servants of foreign aristocrats bent on undermining the revolution. Even though Bolshevik presence had been
90　weak in the Ukraine, Trotsky still saw fit to portray himself as the representative of "the working class of the Ukraine" and the Makhnovists as loyal to the working class only to the degree that they recognized Red Army authority.

---

[1] Serfdom had only been abolished in 1861, and many traces of it remained.
[2] The Bolsheviks were the Communist party that established the Soviet Union.
[3] The Central Powers were Germany, Austria-Hungary, the Ottoman Empire, and Bulgaria. During World War I (which took place from 1914 to 1918), they were fighting against the Allies—France, Russia, Great Britain, and the United States. During the period in question, the Austro-Hungarian Army was occupying much of the Ukraine.
[4] The Russian capital building which, at the time, was occupied by the Bolshevik Party
[5] Karl Marx, the ideological founder of Communism
[6] Vladimir Ilyich Lenin, the leader of the Bolsheviks
[7] Leon Trotsky, one of the leaders of the Bolsheviks
[8] The Bolshevik Army
[9] A conservative army opposed to the revolutionary movements in Russia
[+] The previous alliance between the Makhnovshchina and the Red Army had been broken when the Bolsheviks attacked and devastated the unsuspecting anarchists in a surprise attack.

Proportion of Seats in the Russian Constituent Assembly, 1918

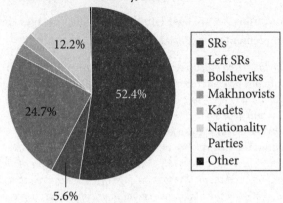

7.　The author of Passage 2 would most likely characterize the Bolsheviks' promise described in Passage 1 as

A)　the reason the Makhnovischina fought alongside the Red Army.

B)　based on theories that had been openly debated.

C)　an example of the Bolsheviks' attempt to control the official view of events.

D)　inspired by Trotsky's wartime writings.

8.　The authors of both passages would most likely agree that

A)　the Bolshevik and Makhnovischina leaders shared many fundamental principles.

B)　the Austro-Hungarian army posed the greatest threat to the Ukranian peasants.

C)　the Makhnovischina were servants of foreign aristocrats.

D)　the Makhnovischina was composed of peasants, intellectuals, and soldiers.

9. It can be reasonably inferred from Passage 2 and the graphic that the Bolsheviks

   A) wielded political power disproportionate to their voting power.

   B) needed to form coalitions to realize their revolutionary promise.

   C) represented a loyal opposition to the ruling SR group.

   D) allied with the Makhnovischina only when necessary to form a majority.

Answers & Explanations for this chapter appear on page 696.

EXTRA PRACTICE

Questions 1-11 are based on the following passages and supplementary material.

Passage 1 is about how scientists use radioisotopes to date artifacts and remains. Passage 2 discusses the varying problems with radioactive contaminants.

Passage 1

Archaeologists often rely on measuring the amounts of different atoms present in an item from a site to determine its age. The identity of an atom
Line depends on how many protons it has in its nucleus;
5 for example, all carbon atoms have 6 protons. Each atom of an element, however, can have a different number of neutrons, so there can be several versions, or isotopes, of each element. Scientists name the isotopes by the total number of protons
10 plus neutrons. For example, a carbon atom with 6 neutrons is carbon-12 while a carbon atom with 7 neutrons is carbon-13.

Some combinations of protons and neutrons are not stable and will change over time. For example,
15 carbon-14, which has 6 protons and 8 neutrons, will slowly change into nitrogen-14, with 7 protons and 7 neutrons. Scientists can directly measure the amount of carbon-12 and carbon-14 in a sample or they can use radiation measurements to calculate these
20 amounts. Each atom of carbon-14 that changes to nitrogen-14 emits radiation. Scientists can measure the rate of emission and use that to calculate the total amount of carbon-14 present in a sample.

Carbon-14 atoms are formed in the atmosphere
25 at the same rate at which they decay. Therefore, the ratio of carbon-12 to carbon-14 atoms in the atmosphere is constant. Living plants and animals have the same ratio of carbon-12 to carbon-14 in their tissues because they are constantly taking in
30 carbon in the form of food or carbon dioxide. After the plant or animal dies, however, it stops taking in carbon and so the amount of carbon-14 atoms in its tissues starts to decrease at a predictable rate.

By measuring the ratio of carbon-12 to carbon-14
35 in a bone, for example, a scientist can determine how long the animal the bone came from has been dead. To determine an object's age this way is called "car-

bon-14 dating." Carbon-14 dating can be performed on any material made by a living organism, such as
40 wood or paper from trees or bones and skin from animals. Materials with ages up to about 50,000 years old can be dated. By finding the age of several objects found at different depths at an archeological dig, the archeologists can then make a timeline for the layers
45 of the site. Objects in the same layer will be about the same age. By using carbon dating for a few objects in a layer, archeologists know the age of other objects in that layer, even if the layer itself cannot be carbon dated.

Passage 2

50 Radioactive materials contain unstable atoms that decay, releasing energy in the form of radiation. The radiation can be harmful to living tissue because it can penetrate into cells and damage their DNA. If an explosion or a leak at a nuclear power plant releases
55 large amounts of radioactive materials, the surrounding area could be hazardous until the amount of radioactive material drops back to normal levels. The amount of danger from the radiation and the amount of time until the areas are safe again depend on
60 how fast the materials emit radiation.

Scientists use the "half-life" of a material to indicate how quickly it decays. The half-life of a material is the amount of time it takes for half of a sample of that material to decay. A mate-
65 rial with a short half-life decays more quickly than a material with a long half-life. For example, iodine-131 and cesium-137 can both be released as a result of an accident at a nuclear power plant. Iodine-131 decays rapidly, with a half-life of 8 days.
70 Cesium-137, however, decays more slowly, with a half-life of 30 years.

If an accident releases iodine-131, therefore, it is a short-term concern. The amount of radiation emitted will be high but will drop rapidly. After
75 two months, less than one percent of the original iodine-131 will remain. An accidental release of

cesium-137, however, is a long-term concern.
The amount of radiation emitted at first will be low
but will drop slowly. It will take about 200 years
80 for the amount of cesium-137 remaining to drop
below one percent. The total amount of radiation
emitted in both cases will be the same, for the same
amount of initial material. The difference lies in
whether the radiation is all released rapidly at high
85 levels in a short time, or is released slowly at low
levels, over a long time span.

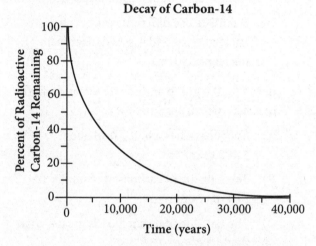

Decay of Carbon-14

This data is from the *Journal of Research of the National Bureau
of Standards*, Vol. 64, No. 4, April 1951, pp. 328 – 333.

1. Based on the information in Passage 1,
   which of the following could be dated using
   carbon-14 dating?

   A) An iron pot found in a cave

   B) A rock at the bottom of a quarry

   C) An arrowhead made from bone

   D) The remains of a house made from stone

2. Which choice provides the best evidence for
   the answer to the previous question?

   A) Lines 10-12 ("For example … carbon-13")

   B) Lines 27-30 ("Living plants … dioxide")

   C) Lines 30-33 ("After the plant … rate")

   D) Lines 38-41 ("Carbon-14 dating …
      animals")

3. As used in line 25, "decay" most nearly means

   A) yield.

   B) deteriorate.

   C) discharge.

   D) circulate.

4. Which statement best describes the
   relationship between carbon-12 and
   carbon-14 in living tissue?

   A) There is more carbon-14 than carbon-12.

   B) There is more carbon-12 than carbon-14.

   C) The ratio of carbon-12 to carbon-14 is
      constant.

   D) The ratio of carbon-12 to carbon-14
      fluctuates greatly.

5. Which choice provides the best evidence for
   the answer to the previous question?

   A) Lines 13-14 ("Some combinations …
      time")

   B) Lines 24-25 ("Carbon-14 atoms … decay")

   C) Lines 27-30 ("Living plants … carbon
      dioxide")

   D) Lines 30-33 ("After the plant … rate")

6. In Passage 2, the author refers to an accident
   that results in the release of iodine-131 as a
   "short-term concern" (line 73) because the
   initial amount of radiation released is

   A) low but will drop slowly.

   B) high but will drop quickly.

   C) low and will drop quickly.

   D) high and will drop slowly.

7. Based on the information in Passage 2, living tissue exposed to radioactive material can

   A) be destroyed by high levels of heat caused by the radiation.

   B) become radioactive itself and damage surrounding tissue.

   C) suffer injury when the cell's components are damaged.

   D) be killed by extra protons released by the radioactive material.

8. As used in line 75, "original" most nearly means

   A) earliest.

   B) unique.

   C) unusual.

   D) critical.

9. According to Passage 2, scientists use the half-life of radioactive material to determine the

   A) amount of danger posed by radiation immediately following a nuclear accident.

   B) likelihood of a nuclear accident involving the release of radioactive material at any given location.

   C) amount of radiation contained in a sample of iodine-131 or cesium-137 used in nuclear reactions.

   D) length of time that must pass until an area is safe after the release of radioactive material.

10. Which generalization about the study of physics is supported by both passages?

    A) The study of atomic and nuclear physics can have many applications in a variety of fields.

    B) The study of physics has helped revolutionize how archaeologists study artifacts.

    C) Scientists use physics to keep people and wildlife safe following a nuclear accident.

    D) Scientists use different concepts to date ancient items and assess danger from nuclear accidents.

11. Based on the graph and the information in the passages, which statement is accurate?

    A) Carbon-14 has a half-life of about 5,400 years.

    B) The half-life of carbon-14 is similar to that of cesium-137.

    C) The half-life of iodine-131 is greater than that of cesium-137.

    D) All radioactive materials have a half-life of 30 to 5,400 years.

UNIT SIX

Writing & Language

BY THE END OF THIS UNIT, YOU WILL BE ABLE TO:

1. Apply the Kaplan Method for Writing & Language

2. Evaluate the effectiveness and clarity of a given passage

3. Identify proper and effective language use

4. Utilize the standard conventions of usage in written English

CHAPTER 16

The Kaplan Methods for Writing & Language and Infographics

CHAPTER OBJECTIVES

By the end of this chapter, you will be able to:

1. Identify issues in a passage and select the correct answer by applying the Kaplan Method for Writing & Language

2. Identify and analyze quantitative information and infographics

3. Synthesize information from infographics and text

SMARTPOINTS

Point Value	SmartPoint Category
Point Builder	The Kaplan Method for Writing & Language
Point Builder	The Kaplan Method for Infographics
10 Points	Quantitative

THE KAPLAN METHOD FOR WRITING & LANGUAGE

The Kaplan Method for Writing & Language is the method you will use to boost your score on the Writing & Language Test. By understanding what the question is looking for, how it relates to the passage, and what questions you should ask yourself on Test Day, you will maximize the number of points you earn. Use the Kaplan Method for Writing & Language for every SAT Writing & Language Test passage and question you encounter, whether practicing, completing your homework, working on a Practice Test, or taking the actual exam on Test Day.

The Kaplan Method for Writing & Language has three steps:

Step 1: Read the passage and identify the issue

- If there's an infographic, apply the Kaplan Method for Infographics

Step 2: Eliminate answer choices that do not address the issue

Step 3: Plug in the remaining answer choices and select the most correct, concise, and relevant one

> **✔ On Test Day**
>
> **The SAT will expect you to be able to recognize errors in organization, pronouns, agreement, comparisons, development, sentence structure, modifiers, verbs, wordiness, style, tone, and syntax.**

Let's take a closer look at each step.

Step 1: Read the passage and identify the issue

This means:

- Rather than reading the whole passage and then answering all of the questions, you can answer questions as you read because they are mostly embedded in the text itself.

- When you see a number, stop reading and look at the question. If you can answer it with what you've read so far, do so. If you need more information, keep reading for context until you can answer the question.

Step 2: Eliminate answer choices that do not address the issue

Eliminating answer choices that do not address the issue:

- Increases your odds of getting the correct answer by removing obviously incorrect answer choices.

Step 3: Plug in the remaining answer choices and select the most correct, concise, and relevant one

Correct, concise, and relevant means that the answer choice you select:

- Makes sense when read with the correction.
- Is as short as possible while retaining the information in the text.
- Relates well to the passage overall.

There is no wrong answer penalty on the SAT. When in doubt, eliminate what you can and then guess. You won't lose points for guessing.

Answer choices should not:

- Change the intended meaning of the original sentence, paragraph, or passage
- Introduce new grammatical errors, even if the answer choice in question resolves the initial issue in the passage

If you have to guess, eliminate answer choices that are clearly wrong and then choose the shortest one—the SAT rewards students who know how to be concise.

You will see four Writing & Language passages on Test Day, each of which will have 11 questions. When you encounter a Writing & Language question, use the Kaplan Method, asking yourself a series of strategic thinking questions.

By asking these strategic thinking questions, you will be able to select the correct answer choice more easily and efficiently. Pausing to ask questions may seem like it takes a lot of time, but it actually saves you time by preventing you from weighing the four answer choices against each other. Better to ask questions that lead you directly to the correct answer than to debate which of four answers seems the least incorrect.

Let's look at the following example of the Kaplan Method for Writing & Language in action in a short test-like passage. The left column contains text and a question similar to what you'll see on the Writing & Language Test on Test Day. The column on the right features the strategic thinking a test expert employs when approaching the passage and question presented.

Question	Strategic Thinking
A 2005 report from the United States Department of Agriculture estimates that the cost of raising a child from birth until age seventeen is approximately $500,000. This cost includes housing, food, clothing, transportation, health care, child care, and education and does, of course, vary considerably. However, with the average cost of having and raising a child set at half a million dollars, and with additional children in the family raising that financial expenditure accordingly, it becomes clear that parenthood should not be entered into lightly. Even for families that plan for children, there may be costs for which they are unprepared. For instance, if a woman chooses to spend the first years of her child's life as a full-time mother and homemaker, she can lose career momentum and end up making a substantially lower salary than a woman with the same background who maintains consistent employment. While these factors should in no way be construed as a recommendation against having children, ❶ if you're planning a family, be ready. 1. A) NO CHANGE B) but think about the problems it might cause. C) they speak to the need for responsible family planning and financial preparation. D) make sure you understand what you're getting into.	**Step 1: Read the passage and identify the issue** The underlined phrase is grammatically correct. When there is no apparent grammatical issue, check style, tone, and syntax. The tone of the underlined portion is much more informal than the tone of the overall passage, as evidenced by the use of the second person ("you"). **Step 2: Eliminate answer choices that do not address the issue** Eliminate A because there is a tone issue in the underlined portion. Eliminate B and D because they still use the second person (it's implied in B with the imperative mood of the verb "think"). **Step 3: Plug in the remaining answer choices and select the most correct, concise, and relevant one** Choice (C) is the only answer choice left and is therefore correct.

THE KAPLAN METHOD FOR INFOGRAPHICS

The SAT Writing & Language Test will contain one or more passages and/or questions that include one or more infographics. Each infographic will convey or expand on information from the passage.

The Kaplan Method for Infographics has three steps:

Step 1: Read the question

Step 2: Examine the infographic

Step 3: Predict and answer

Let's examine these steps a bit more closely.

Step 1: Read the question

Assess the question stem for information that will help you zero in on the specific parts of the infographic that apply to the question.

Step 2: Examine the infographic

Make sure to:

- Circle parts of the infographic that relate directly to the question

- Identify units of measurement, labels, and titles

Step 3: Predict and answer

Just as in Step 3 of the Kaplan Method for Reading Comprehension, do not look at the answer choices until you've used the infographic to make a prediction. Even though the Kaplan Method for Writing & Language does not ask you to predict before you peek, make sure to do so when presented with an infographic question on the SAT Writing & Language Test.

No matter how many infographics you see on the Writing & Language Test on Test Day, make sure you use the Kaplan Method for Infographics for each one so that you maximize your score by answering the associated questions correctly.

SAT experts ask themselves the questions outlined in the previous section as well as other questions that are more specific to the infographic and the passage it accompanies. Remember, infographics vary in format—there can be tables, graphs, charts, and so on—so be flexible when you ask yourself these critical-thinking questions.

As always, asking questions and taking time to assess the given information before answering the test question will increase your chances of selecting the correct answer.

Let's look at how to apply the Kaplan Method for Infographics. This infographic would either represent data described in the passage or present new data that expand on what the passage is about.

The left column contains an infographic similar to the ones you'll see on the Writing & Language Test on Test Day. The column on the right features the strategic thinking a test expert employs when approaching the question and infographic presented.

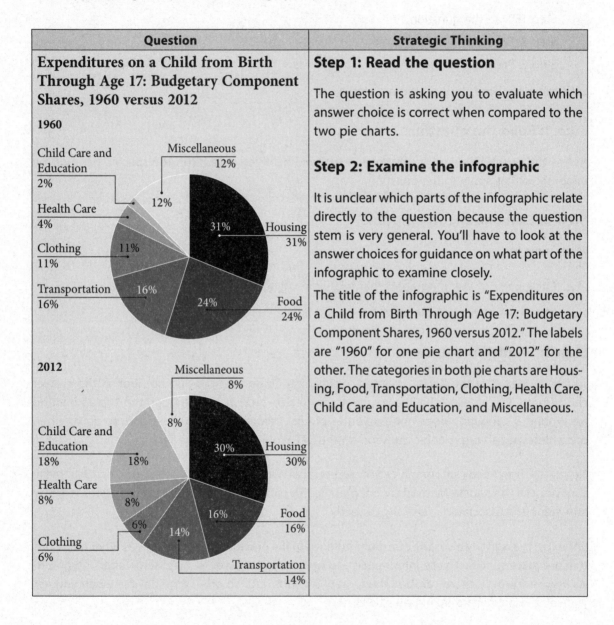

Question	Strategic Thinking
Expenditures on a Child from Birth Through Age 17: Budgetary Component Shares, 1960 versus 2012	**Step 1: Read the question**

Step 1: Read the question

The question is asking you to evaluate which answer choice is correct when compared to the two pie charts.

Step 2: Examine the infographic

It is unclear which parts of the infographic relate directly to the question because the question stem is very general. You'll have to look at the answer choices for guidance on what part of the infographic to examine closely.

The title of the infographic is "Expenditures on a Child from Birth Through Age 17: Budgetary Component Shares, 1960 versus 2012." The labels are "1960" for one pie chart and "2012" for the other. The categories in both pie charts are Housing, Food, Transportation, Clothing, Health Care, Child Care and Education, and Miscellaneous.

1960

Child Care and Education 2%
Miscellaneous 12%
12%
Health Care 4%
31%
Housing 31%
Clothing 11%
11%
Transportation 16%
16%
24%
Food 24%

2012

Miscellaneous 8%
8%
Child Care and Education 18%
18%
Housing 30%
30%
Health Care 8%
8%
16%
Food 16%
Clothing 6%
6%
14%
Transportation 14%

Question	Strategic Thinking
2. Which claim about the cost of raising children is supported by the two pie charts? A) Between 1960 and 2012, the percent of a budget spent on food increased. B) Between 1960 and 2012, the percent of a budget spent on health care decreased. C) Between 1960 and 2012, the percent of a budget spent on transportation experienced the greatest decrease. D) Between 1960 and 2012, the percent of a budget spent on child care and education experienced the greatest increase.	**Step 3: Predict and answer** The percent of a budget spent on food did not increase from 1960 to 2012, as A claims. Rather, it decreased from 24% to 16%. Eliminate A. The percent of a budget spent on health care did not decrease from 1960 to 2012, as B claims. Rather, it increased from 4% to 8%. Eliminate B. The percent of a budget spent on transportation decreased from 16% in 1960 to 14% in 2012. This was not the greatest decrease, as C claims; the decrease of the percent of a budget spent on food was greater. Eliminate C. The percent of a budget spent on child care and education increased from 2% in 1960 to 18% in 2012. This is the greatest increase, as D claims. Choice (D) is correct.

You have seen what kinds of strategic thinking questions SAT experts ask themselves when they encounter Writing & Language Test questions.

Look at the Writing & Language passage excerpt below. There are three questions associated with it. Use the Kaplan Method for Writing & Language to answer the questions. But remember to look at the guiding questions that have been laid out for you—some of the answers have been filled in, but you will have to fill in the answers to others.

Use your answers to the strategic thinking questions to select the correct answer, just as you will on Test Day.

Questions 3-5 are based on the following passage.

Industrial Progress

Is industrial progress a mixed blessing? ❸ <u>Hundred years</u> ago, this question was seldom asked. Science and industry were flooding the world with products that made life easier. But today we know that many industrial processes create pollution that can destroy our environment. Industries produce toxic waste, discharging harmful chemicals directly into lakes, rivers, and the air. One of the results of this pollution that must be managed in order to protect our ecosystems is acid rain.

Air, clouds, and rain containing acids caused by industrial pollution can have terrible effects. Acid droplets in the air can be inhaled, causing illness. From clouds, these acid droplets fall as rain. If natural chemical processes in soils do not deactivate the acids, these acids can accumulate and kill both plant and animal life. In some parts of the Northeast and Midwest, 10 percent of all lakes show dangerous acid levels. In eastern mountains in the United States, large forest tracts have been lost at elevations where trees are regularly bathed in acidic clouds.

Acid rain is caused by industrial processes that release compounds of nitrogen and sulfur. ❹ <u>These pollutants</u> combine with clean air, the results are nitric and sulfuric acids. The main components of acid rain ❺ <u>is</u> oxides of nitrogen and sulfur dioxide, which are emitted from oil- and coal-burning power plants. To reduce acid rain, emissions from these plants, particularly sulfur dioxide, must be reduced. One way is to install machines that remove sulfur dioxide from a plant's emissions. Another is to build new plants modeled on currently experimental designs that produce less sulfur dioxide.

Questions	Strategic Thinking
3. A) NO CHANGE B) A hundred years, give or take, C) One hundred years D) Hundred years or so	**Step 1: Read the passage and identify the issue** *What is the issue?* As written, the underlined portion uses the incorrect form of a number, which is an error in idiom construction. **Step 2: Eliminate answer choices that do not address the issue** *What answer choice(s) can you eliminate?* _____ _____ _____ **Step 3: Plug in the remaining answer choices and select the most correct, concise, and relevant one** *What is the answer?*_____
4. A) NO CHANGE B) Because these pollutants C) When these pollutants D) Where these pollutants	**Step 1: Read the passage and identify the issue** *What is the issue?* While there is nothing necessarily incorrect about the underlined portion, if you keep reading the entire sentence it belongs to, you'll see that it is is a run-on. **Step 2: Eliminate answer choices that do not address the issue** *What answer choice(s) can you eliminate?* _____ _____ _____ **Step 3: Plug in the remaining answer choices and select the most correct, concise, and relevant one** *What is the answer?* _____

Questions	Strategic Thinking
5. A) NO CHANGE B) are C) was D) were	**Step 1: Read the passage and identify the issue** *What is the issue?* The singular verb "is" does not agree with its subject, "the main components." You need a plural verb in the present tense. **Step 2: Eliminate answer choices that do not address the issue** *What answer choice(s) can you eliminate?* _____ _____ _____ **Step 3: Plug in the remaining answer choices and select the most correct, concise, and relevant one** *What is the answer?* _____

Now, try a test-like Writing & Language passage and infographic on your own. Give yourself 5 minutes to read the passage and answer the questions.

Questions 6-13 are based on the following passage and supplementary material.

Jupiter

As the fifth planet from the Sun, and by far the most massive in our solar system at 318 times the mass of Earth, Jupiter has ❻ <u>fascinated and intrigued</u> scientists for centuries. In fact, it was the initial discovery of this massive, gaseous planet that marked the first time astronomers considered the possibility that the movement of other planets was not centered around the Earth. More specifically, when Jupiter was first viewed from Earth by the Italian astronomer Galileo in 1610, four large moons were also spotted in orbit around this enormous planet. It was these moons, now known as the Galilean moons, that provided important evidence for Galileo's outspoken support of Copernicus's heliocentric theory of planetary ❼ <u>movement. Because</u> these moons seemed to revolve around a planet other than Earth.

The first close look at Jupiter came in 1973, when the unmanned NASA probe *Pioneer 10* completed a successful ❽ <u>flyby, and it collected</u> important data regarding the planet's chemical composition and interior structure. ❾ <u>After completing its mission to Jupiter, *Pioneer 10* became the first spacecraft to leave the Solar System.</u> Designated as one of the gas planets—along with Saturn, Uranus, and Neptune—Jupiter is composed of about 90 percent hydrogen and 10 percent helium and has no solid surface, only varying densities of gas. In fact, very little is known about the interior of Jupiter. What is visible when looking at a gas planet like Jupiter is really only the tops of clouds making up the outermost atmosphere, and probes have been able to penetrate only about 90 miles below this layer. However, after analyzing traces of water and minerals

6. A) NO CHANGE
   B) fascinated
   C) intrigued, and fascinated
   D) fascinated intriguing

7. A) NO CHANGE
   B) movement. These
   C) movement. Although
   D) movement because

8. A) NO CHANGE
   B) flyby and it collected
   C) flyby, and collecting
   D) flyby and collected

9. The author is considering omitting the underlined sentence. Should the sentence be kept or omitted?

   A) It should be kept because it adds an interesting detail about the *Pioneer 10* mission.

   B) It should be kept because it provides support for the claim that the mission was successful.

   C) It should be omitted because it shifts the focus of the passage from Jupiter to the *Pioneer 10* mission.

   D) It should be omitted because it does not include information about when *Pioneer 10* left the solar system.

collected from Jupiter's atmosphere, scientists believe that the planet has a core of rocky material amounting to a mass perhaps as much as 15 times that of Earth.

10 Jupiter is like other gaseous planets. Jupiter has high-velocity winds that blow in wide bands of latitude, each moving in an alternate direction. Slight chemical and temperature changes between these bands, and the resulting chemical reactions, are probably responsible for the array of vibrant colors that dominate the planet's appearance. **11** Measurement taken by a number of probes indicate that the powerful winds moving these bands can reach speeds exceeding 400 miles per hour and likely extend thousands of miles below Jupiter's outer atmosphere.

Yet perhaps the most fascinating characteristic of this planet is the rotational speed of the entire globe of gas itself. While Earth takes 24 hours to make a full revolution, Jupiter completes a full revolution **12** in less time, an amazingly short period of time for a planet with a diameter roughly 11 times that of **13** ours. How Jupiter is able to rotate so fast is just one of many mysteries that scientists continue to explore in their efforts to understand our largest neighbor.

10. A) NO CHANGE
    B) Like other gaseous planets,
    C) Jupiter is like other gaseous planets,
    D) Jupiter, like other gaseous planets,

11. A) NO CHANGE
    B) A measurement
    C) The measurement
    D) Measurements

12. Which choice most accurately reflects the data found in the table?
    A) NO CHANGE
    B) in half that time
    C) in fewer than 10 Earth hours
    D) in more time than all the other planets

13. A) NO CHANGE
    B) our own planet
    C) our own
    D) our own planet's

Planets in Our Solar System				
Planet	Period of Revolution Around the Sun (1 planetary year)	Period of Rotation (1 planetary day)	Mass (kg)	Diameter (miles)
Mercury	87.96 Earth days	58.7 Earth days	3.3×10^{23}	3,031 miles
Venus	224.68 Earth days	243 Earth days	4.87×10^{24}	7,521 miles
Earth	365.26 days	24 hours	5.98×10^{24}	7,926 miles
Mars	686.98 Earth days	24.6 Earth hours	6.42×10^{23}	4,222 miles
Jupiter	11.862 Earth years	9.84 Earth hours	1.90×10^{27}	88,729 miles
Saturn	29.456 Earth years	10.2 Earth hours	5.69×10^{26}	74,600 miles
Uranus	84.07 Earth years	17.9 Earth hours	8.68×10^{25}	32,600 miles
Neptune	164.81 Earth years	19.1 Earth hours	1.02×10^{26}	30,200 miles
Pluto (a dwarf planet)	247.7 Earth years	6.39 Earth days	1.29×10^{22}	1,413 miles

Answers & Explanations for this chapter begin on page 705.

EXTRA PRACTICE

Questions 1-11 are based on the following passage and supplementary material.

The Pony Express: Not a Tame Ride

The 19th century saw the Civil War, the California Gold Rush, and the migration of thousands of people to the West along the Oregon Trail. With these events came **❶** the really great and strong need for communication between the original colonies and the new state of California.

❷ William H. Russell, Alexander Majors, and William B. Waddell brought about the solution to this need by creating Leavenworth & Pike's Peak Express Company, which later became known as the Pony Express.

The Pony Express was a system of riders that ran 2,000 miles from St. Joseph, Missouri, to Sacramento, California. Riders, who carried mail in leather satchels, changed every 75 to 100 miles. They changed horses every 10 to 15 miles. **❸** When the Pony Express was its largest, it had a lot of riders who were paid for their services.

1. A) NO CHANGE
   B) the very strong and real need
   C) the need
   D) the strong and real need

2. A) NO CHANGE
   B) William H. Russell
      Alexander Majors and
      William B. Waddell
   C) William H. Russell
      Alexander Majors, and
      William B. Waddell
   D) William H. Russell,
      Alexander Majors, and,
      William B. Waddell

3. Which choice most effectively revises the underlined sentence?
   A) When the Pony Express was at its largest, it was a very glamorous job.
   B) At its largest, the Pony Express had over 150 riders of all ages and they were paid.
   C) When the Pony Express peaked, it employed a lot of riders and the youngest one was named Bronco Charlie Miller.
   D) At its peak, the Pony Express employed over 180 riders who ranged in age from 11 to 50 years old, and earned $50 a month.

Riders changed horses or took a short break at relay posts, or stations: small, simple cabins, with dirt floors and a few stalls for the horses. Riders could get small meals at the ❹ stations, they usually consisted of dried fruit, cured meats, pickles, coffee, and cornmeal. At some bigger stations, known as "home stations," riders were able to enjoy a more relaxed meal, perhaps chat with other riders, and get some sleep.

The relay posts were also a source of employment. Each housed a station keeper who was responsible for having horses saddled and ready when a rider arrived, as well as for logging ❺ accurate records of arrival and departure times. The job of a station keeper was not an easy one. The ❻ stations were located in remote areas, had little access to resources, and were being unprotected from attacks by Native Americans.

❼ Riders often rode through rough, unfamiliar terrain; were exposed to harsh weather; and were susceptible to attack by hostile Native Americans.

4. A) NO CHANGE
   B) stations they usually consisted
   C) stations. They usually consisted
   D) stations yet they usually consisted

5. A) NO CHANGE
   B) lengthy
   C) sorrowful
   D) agreeable

6. A) NO CHANGE
   B) stations were located in remote areas, had little access to resources, and were unprotected
   C) stations were being located in remote areas, had little access to resources, and were unprotected
   D) stations were located in remote areas, having little access to resources, and were unprotected

7. Which choice most effectively establishes the main topic of the paragraph?
   A) The riders' routes were fraught with danger of many kinds.
   B) The Pony Express helped tie California with the rest of the country.
   C) The Pony Express was not successful financially.
   D) Some of the riders died while trying to deliver the mail.

8 <u>As a result of</u> these challenges, only one mail delivery was lost during the Pony Express's 19 months of operation.

Shortly after the first riders of the Pony Express set out on April 3, 1860, Congress approved a bill **9** <u>funding the construction of a transcontinental telegraph line in March, 1860</u>. The result of this bill was the creation of the Overland Telegraph Company of California and the Pacific Telegraph Company of Nevada. Once they were fully **10** <u>invented</u> on October 24, 1861, the Pony Express was no longer needed. Two days later, the Pony Express announced its closure.

Although its existence was a short one, the Pony Express played an important role in the development of **11** <u>the Pacific Coast. It remains</u> an icon of the Wild West.

History of the Pony Express

January–March 1860 ➤	Russell, Majors, and Waddell establish Pony Express mail service.
April 3, 1860 ➤	First riders leave St. Joseph, Missouri, and Sacramento, California.
June 8, 1860 ➤	Congress authorizes building of transcontinental telegraph line.
October 24, 1861 ➤	East and West coasts connected by telegraph line.
October 26, 1861 ➤	Pony Express discontinued.

8. A) NO CHANGE
   B) Despite
   C) However
   D) For instance

9. Which choice completes the sentence with accurate data based on the timeline?
   A) NO CHANGE
   B) funding the construction of a transcontinental telegraph line on June 8, 1860
   C) funding the construction of a transcontinental telegraph line on October 24, 1861
   D) funding the construction of a transcontinental telegraph line in January, 1860

10. A) NO CHANGE
    B) breached
    C) operational
    D) contrasted

11. Which choice most effectively combines the sentences at the underlined portion?
    A) the Pacific Coast, since it remains
    B) the Pacific Coast, however, it remains
    C) the Pacific Coast, that it remains
    D) the Pacific Coast and remains

CHAPTER 17

Development

CHAPTER OBJECTIVES

By the end of this chapter, you will be able to:

1. Evaluate the effectiveness and clarity of a passage's arguments, information, and ideas and determine whether a revision is necessary for the passage to be clear and effective

2. Evaluate information and ideas intended to support claims or points in the passage

3. Identify elements in the passage that are not relevant to the passage's topic and purpose

SMARTPOINTS

Point Value	SmartPoint Category
40 Points	Development

PROPOSITION

Proposition questions ask about how well a writer uses language—arguments, information, and ideas—to express the central purpose of a passage or part of a passage.

You will be asked to add, revise, or retain portions of the passage to communicate key ideas, claims, counterclaims, and topic sentences most clearly and effectively.

To answer Proposition questions, you need to identify the topic and purpose of the passage and focus on the writer's point of view. Ask questions such as:

- What is the central idea of the passage?

- Why did the author write the passage?

- What does the author think about the subject?

- What is the author's tone?

> ✔ **Remember**
>
> **The writer's point of view will be consistent throughout the passage. If the writer supports a certain issue, the correct answer choices will reflect this support and how the author effectively communicates it.**

SUPPORT

Support questions test issues related to information and ideas presented by the writer. You will be asked to evaluate the effectiveness of the facts and details employed by the writer to support claims made in the passage.

Support questions may ask you to keep, change, or add a detail or example. A Support question could ask about an example used to support a central argument or simply a minor detail used to weaken a point made by the author.

To answer Support questions, look around the underlined portion for a clue indicating what kind of support is required. If the example supports a central idea or claim, ask if the example strengthens the author's central idea. Eliminate answer choices that don't fit the context or have a negative or trivial effect on the central idea.

FOCUS

Focus questions require you to assess whether portions of the passage include only the information and ideas relevant to the author's topic and purpose. You may be asked to add, change, or omit text.

You can recognize relevant information and ideas by making sure they match the rest of the passage's topic, scope, and purpose.

> ✔ **Remember**
>
> *Topic* is what the passage is about. *Scope* is the aspect of the broader topic that is the center of the author's focus. *Purpose* is the author's reason for writing.

When answering Focus questions, identify whether the text in question fits the topic, scope, and purpose of the entire passage.

Let's look at the following Writing & Language passage and questions. After the passage, there are two columns. The left column contains test-like questions. The column on the right features the strategic thinking a test expert employs when approaching the passage and questions presented.

Questions 1-4 are based on the following passage.

Dr. Barry Marshall

For hundreds of years, the medical community and conventional wisdom held that ulcers were caused by stress. Strong gastric juices would sometimes burn sores through the lining of the stomach or intestines, causing widely varied symptoms, including internal bleeding, inflammation, and stomach pain. Doctors reasoned that if patients with ulcers changed their daily habits to reduce the level of tension in their lives, altered their diets to avoid foods that would irritate the stomach, and took medicine to moderate the amount of stomach acid, these ulcers would heal. Although the problem often recurred, no one seriously questioned why. ❶ <u>This medical advice remained standard for generations, until Dr. Barry Marshall came along.</u>

Beginning in the 1980s, Marshall, an Australian physician, hypothesized that at least some ulcers were caused by bacteria that often lie dormant in the human stomach. The international medical community scoffed. It was common knowledge, or so Marshall's colleagues believed, that no microbes could survive for long in the highly acidic environment of the stomach. ❷ <u>At medical conferences, the veteran, well-known Marshall was regarded as at best, a maverick, and at worst, a quack.</u> Over several years, he and his fellow researcher, Dr. J. Robin Warren, attempted to isolate and identify the bacteria that caused ulcers. As is the case with many medical discoveries, their breakthrough came about partly by accident, when they left a culture growing in the lab overnight. `3`

After this, to further prove his point, Dr. Marshall took a bold step. Although hospitals frown on such potentially dangerous actions, the doctor experimented on himself by deliberately drinking a flask of the bacteria. Over a two-week period, Marshall developed vague, though not disabling, symptoms, and medical tests showed evidence of ulcers and infection. Other researchers' studies later confirmed that Marshall's and Warren's findings apply to about 90% of all ulcers, which can now be cured by a short course of antibiotics instead of being temporarily managed by antacids.

In 2005, Marshall's bold move earned him and Warren the Nobel Prize in Medicine. `4`

Questions	Strategic Thinking
1. A) NO CHANGE B) This medical advice remains the standard today, despite Dr. Barry Marshall's recent efforts. C) This medical advice remained the standard for generations, until Dr. Barry Marshall developed a cure for the stomach ulcer. D) This medical advice remained standard for generations despite a lack of evidence. That is, until Dr. Barry Marshall proved it with scientific experiments.	**Step 1: Read the passage and identify the issue** The issue is Proposition: The underlined portion is the concluding sentence of a paragraph and should therefore provide a claim central to the passage as a whole. **Step 2: Eliminate answer choices that do not address the issue** Eliminate B because it is untrue according to the rest of the passage. Eliminate C and D because they distort the supporting details provided in the remainder of the passage. **Step 3: Plug in the remaining answer choices and select the most correct, concise, and relevant one** Choice (A) is the only remaining answer choice and is therefore correct.

Questions	Strategic Thinking
2. A) NO CHANGE B) At medical conferences, the young, unknown Marshall was regarded as at best, a maverick, and at worst, a quack. C) At medical conferences, the young, unknown Marshall was regarded as friendly and sociable at after-hours networking events. D) Dr. Marshall mostly avoided medical conferences and symposia.	**Step 1: Read the passage and identify the issue** The issue is Focus because the underlined sentence provides details about Dr. Marshall's character that you need to make sure fit the tone, scope, and purpose of the passage. **Step 2: Eliminate answer choices that do not address the issue** Eliminate A because the surrounding text does not support that Marshall was "veteran" and "well-known." Eliminate C and D because they are irrelevant to the passage as a whole. **Step 3: Plug in the remaining answer choices and select the most correct, concise, and relevant one** Choice (B) is the only remaining answer choice and is therefore correct.

Questions	Strategic Thinking
3. Which additional detail is most appropriate to include at this point in the passage? A) Dr. Marshall was a well-organized man and valued a neat workspace; the misplaced petri dish was almost certainly Dr. Warren's fault. B) The following morning, Marshall and Warren found a vibrant culture of a theretofore overlooked bacteria that they soon realized was an important suspect in the formation of ulcers. C) Marshall's and Warren's research was supported by grants, and by that point they were nearing the exhaustion of their funds. D) What Marshall and Warren discovered in their lab the next day brought them closer to finding the link between bacteria, ulcers, and stress.	**Step 1: Read the passage and identify the issue** The issue is Support. The question stem asks for the answer choice that includes an "appropriate" detail for this point in the passage. Details should support the passage's central idea. **Step 2: Eliminate answer choices that do not address the issue** The preceding paragraph is about Dr. Marshall's first hypothesis, his career and partnership, and the fact that his and Dr. Warren's breakthrough was an accident. Eliminate A because it does not describe why the discovery was accidental. Eliminate C because it does not relate to the discovery. Eliminate D because it is too general. **Step 3: Plug in the remaining answer choices and select the most correct, concise, and relevant one** Choice (B) is the only remaining answer choice and is therefore correct.

Questions	Strategic Thinking
4. Which choice most effectively concludes the passage? A) Dr. Marshall brought his wife to the Nobel Prize ceremony, and she was very proud to witness the public celebration of his work. B) Both of their careers flourished from this point forward, with each earning a tenured, endowed faculty position at a prestigious university. C) Sadly, since 2005, Marshall's and Warren's work has been neglected by the medical and scientific communities, and our understanding of ulcers has not progressed since that time. D) Their important advance, like many other scientific discoveries in history, was a combination of experimentation, persistence, and luck.	**Step 1: Read the passage and identify the issue** The issue is Proposition because the question asks for an effective conclusion for the overall passage. An effective conclusion should contain a summary of the author's central idea and argument. **Step 2: Eliminate answer choices that do not address the issue** Eliminate A and B because they are only details. Eliminate C because it goes beyond the scope of the passage by talking about events since 2005. **Step 3: Plug in the remaining answer choices and select the most correct, concise, and relevant one** Choice (D) is the only remaining answer choice and is therefore correct.

You have seen the ways in which the SAT tests you on Development on the Writing & Language Test and how an SAT expert approaches these types of questions.

Look at the Writing & Language passage excerpt that follows. There are four questions associated with it. Use the Kaplan Method for Writing & Language to answer the questions. Remember to look at the strategic thinking questions that have been laid out for you—some of the answers have been filled in, but you will have to fill in the answers to others.

Use your answers to the strategic thinking questions to select the correct answer, just as you will on Test Day.

Questions 5-8 are based on the following passage.

Human Skin

The skin is the human body's largest organ. An adult's skin comprises between 15 and 20 percent of the total body weight. Each square centimeter has 6 million cells, 5,000 sensory points, 100 sweat glands, and 15 sebaceous glands. The outer layer, the epidermis, consists of rows of cells about 12 to 15 deep and is between .07 and .12 millimeters thick (the thickness of a piece of paper). This top layer **5** has already been studied by countless scientists, and few new discoveries or insights are likely to occur. One square inch of skin contains up to 4.5 m of blood vessels, which have as one of their functions the regulation of body temperature. The skin varies in thickness from .5 mm on the eyelids to 4 mm or more on the palms and the soles.

The skin forms a protective barrier against the action of physical, chemical, and bacterial agents on the deeper tissues and contains the special nerve organs for the various sensations commonly grouped as the sense of touch. The body replaces its skin every month, and because the skin constitutes the first line of defense against dehydration, infection, injuries, and extreme temperature, **6** the skin detoxifies harmful substances with many of the same enzymatic processes the liver uses.

Skin is constantly being regenerated. A cell is born in the lower layer of the skin, called the dermis, which is supplied with blood vessels and nerve endings. For the next two weeks, the cell migrates upward until it reaches the bottom portion of the epidermis, which is the outermost skin layer. The cell then flattens out and continues moving toward the surface until it dies and is shed.

The most important property of the skin is that it provides our sense of touch. All other senses have a definite key organ that can be studied, but the skin is spread over the entire body and cannot be as easily studied. Receptors located at the ends of nerve fibers are used to detect stimuli and convert them into neural impulses to be sent to the brain through the peripheral and central nervous systems. The sense of touch is actually recorded in the dermis (skin) and passed on to the central nervous system.

The most important job of the skin is to protect the inside of the body; it acts like a "shock absorber." If a body falls, the skin protects all of the internal organs. When the skin is broken, **7** there is an elaborate repair system that relies primarily on blood cells, which clot the breach, fight infection, and initiate healing. The skin also acts as a thermostat to regulate body temperature. **8**

Questions	Strategic Thinking

5.   A) NO CHANGE
 	
     B) has already been studied by countless scientists.
 	
     C) is mainly composed of dead cells and thus is not of great interest to scientists.
 	
     D) is mainly composed of dead cells, and these are constantly being replaced by newer cells.
	Step 1: Read the passage and identify the issue
	
	What is the issue?
	Focus. The underlined portion consists of details in the middle of a paragraph.
	
	Step 2: Eliminate answer choices that do not address the issue
	
	What is this paragraph about?
	It introduces the topic of the passage—human skin—and contains many details about said organ.
	
	What answer choice(s) can you eliminate?
	
	_____
	_____
	_____
	_____
	
	Step 3: Plug in the remaining answer choices and select the most correct, concise, and relevant one
	
	What is the answer? _____

Questions	Strategic Thinking
6. A) NO CHANGE B) the skin detoxifies harmful substances in a way scientists are still trying to understand. C) the skin relies on other organs, such as the liver, to detoxify harmful substances with special enzymatic processes. D) requires careful and upkeep and care.	**Step 1: Read the passage and identify the issue** *What is the issue?* Focus. The underlined portion belongs to the last sentence of a body paragraph, which should tie back into the passage's central idea. **Step 2: Eliminate answer choices that do not address the issue** *What is the central idea of the passage?* _____ _____ _____ *What answer choice(s) can you eliminate?* _____ _____ _____ _____ **Step 3: Plug in the remaining answer choices and select the most correct, concise, and relevant one** *What is the answer?* _____

Questions	Strategic Thinking
7. A) NO CHANGE B) immediate medical attention is necessary to protect the internal organs. C) it has its own defense system that immediately goes into repair mode. D) there is an elaborate repair system that relies primarily on red and white blood cells, which clot the breach, fight infection, and initiate healing.	**Step 1: Read the passage and identify the issue** *What is the issue?* Support. *How do you know?* _____ _____ _____ **Step 2: Eliminate answer choices that do not address the issue** *What is the paragraph to which the underlined portion belongs about?* _____ _____ _____ *What answer choice(s) can you eliminate?* _____ _____ _____ _____ **Step 3: Plug in the remaining answer choices and select the most correct, concise, and relevant one** *What is the answer?* _____

Questions	Strategic Thinking
8. Which choice most effectively concludes the passage? A) It is no exaggeration to say that skin is among the most important organs—without it, a body simply cannot continue living. B) Since skin covers the body and is easily visible, it is no wonder that its color and decoration have important cultural meanings. C) However, more important organs do indeed exist and likely deserve more scientific attention than the skin. D) Without the skin's properties, most importantly the sense of touch, life would hardly be worth living.	**Step 1: Read the passage and identify the issue** What is the issue? _____ How do you know? _____ _____ _____ **Step 2: Eliminate answer choices that do not address the issue** What would effectively conclude the passage? _____ _____ _____ What answer choice(s) can you eliminate? _____ _____ _____ _____ **Step 3: Plug in the remaining answer choices and select the most correct, concise, and relevant one** What is the answer? _____

Now, try a test-like Writing & Language passage on your own. Give yourself 5 minutes to read the passage and answer the questions.

Questions 9-16 are based on the following passage.

James Polk

For much of his distinguished career, James Knox Polk followed in the footsteps of Andrew Jackson.[1] [9] In fact, "Young Hickory's"

9. Which detail is most appropriate to include at this point in the passage?

A) Like the fiery Jackson, Polk was born in North Carolina and moved to Tennessee to begin a political career.

B) Both men were fiery, aggressive personalities who hailed from North Carolina and later moved to Tennessee to begin their political careers.

C) Like the fiery Jackson, Polk was born in North Carolina and moved to Tennessee, but unlike Jackson, he did not fight in the War of 1812.

D) Polk, like Jackson, had antipathy toward the Native Americans of the southeastern United States, and his efforts to remove them defined his career.

policies were very similar to Jackson's: **🔟** <u>both men favored lower taxes, championed the frontiersmen, farmers, and workers, and neither was afraid to indulge in Tennessee whisky.</u> Polk, however, did not share Jackson's rather fierce temperament but was instead known for remaining soft-spoken even as he worked energetically toward his goals. Although history will likely always remember the frontier persona of Andrew Jackson, it was Polk who did much more to shape the course of American history.

11 From an early age, Polk suffered ill health that would turn out to be a lifelong affliction. Despite his physical shortcomings, he was an able student and graduated from the University of North Carolina with honors in 1818. Two years later, Polk was admitted to the bar, and in 1823,

10. A) NO CHANGE

B) while they agreed on little regarding taxes or the suffrage of frontiersmen, farmers, and workers, both men were known to indulge in Tennessee whisky.

C) both men favored lower taxes, championed the frontiersmen, farmers, and workers, and opposed the controversial Bank of the United States.

D) both men favored lower taxes, championed the frontiersmen, farmers, and workers, and yet they could not agree on the controversial Bank of the United States.

11. Which choice most effectively introduces this paragraph?

A) The Polk family was poor—James's father had emigrated from Scotland and arrived in the U.S. South penniless.

B) James Polk's parents tried to discourage the draw of politics and law, instead urging their eldest son to become a farmer.

C) Polk married his wife, Sarah Childress, in 1823.

D) Polk was born in Mecklenburg, North Carolina, in 1795 as the oldest of 10 children.

⑫ <u>he married Sarah Childress, the daughter of a prominent planter and merchant from Murfreesboro.</u> From there, he was elected to the U.S. House of Representatives in 1825, serving until 1839. **⑬** <u>Polk was also Speaker of the House from 1835 to 1839.</u>

12. A) NO CHANGE
    B) he married Sarah Childress.
    C) he was elected as governor of Tennessee.
    D) he was elected to the Tennessee House of Representatives.

13. A) NO CHANGE
    B) Polk was also Speaker of the House from 1835 to 1839, an experience that made him wary of wading deeper into national politics.
    C) Polk was also Speaker of the House from 1835 to 1839, a post that catapulted him to a position of prominence in politics.
    D) Polk was also Speaker of the House from 1835 to 1839, an experience that left his already strained constitution exhausted and forced him into a temporary retirement.

After he left Congress to serve as governor of Tennessee in 1839, it became clear that Polk's political aspirations were high indeed. During the 1844 presidential campaign, **⑭** <u>a young Abraham Lincoln threw his support behind Whig Henry Clay instead of the Democratic ex-President Martin van Buren.</u> Both men, as part of their platforms, opposed expansionist policies, and neither intended to annex the independent state of Texas or the Oregon Territory. **⑮** <u>Polk, spurred on by Jackson's advice, recognized</u> that neither candidate had correctly surmised the feelings of the people, so he publicly announced that, as president, he would do his utmost to acquire Texas and Oregon. Polk was the first political "dark horse" in American politics, coming out of nowhere to win the Democratic nomination and the election.

As the eleventh President of the United States, **⑯** <u>Polk pursued an agenda of diverse issues.</u> First, he reached an agreement with England that divided the Oregon Territory, carving out the present-day states of Washington and Oregon. Polk also quickly annexed Texas and provoked war with Mexico to acquire California and the New Mexico territory. While these triumphs were somewhat diminished by controversy from abolitionists who opposed the spread of slavery into new territories, under Polk's leadership the dream of "manifest destiny" became a reality, and the United States fully extended its borders from the Atlantic to the Pacific.

[1] Seventh U.S. President from 1829 to 1837 and War of 1812 hero often referred to as "Old Hickory"

14. A) NO CHANGE
    B) the leading Democratic candidate was ex-President Martin van Buren, and the Whig candidate was Henry Clay.
    C) the issue of slavery's expansion into new territories began its long stint as the most divisive issue to plague national politics.
    D) both the leading Democratic candidate, ex-President Martin van Buren, and the Whig candidate, Henry Clay, sought to campaign under the banner of "Manifest Destiny" and territorial expansion.

15. A) NO CHANGE
    B) Polk, against Jackson's advice, recognized
    C) Polk recognized
    D) Polk, against the wishes of his advisors, recognized

16. A) NO CHANGE
    B) Polk worked tirelessly to expand the borders of the nation.
    C) Polk worked to reign in unchecked expansion of the frontiers.
    D) Polk stopped at nothing short of war to expand the borders of the nation.

Answers & Explanations for this chapter begin on page 710.

EXTRA PRACTICE

Questions 1-11 are based on the following passage.

The Power of the PA

[1] In 1960s America, there were not enough doctors to meet the primary care needs of patients nationwide. Due to the shortage, and in hopes of improving health care and its accessibility, educators sought to establish alternatives to medical school that would effectively equip other health care workers to share more of the physicians' workload. Their project altered health care history: the physician assistant (PA) was born. In 1967, the first PA program ❷ launched at Duke University, notable for its education and sports programs. The coming decades saw the field develop into what is considered today to be one of the most desirable and quickly growing careers in the country.

1. Which choice most effectively establishes the main topic of the paragraph?

   A) Today, physician assistants are vital members of any health care system, but it hasn't always been that way.

   B) For many years, doctors and educators struggled to find a role for the high number of incoming medical students.

   C) The difference between physician assistants and nurse practitioners was often hard to quantify, but then came a shift in health care needs.

   D) Physician assistants had long played a vital role in the medical field, but the PA career didn't become popular until the mid-20th century.

2. A) NO CHANGE

   B) launched at Duke University, noted for its education programs.

   C) launched at the renowned Duke University.

   D) launched at Duke University.

[1] Becoming a PA is simpler than becoming a physician, which usually takes over nine years of higher education and training. [2] Those seeking acceptance into PA programs typically study science or health as undergraduates. [3] Once practicing, PAs are required to maintain proficiency through continued education and a recertification exam every ten years. [4] They also usually ❸ obtain some health-related work experience before applying. [5] ❹ Once accepted to a program, most students will be in their programs for about twenty-seven months. [6] Schooling involves both classroom and field study, and students undergo hundreds of hours in clinical training rotations in order to gain a breadth of supervised experience. [7] Today there are over one hundred and seventy accredited PA programs, most of which award masters degrees to graduates. [8] After graduation, ❺ graduates must complete one final step: passing the national licensure exam. [6]

While physicians can work ❼ anonymously, PAs always work under the supervision of physicians. But like nurse practitioners, another primary care alternative that emerged from the 1960s, PAs can do much of the work commonly expected of a physician. PAs are trained and qualified to meet with, examine, treat, diagnose, and counsel patients. They can prescribe medication, interpret lab data, and help physicians with surgical procedures. ❽ In many ways, PAs lighten the workload for physicians on their teams. This enables clinics, hospitals, and other health care systems to run more efficiently and meet patient needs with greater accuracy and timeliness.

Physician assistants enjoy various options in terms of where they can practice. Almost every field of medicine has positions for those PAs who specialize accordingly. Also, depending on the needs of the physicians ❾ under which PAs work, as well as the particular limitations that might be imposed by a specific state, the requirements and responsibilities of the job can vary.

3. A) NO CHANGE
    B) accrue
    C) perceive
    D) formulate

4. A) NO CHANGE
    B) Once accepted
    C) Once they begin,
    D) Once programs accept them

5. A) NO CHANGE
    B) physicians
    C) PAs
    D) candidates

6. For the sake of cohesion in this paragraph, sentence 3 should be placed
    A) where it is now.
    B) after sentence 5.
    C) before sentence 7.
    D) after sentence 8.

7. A) NO CHANGE
    B) defensively
    C) autonomously
    D) fundamentally

8. A) NO CHANGE
    B) On the other hand
    C) For example
    D) First of all

9. A) NO CHANGE
    B) where PAs work
    C) under whom PAs work
    D) who work under PAs

The past half-century saw the career of physician assistant rise from nascence to become a highly sought-after and still rapidly growing addition to American health care. Projections indicate that within the next decade, the number of employed PAs should increase significantly. **🔟** <u>I believe PAs are an ever-increasing presence</u> in health care, and a powerful influence on the medical world for the better. **11**

10. A) NO CHANGE

    B) PAs are an ever-increasing presence

    C) Doctors believe PAs are an ever-increasing presence

    D) You can believe that PAs are an ever-increasing presence

11. What fact is omitted from this paragraph that would help support the author's claims?

    A) The number of PAs hired over the last half-century

    B) The expected PA-to-patient ratio over the next decade

    C) The number of PA positions compared to the number of nurse practitioner positions

    D) The specific rate at which PAs will be employed over the next decade

CHAPTER 18

Effective Language Use

CHAPTER OBJECTIVES

By the end of this chapter, you will be able to:

1. Revise the text as needed to improve the exactness or content appropriateness of word choice or eliminate wordiness and redundancy

2. Improve the consistency of style and tone with the passage's purpose, as necessary

3. Evaluate the use of sentence structure to accomplish the intended rhetorical purpose of a passage

SMARTPOINTS

Point Value	SmartPoint Category
50 Points	Effective Language Use

PRECISION

On the SAT, precision refers to the exactness and accuracy of the author's choice of words, also known as diction. Precision questions will ask you to revise a text as needed to improve the exactness or content appropriateness of the author's word choice.

Word choice is important because being precise in language use allows an author to effectively and precisely convey his or her thoughts, including the thesis and central arguments.

SAT Precision questions mostly test your knowledge of correct word choice in context. These questions are very similar to the Reading Test's Vocab-in-Context questions, which you can review in chapter 12.

> **✔ Expert Tip**
>
> One common way in which precision is tested is through incorrect pronoun use. Remember to use *who* and *whom* when referring to people; use *that* or *which* to refer to any other nouns.

CONCISION

Remember the third step of the Kaplan Method for Writing & Language: Plug in the remaining answer choices and select the most clear, concise, and relevant one. You must use not only the correct words to convey your ideas but also as few words as possible.

Concision questions will require you to revise text to improve the economy of word choice by eliminating wordiness and redundancy. The SAT tests concision by presenting you with unnecessarily long and complex structures or redundant usage—or sometimes both.

> **✔ On Test Day**
>
> The shortest answer will not always be the correct one; the portion of the passage in question needs to be grammatically correct and retain the intended meaning.

Unnecessarily long and complex structure implies that a sentence uses more words than necessary to make its point, even though it may be grammatically correct. Not every long underlined segment will be a Concision question; sometimes it takes a lot of words to convey meaning. Nevertheless, when a long selection is underlined, you should ask, "Are all of these words necessary? Is there a more concise way to say the same thing?"

Another aspect of concision is redundancy. Redundancy errors occur when two words in the sentence have essentially the same meaning in context or when the meaning of one word is implicit in the meaning of another.

STYLE AND TONE

SAT Style and Tone questions ask you to revise a text to ensure consistency of style and tone or to reflect the author's purpose. You must also confirm that the text's style and tone match its subject and format.

Style and Tone questions will sometimes have question stems that correspond to small numbers in boxes within the passage. Other times, these questions will not have question stems. In the case of the latter, you must determine if the underlined segment matches the general tone of the passage or if one of the other choices is more appropriate in context.

> ✔ **Expert Tip**
>
> If you spot a Style and Tone question at the beginning of a passage, read the passage through before answering it so you can determine overall tone first.

SYNTAX

Questions about syntax will ask you to assess whether different sentence structures accomplish an author's intended rhetorical purpose. In narratives or prose, syntax can enhance intended meaning and contribute toward tone.

> ✔ **Definition**
>
> Syntax refers to the arrangement of words and phrases within a sentence. It dictates how words from different parts of speech are assembled to convey a complete thought.

Sophisticated and academic writing like the kind you'll see on the SAT employs varied kinds of syntax. One way in which syntax is categorized is by sentence type. The following table portrays the four sentence types classified by the clauses they contain.

> ✔ **Definition**
>
> A clause is a part of a sentence containing a subject and a predicate verb.

Sentence Type	Description	Example
Simple	Contains a single, independent clause	I don't like cats.
Compound	Contains two independent clauses that are joined by a coordinating conjunction (e.g., *but, or, and, so*)	I don't like cats, and my sister doesn't like dogs.
Complex	Contains an independent clause plus one or more dependent clauses (a dependent clause starts with a coordinating conjunction such as *that, because, while, although, where, if*)	I don't like cats that scratch the furniture.
Compound-Complex	Contains three or more clauses (of which at least two are independent and one is dependent)	I don't like cats, and my sister doesn't like dogs because they bark.

Let's look at the following Writing & Language passage and questions. After the passage, there are two columns. The left column contains test-like questions. The column on the right features the strategic thinking a test expert employs when approaching the passage and questions presented.

Questions 1-4 are based on the following passage.

Modern Readers

Judging by the types of novels that typically receive the top rankings on contemporary "best seller lists, one would be wise to conclude that the modern book consumer does not enjoy reading ancient mythology. Seemingly, such antiquated stories hold little relevance to the concerns of the modern age. It is a literature not for the ❶ <u>distracted</u> reader immersed in his "everyday" cares but for a more imaginative audience with more universal tastes.

To even begin ❷ <u>to understand or comprehend</u> this issue, we must understand what it is that most readers seek out in the works they read. What is it in a book—a novel, for example—that causes them to continue turning the pages? The answer can be a bit slippery. Is it the psychological realism of the characters? Is it the drama of the events they encounter? Is it the modern author's consciousness of his position as author and the relationship—distant or intimate, serious or playful—that he develops with his readers?

The obvious answer is that it is all of these things. The defining features of the modern story are its complexity and ambivalence. Narrators are not always reliable. Loyalties are often fleeting, and even a character's central motives may undergo a transformation before the story is done. There is no neat conclusion, no

---

definitive redemption or damnation, and not always even a clear message. In this confusion and dislocation, the modern reader sees his own life reflected, complete with all of its ❸ complexity and ambivalence.

In a complex world where the disparate lives of alienated individuals still manage to affect each other on a daily basis, there is a paradoxical credulity extended towards anything murky and unclear. Far from the cosmopolitan savant he would like us to believe he is (to say nothing of the author who writes for him), the modern reader is only able to take comfort in his own confusion. When, for example, George and Jane finish their fairytale courtship and suddenly find themselves unable to live together, the contemporary pop intellectual will ❹ nod his head sagely, and he will think about the relationships in his own life that he didn't understand either.

What escapes the minds of the masses is that, taken past a certain point, realism is not art. Neither unsatisfying conclusions, nor irritating characters, nor obscure motives are indications of the literary talents of the author. The older, mythic characters may be drawn with a broad brush, and may possess a simplicity and singularity of purpose that finds no parallel in day-to-day life, but that simplicity is not a sign of an author lacking in subtlety. Rather, a purposeful author will have purposeful characters. Whether the story is meant to illustrate moral principles, explore character types, or simply entertain, a quality work of art must have a purpose.

Questions	Strategic Thinking
1. A) NO CHANGE B) prosaic C) voracious D) modern	**Step 1: Read the passage and identify the issue** The issue is Word Choice, or Precision. **Step 2: Eliminate answer choices that do not address the issue** Eliminate A because while the "distracted" reader may be "immersed in his cares," "distracted" does not directly contrast the "more imaginative audience with more universal tastes," as indicated by the use of the word "but." Eliminate C because a "voracious" reader is one who reads an enormous amount, not an ordinary amount. Eliminate D because the reader's era has nothing to do with the sentence. **Step 3: Plug in the remaining answer choices and select the most correct, concise, and relevant one** Choice (B) is the only remaining answer choice and is therefore correct.

Questions	Strategic Thinking
2. A) NO CHANGE B) to understand or to comprehend C) to understand and comprehend D) to understand	**Step 1: Read the passage and identify the issue** The issue is Redundancy or Concision because "understand" and "comprehend" have the same meaning. **Step 2: Eliminate answer choices that do not address the issue** Eliminate A because the underlined portion is redundant as written. Eliminate B and C because they do not correct the redundancy issue. **Step 3: Plug in the remaining answer choices and select the most correct, concise, and relevant one** Choice (D) is the only remaining answer choice and is therefore correct.
3. A) NO CHANGE B) ambivalence C) complexity D) ambivalent complexity	**Step 1: Read the passage and identify the issue** The issue is Style and Tone. The style and tone of the passage are authoritative and academic. **Step 2: Eliminate answer choices that do not address the issue** The author uses the underlined phrase previously in the second sentence of the paragraph: "The defining features of the modern story are its complexity and ambivalence." Eliminate B and C because they both remove one of the previously used words. Eliminate D because even though it is more concise, it alters the intended meaning. **Step 3: Plug in the remaining answer choices and select the most correct, concise, and relevant one** Choice (A) is the only remaining answer choice and is therefore correct.

Questions	Strategic Thinking
4. Which choice most effectively combines the sentences at the underlined portion? A) NO CHANGE B) nod his head sagely. He will think about C) nod his head sagely, thinking about D) nod his head sagely, be thinking about	**Step 1: Read the passage and identify the issue** The issue is Syntax. **Step 2: Eliminate answer choices that do not address the issue** Eliminate A because as written, the underlined portion creates a run-on sentence. Eliminate B because it separates the underlined portion into two sentences, which, while grammatically correct, is not the most effective combination because it places distance between the joined content of the two parts. Eliminate D because it is grammatically incorrect. **Step 3: Plug in the remaining answer choices and select the most correct, concise, and relevant one** Choice (C) is the only remaining answer choice and is therefore correct.

You have seen the ways in which the SAT tests you on Effective Language Use on the Writing & Language Test and how an SAT expert approaches these types of questions.

Look at the Writing & Language passage excerpt that follows. There are four questions associated with it. Use the Kaplan Method for Writing & Language to answer the questions. Remember to look at the strategic thinking questions that have been laid out for you—some of the answers have been filled in, but you will have to fill in the answers to others.

Use your answers to the strategic thinking questions to select the correct answer, just as you will on Test Day.

Questions 5-8 are based on the following passage.

Military Nurses

During the American Civil War, Miss Dorothea Dix was in charge of organizing the volunteer nurses who assisted the Union Army. The nurses chosen by Dix were all women, preferably plain ones, and had to dress simply in order to serve. Dorothea Dix's volunteers were the first famous nurses in United States history, but on both the Union and Confederate sides, **5** other health care professionals there that few people knew about were male nurses. However, as the nineteenth century progressed, nursing became increasingly considered "women's work," until, at the turn of the 20th century, female nurses began to organize, unofficially excluding men. The American Nursing Association was formed in 1917, and men were officially not permitted to join until 1930.

One of the **6** major victories of the female-dominated nursing community was to have men **7** denied admission to and excluded from military nursing. Although traditionally, non-volunteer military nurses had been exclusively male, in 1901 the United States Army Nurse Corps was formed, and only women could serve. **8** It is amazing to even think that men couldn't work as military nurses until after the Korean War. Today, depending on the branch of service, anywhere between 35% and 70% of military nurses are men; this is in sharp contrast to the civilian world, where an average of 6% of American nurses are men.

Questions	Strategic Thinking
5. A) NO CHANGE B) few people knew there were other health care professionals about: male nurses C) some health care professionals were male nurses that few people knew about D) there were other health care professionals that few people knew about: male nurses	**Step 1: Read the passage and identify the issue** *What is the issue?* The issue is Syntax because as written, the sentence is hard to follow due to the placement of the words. **Step 2: Eliminate answer choices that do not address the issue** *What answer choice(s) can you eliminate?* Eliminate A, B, and C because they do not correct the Syntax error. **Step 3: Plug in the remaining answer choices and select the most correct, concise, and relevant one** What is the correct answer? _____
6. A) NO CHANGE B) first triumphs C) undisputed wins D) finest achievements	**Step 1: Read the passage and identify the issue** *What is the issue?* Word choice, or Precision. *What does the underlined phrase indicate? Does it fit the context of the passage? Why or why not?* Notice, C and D both mean the same thing as A. Since there can't be three correct answers on the SAT, this should assist you in eliminating several possibilities. **Step 2: Eliminate answer choices that do not address the issue** *What answer choice(s) can you eliminate?* _____ _____ **Step 3: Plug in the remaining answer choices and select the most correct, concise, and relevant one** *What is the correct answer?* _____

Questions	Strategic Thinking
7. A) NO CHANGE B) denied to and excluded from C) excluded from D) denied and excluded from	**Step 1: Read the passage and identify the issue** *What is the issue?* Redundancy, or Concision. *Why is the underlined portion redundant?* _____ _____ _____ _____ _____ **Step 2: Eliminate answer choices that do not address the issue** *What answer choice(s) can you eliminate?* _____ _____ _____ _____ **Step 3: Plug in the remaining answer choices and select the most correct, concise, and relevant one** *What is the correct answer?* _____

Questions	Strategic Thinking
8. A) NO CHANGE B) It was not until after the Korean War that men could once more work as military nurses. C) In this day and age, it is nearly inconceivable that it took until after the Korean War before men could once more exercise their right to work as military nurses. D) Not until after the Korean War could men once more take up the noble calling to serve as military nurses.	**Step 1: Read the passage and identify the issue** *What is the issue?* Style and Tone. *What are the style and tone of the passage?* _____ _____ _____ _____ *Does the underlined portion match the style and tone of the passage? Why or why not?* _____ _____ _____ _____ **Step 2: Eliminate answer choices that do not address the issue** *What answer choice(s) can you eliminate?* _____ _____ _____ _____ _____ **Step 3: Plug in the remaining answer choices and select the most correct, concise, and relevant one** *What is the correct answer?* _____

Now, try a test-like Writing & Language passage on your own. Give yourself 5 minutes to read the passage and answer the questions.

Questions 9-16 are based on the following passage.

Genetically Modified Organisms

Although biotechnology companies and the chronically naïve ⑨ imagine that there is no danger to be feared from genetically modified foods, they overlook a plethora of evidence indicating that we may be gambling with our very lives by continuing to ⑩ interfere and tamper with nature to create these "Frankenfoods." Potential problems range from the relatively minor—increased possibilities of allergic reactions to certain foods, for instance—to the potentially devastating—the complete skewing of the balance of an ecosystem. All of these factors should be carefully considered before ⑪ we choose to risk so much for the possibility of a better tomato.

For example, the cultivation of insect-resistant plants could lead to the reduction or even destruction of certain insect species that naturally feed on those plants. A change in the insect population could have a disastrous impact on ⑫ certain bird species. They rely on the affected insects as their food source. And alterations in the balance of the bird population could have further-reaching consequences, all the way up the food chain. An ecosystem is a delicate thing, and the ripple created by genetically altering one variety of soybean ⑬ will translate into a shock wave of unforeseen repercussions in the long term.

9. A) NO CHANGE
    B) insist
    C) hope
    D) think

10. A) NO CHANGE
    B) thoughtlessly interfere and casually tamper
    C) interfere by casually tampering
    D) tamper

11. A) NO CHANGE
    B) we as a society
    C) those of us who comprise society
    D) the citizens making up our population

12. Which choice most effectively combines the sentences at the underlined portion?
    A) NO CHANGE
    B) certain bird species that rely on the affected insects
    C) certain bird species relying on the affected insects
    D) certain bird species, and they rely on the affected insects

13. A) NO CHANGE
    B) must
    C) would
    D) could

14 <u>The actual impact on the genetically modified organisms themselves, and on those who consume foods produced from genetically modified organisms, also remains to be seen.</u> Some studies have indicated that certain genetically modified foods had negative effects on the digestive systems and cardiac health of rats that consumed those foods in high quantities; although human studies have not been performed, the possibility that tampering with an organism's genetic structure could cause far-reaching health consequences for the people who eat genetically modified foods must be confronted.

14. A) NO CHANGE

B) What also remains to be seen, on both the genetically modified organisms themselves and on those who consume foods produced from genetically modified organisms, is the actual impact.

C) Remaining to be seen is the actual impact on genetically modified organisms themselves and those who consume genetically modified organisms.

D) The actual impact remains to be seen on genetically modified organisms themselves and those who consume genetically modified organisms.

And arguments about the potential for genetic engineering to end world hunger by maximizing the quantity and quality of food grown around the world are based on an **15** essential fallacy: people do not starve because there is a lack of food. People starve because it is more profitable to let food go to waste than to distribute it to the world's impoverished and famine-stricken regions. We have plenty of farmland sitting fallow and plenty of food rotting in warehouses. Many of the agribusinesses arguing that genetically modified foods can solve world hunger are the same companies that accept government subsidies now to limit their production of crops in order to avoid flooding the market. These companies are primarily concerned with profit, and whatever lip service they pay to global well-being, the driving force behind genetically modified organisms and foods is profit, not people. **16** In conclusion, the benefits and risks of any new technology must be carefully considered before implementing that technology.

15. A) NO CHANGE
    B) harmful delusion
    C) fanciful illusion
    D) fundamental untruth

16. A) NO CHANGE
    B) It would be nice if we could trust the very companies that could benefit most from the creation of genetically modified organisms.
    C) Unfortunately, those companies affect so many aspects of modern life that we have no choice but to trust them.
    D) Why would we trust our own well-being and that of the planet to companies recklessly pursuing money at the risk of Mother Earth?

Answers & Explanations for this chapter begin on page 715.

EXTRA PRACTICE

Questions 1-11 are based on the following passage.

Long History, Short Poem: The Haiku

❶ Of the many forms poetry can take, triolet, ballad, ode, and epigram, to name a few, none is quite as briefly beautiful as the Japanese haiku. With a **❷** complex history and a challenging structure, the haiku is as popular as it is difficult to master. Composed of only three lines and 17 or fewer syllables, haiku have been written by some of the world's most prominent poets.

1. A) NO CHANGE
   B) Of the many forms poetry can take—triolet, ballad, ode, and epigram, to name a few—none is quite as briefly beautiful as the Japanese haiku.
   C) Of the many forms poetry can take, triolet, ballad, ode and epigram to name a few—none is quite as briefly beautiful as the Japanese haiku.
   D) Of the many forms poetry can take: triolet, ballad, ode, and epigram to name a few, none is quite as briefly beautiful as the Japanese haiku.

2. A) NO CHANGE
   B) controversial
   C) brief
   D) difficult

3 [1] Pre-Buddhist and early Shinto ceremonies included narrative poems called "uta," or songs. [2] These songs were written about common activities like planting and prayer. [3] The most popular "uta" were "waka," or songs featuring 31 syllables broken into five different lines. [4] Later, the "waka" format was distilled into the 5-7-5-7-7 syllables-per-line format that is still used and recognized today. [5] During the same time period, writers played word games. [6] The syllabic 5-7-5-7-7 structure would remain throughout the work, adhering to the guidelines used in ceremonies and royal court proceedings. [7] They would compose lines of poetry, alternating turns, until long strings of text called "renga" were created. [8] It was not until the 15th and 16th centuries that writers of "renga" broke with tradition and shortened the form, writing "hokku," meaning "first verse." [9] ❹ <u>This name changed into "haiku" over time.</u> **5**

3. Which sentence should be inserted before sentence 1 in order to introduce the topic of the paragraph?

   A) Although the format remained unknown to Americans until the 1950s, haiku dates back as early as the seventh century.

   B) The art of haiku includes specific rules about how lines are to be structured, but these rules are difficult to pin down.

   C) Despite its difficult reputation and the years it takes to master, haiku is highly entertaining.

   D) Haiku is a Japanese poetic art form and many poets enjoy the challenge of writing a poem within its rules.

4. A) NO CHANGE

   B) Omit the sentence

   C) Nobody is quite sure when it became known as "haiku."

   D) These days, we know this word as "haiku."

5. For the sake of the cohesion of this paragraph, sentence 7 should be placed

   A) where it is now.

   B) before sentence 2.

   C) before sentence 6.

   D) after sentence 8.

(6) <u>Previously,</u> hokku master Matsunaga Teitoku began teaching renga in an attempt to ignite a classical renaissance. He founded a writing school where he taught Matsuo Basho, who is now known as one of Japan's most famous writers. Basho traveled throughout Japan writing about nature and his travels.

It is through Basho's many poems that (7) <u>haiku came to be known as being pretty tied up with</u> nature and the seasons. [8] Basho influenced many students of verse over the course of his lifetime and was declared the saint of the haiku in the Shinto religion.

6. A) NO CHANGE

   B) However

   C) In the next century

   D) As a result

7. A) NO CHANGE

   B) haiku transformed into a mode of artistic expression that was irreversibly intertwined with the themes of

   C) haiku became popular because it was seen as having something to do with

   D) haiku developed its common association with

8. Which sentence, if added here, would provide the best support for this paragraph?

   A) However, haiku can be used to communicate many other ideas as well, from love to humor.

   B) His words emphasized contentment and solitary contemplation, ideals linked to Japanese religions.

   C) Basho's poetic influence continues to be felt even now in the work of several modern poets.

   D) For example, a Basho haiku might focus on a frog or on the coming of spring.

It was not until 1827 that the hokku was renamed haiku by Masaoka Shiki. **9** Shiki was a poet, and he most famously shrank the structure of the haiku to its current format of 5-7-5. His work **10** helped Western writers like e. e. cummings and Ezra Pound, but haiku did not become the easily recognizable, popular type of poetry that it is today until writers like Allen Ginsberg and Jack Kerouac popularized it.

These writers were taken by **11** the brevity of the form, but it provided them a new, challenging form of expression while enabling them to share full ideas in such a short form. Both Japanese and American poets continue to use the structures to create snapshots of beauty and calm.

9. A) NO CHANGE
    B) Shiki was a poet who also shrank the structure of the haiku to the current 5-7-5 format.
    C) Shiki was the poet who shrank the structure of the haiku to its current 5-7-5 format.
    D) Shiki was the poet who was also known for shrinking the structure of the haiku to its current format of 5-7-5.

10. A) NO CHANGE
    B) inspired
    C) aided
    D) started

11. A) NO CHANGE
    B) the brevity of the form, it
    C) the brevity of the form, and it
    D) the brevity of the form, as it

CHAPTER 19

Conventions of Usage

CHAPTER OBJECTIVES

By the end of this chapter, you will be able to:

1. Recognize and correct errors in pronoun clarity, grammatical agreement, and logical comparison

2. Distinguish among commonly confused possessive determiners, contractions, and adverbs

3. Recognize and correct incorrectly constructed idioms and frequently misused words

SMARTPOINTS

Point Value	SmartPoint Category
50 Points	Usage

PRONOUNS

A pronoun is ambiguous if its antecedent is either missing or unclear. On the SAT, you must be able to recognize either situation and make the appropriate correction. When you see an underlined pronoun, make sure you can find the specific noun to which it refers.

Missing Antecedent

- When the flight arrived, *they* told the passengers to stay seated until the plane reached the gate. (The pronoun "they" does not have an antecedent in this sentence.)

- When the flight arrived, *the flight crew* told the passengers to stay seated until the plane reached the gate. (Replacing the pronoun with a specific noun clarifies the meaning.)

Unclear Antecedent

- Martha asked Mia to drive Samantha to the airport because *she* was running late. (The pronoun "she" could refer to any of the three people mentioned in the sentence.)

- Because Martha was running late, she asked Mia to drive Samantha to the airport. (By rearranging the sentence, the pronoun "she" unambiguously refers to Martha.)

> ✔ **Definition**
>
> The **antecedent** is the noun that the pronoun replaces or stands in for another part of the sentence. To identify the **antecedent** of a pronoun, check the nouns near the pronoun. Substitute those nouns for the pronoun to see which one makes sense.

AGREEMENT

Pronoun-Antecedent Agreement

Pronouns must agree with their antecedents not only in person and number, but also in gender. Only third-person pronouns make a distinction based on gender.

Gender	Example
Feminine	Because Yvonne had a question, *she* raised her hand.
Masculine	Since *he* had lots of homework, Justin started working right away.
Neuter	The rain started slowly, but then *it* became a downpour.
Unspecified	If a traveler is lost, *he* or *she* should ask for directions.

Pronoun-Case Agreement

There are three pronoun cases:

1. Subjective case: The pronoun is used as the subject.

2. Objective case: The pronoun is used as the object of a verb or a preposition.

3. Possessive case: The pronoun expresses ownership.

Subjective Case	I, you, she, he, it, we, you, they, who
Objective Case	me, you, her, him, it, us, you, them, whom
Possessive Case	my, mine, your, yours, his, her, hers, its, our, ours, their, theirs, whose

> ✔ **Expert Tip**
>
> When there are two pronouns or a noun and a pronoun in a compound structure, drop the other noun to confirm which case to use. For example: *Tom and me walk into town.* Would you say, "Me walk into town"? No, you would say, "I walk into town." Therefore, the correct case is subjective and the original sentence should read *Tom and I walk into town.*

> ✔ **Remember**
>
> Use "who" when you would use "he" or "she." Use "whom" when you would use "him" or "her."

Subject-Verb Agreement

A verb must agree with its subject noun in person and number:

- Singular: A **stamp sticks** to an envelope.
- Plural: **Stamps stick** to envelopes.

The noun closest to a verb may not be its subject: *The **chair** with the cabriole legs **is** an antique.* The noun closest to the verb in this sentence ("is," which is singular) is "legs," which is plural. However, the verb's subject is "chair," so the sentence is correct as written.

Only the conjunction *and* forms a compound subject requiring a plural verb form:

- Danny **and** Jared **are** in the fencing club.
- **Either** Danny or Jared **is** in the fencing club.
- **Neither** Danny nor Jared **is** in the fencing club.

Noun-Number Agreement

Related nouns must be consistent in number:

- *Students* applying for college must submit their *applications* on time. (The sentence refers to multiple students, and they all must submit applications.)

FREQUENTLY CONFUSED WORDS

The English language contains many pairs of words that sound alike but are spelled differently and have different meanings.

ACCEPT/EXCEPT: To *accept* is to take or receive something that is offered: *Dad said he would accept my apology for putting a dent in his new car, but then he grounded me for two weeks.* To *except* is to leave out or exclude: *The soldier was excepted from combat duty because he had poor field vision. Except* is usually used as a preposition that signifies "with the exception of, excluding": *When the receptionist found out that everyone except him had received a raise, he demanded a salary increase as well.*

AFFECT/EFFECT: To *affect* is to have an influence on something: *Al refused to let the rain affect his plans for a picnic, so he sat under an umbrella and ate potato salad.* To *effect* is to bring something about or cause something to happen: *The young activist received an award for effecting a change in her community.* An *effect* is an influence or a result: *The newspaper article about homeless animals had such an effect on Richard that he brought home three kittens from the shelter.* Most often, *affect* is used in its verb form, and *effect* is used in its noun form.

AFFLICT/INFLICT: To *afflict* is to torment or distress someone or something. It usually appears as a passive verb: *Jeff is afflicted with severe migraine headaches.* To *inflict* is to impose punishment or suffering on someone or something: *No one dared displease the king, for he was known to inflict severe punishments on those who upset him.*

ALLUSION/ILLUSION: An *allusion* is an indirect reference to something, a hint: *I remarked that Sally's boyfriend was unusual looking; this allusion to his prominent tattoos did not please Sally.* An *illusion* is a false, misleading, or deceptive appearance: *A magician creates the illusion that something has disappeared by hiding it faster than the eye can follow it.*

EMIGRATE/IMMIGRATE: To *emigrate* is to leave one country for another country. It is usually used with the preposition *from: Many people emigrated from Europe in search of better living conditions.* To *immigrate* is to enter a country to take up permanent residence there. It is usually used with the preposition *to: They immigrated to North America because land was plentiful.*

EMINENT/IMMINENT: Someone who is *eminent* is prominent or outstanding: *The eminent archeologist Dr. Wong has identified the artifact as prehistoric in origin.* Something that is *imminent* is likely to happen soon or is impending: *After being warned that the hurricane's arrival was imminent, beachfront residents left their homes immediately.*

LAY/LIE: To *lay* is to place or put something down, and this verb usually does have a "something"— a direct object—following it: *Before she begins her pictures, Emily lays all of her pencils, brushes, and paints on her worktable to avoid interruptions while she draws and paints.* One form, *laid,* serves as the simple past and the past participle of *lay.* To *lie* is to recline, to be in a lying position or at rest. This verb never takes a direct object: you do not lie anything down. The simple past form of *lie* is *lay;* the past participle is *lain.* Notice that the past form of *lie* is identical with the present form of *lay.* This coincidence complicates the task of distinguishing the related meanings of *lay* and *lie:* *Having laid the picnic cloth under the sycamore, they lay in the shady grass all last Sunday afternoon.*

LEAVE/LET: To *leave* is to depart, to allow something to remain behind after departing, or to allow something to remain as it is. One irregular verb form, *left,* serves as the simple past and the past participle: *I boarded my plane and it left, leaving my baggage behind in Chicago.* When *leave* is used in the third sense—to allow something to remain as it is—and followed by *alone,* this verb does overlap with *let: If parents leave (or let) a baby alone with a new toy, she will understand it as quickly as if they demonstrated how the toy works.* To *let* is to allow or to rent out. These are the verb's core meanings, but it also combines with several different prepositions to produce various specific senses. *Let* is irregular. One form serves as present tense, past tense, and past participle. *The French border police would not let the Dutch tourist pass without a passport.*

RAISE/RISE: *Raise* is a regular verb that means to lift up or to cause to rise or grow, and it usually has a direct object: you *raise* dumbbells, roof beams, tomato plants, or livestock. *Raise* is a completely regular verb. *The trade tariff on imported leather goods raised the prices of Italian shoes.* To *rise* is to get up, to go up, or to be built up. This verb never takes a direct object: you do not *rise* something. The past and past participle forms are irregular; *rose* is the simple past tense, while *risen* is the past participle. *Long-distance commuters must rise early and return home late.*

SET/SIT: The difference between *set* and *sit* is very similar to the difference between *lay* and *lie* and between *raise* and *rise.* To *set* is to put or place something, to settle or arrange it. But *set* takes on other specific meanings when it combines with several different prepositions. *Set* is an irregular verb in that one form serves as present tense, past tense, and past participle. *Set* usually takes a direct object: you *set* a ladder against the fence, a value on family heirlooms, or a date for the family reunion: *The professor set the students' chairs in a semicircle in order to promote open discussion.* To *sit* is to take a seat or to be in a seated position, to rest somewhere, or to occupy a place. This verb does not usually take a direct object, although you can say: *The usher sat us in the center seats of the third row from the stage.* The irregular form *sat* serves as past tense and past participle. This verb does not typically take a direct object. *The beach house sits on a hill at some distance from the shoreline.*

Other pairs of words do not sound alike at all but have similar meanings that are often confused:

AMONG/BETWEEN: The preposition *among* refers to collective arrangements; that is, use it when referring to three or more people or items. *The soccer team shared a whole case of water among themselves. Between* is also a preposition but is used in the presence of only two people or items: *Amy and Tonia split the tasks between them.*

AMOUNT/NUMBER: *Amount* is used in reference to mass nouns (also known as uncountable nouns): *The amount of bravery displayed was awe-inspiring. Number* is used in reference to countable nouns: *The recipe calls for a specific number of chocolate chips.*

FEWER/LESS: *Fewer* should be used when referring to countable objects and concepts: *Diana's yard has fewer squirrels than mine. Less* should be used only with a grammatically singular noun: *Diana's yard has less wildlife than mine.* One common misuse of *less* is a sign you probably encounter frequently at the supermarket: The *10 items or less* sign should actually be *10 items or fewer*, because the items are countable.

MANY/MUCH: *Many* modifies things that can be counted, such as plural nouns: *Samantha has many awards in her collection. Much*, on the other hand, modifies things that cannot be counted, often singular nouns: *Jim has much more money than I do.*

The SAT will also test your ability to correctly use and identify possessive pronouns, contractions, and adverbs:

ITS/IT'S: *Its* is a possessive pronoun like *his* and *hers*: *The rare book would be worth more if its cover weren't ripped. It's* is a contraction that can mean *it is*, *it has*, or *it was*: *It's been a long time since I last saw you.*

THEIR/THEY'RE/THERE: *Their* is a possessive form of the pronoun *they*: *The players respected their coach. They're* is a contraction of *they are*: *The students say they're planning to attend college. There* is used to introduce a sentence or indicate a location: *There was no water in the well when we arrived there.*

THEIRS/THERE'S: *Theirs* is the possessive plural form of the pronoun *they*: *The careless bikers admitted the fault was theirs. There's* is a contraction of *there is* or *there has*: *There's been a lot of rain this summer.*

WHOSE/WHO'S: *Whose* is a possessive pronoun used to refer to people or things: *Whose phone is ringing? Who's* is a contraction of *who is* or *who has*: *Who's planning to join us for dinner?*

COMPARISONS

The SAT will test your ability to recognize and correct improper comparisons. There are three rules governing correct comparisons:

1. Compare Logical Things

   The **price of tea** has risen sharply, while **coffee** has remained the same.

   This sentence incorrectly compares *the price of tea* to *coffee*. The sentence should read: *The* **price of tea** *has risen sharply, while the* **price of coffee** *has remained the same.*

2. Use Parallel Structure

   I prefer **hiking** rather than **to read**.

   This sentence uses the gerund verb form (*hiking*) then switches to the infinitive verb form (*to read*). To correct the sentence, make sure the verb forms are consistent: *I prefer* **to hike** *rather than* **to read**.

3. Structure Comparisons Correctly

   Some students are **better** in reading **than** they are in math.
   Other students are **as** good in math **as** they are in reading.

   Both of these sentences are correctly structured: the first with the use of *better . . . than*, and the second with the use of *as . . . as*.

When comparing like things, use adjectives that match the number of items being compared. When comparing two items or people, use the comparative form of the adjective. When comparing three or more items or people, use the superlative form.

Comparative	Superlative
Use when comparing two items.	Use when comparing three or more items.
better	best
more	most
newer	newest
older	oldest
shorter	shortest
taller	tallest
worse	worst
younger	youngest

IDIOMS

An **idiom** is a combination of words that must be used together to convey either a figurative or literal meaning. Idioms are tested in four ways on the SAT:

1. Proper Preposition Usage in Context

   *The three finalists will compete **for** the grand prize: an all-inclusive cruise to Bali.*
   *Roger will compete **against** Rafael in the final round of the tournament.*
   *I will compete **with** Deborah in the synchronized swimming competition.*

2. Verb Forms

   *The architect likes **to draft** floor plans.*
   *The architect enjoys **drafting** floor plans.*

3. Idiomatic Expressions

   Idiomatic expressions refer to words or phrases that must be used together to be correct.

   *Simone will **either** continue sleeping **or** get up and get ready for school.*
   ***Neither** the principal **nor** the teachers will tolerate tardiness.*
   *This fall, Shari is playing **not only** soccer **but also** field hockey.*

4. Implicit Double Negatives

   Some words imply a negative and therefore cannot be paired with an explicit negative.

   *Janet **cannot hardly** wait for summer vacation.*

   This sentence is incorrect as written. It should read: *Janet **can hardly** wait for summer vacation.*

Frequently Tested Prepositions	Idiomatic Expressions	Words That Can't Be Paired with Negative Words
at	as . . . as	barely
by	between . . . and	hardly
for	both . . . and	scarcely
of	either . . . or	
on	just as . . . so too	
to	neither . . . nor	
with	not only . . . but also	

Let's look at the following example of the Kaplan Method for Writing & Language in action in a short test-like passage. The left column contains text and a question similar to what you'll see on the Writing & Language Test on Test Day. The column on the right features the strategic thinking a test expert employs when approaching the passage and question presented.

Questions 1-4 are based on the following passage.

Akira Kurosawa

What do samurai,[1] cowboys, shogun,[2] gangsters, peasants, and William Shakespeare all have in common? These are just some of the varied influences on the work of Akira Kurosawa (1910–1998), a Japanese film director considered by movie critic Leonard Maltin to be "one of the undisputed giants of cinema." Over his career, Kurosawa's unique blend of Western themes and Eastern settings made him arguably the **❶ more important** Japanese filmmaker in history.

Kurosawa's style reflects his own experiences. As a young man, he studied Western art and literature, deciding to be a painter. However, World War II led Kurosawa to film; he acted as an assistant director of wartime propaganda films in Tokyo. After Japan's surrender in 1945, he took the lessons he learned in Tokyo and began making his own films— **❷ work** that took the values and traditions of the West and reinterpreted them with a Japanese sensibility, using distinctly Japanese settings and characters.

The most famous example of Kurosawa's style is his 1954 film *Seven Samurai*. Although the setting is medieval Japan, with peasants and samurai, its story is influenced by Western films: a group of villagers, terrorized by local bandits, turn to seven down-on-their-luck yet good-hearted samurai for their protection. Like movie cowboys, the samurai are romantic heroes, sure of their morals and battling clear forces of evil. This contrasts with the traditional Japanese version of a samurai as a noble and often distant, symbol of Japan's imperial heritage. To **❸ him**, the film's samurai were distinctly human characters, with both a conscience and the will to act to correct the wrongs around them.

Although Kurosawa's films enjoyed—and still enjoy—a lofty reputation in the West, Japanese audiences have regarded his work with suspicion. By using Western ideals and themes—even reinterpreting Western authors such as William Shakespeare and Fyodor Dostoyevsky—Kurosawa is regarded by many critics and moviegoers in his home country as **❹ neither** original nor particularly Japanese. They see his using Japanese culture as mere "window dressing" applied to what were essentially foreign stories. Ironically, it was Kurosawa's success that opened the door for other, more "Japanese" directors, such as Yasujiro Ozu and Kenji Mizoguchi, to gain a wider audience.

Regardless of the criticism, Kurosawa's effect on Western filmmaking is beyond dispute. Ironically, Kurosawa's films have influenced the very same American movie genres that Kurosawa admired so much. *Seven Samurai* became the basis for the American Western epic *The Magnificent Seven. Yojimbo,* another story of a samurai for hire, strongly influenced the film *A Fistful of Dollars*. Other genres benefited from Kurosawa's work as well; *Rashomon,* a crime story told from different points of view, has influenced almost every crime movie since. Finally, *The Hidden Fortress*, about two peasants escorting a princess during a war, became George Lucas's expressed basis for the science fiction masterpiece *Star Wars.*

[1] samurai: noble warriors of medieval Japan, similar to European knights

[2] shogun: military dictators of Japan from 1603 to 1868

Questions	Strategic Thinking
1. A) NO CHANGE B) important C) most important D) least important	**Step 1: Read the passage and identify the issue** The issue is Comparisons. The underlined portion contains the word "more," which is an adjective used to compare two items. **Step 2: Eliminate answer choices that do not address the issue** Eliminate A because more than two items are being compared. Eliminate B because it eliminates the comparison. Eliminate D because it changes the meaning of the sentence. **Step 3: Plug in the remaining answer choices and select the most correct, concise, and relevant one** Choice (C) is the only remaining answer choice and is therefore correct.
2. A) NO CHANGE B) works C) working D) idea	**Step 1: Read the passage and identify the issue** The issue is Noun Agreement because the underlined word (a singular noun) is a synonym for the word that precedes the dash: "films" (a plural noun). **Step 2: Eliminate answer choices that do not address the issue** Eliminate A because the singular "work" does not agree with the plural "films." Eliminate C because "working" is a verb, not a noun. Eliminate D because it changes the author's meaning. **Step 3: Plug in the remaining answer choices and select the most correct, concise, and relevant one** Choice (B) is the only remaining answer choice and is therefore correct.

Questions	Strategic Thinking
3. A) NO CHANGE B) them C) Kurosawa D) the samurai	**Step 1: Read the passage and identify the issue** The issue is Pronoun Clarity. The underlined pronoun's antecedent is unclear. **Step 2: Eliminate answer choices that do not address the issue** The most likely antecedent of the underlined pronoun "him" is Akira Kurosawa. Eliminate A because it is ambiguous as written. Eliminate B because even though the pronoun is plural, it is still ambiguous. Eliminate D because the pronoun does not refer to "the samurai." **Step 3: Plug in the remaining answer choices and select the most correct, concise, and relevant one** Choice (C) is the only remaining answer choice and is therefore correct.
4. A) NO CHANGE B) either C) never D) both	**Step 1: Read the passage and identify the issue** The issue is Idioms because the underlined word is part of an idiomatic expression. **Step 2: Eliminate answer choices that do not address the issue** "Neither...nor" is a common idiomatic expression. Eliminate B, C, and D because the sentence later uses the word "nor," which means "neither" must precede it. **Step 3: Plug in the remaining answer choices and select the most correct, concise, and relevant one** Choice (A) is the only remaining answer choice and is therefore correct.

You have seen the ways in which the SAT tests you on Usage in Writing & Language passages and the way an SAT expert approaches these types of questions.

Look at the Writing & Language passage excerpt that follows. There are four questions associated with it. Use the Kaplan Method for Writing & Language to answer the questions. Remember to look at the strategic thinking questions that have been laid out for you—some of the answers have been filled in, but you will have to fill in the answers to others.

Use your answers to the strategic thinking questions to select the correct answer, just as you will on Test Day.

Questions 5-8 are based on the following passage.

Opossum

Commonly seen rooting through the trash or slipping down a sewer grate, the opossum is actually one of North America's **⑤** best animals. While its rodent-like body seems unremarkable at first glance, the opossum is actually closely related to the kangaroo and is the only marsupial native to this continent. Indeed, like all female marsupials, the female opossum has a pouch for carrying and nursing her young. After a 12-day gestation period, thought to be the shortest of any marsupial, between 5 and 25 blind and hairless babies instinctively crawl the two inches from the birth canal to the pouch. Upon arrival, they quickly attach themselves to a nipple, drawing constant nourishment from the mother for more than two months.

The distinctive features of the opossum go beyond its surprising relation to the kangaroo. **⑥** It boasts an incredible array of 50 razor-sharp teeth, the most of any mammal in the world. The opossum is also among the most primitive of animals, having lived during the time of the dinosaurs. It has survived for millions of years by adapting to diverse habitats—including dense urban areas—and food supplies. Opossums eat beetles and even earthworms as well as tree roots, eggs, vegetables, and fruit. Today, many opossums that live in areas densely populated by humans survive on garbage and small mice. Opossums thrive in fields and woodlands, but they can also survive by digging a nest under a building or deck.

Of course, the opossum does have vulnerabilities. Its average three-year life span is not unusual for its size, typically between two and three feet long. What is unusual is that opossums continue growing throughout their lifetimes. Such a state of constant development is linked with metabolic limitations **⑦** in the amount of food and energy that can be stored within the opossum's body, requiring that ready food sources be available year-round. In addition, opossums are highly susceptible to the cold, making it rather common to see opossums with frostbitten ears and tails. Nevertheless, opossums have displayed amazing resilience over the years, often surviving attacks from intimidating predators like dogs and even hawks. While the opossum's first reaction when threatened is to begin running to the nearest tree, **⑧** their primary defense is a nervous system reaction that, when sensing danger, throws the opossum's body into a catatonic state that dramatically slows its heart rate. The opossum will then begin to drool and appear dead, another trait that only adds to the fascinating nature of these animals.

Questions	Strategic Thinking
5. A) NO CHANGE B) most unusual C) better D) abnormal	**Step 1: Read the passage and identify the issue** *What is the issue?* Comparisons. The underlined word is a superlative adjective, used to compare three or more items. **Step 2: Eliminate answer choices that do not address the issue** *What answer choice(s) can you eliminate?* _____ _____ _____ _____ **Step 3: Plug in the remaining answer choices and select the most correct, concise, and relevant one** *What is the answer?* _____
6. A) NO CHANGE B) They C) The kangaroo D) The opossum	**Step 1: Read the passage and identify the issue** *What is the issue?* Pronoun clarity. The underlined word is a pronoun that begins a sentence. **Step 2: Eliminate answer choices that do not address the issue** *To what does the underlined pronoun refer?* _____ _____ *What answer choice(s) can you eliminate?* _____ _____ _____ _____ **Step 3: Plug in the remaining answer choices and select the most correct, concise, and relevant one** *What is the answer?* _____

Questions	Strategic Thinking
7. A) NO CHANGE B) with C) on D) for	**Step 1: Read the passage and identify the issue** *What is the issue?* Idioms. The underlined word is a preposition, so the question is likely testing proper preposition usage in context. **Step 2: Eliminate answer choices that do not address the issue** *What answer choice(s) can you eliminate?* _____ _____ _____ _____ **Step 3: Plug in the remaining answer choices and select the most correct, concise, and relevant one** What is the answer? _____
8. A) NO CHANGE B) there C) its D) his	**Step 1: Read the passage and identify the issue** *What is the issue?* Pronoun-antecedent agreement. The underlined word is a pronoun in the middle of a sentence. **Step 2: Eliminate answer choices that do not address the issue** *What is the underlined pronoun's antecedent?* _____ _____ *What answer choice(s) can you eliminate?* _____ _____ _____ _____ **Step 3: Plug in the remaining answer choices and select the most correct, concise, and relevant one** *What is the answer?* _____

Now, try a test-like Writing & Language passage on your own. Give yourself 5 minutes to read the passage and answer the questions.

Questions 9-16 are based on the following passage.

The Hindenburg

Today, airships are seen mostly as advertisements hovering in the sky over sporting events. Such companies as Goodyear®, Metropolitan Life®, and Fuji Film® have all made use of "blimps" in this way. But before World War II, **9** blimps—as well as other lighter-than-air vehicles—were used as modes of transportation. One in particular, the German airship *Hindenburg*, changed the fate of airships forever. In spectacular fashion, the *Hindenburg* revealed the downside of the use of airships in transportation.

Airships enjoyed many advantages in the early twentieth century, and the *Hindenburg* was considered one of a kind. When the 804-foot *Hindenburg* was launched in 1936, it was the **10** large airship in the world. Like most airships of the period, the *Hindenburg* was built with a solid frame that encased a simple balloon filled with a light gas—in this case, hydrogen. In an age when airplanes could not carry more than 10 passengers at a time, **11** they could initially carry 50 passengers, a capacity that was later upgraded to 72.

Despite these advantages, the *Hindenburg* was hampered by many of the same drawbacks as other airships. Tickets to fly in the *Hindenburg* were not affordable for most people. The massive amount of fuel needed to not only fill the balloon **12** and to power **13** it's propellers made this airship very expensive to operate. Even with all of that fuel, the *Hindenburg* flew at a mere 76 miles per hour—a snail's pace considering that it was used for transatlantic passenger service. Because an airship is essentially a balloon with an engine, it is extremely vulnerable to air currents and stormy weather, and the *Hindenburg* was no different.

9. A) NO CHANGE
   B) the blimp
   C) the airship
   D) airplanes

10. A) NO CHANGE
    B) largest
    C) big
    D) larger

11. A) NO CHANGE
    B) it
    C) the *Hindenburg*
    D) he

12. A) NO CHANGE
    B) but also
    C) and also
    D) nor

13. A) NO CHANGE
    B) its
    C) it is
    D) their

The *Hindenburg's* fate, however, rested **14** by the most dangerous characteristic of these airships: hydrogen gas is extremely flammable. Any spark or flame that came near the gas could cause a horrific explosion, which is exactly what happened. On May 6, 1937, as the *Hindenburg* was landing in Lakehurst, New Jersey, it suddenly burst into flames, killing 36 of the 97 passengers and crew on board. This explosion, which ultimately destroyed the airship, was believed to have been caused by a discharge of electricity in the air, which reacted with a small leak in the **15** balloons.

However, when the disaster occurred, the airship was already obsolete as a mode of transportation. By the 1940s, commercial airplanes had advanced in development far beyond the airship's capacity. Today, airplanes cost much less to operate and fly at more than seven times the speed of the *Hindenburg*, and airline tickets are far more affordable. The airship thus became outdated as a mode of passenger service and acquired **16** their modern-day role as an advertising platform.

14. A) NO CHANGE
    B) in
    C) on
    D) with

15. A) NO CHANGE
    B) blimps
    C) hydrogen
    D) balloon

16. A) NO CHANGE
    B) its
    C) it's
    D) they're

Answers & Explanations for this chapter begin on page 722.

EXTRA PRACTICE

Questions 1-11 are based on the following passage and supplementary material.

Batteries Out in the Cold

Many people have trouble starting their cars on a cold winter morning. In a cold car, the engine turns over more slowly, **①** <u>since</u> it sometimes does not turn over at all. Car owners may **②** <u>credit</u> their cold engines, but the real problem is a cold battery.

3 [1] A motor is generally connected to its circuit by using a battery. [2] When a motor is hooked up in a circuit with a battery, electrons move through the circuit, creating a current. [3] Likewise, decreasing the number of electrons moving will decrease the amount of power available. [4] Increasing the number of electrons moving increases the current and so increases the amount of power available to the motor.

1. A) NO CHANGE
   B) and
   C) but
   D) yet

2. A) NO CHANGE
   B) criticize
   C) accuse
   D) blame

3. To enhance the logical sequence of paragraph 2, sentence 3 should be placed
   A) where it is now.
   B) before sentence 1.
   C) before sentence 2.
   D) after sentence 4.

4 **5** <u>A typical car battery, uses lead, and sulfuric acid.</u> At the negative pole, lead reacts with sulfate ions in the solution around it to form lead sulfate, giving off electrons. At the positive pole, lead oxide

4. Which choice most effectively establishes the main topic of the paragraph?

A) Electrons move through a battery as a result of two chemical reactions occurring within the battery, one at each pole.

B) Sulfuric acid can cause burns to the skin, eyes, lungs, and digestive tract, and severe exposure can result in death.

C) In a direct current circuit, one pole is always negative, the other pole is always positive, and the electrons flow in one direction only.

D) Lead sulfate is toxic by inhalation, ingestion, and skin contact; repeated exposure may lead to anemia, kidney damage, and other serious health issues.

5. A) NO CHANGE

B) A typical car battery uses lead, and sulfuric acid.

C) A typical car battery, uses lead and sulfuric acid.

D) A typical car battery uses lead and sulfuric acid.

6 <u>would have reacted</u> with sulfate ions, hydrogen ions, and electrons in the same solution to also form lead sulfate, taking in electrons. The electrons produced at the negative pole flow through the **7** <u>boundary</u> to the positive pole, providing an electric current in the circuit.

8 A battery charger uses the same reactions, but in reverse. As the current flows in the opposite direction, supplied by house current or a generator, the lead sulfate at the positive pole reacts to change back to lead oxide.

Temperature affects the speed of chemical reactions in two ways. For a chemical reaction to happen, the reactants must collide with enough energy to get the reaction going. As the temperature increases, the motion of the reactants increases. The increased motion of the reactants increases the **9** <u>practicality</u> that they will collide and therefore increases the rate of reaction. The amount of energy in the reactants also increases as temperature increases.

6. A) NO CHANGE
   B) did react
   C) reacts
   D) reacted

7. A) NO CHANGE
   B) cycle
   C) circuit
   D) path

8. Which sentence adds supporting information to paragraph 4?
   A) Lead oxide, sometimes called litharge, is an inorganic compound with a formula including lead and oxygen.
   B) At the same time, the lead sulfate at the negative pole reacts to change back to lead metal.
   C) The difference between a house current and a generator is that the generator converts mechanical energy to electrical energy for use in an external circuit.
   D) Using a battery charger incorrectly can be dangerous since a car battery contains chemicals that produce hydrogen, a potentially volatile gas.

9. A) NO CHANGE
   B) way
   C) question
   D) probability

This makes it more likely that any two colliding reactants will have enough energy to react, and so ⑩ its rate of reaction increases.

Low temperatures have the opposite effect from high temperatures. The chemicals in the battery react more slowly at low temperatures, due both to fewer collisions and less energetic collisions, so fewer electrons move through the circuit. A cold battery takes longer to charge and often cannot provide enough energy to start a car. A cold car that will not start will need either additional power from another car to get the motor moving or a source of heat to warm up the battery and speed up the chemical reactions. Research conducted by FleetCarma in Waterloo, Ontario, demonstrates that ⑪ colder temperatures negatively affect the distance electric cars can travel.

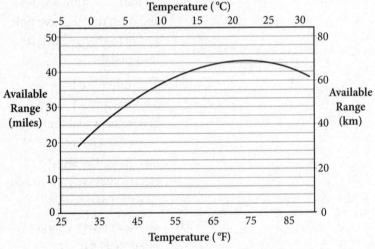

Average Range of Electric Cars as a Function of Temperature

Adapted from research published by FleetCarma, Waterloo, Ontario.

10. A)   NO CHANGE

    B)   it's

    C)   their

    D)   they're

11. Which choice completes the sentence with accurate data based on the graph?

    A)   NO CHANGE

    B)   the number of kilometers an electric car can travel declines as the outside temperature increases.

    C)   temperatures below 15°C make it extremely difficult to start an electric car.

    D)   once the electric car's battery has an alternate heat source by which to start, the distance the car can travel is greatly increased.

PART THREE

The Essay

The Essay

BY THE END OF THIS UNIT, YOU WILL BE ABLE TO:

1. Apply the Kaplan Method for the SAT Essay

2. Use the Kaplan Template for the SAT Essay to create an effective outline

CHAPTER 20

The Kaplan Method for the SAT Essay

CHAPTER OBJECTIVES

By the end of this chapter, you will be able to:

1. Apply the Kaplan Method for the SAT Essay to produce a clear analysis of a source text

SMARTPOINTS

Point Value	SmartPoint Category
Point Builder	The Kaplan Method for the SAT Essay

THE SAT ESSAY IS OPTIONAL. SHOULD YOU WRITE IT?

One of the biggest changes for the 2016 SAT is the fact that the Essay Test is now optional. If you don't want to spend 50 minutes writing an essay, you certainly don't have to. You are free to leave after the final multiple choice section of the test.

However, just because you can leave without completing the Essay Test doesn't mean that you should. If you can state with 100 percent certainty that the colleges to which you are applying do not require the essay component of the SAT, feel free to omit it on Test Day. However, if you are unsure, or don't yet have a finalized list of colleges, Kaplan recommends you complete the Essay Test for the following reasons:

First, consider the fact that the SAT is not an exam you can take in bits and pieces. If you want to take the Essay Test at a later date, you'll have to sit through the entire SAT again. That can translate to a lot of unnecessary stress during your senior year.

Second, if the colleges you apply to don't require you to take the Essay Test, they won't negatively judge you if you do. There is nothing to lose by completing the essay. You might get a great score and add a few more possibilities to your list of potential schools.

Finally, while the Essay Test question on the new SAT will be challenging, it is also standardized. That means you can learn how to write a high-scoring essay by putting in some time, effort, and willingness to practice. This chapter is a great place to start.

THE KAPLAN METHOD FOR THE SAT ESSAY

The SAT Essay, while optional, presents you with a challenge: to read and understand a high-quality source text and write an essay analyzing the author's argument in 50 minutes. By using the Kaplan Method for the SAT Essay, you will be able to make the most out of those 50 minutes and produce a high-scoring written response to a previously published, sophisticated source.

The Kaplan Method for the SAT Essay consists of four steps:

Step 1: Read the source text, taking notes on how the author uses:

- Evidence to support claims
- Reasoning to develop ideas and to connect claims and evidence
- Stylistic or persuasive elements to add power to the ideas expressed

Step 2: Develop an outline of the features you will analyze in your response

Step 3: Write your essay

Step 4: Check your essay for mistakes in grammar, spelling, and clarity

Let's take a closer look at each step.

Step 1: Read the source text, taking notes on how the author uses:

- **evidence to support claims**
- **reasoning to develop ideas and to connect claims and evidence**
- **stylistic or persuasive elements to add power to the ideas expressed**

What is the source text?

The source text for the SAT essay will consist of a passage that is very similar to the passages you'll see in the Reading Test. It will typically be 500–750 words and will deal with topics of general interest in the arts, sciences, and public life. In many cases, the passages will be biased in favor of the author's argument.

While the source text changes from test to test, the directions and essay prompt remain similar. Spend more time reading and understanding the text—the prompt will likely be very similar to other prompts that you've encountered.

What kinds of notes should I take?

The notes you take while reading the source text are similar to those you would take when creating a Passage Map on the Reading Test (see chapter 10). However, these notes will focus on how the author connects central ideas and important details.

Your notes should focus on:

- evidence to support claims (e.g., cited data or statistics, or authoritative sources that support the author's argument)

- reasoning to develop ideas and make connections (e.g., the author explains his logic for using a specific piece of evidence to support a specific claim)

- stylistic or persuasive elements to add power to the ideas expressed (e.g., using figurative language, irony, metaphor, and other elements to appeal to emotions)

In addition to taking notes in the margins of the passage, it is also helpful to underline and circle the following:

- central ideas

- important details

- errors of fact or interpretation

- textual evidence (quotations, paraphrases, or both)

You should spend approximately 10 minutes on Step 1.

Step 2: Develop an outline of the features you will analyze in your response

Why do I need an outline?

Creating an outline before you write your essay is a huge time-saver, which is essential when you have only 50 minutes to complete the SAT Essay Test. Spending the first part of the allotted time effectively (i.e., reading and taking notes on the source text and creating an outline) will lead to a well-organized, more convincing essay. You'll also find that organizing your thoughts ahead of time will enable you to write much more quickly!

What should I put in my outline?

Kaplan has created an efficient and effective template to outline the SAT Essay. The template consists of tasks you should complete and questions you should ask before you begin writing. You do not need to answer the questions in complete sentences—sketch out your notes and use abbreviations that you understand.

The six questions for each body paragraph may seem like a lot, but answering these questions before you write will make the writing itself that much easier.

Using the template will prevent you from encountering a writing or thinking block. With the template and the Kaplan Method, you will know what you want to write about the source text and not waste any time.

The Kaplan Template for the SAT Essay can be found on page 450.

You should spend approximately 8 minutes on Step 2.

> ✔ **On Test Day**
>
> You will not be able to bring these questions with you to Test Day. Therefore, it is important that you memorize the gist and logical flow of the questions well before Test Day so that asking these questions is second nature to you when you sit down to write your essay.

Step 3: Write your essay

After you have read and analyzed the source text, your next goal is to write a cohesive essay that demonstrates your use and command of standard written English. To demonstrate your proficiency, you must:

- Provide your own precise central claim
- Use a variety of sentence structures
- Employ precise word choice
- Maintain a constant and appropriate style and tone

You should spend approximately 30 minutes on Step 3.

Step 4: Check your essay for mistakes in grammar, spelling, and clarity

While a few grammar and spelling mistakes won't drastically harm your SAT Essay score, setting aside some time to proofread can help you catch careless errors that you can easily correct, thereby increasing your Writing score on the SAT Essay.

You should spend the remaining 2 minutes on Step 4.

THE KAPLAN TEMPLATE FOR THE SAT ESSAY

Introductory Paragraph:

To demonstrate that you understand the source text, **paraphrase the author's central idea or claim:** _____

_____

_____

_____

> ✔ **Definition**
>
> Features are the key elements of the essay that you marked in your notes. They could include stylistic techniques, like irony, or data, like statistics, used to bolster a claim.

List the three features you will analyze in your essay.

1. Feature #1

2. Feature #2

3. Feature #3

Body Paragraph Feature #1: _____

Where does the author use this feature? _____

What example(s) of this feature can you cite from the source text (direct quotations or paraphrases)?
_____
_____
_____

How does this example interrelate with the author's central claim? _____
_____
_____

How does this feature affect the author's audience? _____
_____
_____

Does achieving this effect help build the author's argument? Why or why not? _____
_____
_____

What are the function of this feature and example in the overall text? _____
_____
_____

Body Paragraph Feature #2: _____

Where does the author use this feature? _____

What example(s) of this feature can you cite from the source text (direct quotations or paraphrases)?
_____
_____
_____

How does this example interrelate with the author's central claim? _____
_____
_____

How does this feature affect the author's audience? _____
_____
_____

Does achieving this effect help build the author's argument? Why or why not? _____
_____
_____
_____

What are the function of this feature and example in the overall text? _____
_____
_____

Body Paragraph Feature #3: _____

Where does the author use this feature? _____

What example(s) of this feature can you cite from the source text (direct quotations or paraphrases)?
_____
_____
_____

How does this example interrelate with the author's central claim? _____
_____
_____

How does this feature affect the author's audience? _____
_____
_____

Does achieving this effect help build the author's argument? Why or why not? _____
_____
_____
_____

What are the function of this feature and example in the overall text? _____

_____

_____

Conclusion:

What is the author's overall purpose for writing this passage? _____

_____

_____

What is the author's central argument or claim? _____

_____

_____

How did the author build his or her argument or claim? <u>By using Feature #1, Feature #2, and Feature #3.</u>

THE SAT ESSAY PROMPT

As mentioned previously in this chapter, the SAT Essay source text will change from administration to administration, but the prompt will remain largely the same in both format and wording.

Become familiar with the idea behind the prompt and assignment as soon as you can so that on Test Day, you will be able to focus on reading, analyzing, and writing, rather than figuring out what the prompt is asking you to accomplish.

The generic SAT Essay prompt is as follows:

As you read the passage below, consider how [the author] uses

- evidence, such as facts or examples, to support claims.

- reasoning to develop ideas and to connect claims and evidence.

- stylistic or persuasive elements, such as word choice or appeals to emotion, to add power to the ideas expressed.

Source Text Will Appear Here

Write an essay in which you explain how [the author] builds an argument to persuade [his/her] audience that [author's claim]. In your essay, analyze how [the author] uses one or more of the features listed previously (or features of your own choice) to strengthen the logic and persuasiveness of [his/her] argument. Be sure your analysis focuses on the most relevant aspects of the passage.

Your essay should not explain whether you agree with [the author's] claims, but rather explain how [the author] builds an argument to persuade [his/her] audience.

SAT ESSAY SCORING RUBRIC

There are three different scores for the SAT Essay: Reading, Analysis, and Writing. Each category will be scored on a scale of 1 to 4. The scores you receive will range from 2 to 8, as they will be the scores of two raters.

The raters will use the following rubric to determine each area score.

	1	2
Reading	• Demonstrates **little or no comprehension** of the source text • Fails to show an understanding of the text's central idea(s), and may include only details without reference to central idea(s) • May contain numerous errors of fact and/or interpretation with regard to the text • Makes little or no use of textual evidence	• Demonstrates **some comprehension** of the source text • Shows an understanding of the text's central idea(s) but not of important details • May contain errors of fact and/or interpretation with regard to the text • Makes limited and/or haphazard use of textual evidence
Analysis	• Offers **little or no analysis or ineffective analysis** of the source text and demonstrates **little to no understanding** of the analytical task • Identifies without explanation some aspects of the author's use of evidence, reasoning, and/or stylistic and persuasive elements, and/or feature(s) of the student's own choosing • Numerous aspects of analysis are unwarranted based on the text • Contains little or no support for claim(s) or point(s) made, or support is largely irrelevant • May not focus on features of the text that are relevant to addressing the task • Offers no discernible analysis (e.g., is largely or exclusively summary)	• Offers **limited analysis** of the source text and demonstrates only **partial understanding** of the analytical task • Identifies and attempts to describe the author's use of evidence, reasoning, and/or stylistic and persuasive elements, and/or feature(s) of the student's own choosing, but merely asserts rather than explains their importance • One or more aspects of analysis are unwarranted based on the text • Contains little or no support for claim(s) or point(s) made • May lack a clear focus on those features of the text that are most relevant to addressing the task
Writing	• Demonstrates **little or no cohesion** and **inadequate skill** in the use and control of language • May lack a clear central claim or controlling idea • Lacks a recognizable introduction and conclusion; does not have a discernible progression of ideas • Lacks variety in sentence structures; sentence structures may be repetitive; demonstrates general and vague word choice; word choice may be poor or inaccurate; may lack a formal style and objective tone • Shows a weak control of the conventions of standard written English and may contain numerous errors that undermine the quality of writing	• Demonstrates **little or no cohesion** and **limited skill** in the use and control of language • May lack a clear central claim or controlling idea or may deviate from the claim or idea • May include an ineffective introduction and/or conclusion; may demonstrate some progression of ideas within paragraphs but not throughout • Has limited variety in sentence structures; sentence structures may be repetitive; demonstrates general or vague word choice; word choice may be repetitive; may deviate noticeably from a formal style and objective tone • Shows a limited control of the conventions of standard written English and contains errors that detract from the quality of writing and may impede understanding

	3	4
Reading	• Demonstrates **effective comprehension** of the source text • Shows an understanding of the text's central idea(s) and important details • Is free of substantive errors of fact and interpretation with regard to the text • Makes appropriate use of textual evidence	• Demonstrates **thorough comprehension** of the source text • Shows an understanding of the text's central idea(s) and most important details and how they interrelate • Is free of errors of fact or interpretation with regard to the text • Makes skillful use of textual evidence
Analysis	• Offers an **effective analysis** of the source text and demonstrates an **understanding** of the analytical task • Competently evaluates the author's use of evidence, reasoning, and/or stylistic and persuasive elements, and/or feature(s) of the student's own choosing • Contains relevant and sufficient support for claim(s) or point(s) made • Focuses primarily on those features of the text that are most relevant to addressing the task	• Offers an **insightful analysis** of the source text and demonstrates a **sophisticated understanding** of the analytical task • Offers a thorough, well-considered evaluation of the author's use of evidence, reasoning, and/or stylistic and persuasive elements, and/or feature(s) of the student's own choosing • Contains relevant, sufficient, and strategically chosen support for claim(s) or point(s) made • Focuses consistently on those features of the text that are most relevant to addressing the task
Writing	• Is **mostly cohesive** and demonstrates **effective use and control** of language • Includes a central claim or implicit controlling idea • Includes an effective introduction and conclusion; demonstrates a clear progression of ideas both within paragraphs and throughout the essay • Has variety in sentence structures; demonstrates some precise word choice; maintains a formal style and objective tone • Shows a good control of the conventions of standard written English and is free of significant errors that detract from the quality of writing	• Is **cohesive** and demonstrates a **highly effective use and command** of language • Includes a precise central claim • Includes a skillful introduction and conclusion; demonstrates a deliberate and highly effective progression of ideas both within paragraphs and throughout the essay • Has a wide variety of sentence structures; demonstrates a consistent use of precise word choice; maintains a formal style and objective tone • Shows a strong command of the conventions of standard written English and is free or virtually free of errors

Look at the test-like source text and prompt that follows. Notice what kinds of notes an SAT expert takes in the margins of the passage. Then, look at how the SAT expert answers the Kaplan Template questions for the introduction and one of the body paragraphs of his own essay and uses those answers to write those sections.

As you read the passage below, consider how Tony Blair uses

- evidence, such as facts or examples, to support claims.

- reasoning to develop ideas and to connect claims and evidence.

- stylistic or persuasive elements, such as word choice or appeals to emotion, to add power to the ideas expressed.

Adapted from British Prime Minister Tony Blair's speech to American citizens following 9/11/2001.

The only purpose of being in politics is to strive for the values and ideals we believe in: freedom, justice, what we Europeans call solidarity but you might call respect for and help for others. These are the decent democratic values we all avow. But alongside the values we know we need a hard-headed pragmatism—a *realpolitik*— required to give us any chance of translating those values into the practical world we live in.

juxt. btwn. Euro & aud. (U.S.)

The same tension exists in the two views of international affairs. One is utilitarian: each nation maximizes its own self-interest. The other is utopian: we try to create a better world. Today I want to suggest that more than ever before those two views are merging.

ev: util. vs utop. views

I advocate an enlightened self-interest that puts fighting for our values right at the heart of the policies necessary to protect our nations. Engagement in the world on the basis of these values, not isolationism from it, is the hard-headed pragmatism for the 21st century.

Why? In part it is because the countries and people of the world today are more interdependent than ever. In truth, it is very rare today that trouble in one part of the globe remains limited in its effect. Not just in security, but in trade and finance—witness the crisis of 1998 which began in Thailand and ended in Brazil—the world is interlocked.

rhet. ?

ev: 1998 crisis

This is heightened by mass communications and technology. In Queen Victoria's time, reports of battles came back weeks or months after they were won or lost. Today we see them enacted live on the BBC, Sky or CNN. Their very visibility, immediate and in Technicolor, inflames feelings that can spread worldwide across different ethnic, religious, and cultural communities.

ev: Queen Vic. time's reports vs today's

So today, more than ever, "their" problem becomes "our" problem. Instability is contagious and, again today, more than ever, nations, at least most of them, crave stability. That's for a simple reason. Our people want it, because without it, they can't do business and prosper. What brings nations together—what brought them together post–September 11—is the international recognition that the world needs order. Disorder is the enemy of progress.

quotes → irony

The struggle is for stability, for the security within which progress can be made. Of course, countries want to protect their territorial integrity but few are into empire-building. This is especially true of democracies whose people vote for higher living standards and punish governments who don't deliver them. For 2,000 years Europe fought over territory.

ex: 2000 year Eur. fight

Today boundaries are virtually fixed. Governments and people know that any territorial ambition threatens stability, and instability threatens prosperity.

And of course the surest way to stability is through the very values of freedom, democracy and justice. Where these are strong, the people push for moderation and order. Where they are absent, regimes act unchecked by popular accountability and pose a threat; and the threat spreads.

logic & results

So the promotion of these values becomes not just right in itself but part of our long-term security and prosperity. We can't intervene in every case. Not all the wrongs of the world can be put right, but where disorder threatens us all, we should act.

Like it or not, whether you are a utilitarian or a utopian, the world is interdependent. One consequence of this is that foreign and domestic policy are ever more closely interwoven.

what prompted speech

It was September 11 that brought these thoughts into sharper focus. Watching the horror unfold, imagining the almost unimaginable suffering of the thousands of innocent victims of the terror and carnage, the dominant emotion after the obvious feelings of revulsion, sympathy and anger was determination.

juxt. "imagining… unimaginable"

The guts and spirit of the people of New York and America in the aftermath of that terrible day were not just admirable, they were awesome. They were the best riposte to the terrorists that humanity could give and you should be very proud of that. I want you to know too that the British people were with you from the first moment, and we will always be with you at times like those. We are not half-hearted friends and we never will be. But the determination must be not just to pursue those responsible and bring them to justice but to learn from September 11. There is a real danger we forget the lessons of September 11. Human beings recover from tragedy and the memory becomes less fraught. That is a healthy part of living. But we should learn from our experience.

praising aud.

promises

The <u>most obvious lesson is indeed our</u> (interdependence.) For a time our world stood still. Quite apart from our security, the shock impacted on economic confidence, on business, on trade, and it is only now, with the terrorist network on the run, that confidence is really returning. <u>Every nation in the world</u> felt the reverberation of that fateful day. And that <u>has been well illustrated</u> by the role which the United Nations—under Kofi Annan's excellent leadership—has played since September 11.

ex: U.N. & Kofi A.
global effects of 9/11

So if we didn't know it before, we know now: these events and our response to them shape the fate <u>not of one nation but of one world</u>.

For America, it has laid bare the reality. American power affects the world fundamentally. It is there. It is real. It is never irrelevant. It can affect the world for good, or for bad. Stand aside or engage; it never fails to affect.

short sentences

You know I want it engaged. Under President Bush, I am confident it will be and for good. But if that's what I and many others want, it comes at a price for us too. It means we don't shirk our responsibility. It means that when America is fighting for those values, then, however tough, we fight with her. No grandstanding, no offering implausible but impractical advice from the comfort of the touchline, no wishing away the hard not the easy choices, but working together, side by side.

personification of America

Write an essay in which you explain how Tony Blair builds an argument to persuade his audience that imbuing the world with values must be approached pragmatically and universally. In your essay, analyze how Blair uses one or more of the features listed above (or features of your own choice) to strengthen the logic and persuasiveness of his argument. Be sure your analysis focuses on the most relevant aspects of the passage.

Your essay should not explain whether you agree with Blair's claims, but rather explain how Blair builds an argument to persuade his audience.

Now that you've seen what kinds of notes a test expert takes for the SAT Essay source text, look at how he or she does some analysis by using the Kaplan Template to create an outline.

While the following example includes full sentences and quotations from the source text, please know that you should use shorthand and ellipses on Test Day; it's not your outline that's evaluated, but your actual essay.

Introductory Paragraph:

To demonstrate that you understand the source text, **paraphrase the author's central idea or claim**: Because the 21st-century world is interdependent, all nations must fight together for the values of freedom, democracy, and justice.

List the three features you will analyze in your essay.

1. Irony

2. Historical Evidence

3. Juxtaposition

Body Paragraph #1: Irony

Where does the author use this feature?

In the beginning of the sixth paragraph.

What example(s) of this feature can you cite from the source text (direct quotations or paraphrases)?

The use of quotation marks around the words "their" and "our." Also: "Like it or not, whether you are a utilitarian or a utopian, the world is interdependent."

How does this example interrelate with the author's central claim?

By using quotation marks, Blair is suggesting that there is no real difference between "their" problem and "our" problem. The "us versus them" mentality is no more because of the "international recognition that the world needs order."

How does this feature affect the author's audience?

By pointing out the silliness of the "us versus them" mentality, Blair makes his audience realize that different countries with different ideologies can still work together to fight the same battles to achieve the same goals.

Does achieving this effect help build the author's argument? Why or why not?

Yes, because it reinforces a lack of divide and that the world is "interdependent."

What is the function of this feature and example in the overall text?

To serve as a rhetorical reminder or example that one nation's tragedy affects many other nations: "For a time our world stood still . . . Every nation in the world felt the reverberation of that fateful day."

Now, look at how these notes translate into the first two paragraphs of a high-scoring student response to the SAT Essay.

In his speech to American citizens after the events of September 11, 2001, British Prime Minister Tony Blair asserted that because of the interdependent state of the world in the 21st century, all nations must band together in the fight for the values of freedom, democracy, and justice. Blair effectively conveys this argument by using irony, relevant historical examples as evidence, and juxtaposition.

In the beginning of the sixth paragraph, Blair uses quotation marks around the words "their" and "our," stating, "So today, more than ever, 'their' problem becomes 'our' problem." By using quotation marks around these opposing plural pronouns, Blair reveals the irony of the terms in the 21st-century global context. There is no "their" and no "our"—the preconceived notion of an "us versus them" mentality no longer applies to the interdependent state of the world. Blair supports this implication by emphasizing that there is an "international recognition that the world needs order." By highlighting the impracticality of the "us versus them" mentality, Blair convinces his audience that different countries must unite in order to achieve common goals, reinforcing his recurring characterization of the world as "interdependent." The use of irony through the quotation marks serves as a rhetorical reminder or example that one nation's tragedy (like 9/11) is not isolated: "it can affect the world for good, or for bad."

You have seen the kinds of notes SAT experts take and the strategic thinking questions they ask while planning their responses to the SAT Essay source text.

Based on the prompt on pages 456–458, use the Kaplan Template questions to plan an additional body paragraph for the response essay. You may use one of the other two features mentioned on page 459 (Historical Evidence or Juxtaposition) or come up with one of your own to answer the questions for the template.

Body Paragraph Feature: _____

Where does the author use this feature? _____

What example(s) of this feature can you cite from the source text (direct quotations or para-phrases)? _____
_____
_____
_____

How does this example interrelate with the author's central claim? _____
_____
_____
_____

How does this feature affect the author's audience? _____
_____
_____
_____

Does achieving this effect help build the author's argument? Why or why not? _____
_____
_____
_____
_____

What are the function of this feature and example in the overall text? _____
_____
_____
_____

Now, use your answers to the Kaplan Template questions you completed on page 461 to write a full body paragraph on the lines that follow. Give yourself 8 minutes to write the paragraph.

_____

_____

_____

_____

_____

_____

_____

_____

_____

_____

_____

_____

_____

_____

_____

_____

_____

_____

_____

_____

_____

_____

_____

_____

_____

_____

_____

_____

EXTRA PRACTICE

As you read the passage below, consider how Emmeline Pankhurst uses

- evidence, such as facts or examples, to support claims.

- reasoning to develop ideas and to connect claims and evidence.

- stylistic or persuasive elements, such as word choice or appeals to emotion, to add power to the ideas expressed.

Adapted from "Freedom or Death," a speech delivered by Emmeline Pankhurst on November 13, 1913, in Hartford, Connecticut

Mrs. Hepburn, ladies, and gentlemen:

Tonight I am not here to advocate woman suffrage. American suffragists can do that very well for themselves. I am here as a soldier who has temporarily left the field of battle in order to explain what civil war is like when civil war is waged by women. I am here as a person who, according to the law courts of my country, it has been decided, is of no value to the community at all: and I am adjudged because of my life to be a dangerous person.

Now, first of all I want to make you understand the inevitableness of revolution and civil war, even on the part of women, when you reach a certain stage in the development of a community's life. It is quite easy for you to understand the desirability of revolution if I were a man. If an Irish revolutionary had addressed this meeting, and many have addressed meetings all over the United States during the last twenty or thirty years, it would not be necessary for that revolutionary to explain the need of revolution beyond saying that the people of his country were denied—and by people, meaning men—were denied the right of self-government. That would explain the whole situation. If I were a man and I said to you, "I come from a country which professes to have representative institutions and yet denies me, a taxpayer, an inhabitant of the country, representative rights," you would at once understand that that human being, being a man, was justified in the adoption of revolutionary methods to get representative institutions. But since I am a woman it is necessary in the twentieth century to explain why women have adopted revolutionary methods in order to win the rights of citizenship.

You see, in spite of a good deal that we hear about revolutionary methods not being necessary for American women, we women, in trying to make our case clear, always have to make as part of our argument, and urge upon men in our audience the fact—a very simple fact—that women are human beings. I want to put a few political arguments before you—not arguments for the suffrage, because I said when I opened, I didn't mean to do that—but arguments for the adoption of militant methods in order to win political rights.

Suppose the men of Hartford had a grievance, and they laid that grievance before their legislature, and the legislature obstinately refused to listen to them, or to remove their grievance, what would be the proper and the constitutional and the practical way of getting their grievance removed? Well, it is perfectly obvious at the next general election, when the legislature is elected, the men of Hartford would turn out that legislature and elect a new one: entirely change the personnel of an obstinate legislature.

But let the men of Hartford imagine that they were not in the position of being voters at all, that they were governed without their consent being obtained, that the legislature turned an absolutely deaf ear to their demands, what would the men of Hartford do then? They couldn't vote the legislature out. They would have to make a choice of two evils: they would either have to submit indefinitely to an unjust state of affairs, or they would have to rise up and adopt some of the antiquated means by which men in the past got their grievances remedied. We know what happened when your forefathers decided that they must have representation for taxation, many, many years ago. When they felt they couldn't wait any longer, when they laid all the arguments before an obstinate British government that they could think of, and when their arguments were absolutely disregarded, when every other means had failed, they began by the tea party at Boston, and they went on until they had won the independence of the United States of America. That is what happened in the old days.

It is perfectly evident to any logical mind that when you have got the vote, you can get out of any legislature whatever you want, or, if you cannot get it, you can send them about their business and choose other people who will be more attentive to your demands, But, it is clear to the meanest intelligence that if you have not got the vote, you must either submit to laws just or unjust, administration just or unjust, or the time inevitably comes when you will revolt against that injustice and use violent means to put an end to it.

Write an essay in which you explain how Emmeline Pankhurst builds an argument to persuade her audience that violent as well as nonviolent protest tactics are necessary and justifiable to gain political rights for women. In your essay, analyze how Pankhurst uses one or more of the features listed in the box above (or features of your own choice) to strengthen the logic and persuasiveness of her argument. Be sure that your analysis focuses on the most relevant features of the passage.

Your essay should not explain whether you agree with Pankhurst's claims, but rather explain how Pankhurst builds an argument to persuade her audience.

PART FOUR

Practice Test

HOW TO SCORE YOUR PRACTICE TESTS

For each subject area in the practice test, convert your raw score, or the number of questions you answered correctly, to a scaled score using the table below. To get your raw score for Evidence-Based Reading & Writing, add the total number of Reading questions you answered correctly to the total number of Writing questions you answered correctly; for Math, add the number of questions you answered correctly for the Math—No Calculator and Math—Calculator sections.

Evidence-Based Reading and Writing		Math		Evidence-Based Reading and Writing		Math	
TOTAL Raw Score	Scaled Score	Raw Score	Scaled Score	TOTAL Raw Score	Scaled Score	Raw Score	Scaled Score
0	200	0	200	49	490	49	700
1	200	1	220	50	500	50	710
2	210	2	240	51	500	51	720
3	220	3	260	52	510	52	740
4	240	4	290	53	510	53	750
5	260	5	310	54	520	54	760
6	270	6	320	55	520	55	770
7	270	7	330	56	530	56	780
8	290	8	340	57	530	57	790
9	290	9	360	58	540	58	800
10	300	10	370	59	540		
11	300	11	380	60	550		
12	310	12	390	61	550		
13	320	13	400	62	560		
14	320	14	410	63	560		
15	330	15	420	64	570		
16	330	16	430	65	570		
17	340	17	430	66	580		
18	340	18	440	67	580		
19	350	19	450	68	590		
20	350	20	450	69	590		
21	360	21	460	70	600		
22	360	22	470	71	600		
23	370	23	480	72	610		
24	370	24	490	73	610		
25	370	25	500	74	610		
26	380	26	510	75	620		
27	380	27	520	76	620		
28	380	28	530	77	630		
29	380	29	540	78	630		
30	390	30	540	79	640		
31	390	31	550	80	640		
32	400	32	560	81	660		
33	400	33	560	82	660		
34	410	34	570	83	670		
35	410	35	580	84	680		
36	420	36	590	85	690		
37	430	37	600	86	700		
38	430	38	600	87	700		
39	440	39	610	88	710		
40	440	40	620	89	710		
41	450	41	630	90	730		
42	450	42	640	91	740		
43	460	43	640	92	750		
44	460	44	660	93	760		
45	470	45	670	94	780		
46	480	46	670	95	790		
47	480	47	680	96	800		
48	490	48	690				

SAT PRACTICE TEST ANSWER SHEET

Remove (or photocopy) this answer sheet and use it to complete the test. See the answer key following the test when finished.

Start with number 1 for each section. If a section has fewer questions than answer spaces, leave the extra spaces blank.

SECTION 1

1. Ⓐ Ⓑ Ⓒ Ⓓ
2. Ⓐ Ⓑ Ⓒ Ⓓ
3. Ⓐ Ⓑ Ⓒ Ⓓ
4. Ⓐ Ⓑ Ⓒ Ⓓ
5. Ⓐ Ⓑ Ⓒ Ⓓ
6. Ⓐ Ⓑ Ⓒ Ⓓ
7. Ⓐ Ⓑ Ⓒ Ⓓ
8. Ⓐ Ⓑ Ⓒ Ⓓ
9. Ⓐ Ⓑ Ⓒ Ⓓ
10. Ⓐ Ⓑ Ⓒ Ⓓ
11. Ⓐ Ⓑ Ⓒ Ⓓ
12. Ⓐ Ⓑ Ⓒ Ⓓ
13. Ⓐ Ⓑ Ⓒ Ⓓ

14. Ⓐ Ⓑ Ⓒ Ⓓ
15. Ⓐ Ⓑ Ⓒ Ⓓ
16. Ⓐ Ⓑ Ⓒ Ⓓ
17. Ⓐ Ⓑ Ⓒ Ⓓ
18. Ⓐ Ⓑ Ⓒ Ⓓ
19. Ⓐ Ⓑ Ⓒ Ⓓ
20. Ⓐ Ⓑ Ⓒ Ⓓ
21. Ⓐ Ⓑ Ⓒ Ⓓ
22. Ⓐ Ⓑ Ⓒ Ⓓ
23. Ⓐ Ⓑ Ⓒ Ⓓ
24. Ⓐ Ⓑ Ⓒ Ⓓ
25. Ⓐ Ⓑ Ⓒ Ⓓ
26. Ⓐ Ⓑ Ⓒ Ⓓ

27. Ⓐ Ⓑ Ⓒ Ⓓ
28. Ⓐ Ⓑ Ⓒ Ⓓ
29. Ⓐ Ⓑ Ⓒ Ⓓ
30. Ⓐ Ⓑ Ⓒ Ⓓ
31. Ⓐ Ⓑ Ⓒ Ⓓ
32. Ⓐ Ⓑ Ⓒ Ⓓ
33. Ⓐ Ⓑ Ⓒ Ⓓ
34. Ⓐ Ⓑ Ⓒ Ⓓ
35. Ⓐ Ⓑ Ⓒ Ⓓ
36. Ⓐ Ⓑ Ⓒ Ⓓ
37. Ⓐ Ⓑ Ⓒ Ⓓ
38. Ⓐ Ⓑ Ⓒ Ⓓ
39. Ⓐ Ⓑ Ⓒ Ⓓ

40. Ⓐ Ⓑ Ⓒ Ⓓ
41. Ⓐ Ⓑ Ⓒ Ⓓ
42. Ⓐ Ⓑ Ⓒ Ⓓ
43. Ⓐ Ⓑ Ⓒ Ⓓ
44. Ⓐ Ⓑ Ⓒ Ⓓ
45. Ⓐ Ⓑ Ⓒ Ⓓ
46. Ⓐ Ⓑ Ⓒ Ⓓ
47. Ⓐ Ⓑ Ⓒ Ⓓ
48. Ⓐ Ⓑ Ⓒ Ⓓ
49. Ⓐ Ⓑ Ⓒ Ⓓ
50. Ⓐ Ⓑ Ⓒ Ⓓ
51. Ⓐ Ⓑ Ⓒ Ⓓ
52. Ⓐ Ⓑ Ⓒ Ⓓ

right in Section 1

wrong in Section 1

SECTION 2

1. Ⓐ Ⓑ Ⓒ Ⓓ
2. Ⓐ Ⓑ Ⓒ Ⓓ
3. Ⓐ Ⓑ Ⓒ Ⓓ
4. Ⓐ Ⓑ Ⓒ Ⓓ
5. Ⓐ Ⓑ Ⓒ Ⓓ
6. Ⓐ Ⓑ Ⓒ Ⓓ
7. Ⓐ Ⓑ Ⓒ Ⓓ
8. Ⓐ Ⓑ Ⓒ Ⓓ
9. Ⓐ Ⓑ Ⓒ Ⓓ
10. Ⓐ Ⓑ Ⓒ Ⓓ
11. Ⓐ Ⓑ Ⓒ Ⓓ

12. Ⓐ Ⓑ Ⓒ Ⓓ
13. Ⓐ Ⓑ Ⓒ Ⓓ
14. Ⓐ Ⓑ Ⓒ Ⓓ
15. Ⓐ Ⓑ Ⓒ Ⓓ
16. Ⓐ Ⓑ Ⓒ Ⓓ
17. Ⓐ Ⓑ Ⓒ Ⓓ
18. Ⓐ Ⓑ Ⓒ Ⓓ
19. Ⓐ Ⓑ Ⓒ Ⓓ
20. Ⓐ Ⓑ Ⓒ Ⓓ
21. Ⓐ Ⓑ Ⓒ Ⓓ
22. Ⓐ Ⓑ Ⓒ Ⓓ

23. Ⓐ Ⓑ Ⓒ Ⓓ
24. Ⓐ Ⓑ Ⓒ Ⓓ
25. Ⓐ Ⓑ Ⓒ Ⓓ
26. Ⓐ Ⓑ Ⓒ Ⓓ
27. Ⓐ Ⓑ Ⓒ Ⓓ
28. Ⓐ Ⓑ Ⓒ Ⓓ
29. Ⓐ Ⓑ Ⓒ Ⓓ
30. Ⓐ Ⓑ Ⓒ Ⓓ
31. Ⓐ Ⓑ Ⓒ Ⓓ
32. Ⓐ Ⓑ Ⓒ Ⓓ
33. Ⓐ Ⓑ Ⓒ Ⓓ

34. Ⓐ Ⓑ Ⓒ Ⓓ
35. Ⓐ Ⓑ Ⓒ Ⓓ
36. Ⓐ Ⓑ Ⓒ Ⓓ
37. Ⓐ Ⓑ Ⓒ Ⓓ
38. Ⓐ Ⓑ Ⓒ Ⓓ
39. Ⓐ Ⓑ Ⓒ Ⓓ
40. Ⓐ Ⓑ Ⓒ Ⓓ
41. Ⓐ Ⓑ Ⓒ Ⓓ
42. Ⓐ Ⓑ Ⓒ Ⓓ
43. Ⓐ Ⓑ Ⓒ Ⓓ
44. Ⓐ Ⓑ Ⓒ Ⓓ

right in Section 2

wrong in Section 2

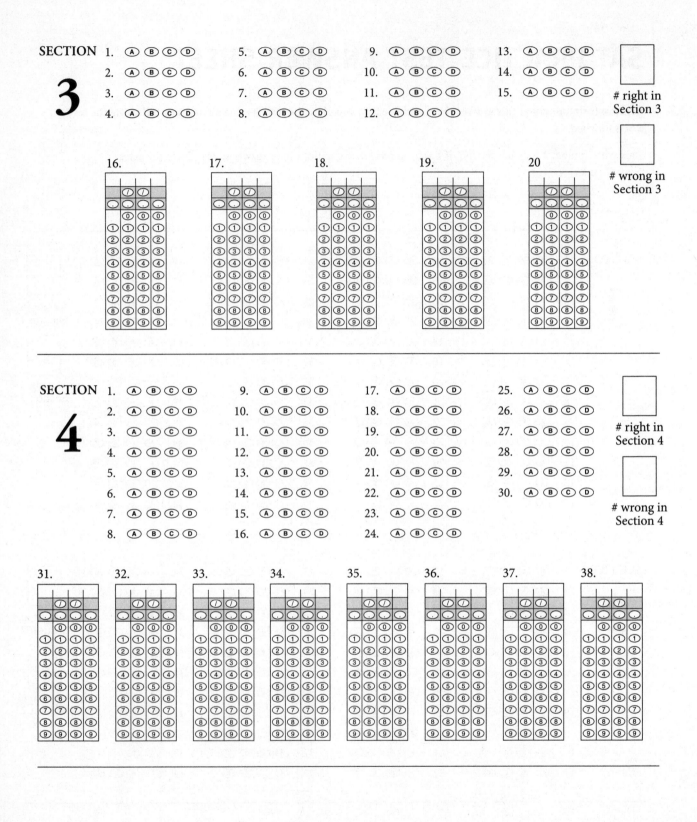

SECTION

3

1. Ⓐ Ⓑ Ⓒ Ⓓ
2. Ⓐ Ⓑ Ⓒ Ⓓ
3. Ⓐ Ⓑ Ⓒ Ⓓ
4. Ⓐ Ⓑ Ⓒ Ⓓ

5. Ⓐ Ⓑ Ⓒ Ⓓ
6. Ⓐ Ⓑ Ⓒ Ⓓ
7. Ⓐ Ⓑ Ⓒ Ⓓ
8. Ⓐ Ⓑ Ⓒ Ⓓ

9. Ⓐ Ⓑ Ⓒ Ⓓ
10. Ⓐ Ⓑ Ⓒ Ⓓ
11. Ⓐ Ⓑ Ⓒ Ⓓ
12. Ⓐ Ⓑ Ⓒ Ⓓ

13. Ⓐ Ⓑ Ⓒ Ⓓ
14. Ⓐ Ⓑ Ⓒ Ⓓ
15. Ⓐ Ⓑ Ⓒ Ⓓ

right in
Section 3

wrong in
Section 3

16. 17. 18. 19. 20

SECTION

4

1. Ⓐ Ⓑ Ⓒ Ⓓ
2. Ⓐ Ⓑ Ⓒ Ⓓ
3. Ⓐ Ⓑ Ⓒ Ⓓ
4. Ⓐ Ⓑ Ⓒ Ⓓ
5. Ⓐ Ⓑ Ⓒ Ⓓ
6. Ⓐ Ⓑ Ⓒ Ⓓ
7. Ⓐ Ⓑ Ⓒ Ⓓ
8. Ⓐ Ⓑ Ⓒ Ⓓ

9. Ⓐ Ⓑ Ⓒ Ⓓ
10. Ⓐ Ⓑ Ⓒ Ⓓ
11. Ⓐ Ⓑ Ⓒ Ⓓ
12. Ⓐ Ⓑ Ⓒ Ⓓ
13. Ⓐ Ⓑ Ⓒ Ⓓ
14. Ⓐ Ⓑ Ⓒ Ⓓ
15. Ⓐ Ⓑ Ⓒ Ⓓ
16. Ⓐ Ⓑ Ⓒ Ⓓ

17. Ⓐ Ⓑ Ⓒ Ⓓ
18. Ⓐ Ⓑ Ⓒ Ⓓ
19. Ⓐ Ⓑ Ⓒ Ⓓ
20. Ⓐ Ⓑ Ⓒ Ⓓ
21. Ⓐ Ⓑ Ⓒ Ⓓ
22. Ⓐ Ⓑ Ⓒ Ⓓ
23. Ⓐ Ⓑ Ⓒ Ⓓ
24. Ⓐ Ⓑ Ⓒ Ⓓ

25. Ⓐ Ⓑ Ⓒ Ⓓ
26. Ⓐ Ⓑ Ⓒ Ⓓ
27. Ⓐ Ⓑ Ⓒ Ⓓ
28. Ⓐ Ⓑ Ⓒ Ⓓ
29. Ⓐ Ⓑ Ⓒ Ⓓ
30. Ⓐ Ⓑ Ⓒ Ⓓ

right in
Section 4

wrong in
Section 4

31. 32. 33. 34. 35. 36. 37. 38.

READING TEST

65 Minutes—52 Questions

Turn to Section 1 of your answer sheet to answer the questions in this section.

Directions: Each passage or pair of passages below is followed by a number of questions. After reading each passage or pair, choose the best answer to each question based on what is stated or implied in the passage or passages and in any accompanying graphics (such as a table or graph).

Questions 1–10 are based on the following passage.

The following passage is adapted from Leo Tolstoy's 1873 novel, Anna Karenina *(translated from the original Russian by Constance Garnett). Prior to this excerpt, one of the major characters, Levin, has realized that he is in love with his longtime friend Kitty Shtcherbatsky.*

At four o'clock, conscious of his throbbing heart, Levin stepped out of a hired sledge at the Zoological Gardens, and turned along the path to the frozen
Line mounds and the skating ground, knowing that he
(5) would certainly find her there, as he had seen the Shtcherbatskys' carriage at the entrance.

It was a bright, frosty day. Rows of carriages, sledges, drivers, and policemen were standing in the approach. Crowds of well-dressed people, with hats
(10) bright in the sun, swarmed about the entrance and along the well-swept little paths between the little houses adorned with carving in the Russian style. The old curly birches of the gardens, all their twigs laden with snow, looked as though freshly decked in
(15) sacred vestments.

He walked along the path towards the skating-ground, and kept saying to himself—"You mustn't be excited, you must be calm. What's the matter with you? What do you want? Be quiet, stupid," he
(20) conjured his heart. And the more he tried to compose himself, the more breathless he found himself. An acquaintance met him and called him by his name, but Levin did not even recognize him. He went towards the mounds, whence came the clank
(25) of the chains of sledges as they slipped down or were dragged up, the rumble of the sliding sledges, and the sounds of merry voices. He walked on a few steps, and the skating-ground lay open before his eyes, and at once, amidst all the skaters, he knew her.

(30) He knew she was there by the rapture and the terror that seized on his heart. She was standing talking to a lady at the opposite end of the ground. There was apparently nothing striking either in her dress or her attitude. But for Levin she was as easy to find
(35) in that crowd as a rose among nettles. Everything was made bright by her. She was the smile that shed light on all round her. "Is it possible I can go over there on the ice, go up to her?" he thought. The place where she stood seemed to him a holy shrine, unap-
(40) proachable, and there was one moment when he was almost retreating, so overwhelmed was he with terror. He had to make an effort to master himself, and to remind himself that people of all sorts were moving about her, and that he too might come there
(45) to skate. He walked down, for a long while avoiding looking at her as at the sun, but seeing her, as one does the sun, without looking.

On that day of the week and at that time of day people of one set, all acquainted with one another,
(50) used to meet on the ice. There were crack skaters there, showing off their skill, and learners clinging to chairs with timid, awkward movements, boys, and elderly people skating with hygienic motives. They seemed to Levin an elect band of blissful beings
(55) because they were here, near her. All the skaters, it seemed, with perfect self-possession, skated towards her, skated by her, even spoke to her, and were happy, quite apart from her, enjoying the capital ice and the fine weather.

(60) Nikolay Shtcherbatsky, Kitty's cousin, in a short jacket and tight trousers, was sitting on a garden seat with his skates on. Seeing Levin, he shouted to him:

"Ah, the first skater in Russia! Been here long?
(65) First-rate ice—do put your skates on."

GO ON TO THE NEXT PAGE

1. According to the passage, how did Levin first know that Kitty was at the Zoological Gardens?

   A) Kitty's carriage was parked near the entrance.

   B) Nikolay said he had been skating with Kitty earlier.

   C) He saw her talking with another woman near the pond.

   D) Kitty invited him to meet her there at a certain time.

2. As used in line 10, "swarmed" most nearly means

   A) invaded.

   B) gathered.

   C) flew.

   D) obstructed.

3. The passage most strongly suggests that which of the following is true of Levin?

   A) He worries about his appearance.

   B) He wishes he were more impressive.

   C) He is an extremely passionate person.

   D) He is wary of his surroundings.

4. Which choice provides the best evidence for the answer to the previous question?

   A) Lines 7–12 ("It was a bright, frosty day . . . in the Russian style")

   B) Lines 22–27 ("An acquaintance met him . . . merry voices")

   C) Lines 38–45 ("The place where . . . there to skate")

   D) Lines 48–53 ("On that day . . . hygienic motives")

5. What theme does the passage communicate through the experiences of Levin?

   A) Love is a powerful emotion.

   B) People long to have company.

   C) Life should be filled with joy.

   D) People are meant to work hard.

6. The passage most strongly suggests that which of the following is true of how Levin appears to others?

   A) People think that Levin looks agitated because of the way he is acting.

   B) People think that Levin is sick because he seems to be feverish.

   C) People think that Levin seems normal because he is doing nothing unusual.

   D) People think that Levin is in trouble because he is not protecting himself emotionally.

7. Which choice provides the best evidence for the answer to the previous question?

   A) Lines 1–6 ("At four o'clock . . . at the entrance")

   B) Lines 9–12 ("Crowds . . . the Russian style")

   C) Lines 23–29 ("He went . . . he knew her")

   D) Lines 60–65 ("Nikolay Shtcherbatsky . . . your skates on")

8. As used in line 20, "conjured" most nearly means

   A) begged.

   B) created.

   C) summoned.

   D) tricked.

GO ON TO THE NEXT PAGE

9. The author's use of the word "throbbing" in line 1 implies that Levin

    A) has cut himself badly.

    B) has a sudden pain in his chest.

    C) is about to collapse.

    D) is in an agitated state.

10. Based on the tone of this passage, what emotion does the author wish the reader to feel about Levin?

    A) Empathy

    B) Cynicism

    C) Hostility

    D) Disgust

Questions 11–20 are based on the following passage.

This passage is adapted from a speech delivered by President Franklin Roosevelt on January 6, 1941, to the United States Congress. In the passage, Roosevelt reveals his intention to preserve and spread American ideals around the world.

The Nation takes great satisfaction and much strength from the things which have been done to make its people conscious of their individual stake
Line in the preservation of democratic life in America.
(5) Those things have toughened the fibre of our people, have renewed their faith and strengthened their devotion to the institutions we make ready to protect.

Certainly this is no time for any of us to stop thinking about the social and economic problems
(10) which are the root cause of the social revolution which is today a supreme factor in the world.

For there is nothing mysterious about the foundations of a healthy and strong democracy. The basic things expected by our people of their political and
(15) economic systems are simple. They are:

• Equality of opportunity for youth and for others.

• Jobs for those who can work.

• Security for those who need it.

• The ending of special privilege for the few.

(20) • The preservation of civil liberties for all.

• The enjoyment of the fruits of scientific progress in a wider and constantly rising standard of living.

These are the simple, basic things that must never be lost sight of in the turmoil and unbelievable com
(25) plexity of our modern world. The inner and abiding strength of our economic and political systems is dependent upon the degree to which they fulfill these expectations.

Many subjects connected with our social econo-
(30) my call for immediate improvement.

As examples:

• We should bring more citizens under the coverage of old-age pensions and unemployment insurance.

• We should widen the opportunities for adequate
(35) medical care.

• We should plan a better system by which persons deserving or needing gainful employment may obtain it.

I have called for personal sacrifice. I am as-
(40) sured of the willingness of almost all Americans to respond to that call.

A part of the sacrifice means the payment of more money in taxes. In my Budget Message I shall recommend that a greater portion of this great de-
(45) fense program be paid for from taxation than we are paying today. No person should try, or be allowed, to get rich out of this program; and the principle of tax payments in accordance with ability to pay should be constantly before our eyes to guide our legislation.

(50) If the Congress maintains these principles, the voters, putting patriotism ahead of pocketbooks, will give you their applause.

In the future days, which we seek to make secure, we look forward to a world founded upon four
(55) essential human freedoms.

The first is freedom of speech and expression—everywhere in the world.

The second is freedom of every person to worship God in his own way—everywhere in the world.

(60) The third is freedom from want—which, translated into world terms, means economic

GO ON TO THE NEXT PAGE

understandings which will secure to every nation a healthy peacetime life for its inhabitants—everywhere in the world.

(65) The fourth is freedom from fear—which, translated into world terms, means a world-wide reduction of armaments to such a point and in such a thorough fashion that no nation will be in a position to commit an act of physical aggression against

(70) any neighbor—anywhere in the world.

That is no vision of a distant millennium. It is a definite basis for a kind of world attainable in our own time and generation. That kind of world is the very antithesis of the so-called new order of

(75) tyranny which the dictators seek to create with the crash of a bomb.

To that new order we oppose the greater conception—the moral order. A good society is able to face schemes of world domination and

(80) foreign revolutions alike without fear.

Since the beginning of our American history, we have been engaged in change—in a perpetual peaceful revolution—a revolution which goes on steadily, quietly adjusting itself to changing

(85) conditions—without the concentration camp or the quick-lime in the ditch. The world order which we seek is the cooperation of free countries, working together in a friendly, civilized society.

This nation has placed its destiny in the hands

(90) and heads and hearts of its millions of free men and women; and its faith in freedom under the guidance of God. Freedom means the supremacy of human rights everywhere. Our support goes to those who struggle to gain those rights or keep them.

(95) Our strength is our unity of purpose. To that high concept there can be no end save victory.

11. Which phrase from the passage most clearly reflects President Roosevelt's purpose in making this speech?

A) Lines 2–4 ("to make . . . democratic life")

B) Lines 8–11 ("to stop thinking . . . the world")

C) Lines 54–55 ("[to] look forward to . . . freedoms")

D) Lines 79–80 ("to face . . . without fear")

12. Which choice provides the best evidence for the answer to the previous question?

A) Lines 13–15 ("The basic things . . . are simple")

B) Lines 29–30 ("Many subjects . . . improvement")

C) Lines 50–52 ("If the Congress . . . applause")

D) Lines 53–55 ("In the future days . . . freedoms")

13. As used in line 39, "sacrifice" most nearly means

A) religious offerings to a deity.

B) service in the military.

C) losses of limbs in battle.

D) surrender of interests to a greater good.

14. The passage most strongly suggests a relationship between which of the following phenomena?

A) Protection of human rights abroad and military service

B) Spread of freedom abroad and defense of democracy at home

C) Defeat of tyrants abroad and establishment of democratic government at home

D) Investment in global democracies abroad and strengthening of patriotism at home

GO ON TO THE NEXT PAGE

15. Which choice provides the best evidence for the answer to the previous question?

    A) Lines 23–28 ("These are . . . expectations")

    B) Lines 50–52 ("If the Congress . . . applause")

    C) Lines 71–76 ("That is no . . . of a bomb")

    D) Lines 92–95 ("Freedom means . . . unity of purpose")

16. In line 51, "pocketbooks" most nearly refers to

    A) local, state, and national taxes.

    B) war debt accumulated by the nation.

    C) citizens' individual monetary interests.

    D) Americans' personal investment in the defense industry.

17. In lines 71–73 ("That is no . . . generation"), President Roosevelt is most likely responding to what implicit counterclaim to his own argument?

    A) The spread of global democracy is idealistic and unrealistic.

    B) The defeat of tyrannical dictators in Europe is implausible.

    C) The commitment of the American people to the war effort is limited.

    D) The resources of the United States are insufficient to wage war abroad.

18. Which choice offers evidence that the spread of global democracy is achievable?

    A) Lines 46–47 ("No person . . . this program")

    B) Lines 54–55 ("we look forward . . . human freedoms")

    C) Lines 81–82 ("Since the beginning . . . in change")

    D) Line 95 ("Our strength . . . purpose")

19. In lines 60–64 ("The third is . . . world"), President Roosevelt sets a precedent by which he would most likely support which of the following policies?

    A) Military defense of political borders

    B) Investment in overseas business ventures

    C) Aid to nations struggling due to conflict and other causes

    D) Reduction of domestic services to spur job growth

20. The author refers to "the so-called new order of tyranny" primarily to

    A) connect the global conflict for human rights to citizens on a personal level.

    B) demonstrate the power of the global opposition to the United States.

    C) offer an alternative vision of the world without democracy.

    D) provide examples of the political and social revolutions underway.

GO ON TO THE NEXT PAGE ▷

Questions 21–31 are based on the following passage and supplementary material.

The United States Constitution has been amended twenty-seven times since its ratification. Rights such as freedom of speech, religion, and press, for example, are granted by the First Amendment. This passage focuses on the Nineteenth Amendment, which gave women the right to vote.

The American political landscape is constantly shifting on a myriad of issues, but the voting process itself has changed over the years as well. Electronic
Line ballot casting, for example, provides the public with
(5) instantaneous results, and statisticians are more accurate than ever at forecasting our next president. Voting has always been viewed as an intrinsic American right and was one of the major reasons for the nation's secession from Britain's monarchical
(10) rule. Unfortunately, although all men were constitutionally deemed "equal," true equality of the sexes was not extended to the voting booths until 1920.

The American women's suffrage movement began in 1848, when Elizabeth Cady Stanton and Lucretia
(15) Mott organized the Seneca Falls Convention. The meeting, initially an attempt to have an open dialogue about women's rights, drew a crowd of nearly three hundred women and included several dozen men. Topics ranged from a woman's role in society
(20) to law, but the issue of voting remained a contentious one. A freed slave named Frederick Douglass spoke eloquently about the importance of women in politics and swayed the opinion of those in attendance. At the end of the convention, one hundred
(25) people signed the Seneca Falls Declaration, which demanded "immediate admission to all the rights and privileges which belong to [women] as citizens of the United States."

Stanton and Mott's first victory came thirty years
(30) later when a constitutional amendment allowing women to vote was proposed to Congress in 1878. Unfortunately, election practices were already a controversial issue, as unfair laws that diminished the African-American vote had been passed during
(35) Reconstruction. Questionable literacy tests and a "vote tax" levied against the poor kept minority turnout to a minimum. And while several states al-

lowed women to vote, federal consensus was hardly as equitable. The rest of the world, however, was
(40) taking note—and women were ready to act.

In 1893, New Zealand allowed women the right to vote, although women could not run for office in New Zealand. Other countries began reviewing and ratifying their own laws as well. The United King-
(45) dom took small steps by allowing married women to vote in local elections in 1894. By 1902, all women in Australia could vote in elections, both local and parliamentary.

The suffrage movement in America slowly built
(50) momentum throughout the early twentieth century and exploded during World War I. President Woodrow Wilson called the fight abroad a war for democracy, which many suffragettes viewed as hypocritical. Democracy, after all, was hardly worth fighting for
(55) when half of a nation's population was disqualified based on gender. Public acts of civil disobedience, rallies, and marches galvanized pro-women advocates while undermining defenders of the status quo. Posters read "Kaiser Wilson" and called into ques-
(60) tion the authenticity of a free country with unjust laws. The cry for equality was impossible to ignore and, in 1919, with the support of President Wilson, Congress passed the Nineteenth Amendment to the Constitution. It was ratified one year later by two-
(65) thirds of the states, effectively changing the Constitution. Only one signatory from the original Seneca Falls Declaration lived long enough to cast her first ballot in a federal election.

America's election laws were far from equal for
(70) all, as tactics to dissuade or prohibit African Americans from effectively voting were still routinely employed. However, the suffrage movement laid the groundwork for future generations. Laws, like people's minds, could change over time. The civil
(75) rights movement in the mid- to late twentieth century brought an end to segregation and so-called Jim Crow laws that stifled African-American advancement. The Voting Rights Act of 1965 was the final nail in the coffin; what emerged was a free nation
(80) guided by elections determined not by skin color or gender, but by the ballot box.

GO ON TO THE NEXT PAGE ⟶

Women's Suffrage in the United States

1848 ➤ Seneca Falls Convention.

1878 ➤ 19th Amendment submitted; not ratified.

1911 ➤ Several states now grant women suffrage.

1914 ➤ Start of World War I.

1917 ➤ Picketing at the White House.

1918 ➤ Amendment passes in the House but fails in the Senate.

1919 ➤ Both the House and Senate pass the amendment.

1920 ➤ 19th Amendment ratified.

21. The stance the author takes in the passage is best described as that of

A) an advocate of women's suffrage proposing a constitutional amendment.

B) a legislator reviewing the arguments for and against women's suffrage.

C) a scholar evaluating the evolution and impact of the women's suffrage movement.

D) a historian summarizing the motivations of women's suffrage leaders.

22. Lines 69–70 ("America's election laws . . . equal for all") most clearly support which explicit claim?

A) The founders of the Constitution did not provide for free and fair elections.

B) The United States still had work to do to secure equal voting rights for some people.

C) Most women in the United States did not want suffrage and equal rights.

D) The women's suffrage movement perpetuated discriminatory voting laws.

23. Which choice provides the best evidence for the answer to the previous question?

A) Lines 13–14 ("The American . . . in 1848")

B) Lines 41–42 ("In 1893 . . . to vote")

C) Lines 63–64 ("Congress . . . the Constitution")

D) Lines 78–79 ("The Voting Rights Act . . . the coffin")

24. As used in line 57, "galvanized" most nearly means

A) displaced.

B) divided.

C) excited.

D) organized.

25. The main rhetorical effect of lines 73–74 ("Laws, like . . . could change") is to

A) connect the success of legislative reform with shifts in public sentiment.

B) dissuade reformers from focusing on grassroots activity rather than political campaigns.

C) evaluate the effectiveness of judicial rulings based on popular response to public polls.

D) reject the need for legal actions and court proceedings to attain social change.

26. As a whole, the passage most strongly suggests which conclusion?

A) American government adapts to the changing needs and ideas of society.

B) The best-organized reform movements are most likely to achieve their goals.

C) The nation is more vulnerable to change during the confusion of wartime.

D) The civil rights movement would not have happened without women suffragists.

GO ON TO THE NEXT PAGE ⟩

27. Which choice provides the best evidence for the answer to the previous question?

    A) Lines 3–7 ("Electronic ballot casting . . . our next president")

    B) Lines 7–10 ("Voting has . . . monarchical rule")

    C) Lines 15–19 ("The meeting . . . dozen men")

    D) Lines 74–78 ("The civil rights . . . advancement")

28. The graphic most clearly illustrates which idea?

    A) The Nineteenth Amendment happened as a result of World War I.

    B) The states slowed reform of national voting rights laws.

    C) Women's suffrage resulted from a slow evolution of events.

    D) Acts of civil disobedience won support for suffrage in Congress.

29. In line 60, the word "authenticity" most nearly means

    A) reliability.

    B) realism.

    C) legitimacy.

    D) truth.

30. The passage suggests that President Wilson contributed to the success of the women's suffrage movement by

    A) circulating government propaganda in support of women's suffrage.

    B) framing the fight in World War I as a fight for democracy and freedom.

    C) engaging in a foreign war to distract the nation from political debate.

    D) working with legislators to write the Nineteenth Amendment.

31. The graphic helps support which statement referred to in the passage?

    A) Early women suffragists did not live to vote in national elections.

    B) The Nineteenth Amendment passed within a few years of its introduction.

    C) A majority of state representatives opposed women's suffrage in 1918.

    D) Many state governments approved suffrage before the federal government did.

Questions 32–42 are based on the following passages.

Passage 1

Coffee is a pillar of the world economy, generating both jobs and profits. The plant produced revenue to the tune of $15.4 billion in 2013 alone.
Line The coffee industry is also one of the world's largest
(5) employers, supporting 26 million employees. Because of the global importance of coffee, scientists at the University at Buffalo and their international colleagues were compelled to sequence the genome of the most popular coffee plant. In the genome lies
(10) the secrets of the bold flavor that people around the world have come to enjoy daily, as well as the caffeine kick that comes along with it. This new genetic information can be used to expand the market by creating new types of coffee varieties. The results of
(15) the study can also safeguard the existing industry. Scientists can now modify the genetic material of the coffee plant. Heartier strains of popular coffee types can be created so that they are resistant to drought, disease, and bugs.
(20)   Researchers began their work by sequencing the genome of the type of coffee that makes up 30 percent of all coffee production. The conclusions drawn from this study will help save money and resources during the coffee production process. Re-
(25) searchers were able to isolate the genetic information of the enzymes in the coffee plant that produce caffeine. With this information, it may be possible to reduce or eliminate caffeine from coffee. This would remove a costly step in the current process

GO ON TO THE NEXT PAGE

(30) of extracting caffeine from the coffee beans, while expanding the coffee market to people who avoid caffeine for health reasons, such as high blood pressure or pregnancy. The same research team plans to sequence the genome of other types of coffee in

(35) the future. It is their hope that the information will benefit the coffee producer, consumer, and also the environment.

Passage 2

The Gibbon Genome Sequencing Consortium has successfully sequenced the genome of the Northern

(40) white-cheeked gibbon. Both gibbons and humans have DNA that changes during the course of their lifetime. Some DNA changes in humans are the result of mutations, which cause cancer and other diseases. The changes in gibbons' DNA have resulted

(45) in many changes to the species over a very short period of time. Although gibbons are close relatives to humans, their DNA changes do not cause disease. Understanding the pattern of the gibbon genome might turn out to be very important to humans. If

(50) these changes in DNA can be understood, scientists may be able to use the information to better understand human disease.

Cancer and other genetic diseases are caused by faulty gene regulation. Scientists have sought to under-

(55) stand human biology through the lens of gibbon DNA structures for some time. Until now, there has simply been too much information to analyze. The endless rearrangements made it difficult to align gibbon DNA to that of humans, but it has finally been accomplished.

(60) Scientists discovered a piece of DNA that is unique to the gibbon species. Gibbons have a specific repeat element, or a piece of DNA that copies itself multiple times throughout the genome. Repeat elements, in both gibbons and humans, are related to the

(65) maintenance of genetic structures. Scientists hope to be able to answer the question "Why can gibbon DNA rearrange itself without causing diseases—unlike humans' DNA?" If this complicated biological question can be solved, scientists may be able to work

(70) backward in order to help stop cancer, heart failure, and other human disease related to genetic repeats.

32. Which of the following best describes the central idea of Passage 1?

A) Advancements in genome sequencing will lead to healthier food options worldwide.

B) Genome sequencing of coffee can increase the profitability of coffee as a commodity.

C) Removing caffeine from coffee will allow more people to drink and enjoy coffee.

D) The coffee trade is an important sector of the global economy.

33. The author of Passage 2 would most likely agree that

A) instead of studying nonhuman animals, scientists should look for a way to stop human DNA from changing when it replicates itself.

B) sequencing the genome of other nonhuman primates could yield results that would be beneficial to people.

C) the benefits of genome sequencing of gibbons and other nonhuman animals does not justify the great expense and resources used.

D) scientists will be able to cure cancer once the mystery is solved of how the DNA of gibbons replicates itself without causing disease.

34. Passage 1 most strongly suggests that

A) the coffee industry will fail without new developments stemming from genome sequencing.

B) newly developed varieties of coffee plants are more expensive for consumers than are existing varieties.

C) future research will lead to developments that could increase the profitability for coffee producers.

D) genome sequencing of coffee plants could help scientists understand diseases that affect humans.

GO ON TO THE NEXT PAGE ▷

35. Which choice provides the best evidence for the answer to the previous question?

    A) Lines 5–9 ("Because of the global . . . coffee plant")

    B) Lines 16–17 ("Scientists can . . . coffee plant")

    C) Lines 20–22 ("Researchers began . . . coffee production")

    D) Lines 28–33 ("This would remove . . . pregnancy")

36. Passage 2 most strongly suggests which of the following?

    A) The genetic makeup of the Northern white-cheeked gibbon is more similar to that of humans than to other primates.

    B) More research is needed before the findings of scientists studying the DNA of gibbons can be used to cure disease in humans.

    C) Many diseases and illnesses that affect humans can only be understood by studying the DNA of plants and other animals.

    D) Cancer and other diseases can be eliminated completely if enough funding is given to scientific research.

37. Which choice provides the best evidence for the answer to the previous question?

    A) Lines 40–44 ("Both gibbons . . . diseases")

    B) Lines 54–56 ("Scientists have sought . . . some time")

    C) Lines 63–65 ("Repeat elements . . . genetic structures")

    D) Lines 68–71 ("If this . . . genetic repeats")

38. Which of the following best summarizes a shared purpose of the two authors?

    A) To explain how genome sequencing in animals and plants can benefit people in unexpected ways

    B) To summarize how genome sequencing has changed the field of medicine and the study of diseases

    C) To inform readers about how scientific research can be applied to improving the world economy

    D) To convince readers to support funding for research in genome sequencing of plants and animals

39. As used in line 8, "compelled" most nearly means

    A) forced.

    B) driven.

    C) required.

    D) constrained.

40. As used in line 65, "maintenance" most nearly means

    A) preservation.

    B) protection.

    C) organization.

    D) repair.

41. Which point is the author of Passage 1 trying to make by using the phrase "a pillar of the world economy" in line 1 to refer to the coffee industry?

    A) Research into the coffee plant is important and should be continued.

    B) The coffee industry plays a significant role in global economics.

    C) Many jobs will be lost if the coffee industry goes into decline.

    D) The coffee industry provides financial stability for millions of people worldwide.

GO ON TO THE NEXT PAGE

42. Which of the following can reasonably be inferred based on the information in both passages?

    A) Studying the genomes of animals closely related to humans can help scientists learn about diseases that affect humans.

    B) Expanding the customer base of the coffee industry will lead to higher profits and increase the stability of the global economy.

    C) The scientists who study coffee and those who study gibbons could learn more by collaborating.

    D) The genomes of other plants and nonhuman animals hold secrets that can benefit people and are worthy of exploration.

Questions 43–52 are based on the following passage and supplementary material.

In 1948, Swiss chemist George de Mestral was impressed with the clinging power of burrs snagged in his dog's fur and on his pant legs after he returned
Line from a hike. While examining the burrs under a
(5) microscope, he observed many hundreds of small fibers that grabbed like hooks. He experimented with replicas of the burrs and eventually invented Velcro,* a synthetic clinging fabric that was first marketed as "the zipperless zipper." In the 1960s,
(10) NASA used de Mestral's invention on space suits, and now, of course, we see it everywhere.

You might say that de Mestral was the father of biomimicry, an increasingly essential field that studies nature, looking for efficiencies in materials and
(15) systems, and asks the question "How can our homes, our electronics, our cities work better?" As one biomimetics company puts it: "Nature is the largest laboratory that ever existed and ever will."

Architecture is one field that is constantly
(20) exploring new ways to incorporate biomimicry. Architects have studied everything from beehives to beaver dams to learn how to best use materials, geometry, and physics in buildings. Termite mounds, for example, very efficiently regulate temperature,

(25) humidity, and airflow, so architects in Zimbabwe are working to apply what they've learned from termite mounds to human-made structures.

Says Michael Pawlyn, author of *Biomimicry in Architecture,* "If you look beyond the nice shapes
(30) in nature and understand the principles behind them, you can find some adaptations that can lead to new, innovative solutions that are radically more resource-efficient. It's the direction we need to take in the coming decades."

(35) Designers in various professional fields are drawing on biomimicry; for example, in optics, scientists have examined the surface of insect eyes in hopes of reducing glare on handheld device screens. Engineers in the field of robotics worked to replicate the
(40) property found in a gecko's feet that allows adhesion to smooth surfaces.

Sometimes what scientists learn from nature isn't more advanced, but simpler. The abalone shrimp, for example, makes its shell out of calcium carbonate,
(45) the same material as soft chalk. It's not a rare or complex substance, but the unique arrangement of the material in the abalone's shell makes it extremely tough. The walls of the shell contain microscopic pieces of calcium carbonate stacked like bricks,
(50) which are bound together using proteins just as concrete mortar is used. The result is a shell three thousand times harder than chalk and as tough as Kevlar* (the material used in bullet-proof vests).

Often it is necessary to look at the nanoscale
(55) structures of a living material's exceptional properties in order to re-create it synthetically. Andrew Parker, an evolutionary biologist, looked at the skin of the thorny devil (a type of lizard) under a scanning electron microscope, in search of the features that let the
(60) animal channel water from its back to its mouth.

Examples like this from the animal world abound. Scientists have learned that colorful birds don't always have pigment in their wings but are sometimes completely brown; it's the layers of keratin
(65) in their wings that produce color. Different colors, which have varying wavelengths, reflect differently through keratin. The discovery of this phenomenon can be put to use in creating paints and cosmetics that won't fade or chip. At the same time, paint for

GO ON TO THE NEXT PAGE ▷

(70) outdoor surfaces can be made tougher by copying the structures found in antler bone. Hearing aids are being designed to capture sound as well as the ears of the *Ormia* fly do. And why can't we have a self-healing material like our own skin? Researchers

(75) at the Beckman Institute at the University of Illinois are creating just that; they call it an "autonomic materials system." A raptor's feathers, a whale's fluke, a mosquito's proboscis—all have functional features we can learn from.

(80)   The driving force behind these innovations, aside from improved performance, is often improved energy efficiency. In a world where nonrenewable energy resources are dwindling and carbon emissions threaten the planet's health, efficiency has

(85) never been more important. Pawlyn agrees: "For me, biomimicry is one of the best sources of innovation to get to a world of zero waste because those are the rules under which biological life has had to exist."

(90)   Biomimicry is a radical field and one whose practitioners need to be radically optimistic, as Pawlyn is when he says, "We could use natural products such as cellulose, or even harvest carbon from the atmosphere to create bio-rock."

Tiny florets in a sunflower's center are arranged in an interlocking spiral, which inspired engineers in the design of this solar power plant. Mirrors positioned at the same angle as the florets bounce light toward the power plant's central tower.

Adapted from David Ferris, "Innovate: Solar Designs from Nature." © 2014 by Sierra Club.

43. The central idea of the passage is primarily concerned with

A) the field of biomimicry, the study of materials and systems found in nature and replicated in ways that benefit people.

B) the work of George de Mestral, the Swiss chemist who invented Velcro® after observing burrs under a microscope.

C) the ways in which architects use termite mounds as models for human-made structures in Zimbabwe.

D) how scientists are seeking ways to improve energy efficiency as nonrenewable energy sources decline.

44. Which choice provides the best evidence for the answer to the previous question?

A) Lines 1–6 ("In 1948 . . . hooks")

B) Lines 12–18 ("You might say . . . ever will'")

C) Lines 23–27 ("Termite mounds . . . structures")

D) Lines 80–85 ("The driving . . . more important")

45. The author includes a quote in paragraph 4 in order to

A) explain why architects are looking to biomimicry for solutions in architecture.

B) provide an argument for more scientists to study biomimicry.

C) give an explanation as to why someone might choose a career in architecture.

D) provide a counterargument to the author's central claim.

GO ON TO THE NEXT PAGE ⟶

46. Based on the information in paragraph 6, how does the shell of an abalone shrimp compare with soft chalk?

    A) The essential building blocks are arranged in a similar manner, but the material that makes up the shell of an abalone shrimp is harder.

    B) Both are made from the same essential building blocks, but the shell of the abalone shrimp is much harder because of the manner in which the materials are arranged.

    C) The essential building blocks of both are the same, but the abalone shrimp shell is harder because the soft chalk lacks a protein binding the materials together.

    D) They are made from different essential building blocks, but they have a similar hardness because the materials are arranged in a similar manner.

47. In paragraph 9, what is the most likely reason that the author included the quote from Pawlyn about efficiency?

    A) To convince readers that Pawlyn is an expert in his field

    B) To prove that great strides are being made in creating products that do not generate waste

    C) To demonstrate the limits of what biomimicry can achieve

    D) To support the statement that energy efficiency "has never been more important"

48. In line 30, "principles" most nearly means

    A) sources.

    B) attitudes.

    C) standards.

    D) theories.

49. It can be reasonably inferred from the passage that

    A) more scientists will utilize solutions developed through biomimicry in the future.

    B) the field of biomimicry will eventually decline as more nonrenewable resources are discovered.

    C) scientists will leave the fields they are currently working in and begin research in biomimicry.

    D) doctors will create a self-healing skin called an "autonomic materials system" using methods based in biomimicry.

50. Which choice provides the best evidence for the answer to the previous question?

    A) Lines 35–38 ("Designers . . . screens")

    B) Lines 54–56 ("Often it is . . . synthetically")

    C) Lines 61–79 ("Examples like . . . learn from")

    D) Lines 89–94 ("Biomimicry . . . bio-rock")

51. As used in line 90, "radical" most nearly means

    A) pervasive.

    B) drastic.

    C) essential.

    D) revolutionary.

52. The graphic and caption that accompany this passage help illustrate how biomimicry can be used to

    A) make a solar plant more attractive.

    B) decrease waste generated by energy sources.

    C) improve the efficiency of existing models.

    D) replicate a pattern common in nature.

WRITING AND LANGUAGE TEST

35 Minutes—44 Questions

Turn to Section 2 of your answer sheet to answer the questions in this section.

Directions: Each passage below is accompanied by a number of questions. For some questions, you will consider how the passage might be revised to improve the expression of ideas. For other questions, you will consider how the passage might be edited to correct errors in sentence structure, usage, or punctuation. A passage or a question may be accompanied by one or more graphics (such as a table or graph) that you will consider as you make revising and editing decisions.

Some questions will direct you to an underlined portion of a passage. Other questions will direct you to a location in a passage or ask you to think about the passage as a whole.

After reading each passage, choose the answer to each question that most effectively improves the quality of writing in the passage or that makes the passage conform to the conventions of standard written English. Many questions include a "NO CHANGE" option. Choose that option if you think the best choice is to leave the relevant portion of the passage as it is.

Questions 1–11 are based on the following passage.

The Age of the Librarian

When Kristen Harris ❶ is in college, she worked in her university's library and was constantly told, "You really should be studying to be a librarian; this is ❷ your home" however Harris was pursuing a bachelor's degree in elementary education at the time. Little did she realize that becoming a school librarian was indeed ❸ elective. During the 21st century, the age of information, what could be more necessary than an individual trained to gather, process, and disseminate information? So, after teaching children in the classroom, Harris went back to school to earn her Master of Library Science degree.

1. A) NO CHANGE
    B) has been
    C) was
    D) had been

2. A) NO CHANGE
    B) your home," however Harris
    C) your home."; However Harris
    D) your home." However, Harris

3. A) NO CHANGE
    B) imminent
    C) threatening
    D) optional

GO ON TO THE NEXT PAGE ⟹

Today, Harris is preparing a story time for a group of young students. As it has done with everything else, the technology revolution has elevated the school library to "Library 2.0," and Harris's tablet-integrated story time begins when she projects images for *The Very Cranky Bear* onto a projector screen. As a child, Harris got excited whenever a puppet appeared during story time, but now she uses an interactive app (application software) to enhance her own story time and ❹ integrate this next generation of children.

As she introduces the children to the problem of cheering up a cranky ❺ bear, Harris sees Miguel scouring the library shelves for another book by a popular author. ❻ Miguel had said asking Harris for a book two weeks earlier "If you have any funny stories, I like those."

4. A) NO CHANGE
   B) enervate
   C) energize
   D) elucidate

5. A) NO CHANGE
   B) bear; Harris sees Miguel
   C) bear: Harris sees Miguel
   D) bear Harris sees Miguel

6. A) NO CHANGE
   B) Miguel had said, "If you have any funny stories, I like those, "asking Harris for a book two weeks earlier.
   C) Asking Harris for a book two weeks earlier, Miguel had said, "If you have any funny stories, I like those."
   D) Miguel asked Harris for a book two weeks earlier had said, "If you have any funny stories, I like those."

"It will always be satisfying," reflects Harris, "the act of finding books for students and having them return to say, 'I really liked that one. Are there any more by that author?'"

[7] These days, Harris would call herself a media mentor as much as a librarian because she regularly visits her favorite websites for reviews of apps and other digital tools to suggest to students and parents. Librarians have always been an important resource for families in a community, but this importance has grown exponentially because of the advent of technology. Librarians are offering guidance about new media to address the changing information needs in our communities. Furthermore, libraries are becoming increasingly technology driven, for example,

7. Which sentence could be added to the paragraph to most effectively establish its main idea?

A) Harris maintains active profiles on multiple social media networks to better connect with her students.

B) The role of the school librarian has changed rapidly to meet the needs of students who are digital citizens.

C) Librarians still perform many traditional tasks such as putting great literature in the hands of their students.

D) In the future, many school libraries are unlikely to have books on the shelves because students prefer electronic media.

8 enabling access to collections of other libraries, offering remote access to databases, or they house video production studios. So, in Harris's opinion, librarians must be masters of the digital world. **9**

Harris finishes her story time and heads across the library. A young student stops her and asks, "Ms. Harris, what's new in the library?"

8. A) NO CHANGE

   B) by enabling access to collections of other libraries, offering remote access to databases, or by housing video production studios.

   C) they enable access to collections of other libraries, offering remote access to databases, or they house video production studios.

   D) enabling access to collections of other libraries, offering remote access to databases, or housing video production studios.

9. Which sentence would provide evidence to effectively support the main idea of the paragraph?

   A) Harris sponsors a weekly "Fun Read" book discussion club that is well attended by many of the students at her school.

   B) Librarians continue to help students and teachers locate the perfect book in the library's collection.

   C) Teachers frequently ask Harris to recommend educational apps to support early literacy for their students.

   D) Many parents are concerned with online safety and digital citizenship due to the proliferation of social media.

GO ON TO THE NEXT PAGE

(10) She chuckles and thinks about the many collections, services, and programs their school library offers. "Have you seen the Trendy 10 list? You read the books on the list and blog **(11)** your ideas about them. I'll set you up with a password and username so you can blog," says Harris. In this library full of information, she's the gatekeeper.

Questions 12–22 are based on the following passage.

Unforeseen Consequences: The Dark Side of the Industrial Revolution

There is no doubt that the Industrial Revolution guided America through the nascent stages of independence **(12)** and into being a robust economic powerhouse. Inventions like the cotton gin revolutionized the textile industry, and the steam engine ushered in the advent of expeditious cross-country distribution.

The Industrial Revolution marked a shift from an agrarian to an industry-centered society. People eschewed farming in favor of **(13)** more lucrative enterprises in urban areas which put a strain on existing local resources. Necessary goods such as **(14)** food crops, vegetables, and meat products also had to be shipped in order to meet the dietary needs of a consolidated population. And because there were fewer people farming, food had to travel farther and in higher quantities to meet demand. Issues like carbon dioxide emissions, therefore, arose not only as byproducts of industrial production but also from the delivery of these products. As a result, booming metropolises needed additional lumber, metal, and coal shipped from rural areas to sustain population and industrial growth.

10. A) NO CHANGE
    B) He chuckles
    C) Harris chuckles
    D) They chuckle

11. A) NO CHANGE
    B) they're
    C) you're
    D) their

12. A) NO CHANGE
    B) and into the role of a robust economic powerhouse
    C) and turned into a robust economic powerhouse
    D) and then became a robust economic powerhouse

13. A) NO CHANGE
    B) more lucrative enterprises in urban areas, which put a strain on
    C) more lucrative enterprises in urban areas; which put a strain on
    D) more lucrative enterprises in urban areas. Which put a strain on

14. A) NO CHANGE
    B) food
    C) food crops
    D) vegetables and meat products

GO ON TO THE NEXT PAGE ▷

15 [1] The negative effects of such expansion on humans were immediately apparent. Improper water sanitization led to cholera outbreaks in big cities. [2] Miners suffered from black lung after spending hours harvesting coal in dark caverns. [3] Combusted fossil fuels **16** <u>released unprecedented amounts of human-made carbon dioxide into the air</u>, resulting in respiratory ailments. [4] The fact remains that smog, now an internationally recognized buzzword, simply did not exist before the factories that produced it.

The critical impact on the environment must also **17** <u>be taken into account. Proper regulations</u> were either not in place or not enforced.

15. To effectively transition from paragraph 2, which sentence should begin paragraph 3?

A) Sentence 1

B) Sentence 2

C) Sentence 3

D) Sentence 4

16. Which graphic would best support the underlined claim?

A) A line graph plotting an increase in atmospheric carbon dioxide over time

B) A pie chart comparing the present percentages of carbon dioxide and other atmospheric gases

C) A timeline tracking carbon dioxide emissions testing dates

D) A bar graph showing levels of atmospheric carbon dioxide in different locations

17. Which choice most effectively combines the sentences at the underlined portion?

A) be taken into account, and proper regulations

B) be taken into account since without proper regulations

C) be taken into account, as proper regulations

D) be taken into account; however, proper regulations

Industrial waste was often disposed of in the nearest river or buried in landfills, where it ⓲ <u>polluted</u> groundwater essential for wildlife to thrive. Deforestation across the United States served the dual purpose of providing inhabitable land and wood, but it also caused animals to migrate or die out completely.

Although the Industrial Revolution heralded an age of consumer ease and excess, it also invited a cyclical process of destruction and reduced resources. ⓳ <u>Greenhouse gases were released into the atmosphere.</u> Numerous health problems caused by ⓴ <u>depressing</u> working conditions prevented rural emigrants from thriving. And the environment that had cradled humankind since its inception was slowly being ㉑ <u>degraded.</u> <u>All</u> in the name of progress. 22

18. A) NO CHANGE
    B) disturbed
    C) drained
    D) enhanced

19. Which choice should be added to the end of the underlined sentence to better support the claim in the preceding sentence?

    A) NO CHANGE
    B) while carbon dioxide-consuming trees were cut down to make way for new living spaces.
    C) and caused an increase in global temperatures as well as a rise in coastal sea levels.
    D) faster than they could be absorbed by the atmosphere's shrinking ozone layer.

20. A) NO CHANGE
    B) urban
    C) substandard
    D) developing

21. A) NO CHANGE
    B) degraded; all
    C) degraded! All
    D) degraded—all

GO ON TO THE NEXT PAGE ⇨

22. Which choice most effectively states the central idea of the essay on the previous page?

A) The Industrial Revolution created a new consumer society that replaced the existing farming society.

B) Politicians and historians today disagree about the true consequences of the Industrial Revolution.

C) Although some analysts suggest that industrialization had many problems, its immense benefits outweigh these concerns.

D) Unfortunately, progress came at the expense of environmental and ecological preservation and may well have ruined the future that once looked so bright.

Questions 23–33 are based on the following passage.

Remembering Freud

Psychology has grown momentously over the past century, largely due to the influence of Sigmund Freud, a pioneer of the field. This Austrian-born neurologist founded the practice of psychoanalysis and 23 began scientific study of the unconscious mind. 24 Since his career which ended in the mid-twentieth century, Freud has remained a common cultural and scientific reference point.

23. A) NO CHANGE
    B) continued
    C) spearheaded
    D) led to

24. A) NO CHANGE
    B) Since his career, which ended in the mid-twentieth century, Freud has remained
    C) Since his career ending in the mid-twentieth century; Freud has remained
    D) Since his career (ending in the mid-twentieth century) Freud has remained

GO ON TO THE NEXT PAGE →

25 Even the abiding popularity of terms such as "id," "ego," or talking about a "Freudian slip" serves to indicate how this psychologist lingers powerfully in Western memory.

As neuroscience has progressed, many early practices and theories, including some of Freud's, have been dismissed as outdated, unscientific, or even harmful. Much of Freud's theory, clinical practice, and even lifestyle are now discredited. But when considered in his historical context, alongside the astounding progress catalyzed by his work, Freud's contribution was significant indeed.

26 Because he is now widely referred to as the Father of Psychoanalysis, Freud was among the first to develop the now-commonplace psychological method of inviting patients to freely speak. For Freud, this was both study and treatment. It helped doctors to understand patients, but more importantly it helped patients to understand themselves. Freud employed the classic (now largely outdated) psychiatric style in which the patient lies face-up on a clinical bed, allegedly enabling access to deep **27** parts of the mind. These recesses, better known as the unconscious or subconscious, fascinated Freud.

25. A) NO CHANGE
   B) Even the abiding popularity of terms such as the "id," "ego," or a "Freudian slip"
   C) Even the abiding popularity of terms such as talking about an "id," "ego," or "Freudian slip"
   D) Even the abiding popularity of terms such as "id," "ego," or "Freudian slip"

26. A) NO CHANGE
   B) Widely remembered as the Father of Psychoanalysis, Freud was among the first to develop the now-commonplace psychological method of inviting patients to freely speak.
   C) Freud was among the first to develop the now-commonplace psychological method of inviting patients to freely speak, which is why he is now widely remembered as the Father of Psychoanalysis.
   D) Although he is widely remembered as the Father of Psychoanalysis, Freud was among the first to develop the now-commonplace psychological method of inviting patients to freely speak.

27. A) NO CHANGE
   B) recesses
   C) places
   D) components

GO ON TO THE NEXT PAGE

28 He believed that uncovering repressed memories, was necessary for recovery. For Freud, understanding the activity of the innermost mind was essential. **29** In dealing with the conditions of patients, like neurosis or other psychological trauma, he suspected that there was a great deal going on beneath the "surface" of the psyche. He thought it was possible to reunite external, or conscious, thought with the internal,

28. A) NO CHANGE
    B) He believed that uncovering repressed memories, being necessary for recovery.
    C) He believed that uncovering repressed memories was necessary for recovery.
    D) He believed that uncovering, repressed memories was necessary for recovery.

29. A) NO CHANGE
    B) In dealing with patients' conditions, like neurosis or other psychological trauma, he suspected that
    C) In dealing with patients like neurosis or other psychological trauma conditions he suspected that
    D) He suspected that, in dealing with patients' conditions like neurosis or other psychological trauma,

or unconscious. **30** Moreover, the method of inviting patients to speak and process their thoughts aloud remains central to today's psychological practice.

Freud altered the course of twentieth-century medicine by initiating what would become a grand, global conversation about the **31** still vastly mysterious human mind before Freud, medicine had barely scratched the surface in understanding mental health. Patients were met with very few answers, let alone recovery protocols. **32** Through trial and error—scientific method in action—Freud's finding of a method that seemed to work.

30. Which detail would provide the best support for the ideas presented in this section?

A) At the same time that Freud practiced, many people were interested in spiritualism.

B) Freud lived and worked mostly in London although he had originally trained in Austria.

C) While some of Freud's more unusual practices have been criticized or abandoned, his interest in the unconscious altered the trajectory of the field.

D) Psychologists today employ many theories, not just those developed by Freud.

31. A) NO CHANGE

B) still vastly mysterious human mind. Before Freud, medicine

C) still vastly mysterious human mind, before Freud, medicine

D) still vastly mysterious human mind before Freud. Medicine

32. A) NO CHANGE

B) Through trial and error—scientific method in action—Freud's finding a method that seems to work.

C) Through trial and error—scientific method in action—Freud finds a method that seemed to work.

D) Through trial and error—scientific method in action—Freud found a method that seemed to work.

GO ON TO THE NEXT PAGE

Since then, decades of ever-sharpening science have used his work as a launching pad. Therefore, as long as occasions arise to celebrate the progress of ❸❸ the field, Sigmund Freud will be remembered for groundbreaking work that enabled countless advances.

Questions 34–44 are based on the following passage and supplementary material.

Success in Montreal

The Montreal Protocol on Substances That Deplete the Ozone Layer is an international treaty that was created to ensure that steps would be taken to reverse damage to Earth's ozone layer and ❸❹ preventing future damage. ❸❺ It was signed in 1987. This document created restrictions on chemicals that were known to be dangerous to the protective barrier that the ozone layer offers Earth. Without the ozone layer, the sun's dangerous UV rays would alter our climate so drastically, life on land and in water would cease to exist.

33. A) NO CHANGE
    B) the field; Sigmund Freud will be remembered for ground-breaking work that
    C) the field Sigmund Freud will be remembered for ground-breaking work that
    D) the field Sigmund Freud will be remembered for ground-breaking work, and that

34. A) NO CHANGE
    B) to prevent
    C) prevented
    D) was preventing

35. Which choice most effectively combines the sentences in the underlined portion?
    A) Signed in 1987, this document
    B) Because it was signed in 1987, this document
    C) It was signed in 1987, and this document
    D) It was signed in 1987 so this document

GO ON TO THE NEXT PAGE

A hole in Earth's ozone layer was discovered over Antarctica 🕘 <u>as long as two years prior</u> to the signing of the treaty. The discovery brought the human impact on the environment to the forefront of 🕘 <u>international conversation, the massive hole</u> was evidence that a global response was necessary and that large-scale action was needed. The Montreal Protocol became effective January 1, 1989, and nearly 100 gases deemed dangerous to the ozone layer have been phased out. As a result, 🕘 <u>the size of the ozone hole decreased significantly during the 1990s.</u>

Now that a substantial amount of time has passed since the treaty was put into place, the effects can begin to be 🕘 <u>looked at</u>. As a part of the treaty, the Montreal Protocol's Scientific Assessment Panel was created to gauge 🕘 <u>their</u> effect on the hole in the ozone layer.

36. A) NO CHANGE
    B) long ago, two years prior
    C) two years prior
    D) years prior

37. A) NO CHANGE
    B) international conversation, yet the massive hole
    C) international conversation. The massive hole
    D) international conversation, so the massive hole

38. Which choice completes the sentence with accurate data based on the graphic?
    A) NO CHANGE
    B) the average size of the ozone hole leveled off beginning in the 1990s.
    C) the average size of the ozone hole decreased beginning in the 2000s.
    D) the average size of the ozone hole increased beginning in the 1980s.

39. A) NO CHANGE
    B) controlled
    C) measured
    D) governed

40. A) NO CHANGE
    B) its
    C) it's
    D) there

GO ON TO THE NEXT PAGE

The Panel has since reported the results every four years. The Panel predicts that the ozone layer will return to its former state of health by 2060-2075. `41`

While the treaty is already an obvious success, work continues to ensure that human strides in technology and industry do not reverse the healing process. The Montreal Protocol's Multilateral Fund was established to help developing countries transition away from the consumption and production of harmful chemicals. So far, over $3 billion has been invested by the Fund. The developing countries are referred to as "Article 5 countries." `42`

41. Which choice could be added to paragraph 3 to most effectively convey its central idea?

A) It is the Panel's current estimation that the ozone layer is beginning to heal, but the rate of progress is slow.

B) The Panel meets once a year to assess the increase or decrease of each gas that has been identified as dangerous.

C) Of much concern to the Panel was the effect of ultraviolet radiation on the ozone layer.

D) The Panel has recently updated procedures for the nomination and selection of its membership.

42. Which sentence in paragraph 4 provides the least support for the central idea of the paragraph?

A) While the treaty is already an obvious success, work continues to ensure that human strides in technology and industry do not reverse the healing process.

B) The Montreal Protocol's Multilateral Fund was established to help developing countries transition away from the consumption and production of harmful chemicals.

C) So far, over $3 billion has been invested by the Fund.

D) The developing countries are referred to as "Article 5 countries."

GO ON TO THE NEXT PAGE

[1] The Montreal Protocol is a living document. [2] A current amendment proposition has been put forth by the United States, Mexico, and Canada jointly. [3] It aims to cut down on harmful gases that were put into use as an alternative to the gases specified in the original Montreal Protocol treaty. [4] It has been amended four times since its inception. [5] Combating the erosion of our ozone layer will take time and flexibility, but the research is clear: If humans stay conscious of what we emit into the atmosphere, we can not only stall the damage we have done in the past, but we can **43** change it. **44**

43. A) NO CHANGE
    B) switch
    C) invert
    D) reverse

44. For the sake of cohesion of this paragraph, sentence 4 should be placed

    A) where it is now.
    B) before sentence 1.
    C) after sentence 1.
    D) before sentence 3.

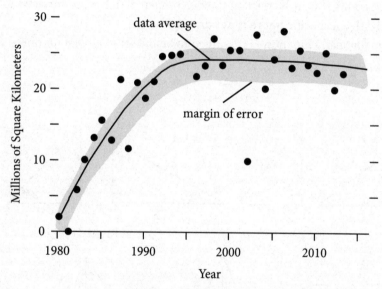

Size of Ozone Hole

Adapted from Ozone Hole Watch, NASA Goddard Space Flight Center.

MATH TEST

25 Minutes—20 Questions

NO-CALCULATOR SECTION

Turn to Section 3 of your answer sheet to answer the questions in this section.

Directions: For this section, solve each problem and decide which is the best of the choices given. Fill in the corresponding oval on the answer sheet. You may use any available space for scratch work.

Notes:

1. Calculator use is NOT permitted.
2. All numbers used are real numbers.
3. All figures used are necessary to solving the problems that they accompany. All figures are drawn to scale EXCEPT when it is stated that a specific figure is not drawn to scale.
4. Unless stated otherwise, the domain of any function f is assumed to be the set of all real numbers x, for which $f(x)$ is a real number.

Information:

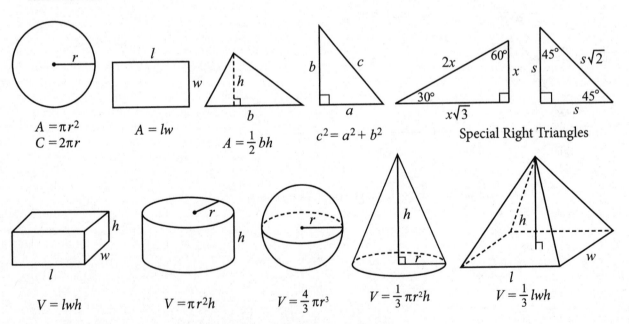

$A = \pi r^2$
$C = 2\pi r$

$A = lw$

$A = \frac{1}{2}bh$

$c^2 = a^2 + b^2$

Special Right Triangles

$V = lwh$

$V = \pi r^2 h$

$V = \frac{4}{3}\pi r^3$

$V = \frac{1}{3}\pi r^2 h$

$V = \frac{1}{3}lwh$

The sum of the degree measures of the angles in a triangle is 180.

The number of degrees of arc in a circle is 360.

The number of radians of arc in a cirlce is 2π.

GO ON TO THE NEXT PAGE

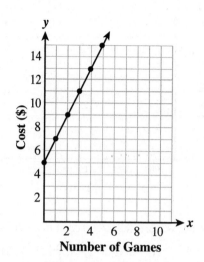

Number of Games

1. The graph above shows the amount that a new, high-tech video arcade charges its customers. What could the *y*-intercept of this graph represent?

   A) The cost of playing 5 games

   B) The cost per game, which is $5

   C) The entrance fee to enter the arcade

   D) The number of games that are played

$$\frac{3x}{x+5} \div \frac{6}{4x+20}$$

2. Which of the following is equivalent to the expression above, given that $x \neq -5$?

   A) $2x$

   B) $\dfrac{x}{2}$

   C) $\dfrac{9x}{2}$

   D) $2x + 4$

$$(x+3)^2 + (y+1)^2 = 25$$

3. The graph of the equation above is a circle. What is the area, in square units, of the circle?

   A) 4π

   B) 5π

   C) 16π

   D) 25π

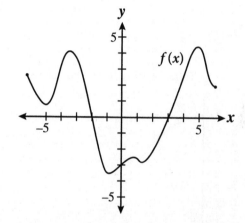

4. The figure above shows the graph of $f(x)$. For which value(s) of x does $f(x)$ equal 0?

   A) 3 only

   B) −3 only

   C) −2 and 3

   D) −3, −2, and 3

GO ON TO THE NEXT PAGE

$$\frac{4(d+3)-9}{8}=\frac{10-(2-d)}{6}$$

5. In the equation above, what is the value of *d*?

A) $\dfrac{23}{16}$

B) $\dfrac{23}{8}$

C) $\dfrac{25}{8}$

D) $\dfrac{25}{4}$

Total Fertility Rate, 1960-2010

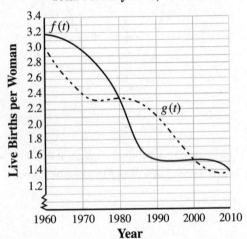

Source: Data from Eurostat.

6. One indicator of a declining economy is a continued decline in birth rates. In 2010, birth rates in Europe were at an all-time low, with the average number of children that a woman has in her lifetime at well below two. In the figure above, *f*(*t*) represents birth rates for Portugal between 1960 and 2010, and *g*(*t*) represents birth rates in Slovakia for the same time period. For which value(s) of *t* is *f*(*t*) > *g*(*t*)?

A) 1960 < *t* < 1980 only

B) 1980 < *t* < 2000 only

C) 1960 < *t* < 1980 and 1990 < *t* < 2000

D) 1960 < *t* < 1980 and 2000 < *t* < 2010

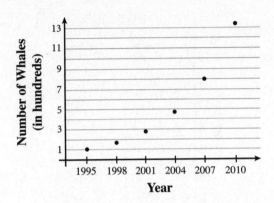

7. The blue whale is the largest creature in the world and has been found in every ocean in the world. A marine biologist surveyed the blue whale population in Monterey Bay, off the coast of California, every three years between 1995 and 2010. The figure above shows her results. If *w* is the number of blue whales present in Monterey Bay and *t* is the number of years since the study began in 1995, which of the following equations best represents the blue whale population of Monterey Bay?

A) $w = 100 + 2t$

B) $w = 100 + \dfrac{t^2}{4}$

C) $w = 100 \times 2^t$

D) $w = 100 \times 2^{\frac{t}{4}}$

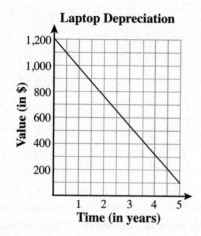

Laptop Depreciation

8. The figure above shows the straight-line deprecia-tion of a laptop computer over the first five years of its use. According to the figure, what is the average rate of change in dollars per year of the value of the computer over the five-year period?

A) −1,100

B) −220

C) −100

D) 100

9. What is the coefficient of x^2 when $6x^2 - \dfrac{2}{5}x + 1$ is multiplied by $10x + \dfrac{1}{3}$?

A) −4

B) −2

C) 2

D) 4

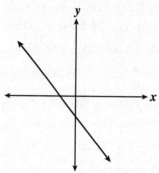

10. The graph above could represent which of the fol-lowing equations?

A) $-6x - 4y = 5$

B) $-6x - 4y = -5$

C) $-6x + 4y = 5$

D) $-6x + 4y = -5$

$$\begin{cases} \dfrac{3}{4}x - \dfrac{1}{2}y = 12 \\ kx - 2y = 22 \end{cases}$$

11. If the system of linear equations above has no solu-tion, and k is a constant, what is the value of k?

A) $-\dfrac{4}{3}$

B) $-\dfrac{3}{4}$

C) 3

D) 4

GO ON TO THE NEXT PAGE

12. In Delray Beach, Florida, you can take a luxury golf cart ride around downtown. The driver charges $4 for the first $\frac{1}{4}$ mile, plus $1.50 for each additional $\frac{1}{2}$ mile. Which inequality represents the number of miles, m, that you could ride and pay no more than $10?

A) $3.25 + 1.5m \leq 10$

B) $3.25 + 3m \leq 10$

C) $4 + 1.5m \leq 10$

D) $4 + 3m \leq 10$

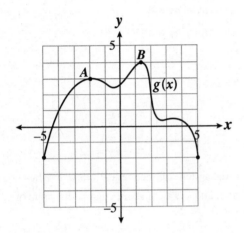

13. The graph of $g(x)$ is shown in the figure above. If $h(x) = -g(x) + 1$, which of the following statements is true?

A) The range of $h(x)$ is $-3 \leq y \leq 3$.

B) The minimum value of $h(x)$ is -4.

C) The coordinates of point A on the function $h(x)$ are $(2, 4)$.

D) The graph of $h(x)$ is increasing between $x = -5$ and $x = -2$.

14. If $a + bi$ represents the complex number that results from multiplying $3 + 2i$ times $5 - i$, what is the value of a?

A) 2

B) 13

C) 15

D) 17

$$\frac{1}{x} + \frac{4}{x} = \frac{1}{72}$$

15. In order to create safe drinking water, cities and towns use water treatment facilities to remove contaminants from surface water and groundwater. Suppose a town has a treatment plant but decides to build a second, more efficient facility. The new treatment plant can filter the water in the reservoir four times as quickly as the older facility. Working together, the two facilities can filter all the water in the reservoir in 72 hours. The equation above represents the scenario. Which of the following describes what the term $\frac{1}{x}$ represents?

A) The portion of the water the older treatment plant can filter in 1 hour

B) The time it takes the older treatment plant to filter the water in the reservoir

C) The time it takes the older treatment plant to filter $\frac{1}{72}$ of the water in the reservoir

D) The portion of the water the new treatment plant can filter in 4 hours

GO ON TO THE NEXT PAGE

Directions: For questions 16-20, solve the problem and enter your answer in the grid, as described below, on the answer sheet.

1. Although not required, it is suggested that you write your answer in the boxes at the top of the columns to help you fill in the circles accurately. You will receive credit only if the circles are filled in correctly.

2. Mark no more than one circle in any column.

3. No question has a negative answer.

4. Some problems may have more than one correct answer. In such cases, grid only one answer.

5. **Mixed numbers** such as $3\frac{1}{2}$ must be gridded as 3.5 or $\frac{7}{2}$.
    (If $3\frac{1}{2}$ is entered into the grid as $\boxed{3\;1\;/\;2}$, it will be interpreted as $\frac{31}{2}$, not $3\frac{1}{2}$).

6. **Decimal answers:** If you obtain a decimal answer with more digits than the grid can accommodate, it may be either rounded or truncated, but it must fill the entire grid.

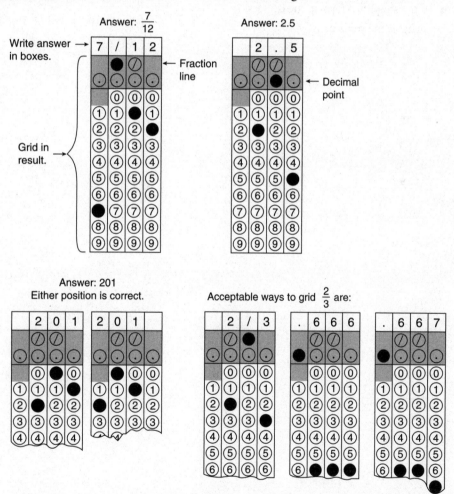

16. If $\dfrac{1}{4}x = 5 - \dfrac{1}{2}y$, what is the value of $x + 2y$?

$$\begin{cases} x + 3y \le 18 \\ 2x - 3y \le 9 \end{cases}$$

17. If (a, b) is a point in the solution region for the system of inequalities shown above and $a = 6$, what is the minimum possible value for b?

$$\frac{\sqrt{x} \cdot x^{\frac{5}{6}} \cdot x}{\sqrt[3]{x}}$$

18. If x^n is the simplified form of the expression above, what is the value of n?

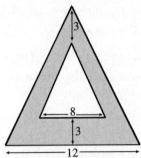

Note: Figure not drawn to scale.

19. In the figure above, the area of the shaded region is 52 square units. What is the height of the larger triangle?

20. If $y = ax^2 + bx + c$ passes through the points $(-3, 10)$, $(0, 1)$, and $(2, 15)$, what is the value of $a + b + c$?

MATH TEST

55 Minutes—38 Questions

CALCULATOR SECTION

Turn to Section 4 of your answer sheet to answer the questions in this section.

Directions: For this section, solve each problem and decide which is the best of the choices given. Fill in the corresponding oval on the answer sheet. You may use any available space for scratch work.

Notes:

1. Calculator use is permitted.
2. All numbers used are real numbers.
3. All figures used are necessary to solving the problems that they accompany. All figures are drawn to scale EXCEPT when it is stated that a specific figure is not drawn to scale.
4. Unless stated otherwise, the domain of any function f is assumed to be the set of all real numbers x, for which $f(x)$ is a real number.

Information:

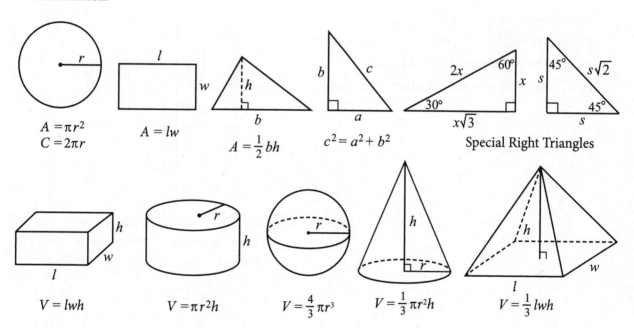

$A = \pi r^2$
$C = 2\pi r$

$A = lw$

$A = \frac{1}{2} bh$

$c^2 = a^2 + b^2$

Special Right Triangles

$V = lwh$

$V = \pi r^2 h$

$V = \frac{4}{3} \pi r^3$

$V = \frac{1}{3} \pi r^2 h$

$V = \frac{1}{3} lwh$

The sum of the degree measures of the angles in a triangle is 180.

The number of degrees of arc in a circle is 360.

The number of radians of arc in a cirlce is 2π.

GO ON TO THE NEXT PAGE

1. Oceans, seas, and bays represent about 96.5% of Earth's water, including the water found in our atmosphere. If the volume of the water contained in oceans, seas, and bays is about 321,000,000 cubic miles, which of the following best represents the approximate volume, in cubic miles, of all the world's water?

   A) 308,160,000

   B) 309,765,000

   C) 332,642,000

   D) 334,375,000

2. An electrician charges a one-time site visit fee to evaluate a potential job. If the electrician accepts the job, he charges an hourly rate plus the cost of any materials needed to complete the job. The electrician also charges for tax, but only on the cost of the materials. If the total cost of completing a job that takes h hours is given by the function $C(h) = 45h + 1.06(82.5) + 75$, then the term $1.06(82.5)$ represents

   A) the hourly rate.

   B) the site visit fee.

   C) the cost of the materials, including tax.

   D) the cost of the materials, not including tax.

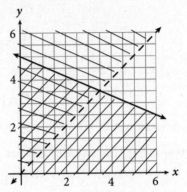

3. The figure above shows the solution set for the system $\begin{cases} y > x \\ y \le -\dfrac{3}{7}x + 5 \end{cases}$. Which of the following is not a solution to the system?

   A) (0, 3)

   B) (1, 2)

   C) (2, 4)

   D) (3, 3)

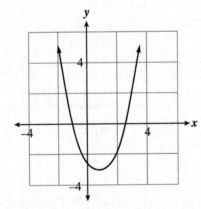

4. Each of the following quadratic equations represents the graph shown above. Which equation reveals the exact values of the x-intercepts of the graph?

   A) $y = \dfrac{1}{2}(2x - 5)(x + 1)$

   B) $y = x^2 - \dfrac{3}{2}x - \dfrac{5}{2}$

   C) $y + \dfrac{49}{16} = \left(x - \dfrac{3}{4}\right)^2$

   D) $y = \left(x - \dfrac{3}{4}\right)^2 - \dfrac{49}{16}$

GO ON TO THE NEXT PAGE

National Government Concerns

Average Annual Gas Prices

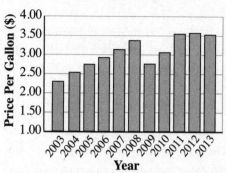

Data from U.S. Energy Information Administration.

5. Margo surveyed all the students in the government classes at her school to see what they thought should be the most important concern of a national government. The results of the survey are shown in the figure above. If the ratio of students who answered "Foreign Policy" to those who answered "Environment" was 5:3, what percentage of the students answered "Environment"?

A) 16%

B) 21%

C) 24%

D) 35%

6. Marco needs to buy several white dress shirts for his new job. He finds one he likes for $35 that is on sale for 40% off. He also likes a black tie that costs $21. Which of the following represents the total cost, not including tax, if Marco buys x of the white shirts that are on sale and two of the black ties?

A) $C = 14x + 42$

B) $C = 21x + 21$

C) $C = 21x + 42$

D) $C = 35x + 42$

7. The figure above shows the average annual gas prices in the United States from 2003 to 2013. Based on the information shown, which of the following conclusions is valid?

A) A gallon of gas cost more in 2008 than in 2013.

B) The price more than doubled between 2003 and 2013.

C) The drop in price from 2008 to 2009 was more than $1.00 per gallon.

D) The overall change in price was greater between 2003 and 2008 than it was between 2008 and 2013.

$$\begin{cases} -2x + 5y = 1 \\ 7x - 10y = -11 \end{cases}$$

8. If (x, y) is a solution to the system of equations above, what is the sum of x and y?

A) $-\dfrac{137}{30}$

B) -4

C) $-\dfrac{10}{3}$

D) -3

GO ON TO THE NEXT PAGE ▷

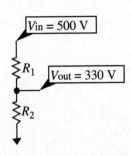

$V_{in} = 500$ V

R_1

$V_{out} = 330$ V

R_2

9. A voltage divider is a simple circuit that converts a large voltage into a smaller one. The figure above shows a voltage divider that consists of two resistors that together have a total resistance of 294 ohms. To produce the desired voltage of 330 volts, R2 must be 6 ohms less than twice R1. Solving which of the following systems of equations gives the individual resistance for R1 and R2?

A) $\begin{cases} R_2 = 2R_1 - 6 \\ R_1 + R_2 = 294 \end{cases}$

B) $\begin{cases} R_1 = 2R_2 + 6 \\ R_1 + R_2 = 294 \end{cases}$

C) $\begin{cases} R_2 = 2R_1 - 6 \\ R_1 + R_2 = \dfrac{294}{330} \end{cases}$

D) $\begin{cases} R_1 = 2R_2 + 6 \\ R_1 + R_2 = 330(294) \end{cases}$

10. If $\dfrac{2}{5}(5x) + 2(x-1) = 4(x+1) - 2$, what is the value of x?

A) $x = -2$

B) $x = 2$

C) There is no value of x for which the equation is true.

D) There are infinitely many values of x for which the equation is true.

11. Crude oil is being transferred from a full rectangular storage container with dimensions 4 meters by 9 meters by 10 meters into a cylindrical transportation container that has a diameter of 6 meters. What is the minimum possible length for a transportation container that will hold all of the oil?

A) 40π

B) $\dfrac{40}{\pi}$

C) 60π

D) $\dfrac{120}{\pi}$

12. The percent increase from 5 to 12 is equal to the percent increase from 12 to what number?

A) 16.8

B) 19.0

C) 26.6

D) 28.8

$$b = \frac{L}{4\pi d^2}$$

13. The brightness of a celestial body, like a star, decreases as you move away from it. In contrast, the luminosity of a celestial body is a constant number that represents its intrinsic brightness. The inverse square law, shown above, is used to find the brightness, b, of a celestial body when you know its luminosity, L, and the distance, d, in meters to the body. Which equation shows the distance to a celestial body, given its brightness and luminosity?

A) $d = \dfrac{1}{2}\sqrt{\dfrac{L}{\pi b}}$

B) $d = \sqrt{\dfrac{L}{2\pi b}}$

C) $d = \dfrac{\sqrt{L}}{2\pi b}$

D) $d = \dfrac{L}{2\sqrt{\pi b}}$

GO ON TO THE NEXT PAGE

Questions 14 and 15 refer to the following information.

Each month, the Bureau of Labor Statistics conducts a survey called the Current Population Survey (CPS) to measure unemployment in the United States. Across the country, about 60,000 households are included in the survey sample. These households are grouped by geographic region. A summary of the January 2014 survey results for male respondents in one geographic region is shown in the table below.

Age Group	Employed	Unemployed	Not in the Labor Force	Total
16 to 19	8	5	10	23
20 to 24	26	7	23	56
25 to 34	142	11	28	157
35 to 44	144	8	32	164
45 to 54	66	6	26	98
Over 54	65	7	36	152
Total	451	44	155	650

14. According to the data in the table, for which age group did the smallest percentage of men report that they were unemployed in January 2014?

    A) 20 to 24 years

    B) 35 to 44 years

    C) 45 to 54 years

    D) Over 54 years

15. If one unemployed man from this sample is chosen at random for a follow-up survey, what is the probability that he will be between the ages of 45 and 54?

    A) 6.0%

    B) 13.6%

    C) 15.1%

    D) 44.9%

GO ON TO THE NEXT PAGE

16. Which of the following are solutions to the quadratic equation $(x-1)^2 = \dfrac{4}{9}$?

   A) $x = -\dfrac{5}{3}, x = \dfrac{5}{3}$

   B) $x = \dfrac{1}{3}, x = \dfrac{5}{3}$

   C) $x = \dfrac{5}{9}, x = \dfrac{13}{9}$

   D) $x = 1 \pm \sqrt{\dfrac{2}{3}}$

17. Damien is throwing darts. He has a total of 6 darts to throw. He gets 5 points for each dart that lands in a blue ring and 10 points for each dart that lands in a red ring. If x of his darts land in a blue ring and the rest land in a red ring, which expression represents his total score?

   A) $10x$

   B) $10x + 5$

   C) $5x + 30$

   D) $60 - 5x$

18. Red tide is a form of harmful algae that releases toxins as it breaks down in the environment. A marine biologist is testing a new spray, composed of clay and water, hoping to kill the red tide that almost completely covers a beach in southern Florida. He applies the spray to a representative sample of 200 square feet of the beach. By the end of the week, 184 square feet of the beach is free of the red tide. Based on these results, and assuming the same general conditions, how much of the 10,000-square-foot beach would still be covered by red tide if the spray had been used on the entire area?

   A) 800 sq ft

   B) 920 sq ft

   C) 8,000 sq ft

   D) 9,200 sq ft

$$\begin{cases} y = \dfrac{1}{2}x - 2 \\ y = -x^2 + 1 \end{cases}$$

19. If (a, b) is a solution to the system of equations above, which of the following could be the value of b?

   A) −3

   B) −2

   C) 1

   D) 2

20. Given the function $g(x) = \dfrac{2}{3}x + 7$, what domain value corresponds to the range value of 3?

   A) −6

   B) −2

   C) 6

   D) 9

21. A landscaper buys a new commercial-grade lawn mower that costs $2,800. Based on past experience, he expects it to last about 8 years, and then he can sell it for scrap metal with a salvage value of about $240. Assuming the value of the lawn mower depreciates at a constant rate, which equation could be used to find its approximate value after x years, given that $x < 8$?

   A) $y = -8x + 2,560$

   B) $y = -240x + 2,800$

   C) $y = -320x + 2,800$

   D) $y = 240x - 2,560$

GO ON TO THE NEXT PAGE

22. A microbiologist is studying the effects of a new antibiotic on a culture of 20,000 bacteria. When the antibiotic is added to the culture, the number of bacteria is reduced by half every hour. What kind of function best models the number of bacteria remaining in the culture after the antibiotic is added?

    A) A linear function

    B) A quadratic function

    C) A polynomial function

    D) An exponential function

23. An airline company purchased two new airplanes. One can travel at speeds of up to 600 miles per hour and the other at speeds of up to 720 miles per hour. How many more miles can the faster airplane travel in 12 seconds than the slower airplane?

    A) $\dfrac{1}{30}$

    B) $\dfrac{2}{5}$

    C) 2

    D) 30

State	Minimum Wage per Hour
Idaho	$7.25
Montana	$7.90
Oregon	$9.10
Washington	$9.32

24. When bordering states offer a higher minimum wage, workers often commute across state lines in order to earn a better living. The table above shows the 2014 minimum wages for several states that share a border. Assuming an average workweek of between 35 and 40 hours, which inequality represents how much more a worker who earns minimum wage can earn per week in Oregon than in Idaho?

    A) $x \geq 1.85$

    B) $7.25 \leq x \leq 9.10$

    C) $64.75 \leq x \leq 74$

    D) $253.75 \leq x \leq 364$

25. In the United States, the maintenance and construction of airports, transit systems, and major roads is largely funded through a federal excise tax on gasoline. Based on the 2011 statistics given below, how much did the average household pay per year in federal gasoline taxes?

    • The federal gasoline tax rate was 18.4 cents per gallon.

    • The average motor vehicle was driven approximately 11,340 miles per year.

    • The national average fuel economy for noncommercial vehicles was 21.4 miles per gallon.

    • The average American household owned 1.75 vehicles.

    A) $55.73

    B) $68.91

    C) $97.52

    D) $170.63

GO ON TO THE NEXT PAGE

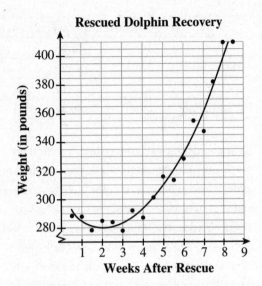

26. Following the catastrophic oil spill in the Gulf of Mexico in April of 2010, more than 900 bottlenose dolphins were found dead or stranded in the oil spill area. The figure above shows the weight of a rescued dolphin during its recovery. Based on the quadratic model fit to the data shown, which of the following is the closest to the average rate of change in the dolphin's weight between week 2 and week 8 of its recovery?

A) 4 pounds per week

B) 16 pounds per week

C) 20 pounds per week

D) 40 pounds per week

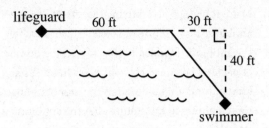

27. As shown in the figure above, a lifeguard sees a struggling swimmer who is 40 feet from the beach. The lifeguard runs 60 feet along the edge of the water at a speed of 12 feet per second. He pauses for 1 second to locate the swimmer again, and then dives into the water and swims along a diagonal path to the swimmer at a speed of 5 feet per second. How many seconds go by between the time the lifeguard sees the struggling swimmer and the time he reaches the swimmer?

A) 16

B) 22

C) 50

D) 56

28. What was the initial amount of gasoline in a fuel trailer, in gallons, if there are now x gallons, y gallons were pumped into a storage tank, and then 50 gallons were added to the trailer?

A) $x + y + 50$

B) $x + y - 50$

C) $y - x + 50$

D) $x - y - 50$

U.S. Foreign Trade, 2014

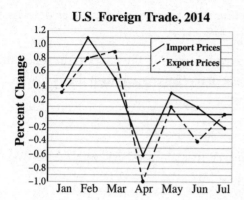

29. The figure above shows the net change, as a percentage, for U.S. import and export prices from January to July 2014 as reported by the Bureau of Labor Statistics. For example, U.S. import prices declined 0.2 percent in July while export prices remained unchanged for that month. Based on this information, which of the following statements is true for the time period shown in the figure?

A) On average, export prices increased more than import prices.

B) Import prices showed an increase more often than export prices.

C) Import prices showed the greatest change between two consecutive months.

D) From January to July, import prices showed a greater overall decrease than export prices.

$$\frac{3.86}{x} + \frac{180.2}{10x} + \frac{42.2}{5x}$$

30. The Ironman Triathlon originated in Hawaii in 1978. The format of the Ironman has not changed since then: it consists of a 3.86-km swim, a 180.2-km bicycle ride, and a 42.2-km run, all raced in that order and without a break. Suppose an athlete bikes 10 times as fast as he swims and runs 5 times as fast as he swims. The variable x in the expression above represents the rate at which the athlete swims, and the whole expression represents the number of hours that it takes him to complete the race. If it takes him 16.2 hours to complete the race, how many kilometers did he swim in 1 hour?

A) 0.85

B) 1.01

C) 1.17

D) 1.87

GO ON TO THE NEXT PAGE

Directions: For questions 31-38, solve the problem and enter your answer in the grid, as described below, on the answer sheet.

1. Although not required, it is suggested that you write your answer in the boxes at the top of the columns to help you fill in the circles accurately. You will receive credit only if the circles are filled in correctly.

2. Mark no more than one circle in any column.

3. No question has a negative answer.

4. Some problems may have more than one correct answer. In such cases, grid only one answer.

5. **Mixed numbers** such as $3\frac{1}{2}$ must be gridded as 3.5 or $\frac{7}{2}$.
   (If $3\frac{1}{2}$ is entered into the grid as $\boxed{3\,1\,/\,2}$, it will be interpreted as $\frac{31}{2}$, not $3\frac{1}{2}$).

6. **Decimal answers:** If you obtain a decimal answer with more digits than the grid can accommodate, it may be either rounded or truncated, but it must fill the entire grid.

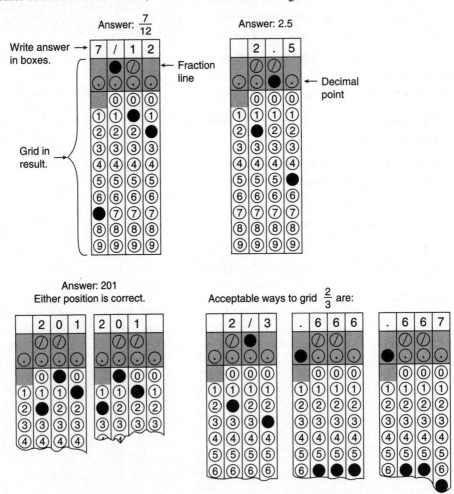

GO ON TO THE NEXT PAGE ⇒

31. What value of x satisfies the equation
$$\frac{2}{3}(5x+7)=8x\ ?$$

32. Some doctors base the dosage of a drug to be given to a patient on the patient's body surface area (BSA). The most commonly used formula for calculating BSA is $BSA = \sqrt{\dfrac{wh}{3,600}}$, where w is the patient's weight (in kg), h is the patient's height (in cm), and BSA is measured in square meters. How tall (in cm) is a patient who weighs 150 kg and has a BSA of $2\sqrt{2}$ m²?

33. If $-\dfrac{3}{2} < -2m + 1 < -\dfrac{7}{5}$, what is one possible value of $10m - 5$?

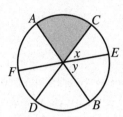

34. In the figure above, $\overline{AB}$, $\overline{CD}$, and $\overline{EF}$ are diameters of the circle. If $y = 2x - 12$, and the shaded area is $\dfrac{1}{5}$ of the circle, what is the value of x?

35. If the slope of a line is $-\dfrac{7}{4}$ and a point on the line is $(4, 7)$, what is the y-intercept of the line?

36. Rory left home and drove straight to the airport at an average speed of 45 miles per hour. He returned home along the same route, but traffic slowed him down and he only averaged 30 miles per hour on the return trip. If his total travel time was 2 hours and 30 minutes, how far is it, in miles, from Rory's house to the airport?

Questions 37 and 38 refer to the following information.

Chemical Makeup of One Mole of Chloroform

Element	Number of Moles	Mass per Mole (grams)
Carbon	1	12.011
Hydrogen	1	1.008
Chlorine	3	35.453

A chemical solvent is a substance that dissolves another to form a solution. For example, water is a solvent for sugar. Unfortunately, many chemical solvents are hazardous to the environment. One eco-friendly chemical solvent is chloroform, also known as trichloromethane ($CHCl_3$). The table above shows the chemical makeup of one mole of chloroform.

37. Carbon makes up what percent of the mass of one mole of chloroform? Round your answer to the nearest whole percent and ignore the percent sign when entering your answer.

38. If a chemist starts with 1,000 grams of chloroform and uses 522.5 grams, how many moles of chlorine are left?

IF YOU FINISH BEFORE TIME IS CALLED, YOU MAY CHECK YOUR WORK ON THIS SECTION ONLY. DO NOT TURN TO ANY OTHER SECTION IN THE TEST.   **STOP**

ESSAY TEST

50 minutes

The essay gives you an opportunity to show how effectively you can read and comprehend a passage and write an essay analyzing the passage. In your essay, you should demonstrate that you have read the passage carefully, present a clear and logical analysis, and use language precisely.

Your essay must be written on the lines provided in your answer booklet; except for the planning page of the answer booklet, you will receive no other paper on which to write. You will have enough space if you write on every line, avoid wide margins, and keep your handwriting to a reasonable size. Remember that people who are not familiar with your handwriting will read what you write. Try to write or print so that what you are writing is legible to those readers.

You have 50 minutes to read the passage and write an essay in response to the prompt provided inside this booklet.

1. Do not write your essay in this booklet. Only what you write on the lined pages of your answer booklet will be evaluated.
2. An off-topic essay will not be evaluated.

As you read the passage below, consider how Morris uses

- evidence, such as facts or examples, to support claims.

- reasoning to develop ideas and to connect claims and evidence.

- stylistic or persuasive elements, such as word choice or appeals to emotion, to add power to the ideas expressed.

This passage is adapted from Elisabeth Woodbridge Morris's essay "The Tyranny of Things." In this portion, Morris paints a portrait of American consumerism in 1917 and offers a distinct perspective on the joy of freedom from "things, things, things."

Two fifteen-year-old girls stood eyeing one another on first acquaintance. Finally one little girl said, "Which do you like best, people or things?" The other little girl said, "Things." They were friends at once.

I suppose we all go through a phase when we like things best; and not only like them, but want to possess them under our hand. The passion for accumulation is upon us. We make "collections," we fill our rooms, our walls, our tables, our desks, with things, things, things.

Many people never pass out of this phase. They never see a flower without wanting to pick it and put it in a vase, they never enjoy a book without wanting to own it, nor a picture without wanting to hang it on their walls. They keep photographs of all their friends and Kodak albums of all the places they visit, they save all their theater programmes and dinner cards, they bring home all their alpenstocks.* Their houses are filled with an undigested mass of things, like the terminal moraine where a glacier dumps at length everything it has picked up during its progress through the lands.

But to some of us a day comes when we begin to grow weary of things. We realize that we do not possess them; they possess us. Our books are a burden to us, our pictures have destroyed every restful wall-space,

---

* alpenstocks: strong pointed poles used by mountain climbers

GO ON TO THE NEXT PAGE ⟶

our china is a care, our photographs drive us mad, our programmes and alpenstocks fill us with loathing. We feel stifled with the sense of things, and our problem becomes, not how much we can accumulate, but how much we can do without. We send our books to the village library, and our pictures to the college settlement. Such things as we cannot give away, and have not the courage to destroy, we stack in the garret, where they lie huddled in dim and dusty heaps, removed from our sight, to be sure, yet still faintly importunate.

Then, as we breathe more freely in the clear space that we have made for ourselves, we grow aware that we must not relax our vigilance, or we shall be once more overwhelmed. . . .

It extends to all our doings. For every event there is a "souvenir." We cannot go to luncheon and meet our friends but we must receive a token to carry away. Even our children cannot have a birthday party, and play games, and eat good things, and be happy. The host must receive gifts from every little guest, and provide in return some little remembrance for each to take home. Truly, on all sides we are beset, and we go lumbering along through life like a ship encrusted with barnacles, which can never cut the waves clean and sure and swift until she has been

scraped bare again. And there seems little hope for us this side our last port.

And to think that there was a time when folk had not even that hope! When a man's possessions were burned with him, so that he might, forsooth, have them all about him in the next world! Suffocating thought! To think one could not even then be clear of things, and make at least a fresh start! That must, indeed, have been in the childhood of the race.

Once upon a time, when I was very tired, I chanced to go away to a little house by the sea. . . . There was nothing in the house to demand care, to claim attention, to cumber my consciousness with its insistent, unchanging companionship. There was nothing but a shelter, and outside, the fields and marshes, the shore and the sea. These did not have to be taken down and put up and arranged and dusted and cared for. They were not things at all, they were powers, presences. . . .

If we could but free ourselves once for all, how simple life might become! One of my friends, who, with six young children and only one servant, keeps a spotless house and a soul serene, told me once how she did it. "My dear, once a month I give away every single thing in the house that we do not imperatively need. It sounds wasteful, but I don't believe it really is. . . ."

Write an essay in which you explain how Morris builds an argument to persuade her audience that possessions are oppressive. In your essay, analyze how Morris uses one or more of the listed features in the box above (or features of your own choice) to strengthen the logic and persuasiveness of her argument. Be sure that your analysis focuses on the most relevant features of the passage.

Your essay should not explain whether you agree with Morris's claims, but rather explain how Morris builds an argument to persuade her audience.

ANSWER KEY
READING TEST

1. A	14. B	27. D	40. A
2. B	15. D	28. C	41. B
3. C	16. C	29. C	42. D
4. C	17. A	30. B	43. A
5. A	18. D	31. D	44. B
6. C	19. C	32. B	45. A
7. D	20. C	33. B	46. B
8. A	21. C	34. C	47. D
9. D	22. B	35. D	48. D
10. A	23. D	36. B	49. A
11. A	24. C	37. D	50. C
12. D	25. A	38. A	51. D
13. D	26. A	39. B	52. C

WRITING AND LANGUAGE TEST

1. C	12. B	23. C	34. B
2. D	13. B	24. B	35. A
3. B	14. B	25. D	36. C
4. C	15. A	26. B	37. C
5. A	16. A	27. B	38. B
6. C	17. C	28. C	39. C
7. B	18. A	29. B	40. B
8. D	19. B	30. C	41. A
9. C	20. C	31. B	42. D
10. C	21. D	32. D	43. D
11. A	22. D	33. A	44. C

MATH—NO CALCULATOR

1. C	6. D	11. C	16. 20
2. A	7. D	12. B	17. 1
3. D	8. B	13. A	18. 2
4. C	9. B	14. D	19. 14
5. B	10. A	15. A	20. 6

MATH—CALCULATOR

1. C	11. B	21. C	31. 1
2. C	12. D	22. D	32. 192
3. D	13. A	23. B	33. $7 < x < 7.5$
4. A	14. D	24. C	34. 40
5. B	15. B	25. D	35. 14
6. C	16. B	26. C	36. 45
7. D	17. D	27. A	37. 10
8. B	18. A	28. B	38. 12
9. A	19. A	29. B	
10. C	20. A	30. D	

ANSWERS AND EXPLANATIONS

READING TEST

Anna Karenina

1. A

Difficulty: Easy

Category: Reading / Detail

Strategic Advice: Make sure to read the passage closely so events are clearly understood.

Getting to the Answer: The first paragraph explicitly states how Levin knew that Kitty was there. Choice (A) matches the information stated in the passage.

2. B

Difficulty: Medium

Category: Reading / Vocab-in-Context

Strategic Advice: Use context clues to help you distinguish the shades of meaning each word has.

Getting to the Answer: Two of the answer choices have a somewhat negative connotation. The author is not describing the scene in a negative way. In this passage, the word "swarmed" means "gathered." Therefore, (B) is the correct answer. The other words' connotations do not fit with the context of the sentence.

3. C

Difficulty: Hard

Category: Reading / Inference

Strategic Advice: Look for clues in the text that suggest what Levin is like.

Getting to the Answer: Emotionally charged phrases, such as "the rapture and the terror that seized on

his heart," help reveal Levin's personality. Choice (C) reflects the depiction of Levin as a passionate person.

4. C

Difficulty: Hard

Category: Reading / Command of Evidence

Strategic Advice: Eliminate answer choices that don't include a description of Levin.

Getting to the Answer: Because the excerpt focuses on Levin's feelings toward Kitty, evidence of the kind of person he is will probably reflect this. Choice (C) provides the best evidence.

5. A

Difficulty: Medium

Category: Reading / Global

Strategic Advice: The central theme of a passage is the insight about life that the author is trying to get across to the reader. Eliminate any themes that are not revealed by the experiences of Levin.

Getting to the Answer: Though you may personally agree with more than one of the themes presented, (A) is only one answer choice that is supported by details in the passage. Levin's feelings and actions support this theme.

6. C

Difficulty: Medium

Category: Reading / Inference

Strategic Advice: Examine the passage to see what other characters do in response to Levin.

Getting to the Answer: The other skaters go about their business. Most take little notice of Levin. Therefore, (C) is the correct answer.

7. D
Difficulty: Medium

Category: Reading / Command of Evidence

Strategic Advice: Reread each quote in the context of the passage. This will help you decide the correct answer.

Getting to the Answer: Of all the answer choices, Nikolay's way of greeting Levin is the strongest evidence that people think Levin seems normal. Choice (D) is the correct answer.

8. A
Difficulty: Medium

Category: Reading / Vocab-in-Context

Strategic Advice: The context of the passage can help reveal the meaning of the word. Insert each choice in the sentence to see which one makes the most sense.

Getting to the Answer: Levin speaks directly to his heart, asking it to behave. Choice (A), "begged," comes closest to meaning the same thing as "conjured" in this context.

9. D
Difficulty: Medium

Category: Reading / Rhetoric

Strategic Advice: Think about the entire scene described in the passage and decide why the author chose to describe Levin's heart as "throbbing."

Getting to the Answer: Choice (D) is the correct answer. The author chose this word to capture Levin's agitated state.

10. A
Difficulty: Hard

Category: Reading / Rhetoric

Strategic Advice: Eliminate answer choices that are clearly not representative of the author's feelings, or attitude, about Levin.

Getting to the Answer: The author presents Levin's situation as one that is painful. The passage's tone suggests that Levin is worthy of the reader's empathy. Choice (A) fits this tone.

Franklin Delano Roosevelt Speech

11. A
Difficulty: Hard

Category: Reading / Rhetoric

Strategic Advice: Watch out for choices that indicate broad supporting goals. The correct answer will reflect the specific intent of President Roosevelt in giving this address.

Getting to the Answer: The introduction to the passage states that President Roosevelt reveals his intention to preserve and spread American democratic ideals. Roosevelt's remarks regarding taxation, patriotism, and sacrifice suggest that he wishes to gain the support of the American people for these goals and to persuade them to connect the fight for global democracy with their own democratic interests. Choice (A) makes clear the president's purpose in winning citizens' support for the battles abroad.

12. D
Difficulty: Hard

Category: Reading / Command of Evidence

Strategic Advice: Be careful of choices that do not provide direct evidence to support the president's purpose. The correct answer will relate specifically to the stated purpose, or intent, of the passage.

Getting to the Answer: President Roosevelt makes clear that his intention is to provide support for global efforts to end tyranny and spread democracy and to garner the support of the American people for these goals. In the previous question, his stated purpose is "to make its people conscious of their individual stake in the preservation of democratic life in America." The two elements of that purpose are the American people and the preservation of democratic life. Only (D) provides direct evidence for the previous question.

13. D
Difficulty: Easy

Category: Reading / Vocab-in-Context

Strategic Advice: All answer choices are alternate meanings of the word "sacrifice." The correct answer will relate directly to the context of the passage.

Getting to the Answer: Despite the fact that Roosevelt gave the speech on the eve of America's involvement in World War II, neither B nor C is the meaning he's after. Roosevelt also mentions paying more taxes as a form of sacrifice in lines 42-43. Choice (D), "surrender of interests to a greater good," is the correct answer.

14. B
Difficulty: Hard

Category: Reading / Inference

Strategic Advice: Keep in mind that you're looking for a relationship that is suggested, not stated. To reach the correct answer, you must infer, or make a logical guess, based on information in the passage.

Getting to the Answer: The correct answer will provide support for the stated purpose of the passage while demonstrating a logical relationship. Choice (B) provides support for the stated goal of winning support among U.S. citizens for the spread of democracy abroad. It does so by suggesting that the security of U.S. democracy depends on the advancement of human rights and freedoms globally.

15. D
Difficulty: Medium

Category: Reading / Command of Evidence

Strategic Advice: Avoid answers that provide evidence for incorrect answers to the previous question. The correct answer will use language reflective of the correct answer above to demonstrate a relationship.

Getting to the Answer: Principles and ideas such as democracy, freedom, and protection of human

rights are used interchangeably throughout Roosevelt's speech. The lines in (D) draw the connection between freedom at home and freedom everywhere.

16. C
Difficulty: Easy

Category: Reading / Vocab-in-Context

Strategic Advice: Substitute each answer choice for the word in question and decide which one fits the context provided in the passage.

Getting to the Answer: In the context of the passage, (C) works best. It draws a distinction between individual citizens' monetary interests, or their pocketbooks, and the cause of patriotism, or the greater good.

17. A
Difficulty: Medium

Category: Reading / Rhetoric

Strategic Advice: Keep in mind that the correct answer will relate directly to the meaning of the elements in the identified lines.

Getting to the Answer: President Roosevelt is arguing against those who would oppose the overarching goal of his speech, namely to recruit American public support for the war effort and the spread of democracy overseas. Choice (A) fits best; Roosevelt asserts that his goals are realistic and attainable, not just idealistic visions, as his opponents might claim.

18. D
Difficulty: Medium

Category: Reading / Rhetoric

Strategic Advice: Be wary of answers like A and B that seem to offer specific advice or state specific goals relevant to the purpose of the passage without suggesting how those goals might be achieved. The correct answer will offer a tool, a condition, or another asset for achieving the passage's claim—in this case, the spread of democracy.

Getting to the Answer: The previous question identifies that President Roosevelt considers the spread of global democracy achievable. This question asks you to identify how the president envisions achieving that purpose. Choice (D) matches the intent. In this line, President Roosevelt identifies "our unity of purpose" as an asset that will help achieve his goal.

19. C
Difficulty: Hard

Category: Reading / Inference

Strategic Advice: Be careful of answers that cite other policies that the president might support that are not related to the lines quoted. The correct answer will relate directly to the specific lines in question.

Getting to the Answer: In this speech, Roosevelt identifies four freedoms that he views the United States as obligated to defend. The freedom from want signifies a commitment to helping struggling populations at home and abroad. Choice (C) fits. The president urges economic understandings among nations to help those in need.

20. C
Difficulty: Medium

Category: Reading / Rhetoric

Strategic Advice: Be careful of answers like A that offer other viable uses of rhetoric within the larger passage. The correct answer will relate specifically to the text cited in the question.

Getting to the Answer: Roosevelt suggests that the preservation of American freedoms cannot exist without the preservation of human rights on a global scale. To cement this connection, he contrasts democratic movements with tyrannical movements occurring in the world. Choice (C) is the correct answer. President Roosevelt references "the so-called new order of tyranny" in order to show what might happen should the United States and the American people not support other nations in their fight against such tyranny.

Women's Suffrage

21. C
Difficulty: Medium

Category: Reading / Rhetoric

Strategic Advice: Keep in mind that the "stance" of an author refers to his or her perspective or attitude toward the topic written about.

Getting to the Answer: The passage is written by a secondary source, such as a scholar or a historian, who is looking back on the events that led to the adoption of the Nineteenth Amendment. It is not written by a primary source, such as a legislator or an advocate in the midst of the movement's events. For this reason, (C) is the correct answer. The author of the passage is most clearly a scholar evaluating not just the motivation of women's suffrage leaders but the key events and impact of the movement as a whole.

22. B
Difficulty: Hard

Category: Reading / Rhetoric

Strategic Advice: Avoid answers like A that refer to related issues not relevant to the passage's purpose and answers like D that go too far. The correct answer will identify a claim made explicitly in the quote.

Getting to the Answer: In the quote, the author notes that election laws following passage of the Nineteenth Amendment did not secure equal voting rights for all. From this statement, it is fairly clear that other groups of people still needed support for their voting rights. Answer (B) is correct.

23. D
Difficulty: Medium

Category: Reading / Command of Evidence

Strategic Advice: Reread the line quoted in the previous question and notice that it occurs in the passage after ratification of the Nineteenth Amendment.

Therefore, the evidence you're looking for will refer to an event that came later.

Getting to the Answer: The author suggests that the Nineteenth Amendment did not win equal voting rights for all citizens but that it did serve as an important step on the way to free and fair elections. Choice (D) demonstrates that a later event expanded voting rights further, to citizens regardless not only of gender but also of race.

24. C
Difficulty: Easy

Category: Reading / Vocab-in-Context

Strategic Advice: Consider the events that are being described in the paragraph in which the word appears. This will help you choose the best answer.

Getting to the Answer: It's clear in this paragraph that the women's suffrage movement was gaining momentum at this time. Events and tactics excited those who supported the movement and attracted more supporters. Therefore, (C) reflects the correct meaning of "galvanized."

25. A
Difficulty: Hard

Category: Reading / Rhetoric

Strategic Advice: Carefully review the paragraph in which the line appears before choosing the best answer.

Getting to the Answer: Choice (A) demonstrates the connection between successfully changing one element (people's minds) in order to change the other (laws).

26. A
Difficulty: Hard

Category: Reading / Inference

Strategic Advice: Be wary of answers like D that go too far in asserting unsubstantiated causal

relationships. The correct answer will reference an idea or a relationship that is supported by the content of the passage.

Getting to the Answer: Choice (A) expresses the idea implicit in the passage that the American government responds, sometimes slowly, to the changing needs and sentiments of the American people.

27. D
Difficulty: Hard

Category: Reading / Command of Evidence

Strategic Advice: Watch for answers like A and C that cite specific changes or examples that might seem to support the implicit meaning but do not go far enough. The correct answer will reflect the full relationship or idea described in the implicit meaning.

Getting to the Answer: The correct answer to the previous question states the idea implicit in the passage that the government responds and adapts to changes in U.S. society. This suggests a change that takes place over time. Choice (D) demonstrates the idea that both society and the government have changed over time as the civil rights movement of the late twentieth century overcame social and legal inequalities inherited from earlier in the nation's history.

28. C
Difficulty: Medium

Category: Reading / Detail

Strategic Advice: Be careful of answers that aren't backed by sufficient evidence in the graphic.

Getting to the Answer: The graphic shows proof that women's suffrage unfolded through a series of events over a long period of time. Choice (C) is the correct answer.

29. C
Difficulty: Medium

Category: Reading / Vocab-in-Context

Strategic Advice: Read the sentence in which the word appears. The correct answer should be interchangeable with the word.

Getting to the Answer: The passage states that "Posters . . . called into question the authenticity of a free country with unjust laws." Choice (C) is the correct answer, as "legitimacy" refers to something that is in accordance with established rules or principles.

30. B
Difficulty: Medium

Category: Reading / Inference

Strategic Advice: Be cautious about answers that state true events but that do not directly relate to the content of the question.

Getting to the Answer: Choice (B) is the correct answer. Wilson's framing of the conflict abroad as a fight for democracy and freedom helped women suffragists draw attention to the fact that the U.S. government was fighting for justice abroad while denying justice at home.

31. D
Difficulty: Medium

Category: Reading / Synthesis

Strategic Advice: A question like this is asking you to compare information provided in the graphic with information provided in the passage text. Consider each answer choice as you make your comparison.

Getting to the Answer: Choice (D) is the correct answer. Both the graphic and the passage indicate that women's suffrage gained early victories in several states quite a few years before becoming law at the federal level through passage of the Nineteenth Amendment.

Paired Passages—Genomes

32. B
Difficulty: Medium

Category: Reading / Global

Strategic Advice: Look for the answer choice that describes an idea supported throughout the passage rather than a specific detail.

Getting to the Answer: Collectively, the details in the passage support the idea that the coffee market can be expanded and the profits generated from coffee sales can be increased by applying information gained in sequencing the genome of coffee plants. Choice (B) is the correct answer.

33. B
Difficulty: Hard

Category: Reading / Rhetoric

Strategic Advice: Avoid answers that are not directly supported by evidence in the passage.

Getting to the Answer: Eliminate answers such as A and C, which are not supported by the main idea of the passage. In contrast, there is evidential support for (B). The author would most likely agree that studying other nonhuman primates could be beneficial to people.

34. C
Difficulty: Medium

Category: Reading / Inference

Strategic Advice: Watch out for answer choices that seem plausible but are not directly implied by the evidence in the passage.

Getting to the Answer: Choice (C) is the correct answer. In the last paragraph, the author discusses how research that is currently being conducted could impact the future of coffee production.

35. D

Difficulty: Medium

Category: Reading / Command of Evidence

Strategic Advice: Look back at the previous question. Find the lines from the passage that describe research that could increase the profitability of coffee for producers.

Getting to the Answer: Choice (D) is the correct answer. In the last paragraph, the author describes how current research could lead to a way to produce coffee plants without caffeine in a more cost-effective manner.

36. B

Difficulty: Hard

Category: Reading / Inference

Strategic Advice: Eliminate any answer choices that may sound plausible but take the information presented in the passage too far.

Getting to the Answer: The passage states that the research being conducted on the DNA of gibbons could provide scientists with a way to start figuring out how to prevent cancer and other human ailments. Choice (B) is the correct answer.

37. D

Difficulty: Medium

Category: Reading / Command of Evidence

Strategic Advice: Look at your answer for the previous question. Skim the passage to find the paragraph you used to select your answer.

Getting to the Answer: Choice (D) is the quote from the passage that directly supports the idea that more research would be needed before current findings could be applied to curing diseases in humans.

38. A

Difficulty: Medium

Category: Reading / Rhetoric

Strategic Advice: Remember that you're looking for a statement that expresses the purposes of both passages, not just one.

Getting to the Answer: Both passages discuss how sequencing the genome of a nonhuman organism can benefit people. Therefore, (A) is the correct answer.

39. B

Difficulty: Medium

Category: Reading / Vocab-in-Context

Strategic Advice: Be careful of answer choices that are synonyms for "compelled" but do not make sense in the context in which they're used in the passage.

Getting to the Answer: Choice (B) makes the most sense in context. The scientists felt driven to pursue genome sequencing of the coffee plant.

40. A

Difficulty: Easy

Category: Reading / Vocab-in-Context

Strategic Advice: Replace the word in the sentence with each answer choice and eliminate those that do not make sense in context.

Getting to the Answer: In the context, (A) makes the most sense. "Maintenance" most nearly means "preservation."

41. B

Difficulty: Hard

Category: Reading / Rhetoric

Strategic Advice: Be careful of answer choices that are not directly related to the phrase being considered.

Getting to the Answer: The author of Passage 1 is making a generalization about the coffee industry in order to introduce the main topic to the reader. The author uses the phrase a "pillar of the world economy" to show that the coffee industry plays a vital role in the world economy. Choice (B) is the correct answer.

42. D

Difficulty: Hard

Category: Reading / Synthesis

Strategic Advice: Be careful of answer choices that make inferences based on only one of the passages.

Getting to the Answer: Each passage describes a way that genome sequencing of an organism other than a human has benefited people. Therefore, (D) is the correct answer.

Biomimicry Passage

43. A

Difficulty: Medium

Category: Reading / Global

Strategic Advice: Look for the answer choice that describes an idea supported throughout the passage rather than a specific detail.

Getting to the Answer: The passage cites several examples of biomimicry, the study of how materials and systems found in nature can be replicated to benefit humans. Therefore, (A) is the best summary of the central idea of the passage.

44. B

Difficulty: Medium

Category: Reading / Command of Evidence

Strategic Advice: Think back to why you chose your answer to the previous question. This will help you pick the correct quote as evidence.

Getting to the Answer: Choice (B) is the correct answer because it provides evidence for the central idea that the author presents about the field of biomimicry.

45. A

Difficulty: Hard

Category: Reading / Rhetoric

Strategic Advice: Think about the main idea of the quote. Eliminate any answer choices that don't support this main idea.

Getting to the Answer: The quote explains why architects turn to biomimicry for solutions in their work. Choice (A) is the correct answer.

46. B

Difficulty: Medium

Category: Reading / Inference

Strategic Advice: Reread the paragraph that the question is asking about. Look for specific details about the abalone shrimp shell and soft chalk.

Getting to the Answer: The passage clearly states that the abalone shrimp shell is harder than soft chalk because of the way the basic material composing each is arranged, so (B) is the correct answer.

47. D

Difficulty: Medium

Category: Reading / Rhetoric

Strategic Advice: In order to understand why an author includes a quote from another person, examine the surrounding sentences. This often makes clear the author's reason for including the quotation.

Getting to the Answer: The author includes the quote from Pawlyn to support and strengthen his or her own view that energy efficiency "has never been more important." Therefore, (D) is the correct answer.

48. D
Difficulty: Easy

Category: Reading / Vocab-in-Context

Strategic Advice: Replace the word in question with each of the answer choices. This will help you eliminate the ones that don't make sense in the context.

Getting to the Answer: Choice (D), "theories," is the only answer choice that makes sense in this context.

49. A
Difficulty: Medium

Category: Reading / Inference

Strategic Advice: Keep in mind that you're being asked to make an inference, a logical guess based on information in the passage. Therefore, the correct answer is not stated in a passage.

Getting to the Answer: The variety of examples of biomimicry mentioned in the passage make it reasonable to infer that more scientists will utilize solutions developed through biomimicry in the future. Choice (A) is the correct answer.

50. C
Difficulty: Medium

Category: Reading / Command of Evidence

Strategic Advice: Reread each quotation in the context of the passage. Consider which one is the best evidence to support the inference made in the previous question.

Getting to the Answer: The examples cited in (C) provide strong evidence for the inference that more scientists will probably make use of biomimicry in years to come.

51. D
Difficulty: Medium

Category: Reading / Vocab-in-Context

Strategic Advice: Eliminate answer choices that are synonyms for the word in question but do not work in the context of the sentence.

Getting to the Answer: Because biomimicry is such an innovative approach, it makes sense that the meaning of "radical" in this context is closest to (D), "revolutionary."

52. C
Difficulty: Hard

Category: Reading / Synthesis

Strategic Advice: Remember that a graphic might not refer to something explicitly stated in the passage. Instead, it often provides a visual example of how an important concept discussed in the passage works.

Getting to the Answer: The graphic and its caption help illustrate an example of biomimicry not mentioned in the passage: that of a solar power plant designed to mimic the arrangement of petals in a sunflower. This directs more energy toward the power plant's central tower and improves the efficiency of the power plant. Choice (C) is the correct answer.

WRITING AND LANGUAGE TEST

The Age of the Librarian

1. C
Difficulty: Easy

Category: Writing & Language / Shifts in Construction

Strategic Advice: Examine the verb tense in the rest of the sentence. This will help you find the correct answer.

Getting to the Answer: As written, the sentence switches verb tense midsentence. Other verbs in the sentence, "worked" and "was," indicate that the events happened in the past. Choice (C) is the correct choice because it correctly uses the past tense of the target verb.

2. D
Difficulty: Medium

Category: Writing & Language / Punctuation

Strategic Advice: Pay attention to the quotation marks. Make sure a complete sentence is properly punctuated within the quotation marks.

Getting to the Answer: Reading through the sentence and the answer choices shows that two issues might need correcting. The sentence inside the quotation marks is a complete sentence. The correct answer needs to punctuate that sentence before closing the quote. Additionally, "however" is being used as a connector or transition word and needs to be followed by a comma after beginning the new sentence. Choice (D) appropriately uses a period prior to the end quotes and correctly inserts a comma after the transition "However."

3. B
Difficulty: Medium

Category: Writing & Language / Effective Language Use

Strategic Advice: Watch out for choices that distort the tone of the passage.

Getting to the Answer: The passage suggests that people expected or anticipated that Harris would become a librarian. Evidence for this idea is found in the statement that she was "constantly told" that she "should be studying to be a librarian." Harris was certainly aware that people anticipated this course of study for her, but the presence of the phrase "Little did she realize" tells you that she didn't expect to become one. The correct choice is (B), "imminent," meaning that becoming a librarian was about to occur despite her own expectations.

4. C
Difficulty: Hard

Category: Writing & Language / Effective Language Use

Strategic Advice: Read the sentence carefully for context clues. Also, think about the tone of what is being described. This will help you choose the best answer.

Getting to the Answer: Given the phrasing of the sentence, the answer must be close in meaning to "excited," which is used earlier in the sentence. Therefore, (C) is the correct answer.

5. A
Difficulty: Medium

Category: Writing & Language / Punctuation

Strategic Advice: Determine whether a clause is independent or dependent to decide between a comma and a semicolon.

Getting to the Answer: Choice (A) is the correct answer. The sentence is correctly punctuated as written because it uses a comma at the end of the introductory clause.

6. C

Difficulty: Medium

Category: Writing & Language / Sentence Formation

Strategic Advice: Read the sentence carefully. The sentence sounds clunky and awkward. Look for an answer choice that makes the sentence clear and easy to understand. Notice that the word "asking" is part of a participial phrase that modifies "Miguel."

Getting to the Answer: A participial phrase should be placed as close as possible to the noun it modifies. When a participial phrase begins a sentence, it should be set off with a comma.

Choice (C) is correct. The placement of commas and modifiers makes the content easy to understand, and the sentence is free of grammatical or punctuation errors.

7. B

Difficulty: Medium

Category: Writing & Language / Development

Strategic Advice: Read the entire paragraph carefully and predict the main idea. Then look for a close match with your prediction.

Getting to the Answer: The paragraph discusses how the role of librarian has changed due to an increased use of technology. Choice (B) is the correct answer, as it explicitly addresses the changing role of the librarian due to technology.

8. D

Difficulty: Medium

Category: Writing & Language / Sentence Formation

Strategic Advice: Read the sentence and note the series of examples. A series should have parallel structure.

Getting to the Answer: The sentence is not correct as written. The items in the series switch forms from participial phrases beginning with "enabling" and "offering" to "they house." All of the items need to fit the same pattern or form. Choice (D) is correct because it appropriately begins each item in the series with a participle.

9. C

Difficulty: Hard

Category: Writing & Language / Development

Strategic Advice: Don't be fooled by answer choices that are true statements but do not directly support the main idea of the paragraph.

Getting to the Answer: The paragraph concerns how the role of librarian has changed due to an increased use of technology. The correct answer needs to support the idea that librarians work with technology in new ways. Choice (C) works best. It offers a specific example of how teachers look to the librarian to be a "media mentor" and illustrates this new role for school librarians.

10. C

Difficulty: Easy

Category: Writing & Language / Usage

Strategic Advice: Read the sentence prior to the pronoun and determine whom the pronoun is referencing. Pronouns should not be ambiguous, and they must match the verb in number.

Getting to the Answer: The sentence is ambiguous as written. "She" would presumably refer back to the "young student" but it seems unlikely that the student would be laughing and thinking about the collections in the library after asking the librarian a question. Choice (C) is the best choice. It clearly indicates the subject of the sentence (Harris) and avoids ambiguity.

11. A

Difficulty: Medium

Category: Writing & Language / Usage

Strategic Advice: Figure out whom the pronoun refers to and make sure it matches the antecedent in number. Watch out for confusing contractions and possessives.

Getting to the Answer: The pronoun in the sentence needs to indicate who will have the ideas. Harris is talking to a single student, so you will need a singular possessive pronoun.

Choice (A) is correct. As it is, the sentence correctly uses a singular possessive pronoun.

Unforeseen Consequences: The Dark Side of the Industrial Revolution

12. B

Difficulty: Medium

Category: Writing & Language / Sentence Formation

Strategic Advice: Be careful of answers that sound correct when they stand alone but do not conform to the structure of the sentence as a whole.

Getting to the Answer: The existing text is incorrect, as it does not maintain parallel structure. Choice (B) is the correct answer, as it maintains the parallel structure of preposition ("into") + noun ("the role").

13. B

Difficulty: Easy

Category: Writing & Language / Punctuation

Strategic Advice: Eliminate answers that confuse the usage of commas and semicolons.

Getting to the Answer: Choice (B) is correct. Without the comma, the following clause modifies "urban areas" when it should modify the entire preceding clause.

14. B

Difficulty: Medium

Category: Writing & Language / Effective Language Use

Strategic Advice: Avoid choices that are redundant and imprecise. The correct answer will use the clearest, most concise terminology to communicate the idea.

Getting to the Answer: Choice (B) is correct. It is the most concise—and clearest—word choice. The other choices use more words than necessary to convey meaning.

15. A

Difficulty: Medium

Category: Writing & Language / Organization

Strategic Advice: The first sentence should function as a transition between ideas in the previous paragraph and ideas in the current paragraph.

Getting to the Answer: Choice (A) makes sense. This choice connects ideas from the previous paragraph with the content of paragraph 3. The sentences that follow provide details to support that introductory idea.

16. A

Difficulty: Hard

Category: Writing & Language / Development

Strategic Advice: Eliminate answers like B that fail to directly support the cited sentence.

Getting to the Answer: The underlined sentence references "unprecedented amounts of human-made carbon dioxide into the air." This suggests an increase in the amount of carbon dioxide in the atmosphere over time. Therefore, (A) is the correct answer.

17. C
Difficulty: Medium

Category: Writing & Language / Effective Language Use

Strategic Advice: Choose the answer that presents the correct relationship between ideas.

Getting to the Answer: Choice (C) is correct. It shows the causal relationship without adding unnecessary verbiage.

18. A
Difficulty: Easy

Category: Writing & Language / Effective Language Use

Strategic Advice: Plug in the answer choices and select the one that reflects a specific meaning relevant to the sentence.

Getting to the Answer: The paragraph focuses on the negative effects of industrialization and waste production. Therefore, (A) is the correct answer.

19. B
Difficulty: Hard

Category: Writing & Language / Development

Strategic Advice: Be careful of choices that relate to the underlined portion of the text without showing clearly how the underlined portion supports the full implication of the preceding sentence.

Getting to the Answer: The paragraph explains that industrialization resulted in the destruction of resources. The correct answer, (B), serves as clear evidence of the "process of destruction and reduced resources."

20. C
Difficulty: Medium

Category: Writing & Language / Effective Language Use

Strategic Advice: Be careful of answers that make sense but do not fully support the meaning of the content. The correct answer will not only flow logically but will also reflect the precise purpose and meaning of the larger sentence and paragraph.

Getting to the Answer: Choice (C) is the correct answer. "Substandard" communicates clearly that the working conditions were the cause of the health problems.

21. D
Difficulty: Medium

Category: Writing & Language / Sentence Formation

Strategic Advice: Eliminate choices that result in sentence fragments or fragmented clauses. The correct answer will maintain appropriate syntax without misusing punctuation.

Getting to the Answer: Choice (D) is correct. It sets off the dependent clause without using incorrect punctuation to signal a hard break before an independent clause or second complete sentence.

22. D
Difficulty: Hard

Category: Writing & Language / Development

Strategic Advice: Avoid answers that draw on similar ideas but combine those ideas in a way that communicates a proposition not supported by the essay as a whole. The correct answer will make sense within the larger context of the essay.

Getting to the Answer: The central idea of the entire essay is that industrialization and progress came at a cost that made the promise of a bright future difficult to fulfill. Choice (D) is the correct answer.

Remembering Freud

23. C
Difficulty: Hard

Category: Writing & Language / Effective Language Use

Strategic Advice: Consider the fact that there may be a choice that helps make the meaning of the sentence very precise.

Getting to the Answer: Choice (C) most accurately indicates that Freud led a whole movement.

24. B
Difficulty: Medium

Category: Writing & Language / Punctuation

Strategic Advice: Plug in each answer choice and select the one that seems most correct.

Getting to the Answer: Choice (B) makes it clear to the reader that this is extra information modifying the word "career."

25. D
Difficulty: Medium

Category: Writing & Language / Sentence Formation

Strategic Advice: Remember that in a list, all things listed should be presented with the same grammatical structure.

Getting to the Answer: "Id," "ego," and "Freudian slip" are all nouns. Choice (D) is the correct answer because it uses a parallel structure for all three nouns.

26. B
Difficulty: Hard

Category: Writing & Language / Development

Strategic Advice: Notice that the underlined sentence is the first sentence in the paragraph. Think about which choice would make the best topic sentence, given the content of the rest of the paragraph.

Getting to the Answer: Choice (B) correctly makes the free-speaking technique the focus of the paragraph's topic sentence, while suggesting that the technique was radical enough to earn Freud his title.

27. B
Difficulty: Medium

Category: Writing & Language / Effective Language Use

Strategic Advice: Eliminate any choices that don't seem as precise as others.

Getting to the Answer: Choice (B) is correct. The word "recesses" is more precise; it connotes smaller parts of the brain and a sense of being hidden.

28. C
Difficulty: Easy

Category: Writing & Language / Punctuation

Strategic Advice: Try reading the sentence in question aloud. This often helps you get a good sense of whether or not a comma is needed.

Getting to the Answer: Choice (C) would fit here. The sentence eliminates the unneeded comma and is a correct sentence.

29. B
Difficulty: Hard

Category: Writing & Language / Sentence Formation

Strategic Advice: Remember that a modifier should be adjacent to the noun it is modifying and set off by punctuation.

Getting to the Answer: Choice (B) is correct. The modifier "like neurosis or other psychological trauma" should come directly after "conditions."

30. C
Difficulty: Hard

Category: Writing & Language / Development

Strategic Advice: Consider how this sentence relates to the one before it and the one that follows it. Does it offer strong support of the connecting ideas?

Getting to the Answer: This section discussed the development and lasting influence of Freud's ideas. The best supporting sentence will provide details connecting these concepts. Choice (C) is correct. It emphasizes that Freud developed new ideas that have had a lasting influence on psychological practices.

31. B
Difficulty: Medium

Category: Writing & Language / Sentence Formation

Strategic Advice: Notice that you are dealing with a run-on sentence. Identify the point in the run-on where it appears two sentences have been fused together.

Getting to the Answer: Choice (B) is correct. This choice splits the run-on sentence into two separate, grammatical sentences.

32. D
Difficulty: Easy

Category: Writing & Language / Sentence Formation

Strategic Advice: Eliminate answer choices that are not complete sentences or do not maintain the correct verb tense.

Getting to the Answer: Choice (D) correctly changes the phrase "Freud's finding of a method" to "Freud found a method," making the sentence complete. It also corrects the verb tense.

33. A
Difficulty: Hard

Category: Writing & Language / Sentence Formation

Strategic Advice: Recall that when a dependent clause precedes an independent clause, it should be set off with a comma.

Getting to the Answer: Choice (A) is the best choice. Although lengthy, the dependent clause in the sentence ("So as long as occasions arise . . . ") is correctly combined with its independent clause ("Sigmund Freud will be remembered . . . ") by use of a comma.

Success in Montreal

34. B
Difficulty: Easy

Category: Writing & Language / Sentence Formation

Strategic Advice: Always check whether two or more verbs that serve the same function have a parallel structure.

Getting to the Answer: Choice (B) is correct. "To prevent" is in the infinitive form like the first verb in the sentence, "to reverse."

35. A
Difficulty: Hard

Category: Writing & Language / Effective Language Use

Strategic Advice: Look for the choice that most concisely and correctly joins the two sentences.

Getting to the Answer: Choice (A) is the best fit. This option joins the sentences concisely and correctly.

36. C
Difficulty: Medium

Category: Writing & Language / Effective Language Use

Strategic Advice: Remember that the best answer is the most concise and effective way of stating the information while ensuring that the information is complete.

Getting to the Answer: Choice (C) works best here. It uses the fewest necessary words to convey the complete information.

37. C
Difficulty: Medium

Category: Writing & Language / Sentence Formation

Strategic Advice: Eliminate any choices that use transition words inappropriately.

Getting to the Answer: Two complete thoughts should be separated into two different sentences. Therefore, (C) is the best choice.

38. B
Difficulty: Hard

Category: Writing & Language / Quantitative

Strategic Advice: Examine the graphic for details that suggest which answer is correct.

Getting to the Answer: Choice (B) accurately reflects the information in the graphic. Beginning in the 1990s, the size of the ozone hole began to level off.

39. C
Difficulty: Medium

Category: Writing & Language / Effective Language Use

Strategic Advice: Check each word to see how it fits with the context of the sentence.

Getting to the Answer: While all of the words have similar meanings, only one fits the context of the paragraph. Choice (C), "measured," has a connotation that corresponds to "gauge" in the following sentence.

40. B
Difficulty: Easy

Category: Writing & Language / Usage

Strategic Advice: Remember that the possessive form must agree with its antecedent.

Getting to the Answer: The correct answer will reflect the gender and number of its antecedent; in this case, the word "treaty." Therefore, (B) is correct.

41. A
Difficulty: Hard

Category: Writing & Language / Development

Strategic Advice: To find the central idea of a paragraph, identify important details and then summarize them in a sentence or two. Then find the choice that is the closest to your summary.

Getting to the Answer: Choice (A) most clearly states the paragraph's central idea.

42. D
Difficulty: Medium

Category: Writing & Language / Development

Strategic Advice: To find the correct answer, first determine the central idea of the paragraph.

Getting to the Answer: Choice (D) is the least essential sentence in the paragraph, so it is the correct answer.

43. D
Difficulty: Medium

Category: Writing & Language / Effective Language Use

Strategic Advice: Context clues tell which word is appropriate in the sentence. Check to see which word fits best in the sentence.

Getting to the Answer: The word "reverse," (D), fits with the context of the sentence and connotes a more precise action than does "change."

44. C
Difficulty: Hard

Category: Writing & Language / Organization

Strategic Advice: Examine the entire paragraph. Decide whether the sentence provides more information about a topic mentioned in one of the other sentences.

Getting to the Answer: This sentence provides more information related to sentence 1, "The Montreal Protocol is a living document"; it describes how the document is "living." Choice (C) is the correct answer.

MATH TEST: NO-CALCULATOR SECTION

1. C
Difficulty: Easy

Category: Heart of Algebra / Linear Equations

Strategic Advice: To determine what the y-intercept could mean in the context of a word problem, examine the labels on the graph and note what each axis represents.

Getting to the Answer: According to the labels, the y-axis represents cost, and the x-axis represents the number of games played. The y-intercept, (0, 5), has an x-value of 0, which means zero games were played, yet there is still a cost of $5. The cost must represent a flat fee that is charged before any games are played, such as an entrance fee to enter the arcade.

2. A
Difficulty: Easy

Category: Passport to Advanced Math / Exponents

Strategic Advice: To divide one rational expression by another, multiply the first expression by the reciprocal (the flip) of the second expression.

Getting to the Answer: Rewrite the division as multiplication, factor any factorable expressions, and then simplify if possible.

$$\frac{3x}{x+5} \div \frac{6}{4x+20} = \frac{3x}{x+5} \cdot \frac{4x+20}{6}$$
$$= \frac{3x}{x\!\!\!\!\diagup+5} \cdot \frac{4\,(x\!\!\!\!\diagup+5)}{6}$$
$$= \frac{12x}{6}$$
$$= 2x$$

Note that the question also states that $x \neq -5$. This doesn't affect your answer—it is simply stated because the denominators of rational expressions cannot equal 0.

3. D
Difficulty: Easy

Category: Additional Topics in Math / Geometry

Strategic Advice: When the equation of a circle is written in the form $(x - h)^2 + (y - k)^2 = r^2$, the point (h, k) represents the center of the circle on a coordinate plane, and r represents the length of the radius.

Getting to the Answer: To find the area of a circle, use the formula, $A = \pi r^2$. In the equation given in the question, r^2 is the constant on the right-hand side (25)—you don't even need to solve for r because the area formula involves r^2, not r. So, the area is $\pi(25)$ or 25π.

4. C
Difficulty: Easy

Category: Passport to Advanced Math / Functions

Strategic Advice: When using function notation, $f(x)$ is simply another way of saying y, so this question is asking you to find the values of x for which $y = 0$, or in other words, where the graph crosses the x-axis.

Getting to the Answer: The graph crosses the x-axis at the points (–2, 0) and (3, 0), so the values of x for which $f(x) = 0$ are –2 and 3.

5. B

Difficulty: Medium

Category: Heart of Algebra / Linear Equations

Strategic Advice: Choose the best strategy to answer the question. You could start by cross-multiplying to get rid of the denominators, but simplifying the numerators first will make the calculations easier.

Getting to the Answer:

$$\frac{4(d+3)-9}{8} = \frac{10-(2-d)}{6}$$

$$\frac{4d+12-9}{8} = \frac{10-2+d}{6}$$

$$\frac{4d+3}{8} = \frac{8+d}{6}$$

$$6(4d+3) = 8(8+d)$$

$$24d+18 = 64+8d$$

$$16d = 46$$

$$d = \frac{46}{16} = \frac{23}{8}$$

6. D

Difficulty: Medium

Category: Passport to Advanced Math / Functions

Strategic Advice: This is a crossover question, so quickly skim the first couple of sentences. Then look for the relevant information in the last couple of sentences. It may also help to circle the portions of the graph that meet the given requirement.

Getting to the Answer: Because *greater* means *higher* on a graph, the statement $f(t) > g(t)$ translates to "Where is $f(t)$ above $g(t)$?" The solid curve represents f and the dashed curve represents g, so $f > g$ between the years 1960 and 1980 and again between the years 2000 and 2010. Look for these time intervals in the answer choices: $1960 < t < 1980$ and $2000 < t < 2010$.

7. D

Difficulty: Medium

Category: Passport to Advanced Math / Scatterplots

Strategic Advice: Use the shape of the data to predict the type of equation that might be used as a model. Then, use specific values from the graph to choose the correct equation.

Getting to the Answer: According to the graph, the population of the whales grew slowly at first and then more quickly. This means that an exponential model is probably the best fit, so you can eliminate A (linear) and B (quadratic). The remaining equations are both exponential, so choose a data point and see which equation is the closest fit. Be careful—the vertical axis represents *hundreds* of whales, and the question states that t represents the number of years since the study began, so $t = 0$ for 1995, $t = 3$ for 1998, and so on. If you use the data for 1995, which is the point (0, 100), the results are the same for both equations, so choose a different point. Using the data for 2007, $t = 2007 - 1995 = 12$, and the number of whales was 800. Substitute these values into C and D to see which one is true. Choice C is not true because $800 \neq 100 \times 2^{12}$. Choice (D) is correct because $800 = 100 \times 2^{\frac{12}{4}} = 100 \times 2^3 = 100 \times 8$ is true.

8. B

Difficulty: Medium

Category: Heart of Algebra / Linear Equations

Strategic Advice: Average rate of change is the same as slope, so use the slope formula.

Getting to the Answer: To find the average rate of change over the 5-year period, find the slope between the starting point (0, 1,200) and the ending point (5, 100).

$$m = \frac{y_2 - y_1}{x_2 - x_1} = \frac{100 - 1,200}{5 - 0} = \frac{-1,100}{5} = -220$$

The average rate of change is negative because the laptop decreases in value over time.

Note: Because the question involves *straight-line* depreciation, you could have used any two points on the graph to find the slope. As a general rule, however, you should use the endpoints of the given time interval.

9. B

Difficulty: Medium

Category: Passport to Advanced Math / Exponents

Strategic Advice: When multiplying polynomials, carefully multiply each term in the first factor by each term in the second factor. This question doesn't ask for the entire product, so check to make sure you answered the right question (the coefficient of x^2).

Getting to the Answer:

$$\left(6x^2 - \frac{2}{5}x + 1\right)\left(10x + \frac{1}{3}\right)$$
$$= 6x^2\left(10x + \frac{1}{3}\right) - \frac{2}{5}x\left(10x + \frac{1}{3}\right) + 1\left(10x + \frac{1}{3}\right)$$
$$= 60x^3 + 2x^2 - 4x^2 - \frac{2}{15}x + 10x + \frac{1}{3}$$

The coefficient of x^2 is $2 + (-4) = -2$.

10. A

Difficulty: Medium

Category: Heart of Algebra / Linear Equations

Strategic Advice: Notice that there are no grid lines and no numbers on the axes. This is a great clue that the numbers in the equations don't actually matter.

Getting to the Answer: The line is decreasing, so the slope (m) is negative. The line crosses the y-axis below 0, so the y-intercept (b) is also negative. Put each answer choice in slope-intercept form, one at a time, and examine the signs of m and b. Begin with A:

$$-6x - 4y = 5$$
$$-4y = 6x + 5$$
$$y = \frac{6x}{-4} + \frac{5}{-4}$$
$$y = -\frac{3}{2}x - \frac{5}{4}$$

You don't need to check any of the other equations. Choice (A) has a negative slope and a negative y-intercept, so it is the correct equation.

11. C

Difficulty: Hard

Category: Heart of Algebra / Systems of Linear Equations

Strategic Advice: Graphically, a system of linear equations that has no solution indicates two parallel lines or, in other words, two lines that have the same slope. So, write each of the equations in slope-intercept form ($y = mx + b$) and set their slopes (m) equal to each other to solve for k. Before finding the slopes, multiply the top equation by 4 to make it easier to manipulate.

Getting to the Answer:

$$4\left(\frac{3}{4}x - \frac{1}{2}y = 12\right) \rightarrow 3x - 2y = 48 \rightarrow y = \frac{3}{2}x - 24$$
$$kx - 2y = 22 \rightarrow -2y = -kx + 22 \rightarrow y = \frac{k}{2}x - 11$$

The slope of the first line is $\frac{3}{2}$, and the slope of the second line is $\frac{k}{2}$. Set them equal and solve for k.

$$\frac{3}{2} = \frac{k}{2}$$
$$2(3) = 2(k)$$
$$6 = 2k$$
$$3 = k$$

12. B

Difficulty: Hard

Category: Heart of Algebra / Inequalities

Strategic Advice: Pay careful attention to units, particularly when a question involves rates. The $4.00 for the first $\frac{1}{4}$ mile is a flat fee. Before you write the inequality, you need to find the per-mile rate for the remaining miles.

Getting to the Answer: The driver charges $4.00 for the first $\frac{1}{4}$ mile, which is a flat fee, so write 4. The additional charge is $1.50 per $\frac{1}{2}$ mile, or 1.50 times 2 = $3.00 per mile. The number of miles after the first $\frac{1}{4}$ mile is $m - \frac{1}{4}$, so the cost of the trip, not including the first $\frac{1}{4}$ mile, is $3\left(m - \frac{1}{4}\right)$. This means the cost of the whole trip is $4 + 3\left(m - \frac{1}{4}\right)$. The clue "no more than $10" means that much or less, so use the symbol $\le$. The inequality is $4 + 3\left(m - \frac{1}{4}\right) \le 10$, which simplifies to $3.25 + 3m \le 10$.

13. A

Difficulty: Hard

Category: Passport to Advanced Math / Functions

Strategic Advice: Think about how the transformations affect the graph of $g(x)$ and draw a sketch of $h(x)$ on the same grid. Compare the new graph to each of the answer choices until you find one that is true.

Getting to the Answer: The graph of $h(x) = -g(x) + 1$ is a vertical reflection of $g(x)$, over the x-axis, that is then shifted up 1 unit. The graph looks like the dashed line in the following graph:

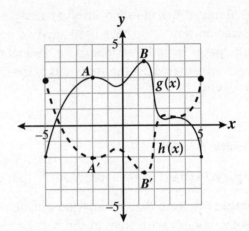

Now, compare the dashed line to each of the answer choices: the range of $h(x)$ is the set of y-values from lowest to highest (based on the dashed line). The lowest point occurs at point B' and has a y-value of −3; the highest value occurs at both ends of the graph and is 3, so the range is $-3 \le y \le 3$. This means (A) is correct and you can move on to the next question. Don't waste valuable time checking the other answer choices unless you are not sure about the range. (Choice B: The minimum value of $h(x)$ is −3, not −4. Choice C: The coordinates of point A on $h(x)$ are (−2, −2), not (2, 4). Choice D: the graph of $h(x)$ is decreasing, not increasing, between $x = -5$ and $x = -2$.)

14. D

Difficulty: Medium

Category: Additional Topics in Math / Imaginary Numbers

Strategic Advice: Multiply the two complex numbers just as you would two binomials (using FOIL). Then, combine like terms and use the definition $i^2 = -1$ to simplify the result.

Getting to the Answer:

$$(3+2i)(5-i)=3(5-i)+2i(5-i)$$
$$=15-3i+10i-2i^2$$
$$=15+7i-2(-1)$$
$$=15+7i+2$$
$$=17+7i$$

The question asks for a in $a + bi$, so the correct answer is 17.

15. A
Difficulty: Hard

Category: Passport to Advanced Math / Exponents

Strategic Advice: Think of the rate given in the question in terms of the constant term you see on the right-hand side of the equation. Working together, the two treatment plants can filter the water in 72 hours. This is equivalent to saying that they can filter $\frac{1}{72}$ of the water in 1 hour.

Getting to the Answer: If $\frac{1}{72}$ is the portion of the water the two treatment plants can filter *together*, then each term on the left side of the equation represents the portion that each plant can filter *individually* in 1 hour. Because the new facility is 4 times as fast as the older facility, $\frac{4}{x}$ represents the portion of the water the new plant can filter in 1 hour, and $\frac{1}{x}$ represents the portion of the water the older plant can filter in 1 hour.

16. 20
Difficulty: Medium

Category: Heart of Algebra / Linear Equations

Strategic Advice: Only one equation is given, and it has two variables. This means that you don't have enough information to solve for either variable. Instead, look for the relationship between the variable terms in the equation and those in the expression that you are trying to find, $x + 2y$.

Getting to the Answer: First, move the y-term to the left side of the equation to make it look more like the expression you are trying to find. The expression doesn't have fractions, so clear the fractions in the equation by multiplying both sides by 4. This yields the expression that you are looking for, $x + 2y$, so no further work is required—just read the value on the right-hand side of the equation. The answer is 20.

$$\frac{1}{4}x=5-\frac{1}{2}y$$
$$\frac{1}{4}x+\frac{1}{2}y=5$$
$$4\left(\frac{1}{4}x+\frac{1}{2}y\right)=4(5)$$
$$x+2y=20$$

17. 1
Difficulty: Medium

Category: Heart of Algebra / Inequalities

Strategic Advice: This question is extremely difficult to answer unless you draw a sketch. It doesn't have to be perfect—you just need to get an idea of where the solution region is. Don't forget to flip the inequality symbol when you graph the second equation.

Getting to the Answer: Sketch the system.

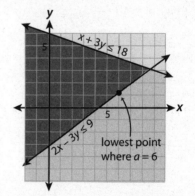

If (a, b) is a solution to the system, then a is the x-coordinate of any point in the darkest shaded region and b is the corresponding y-coordinate. When $a = 6$, the minimum possible value for b lies on the lower boundary line, $2x - 3y \le 9$. It looks like the y-coordinate is 1, but to be sure, substitute $x = 6$ into the equation and solve for y. You can use $=$ in the equation, instead of the inequality symbol, because you are finding a point on the boundary line.

$$2x - 3y = 9$$
$$2(6) - 3y = 9$$
$$12 - 3y = 9$$
$$-3y = -3$$
$$y = 1$$

18. 2

Difficulty: Hard

Category: Passport to Advanced Math / Exponents

Strategic Advice: Rewrite the radicals as fraction exponents: $\sqrt{x} = x^{\frac{1}{2}}$ and $\sqrt[3]{x} = x^{\frac{1}{3}}$.

Getting to the Answer: Write each factor in the expression in exponential form. Then use the rules of exponents to simplify the expression. Add the exponents of the factors that are being multiplied and subtract the exponent of the factor that is being divided:

$$\frac{\sqrt{x} \cdot x^{\frac{5}{6}} \cdot x}{\sqrt[3]{x}} = \frac{x^{\frac{1}{2}} \cdot x^{\frac{5}{6}} \cdot x^{1}}{x^{\frac{1}{3}}}$$

$$= x^{\frac{1}{2} + \frac{5}{6} + \frac{1}{1} - \frac{1}{3}}$$

$$= x^{\frac{3}{6} + \frac{5}{6} + \frac{6}{6} - \frac{2}{6}}$$

$$= x^{\frac{12}{6}} = x^2$$

Because n is the power of x, the value of n is 2.

19. 14

Difficulty: Hard

Category: Additional Topics in Math / Geometry

Strategic Advice: The shaded region is the area of the larger triangle minus the area of the smaller triangle. Set up and solve an equation using the information from the figure. Before you grid in your answer, check that you answered the right question (height of larger triangle).

Getting to the Answer: You don't know the height of the smaller triangle, so call it h. You do know the area of the shaded region—it's 52 square units.

Larger triangle: base = 12; height = $h + 3 + 3$

Smaller triangle: base = 8; height = h

Shaded area = large area – small area

$$52 = \left[\left(\frac{1}{2} \right)(12)(h + 6) \right] - \left[\left(\frac{1}{2} \right)(8)(h) \right]$$
$$52 = 6(h + 6) - 4h$$
$$52 = 6h + 36 - 4h$$
$$52 = 2h + 36$$
$$16 = 2h$$
$$8 = h$$

The question asks for the height of the *larger* triangle, so the correct answer is $8 + 3 + 3 = 14$.

20. 6

Difficulty: Hard

Category: Passport to Advanced Math / Quadratics

Strategic Advice: The highest power of x in the equation is 2, so the function is quadratic. Writing quadratic equations can be tricky and time-consuming. If you know the roots, you can use factors to write the equation. If you don't know the roots, you need to create a system of equations to find the coefficients of the variable terms.

Getting to the Answer: You don't know the roots of this equation, so start with the point that has the easiest values to work with, (0, 1), and substitute them into the equation $y = ax^2 + bx + c$.

$$1 = a(0)^2 + b(0) + c$$

$$1 = c$$

Now your equation looks like $y = ax^2 + bx + 1$. Next, use the other two points to create a system of two equations in two variables.

$$(-3, 10) \rightarrow 10 = a(-3)^2 + b(-3) + 1 \rightarrow 9 = 9a - 3b$$

$$(2, 15) \rightarrow 15 = a(2)^2 + b(2) + 1 \rightarrow 14 = 4a + 2b$$

You now have a system of equations to solve. None of the variables has a coefficient of 1, so use elimination to solve the system. If you multiply the top equation by 2 and the bottom equation by 3, the b-terms will eliminate each other.

$$2[9a - 3b = 9] \rightarrow 18a - 6b = 18$$
$$3[4a + 2b = 14] \rightarrow \underline{12a + 6b = 42}$$
$$30a = 60$$
$$a = 2$$

Now, find b by substituting $a = 2$ into either of the original equations. Using the top equation, you get:

$$9(2) - 3b = 9$$
$$18 - 3b = 9$$
$$-3b = -9$$
$$b = 3$$

The value of $a + b + c$ is $2 + 3 + 1 = 6$.

MATH TEST: CALCULATOR SECTION

1. C
Difficulty: Easy

Category: Problem Solving and Data Analysis / Rates, Ratios, Proportions, and Percentages

Strategic Advice: You can use the formula $\text{Percent} = \dfrac{\text{Part}}{\text{Whole}} \times 100\%$ whenever you know two out of the three quantities.

Getting to the Answer: The clue "all" tells you that the "whole" is what you don't know. The percent is 96.5, and the part is 321,000,000.

$$96.5 = \frac{321,000,000}{w} \times 100\%$$
$$96.5w = 32,100,000,000$$
$$w = \frac{32,100,000,000}{96.5}$$
$$w = 332,642,487$$

The answer choices are rounded to the nearest thousand, so the answer is 332,642,000.

2. C
Difficulty: Easy

Category: Heart of Algebra / Linear Equations

Strategic Advice: A *one-time* fee does not depend on the variable and is therefore a constant. A unit rate, however, is always multiplied by the independent variable.

Getting to the Answer: The total cost consists of the site visit fee (a constant), an hourly cost (which depends on the number of hours), and the cost of the materials (which are taxed). The constant in the equation is 75 and is therefore the site visit fee; 45 is being multiplied by h (the number of hours), so $45 must be the hourly rate. That leaves the remaining term, 1.06(82.5), which must be the cost of the materials ($82.50) plus a 6% tax.

3. D

Difficulty: Easy

Category: Heart of Algebra / Inequalities

Strategic Advice: The intersection (overlap) of the two shaded regions is the solution to the system of inequalities. Check each point to see whether it lies in the region with the darkest shading. Don't forget to check that you answered the right question—you are looking for the point that is *not* a solution to the system.

Getting to the Answer: Each of the first three points clearly lies in the overlap. The point (3, 3) looks like it lies on the dashed line, which means it is *not* included in the solution. To check this, plug (3, 3) into the easier inequality: $3 \not> 3$ (3 is equal to itself, not greater than itself), so (D) is correct.

4. A

Difficulty: Easy

Category: Passport to Advanced Math / Quadratics

Strategic Advice: Quadratic equations can be written in several forms, each of which reveals something special about the graph. For example, the vertex form of a quadratic equation gives the minimum or maximum value of the function, while the standard form reveals the y-intercept.

Getting to the Answer: The factored form of a quadratic equation reveals the solutions to the equation, which graphically represent the x-intercepts. Choice (A) is the only equation written in this form and therefore must be correct. You can set each factor equal to 0 and solve to find that the x-intercepts of the graph are $x = \frac{5}{2}$ and $x = -1$.

5. B

Difficulty: Easy

Category: Problem Solving and Data Analysis / Rates, Ratios, Proportions, and Percentages

Strategic Advice: Break the question into steps. Before you can use the ratio, you need to find the percent of the students who answered either "Foreign Policy" or "Environment."

Getting to the Answer: The ratio given in the question is 5:3, so write this as 5 parts "Foreign Policy" and 3 parts "Environment." You don't know how big a *part* is, so call it x. This means that $5x + 3x =$ the percent of the students who answered either "Foreign Policy" or "Environment," which is 100% – all the other answers:

$$100 - (16 + 14 + 9 + 5) = 100 - 44 = 56$$
$$5x + 3x = 56$$
$$8x = 56$$
$$x = 7$$

Each part has a value of 7, and 3 parts answered "Environment," so the correct percentage is $3(7) = 21\%$.

6. C

Difficulty: Easy

Category: Heart of Algebra / Linear Equations

Strategic Advice: Don't peek at the answers. They may confuse you because the numbers look different from the ones given in the question. Instead, write your own equation in words first and then translate from English to math.

Getting to the Answer: Keep in mind that the shirts are on sale but the tie is not. The shirts are 40% off, which means that Marco only pays 100 – 40 = 60% of the price, or 0.6(35).

$$\text{Cost} = (\text{Shirt price times how many}) \text{ plus } (\text{Tie price times how many})$$

$$C = 0.6(35)x + 21(2)$$

This is not one of the answer choices, so simplify to get $C = 21x + 42$.

There are variables in the answer choices, so you could also use the Picking Numbers strategy to answer this question.

7. D

Difficulty: Easy

Category: Problem Solving and Data Analysis / Statistics and Probability

Strategic Advice: Your only choice for this question is to compare each statement to the figure. Don't waste time trying to figure out the exact value for each bar—an estimate is good enough to determine whether each statement is true.

Getting to the Answer: Choice A is incorrect because the price in 2008 was slightly less (not more) than $3.50, while the price in 2013 was right around $3.50. Choice B is incorrect because the price in 2003 was more than $2.00, and the price in 2013 was not more than twice that ($4.00). Choice C is incorrect because the price in 2008 was about $3.25 and the price in 2009 was about $2.75—this is not a difference of more than $1.00. This means (D) must be correct. You don't have to check it—just move on. (Between 2003 and 2008, the change in price was about $3.40 − $2.30 = $1.10; between 2008 and 2013, the change in price was only about $3.50 − $3.40 = $0.10; the change in price was greater between 2003 and 2008.)

8. B

Difficulty: Medium

Category: Heart of Algebra / Systems of Linear Equations

Strategic Advice: Because none of the variable terms has a coefficient of 1, solve the system of equations using elimination by addition (combining the equations). Before you choose an answer, check that you answered the right question (the sum of x and y).

Getting to the Answer: Multiply the top equation by 2 to eliminate the terms that have y's in them.

$$2[-2x+5y=1] \rightarrow -4x+10y=2$$
$$7x-10y=-11 \rightarrow \underline{7x-10y=-11}$$
$$3x \quad\quad =-9$$
$$x \quad\quad =-3$$

Now, substitute the result into either of the original equations and simplify to find y:

$$-2x+5y=1$$
$$-2(-3)+5y=1$$
$$6+5y=1$$
$$5y=-5$$
$$y=-1$$

The question asks for the *sum*, so add x and y to get $-3 + (-1) = -4$.

9. A

Difficulty: Medium

Category: Heart of Algebra / Systems of Linear Equations

Strategic Advice: Take a quick peek at the answers just to see what variables are being used, but don't study the equations. Instead, write your own system using the same variables as given in the answer choices.

Getting to the Answer: One of the equations in the system should represent the sum of the two resistors ($R_1 + R_2$), which is equal to 294. This means you can eliminate C and D. The second equation needs to satisfy the condition that R_2 is 6 less than twice R_1, or $R_2 = 2R_1 - 6$. This means (A) is correct.

10. C

Difficulty: Medium

Category: Heart of Algebra / Linear Equations

Strategic Advice: Use the distributive property to simplify each of the terms that contains parentheses. Then use inverse operations to solve for x.

Getting to the Answer:

$$\frac{2}{5}\left(5x\right)+2(x-1)=4(x+1)-2$$
$$2x+2x-2=4x+4-2$$
$$4x-2=4x+2$$
$$-2\neq2$$

All of the variable terms cancel out, and the resulting numerical statement is false (because negative 2 does not equal positive 2), so there is no solution to the equation. Put another way, there is no value of x for which the equation is true.

11. B
Difficulty: Medium

Category: Additional Topics in Math / Geometry

Strategic Advice: Think about this question logically before you start writing things down—after it's transferred, the volume of the oil in the cylindrical container will be the same volume as the rectangular container, so you need to set the two volumes equal and solve for h.

Getting to the Answer: The volume of the rectangular container is $4 \times 9 \times 10$, or 360 cubic meters. The volume of a cylinder equals the area of its base times its height, or $\pi r^2 h$. Because the diameter is 6 meters, the radius, r, is half that, or 3 meters. Now we're ready to set up an equation and solve for h (which is the height of the cylinder, or in this case, the length of the transportation container):

Volume of oil = Volume of rectangular container
$$\pi(3)^2 h = 360$$
$$9\pi h = 360$$
$$h = \frac{360}{9\pi} = \frac{40}{\pi}$$

12. D
Difficulty: Medium

Category: Problem Solving and Data Analysis / Rates, Ratios, Proportions, and Percentages

Strategic Advice: Even though this question uses the word *percent*, you are never asked to find the actual percent itself. Set this question up as a proportion to get the answer more quickly. Remember, percent change equals amount of change divided by the original amount.

Getting to the Answer:

$$\frac{12-5}{5}=\frac{x-12}{12}$$
$$\frac{7}{5}=\frac{x-12}{12}$$
$$12(7)=5(x-12)$$
$$84=5x-60$$
$$144=5x$$
$$28.8=x$$

13. A
Difficulty: Medium

Category: Passport to Advanced Math / Exponents

Strategic Advice: Don't spend too much time reading the scientific explanation of the equation. Focus on the question at the very end—it's just asking you to solve the equation for d.

Getting to the Answer: First, cross-multiply to get rid of the denominator. Then, divide both sides of the equation by $4\pi b$ to isolate d^2. Finally, take the square root of both sides to find d.

$$b(4\pi d^2) = L$$

$$\frac{b(4\pi d^2)}{4\pi b} = \frac{L}{4\pi b}$$

$$d^2 = \frac{L}{4\pi b}$$

$$\sqrt{d^2} = \sqrt{\frac{L}{4\pi b}}$$

$$d = \sqrt{\frac{L}{4\pi b}}$$

Unfortunately, this is not one of the answer choices, so you'll need to simplify further. You can take the square root of 4 (it's 2), but be careful—it's in the denominator of the fraction, so it comes out of the square root as $\frac{1}{2}$. The simplified equation is $d = \frac{1}{2}\sqrt{\frac{L}{\pi b}}$.

14. D
Difficulty: Easy

Category: Problem Solving and Data Analysis / Statistics and Probability

Strategic Advice: You do not need to use all of the information presented in the table to find the answer. Read the question carefully to make sure you use only what you need.

Getting to the Answer: To calculate the percentage of men in each age group who reported being unemployed in January 2014, divide the number in *that* age group who were unemployed by the total number in *that* age group. There are six age groups but only four answer choices, so don't waste time on the age groups that aren't represented. Choice (D) is correct because $7 \div 152 \approx 0.046 = 4.6\%$, which is a lower percentage than that for any other age group (20 to 24 = 12.5%; 35 to 44 = 4.9%; 45 to 54 = 6.1%).

15. B
Difficulty: Medium

Category: Problem Solving and Data Analysis / Statistics and Probability

Strategic Advice: The follow-up survey targets only those respondents who said they were unemployed, so focus on that column in the table.

Getting to the Answer: There were 6 respondents out of 44 unemployed males who were between the ages of 45 and 54, so the probability is $\frac{6}{44} = 0.1\overline{36}$, or about 13.6%.

16. B
Difficulty: Medium

Category: Passport to Advanced Math / Quadratics

Strategic Advice: Taking the square root is the inverse operation of squaring, and both sides of the equation are already perfect squares, so take their square roots. Then solve the resulting equations. Remember, there will be two equations to solve.

Getting to the Answer:

$$(x-1)^2 = \frac{4}{9}$$

$$\sqrt{(x-1)^2} = \sqrt{\frac{4}{9}}$$

$$x - 1 = \pm\frac{\sqrt{4}}{\sqrt{9}}$$

$$x = 1 \pm \frac{2}{3}$$

Now, simplify each equation: $x = 1 + \frac{2}{3} = \frac{3}{3} + \frac{2}{3} = \frac{5}{3}$ and $x = 1 - \frac{2}{3} = \frac{3}{3} - \frac{2}{3} = \frac{1}{3}$.

17. D
Difficulty: Medium

Category: Heart of Algebra / Linear Equations

Strategic Advice: The key to answering this question is to determine how many darts land in each color ring. If there are 6 darts total and x land in a blue ring, the rest, or $6 - x$, must land in a red ring.

Getting to the Answer: Write the expression in words first: points per blue ring (5) times number of darts in blue ring (x), plus points per red ring (10) times number of darts in red ring ($6 − x$). Now, translate the words into numbers, variables, and operations: $5x + 10(6 − x)$. This is not one of the answer choices, so simplify the expression by distributing the 10 and then combining like terms: $5x + 10(6 − x) = 5x + 60 − 10x = 60 − 5x$.

18. A

Difficulty: Medium

Category: Problem Solving and Data Analysis / Statistics and Probability

Strategic Advice: This is a science crossover question. Read the first two sentences quickly—they are simply describing the context of the question. The last two sentences pose the question, so read those more carefully.

Getting to the Answer: In the sample, 184 out of 200 square feet were free of red tide after applying the spray. This is $\frac{184}{200} = 0.92 = 92\%$ of the area. For the whole beach, $0.92(10{,}000) = 9{,}200$ square feet should be free of the red tide. Be careful—this is *not* the answer. The question asks how much of the beach would still be covered by red tide, so subtract to get $10{,}000 − 9{,}200 = 800$ square feet.

19. A

Difficulty: Medium

Category: Passport to Advanced Math / Quadratics

Strategic Advice: The solution to a system of equations is the point(s) where their graphs intersect. You can solve the system algebraically by setting the equations equal to each other, or you can solve it graphically using your calculator. Use whichever method gets you to the answer more quickly.

Getting to the Answer: Both equations are given in calculator-friendly format ($y = ...$), so graphing them is probably the more efficient approach. The graph looks like:

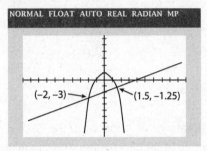

The solution point in the question is given as (a, b), so b represents the y-coordinate of the solution. The y-coordinates of the points of intersection are −3 and −1.25, so choice (A) is correct.

20. A

Difficulty: Medium

Category: Passport to Advanced Math / Functions

Strategic Advice: Don't answer this question too quickly—you may be tempted to substitute 3 for x, but 3 is the output (range), not the input (domain).

Getting to the Answer: The given range value is an output value, so substitute 3 for $g(x)$ and use inverse operations to solve for x, which is the corresponding domain value.

$$g(x) = \frac{2}{3}x + 7$$
$$3 = \frac{2}{3}x + 7$$
$$-4 = \frac{2}{3}x$$
$$-12 = 2x$$
$$-6 = x$$

You could also graph the function and find the value of x (the domain value) for which the value of y (the range value) is 3. The point on the graph is (−6, 3).

21. C
Difficulty: Medium

Category: Heart of Algebra / Linear Equations

Strategic Advice: Don't peek at the answers. Write your own equation using the initial cost and the rate of change in the value of the lawn mower. Remember —when something changes at a constant rate, it can be represented by a linear equation.

Getting to the Answer: When a linear equation in the form $y = mx + b$ is used to model a real-world scenario, m represents the constant rate of change, and b represents the starting amount. Here, the starting amount is easy—it's the purchase price, $2,800. To find the rate of change, think of the initial cost as the value at 0 years, or the point (0, 2,800), and the salvage amount as the value at 8 years, or the point (8, 240). Substitute these points into the slope formula to find that $m = \dfrac{y_2 - y_1}{x_2 - x_1} = \dfrac{240 - 2,800}{8 - 0} = \dfrac{-2,560}{8} = -320$, so the equation is $y = -320x + 2,800$.

22. D
Difficulty: Medium

Category: Problem Solving and Data Analysis / Functions

Strategic Advice: Determine whether the change in the number of bacteria is a common difference (linear function) or a common ratio (exponential function) or if the number of bacteria changes direction (quadratic or polynomial function).

Getting to the Answer: The question tells you that the number of bacteria is reduced by half every hour after the antibiotic is applied. The microbiologist started with 20,000, so after one hour, there are 10,000 left, or $20,000 \times \dfrac{1}{2}$. After 2 hours, there are 5,000 left, or $20,000 \times \dfrac{1}{2} \times \dfrac{1}{2}$, and so on. The change in the number of bacteria is a common ratio $\left(\dfrac{1}{2}\right)$,

so the best model is an exponential function of the form $y = a\left(\dfrac{1}{2}\right)^x$. In this scenario, a is 20,000.

23. B
Difficulty: Medium

Category: Problem Solving and Data Analysis / Rates, Ratios, Proportions, and Percentages

Strategic Advice: Let the units in this question guide you to the solution. The speeds of the airplanes are given in miles per hour, but the question asks about the number of miles each airplane can travel in 12 seconds, so convert miles per hour to miles per second.

Getting to the Answer:

Slower airplane:

$$\dfrac{600 \text{ mi}}{\cancel{hr}} \times \dfrac{1 \cancel{hr}}{60 \cancel{min}} \times \dfrac{1 \cancel{min}}{60 \cancel{sec}} \times 12 \cancel{sec} = 2 \text{ mi}$$

Faster airplane:

$$\dfrac{720 \text{ mi}}{\cancel{hr}} \times \dfrac{1 \cancel{hr}}{60 \cancel{min}} \times \dfrac{1 \cancel{min}}{60 \cancel{sec}} \times 12 \cancel{sec} = 2.4 \text{ mi}$$

The faster plane can travel $2.4 - 2 = 0.4$ miles farther, which is the same as $\dfrac{2}{5}$ miles.

24. C
Difficulty: Medium

Category: Heart of Algebra / Inequalities

Strategic Advice: The best way to answer this question is to pretend you are the worker. How much more would you earn for one hour in Oregon than in Idaho? If you worked 35 hours per week, how much more would this be? If you worked 40 hours per week, how much more would this be?

Getting to the Answer: Based on the data in the table, a worker would earn $9.10 − $7.25 = $1.85 more for one hour of work in Oregon than in Idaho.

If he worked 35 hours per week, he would earn 35(1.85) = $64.75 more. If he worked 40 hours per week, he would earn 40(1.85) = $74 more. So, the worker would earn somewhere between $64.75 and $74 more per week, which can be expressed as the compound inequality $64.75 \le x \le 74$.

25. D
Difficulty: Medium

Category: Problem Solving and Data Analysis / Rates, Ratios, Proportions, and Percentages

Strategic Advice: This is another question where the units can help you find the answer. Use the number of vehicles owned to find the total number of miles driven to find the total number of gallons of gas used to find the total tax paid. Phew!

Getting to the Answer:

$$1.75 \text{ vehicles} \times \frac{11{,}340 \text{ miles}}{\text{vehicle}} = 19{,}845 \text{ miles}$$

$$19{,}845 \text{ miles} \times \frac{1 \text{ gallon of gas}}{21.4 \text{ miles}} = 927.336 \text{ gallons}$$

$$927.336 \text{ gallons} \times \frac{\$0.184}{\text{gallon}} = \$170.63$$

26. C
Difficulty: Medium

Category: Problem Solving and Data Analysis / Scatterplots

Strategic Advice: The average rate of change of a function over a given interval, from a to b, compares the change in the outputs, $f(b) - f(a)$, to the change in the inputs, $b - a$. In other words, it is the slope of the line that connects the endpoints of the interval, so you can use the slope formula.

Getting to the Answer: Look at the quadratic model, not the data points, to find that the endpoints of the given interval, week 2 to week 8, are (2, 280) and (8, 400). The average rate of change is $\frac{400 - 280}{8 - 2} = \frac{120}{6} = 20$.

On average, the dolphin's weight increased by 20 pounds per week.

27. A
Difficulty: Hard

Category: Additional Topics in Math / Geometry

Strategic Advice: In this question, information is given in both the diagram and the text. You need to relate the text to the diagram, one piece of information at a time, to calculate how long the lifeguard ran along the beach and how long he swam. Before you find the swim time, you need to know how *far* he swam.

Getting to the Answer: Whenever you see a right triangle symbol in a diagram, you should think Pythagorean theorem or, in this question, special right triangles. All multiples of 3-4-5 triangles are right triangles, so the length of the lifeguard's swim is the hypotenuse of a 30-40-50 triangle, or 50 feet. Add this number to the diagram. Now calculate the times using the distances and the speeds given. Don't forget the 1 second that the lifeguard paused.

$$\text{Run time} = 60 \text{ ft} \times \frac{1 \text{ sec}}{12 \text{ ft}} = \frac{60}{12} = 5 \text{ sec}$$

Pause time = 1 sec

$$\text{Swim time} = 50 \text{ ft} \times \frac{1 \text{ sec}}{5 \text{ ft}} = \frac{50}{5} = 10 \text{ sec}$$

Total time = 5 + 1 + 10 = 16 seconds

28. B
Difficulty: Hard

Category: Heart of Algebra / Linear Equations

Strategic Advice: Write an equation in words first and then translate from English to math. Finally, rearrange your equation to find what you're interested in, which is the initial amount of gasoline.

Getting to the Answer: Call the initial amount A. After you've written your equation, solve for A.

Amount now (x) = Initial amount (A) minus y, plus 50

$$x = A - y + 50$$
$$x + y - 50 = A$$

The initial amount was $x + y - 50$ gallons. Note that you could also use Picking Numbers to answer this question.

29. B
Difficulty: Hard

Category: Problem Solving and Data Analysis / Statistics and Probability

Strategic Advice: When a question involves reading data from a graph, it is sometimes better to skip an answer choice if it involves long calculations. Skim the answer choices for this question—A involves finding two averages, each of which is composed of 7 data values. Skip this choice for now.

Getting to the Answer: Start with (B). Be careful—you are not looking for places where the line segments are increasing. The y-axis already represents the change in prices, so you are simply counting the number of positive values for the imports (5) and for the exports (4). There are more for the imports, so (B) is correct and you don't need to check any of the other statements. Move on to the next question.

30. D
Difficulty: Hard

Category: Passport to Advanced Math / Exponents

Strategic Advice: The key to answering this question is deciding what you're trying to find. The question tells you that x represents the athlete's swim rate and you are looking for the number of kilometers he swam in one hour—these are the same thing. If you find x (in kilometers per hour), you will know how many kilometers he swam in one hour.

Getting to the Answer: Set the equation equal to the total time, 16.2, and solve for x. To do this, write the variable terms over a common denominator, $10x$, and combine them into a single term. Then cross-multiply and go from there.

$$16.2 = \frac{10}{10}\left(\frac{3.86}{x}\right) + \frac{180.2}{10x} + \frac{2}{2}\left(\frac{42.2}{5x}\right)$$
$$16.2 = \frac{38.6}{10x} + \frac{180.2}{10x} + \frac{84.4}{10x}$$
$$16.2 = \frac{303.2}{10x}$$
$$10x(16.2) = 303.2$$
$$162x = 303.2$$
$$x = \frac{303.2}{162} \approx 1.87$$

31. 1
Difficulty: Easy

Category: Heart of Algebra / Linear Equations

Strategic Advice: Choose the best strategy to answer the question. If you distribute the $\frac{2}{3}$, it creates messy calculations. Instead, clear the fraction by multiplying both sides of the equation by 3. Then use the distributive property and inverse operations to solve for x.

Getting to the Answer:

$$\frac{2}{3}(5x + 7) = 8x$$
$$\cancel{3} \cdot \frac{2}{\cancel{3}}(5x + 7) = 3 \cdot 8x$$
$$2(5x + 7) = 24x$$
$$10x + 14 = 24x$$
$$14 = 14x$$
$$1 = x$$

32. 192
Difficulty: Medium

Category: Passport to Advanced Math / Exponents

Strategic Advice: This looks like a word problem, but don't let it intimidate you. Once you read it, you'll see that it boils down to substituting a few given values for the variables and solving the equation.

Getting to the Answer: Before you start substituting values, quickly check that the units given match the units required to use the equation—they do, so proceed. The patient's weight (w) is 150 and the patient's BSA is $2\sqrt{2}$, so the equation becomes $2\sqrt{2} = \sqrt{\dfrac{150h}{3,600}}$. The only variable left in the equation is h, and you are trying to find the patient's height, so you're ready to solve the equation. To do this, square both sides of the equation and then continue using inverse operations. Be careful when you square the left side—you must square both the 2 and the root 2.

$$2\sqrt{2} = \sqrt{\frac{150h}{3,600}}$$

$$\left(2\sqrt{2}\right)^2 = \left(\sqrt{\frac{150h}{3,600}}\right)^2$$

$$2^2\left(\sqrt{2}\right)^2 = \frac{150h}{3,600}$$

$$4(2) = \frac{150h}{3,600}$$

$$28,800 = 150h$$

$$192 = h$$

33. Any value greater than 7 and less than 7.5
Difficulty: Medium

Category: Heart of Algebra / Inequalities

Strategic Advice: You could solve the compound inequality for m and substitute the result into the expression $10m - 5$, but there is a quicker way to answer this question. Look for a relationship between what you're given, the possible values of $-2m + 1$, and what you're looking for, the possible values of $10m - 5$.

Getting to the Answer: Notice that $10m - 5$ is -5 times the expression $-2m + 1$. This means you can answer the question by multiplying all three pieces of the inequality by -5. (Don't forget to flip the inequality symbols because you are multiplying by a negative number.) Then write the inequality with increasing values from left to right.

$$-5\left(-\frac{3}{2}\right) < -5(-2m+1) < -5\left(-\frac{7}{5}\right)$$

$$\frac{15}{2} > 10m - 5 > 7$$

$$7 < 10m - 5 < 7.5$$

You can enter any value between (but not including) 7 and 7.5, such as 7.1 or 7.2.

34. 40
Difficulty: Hard

Category: Additional Topics in Math / Geometry

Strategic Advice: Since $\overline{AB}$, $\overline{CD}$, and $\overline{EF}$ are diameters, the sum of x, y, and the interior angle of the shaded region is 180 degrees. The question tells you that the shaded region is $\dfrac{1}{5}$ of the circle, so the interior angle must equal $\dfrac{1}{5}$ of the degrees in the whole circle, or $\dfrac{1}{5}$ of 360.

Getting to the Answer: Use what you know about y (that it is equal to $2x - 12$) and what you know about the shaded region (that it is $\dfrac{1}{5}$ of 360 degrees) to write and solve an equation.

$$x + y + \frac{1}{5}(360) = 180$$

$$x + (2x - 12) + 72 = 180$$

$$3x + 60 = 180$$

$$3x = 120$$

$$x = 40$$

35. 14
Difficulty: Hard

Category: Heart of Algebra / Linear Equations

Strategic Advice: When you know the slope and one point on a line, you can use $y = mx + b$ to write the equation. Substitute the slope for m and the coordinates of the point for x and y and then solve for b, the y-intercept of the line.

Getting to the Answer: The slope is given as $-\dfrac{7}{4}$, so substitute this for m. The point is given as $(4, 7)$, so $x = 4$ and $y = 7$. Now, find b.

$$y = mx + b$$

$$7 = -\frac{7}{\cancel{4}}(\cancel{4}) + b$$

$$7 = -7 + b$$

$$14 = b$$

The *y*-intercept of the line is 14.

You could also very carefully graph the line using the given point and the slope. Start at (4, 7) and move toward the *y*-axis by rising 7 and running *to the left* 4 (because the slope is negative). You should land at the point (0, 14).

36. 45
Difficulty: Hard

Category: Problem Solving and Data Analysis / Rates, Ratios, Proportions, and Percentages

Strategic Advice: Make a chart that represents rate, time, and distance and fill in what you know. Then use your table to solve for distance. If it took Rory *t* hours to get to the airport, and the total trip took 2 hours and 30 minutes (or 2.5 hours), how long (in terms of *t*) did the return trip take?

Getting to the Answer:

	Rate	Time	Distance
To airport	45 mph	*t*	*d*
Back to home	30 mph	2.5 − *t*	*d*

Now use the formula $d = r \times t$ for both parts of the trip: $d = 45t$ and $d = 30(2.5 - t)$. Because both are equal to *d*, you can set them equal to each other and solve for *t*:

$$45t = 30(2.5 - t)$$
$$45t = 75 - 30t$$
$$75t = 75$$
$$t = 1$$

Now plug back in to solve for *d*:

$$d = 45t$$
$$d = 45(1)$$
$$d = 45$$

37. 10
Difficulty: Medium

Category: Problem Solving and Data Analysis / Rates, Ratios, Proportions, and Percentages

Strategic Advice: You don't need to know chemistry to answer this question. All the information you need is in the table. Use the formula

$$\text{Percent} = \frac{\text{Part}}{\text{Whole}} \times 100\%.$$

Getting to the Answer: To use the formula, find the part of the mass represented by the carbon; there is 1 mole of carbon, and it has a mass of 12.011 grams. Next, find the whole mass of the mole of chloroform; 1 mole carbon (12.011 g) + 1 mole hydrogen (1.008 g) + 3 moles chlorine (3 × 35.453 = 106.359 g) = 12.011 + 1.008 + 106.359 = 119.378. Now use the formula:

$$\text{Percent} = \frac{12.011}{119.378} \times 100\%$$
$$= 0.10053 \times 100\%$$
$$= 10.053\%$$

Before you grid in your answer, make sure you follow the directions—round to the nearest whole percent, which is 10.

38. 12
Difficulty: Hard

Category: Problem Solving and Data Analysis / Rates, Ratios, Proportions, and Percentages

Strategic Advice: This part of the question contains several steps. Think about the units given in the question and how you can use what you know to find what you need.

Getting to the Answer: Start with grams of chloroform; the chemist starts with 1,000 and uses 522.5, so there are 1,000 − 522.5 = 477.5 grams left. From the previous question you know that 1 mole of chloroform has a mass of 119.378 grams, so there are 477.5 ÷ 119.378 = 3.999, or about 4 moles of chloroform left. Be careful—you're not finished yet. The question asks for the number of moles of *chlorine*, not chloroform. According to the table, each mole of chloroform contains 3 moles of chlorine, so there are 4 × 3 = 12 moles of chlorine left.

ESSAY TEST RUBRIC

The Essay Demonstrates...

4—Advanced	• **(Reading)** A strong ability to comprehend the source text, including its central ideas and important details and how they interrelate; and effectively use evidence (quotations, paraphrases, or both) from the source text.
	• **(Analysis)** A strong ability to evaluate the author's use of evidence, reasoning, and/ or stylistic and persuasive elements, and/or other features of the student's own choosing; make good use of relevant, sufficient, and strategically chosen support for the claims or points made in the student's essay; and focus consistently on features of the source text that are most relevant to addressing the task.
	• **(Writing)** A strong ability to provide a precise central claim; create an effective organization that includes an introduction and conclusion, as well as a clear progression of ideas; successfully employ a variety of sentence structures; use precise word choice; maintain a formal style and objective tone; and show command of the conventions of standard written English so that the essay is free of errors.
3—Proficient	• **(Reading)** Satisfactory ability to comprehend the source text, including its central ideas and important details and how they interrelate; and use evidence (quotations, paraphrases, or both) from the source text.
	• **(Analysis)** Satisfactory ability to evaluate the author's use of evidence, reasoning, and/or stylistic and persuasive elements, and/or other features of the student's own choosing; make use of relevant and sufficient support for the claims or points made in the student's essay; and focus primarily on features of the source text that are most relevant to addressing the task.
	• **(Writing)** Satisfactory ability to provide a central claim; create an organization that includes an introduction and conclusion, as well as a clear progression of ideas; employ a variety of sentence structures; use precise word choice; maintain an appropriate formal style and objective tone; and show control of the conventions of standard written English so that the essay is free of significant errors.
2—Partial	• **(Reading)** Limited ability to comprehend the source text, including its central ideas and important details and how they interrelate; and use evidence (quotations, paraphrases, or both) from the source text.
	• **(Analysis)** Limited ability to evaluate the author's use of evidence, reasoning, and/ or stylistic and persuasive elements, and/or other features of the student's own choosing; make use of support for the claims or points made in the student's essay; and focus on relevant features of the source text.
	• **(Writing)** Limited ability to provide a central claim; create an effective organization for ideas; employ a variety of sentence structures; use precise word choice; maintain an appropriate style and tone; or show control of the conventions of standard written English, resulting in certain errors that detract from the quality of the writing.

1—Inadequate	• **(Reading)** Little or no ability to comprehend the source text or use evidence from the source text.
	• **(Analysis)** Little or no ability to evaluate the author's use of evidence, reasoning, and/or stylistic and persuasive elements; choose support for claims or points; or focus on relevant features of the source text.
	• **(Writing)** Little or no ability to provide a central claim, organization, or progression of ideas; employ a variety of sentence structures; use precise word choice; maintain an appropriate style and tone; or show control of the conventions of standard written English, resulting in numerous errors that undermine the quality of the writing.

SAMPLE ESSAY RESPONSE #1 (ADVANCED SCORE)

As anyone knows who has had to help their family move house, find a textbook in a cluttered room, or even just clean a crowded apartment, possessions can have a huge amount of power over people. Far from being simply objects that we enjoy or that bring us pleasure, it can sometimes feel that our possessions oppress us. This is the point Morris eloquently makes in her essay "The Tyranny of Things." By using anecdotes, examples, reasoning, and powerful imagery, Morris argues that the very things we cherish are nearly crushing the life out of us.

The author begins by relating an anecdote about two teenagers becoming fast friends over their love of things. It is a touching moment, one to which readers can easily relate; even Morris herself says that we all probably go through this phase. This helps establish her credibility with readers, because her examples make sense to them. Gradually, however, Morris makes it clear that this touching moment has a sinister side—the love of things will only result in resentment.

Morris reasons that while it's natural to go through a phase of wanting objects, it is unhealthy to remain in this state. "Many people never pass out of this phase," she writes ominously. "They never see a flower without wanting to pick it . . . they bring home all their alpenstocks." It begins to sound obsessive, this need to control things. Morris goes on to develop her argument by suggesting that possessions are metaphorically suffocating us. She makes the idea of too many possessions sound repulsive by describing them as "an undigested mass of things." The things almost take on a kind of life force, according to Morris: "they possess us." They "have destroyed" our empty spaces and we feel "stifled."

Another way Morris supports her argument is by giving examples of the unnecessary "tokens" associated with social occasions. She describes how at events, luncheons, and parties, gifts are given and received. She then uses powerful negative imagery to describe the effects of these gifts, comparing the recipient to a "ship encrusted with barnacles" that needs to be "scraped bare again." This language suggests that the gifts are burdensome and even harmful.

By contrast, the imagery Morris uses to describe a simple life filled with fewer things is imagery of ease and relaxation. "We breathe more freely in the clear space that we have made for ourselves," she writes. It is not just that we have literally regained control from our possessions and are now acting rather than being acted upon; it is that we are physically more at ease.

In her conclusion, Morris longs for a day when we can live more simply, with fewer possessions. She describes a "house by the sea" that was simple and empty; it did not "demand care" or "claim attention" or otherwise act upon her. Her wish is that "we could but free ourselves" from the tyranny of things that she feels is draining us of our freedom. And at this point, it is likely the reader's wish, too.

SAMPLE ESSAY RESPONSE #2 (PROFICIENT SCORE)

Although as people we like to think of ourselves as owners of things, in fact it can sometimes feel like the things we own end up owning us. At least this is what Morris argues in her essay "The Tyranny of Things." Through her use of evidence, reasoning, and word choice, she makes a strong argument that we should own fewer things if we ever want to be truly happy.

Morris tells a story about two teenage girls who instantly know they will be friends because they both like things. They are not happy just to be. They have to own things. It's like their own experiences aren't enough for them. But Morris says that this is bad for people, because they will end up feeling like their possessions own them.

Morris's reasoning is that we can basically get control back over our own lives if we stop needing things so much. If we have too many things, "they possess us." So we have to get rid of things, and then we can feel better. At least these days we aren't buried with our things anymore, like they were in the olden days.

The word choices in the essay are interesting. She talks about the way things become a problem for us: "our books are a burden to us, our pictures have destroyed every restful wall-space, our china is a care." By using a lot of repetition, it shows how powerful things are.

Morris's essay encourages people to free themselves from their things. If they do so, they will be happier. Through her personal anecdotes, reasoning, and repetitive word choices, she makes her essay very powerful.

PART FIVE

Answers & Explanations

CHAPTER 1

PREPARE

1. D
Difficulty: Medium

Category: Heart of Algebra / Linear Equations

Strategic Advice: Simplify as much as possible, then isolate the variable.

Getting to the Answer: Begin by combining like terms on both sides of the equation. Once complete, solve for z.

$$\frac{4+z-(3+2z)}{6}=\frac{-z-3(5-2)}{7}$$

$$\frac{1-z}{6}=\frac{-z-9}{7}$$

$$7-7z=-6z-54$$

$$-z=-61$$

$$z=61$$

(D) is correct.

2. B
Difficulty: Easy

Category: Heart of Algebra / Linear Equations

Strategic Advice: Straightforward math works well on simple equations like this one.

Getting to the Answer: Combine like terms, then solve for y.

$$3y+2y-4=-25$$

$$5y-4=-25$$

$$5y=-21$$

$$y=-\frac{21}{5}$$

Choice (B) is correct.

3. C
Difficulty: Easy

Category: Heart of Algebra / Linear Equations

Strategic Advice: Before choosing the "cannot be determined" option, check to see if the y terms will cancel.

Getting to the Answer: Divide both sides by 3, then combine like terms. The y terms will drop out, leaving one equation with one variable. Once there, solve for x as usual.

$$3(y-8)+3(6x+2)=24+3y$$

$$y-8+6x+2=8+y$$

$$-8+6x+2=8$$

$$-6+6x=8$$

$$6x=14$$

$$x=\frac{14}{6}=2.33$$

Your answers are in decimal form, so don't waste time trying to reduce $\frac{14}{6}$; just plug it into your calculator. (C) is the correct answer.

4. A
Difficulty: Medium

Category: Heart of Algebra / Linear Equations

Strategic Advice: Wordy questions call for the Kaplan Strategy for Translating English into Math.

Getting to the Answer: Use the route labels for your variables, then break off phrases from the question stem for translation into math. "Route A is 1.5 times longer than Route B" becomes $A = 1.5B$, and "[Route A is] $\frac{3}{4}$ the length of Route C" becomes $A=\frac{3}{4}C$. You're told C is 3 km, so plug this into the second equation to solve for A; you'll find $A=\frac{9}{4}=2.25$ km.

Plug this value into the first equation to get B: $2.25 = 1.5B \rightarrow B = \dfrac{2.25}{1.5} = 1.5$ km. But you're not done yet! Subtract B from A to get your answer, 0.75 km, which matches (A).

5. B

Difficulty: Medium

Category: Heart of Algebra / Linear Equations

Strategic Advice: No real math acrobatics here, but the Kaplan Method for Math will still prove useful.

Getting to the Answer: You're asked to identify the line that the one described in the question stem will never intersect. Lines that never intersect are parallel and therefore have identical slopes, so start by finding the slope of the line whose two coordinate pairs are given. You'll find $m = \dfrac{1-0}{0-(-\frac{2}{5})} = \dfrac{1}{\frac{2}{5}} = \dfrac{5}{2}$;

C and D have negative slopes, so eliminate them. Next, find the slopes of A and B. No need to use the slope formula; counting units on the graphs will be faster. The slope of A is $\dfrac{2}{5}$, and the slope of B is $\dfrac{5}{2}$. Therefore, (B) is correct.

6. A

Difficulty: Easy

Category: Heart of Algebra / Linear Equations

Strategic Advice: Don't get bogged down by the prose; zero in on what you need to answer the question posed.

Getting to the Answer: The last two sentences of the question stem are all you need to answer this; you need the equation of the line shown. Start by finding the slope of the line by picking a pair of points, such as (40, 0) and (65, 100): $m = \dfrac{100 - 0}{65 - 40} = \dfrac{100}{25} = 4$.

B and C have slopes other than 4, so eliminate them. A and D have y-intercepts of −160 and 40, respectively. According to the graph, 40 cannot be the y-intercept because the line does not intersect the y-axis at 40. Therefore, the answer must be (A).

7. C

Difficulty: Medium

Category: Heart of Algebra / Linear Equations

Strategic Advice: Think carefully about the general importance of the slope of a line.

Getting to the Answer: A line's slope is always a rate of change of some sort, so you can eliminate B and D. Now turn to A and C; the way they describe the relationship between exam performance and time spent on the exam is different. The graph indicates time spent on the exam is the independent variable, so exam performance depends on it. The only choice that correctly describes this relationship is (C).

PRACTICE

8. D

Difficulty: Hard

Category: Heart of Algebra / Linear Equations

Strategic Advice: Mind the order in which the changes to the graph occur.

Getting to the Answer: The question states that the downward shift of 2 units occurs first, making the new y-intercept $-\dfrac{3}{2}$. A reflection over the x-axis follows, which changes the y-intercept to $\dfrac{3}{2}$ and makes the slope $\dfrac{7}{4}$. The only graph that correctly depicts these changes is (D). Beware C; this results from a reflection over the *y*-axis, not the *x*-axis. The graphs below visualize each change.

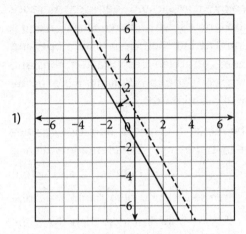

1)

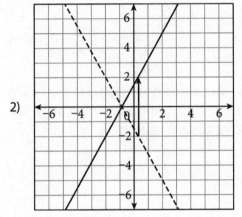

2)

9. C

Difficulty: Medium

Category: Heart of Algebra / Linear Equations

Strategic Advice: Look closely; buried in the text are two sets of coordinates you can use.

Getting to the Answer: The question states that admission was $2 when the admission charge was first implemented and increased to $2.50 after 3 years, making your coordinates (0, 2) and (3, 2.5). The slope of the line passing through these is $m = \frac{2.5 - 2}{3 - 0} = \frac{0.5}{3} = \frac{1}{6}$. Eliminate A and D. Because the admission fee started at $2, 2 is the *y*-intercept, so the full equation is $y = \frac{c}{6} + 2$. (C) is correct.

Because the question says "three years ago," it's tempting to use (–3, 2) and (0, 2.5) as your coordinates. Think about what that would mean: The first admission charge would be $2.50, as it's impossible to have a negative year. This contradicts the question stem, so B is incorrect.

PERFORM

10. A

Difficulty: Easy

Category: Heart of Algebra / Linear Equations

Strategic Advice: Think about what happens to the slope of a line if you're merely moving the line around the coordinate plane.

Getting to the Answer: Any shift of a line, whether it's up, down, left, right, or some combination thereof, will never change the line's slope. The slope will remain –5, which is (A).

11. 36

Difficulty: Medium

Category: Heart of Algebra / Linear Equations

Strategic Advice: That you're asked to find an expression rather than a variable value means there's likely a shortcut.

Getting to the Answer: Start by eliminating the fractions. A common multiple of 4 and 3 is 12, so multiply both sides of the equation by that. Once the fractions are gone, manipulate the equation until you have $2c + \frac{9}{2}y$ isolated.

$$12\left(\frac{3}{4}y = 6 - \frac{1}{3}c\right)$$
$$9y = 72 - 4c$$
$$4c + 9y = 72$$
$$2c + \frac{9}{2}y = 36$$

Grid in 36, the correct answer.

12. A

Difficulty: Hard

Category: Heart of Algebra / Linear Equations

Strategic Advice: Don't panic over the presence of *m*. Just solve for *y*, then think about what kind of graph it can have.

Getting to the Answer: Start by distributing *m* on the right, then move all terms to the left.

$$x - y = m(2x + y)$$

$$x - y = 2mx + my$$

$$x - 2mx - y - my = 0$$

Continue by factoring out *x* and *y*, then move any terms without *y* back to the right.

$$x(1 - 2m) + y(-1 - m) = 0$$

$$y(-1 - m) = -x(1 - 2m)$$

Divide by (–1–*m*), then factor out –1 from the denominator and cancel.

$$y = \frac{-x(1-2m)}{(-1-m)} = \frac{-x(1-2m)}{-(1+m)} = \frac{x(1-2m)}{(1+m)}$$

Don't worry about how messy the right side looks yet; for now, you just need to realize that it's merely *x* multiplied by a complicated coefficient. Because the equation is now solved for *y*, you have an equation of a line: The big coefficient is the slope, and because there's no added (or subtracted) constant, the *y*-intercept is 0. You can eliminate B (not a line) and D (*b* ≠ 0) based on this.

Examine the remaining choices more closely: They only differ in slope sign. To determine which is correct, pick a value for *m* between 0 and $\frac{1}{2}$ (but not 0 or $\frac{1}{2}$ themselves), and plug it into the slope expression. If $k = \frac{1}{4}$, for instance, then the slope

would be $\dfrac{(1 - 2 \times \frac{1}{4})}{(1 + \frac{1}{4})} = \dfrac{(1 - \frac{1}{2})}{\frac{5}{4}} = \dfrac{1}{2} \times \dfrac{4}{5} = \dfrac{2}{5}$, which

is a positive value. Because the slope of this line must be positive, (A), which is the only remaining choice with a positive slope, is correct.

EXTRA PRACTICE

1. C
Difficulty: Easy

Category: Heart of Algebra / Linear Equations

Strategic Advice: Look at the variables in each equation. When written in exponent form (no radicals and no variables in the denominator of a fraction), in which equation would all the exponents be 1?

Getting to the Answer: You can eliminate D right away because the exponent on x is 2. When written in exponent form, the other equations look like:

Choice A: $y = 3x^{-1}$ (not linear because of the -1 power)

Choice B: $x^{\frac{1}{2}} + y = 0$ (not linear because of the $\frac{1}{2}$ power)

Choice (C): $\frac{1}{2}x - \frac{5}{8}y = 11$ (linear)

2. B
Difficulty: Easy

Category: Heart of Algebra / Linear Equations

Strategic Advice: For the equations, look at the exponents on the variables. Are they all 1? For the table, check to see if the change in the y-values compared to the change in the x-values is constant for each pair of values.

Getting to the Answer: The table in (B) does not represent a linear relationship because the x-values change by +4 each time, while the y-values change by −10 then −8 then +8 then +10. A linear relationship has a constant rate of change, which means it is either always increasing or always decreasing, and by the same amount. This data clearly changes direction and is therefore not linear, so (B) is correct.

3. A
Difficulty: Easy

Category: Heart of Algebra / Linear Equations

Strategic Advice: Write the equation in words first and then translate from English into math.

Getting to the Answer: The total cost, c, is the weight of the potatoes in pounds, p, multiplied by the sale price because the purchase is made on Friday: $\$0.90 \times (100 - 30)\% = 0.9 \times 0.7 = 0.63$. This gives the first part of the expression: $0.63p$. Now, add the cost of two cantaloupes, $3.50 \times 2 = 7$, to get the equation $c = 0.63p + 7$, which is (A).

You could also Pick Numbers to answer this question—pick a number for the weight of the potatoes and calculate how much they would cost (on sale) and add the cost of two cantaloupes. Then find the equation that gives the same amount when you substitute the number you picked.

4. C
Difficulty: Easy

Category: Heart of Algebra / Linear Equations

Strategic Advice: The total cost of the two kinds of items is the cost of the paintbrushes multiplied by the number purchased plus the cost of the canvases multiplied by the number purchased. Because a canvas cost "6 times" the cost of a paintbrush, a canvas costs 6($1.50) = $9.

Getting to the Answer:
Total cost of paintbrushes: $1.50 \times p$ or $1.5p$
Total cost of canvases: $9 \times c$ or $9c$
Sum of both: $9c + 1.5p$
Therefore, (C) is correct.

5. D

Difficulty: Easy

Category: Heart of Algebra / Linear Equations

Strategic Advice: Think about whether 0.004 is a constant in the equation or a coefficient that is multiplied by the independent variable.

Getting to the Answer: The total bill consists of a flat tax (the local impact fee) and some part (or percent) of the market value of the volume of gas extracted. The local impact fee is a one-time fee that does not depend on the amount of gas extracted and therefore should not be multiplied by *v*. This means that 50,000 is the local impact fee. The other expression in the equation, 0.004*v*, represents the severance tax times the market value of the volume of gas extracted (which the question tells you is *v*). Therefore, 0.004 could represent the amount of the severance tax as a percentage (0.4%), which is (D).

6. C

Difficulty: Easy

Category: Heart of Algebra / Linear Equations

Strategic Advice: Try to picture in your head what "increase in property values starts to slow down" would look like. It doesn't say the values start to decrease, but rather that the increase is not as fast.

Getting to the Answer: An increasing line (one with a positive slope) indicates increasing property values. The steepness of the line (the actual *value* of the slope) indicates how fast the values are increasing. The second line segment in the graph (between $t = 8$ and $t = 16$) still shows a positive slope, but one that is less steep than the first segment, so the increase in property values starts to slow down at $t = 8$, which is the year $2014 + 8 = 2022$, (C).

7. B

Difficulty: Easy

Category: Heart of Algebra / Linear Equations

Strategic Advice: Read the axis labels carefully. The *y*-intercept is the point at which $x = 0$, which means the number of songs purchased is 0.

Getting to the Answer: The *y*-intercept is (0, 20). This means the cost is $20 before buying any songs, and therefore most likely represents a flat membership fee for joining the service, which means (B) is correct.

8. D

Difficulty: Medium

Category: Heart of Algebra / Linear Equations

Strategic Advice: Let *x* be the number of surfboards Jon sells in a month. Write a linear equation that represents the scenario and then solve for *x*.

Getting to the Answer: Sales must equal expenses for the store to break even. Jon's sales are equal to the selling price ($120) times the number of surfboards he sells (*x*), so write 120*x* on one side of the equal sign. His monthly expenses are his fixed expenses ($3,600) plus the amount he paid for each surfboard ($80) times the number of surfboards (*x*), so write 3,600 + 80*x* on the other side of the equal sign. Then, solve for *x*.

$$120x = 3,600 + 80x$$
$$40x = 3,600$$
$$x = 90$$

Therefore, (D) is correct.

9. A

Difficulty: Medium

Category: Heart of Algebra / Linear Equations

Strategic Advice: This question has multiple fractions, so clear the $\frac{8}{5}$ by multiplying both sides of the equation by its reciprocal, $\frac{5}{8}$. Then, because the answers are given in decimal form, change the other fraction to a decimal by dividing the numerator by the denominator.

Getting to the Answer:

$$\frac{8}{5}\left(x+\frac{33}{12}\right)=16$$

$$\frac{5}{8}\cdot\frac{8}{5}\left[\left(x+\frac{33}{12}\right)\right]=\frac{5}{8}\cdot16$$

$$x+2.75=10$$

$$x=7.25$$

Choice (A) is correct.

10. D

Difficulty: Medium

Category: Heart of Algebra / Linear Equations

Strategic Advice: You could start by cross-multiplying, but there are so many terms and parentheses that you are likely to forget to distribute a factor. Instead, simplify the numerators first. Don't forget to distribute the negative to both terms inside the parentheses on the right-hand side of the equation.

Getting to the Answer: Simplify the numerators, cross-multiply, and then solve for n using inverse operations. Don't try to do steps in your head—writing each step down will keep you organized.

$$\frac{3(n-2)+5}{4}=\frac{11-(7-n)}{6}$$

$$\frac{3n-6+5}{4}=\frac{11-7+n}{6}$$

$$\frac{3n-1}{4}=\frac{4+n}{6}$$

$$6(3n-1)=4(4+n)$$

$$18n-6=16+4n$$

$$14n=22$$

$$n=\frac{22}{14}=\frac{11}{7}$$

Choice (D) is correct.

11. D

Difficulty: Medium

Category: Heart of Algebra / Linear Equations

Strategic Advice: Take a quick peek at the answer choices. The equations are given in slope-intercept form, so start by finding the slope.

Getting to the Answer: Find the slope by substituting two pairs of values from the table (try to pick easy ones if possible) into the slope formula, $m=\frac{y_2-y_1}{x_2-x_1}$. Keep in mind that the projected number of pounds sold *depends* on the price, so the price is the independent variable (x) and the projected number is the dependent variable (y). Using the points (1.2, 15,000) and (2, 5,000), the slope is:

$$m=\frac{5,000-15,000}{2-1.20}$$

$$m=\frac{-10,000}{0.8}$$

$$m=-12,500$$

This means you can eliminate A and B because the slope is not correct. Don't let B fool you—the projected number of pounds sold goes *down* as the price goes *up*, so there is an inverse relationship, which means the slope must be negative. To choose between C and (D), you could find the *y*-intercept of the line, but this is a fairly time-intensive process. Instead, choose the easiest pair of values from the table, (2, 5,000), and substitute into C and (D) only. Choice (D) is correct because 5,000 = −12,500(2) + 30,000 is a true statement.

12. C

Difficulty: Medium

Category: Heart of Algebra / Linear Equations

Strategic Advice: It takes too much time to think about and then compare each answer choice to the scenario. Instead, figure out what each part of the equation most likely represents, and look for the answer choice that matches.

Getting to the Answer: Because the equation represents the balance if Henry deposits his paycheck for *x* weeks, then his paycheck amount must be multiplied by the number of weeks he works. The only two factors in the equation being multiplied are 360 and *x*, so 360 must be the amount of his paycheck. This means you can eliminate A and D. The other number in the equation, −126.13, is a constant, which represents a starting amount. Because the constant is negative, Henry must have had a negative balance in his account before setting up the direct deposit, which means he had overdrawn the account. Thus, (C) is correct.

13. B
Difficulty: Medium

Category: Heart of Algebra / Linear Equations

Strategic Advice: There is not a lot of information to go on here, so start by determining the relationship between the number given in the question, 54,000, and the number in the equation, 2,250.

Getting to the Answer: Because 54,000 ÷ 2,250 = 24 and there are 24 hours in a day, 2,250 is the number of pages the press can print in 1 hour. If the press can print 2,250 in 1 hour, then it can print 2,250 times *x* in *x* hours. This means the function $f(x) = 2,250x$ represents the number of pages the press can print in *x* hours, which means (B) is correct.

14. A
Difficulty: Medium

Category: Heart of Algebra / Linear Equations

Strategic Advice: In this scenario, both the flat fee for serving the food and the per-person rate are likely to be fixed amounts (determined by the catering company), while the number of people attending Nadim's party is likely to be a variable amount.

Getting to the Answer: The total cost is the dependent variable and is calculated by multiplying the per person rate by the number of people attending

and then adding the flat serving fee. So the total cost is represented by *y*. Because the flat serving fee and the per person rate are likely to be fixed amounts, they should be represented by numbers in the equations, 300 and 11, respectively. The total cost depends on the number of people attending, so the number of people is the independent variable and is most likely represented by *x*. Therefore, (A) is correct.

15. A
Difficulty: Medium

Category: Heart of Algebra / Linear Equations

Strategic Advice: A line with an undefined slope is a vertical line (a horizontal line has a slope of 0 because it is flat), so look for an equation that represents a vertical line.

Getting to the Answer: Start with the first equation. If *x* = 3 is the only thing you have to go on, choose a few points with an *x*-coordinate of 3, such as (3, 0), (3, 1), and (3, 2). Plot these points and draw a line through them to see that the graph is a vertical line and therefore has an undefined slope. There is no need to check the other equations. Choice (A) is correct.

16. C
Difficulty: Medium

Category: Heart of Algebra / Linear Equations

Strategic Advice: Use the graph to identify the *y*-intercept and the slope of the line, and then write an equation in slope-intercept form, $y = mx + b$. Once you have your equation, look for the answer choice that matches.

Getting to the Answer: The line crosses the *y*-axis at (0, −4) so the *y*-intercept (*b*) is −4. The line rises vertically 1 unit for every 3 units that it runs to the right, so the slope (*m*) is $\frac{1}{3}$. The equation of the line is $y = \frac{1}{3}x - 4$, which matches (C).

You could also graph each of the answer choices in your calculator to see which one matches the given graph, but this is not the most time-efficient strategy. You also have to be very careful when entering fractions—to graph (C), for example, you would enter $(1/3)x - 4$.

17. B

Difficulty: Medium

Category: Heart of Algebra / Linear Equations

Strategic Advice: Quickly scan the answer choices—they are written as inequalities, so you'll need to translate them into something that makes more sense to you. Use the fact that "< 0" means *negative* and "> 0" means *positive*.

Getting to the Answer: When a linear equation is written in the form $y = mx + b$, the variable m represents the slope of the line and b represents the y-intercept of the line. Look at the graph—the line is decreasing (going down from left to right), so the slope is negative ($m < 0$). This means you can eliminate C and D. Now look at the y-intercept—it is above the x-axis and is therefore positive ($b > 0$), which means (B) is correct.

18. A

Difficulty: Medium

Category: Heart of Algebra / Linear Equations

Strategic Advice: There are no axis labels or numbers on the graph, so quickly skim the answer choices to get the right context.

Getting to the Answer: Regardless of the scenario presented or the missing axis labels, the slope of the line tells you the answer. The line is decreasing from left to right, so it has a negative slope. This means there is an inverse relationship between the amount of algae and the number of fish. In other words, as one increases, the other must decrease, so (A) must be correct.

19. B

Difficulty: Medium

Category: Heart of Algebra / Linear Equations

Strategic Advice: You could find the unit rate by calculating the slope of the line using two of the points shown on the graph, but it may be quicker to simply read the answer from the graph.

Getting to the Answer: The x-axis represents the number of lightbulbs, so find 1 on the x-axis and trace up to where it meets the graph of the line. The y-value is somewhere between $1 and $2, so the only possible correct answer choice is $1.80.

Finding the slope should result in the same answer—the graph rises 9 units and runs 5 units from one point to the next, so the slope is $\frac{9}{5}$, or 1.80, which means (B) is correct.

20. C

Difficulty: Hard

Category: Heart of Algebra / Linear Equations

Strategic Advice: Let v represent the number of visits. The question asks when the two memberships will cost the same, so write an equation that sets the total membership costs equal to each other.

Getting to the Answer: The first membership type costs $325 for unlimited visits, so write 325 on one side of the equal sign. The second type costs $8 per visit (not including the first 5 visits), or $8(v - 5)$, plus a flat $125 enrollment fee, so write $8(v - 5) + 125$ on the other side of the equal sign. Use inverse operations to solve for v.

$$325 = 8(v - 5) + 125$$
$$325 = 8v - 40 + 125$$
$$240 = 8v$$
$$30 = v$$

Choice (C) is correct.

21. D

Difficulty: Hard

Category: Heart of Algebra / Linear Equations

Strategic Advice: When solving a linear equation that has no solution, the variable terms will cancel out and you will be left with a false statement that consists of two numbers that are not equal to each other.

Getting to the Answer: First, check to see if the variables cancel out. In A and B, they don't, so eliminate these choices. To decide between C and (D), check the constant after both sides of the equation have been simplified. If the constants are equal, then the equation has an infinite number of solutions (because a number is always equal to itself). If they are not equal, then the equation has no solution. Choice (D) is correct because:

$$6\left(\frac{2}{3}x+5\right)=4x+5$$
$$4x+30=4x+5$$
$$30\neq5$$

22. D

Difficulty: Hard

Category: Heart of Algebra / Linear Equations

Strategic Advice: When solving a linear equation that has infinitely many solutions, the variable terms will cancel out leaving a number that is equal to itself (which is always true).

Getting to the Answer: Start by simplifying both sides of the equation using the distributive property.

$$2\left(x-\frac{5}{2}\right)=c\left(\frac{4}{5}x-2\right)$$
$$2x-5=\frac{4c}{5}x-2c$$

Because the constant terms must be equal, set $-5=-2c$ and solve for c to get $c=\frac{5}{2}$, which means (D) is correct.

If this were a Grid-in question, you could check your answer by setting the two variable terms equal to each other and solving for c—the result is the same.

23. B

Difficulty: Hard

Category: Heart of Algebra / Linear Equations

Strategic Advice: Do not automatically assume that an equation has *no solution* or *infinite solutions* just because those choices are given as possible answers. This question can be simplified quite a bit by clearing the fractions first. To do this, multiply both sides of the equation by the least common denominator, 12. Then solve for h using inverse operations.

Getting to the Answer:

$$\frac{1}{4}(10h)-\frac{3}{2}(h+1)=-\frac{2}{3}\left(\frac{9}{2}h\right)+6$$
$$12\left[\frac{1}{4}(10h)\right]-12\left[\frac{3}{2}(h+1)\right]=12\left[-\frac{2}{3}\left(\frac{9}{2}h\right)\right]+12[6]$$
$$3(10h)-18(h+1)=-4(9h)+72$$
$$30h-18h-18=-36h+72$$
$$12h-18=-36h+72$$
$$48h=90$$
$$h=\frac{90}{48}=\frac{15}{8}$$

Choice (B) is correct.

24. C

Difficulty: Hard

Category: Heart of Algebra / Linear Equations

Strategic Advice: Pay careful attention to the units. They will lead you to the correct answer.

Getting to the Answer: Here, the units change in the question from seconds to minutes. The light blinks once every 3.5 *seconds*, which is equivalent to $\dfrac{1\,\text{blink}}{3.5\,\cancel{\text{seconds}}} \times \dfrac{60\,\cancel{\text{seconds}}}{1\,\text{minute}} = \dfrac{60\,\text{blinks}}{3.5\,\text{minutes}}$. Over the course of *m* minutes, the light will blink *m* times that amount, or $\dfrac{60m}{3.5}$ times, so the correct equation is $f(m) = \dfrac{60m}{3.5}$. Therefore, (C) is correct.

25. B

Difficulty: Hard

Category: Heart of Algebra / Linear Equations

Strategic Advice: The key to answering this question is determining how many jumps land across each line. If Vera gets 7 jumps total and *x* jumps land over the farther line, the rest, or 7 − *x*, must land over the closer line.

Getting to the Answer: Try writing the expression in words first: points per farther line (10) times number of jumps landing over the farther line (*x*), plus points per closer line (5) times number of jumps landing over the closer line (7 − *x*). Now, translate the words to numbers, variables, and operations: $10x + 5(7 − x)$. This is not one of the answer choices, so simplify the expression by distributing the 5 and then combining like terms: $10x + 5(7 − x) = 10x + 35 − 5x = 5x + 35$, so the function is $f(x) = 5x + 35$, making (B) correct.

26. D

Difficulty: Hard

Category: Heart of Algebra / Linear Equations

Strategic Advice: Consider each choice systematically.

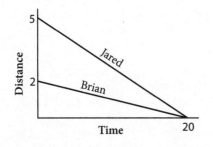

Getting to the Answer: Use the numbers to help you evaluate each statement. It took Brian and Jared each 20 minutes to bike home so A and B are false. Jared biked 5 miles in 20 minutes, while Brian only biked 2 miles in 20 minutes; their rates are not the same, so C is false. This means (D) must be true. Jared starts out farther away than Brian, so Jared must have biked at a faster rate to arrive home in the same amount of time.

27. B

Difficulty: Hard

Category: Heart of Algebra / Linear Equations

Strategic Advice: You aren't given any numbers in this question, so make some up. Sketch a quick graph of any simple linear equation that has a positive *y*-intercept (because it is given that *b* > 0). Then, change the sign of the *y*-intercept and sketch the new graph on the same coordinate plane.

Getting to the Answer: Pick a simple equation that you can sketch quickly, such as $y = x + 3$, and then change the sign of *b*. The new equation is $y = x − 3$. Sketch both graphs. The second line is shifted down 3 units, twice, or *b* × 2 units. If you're not convinced, try another pair of equations. Choice (B) is correct.

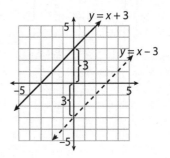

28. D

Difficulty: Hard

Category: Heart of Algebra / Linear Equations

Strategic Advice: Compare the differences in the two lines to the statements in the answer choices.

Pay careful attention to which line represents before the law (the solid line) and which represents after the law (the dashed line).

Getting to the Answer: The y-intercept of both lines is the same. The key difference between the lines is their slopes. The solid line (pre-law) has a steeper slope, while the dashed line has a more gradual slope, so you can eliminate C. The slope of each line is negative (falling from left to right), so even after the proposed law is implemented, the population is still expected to decline, which means you can eliminate B. Because the dashed line's slope is more gradual, the decline in the population is slowing down (decelerating, not accelerating), so you can eliminate A. This means (D) is correct.

29. 18

Difficulty: Medium

Category: Heart of Algebra / Linear Equations

Strategic Advice: Clear the fractions first by multiplying both sides of the equation by 8. Then solve for x using inverse operations.

Getting to the Answer:

$$\frac{7}{8}(n-6) = \frac{21}{2}$$

$$8\left[\frac{7}{8}(n-6)\right] = 8\left[\frac{21}{2}\right]$$

$$7(n-6) = 4(21)$$

$$7n - 42 = 84$$

$$7n = 126$$

$$n = 18$$

30. 1/4

Difficulty: Medium

Category: Heart of Algebra / Linear Equations

Strategic Advice: Start by finding the equation of each line using their slopes and y-intercepts, and then compare the equations.

Getting to the Answer: First, determine the equation for line A. Remember that slope is equal to rise over run, so count the change in y and the change in x from one point on the line to the next. The slope is $\frac{2}{1}$, or just 2. Next, find the y-intercept: −12. Now find the equation for line B: the slope is $\frac{1}{2}$ and the y-intercept is −3. So the equations are:

Line A: $y = 2x - 12$

Line B: $y = \frac{1}{2}x - 3$

Don't be tempted to say k = 4. Notice that the numbers in the equation for line A are larger, so k must be a fraction, $\frac{1}{4}$.

$$\frac{1}{4}(2x - 12) \rightarrow \frac{1}{2}x - 3$$

THIS PAGE INTENTIONALLY LEFT BLANK

CHAPTER 2

PREPARE

1. B
Difficulty: Easy

Category: Heart of Algebra / Linear Equations

Strategic Advice: Don't just use substitution: Check to see if one of the equations can be easily manipulated for use with another method.

Getting to the Answer: Start by combining like terms in the second equation, then use combination to solve for x. No additional manipulation is necessary to eliminate the y terms.

$$\begin{array}{r} 28x - 5y = 36 \\ +\quad 15x + 5y = 50 \\ \hline 43x = 86 \\ x = 2 \end{array}$$

Choice (B) is correct.

2. D
Difficulty: Medium

Category: Heart of Algebra / Linear Equations

Strategic Advice: The question states that there is no solution; use that to your advantage. Also keep in mind what the question is asking, as it requests something other than k.

Getting to the Answer: A system of equations with no solution means that the two equations have identical x coefficients and identical y coefficients and are equal to two different constants. First, rearrange the second equation to $-kx + 6y = -42$ so that variables and constants are properly aligned with those of the first equation. Divide both sides by -2 to get $\frac{k}{2}x - 3y = 21$. The coefficient of x in the

first equation is 5, so $\frac{k}{2} = 5$. Therefore, k must be 10. The question asks for $2k$, so multiply by 2 to get $2k = 20$, which is (D).

3. 9/2 or 4.5
Difficulty: Medium

Category: Heart of Algebra / Linear Equations

Strategic Advice: Substitution will get you the answer, but there's a faster route.

Getting to the Answer: Clear the fractions from the first equation by multiplying it by 4, then set up to solve using combination.

$$\begin{array}{r} x + 8y = 11 \\ +\quad -x - 6y = 7 \\ \hline 2y = 18 \\ y = 9 \end{array}$$

Take half of 9 to get $\frac{9}{2}$, then grid in 9/2 or 4.5.

4. D
Difficulty: Easy

Category: Heart of Algebra / Linear Equations

Strategic Advice: If you're not asked for an individual variable, look for a shortcut.

Getting to the Answer: The question asks for $b + c$, so don't waste your time finding the variables individually. After rearranging the equations so that variables and constants are aligned, you can add them together:

$$\begin{array}{r} -2b + 7c = 15 \\ +3b - 6c = 2 \\ \hline b + c = 17 \end{array}$$

This matches choice (D).

5. A

Difficulty: Medium

Category: Heart of Algebra / Linear Equations

Strategic Advice: Another wordy question means another chance to use the Kaplan Strategy for Translating English into Math.

Getting to the Answer: First, define your variables logically: t for tiny pandas, g for giant pandas. You're given the cost of each, as well as the number of each sold and the total revenue generated. Next, write the system of equations that represents the information given:

$$t + g = 29$$
$$3.5t + 14g = 217$$

Multiplying the top equation by −14 allows you to solve for t by combination:

$$
\begin{array}{r}
-14t - 14g = -406 \\
+ \quad 3.5t + 14g = 217 \\
\hline
-10.5t = -189 \\
t = 18
\end{array}
$$

Solving for t gives 18, which eliminates B and C. Plugging this value back into the first equation allows you to find g, which is 11. (A) is the only choice with these values.

6. C

Difficulty: Medium

Category: Heart of Algebra / Linear Equations

Strategic Advice: Word problems that do not require you to actually solve a system of equations are a quick way to earn points; just follow the Kaplan Strategy for Translating English into Math.

Getting to the Answer: Since you're given the variables (r for resident and n for nonresident), the only thing left for you to do here is break the wording apart into phrases and translate into math. Residents pay \$421 in fees ($421r$), and nonresidents pay \$879 in fees ($879n$). Add together both student types to get the first equation: $r + n = 1,980$. Piece together the fee amounts into your second equation, which will be $421r + 879n = 1,170,210$. Only (C) contains both of those equations.

PRACTICE

7. A

Difficulty: Medium

Category: Heart of Algebra / Linear Equations

Strategic Advice: Use the Kaplan Strategy for Translating English into Math to make sense of the prose.

Getting to the Answer: First, define your variables: w for wooden and c for crystal are good choices. Breaking apart the question, you know the jewelry artist bought 127 beads total. You're also told each wooden bead costs \$0.20 ($0.2w$) and each crystal bead costs \$0.50 ($0.5c$), as well as the fact that she spent \$41 total. You'll have two equations: one relating the number of wooden beads and crystal beads, and a second relating the costs associated with each.

$$w + c = 127$$
$$0.2w + 0.5c = 41$$

Either combination or substitution is a good choice for solving this system. Both are shown here:

Combination

$$-0.5(w + c = 127) \rightarrow -0.5w - 0.5c = -63.5$$

$$
\begin{array}{r}
-0.5w - 0.5c = -63.5 \\
+ \quad 0.2w + 0.5c = 41 \\
\hline
-0.3w = -22.5 \\
w = 75
\end{array}
$$

$$75 + c = 127 \rightarrow c = 52$$

Substitution

$$w + c = 127 \rightarrow c = 127 - w$$
$$0.2w + 0.5(127 - w) = 41$$
$$0.2w + 63.5 - 0.5w = 41$$
$$-0.3w = -22.5$$
$$w = 75$$
$$75 + c = 127 \rightarrow c = 52$$

Be careful here: The question asks for the difference in amount spent on each type of bead, not the difference in quantity of each type. Multiply the bead counts by the correct pricing to get $15 for the wooden beads and $26 for the crystal beads. Take the difference to get $11, which is (A).

8. 59

Difficulty: Medium

Category: Heart of Algebra / Linear Equations

Strategic Advice: Once again, you're asked for an expression instead of a variable; utilize the same tactics you've used for similar questions.

Getting to the Answer: Start by rearranging the two equations so that variables and constants are aligned:

$$x + y = -15$$
$$\frac{x}{2} + \frac{5y}{2} = 37$$

Clear out the fractions, and then combine:

$$2\left(\frac{x}{2} + \frac{5y}{2} = 37\right) \rightarrow x + 5y = 74$$
$$\begin{array}{r} x + y = -15 \\ + x + 5y = 74 \\ \hline 2x + 6y = 59 \end{array}$$

You're done! Grid in 59 and move on.

PERFORM

9. B

Difficulty: Hard

Category: Heart of Algebra / Linear Equations

Strategic Advice: A system of equations with infinitely many solutions describes a single line. Therefore, the equations are dependent, and correct manipulation of one will yield the other.

Getting to the Answer: Because q is the x coefficient in the second equation, look for a way to make the y coefficient equal to the one in the first equation. This can be done by multiplying the second equation by -9: $-9(qx - \frac{y}{3} = -2) \rightarrow -9qx + 3y = 18$. The y-terms and constants of the second equation now match those of the first; all that's left is to set the x coefficients equal to each other and solve for q: $-9q = 6 \rightarrow q = -\frac{6}{9} = -\frac{2}{3}$. (B) is correct.

10. 3/17

Difficulty: Medium

Category: Heart of Algebra / Linear Equations

Strategic Advice: Don't be intimidated by the bigger numbers; the rules of systems of equations still apply. Mind what the question asks, too.

Getting to the Answer: Using combination will make life easier. A common multiple of 5 and 12, the x coefficients, is 60, so multiply by the appropriate factors, remembering to make one of them negative:

$$-5(12x + 15y = 249) \rightarrow -60x - 75y = -1,245$$
$$12(5x + 13y = 124) \rightarrow 60x + 156y = 1,488$$

Combine as usual:

$$\begin{array}{r} -60x - 75y = -1,245 \\ + 60x + 156y = 1,488 \\ \hline 81y = 243 \\ y = 3 \end{array}$$

Don't stop yet; you need x so you can determine $\dfrac{y}{x}$. Substitute 3 for y in one of the original equations:

$$5x + 13(3) = 124$$
$$5x + 39 = 124$$
$$5x = 85$$
$$x = 17$$

Plug your x- and y-values into the expression you need, $\dfrac{y}{x}$, to get $\dfrac{3}{17}$. Grid in 3/17.

11. C

Difficulty: Hard

Category: Heart of Algebra / Linear Equations

Strategic Advice: You can write equations to represent profits generated from each pizza type.

Getting to the Answer: You're told The Works sells for $17 each and that its ingredients cost the pizzeria $450 per week. This means profit generated by this pizza's sales are represented by the equation $y = 17x - 450$. Profits from The Hawaiian are analogous: Each one sells for $13, but the pizzeria loses $310 to pay for ingredients each week. Therefore, profits from this pizza are represented by $y = 13x - 310$. To determine where profits from one pizza overtake the other, set the two equations equal to each other and solve:

$$17x - 450 = 13x - 310$$
$$4x = 140$$
$$x = 35$$

Although ingredients for The Works cost more, the pizza's higher price tag means its profits will eventually surpass those of The Hawaiian. This will occur after the pizzeria sells 35 of each, making (C) correct. Beware D; 145 is the y-value when $x = 35$.

EXTRA PRACTICE

1. D
Difficulty: Easy

Category: Heart of Algebra / Systems of Linear Equations

Strategic Advice: The word "and" in this question tells you that you're dealing with a system of equations.

Whenever a question involves a system, quickly compare the two equations. Sometimes, writing the equations vertically gives you a clue about how to solve it.

$$\begin{cases} 2x - 3y = 14 \\ 5x + 3y = 21 \end{cases}$$

This system is already set up perfectly to solve using elimination by addition (also known as combination) because the y-terms ($-3y$ and $3y$) are opposites.

Getting to the Answer: Add the two equations to cancel $-3y$ and $3y$. Then solve the resulting equation for x. Remember, the question only asks for the value of x, so you don't need to substitute x back into the equation and solve for y.

$$\begin{aligned} 2x - \cancel{3y} &= 14 \\ + 5x + \cancel{3y} &= 21 \\ \hline 7x &= 35 \\ x &= 5 \end{aligned}$$

Choice (D) is correct.

2. B
Difficulty: Easy

Category: Heart of Algebra / Systems of Linear Equations

Strategic Advice: Whenever a question gives you information about a total number of items and a total cost of those items, you should write one equation that represents the total *number* (here, the number of meals), and a second equation that represents the total *cost* (here, the school's total bill).

Getting to the Answer: The number of people who ordered veggie burgers plus the number who ordered roast beef sandwiches equals the total number of people, 56, so one equation is $v + r = 56$. This means you can eliminate A and D. Now, write the cost equation: cost per veggie burger (4.5) times number ordered (v) plus cost per roast beef sandwich (6.25) times number ordered (r) equals the total bill ($308). The cost equation is $4.5v + 6.25r = 308$. Together, these two equations form the system in (B).

Don't let C fool you—there are two choices of meals, but this does not impact the total amount of the bill.

3. C
Difficulty: Medium

Category: Heart of Algebra / Systems of Linear Equations

Strategic Advice: Because x has a coefficient of 1 in the second equation, solve the system using substitution. Before you select your answer, make sure you found the right quantity (the difference of x and y).

Getting to the Answer: First, solve the second equation for x and substitute the result into the first equation and solve for y.

$$\begin{aligned} x - 5y &= 2 \\ x &= 2 + 5y \\ 4(2 + 5y) + 3y &= 14 - y \\ 8 + 20y + 3y &= 14 - y \\ 8 + 23y &= 14 - y \\ 24y &= 6 \\ y &= \frac{6}{24} = \frac{1}{4} \end{aligned}$$

Next, substitute this value back into $x = 2 + 5y$ and simplify.

$$x = 2 + 5\left(\frac{1}{4}\right)$$
$$x = \frac{8}{4} + \frac{5}{4}$$
$$x = \frac{13}{4}$$

Finally, subtract $x - y$ to find the difference.

$$\frac{13}{4} - \frac{1}{4} = \frac{12}{4} = 3$$

4. C

Difficulty: Medium

Category: Heart of Algebra / Systems of Linear Equations

Strategic Advice: Skim the answer choices. They are talking about systems with no solution and infinite solutions. Picture the graphs of both.

Getting to the Answer: Graphically, a system of linear equations that has no solution consists of two parallel lines that will never intersect. They have the same slope but different y-intercepts. A system of linear equations that has infinite solutions is actually the same line, just represented in different ways. Graphically, one line would sit on top of the other, intersecting itself an infinite number of times. These lines would have the same slope *and* the same y-intercept. Without additional information, it is not possible to determine whether the system that Charlie graphed has no solutions or an infinite number of solutions. Therefore, the solution to Charlie's system of equations depends on the y-intercepts of the lines and (C) is correct.

5. C

Difficulty: Medium

Category: Heart of Algebra / Systems of Linear Equations

Strategic Advice: If the graphs intersect at $(-3, 1)$, then the solution to the system is $x = -3$ and $y = 1$. This means you can substitute these values into both equations and go from there.

Getting to the Answer: Substitute the values of x and y into each equation and solve for h and k. Then, divide k by h.

$$
\begin{array}{ll}
hx - 4y = -10 & kx + 3y = -15 \\
h(-3) - 4(1) = -10 & k(-3) + 3(1) = -15 \\
-3h - 4 = -10 & -3k + 3 = -15 \\
-3h = -6 & -3k = -18 \\
h = 2 & k = 6
\end{array}
$$

So, $\frac{k}{h} = \frac{6}{2} = 3$, making (C) correct.

6. D

Difficulty: Hard

Category: Heart of Algebra / Systems of Linear Equations

Strategic Advice: The easiest way to answer this question is to think about how the graphs of the equations would look. Graphically, a system of linear equations that has no solution indicates two parallel lines, or in other words, two lines that have the same slope but different y-intercepts.

Getting to the Answer: In a system with no solutions, the x- and y-coefficients must be the same. The two y-coefficients are $-\frac{2}{3}$ and -8. To make $-\frac{2}{3}$ equal -8, multiply by 12. Then $\frac{1}{2}x$ becomes $6x$. Since the other x-coefficient is a, it must be that $a = 6$.

7. C
Difficulty: Hard

Category: Heart of Algebra / Systems of Linear Equations

Strategic Advice: Create a system of linear equations where x represents the number of packs with 8 plates and y represents the number of packs with 12 plates. Before selecting your final answer, make sure you are answering the right question (how many plates would a customer have who bought all of the packs of 12).

Getting to the Answer: The first equation should represent the total number of *packs*, each with 8 or 12 plates, or $e + t = 54$. The second equation should represent the total number of *plates*. Because e represents packs with 8 plates and t represents packs with 12 plates, the second equation should be $8e + 12t = 496$. Now solve the system using substitution (or combination if it is faster for you). Solve the first equation for either variable and substitute the result into the second equation.

$$e + t = 546$$
$$e = 54 - t$$
$$8(54 - t) + 12t = 496$$
$$432 - 8t + 12t = 496$$
$$432 + 4t = 496$$
$$4t = 64$$
$$t = 16$$

So 16 packs have 12 plates. The question asks about packs of 12, so you don't need to find the value of e. But you are not done yet. The problem asks how many *plates* a customer would buy if he or she buys all of the packs of 12 the store has, not just the *number of packs*. The customer would buy $16 \times 12 = 192$ plates, which is (C).

8. D
Difficulty: Hard

Category: Heart of Algebra / Systems of Linear Equations

Strategic Advice: A system of linear equations has infinitely many solutions if both lines in the system have the same slope and the same y-intercept (in other words, they are the same line).

Getting to the Answer: When a system has infinitely many solutions, the x- and y-coefficients of the two equations must be the same. Use the x-coefficients here: To turn $\frac{1}{2}$ into 3, multiply by 6. So c becomes 6c, and $6c = -6$. Thus $c = -1$.

Choice (D) is correct.

9. 8
Difficulty: Hard

Category: Heart of Algebra / Systems of Linear Equations

Strategic Advice: The solution to the system is the point that both tables will have in common, but the tables, as given, do not share any points. You could use the data to write the equation of each line and then solve the system, but this will use up valuable time on Test Day. Instead, whenever data is presented in a table, look for patterns that can be extended.

Getting to the Answer: In the table on the left, the x-values increase by 2 each time and the y-values decrease by 2. In the table on the right, the x-values increase by 4 each time and the y-values increase by 1. Use these patterns to continue the tables.

Equation 1		Equation 2	
x	**y**	**x**	**y**
−2	6	−8	−8
0	4	−4	−7
2	2	0	−6
4	0	4	−5
6	−2	**8**	**−4**
8	**−4**	12	−3

The point (8, −4) satisfies both equations, so the x-coordinate of the solution to the system is 8.

CHAPTER 3

PREPARE

1. A
Difficulty: Easy

Category: Problem Solving and Data Analysis / Rates, Ratios, Proportions, and Percentages

Strategic Advice: Map out your route from starting units to end units, being mindful of the fact that you have area units.

Getting to the Answer: Your starting quantity is in ft^3, and your desired quantity should be in m^3. The only conversion factor you need is 1 m ≈ 3.28 ft. Setting up your route to m^3, you get $\frac{700 \text{ ft}^3}{1} \times \frac{1 \text{ m}}{3.28 \text{ ft}} \times \frac{1 \text{ m}}{3.28 \text{ ft}} \times \frac{1 \text{ m}}{3.28 \text{ ft}} = \frac{700}{(3.28)^3}\text{m} \approx$ 19.84 m^3, which matches (A).

2. 150
Difficulty: Easy

Category: Problem Solving and Data Analysis / Rates, Ratios, Proportions, and Percentages / Multi-Part Math

Strategic Advice: Identify the units of the starting and desired quantities, then use the given relationships (and those you already know) to plan a route to the answer.

Getting to the Answer: The starting quantity is 2.43 TB, and you need to convert this to hours. Using the correct conversion factors, your calculation is as follows:

$2.43 \text{ TB} \times \frac{10^6 \text{ MB}}{1 \text{ TB}} \times \frac{1 \text{ s}}{4.5 \text{ MB}} \times \frac{1 \text{ min}}{60 \text{ s}} \times \frac{1 \text{ h}}{60 \text{ min}} = 150 \text{ h}$

3. 103
Difficulty: Medium

Strategic Advice: Find the new rate using your percentage expertise, then convert with the factor-label method.

Getting to the Answer: Using the percent three-part formula, you'll find the New York team's software is 1.4×4.5=6.3 MB/s; analogously, Boston's team's software contributes 0.8 × 4.5 = 3.6 MB/s:

$2.43 \text{ TB} \times \frac{10^6 \text{ MB}}{1 \text{ TB}} \times \frac{1 \text{ s}}{14.4 \text{ MB}} \times \frac{1 \text{ min}}{60 \text{ s}} \times \frac{1 \text{ h}}{60 \text{ min}} = 46.875 \text{ h}$.

Subtract this value from the original 150h to get 103.125 h; rounding to the nearest hour gives 103.

4. B
Difficulty: Medium

Category: Problem Solving and Data Analysis / Rates, Ratios, Proportions, and Percentages

Strategic Advice: Look for a way to consolidate the two given ratios into one, and ensure you provide the ratio requested.

Getting to the Answer: The first paint can has a red:blue (R:B) ratio of 25:60; and the second can's ratio, yellow:blue:white (Y:B:W), is 30:70:15. Reduce the ratios to make the math easier. R:B becomes 5:12, and Y:B:W becomes 6:14:3. These cannot be combined as they are, so you need a common factor to link them. Blue is the term common to both ratios; look for a small common multiple of the blue components, 12 and 14. Using 84 as the common multiple, determine factors that, when multiplied by the ratios, turn both blue components into 84. For R:B, the calculation is 7×(5:12)=35:84. Repeating for Y:B:W, you get 6×(6:14:3)=36:84:18. The combined ratio R:B:Y:W becomes 35:84:36:18, making R:W 35:18. The question asks for the ratio of white to red, so flip your ratio to get 18:35, which is (B).

5. C
Difficulty: Easy

Category: Problem Solving and Data Analysis / Rates, Ratios, Proportions, and Percentages

Strategic Advice: Finding 10% of 240 will reduce the number of calculations you'll need to do.

Getting to the Answer: You know Kristina will make 240 oz of each juice blend; 10% of 240 oz is 24 oz. Because each desired percentage is a multiple of 10, you only need to multiply 24 by the appropriate number to get the juice volume for each blend. Therefore, 20% is 48 oz, 40% is 96 oz, 50% is 120 oz, 60% is 144 oz, and 80% is 192 oz. The sum of these five volumes is 600 oz, but you're not done yet. Divide by the volume of one juice bottle, 32 oz, to get 18.75 bottles. Round up to 19; the correct answer is (C).

6. 59

Difficulty: Medium

Category: Problem Solving and Data Analysis / Rates, Ratios, Proportions, Percentages

Strategic Advice: It's easy to switch on autopilot and do five separate cost increase calculations, but you can get away with just one (and subsequently save time).

Getting to the Answer: First, determine the total increase from 2014-15 through 2019-20: $15,564 − $12,192 = $3,372. Dividing $3,372 by 5 (the number of increases) gives $674.40, the average increase per year. To find what portion of this amount is fees, determine 8.75% of $674.40: 0.0875 × $674.40 = $59.01. Rounded to the nearest dollar, the correct answer is 59.

7. 44

Difficulty: Medium

Strategic Advice: Determine the total increase over the entire period (including the extension), and use this to find the percent increase in cost.

Getting to the Answer: Three academic years will pass after the end of the initial five year increase period (2020-21, 2021-22, 2022-23), so multiply the average yearly increase you found in part 1 by 3 to get $674.40 × 3 = $2,023.20. Add this to $3,372, the increase through 2019-20, to get the total increase over this entire period, which is $5,395.20. Divide this by the pre-increase implementation cost (from 2014-15), and multiply this result by 100 to find the percent change: $\frac{\$5395.20}{\$12192} \times 100 = 44.252\%$. Round to 44.

PRACTICE

8. C

Difficulty: Easy

Category: Problem Solving and Data Analysis / Rates, Ratios, Proportions, and Percentages

Strategic Advice: You have a couple rates, but you need to manipulate them slightly before using them in the DIRT equation.

Getting to the Answer: Start by changing the given rates to unit rates. For the 5-second interval, $r_5 = 1$ car per 5 s = 0.2 cars/s. The 8-second interval becomes $r_8 = 1$ car per 8 s = 0.125 cars/s. Next, convert the time window into seconds to match your rates: $3 \text{ h} \times \dfrac{60 \text{ min}}{1 \text{ h}} \times \dfrac{60 \text{ h}}{1 \text{ min}} = 10{,}800$ s. Now you can use the DIRT equation to find the number of cars allowed through at each interval.

5 seconds: $d_5 = 0.2$ cars/s $\times$ 10,800 s = 2,160 cars
8 seconds: $d_8 = 0.125$ cars/s $\times$ 10,800 s = 1,350 cars

Subtracting these gives 2,160 − 1,350 = 810 more cars, which is (C).

9. D

Difficulty: Hard

Category: Problem Solving and Data Analysis / Rates, Ratios, Proportions, and Percentages

Strategic Advice: Read carefully to ensure you do your calculations correctly and in the order specified.

Getting to the Answer: Murray starts with $75,400 per year. The first deduction is the 20% 401(k) contribution. Using the percent three-part formula, you'll find Murray has $0.8 \times \$75{,}400 = \$60{,}320$ left. He pays $150 per month for insurance, which is $1,800 per year. This leaves $58,520 pre-tax. Taxes are trickier, so work carefully. State taxes are easy; just take 4.5% of the pre-tax total: $0.045 \times \$58{,}520 = \$2{,}633.40$.

Federal taxes involve three separate calculations as follows:

$$10\% \text{ bracket: } 0.1 \times \$9{,}225 = \$922.50$$
$$15\% \text{ bracket: } 0.15 \times (\$37{,}450 - \$9{,}226) = \$4{,}233.60$$
$$25\% \text{ bracket: } 0.25 \times (\$58{,}520 - \$37{,}451) = \$5{,}267.25$$

Adding up all of Murray's tax liability gives $13,056.75. Subtract this from his pre-tax total to get $45,463.25. Don't stop yet! The question asks for Murray's biweekly pay. Divide $45,463.25 by 26, the number of pay periods in one year, to get $1,748.59. (D) is the correct choice.

10. 7/16

Difficulty: Hard

Category: Problem Solving and Data Analysis / Rates, Ratios, Proportions, and Percentages / Multi-Part Math

Strategic Advice: The question asks for a fraction, a relative quantity, so don't panic about not having exact dimensions for the squares. Pick your own instead.

Getting to the Answer: Start by labeling each square for clarity.

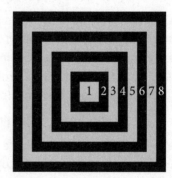

Pick a side length for square 1; 1 in. is an excellent choice. This means its area is 1 in.^{2} If the square edges are 0.5 in. apart, that means square 2 has a side length of 1 + 0.5 + 0.5 = 2 in., square 3 has a side length of 2 + 0.5 + 0.5 = 3 in., and so on. This translates to areas of 1, 4, 9, 16, 25, 36, 49, and 64 (all in.^{2}). But don't forget you need to subtract the square within each to get the true areas! You'll get the following:

$$\text{sq. 1 (gray)} = 1 \text{ in.}^2$$
$$\text{sq. 2 (black)} = 2^2 - 1 = 3 \text{ in.}^2$$
$$\text{sq. 3 (gray)} = 3^2 - 4 = 5 \text{ in.}^2$$
$$\text{sq. 4 (black)} = 4^2 - 9 = 7 \text{ in.}^2$$
$$\text{sq. 5 (gray)} = 5^2 - 16 = 9 \text{ in.}^2$$
$$\text{sq. 6 (black)} = 6^2 - 25 = 11 \text{ in.}^2$$
$$\text{sq. 7 (gray)} = 7^2 - 36 = 13 \text{ in.}^2$$
$$\text{sq. 8 (black)} = 8^2 - 49 = 15 \text{ in.}^2$$

After a few calculations you might start to see a pattern; if so, great! You can shave off a few seconds of number crunching. Now add up the gray squares to get 28, then divide by the area of the whole plate (64) to get $\frac{28}{64} = \frac{7}{16}$. Grid in 7/16, then move to part 2.

11. 10/9
Difficulty: Medium

Strategic Advice: You've already done most of the work for this part; look closely at your work for the first part to see what you can reuse.

Getting to the Answer: Finding the large plate black fraction is easy; just subtract the large plate gray fraction from 1 to get $\frac{9}{16}$. Because the small plate is just a smaller version of the large plate with only four squares, you can use your calculations for squares 1-4 from part 1 here. Squares 1 and 3 (gray) comprise 6 in.^{2}, and squares 2 and 4 (black) comprise 10 in.^{2}. This means the small plate black fraction is $\frac{10}{16} = \frac{5}{8}$. To find how many times more black glaze is on the small plate, divide the small plate black fraction by its large plate counterpart: $\frac{5}{8} \div \frac{9}{16} = \frac{5}{8} \times \frac{16}{9} = \frac{10}{9}$. Grid in 10/9, and you're done!

PERFORM

12. A
Difficulty: Easy

Category: Problem Solving and Data Analysis / Rates, Ratios, Proportions, and Percentages

Strategic Advice: Convert all four rates into the same units before comparing.

Getting to the Answer: You might think you should convert each price into cost per banana, but a closer look reveals that all but one price already uses weight. Save time by converting the units into cost per pound; the order will be no different than if you did cost per banana. Use the banana-pound relationship to convert each price into cost per pound. FoodCo's price is already per pound, so no work is needed there. Bob's charges $0.29 per banana, which becomes $\frac{\$0.29}{1 \text{ banana}} \times \frac{1 \text{ banana}}{\frac{1}{3} \text{ lb}} = \frac{\$0.90}{1 \text{ lb}}$. Acme's price is $1.50 for 2 lb or $0.75 per pound. The deal at Stu's means you pay $1.95 for 4 lb, which is $0.4875 per pound. Therefore, the correct order is Bob's, Acme, FoodCo, Stu's; which matches (A).

13. 18.2
Difficulty: Easy

Category: Problem Solving and Data Analysis / Rates, Ratios, Proportions, and Percentages

Strategic Advice: Start by drawing a diagram to make sense of the situation.

Getting to the Answer: The ziplines make up hypotenuses of two right triangles. Because the two zipline setups are proportional, the triangles are similar.

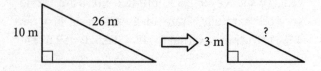

You can use a proportion to solve for the length of the kids' zipline: $\frac{10}{26} = \frac{3}{x}$. Solving for x gives 7.8 m. But you're not done yet! The question asks for the difference in zipline length, so subtract 7.8 from 26 to get 18.2, the correct answer.

14. 166
Difficulty: Medium

Category: Problem Solving and Data Analysis / Rates, Ratios, Proportions, and Percentages / Multi-Part Math

Strategic Advice: Identify the units of your start and end quantities, then string together the proper conversion factors.

Getting to the Answer: You know Mark will drive 960 miles over the course of his trip, and you need to determine what he should budget for fuel. The full conversion is as follows:

$$960 \text{ mi} \times \frac{1 \text{ gal}}{40 \text{ mi}} \times \frac{3.785 \text{ L}}{1 \text{ gal}} \times \frac{1.20 \text{ GBP}}{1 \text{ L}} \times \frac{1.52 \text{ USD}}{1 \text{ GBP}} =$$

165.69 USD. Round to 166 per the question instructions.

15. 17
Difficulty: Medium

Strategic Advice: Determine Mark's fuel cost with the offer, then compare it to the original.

Getting to the Answer: If you stopped your calculations in part 1 after the gallon-to-liter conversion, you would find that Mark will use 90.84 L of fuel. At the new fuel price, Mark would pay 90.84 × 0.75 = 68.13 GBP for fuel. Add the 30 GBP cost for the rate reduction to get 98.13 GBP. Use the GBP-USD conversion to get 149.15 USD. Subtracting this from 166 gives 16.85, which is rounded to 17.

EXTRA PRACTICE

1. A

Difficulty: Easy

Category: Problem Solving and Data Analysis / Rates, Ratios, Proportions, and Percentages

Strategic Advice: When a question involves several rates, break it into separate, manageable pieces and deal with each in turn.

Getting to the Answer: When the car is driven off the lot, it immediately loses $12,000 in value, regardless of how far it is driven, so the after-purchase value is $35,000 – $12,000 = $23,000. The first 50,000 miles *reduce* the car's value by $0.15 each, or 50,000(–$0.15) = –$7,500. Now the car's value is $23,000 – $7,500 = $15,500. Any miles driven over 50,000 reduce the value by $0.10 per mile, and the car is driven for 92,000 miles, which is 42,000 over 50,000. This means the car depreciates another 42,000(–0.10) = –$4,200. The value of the car after being driven 92,000 miles is $15,500 – $4,200 = $11,300, which matches (A).

2. D

Difficulty: Easy

Category: Problem Solving and Data Analysis / Rates, Ratios, Proportions, and Percentages

Strategic Advice: To answer a question that says "directly proportional," set two ratios equal to each other and solve for the missing amount. Don't forget—match the units in the numerators and in the denominators on both sides of the proportion.

Getting to the Answer: Because the first rate is given in minutes, write 1 hour as 60 minutes. Let t equal the number of topics the teacher can cover

in a 60-minute period. Set up a proportion and solve for t:

$$\frac{9 \text{ topics}}{45 \text{ minutes}} = \frac{t \text{ topics}}{60 \text{ minutes}}$$
$$9(60) = 45(t)$$
$$540 = 45t$$
$$12 = t$$

Choice (D) is correct.

3. C

Difficulty: Easy

Category: Problem Solving and Data Analysis / Rates, Ratios, Proportions, and Percentages

Strategic Advice: It can be confusing to decide which operation to perform when dealing with conversions, especially when the conversions involve decimals. Think about how your answer should look first. A person weighs *less* on the moon, so he or she should weigh *more* on Earth. This means your answer must be greater than 29, so you can eliminate A right away.

Getting to the Answer: The easiest way to convert the units and keep them straight is to set up a proportion.

$$\frac{0.166 \text{ lb on moon}}{1 \text{ lb on Earth}} = \frac{29 \text{ lb on moon}}{p \text{ lb on Earth}}$$
$$29(1) = 0.166p$$
$$\frac{29}{0.166} = \frac{\cancel{0.166}p}{\cancel{0.166}}$$
$$174.7 \approx p$$

The man weighs about 175 pounds on Earth. Choice (C) is correct.

4. A

Difficulty: Easy

Category: Problem Solving and Data Analysis / Rates, Ratios, Proportions, and Percentages

Strategic Advice: Whenever multiple rates are given, pay very careful attention to the units. As you read the question, decide how and when you will need to convert units. Use the factor label method as needed.

Getting to the Answer: The answer choices are given in hours and minutes, so start by converting the given typing rate from words per second to words per minute:

$$\frac{3.75 \text{ words}}{1 \text{ second}} \times \frac{60 \text{ seconds}}{1 \text{ minutes}} = \frac{225 \text{ words}}{1 \text{ minute}}$$

Next, find the number of words in the 25-page transcript:

$$\frac{675 \text{ words}}{1 \text{ page}} \times 25 \text{ pages} = 16{,}875 \text{ words}$$

Finally, let m be the number of minutes it takes the court reporter to type the whole transcript. Set up a proportion and solve for m.

$$\frac{225 \text{ words}}{1 \text{ minute}} = \frac{16{,}875 \text{ words}}{m \text{ minutes}}$$
$$225m = 16{,}875$$
$$m = 75$$

Because 75 minutes is not an answer choice, convert it to hours and minutes: 75 minutes = 1 hour, 15 minutes, making (A) the correct answer.

5. C
Difficulty: Medium

Category: Problem Solving and Data Analysis / Rates, Ratios, Proportions, and Percentages

Strategic Advice: Don't let the three-way ratio scare you. You can solve this problem just like any other ratio question.

Getting to the Answer: Set up an equation using *parts*: 35 parts of the vote were for Taft, 41 parts were for Roosevelt, and 63 parts were for Wilson.

You don't know how big a part is, so call it x. Now, write and solve an equation:

$$35x + 41x + 63x = 208{,}500$$
$$139x = 208{,}500$$
$$x = 1{,}500$$

Look back at the ratio—35 parts of the vote were for Taft, so the number of votes cast for Taft was $35(1{,}500) = 52{,}500$, which matches (C).

6. B
Difficulty: Medium

Category: Problem Solving and Data Analysis / Rates, Ratios, Proportions, and Percentages

Strategic Advice: This is a typical proportion question. Use words first to write the proportion. Then translate from English into math.

Getting to the Answer: Let n equal the number of people tested. Set up a proportion and solve for n. Be sure to match the units in the numerators and in the denominators on both sides of the proportion.

$$\frac{\text{false positives}}{\text{number tested}} = \frac{\text{false positives}}{\text{number tested}}$$
$$\frac{6}{3{,}500} = \frac{27}{n}$$
$$6n = 27(3{,}500)$$
$$6n = 94{,}500$$
$$n = 15{,}750$$

This means (B) is correct.

7. C
Difficulty: Medium

Category: Problem Solving and Data Analysis / Rates, Ratios, Proportions, and Percentages

Strategic Advice: Think about this question for a few seconds before you start, and make a plan for solving it. The question is asking for the discounted hourly rate, which is the rate *after* the one free hour and *after* the 10 hours at the $30 rate. Make sure you subtract these numbers from the total number of hours of tutoring the client paid for before you find the discounted rate.

Getting to the Answer: Start with the hours. The client received 25 hours of tutoring, of which 1 hour was free. So, the client paid for 24 hours of tutoring. The first 10 hours were at a different rate than the discounted rate, so subtract these to find that the client paid the discounted rate for $24 - 10 = 14$ hours. Now look at the money: The first 10 hours the client was actually billed for cost $30 per hour for a total of $300, so subtract this from the total amount paid to get $664 - $300 = $364. This is the amount charged for the 14 discounted hours. Divide this amount by the number of hours billed at the discounted rate to get $364 \div 14 = 26 per hour, making (C) the correct choice.

8. D
Difficulty: Medium

Category: Problem Solving and Data Analysis / Rates, Ratios, Proportions, and Percentages

Strategic Advice: You can use the formula Percent = $\frac{\text{Part}}{\text{Whole}} \times 100\%$ to answer this question. But be careful—you have been given several pieces of information, so you'll need to be organized.

Getting to the Answer: First, find the number of people at each location who responded favorably using the formula. Start with the first location: $125 \times 0.224 = 28$. Move on to the second location: $272 \times 0.375 = 102$. Next, find the total number of people that were surveyed at both locations ($125 + 272 = 397$) and the total number who responded favorably ($28 + 102 = 130$). Finally, find the percent of people who responded favorably by using the formula one more time:

$$397 \times \text{Percent} = 130 \times 100\%$$
$$\text{Percent} = 130 \div 397 \times 100\%$$
$$\text{Percent} = 0.3274 \times 100\%$$
$$\text{Percent} = 32.7\%$$

Of all the people surveyed, about 32.7% responded favorably, making (D) the correct answer.

9. A
Difficulty: Medium

Category: Problem Solving and Data Analysis / Rates, Ratios, Proportions, and Percentages

Strategic Advice: Let the units in this question guide you to the solution. The cooking rates of the ovens are given in pounds per hour, but the question asks about the number of ounces each oven can cook in 10 minutes, so convert pounds per hour to ounces per minute. Use the factor-label method.

Getting to the Answer: Start by converting pounds to ounces. There are 16 ounces in one pound, so 3 pounds is 48 ounces and 4.5 pounds is 72 ounces. Now convert the hours to minutes:

Oven at 350°:

$$\frac{48 \text{ oz}}{1 \text{ hr}} \times \frac{1 \text{ hr}}{60 \text{ min}} \times 10 \text{ min} = 8 \text{ oz}$$

Oven at 450°:

$$\frac{72 \text{ oz}}{1 \text{ hr}} \times \frac{1 \text{ hr}}{60 \text{ min}} \times 10 \text{ min} = 12 \text{ oz}$$

In 10 minutes, the oven at 450° can cook $12 - 8 = 4$ ounces more than the oven at 350°, making (A) the correct answer.

10. B
Difficulty: Medium

Category: Problem Solving and Data Analysis / Rates, Ratios, Proportions, and Percentages

Strategic Advice: Before you start, think about where this question is. It is not near the beginning of the homework, so it is probably not an easy problem. This means it won't be as simple as converting 20°C to degrees Fahrenheit using the formula.

Getting to the Answer: The question says temperatures can vary by 20°C during a single day. This is not the same as saying the temperature itself is 20°, so you can't just convert the temperature to Fahrenheit. You aren't given exact numbers, just a range, so you'll need to pick some convenient numbers for yourself. You might know (or can tell from the formula) that 0°C is equal to 32°F. So pick 0°C and 20°C. Convert each of these to Fahrenheit and then find the difference.

$$F = \frac{9}{5}(C) + 32$$

$$F_{at\,0} = \frac{9}{5}(0) + 32$$

$$= 0 + 32$$

$$= 32$$

$$F_{at\,20} = \frac{9}{5}(20) + 32$$

$$= 36 + 32$$

$$= 68$$

0°C = 32°F and 20°C = 68°F, which means a change in temperature of 20°C is equivalent to a change of 68° − 32° = 36°F, which is (B).

You could also recognize from the formula that Fahrenheit measurements are exactly $\frac{9}{5}$ of Celsius measurements, so you could multiply 20 by $\frac{9}{5}$ to arrive at 36 as well.

11. B

Difficulty: Medium

Category: Problem Solving and Data Analysis / Rates, Ratios, Proportions, and Percentages

Strategic Advice: Don't let all the technical words in this question overwhelm you. Solve it step-by-step examining the units as you go. Use the factor label method to help you stay organized.

Getting to the Answer: *Step 1:* Determine the number of megabytes the company can upload in 1 evening (4 hours):

$$\frac{12\ MB}{1\ sec} \times \frac{60\ sec}{1\ min} \times \frac{60\ min}{1\ hr} \times \frac{4\ hr}{1\ evening} = \frac{172,800\ MB}{1\ evening}$$

Step 2: Convert this amount to gigabytes (because the information about the scans is given in gigabytes, not megabytes):

$$172,800\ MB \times \frac{1\ GB}{1,024\ MB} = 168.75\ GB$$

Step 3: Each video file is about 4.5 gigabytes, so divide by 4.5 to determine how many videos the company can upload to the cloud using its internet service provider: 168.75 ÷ 4.5 = 37.5 videos. Remember, you should round this number down to 37, because the question asks for the maximum number the company can upload and it cannot complete the 38th video upload in the time allowed. The correct answer is (B).

12. D

Difficulty: Hard

Category: Problem Solving and Data Analysis / Rates, Ratios, Proportions, and Percentages

Strategic Advice: The key to answering this question is translating from English into math. Start by assigning a variable to what you're looking for.

Getting to the Answer: Let m be the number of months the customer has subscribed to the service. The first month costs a dollars and the remaining months $(m - 1)$ are charged at a rate of b dollars per month. So, the total charge for the service so far is $a + b(m - 1)$. Set this equal to the amount the customer has paid and solve for m. Note that you're not going to get a nice number answer, because the question doesn't give you the actual rates.

$$a + b(m - 1) = 108.60$$
$$a + bm - b = 108.60$$
$$bm = 108.60 - a + b$$
$$m = \frac{108.60 - a + b}{b}$$

The expression for m matches the one in (D).

13. C

Difficulty: Hard

Category: Problem Solving and Data Analysis / Rates, Ratios, Proportions, and Percentages

Strategic Advice: This is a question where you will need to work backward. Normally, when there is a sale, you take the original price and multiply it by the discount to find the amount the shopper paid. But here, you know how much she paid and one discount amount, but not the other, so to work backward, you'll need to divide.

Getting to the Answer: Divide the amount Margo paid, $41.85, by 0.9 (because the discount for using her store credit card was 10%, or 0.1). This will tell you how much she would have paid if she hadn't used her store credit card: $41.85 ÷ 0.9 = $46.50. To find the amount of the sale discount, divide this by the original price: $46.50 ÷ $62.00 = 0.75, which means she paid 75% of the price, or in other words, the discount was 25%, making (C) the correct choice.

You could also try each answer choice, one at a time, but this will use up valuable time on Test Day.

14. D

Difficulty: Hard

Category: Problem Solving and Data Analysis / Rates, Ratios, Proportions, and Percentages

Strategic Advice: Draw a chart or diagram detailing the various price reductions for each two weeks.

Getting to the Answer:

Length of Time on Market	% of Most Recent Price	Resulting Price
List Price	–	$200,000.00
After 2 weeks	100% – 5% = 95%	$190,000.00
After 4 weeks	100% – 5% = 95%	$180,500.00
After 6 weeks	100% – 3% = 97%	$175,085.00
After 8 weeks	100% – 3% = 97%	$169,832.45

You can stop here because the item was sold after 9 weeks and the next price reduction would have been at 10 weeks, so the selling price was $169,832.45, which is (D).

15. B

Difficulty: Hard

Category: Problem Solving and Data Analysis / Rates, Ratios, Proportions, and Percentages

Strategic Advice: Pay careful attention to the units. You need to convert all of the dimensions to inches, and then find the scale factor. You'll have to start with the skull because it's the only part of the T-rex for which you know both the actual length and the model length. Before selecting your answer, make sure you found the right quantity (the difference between the scale model's length and its height).

Getting to the Answer: There are 12 inches in one foot, so Sue's skull length was $12 \times 5 = 60$ inches and the model skull is $3 \times 12 = 36 + 1.5 = 37.5$ inches. Find the scale factor by writing this as a fraction. Multiply both numbers by 10 to get rid of the decimal and then simplify the ratio:

$$\frac{37.5}{60} = \frac{375}{600} = \frac{5}{8}$$

This means the scale factor is $\frac{5}{8}$. You might be tempted to now find the scale model's length and height by multiplying 40 and 13 by $\frac{5}{8}$, but this would waste valuable time. Because the model is a $\frac{5}{8}$ scale model, the difference between the model's length and height will be exactly $\frac{5}{8}$ of the difference between Sue's actual length and height, which is $40 - 13 = 27$ feet. Multiply 27 by $\frac{5}{8}$ to find that the difference between the length and height of the model should be 16.875 feet, or 16 feet, 10.5 inches, which matches (B).

16. C

Difficulty: Medium

Category: Problem Solving and Data Analysis / Rates, Ratios, Proportions, and Percentages

Strategic Advice: This is another question where the units can help you find the answer. Use the number of employees to find the total number of miles driven to find the total number of gallons of gas used. Then you can write an equation, with r equal to the reimbursement rate, and set it equal to the amount of total reimbursements paid.

Getting to the Answer:

$$126 \text{ employees} \times \frac{12{,}250 \text{ mi}}{\text{employee}} = 1{,}543{,}500 \text{ mi}$$

$$1{,}543{,}500 \text{ mi} \times \frac{1 \text{ gal of gas}}{22.5 \text{ miles}} = 68{,}600 \text{ gal}$$

$$68{,}600r = \$96{,}040.00$$
$$r = \$1.40$$

The reimbursement rate was \$1.40 per gallon, which is (C).

17. 14

Difficulty: Easy

Category: Problem Solving and Data Analysis / Rates, Ratios, Proportions, and Percentages

Strategic Advice: Identify the information you are given and figure out what you still need to answer the question—you need to know how long each person took to read their book.

Getting to the Answer: You know the length of Betsy's book and the rate at which she reads. You need to know how many minutes she reads.

$$\frac{116 \text{ pg}}{1 \text{ book}} \times \frac{1.5 \text{ min}}{1 \text{ pg}} = 116 \times 1.5 = 174$$

It takes Betsy 174 minutes to read her book. You know Raymond starts reading at 8:30 AM and reads until 11:38 AM, which is 11:38 − 8:30 = 3 hours, 8 minutes, or 188 minutes. It takes Raymond 188 − 174 = 14 minutes longer to read his book.

18. 4

Difficulty: Easy

Category: Problem Solving and Data Analysis / Rates, Ratios, Proportions, and Percentages

Strategic Advice: Lining up the units so that they cancel nicely is the key to answering this question.

Getting to the Answer: Katrina already knows how much cardboard she needs; she just doesn't have the amount in the proper units. All this question is asking you to do is convert 576 *square* inches to *square* feet.

$$\frac{576 \text{ in.}^2}{1} \times \frac{1 \text{ ft}}{12 \text{ in.}} \times \frac{1 \text{ ft}}{12 \text{ in.}} = \frac{576}{144} \text{ ft}^2 = 4 \text{ ft}^2$$

19. 540

Difficulty: Medium

Category: Problem Solving and Data Analysis / Rates, Ratios, Proportions, and Percentages

Strategic Advice: Break the questions into steps. First, find how long it took the employee to collect samples from one house, and then use that amount to find how long it should take the employee to collect samples from all of the houses.

Getting to the Answer: The employee *started* the 1st house at 9:00 and the 6th house at 10:00, so it took him 1 hour, or 60 minutes, to collect samples from 5 houses. This gives a unit rate of 60 ÷ 5 = 12 minutes per house. Multiply the unit rate by the number of houses in the subdivision (45) to get 12 × 45 = 540 minutes to collect samples from all the houses.

20. 1000

Difficulty: Medium

Category: Problem Solving and Data Analysis / Rates, Ratios, Proportions, and Percentages

Strategic Advice: The distance on the students' maps is 2.5 inches, but you can't just multiply this by the scale because the maps the students have are $\frac{1}{4}$ the size of the wall map, so the scale isn't the same. You must first determine how long 2.5 inches on the student map is on the wall map.

Getting to the Answer: If the student map is $\frac{1}{4}$ the size of the wall map, then 2.5 inches on the student map would be 2.5 × 4 = 10 inches on the wall map. Now set up a proportion to find the actual distance between the cities using the scale of the wall map:

$$\frac{1}{100} = \frac{10}{x}$$
$$x = 1,000$$

The correct answer is 1000.

21. 76.5

Difficulty: Medium

Category: Problem Solving and Data Analysis / Rates, Ratios, Proportions, and Percentages

Strategic Advice: This question is tricky. The interest (after being rounded down) is added to the account at the end of each year. The next year, the new, higher amount is the amount that will earn interest.

Getting to the Answer: Start by multiplying the principal by the interest rate:

$$1,500 \times 0.01 = 15$$

Now add this to the principal:

$$1,500 + 15 = 1,515$$

This is the amount that will earn interest in the next year. Repeat this process for 4 more years. Multiply the principal by the interest rate, round the interest

down to the nearest cent, and then add it to the principal to use for the next year's calculation.

Year two:
$$1,515 \times 0.01 = 15.15$$
$$1,515 + 15.15 = 1,530.15$$
Year three:
$$1,530.15 \times 0.01 = 15.3015 \rightarrow 15.30$$
$$1,530.15 + 15.30 = 1,545.45$$
Year four:
$$1,545.45 \times 0.01 = 15.4545 \rightarrow 15.45$$
$$1,545.45 + 15.45 = 1,560.90$$
Year five:
$$1,560.90 \times 0.01 = 15.609 \rightarrow 15.60$$
$$1,560.90 + 15.60 = 1,576.50$$

Over five years, the account earned $1,576.50 – $1,500 = $76.50 in interest. Enter this as 76.5.

Be careful here—you might be tempted to use the exponential function $f(5) = 1,500(1.01)^5$ to arrive at the answer more quickly. However, the question specifically states that the interest is rounded down to the nearest whole cent each year, which changes the answer by just a couple of cents.

22. 40

Difficulty: Hard

Category: Problem Solving and Data Analysis / Rates, Ratios, Proportions, and Percentages

Strategic Advice: Start by determining what the question is asking. You need to find the net change in the power allocated to Grid 1 over the course of a day. To do this, you need to know how much the grid was allocated at the beginning of the day and how much at the end.

Getting to the Answer: You aren't given a concrete starting point (or units of power), so simply pick a starting number. The best number to use when dealing with percents is 100. First, find how much power the grid was allocated after the first 20% increase: 100 × 1.2 = 120. Next, find the amount after the 10% decrease: 120 × 0.9 = 108. Finally, find the amount after the last 30% increase: 108 × 1.3 = 140.4, which is 140.4 − 100 = 40.4 more than it started the day with. To find the percent change, use the formula Percent change = $\dfrac{\text{Amount of change}}{\text{Original amount}}$ to get $\dfrac{40.4}{100} = 0.404$. Rounded to the nearest whole percent, this is 40 percent.

23. 50

Difficulty: Medium

Category: Problem Solving and Data Analysis / Rates, Ratios, Proportions, and Percentages

Strategic Advice: Break this problem into short steps. Step one: Find the total number of drips needed to deliver 800 mL of medication. Step two: Divide this by the number of hours, 8, over which the meds will be delivered. Step three: Divide the result by 60 to convert the rate to drips per minute.

Getting to the Answer: *Step one*: Find the total number of drips needed by multiplying the amount of medication prescribed, 800 mL, by the number of drips needed to deliver 1 mL: 800 × 30 = 24,000 drips.

Step two: Divide this number by 8 to find how many drips per hour are needed: 24,000 ÷ 8 = 3,000 drips per hour.

Step three: Divide this by 60 (because there are 60 minutes in one hour) to convert drips per hour to drips per minute: 3,000 ÷ 60 = 50 drips per minute.

24. 10.5

Difficulty: Medium

Category: Problem Solving and Data Analysis / Rates, Ratios, Proportions, and Percentages

Strategic Advice: Questions that involve distance, rate, and time can almost always be solved using the DIRT formula, Distance = Rate × Time.

Getting to the Answer: For each of the three friends, you know how long they traveled and their

rate. Use the formula to find the distance for each one. But be careful—the rates are given in miles per hour, which means you must use hours, not minutes, for the times.

Andrea:
30 minutes = 0.5 hours
Distance = 3 × 0.5 = 1.5 miles
Kellan:
45 minutes = 0.75 hours
Distance = 14 × 0.75 = 10.5 miles
Joelle:
15 minutes = 0.25 hours
Distance = 35 × 0.25 = 8.75 miles

Kellan lives the farthest away at 10.5 miles. An important note here—the question did not tell you to round and the entire answer fits in the grid, so you MUST grid the answer in as 10.5. However, had you gotten an answer like 10.57 (which wouldn't fit in the grid), then you could either round to 10.6 or truncate (cut off) the answer at 10.5 because it would still fill the entire grid.

25. 731

Difficulty: Hard

Category: Problem Solving and Data Analysis / Rates, Ratios, Proportions, and Percentages

Strategic Advice: When answering questions that share information, you can almost always save yourself some time by using amounts you found in the first question to answer the second one. You will need to find the total amount of time Kellan was travelling, and then subtract that from his arrival time.

Getting to the Answer: In the previous question, you already found that Andrea's house is 1.5 miles from the restaurant. Use the DIRT formula to determine how long Kellan walked with Andrea:

$$1.5 = 2.5 \times \text{time}$$
$$1.5 = 2.5t$$
$$0.6 = t$$

They walked for 0.6 hours, or $60 \times 0.6 = 36$ minutes. Now calculate how long Kellan biked. Again, you have the distance and the rate, so you need to use the formula to find the time:

$$12 = 15 \times \text{time}$$
$$12 = 15t$$
$$0.8 = t$$

Kellan biked for 0.8 hours, or $60 \times 0.8 = 48$ minutes. So Kellan traveled for a total of $36 + 48 = 84$ minutes, or 1 hour, 24 minutes. Don't forget that they arrived 5 minutes early, or at 8:55. So Kellan must have left his house at 8:55 – 1 hour = 7:55 – 24 minutes = 7:31 AM. Enter this as 731.

26. 660
Difficulty: Easy

Category: Problem Solving and Data Analysis / Rates, Ratios, Proportions, and Percentages

Strategic Advice: Break this question into short steps. Find the amount of the hostess share for one evening. Multiply this by the number of evenings per week, 5, and then the number of weeks, 4. Do this for each restaurant, and then subtract to find the difference.

Getting to the Answer:

Restaurant A:	*Restaurant B:*
$0.07 \times \$1,100 = \$77$	$0.04 \times \$1,100 = \$44$
$\$77 \times 5 = 385$	$\$44 \times 5 = \$220$
$\$385 \times 4 = \$1,540$	$\$220 \times 4 = \$880$

Mia would make $\$1,540 - \$880 = \$660$ more at Restaurant A.

27. 75
Difficulty: Hard

Category: Problem Solving and Data Analysis / Rates, Ratios, Proportions, and Percentages

Strategic Advice: This question requires multiple steps and multiple formulas, so make a plan before you dive in. The formula for percent increase is

$$\text{Percent increase} = \frac{\text{Final amount} \times \text{Original amount}}{\text{Original amount}}.$$

This tells you that you need the final amount in tips that Restaurant B needs to bring in to be equal to Restaurant A, which will depend on the amount in tips Restaurant A brings in. You'll need to use the percent formula (Percent × Whole = Part) to determine what amount would be required at 4% for the hostess share to be equal.

Getting to the Answer: The hostess tip share for one evening at Restaurant A is $\$1,100 \times 0.07 = \$77$. Use this amount to find the final amount of tips, t, Restaurant B needs:

$$0.04 \times t = 77$$
$$0.04t = 77$$
$$t = \$1,925$$

Now use the percent increase formula:

$$\text{Percent increase} = \frac{1,925 - 1,100}{1,100}$$
$$= \frac{825}{1,100}$$
$$= 0.75$$

The percent increase needed is 75%. Per the question's instructions, enter this as 75 (not .75).

28. 45.5
Difficulty: Medium

Category: Problem Solving and Data Analysis / Rates, Ratios, Proportions, and Percentages

Strategic Advice: Use the formula, $\text{Percent} = \frac{\text{Part}}{\text{Whole}} \times 100$. You'll need to do some preliminary calculations to find the *whole*.

Getting to the Answer: The *part* of the budget represented by the textbook is $24.99. The total cost of all the supplies (or the *whole*) is 1 textbook ($24.99) + 5 notebooks (5 × $3.78 = $18.90) + 20 pencils (20 × $0.55 = $11.00) = $54.89. Now use the formula:

$$\text{Percent} = \frac{24.99}{54.89} \times 100$$
$$= 0.45527 \times 100$$
$$= 45.527$$

Before you grid in your answer, make sure you followed the directions—round to the nearest tenth of a percent and ignore the percent sign, which is 45.5.

29. 100
Difficulty: Hard

Category: Problem Solving and Data Analysis / Rates, Ratios, Proportions, and Percentages

Strategic Advice: This question contains several steps. Be careful—there are lots of calculations that involve decimals, and you shouldn't round until the very end.

Getting to the Answer: Start with the total cost of the year's supplies: $988.02. After taking inventory, Bridget knows she has used $713.57 worth of supplies, which means she should have $988.02 − $713.57 = $274.45 worth of supplies left. From the previous question, you know that 1 textbook, 5 notebooks, and 20 pencils together cost $54.89, which means Bridget has $274.45 ÷ $54.89 = 5 sets of the initial supplies left. Don't grid in this amount because you're not finished yet! The question asks for the *number of pencils* left. According to the table, each order (set) contains 20 pencils, so there should be 5 × 20 = 100 pencils left.

CHAPTER 4

PREPARE

1. B
Difficulty: Easy

Category: Problem Solving and Data Analysis / Scatterplots

Strategic Advice: Use a line of best fit to determine whether a correlation exists.

Getting to the Answer: Draw a line of best fit through the data points. You'll see that as farm size increases, the number of farms decreases, which indicates a negative correlation. The majority of the data points are fairly close to the line of best fit, which means the correlation is strong. Therefore, (B) must be correct.

2. C
Difficulty: Easy

Category: Problem Solving and Data Analysis / Scatterplots

Strategic Advice: Identify the type of growth/decay occurring to determine the type of equation you need.

Getting to the Answer: Because the no-show count and group size do not change, you can assume Tracy's account balance will increase at a constant rate, indicating a linear equation. You can therefore eliminate A and B. Identify the last class Tracy missed, and draw a line of best fit through that and any points after it. Extend the line to the y-axis; you'll see the y-intercept is 11. Of the remaining choices, only (C) has this y-intercept, so it must be correct.

3. B
Difficulty: Medium

Category: Problem Solving and Data Analysis / Scatterplots

Strategic Advice: Address each piece of the question individually. Pay attention to the axis labels when interpreting the infographic.

Getting to the Answer: The 2001 formula plot has a slight curve that straightens as wind speed increases. Extend the line to reflect this trend; once complete, draw a straight line from 40 mph on the x-axis to the extended 2001 formula plot (a straight edge such as a piece of scratch paper will help). Then draw a horizontal line from the intersection of the 2001 formula line and the vertical line to the y-axis; you'll see that the corresponding wind chill is −30°F. C and D have different wind chill values, so eliminate them.

The horizontal line that you drew to find the wind chill factor intersects a data point on the 1939 formula plot. Draw a vertical line from that point to the x-axis; you'll find that in 1939, a wind speed of approximately 15 mph would yield a wind chill of −30°F. Therefore, the correct answer is (B).

PRACTICE

4. C
Difficulty: Easy

Category: Problem Solving and Data Analysis / Scatterplots

Strategic Advice: Examine the equation to determine the type of plot it will produce.

Getting to the Answer: When the exponent in an equation is a variable, the graph of the equation is exponential, so eliminate choices A and B. To distinguish between the remaining choices, pick an easy-to-use value to plug into the given equation for x (e.g., 0). You'll see that when x = 0, y should equal 5, which matches the graph in (C).

5. 2

Difficulty: Medium

Category: Problem Solving and Data Analysis / Scatterplots

Strategic Advice: You're asked for a rate; this means finding the slope of the line of best fit.

Getting to the Answer: Start by picking a pair of points, preferably where the line of best fit passes through a gridline intersection to minimize error. The points (50, 20) and (100, 40) are good choices. Determine the slope: $m = \dfrac{y_2 - y_1}{x_2 - x_1} = \dfrac{40 - 20}{100 - 50} = \dfrac{20}{50} = \dfrac{2}{5}$. Don't grid in $\dfrac{2}{5}$, though. Remember what you're being asked: You need the road clearing duration increase for a 5% increase in snowpack water content, not 1%. Multiply $\dfrac{2}{5}$ by 5, which yields 2.

6. 99.2

Difficulty: Medium

Strategic Advice: The slope you derived in the previous part will aid you here.

Getting to the Answer: The line of best fit on the scatterplot intersects the y-axis at (0, 0). Therefore, the equation of the line of best fit is $y = \dfrac{2}{5}x$. Plug 248 in for x and solve for y:

$$y = \dfrac{2}{5} \times 248$$

$$y = \dfrac{496}{5} = 99.2$$

The road clearing time at 248% snowpack water content will take 99.2 days.

PERFORM

7. A

Difficulty: Easy

Category: Problem Solving and Data Analysis / Scatterplots

Strategic Advice: Translate English to Math to make quick work of this question.

Getting to the Answer: The question asks for a rate of change, which means you'll need the slope of the line of best fit. Pick a pair of points to use in the slope formula, such as (1998, 20) and (2012, 90):

$$m = \dfrac{y_2 - y_1}{x_2 - x_1} = \dfrac{90 - 20}{2012 - 1998} = \dfrac{70}{14} = 5.$$ (A) is correct.

8. A

Difficulty: Easy

Category: Problem Solving and Data Analysis / Scatterplots

Strategic Advice: Identify the type of change described in the question to narrow down your choices.

Getting to the Answer: If the number of smartphone users increases by 35% each year, then the amount of the increase is variable (because it's 35% of a bigger number each time), indicating nonlinear (exponential) growth. Eliminate C and D. Recall that when assembling an exponential growth model, r (the rate) must be in decimal form. Therefore, the number raised to the power of x should be $1 + 0.35$ or 1.35. (A) is the only choice that fits these criteria.

9. D

Difficulty: Medium

Category: Problem Solving and Data Analysis / Scatterplots

Strategic Advice: Compare each statement to the infographic one at a time, eliminating true statements as you work.

Getting to the Answer: Start with A: According to the infographic, Strain 1's OD600 was always higher than that of Strain 2, which is consistent with the statement. Eliminate A. B states that Strain 2's growth rate overtook Strain 1's at hour 50, which is consistent with the infographic; eliminate it. C requires math, so skip it for now. (D) states that Strain 1's growth rate was greater than Strain 2's. Although Strain 1's growth rate was greater for part of the monitored period, it is not greater for the entire period (because the slope of Strain 1's curve is not steeper than that of Strain 2's curve for every line segment on the graph), which makes (D) false and, therefore, correct.

EXTRA PRACTICE

1. C

Difficulty: Easy

Category: Problem Solving and Data Analysis / Scatterplots

Strategic Advice: Correlation means that there is a discernible relationship between two or more variables. A positive correlation means that as one variable increases, so does the other variable. A negative correlation means that as one variable increases, the other decreases. The closer the relationship is, the stronger the correlation.

Getting to the Answer: Take a quick peek at the answer choices and picture or draw a sketch of each one. *Linear* indicates that the data follows the path of a straight line. *Positive* means rising from left to right. Finally, *strong* means the relationship is a close one, but not perfect, so the data points should be fairly close to, but not exactly on, the line; choice (C) is correct.

2. A

Difficulty: Easy

Category: Problem Solving and Data Analysis / Scatterplots

Strategic Advice: A line with a downward slant has a negative slope, so you can immediately eliminate C and D. To choose between (A) and B, recall that slope is a ratio that compares vertical change (rise) to horizontal change (run).

Getting to the Answer: Mark the bordered area using equal measures and then estimate the slope of a line drawn through the center of the points as shown.

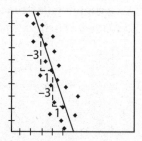

The line appears to fall 3 units and run 1 unit, so a good estimate for the slope is –3, making (A) correct. Note that you could also use what you know about slope to answer the question—lines that have fractional slopes, between –1 and 1, are not steep lines, which means B can't be correct.

3. C

Difficulty: Easy

Category: Problem Solving and Data Analysis / Scatterplots

Strategic Advice: A regression equation is the equation of the line (or curve) that best fits the data. A *linear* regression is used to model data that follows the path of a straight line.

Getting to the Answer: In the equation given, a represents the slope of the linear regression (the line of best fit), so you are looking for data that is linear (looks like a line) and is decreasing, or falling from left to right ($a < 0$ means a is negative). You can eliminate A and D because the data is not linear (A is quadratic and D is exponential). You can also eliminate B because the data is increasing (rising from left to right). This means (C) is correct.

4. A

Difficulty: Easy

Category: Problem Solving and Data Analysis / Scatterplots

Strategic Advice: When an exponential equation is written in the form $y = x_0(1 + r)^x$, x_0 gives the y-intercept of the equation's graph. To answer this question, you need to think about what the y-intercept would represent in the context described.

Getting to the Answer: Whenever time is involved in a relationship that is modeled by an equation or a graph, it is always the independent variable and therefore graphed on the x-axis. Therefore, for this question, population would be graphed on the y-axis, so x_0 most likely represents the population when the time elapsed was zero, or in other words, in the year that Adriana was born, making (A) correct.

5. D

Difficulty: Medium

Category: Problem Solving and Data Analysis / Scatterplots

Strategic Advice: A line that "represents the trend of the data" is another way of saying best-fit line.

Getting to the Answer: The trend of the data is clearly linear because the path of the dots does not turn around or curve, so draw a best-fit line on the graph. Remember, about half of the points should be above the line and half below.

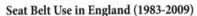

Seat Belt Use in England (1983-2009)

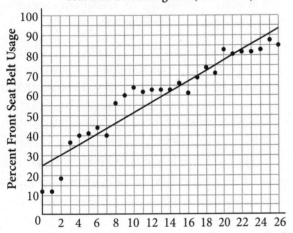

Years After Seat Belt Law Enacted

If you draw your best-fit line all the way to the *y*-axis, you'll save yourself a step by finding the *y*-intercept just by looking at the scatterplot. For this graph, it's about 25. This means you can eliminate B and C. To choose between A and (D), find the approximate slope using two points that lie on (or very close to) the best-fit line. You can use the *y*-intercept, (0, 25), as one of the points to save time and estimate the second, such as (21, 80). Use the slope formula to find the slope:

$$m = \frac{y_2 - y_1}{x_2 - x_1} = \frac{80 - 25}{21 - 0} = \frac{55}{21} = 2.62$$

The result is very close to the slope in (D), making it the correct answer.

6. A

Difficulty: Medium

Category: Problem Solving and Data Analysis / Scatterplots

Strategic Advice: Examine the graph, paying careful attention to units and labels. The average rate of change is the same as the slope of the best-fit line. The data is decreasing (going down from left to right) so you can immediately eliminate C and D.

Getting to the Answer: Find the slope of the best-fit line using the slope formula, $m = \frac{y_2 - y_1}{x_2 - x_1}$, and any two points that lie on (or very close to) the line. Using the two points (5, 14) and (10, 8), the average rate of change is about $\frac{8 - 14}{10 - 5} = \frac{-6}{5} = -1.2$, which matches (A).

7. A

Difficulty: Medium

Category: Problem Solving and Data Analysis / Scatterplots

Strategic Advice: Determine whether the predicted change in the interest rate is a common difference (linear function) or a common ratio (exponential function), or if it changes direction (quadratic or polynomial function).

Getting to the Answer: The company predicts that every six months, the Federal Reserve will *raise* rates by 0.25 percentage points. Interest rates are already expressed as percentages, so raising the rates by 0.25 percentage points means *adding* a quarter of a percent every six months. It does not mean it will increase *by* 0.25% every six months. The function therefore involves a common difference, so the best model would be a linear function, which is (A).

8. C

Difficulty: Medium

Category: Problem Solving and Data Analysis / Scatterplots

Strategic Advice: It is a good idea to familiarize yourself with statistics vocabulary before Test Day. "Correlation" simply means relationship. The word "weak" refers to the strength of the relationship (how close the data lies to the line of best fit), which has no effect on slope.

Getting to the Answer: Be careful not to confuse slope and strength. The fact that a data set shows a weak correlation does not give you any information about the magnitude of the slope. This means you can eliminate A and B. Also, keep in mind that the terms "weak" and "negative" are not related, but rather are two independent descriptors of the correlation. So the fact that the rate of change is negative has nothing to do with the strength of the correlation. In a weak correlation, the data points will loosely follow the line of best fit, making (C) the correct answer.

9. B

Difficulty: Medium

Category: Problem Solving and Data Analysis / Scatterplots

Strategic Advice: Sometimes, a question looks easier than it actually is, and deserves a second read once you've skimmed the answer choices. Remember, correlation does not prove causation, and as a general rule, conclusions can only be drawn about the population studied, not about all populations.

Getting to the Answer: The data points are scattered and do not form any discernible pattern. This means there is no correlation, which is another way of saying the two variables aren't related, so you can eliminate D. You can also eliminate C because the HR representative *is* able to draw a conclusion— that there is no relationship. To choose between A and (B), recall that when you analyze data from a

given population (the employees at that particular company), you can only draw conclusions about that population, not about employee populations in general. Therefore, (B) is correct.

10. D

Difficulty: Easy

Category: Problem Solving and Data Analysis / Scatterplots

Strategic Advice: The value of r^2 describes how well a certain type of regression line (also called a trend line or line of best fit) fits a data set. The closer r^2 is to 1, the better the fit. Ensure you've answered the right question before moving on.

Getting to the Answer: You need not know specific data points in order to answer this question, so you can immediately eliminate D. The question asks for the regression line type that is least (not most) appropriate, so look for the one with the lowest r^2 value. The exponential regression line has the lowest r^2 value (0.623), so (C) is the correct answer.

11. 3

Difficulty: Easy

Category: Problem Solving and Data Analysis / Scatterplots

Strategic Advice: Percent error gives the deviation of an actual value from an expected value. Graphically, this is determined by how far from the line of best fit the data point sits.

Getting to the Answer: You don't need to find the percent error of every point (or even a single point) to answer this question. Instead, you just need to understand that the point with the greatest percent error from the mean of the data is the point that is farthest from the line of best fit. Use the gridlines on the graph to find the point. The point (9, 3) is 4 full gridlines away from the line of best fit, which is farther than any other data point. The question asks for the y-value of this point, so the correct answer is 3.

12. 18

Difficulty: Medium

Category: Problem Solving and Data Analysis / Scatterplots

Strategic Advice: Because the y-value of the graph when x = 3,400 is not shown, this is a question for which a mathematical solution is necessary; extending the line of best fit will not provide an accurate enough answer.

Getting to the Answer: The equation of the model is given as $y=-\dfrac{1}{200}x+35$. Miles over recommended servicing are graphed along the x-axis, so substitute 3,400 for x to find the answer: $y=-\dfrac{1}{200}(3,400)+35=-17+35=18$ miles per gallon.

13. 2

Difficulty: Easy

Category: Problem Solving and Data Analysis / Scatterplots

Strategic Advice: Being able to read information from an infographic is an important skill, and will surely earn you points on Test Day.

Getting to the Answer: Examine the graph, including the axis labels and numbering. Each vertical gridline represents 5 eggs, so look to see how many data points are more than a complete grid space away from the line of best fit. Only 2 are more than 5 away—the first data point and the one between 30 and 35 weeks, making 2 the correct answer.

14. 57

Difficulty: Medium

Category: Problem Solving and Data Analysis / Scatterplots

Strategic Advice: This is a Grid-in question, so you can't just use the graph to estimate the y-value when x = 36. Instead, you need to find the equation of the line of best fit, and then substitute 36 for x and simplify. However, if you are running out of time on Test Day, at least take a guess based on the line of best fit—at x = 36, the y-value looks like it is either 56 or 57.

Getting to the Answer: First, determine the equation of the line of best fit. Start with the slope—you could pick two points on the line and use the slope formula, or you could count the rise and the run. The latter is easier in this question. Beginning at the point (0, 75), the line falls 5 units and runs 10 units to the first point on the line, so the slope is $\dfrac{-5}{10}=-\dfrac{1}{2}$. This means that the equation looks like $y=-\dfrac{1}{2}x+b$. Next, find the y-intercept. You can see clearly from the graph that it is approximately 75.

The equation is $y=-\dfrac{1}{2}x+75$. Now, substitute 36 for x and simplify to find y:

$$y=-\dfrac{1}{2}(36)+75$$
$$y=-18+75$$
$$y=57$$

The correct answer is 57 (which, by the way, was one of the two guesses).

15. 15

Difficulty: Hard

Category: Problem Solving and Data Analysis / Scatterplots

Strategic Advice: Percent error shows the deviation of an actual value from an expected value. The formula for percent error is $\dfrac{\left|\text{Expected Value} - \text{Actual Value}\right|}{\text{Expected Value}}$.

To find the expected value, you'll need to use the

equation of the line of best fit that you found in the previous question, which is often the case when questions are grouped together as a set.

Getting to the Answer: Substitute 20 for x in the equation for the line of best fit and simplify to find the expected number of eggs:

$$y = -\frac{1}{2}(20) + 75$$
$$y = -10 + 75$$
$$y = 65$$

The farmer's flock laid 55 eggs, so the percent error is: $\dfrac{|65-55|}{65} = \dfrac{10}{65} \approx 0.15 = 15\%$

CHAPTER 5

PREPARE

1. B
Difficulty: Easy

Category: Problem Solving and Data Analysis / Statistics and Probability

Strategic Advice: Focus on the rows of the table that you need, and block out the rest.

Getting to the Answer: The trickiest part of this question is understanding what is being asked. What you need is the shop that had the most Tuesday sales *as a fraction of its total sales*. For each shop, divide the number of books it sold on Tuesday by the number of books it sold all week. You can use your calculator to speed up this step.

Bob's Books: $\dfrac{\text{Tuesday total}}{\text{weekly total}} = \dfrac{8}{53} \approx 0.1509$

Nalia's Novels: $\dfrac{\text{Tuesday total}}{\text{weekly total}} = \dfrac{13}{55} \approx 0.2364$

Tumiko's Tomes: $\dfrac{\text{Tuesday total}}{\text{weekly total}} = \dfrac{15}{66} \approx 0.2273$

Vladimir's Volumes: $\dfrac{\text{Tuesday total}}{\text{weekly total}} = \dfrac{13}{58} \approx 0.2241$

The greatest portion of Tuesday sales belongs to Nalia's Novels, so (B) is correct.

2. C
Difficulty: Medium

Category: Problem Solving and Data Analysis / Statistics and Probability

Strategic Advice: When pulling data from the table, make sure you use the correct columns and rows.

Getting to the Answer: Add the number of books sold by Tumiko and Vladimir on Monday, Wednesday, and Friday; then divide the result by the total number of books sold on those days.

Tumiko's and Vladimir's M/W/F sales: $(15 + 12) + (12 + 14) + (10 + 9) = 72$

Total M/W/F sales: $48 + 49 + 39 = 136$

Divide Tumiko's and Vladimir's M/W/F sales by total M/W/F sales to get $\dfrac{72}{136}$, which simplifies to $\dfrac{9}{17}$. Choice (C) is correct.

3. D
Difficulty: Medium

Category: Problem Solving and Data Analysis / Statistics and Probability

Strategic Advice: The answer choices are unsimplified expressions rather than simple values. Don't waste time performing unnecessary calculations!

Getting to the Answer: To find the probability of two events occurring, calculate and then multiply the individual probabilities. The word "both" in the question is your clue that you will need to multiply the individual probabilities. The probability of choosing a sophomore who doesn't prefer strategy games is $\dfrac{493-140}{493} = \dfrac{353}{493}$, and the probability of choosing a senior who doesn't prefer strategy games is $\dfrac{509-148}{509} = \dfrac{361}{509}$. This means the probability of both occurring is $\dfrac{353}{493} \times \dfrac{361}{509}$. Don't do any more math; this is as far as you need to go! Choice (D) is correct.

4. A
Difficulty: Medium

Category: Problem Solving and Data Analysis / Statistics and Probability

Strategic Advice: Don't be intimidated by the verbose nature of this question. Look for key details, and think about the conclusions that you can draw based only on what's given.

Getting to the Answer: The question stem states that the study only utilized high school students in Dallas; consequently, you cannot assume that the findings will apply to all of Texas. Eliminate B and D. Although you know that the study found a correlation between video game time and GPA, there is no evidence to support one directly causing the other. You can therefore eliminate C, leaving (A) as the correct answer.

5. A

Difficulty: Hard

Category: Problem Solving and Data Analysis / Statistics and Probability

Strategic Advice: Pay attention to numeric keywords such as "at least" to make sure you don't count the wrong items when setting up the probability formula.

Getting to the Answer: Start with the fundamental probability formula: $P = \dfrac{\text{number desired}}{\text{number possible}}$. There are five coin flips, each with two possibilities, so the total number of outcomes is $2 \times 2 \times 2 \times 2 \times 2 = 2^5 = 32$. Because at least four of the five flips must be heads, simply writing out all desired outcomes won't take much time.

$$
\begin{array}{c}
H\ H\ H\ H\ H \\
H\ H\ H\ H\ T \\
H\ H\ H\ T\ H \\
H\ H\ T\ H\ H \\
H\ T\ H\ H\ H \\
T\ H\ H\ H\ H
\end{array}
$$

There are six outcomes for which at least four of the flips are heads, so the answer is $\dfrac{6}{32} = \dfrac{3}{16}$. Choice (A) is correct.

6. 700

Difficulty: Easy

Category: Problem Solving and Data Analysis / Statistics and Probability / Multi-Part Math

Strategic Advice: Identify the pieces of the pie graph you need, and then convert from the percent to the total.

Getting to the Answer: You know from the infographic that 21% (5% + 16%) of the visitors were *not* aged 20 or older. This means that 100% − 21% = 79% were aged 20+. Given that the number of visitors aged 20+ was 553, use the three-part percent formula to calculate the total:

$$
\text{total} \times 79\% = 553
$$
$$
\text{total} = \frac{553}{0.79} = 700
$$

7. 2030

Difficulty: Medium

Strategic Advice: Part of your calculations were done in the previous question; use that to save time.

Getting to the Answer: From part 1 you know that the total number of visitors in 2014 was 700. According to the infographic, 25% of all the visitors were aged 40-49, and 8% were aged 50+. This means that $0.25 \times 700 = 175$ attendees were aged 40-49, and $0.08 \times 700 = 56$ were aged 50+. The visitors aged 40-49 paid $175 \times \$10 = \$1,750$ for their tickets, and the visitors aged 50+ paid $56 \times \$5 = \$280$ for their tickets. The total revenue for the two groups was therefore $\$1,750 + \$280 = \$2,030$. Grid in 2030.

8. C

Difficulty: Hard

Category: Problem Solving and Data Analysis / Statistics and Probability

Strategic Advice: No math is required for this question, but you do need to think critically about averages.

Getting to the Answer: You know that *m* is the average age of the males, *f* is the average age of the females, *a* is the overall average, and 65% of the members are males. Because there are more males than females, the overall average age must be closer to the male average than to the female average. In other words, *a* is closer to *m* than to *f*. The expression $\dfrac{m+f}{2}$ appears in all of the choices. This is the average of m and f. You don't know which of m or f is greater, so there are two ways to visualize all of this information on a number line. The first assumes that $m < f$; the second assumes that $m > f$:

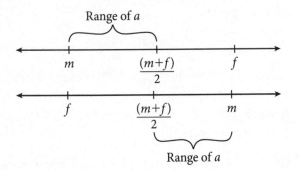

Examine the top number line carefully to see that the only choice consistent with the visualization is (C): when m is less than f, the value of a is less than the average age of both groups.

PRACTICE

9. B
Difficulty: Medium

Category: Problem Solving and Data Analysis / Statistics and Probability

Strategic Advice: You need to have an understanding of data shapes and normal distribution in order to answer this question.

Getting to the Answer: The professor starts with a normal distribution; when the new data are added, the distribution changes:

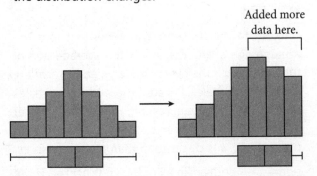

Added more data here.

The new distribution is skewed to the left (in the direction of the graph's tail, not in the direction of its biggest bump), and the median has increased. Although the range of the new data alone might be smaller than the original set, when all data are combined, the range will not have changed from the original data. The correct answer is (B).

10. 28.7
Difficulty: Easy

Category: Problem Solving and Data Analysis / Statistics and Probability / Multi-Part Math

Strategic Advice: Remember which ratings are considered "bad" when doing your calculations, and make sure your work reflects this.

Getting to the Answer: To be considered "bad," a game must have a rating of 1 or 2. Begin by counting the number of "bad" games. There are $5 + 3 + 3 = 11$ games with a rating of 1 and $17 + 12 + 10 = 39$ games with a rating of 2. That's a total of $11 + 39 = 50$ games. Divide this by the total number of games and multiply by 100: $\frac{50}{61+54+59} \times 100 = 28.7\%$. Grid in 28.7.

11. 11.9
Difficulty: Medium

Strategic Advice: The total game count will decrease after the games' removal; keep this in mind when working toward the answer.

Getting to the Answer: You know from part 1 that 50 games are "bad." Reducing this number by 50% is the same as halving it, meaning there will be 25 remaining "bad" games after the removal. Subtract this from the original total game count ($61 + 54 + 59 = 174$) to get the new total, which is 149. Divide the new "bad" count by this total, and then multiply by 100 as you did before: $\frac{25}{149} \times 100 = 16.8\%$. Subtracting the new percentage from the old one gives $28.7\% - 16.8\% = 11.9\%$. Grid in 11.9.

PERFORM

12. D
Difficulty: Medium

Category: Problem Solving and Data Analysis / Statistics and Probability

Strategic Advice: Consider finding the probability of *not* selecting one of the puzzles specified, as there will be fewer dots to count. You can then subtract that probability from 1.

Getting to the Answer: There are only three puzzles that *didn't* take Rolff fewer than 100 seconds to solve. Of these, 2 do *not* have fewer than 6 clues. Therefore, the probability that the conditions *won't* be met is $\frac{2}{20} = 0.1$. This isn't what you're asked to find, so don't stop yet. Subtract 0.1 from 1 to get 0.9. Multiply this by 100 to get 90%; (D) is correct.

13. B
Difficulty: Easy

Category: Problem Solving and Data Analysis / Statistics and Probability

Strategic Advice: Remember the difference between mean and standard deviation: the former is a measure of center; the latter, a measure of spread.

Getting to the Answer: The four answers all involve consistency, which means the explanation should involve standard deviation. Based on this, you can eliminate A and D. Higher consistency means lower standard deviation (and vice versa); the only choice that reflects this—and correctly represents the data in the table—is (B).

14. 594
Difficulty: Medium

Category: Problem Solving and Data Analysis / Statistics and Probability / Multi-Part Math

Strategic Advice: Identify Wilhelmina and Alexandra's hat contributions from the table, and then extrapolate to find how many solid-colored hats they should knit for Spirit Week.

Getting to the Answer: According to the table, Wilhelmina will be responsible for $\frac{24}{60}$ of the hats, and Alexandra will knit $\frac{9}{60}$ of them. The knitting club needs to knit 1,800 hats total, 60% of which should be solid-colored per the survey results. This means that $0.6 \times 1,800 = 1,080$ hats should be solid-colored. Add together the fractions for Wilhelmina and Alexandra to get $\frac{33}{60}$. Multiplying this by the total number of solid-colored hats will yield the number that Wilhelmina and Alexandra will knit: $\frac{33}{60} \times 1,080 = 594$.

15. 282
Difficulty: Medium

Strategic Advice: Read carefully; you're asked about the two other club members' Spirit Week production here, and the question is not limited to solid-colored hats.

Getting to the Answer: Work through this one step at a time. 20% of 1,800 hats = 360 hats with emblems and therefore 360 prize scarves.

The two boys make $\frac{33}{60}$ of the 360 hats = 162 hats.

The two boys make $\frac{11}{33} = \frac{1}{3}$ of the 360 scarves = 120 scarves. They are responsible for 162 + 120 = 282 of these items.

EXTRA PRACTICE

1. B
Difficulty: Easy

Category: Problem Solving and Data Analysis / Statistics and Probability

Strategic Advice: Don't spend too much time reading the description of the study. Focus on the information provided in the table.

Getting to the Answer: The question only asks about participants who were outside a healthy weight range, so focus on this row: 38 out of the 74 participants who were outside a healthy weight range ate breakfast one or fewer times per week. This represents $\frac{38}{74} = .51351$, or 51.35%, which matches (B).

2. D
Difficulty: Medium

Category: Problem Solving and Data Analysis / Statistics and Probability

Strategic Advice: Using the results of a sample study to make predictions about a larger population almost always involves multiplying the total number in the population by a percentage.

Getting to the Answer: The question asks about employees who eat breakfast every weekday, so focus on the "5-7 times per week" column in the table. Assuming the participants in the study were a good representative sample, 36 out of 45, or 80%, of the 3,000 employees are likely to be within a healthy weight range. Multiply 0.8 × 3,000 to arrive at 2,400, which is (D).

3. D
Difficulty: Easy

Category: Problem Solving and Data Analysis / Statistics and Probability

Strategic Advice: When considering the validity of a study, always look for possible sources of bias. In other words, look for things that might skew the results in either direction.

Getting to the Answer: Because the shoe is specifically targeted toward athletes, but is sold in regular shoe stores, conducting the survey outside gyms and sporting goods stores is likely to skew the results. The respondents are already interested in athletics and so are likely to respond more positively than the average shoe store shopper. Therefore, the data from the survey likely overestimates the number of people interested in the new product, making (D) the correct answer.

4. B
Difficulty: Easy

Category: Problem Solving and Data Analysis / Statistics and Probability

Strategic Advice: The mean of a set of numbers is the same as the average, which is the sum of the numbers divided by the amount of numbers.

Getting to the Answer: Use the graph to find the sum of the GPA values, and then calculate the mean. Read the graph carefully—each gridline represents one student. To save time, multiply the frequency in each category by the GPA value and then divide by the total number of students: (10 × 4) + (36 × 3) + (28 × 2) + (8 × 1) + (2 × 0) = 212 ÷ 84 = 2.523, or about 2.5, which is (B).

5. C
Difficulty: Easy

Category: Problem Solving and Data Analysis / Statistics and Probability

Strategic Advice: Think about what each term means: The mean of a data set is the average; the mode is the most commonly occurring data point; the median is the data point in the center when arranged in order from least to greatest; and the standard deviation is a description of how far the data points, as a whole, vary from the mean.

Getting to the Answer: You can eliminate D right away because standard deviation is a measure of spread, not a measure of center. You can also eliminate A because you calculated the mean in the previous question, and it was 2.5, which is less than 3.0. To choose between B and (C), you only need to find the median, because the mode is included in both answer choices. You don't have to list out all 84 scores and find the one in the center; instead, think about it logically. There are 10 + 36 = 46 grades that were a 4.0 or a 3.0, which is more than half of 84, so the median is 3.0. This means either the mode or the median could be used, making (C) correct.

6. B
Difficulty: Medium

Category: Problem Solving and Data Analysis / Statistics and Probability

Strategic Advice: You do not need to use all of the information presented in the table to find the answer. Read the question carefully to make sure you use only what you need.

Getting to the Answer: To calculate the percentage of people in each age group with a healthy blood sugar level (<100), divide the number of people in *that* age group with a healthy blood sugar level by the total number of participants in *that* age group. Choice (B) is correct because $16 \div 98 \approx 0.1633 = 16.33\%$, which is a lower percentage than in the other age groups (18-25 = 18.75%, 36-45 = 20.21%, and Older than 45 = 20%).

7. D
Difficulty: Hard

Category: Problem Solving and Data Analysis / Statistics and Probability

Strategic Advice: This question requires you to read the table carefully. The first criterion is fairly straightforward—you're looking for a participant with a blood sugar level in the 100-125 range, so focus on that column in the table. The second criterion is a bit trickier—*at least 36 years old* means 36 years old or older, so you'll need to use the values in the rows for 36-45, and Older than 45.

Getting to the Answer: Of the 300 participants, there were 35 in the 36-45 age group who were considered at risk, and 27 in the Older than 45 age group, resulting in a total of 35 + 27 = 62 out of 300 participants. The probability of randomly selecting one participant from either of these two groups is $\frac{62}{300}$, which reduces to $\frac{31}{150}$, or (D).

8. A
Difficulty: Medium

Category: Problem Solving and Data Analysis / Statistics and Probability

Strategic Advice: You aren't given the number of vehicles on the lot, but you don't need this information to answer the question because it is asking for a probability, which is a fraction.

Getting to the Answer: Don't neglect the 50% at the beginning of the question just because it is presented in a different form. Instead, convert 50% to a fraction $\left(\frac{1}{2}\right)$ and then think logically—the final probability is $\frac{1}{3}$ of $\frac{3}{4}$ of $\frac{1}{2}$. In math, "of" means multiply, so the probability of randomly choosing a vehicle that is a car with an automatic transmission and a leather interior is $\frac{1}{2} \times \frac{\cancel{3}}{4} \times \frac{1}{\cancel{3}} = \frac{1}{8}$. This means (A) is correct.

9. C
Difficulty: Medium

Category: Problem Solving and Data Analysis / Statistics and Probability

Strategic Advice: A good representative sample is not only random, but also a good representation of the population in question. Here, the senator wants to know about the people who might vote for him.

Getting to the Answer: If the senator is only concerned about people who might vote for him, then the survey only needs to focus on people who can vote. Not all citizens can or choose to vote. Additionally, not everyone in the entire country votes for every senator, so he only needs to focus on voters in his district, making (C) correct.

10. C
Difficulty: Medium

Category: Problem Solving and Data Analysis / Statistics and Probability

Strategic Advice: A good representative sample is not only random, but also a good representation of the population in question. Here, the population in question is tablet owners.

Getting to the Answer: Not everyone who shops at an electronics store owns a tablet. Customers who bought other items, such as laptops, TVs, or MP3 players are likely to make up at least a portion of the surveys distributed with customers' purchases. This means that, despite being randomly selected, the sample is unlikely to be a good representative sample because there is no way to verify whether the responders to the survey actually own a tablet. Therefore, (C) is correct.

11. B
Difficulty: Medium

Category: Problem Solving and Data Analysis / Statistics and Probability

Strategic Advice: Read infographics carefully. Look for patterns in the data that may help you answer the question.

Getting to the Answer: According to the graph, Charlie has been paying down his debt at a rate of

$500 per month. To reach 25% utilization, he needs to get down to $10,000 × 0.25 = $2,500, which means he needs to pay off $10,000 − $2,500 = $7,500. To do this it would take $7,500 ÷ $500 = 15 months, making (B) the correct answer.

12. D
Difficulty: Medium

Category: Problem Solving and Data Analysis / Statistics and Probability

Strategic Advice: Look carefully at the infographic's axes. The number of states correctly named is plotted along the horizontal axis, while the frequency (or number of contestants) is plotted along the vertical axis.

Getting to the Answer: Look at the vertical axis— the frequency tells you the number of contestants who named each number of states. This means 1 contestant named only 1 state, 1 contestant named 2 states, 5 contestants named 3 states, and so on. To answer the question, add all the frequencies to find the total number of contestants: $1 + 1 + 5 + 6 + 4 + 0 + 2 + 1 = 20$, which is (D).

13. D
Difficulty: Medium

Category: Problem Solving and Data Analysis / Statistics and Probability

Strategic Advice: Understanding how averages and sums are connected is the key to answering a question like this. If the average of 14 numbers is 6, then the sum of the 14 numbers must be 84 (because $84 ÷ 14 = 6$).

Getting to the Answer: Use the dot plot to find the total number of appliances the salesman has already sold. Then, subtract this amount from 84. The salesman has already sold $3(2) + 4(3) + 5 + 6(3) + 7 + 8 + 10(2) = 76$ appliances, so he needs to sell $84 − 76 = 8$ appliances on the 14th day to reach his goal. This means (D) is correct.

14. B

Difficulty: Hard

Category: Problem Solving and Data Analysis / Statistics and Probability

Strategic Advice: Work through a question like this one step at a time. Start by using the sample survey to find the percentage of respondents that say they would join a gym if one were located in their area.

Getting to the Answer: According to the sample survey, $\frac{40}{300}$ say they would join the gym. But the gym estimates that only 30% of these respondents would *actually* join, so multiply 40 by 30% to find that the gym can expect $\frac{12}{300} = 0.04 = 4\%$ of the respondents to join Muscles. Multiply this by the total number of residents: 12,600 × 0.04 = 504 residents, so (B) is correct.

15. A

Difficulty: Medium

Category: Problem Solving and Data Analysis / Statistics and Probability

Strategic Advice: Don't let all the numbers in the table intimidate you. You're not expected to calculate anything. All the information you need is already provided for you in the table, so quickly skim the answer choices to see what you're interested in.

Getting to the Answer: The keywords in the question are *average* and *consistently*. The average is the mean and the consistency relates to how spread out each branch's profits are. First, find the branch with the lowest mean profit. This is Branch A, so you can eliminate choices C and D. Standard deviation is a measure of spread, so now focus on that row only. Think about what standard deviation tells you. A lower standard deviation indicates that profits are less spread out and therefore more consistent. Likewise, a higher standard deviation indicates that profits are more spread out and therefore less consistent. Notice the opposite nature of this relationship:

lower standard deviation = more consistent; higher standard deviation = less consistent. Choice (A) is correct because the standard deviation of Branch C's quarterly profits is the *highest*, which means it performed the *least* consistently.

16. 2/5 or .4

Difficulty: Easy

Category: Problem Solving and Data Analysis / Statistics and Probability

Strategic Advice: Read the question carefully. You may not agree with the host's method of determining which entertainer is the most popular (because they did not account for weather, people attending on multiple days, etc.), but your job is to use the definition of "popularity rating" to answer the question.

Getting to the Answer: Take a second to think about the quickest way to answer the question— you're not asked to find the popularity rating of each performer and then compare them. Based on the host's definition, you can pick the most popular performer by simply looking at the numbers in the table. More people attended on day 3, so find the popularity rating for Entertainer C: 1,600 people attended on that day out of a total of 1,280 + 1,120 + 1,600 = 4,000 festival goers, so Entertainer C's popularity rating is $\frac{1,600}{4,000} = \frac{2}{5}$, or .4.

17. 300

Difficulty: Easy

Category: Problem Solving and Data Analysis / Statistics and Probability

Strategic Advice: Read the graph carefully, including the key at the bottom indicating that each bar represents 15 minutes.

Getting to the Answer: The question states that only stage 3 is considered *deep* sleep, and the question asks how much time was spent in *light* sleep. You could count all of the bars that don't represent stage 3, but it would be faster to count the bars that do and subtract. There are 12 bars that represent stage 3, which means the person spent 12 × 15 = 180 minutes in deep sleep. The study was for 8 hours, or 480 minutes, so the person spent 480 − 180 = 300 minutes in light sleep.

18. 3/8 or .375
Difficulty: Medium

Category: Problem Solving and Data Analysis / Statistics and Probability

Strategic Advice: Remember, probability compares the number of desired outcomes (here, the number of 15-minute periods with a sleep stage of 3) with the total number of possible outcomes (here, the total number of 15-minute periods over the course of the 8 hours).

Getting to the Answer: The opening paragraph tells you that the total amount of sleep is 8 hours. In the previous question, you calculated that 180 minutes, or 3 hours are spent in deep sleep. Therefore, the probability would be $\dfrac{3 \text{ hours}}{8 \text{ hours}}$ or $\dfrac{3}{8}$.

19. 81
Difficulty: Easy

Category: Problem Solving and Data Analysis / Statistics and Probability

Strategic Advice: Read the question carefully, identifying the information from the table that you will need. You only need to be concerned with the "Total" row for this question.

Getting to the Answer: There are sixty-one 3-bedroom houses and sixty-four 4-bedroom houses, so there are 61 + 64 = 125 total houses in the development that have 3 or more bedrooms. There are 154 houses in all, which means that 125 ÷ 154 = 0.8117 or approximately 81% of all the houses should receive flyers.

20. .608
Difficulty: Medium

Category: Problem Solving and Data Analysis / Statistics and Probability

Strategic Advice: Sometimes, a question requires more concentration than calculation. In this question, you need to first identify the two categories in the table to which the daycare center will send the invitation. Once you do that, the rest is easy.

Getting to the Answer: The categories to which the daycare center plans to send an invitation are limited to the 3- and 4-bedroom houses (because those are the ones that already received the flyer), so focus on those two columns. The two categories with the most houses are Townhouses/3-bedroom and Single-Family/4-bedroom, with a total of 42 + 34 = 76 houses. You determined in the previous question that there were 125 houses to which the daycare sent flyers, so the probability of randomly selecting one from the two specified groups is $\dfrac{76}{125} = .608$.

21. 15
Difficulty: Medium

Category: Problem Solving and Data Analysis / Statistics and Probability

Strategic Advice: Think about what the infographic shows: dollar amounts that consumers are willing to pay for the store brand version versus the brand name version and the numbers of corresponding consumers (given by the heights of the bars). The question asks *on average* how many more cents consumers are willing to pay, so you will need to find a weighted average for each version of the product.

Getting to the Answer: Start with the store brand. Multiply each dollar amount by the height of the corresponding bar:

$$5 \times 68 = 340$$
$$6 \times 56 = 336$$
$$7 \times 48 = 336$$
$$8 \times 32 = 256$$
$$9 \times 30 = 270$$
$$10 \times 14 = 140$$

Next, add them all together: $1,678. Now, divide this number by the total number of respondents (68 + 56 + 48 + 32 + 30 + 14 = 248): 1,678 ÷ 248 = 6.766, which means *on average* consumers are willing to pay $6.77 for the store brand version of the product. Repeat this process for the brand name version.

$$5 \times 85 = 425$$
$$6 \times 79 = 474$$
$$7 \times 64 = 448$$
$$8 \times 55 = 440$$
$$9 \times 42 = 378$$
$$10 \times 27 = 270$$

Add them all together to get 2,435, and divide by the number of respondents (85 + 79 + 64 + 55 + 42 + 27 = 352) to arrive at 2,435 ÷ 352 = 6.917, or $6.92. *On average*, consumers are willing to pay $6.92 – $6.77 = $0.15, or 15 more cents for the brand name version than the store brand version.

> ✔ **Note**
>
> The preceding calculation can be quite time-consuming. If you are familiar with the weighted average formula, consider using it!
>
> Weighted Average = $w_1x_1 + w_2x_2 + w_3x_3$ ...
>
> Remember, w represents the percent occurrence (in decimal form) of each value, and x represents each value.

22. 1/3 or **.333**
Difficulty: Hard

Category: Problem Solving and Data Analysis / Statistics and Probability

Strategic Advice: In this question, you need to calculate a probability, which means you need to know the total (all the respondents in the survey) and the portion (respondents who are willing to pay at least $8) about which the question asks.

Getting to the Answer: First, find the number of respondents willing to pay at least $8 (which means $8 or more). Be careful—the question doesn't specify store brand or brand name, so use both versions of the product:

$$32 + 55 + 30 + 42 + 14 + 27 = 200$$

Now, find the total number of people in the survey. Again, the question doesn't specify store brand or brand name. You know from the previous question that 248 people responded to the store brand survey and 352 responded to the name brand survey, for a total of 600 respondents. This means the probability that a randomly chosen respondent is willing to pay at least $8 is $\frac{200}{600}$ or $\frac{1}{3}$.

CHAPTER 6

PREPARE

1. A
Difficulty: Easy

Category: Passport to Advanced Math / Exponents

Strategic Advice: Remember your exponent rules and what they do and do not allow.

Getting to the Answer: You can't simplify the expression as it's written, so break it into two fractions first. You can then subtract the exponents of the z terms in each fraction. Once finished, combine the two new fractions back into one. The work for these steps is shown here.

$$\frac{z^{570} - z^{480}}{2z^{30}} = \frac{z^{570}}{2z^{30}} - \frac{z^{480}}{2z^{30}}$$

$$\frac{z^{570}}{2z^{30}} - \frac{z^{480}}{2z^{30}} = \frac{z^{570-30}}{2} - \frac{z^{480-30}}{2}$$

$$\frac{z^{540}}{2} - \frac{z^{450}}{2} = \frac{z^{540} - z^{450}}{2}$$

(A) is the correct answer.

2. B
Difficulty: Easy

Category: Passport to Advanced Math / Exponents

Strategic Advice: Work with each component of the expression one at a time to minimize the chance of careless errors.

Getting to the Answer: Move the expression in parentheses to the denominator to make the sign of the exponent outside positive; do not change the signs of the exponents inside the parentheses. Next, distribute the exponent as usual. Divide the 2 into

−64, and move k^{-12} back to the numerator. Work for all steps is shown below.

$$2(-4j^3k^{-4})^{-3}$$

$$\frac{2}{(-4j^3k^{-4})^3}$$

$$\frac{\cancel{2}}{-\cancel{64}\, j^9 k^{-12}}$$

$$-\frac{k^{12}}{32j^9}$$

Choice (B) is the correct answer.

3. 9
Difficulty: Medium

Category: Passport to Advanced Math / Exponents

Strategic Advice: If you don't immediately see an obvious simplification route, look for links between different parts of the expression to help with rewriting it.

Getting to the Answer: Notice that $27 = 3^3$ and $81 = 3^4$. You can therefore rewrite the given expression as $\frac{3^5 \times (3^3)^3}{(3^4)^3}$, which becomes $\frac{3^5 \times 3^9}{3^{12}} = \frac{3^{14}}{3^{12}}$. Subtract the exponents to get 3^2, which becomes 9, the correct answer.

4. C
Difficulty: Medium

Category: Passport to Advanced Math / Exponents

Strategic Advice: Focus on the statements that appear easiest to verify first, and fight the urge to automatically lunge for the answer that "looks" false. Remember, you only need one example of a statement being true to eliminate it.

Getting to the Answer: D doesn't involve any math, so examine that one first. When a negative fraction is squared, the sign of the result is positive, so D is incorrect. Try C next: As you raise a negative fraction to higher powers, the absolute value of the result will decrease. This contradicts the inequality in (C) regardless of the value you pick for x, so it is the correct answer.

Picking Numbers is a quick route for checking A and B. Suppose $x = -\dfrac{1}{4}$ and $a = -4$: ax would equal 1, and $\sqrt{ax}$ would also equal 1, making A a true statement using these values. If $x = -\dfrac{1}{4}$ and $a = -16$, ax would equal 4, and $\sqrt{ax}$ would equal 2, which makes B true using these values.

5. A

Difficulty: Hard

Category: Passport to Advanced Math / Exponents

Strategic Advice: You can't simplify an expression that has different roots (in this case, third and sixth). Rewrite the expression with fraction exponents first, and then use exponent rules to simplify it.

Getting to the Answer: The rule for fraction exponents is "power over root"; use this to rewrite the expression.

$$\frac{\sqrt[6]{x^{10}y^{12}}}{\sqrt[3]{x^5y^6}} = \frac{x^{\frac{10}{6}}y^{\frac{12}{6}}}{x^{\frac{5}{3}}y^{\frac{6}{3}}}$$

When dividing like bases, subtract the exponents. Find common denominators as needed.

$$x^{\frac{10}{6}-\frac{5}{3}}y^{\frac{12}{6}-\frac{6}{3}} = x^{\frac{10}{6}-\frac{10}{6}}y^{\frac{12}{6}-\frac{12}{6}} = x^0y^0$$

Any number raised to the zero power becomes 1, so the expression becomes $1 \times 1 = 1$. (A) is correct.

6. D

Difficulty: Medium

Category: Passport to Advanced Math / Exponents

Strategic Advice: Remember how multiplicity of zeros works: the number of times a zero's corresponding binomial factor appears in a polynomial

equation dictates whether it is a simple zero, a double zero, etc.

Getting to the Answer: You're told that y has two zeros: one simple and one triple. This means you need one binomial expression raised to the first power and one raised to the third (because the latter is repeated three times). Eliminate B and C. Now examine the remaining choices; mental math reveals that they both have 4 and -4 as roots. The binomial leading to $x = -4$ should be raised to the third power, and the one that yields $x = 4$ should be raised to the first. Only (D) meets this criterion.

7. C

Difficulty: Medium

Category: Passport to Advanced Math / Exponents

Strategic Advice: Factor and cancel as much as you can, remembering the rules of simplifying rational expressions as you do so (meaning no canceling terms that are added or subtracted!).

Getting to the Answer: Start by factoring out the GCF of the two terms in the numerator, and then repeat with the denominator. The expressions left in both sets of parentheses are identical (once you apply the commutative property of addition), so you can cancel them.

$$\frac{27m^4n^3 + 6mn^2}{18m^2n + 81m^5n^2} = \frac{3mn^2(9m^3n + 2)}{9m^2n(2 + 9m^3n)}$$

Once here, you'll see that the GCF of the new numerator and denominator is $3mn$. Factor this out and cancel.

$$\frac{3mn^2}{9m^2n} = \frac{3mn(n)}{3mn(3m)}$$

The simplified expression is $\dfrac{n}{3m}$, which matches (C).

8. 7958

Difficulty: Medium

Category: Problem Solving and Data Analysis / Exponents

Strategic Advice: Word problems are always great opportunities to use the Kaplan Strategy for Translating English into Math. You'll have decimals early on and throughout your calculations, but do not round until the very end.

Getting to the Answer: The nice thing about this question is that some of the steps have been done for you: You already know your variables and are given an equation that relates them. All you need to do is plug in the appropriate values. You're told that $P = 300{,}000$, $r = \dfrac{0.03375}{12} = 0.0028125$ (because r is the monthly interest rate, not the annual rate), and $N = 12 \times 30 = 360$. Plug these values into the formula $m = \dfrac{Pr}{1 - (1+r)^{-N}}$, and then solve for m as shown below.

$$m = \frac{300000 \times 0.0028125}{1 - (1 + 0.0028125)^{-360}}$$

$$m = \frac{843.75}{1 - (1.0028125)^{-360}}$$

$$m = \frac{843.75}{0.6362}$$

$$m = 1{,}326.29$$

Don't stop yet! The question asks for the amount paid for the mortgage after six months, so multiply 1,326.2886 by 6 to get 7,957.7318. Round to 7958, and you're done!

Note that if you rounded 1,326.29 to 1,326, your answer would be off. Avoid rounding until you have your final answer

PRACTICE

9. D

Difficulty: Hard

Category: Passport to Advanced Math / Exponents

Strategic Advice: Don't stress over wordiness or bizarre science jargon in questions like this. All you need to do is solve for the correct variable.

Getting to the Answer: Relative velocity is represented by v, so that's the variable you need to isolate. The manipulation sequence is shown here.

$$\gamma = \frac{1}{\sqrt{1 - \dfrac{v^2}{c^2}}}$$

$$\gamma \sqrt{1 - \frac{v^2}{c^2}} = 1$$

$$\sqrt{1 - \frac{v^2}{c^2}} = \frac{1}{\gamma}$$

$$1 - \frac{v^2}{c^2} = \frac{1}{\gamma^2}$$

$$-\frac{v^2}{c^2} = \frac{1}{\gamma^2} - 1$$

$$v^2 = -c^2 \left(\frac{1}{\gamma^2} - 1 \right)$$

$$v = c\sqrt{1 - \frac{1}{\gamma^2}}$$

The correct answer is (D).

10. B

Difficulty: Medium

Category: Passport to Advanced Math / Exponents

Strategic Advice: Resist the urge to break the expression into two separate radicals; it will likely lead you to an incorrect answer! Look for a common factor instead.

Getting to the Answer: The GCF of the two expressions under the radical is $g^4 h^3$; factoring this out yields $\sqrt[3]{g^4 h^3 (g^2 - 27)}$. You can now pull a g and an h out from under the radical to obtain $gh\sqrt[3]{g(g^2 - 27)}$, which cannot be further simplified except for redistribution of g, which yields $gh\sqrt[3]{g^3 - 27g}$, making (B) correct. Note that $\sqrt[3]{g^3 - 27g}$ *does not* become $g - 3\sqrt[3]{g}$, as you cannot split the expression into two radicals.

11. D
Difficulty: Medium

Category: Passport to Advanced Math / Exponents

Strategic Advice: If you look closely, you'll notice you can do most of the math without a calculator by manipulating the exponents. For example, to convert 7.5×10^3 to a product of 10^6 and another number, move the decimal point in 7.5 three places to the left (the number of times you want to increase the exponent on 10), and write "$\times 10^6$" after it.

Getting to the Answer: Start by setting up a ratio that compares RBC count to total blood cell count. Manipulate the quantities to make all the exponents the same, factor out 10^6, and then add the quantities in parentheses together. Once there, you can use exponent rules to simplify your equation. Divide through and multiply by 100 to get the RBC component as a percentage. Work is shown here.

$$RBC = \frac{5.4 \times 10^6}{5.4 \times 10^6 + 7.5 \times 10^3 + 3.5 \times 10^5}$$

$$RBC = \frac{5.4 \times 10^6}{5.4 \times 10^6 + 0.0075 \times 10^6 + 0.35 \times 10^6}$$

$$RBC = \frac{5.4 \times 10^6}{10^6 (5.4 + 0.0075 + 0.35)}$$

$$RBC = \frac{5.4}{5.7575}$$

Note that the answer choices are, for the most part, far apart. Because 5.4 is relatively close to 5.7575, you can conclude with confidence that the correct answer is likely close to 100%. Therefore, (D) is the correct answer. If this question is in the calculator section, you can plug the numbers into your calculator to check:

$$\% \ RBC = \frac{5.4}{5.7575} \times 100 \approx 93.79\%$$

Choice (D) is still correct.

PERFORM

12. C
Difficulty: Medium

Category: Passport to Advanced Math / Exponents

Strategic Advice: Don't attempt to combine several steps when manipulating the equation; it's very easy for a small error to go unnoticed if you do so.

Getting to the Answer: Begin by moving all terms that don't contain an a to one side of the equation. Once there, multiply both sides by 2 to eliminate the fraction, and then divide by t^2 to isolate a. The manipulation sequence is shown here.

$$h = \frac{1}{2}at^2 + v_0 t + h_0$$

$$h - v_0 t - h_0 = \frac{1}{2}at^2$$

$$at^2 = 2(h - v_0 t - h_0)$$

$$a = \frac{2(h - v_0 t - h_0)}{t^2}$$

(C) is the correct answer.

13. A
Difficulty: Hard

Category: Passport to Advanced Math / Exponents

Strategic Advice: Remember to distribute properly when multiplying expressions.

Getting to the Answer: Start by simplifying the radicals: 72 is the product of 2 and 36, so $\sqrt{72} = 6\sqrt{2}$. You can then factor 3 out of the numerator and denominator to yield $\dfrac{3(1+2\sqrt{2})}{3(1-2\sqrt{2})}$. Cancel the 3s, and you're left with $\dfrac{1+2\sqrt{2}}{1-2\sqrt{2}}$. You can't leave a radical in the denominator, so you'll need to rationalize it. The conjugate of the denominator is $1+2\sqrt{2}$, so multiply the entire expression by $\dfrac{1+2\sqrt{2}}{1+2\sqrt{2}}$, and then simplify as usual (think FOIL):

$$\frac{1+2\sqrt{2}}{1-2\sqrt{2}} \times \frac{1+2\sqrt{2}}{1+2\sqrt{2}}$$

$$\frac{1+2\sqrt{2}+2\sqrt{2}+8}{(1-2\sqrt{2})(1+2\sqrt{2})}$$

$$\frac{1+2\sqrt{2}+2\sqrt{2}+8}{1+2\sqrt{2}-2\sqrt{2}-8}$$

$$\frac{9+4\sqrt{2}}{-7}$$

This expression matches (A).

14. 41

Difficulty: Hard

Category: Passport to Advanced Math / Exponents

Strategic Advice: This is the same formula you used in a previous question in this chapter; you're just looking for a different variable this time.

Getting to the Answer: Like in question 8, you're given all the variables you need and an equation that relates them. All you need to do is plug the given values into the correct locations ($m = 200$, $r = \dfrac{0.015}{12}$, $N = 60$) and solve for what's missing (P in this case). Decimals are truncated for brevity here, but no rounding was done until the final step.

$$m = \frac{Pr}{1-(1+r)^{-N}}$$

$$200 = \frac{P \times \dfrac{0.015}{12}}{1-\left(1+\dfrac{0.015}{12}\right)^{-60}}$$

$$200 = \frac{0.00125P}{1-(1+0.00125)^{-60}}$$

$$200 = \frac{0.00125P}{1-(1.00125)^{-60}}$$

$$200 = \frac{0.00125P}{1-0.9278}$$

$$14.4426 = 0.00125P$$

$$P = 11{,}554.0987$$

Subtract P from the total price (19,560) to obtain Teri's down payment. Divide this by 19,560 and multiply by 100 to arrive at 40.93%. Rounded properly, the correct answer is 41.

EXTRA PRACTICE

1. C

Difficulty: Easy

Category: Passport to Advanced Math / Exponents

Strategic Advice: A variable that has a fraction exponent can be written as a radical expression by writing the numerator as the power of the radicand and denominator as the degree of the root. You can remember this using the phrase "power over root." For example, $x^{\frac{2}{3}} = \sqrt[3]{x^2}$.

Getting to the Answer: Follow the standard order of operations—deal with the exponent first, and then attach the negative sign (because a negative in front of an expression means multiplication by –1). The variable x is being raised to the $\frac{1}{4}$ power, so rewrite the term as a radical expression with 4 as the degree of the root and 1 as the power to which the radicand, x, is being raised.

$$x^{\frac{1}{4}} = \sqrt[4]{x^1} = \sqrt[4]{x}$$

Now attach the negative to arrive at the correct answer, $-\sqrt[4]{x}$, which is (C).

2. C

Difficulty: Easy

Category: Passport to Advanced Math / Exponents

Strategic Advice: Solve equations containing radical expressions the same way you solve any other equation: isolate the variable using inverse operations.

Getting to the Answer: To get rid of the fraction, multiply both sides of the equation by 2. Then, divide by 7 to isolate the radical. Finally, square both sides to get rid of the radical and isolate x.

$$2 \cdot \left(\frac{7\sqrt{x}}{2} = 14 \right)$$
$$7\sqrt{x} = 28$$
$$\sqrt{x} = 4$$
$$(\sqrt{x})^2 = 4^2$$
$$x = 16$$

This means (C) is correct. You could also work backwards to answer this question, but only if you're comfortable finding square roots without a calculator.

3. B

Difficulty: Easy

Category: Passport to Advanced Math / Exponents

Strategic Advice: When you're asked to simplify a rational expression, look for common factors that can be divided out of the numerator and the denominator. If you find any common factors, you can cancel them. Keep in mind that you cannot cancel individual terms.

Getting to the Answer: Factor a 4 from the numerator and the denominator, and then cancel the $\frac{4}{4}$.

$$\frac{4x+8y}{24x-12}$$
$$= \frac{\cancel{4}(1x+2y)}{\cancel{4}(6x-3)}$$
$$= \frac{x+2y}{6x-3}$$

This matches (B).

4. D

Difficulty: Easy

Category: Passport to Advanced Math / Exponents

Strategic Advice: Distribute each term in the first factor to each term in the second factor (FOIL). Be careful with the signs.

Getting to the Answer:

$$(-x + 6)(2x - 3) = -x(2x - 3) + 6(2x - 3)$$
$$= -2x^2 + 3x + 12x - 18$$
$$= -2x^2 + 15x - 18$$

Be careful—the question asks for the coefficient of x, not x^2, so the answer is 15, which is (D).

5. C
Difficulty: Easy

Category: Passport to Advanced Math / Exponents

Strategic Advice: When the denominators of rational expressions are the same, you can combine the numerators and keep the same denominator, just like you do when adding or subtracting plain fractions.

Getting to the Answer: First, write the question as a subtraction problem. Pay careful attention to which expression is being subtracted.

$$\frac{8x-5}{x-1} - \frac{3x+7}{x-1}$$

The terms in the expression have the same denominator, $x - 1$, so their numerators can be subtracted. Simply combine like terms and keep the denominator the same. Don't forget to distribute the negative to both $3x$ and 7.

$$\frac{8x-5}{x-1} - \frac{3x+7}{x-1} = \frac{8x-5-3x-7}{x-1} = \frac{5x-12}{x-1}$$

The reduced expression matches (C).

6. D
Difficulty: Medium

Category: Passport to Advanced Math / Exponents

Strategic Advice: A *double zero* occurs in a polynomial when a factor is repeated, or in other words, squared. For example, the factor $(x - a)$ produces a simple zero at $x = a$, while $(x - b)^2$ produces a double zero at $x = b$. Graphically, this means that the polynomial *crosses* the axis at $x = a$, but just *touches* the x-axis (and then turns around) at $x = b$.

Getting to the Answer: The polynomial has a simple zero at $x = -3$, which corresponds to a factor of $(x + 3)$. The double zero at $x = \frac{5}{4}$ results from a repeated (squared) factor, so you can eliminate A and C. To choose between B and (D), set each factor equal to 0, and then use inverse operations to solve for x (mentally if possible). Choice (D) is correct because:

$$4x - 5 = 0$$
$$4x = 5$$
$$x = \frac{5}{4}$$

7. B
Difficulty: Medium

Category: Passport to Advanced Math / Exponents

Strategic Advice: Don't let all the scientific terminology intimidate you. All you need to do is to solve the equation for T using inverse operations.

Getting to the Answer: Start by getting T out of the denominator of the fraction. To do this, multiply both sides of the equation by T, and then divide both sides by v.

$$v = \frac{2\pi r}{T}$$
$$T \times (v) = \left(\frac{2\pi r}{T}\right) \times T$$
$$Tv = 2\pi r$$
$$T = \frac{2\pi r}{v}$$

Choice (B) is the correct answer.

8. B

Difficulty: Medium

Category: Passport to Advanced Math / Exponents

Strategic Advice: This question would probably be fairly easy if you were allowed to use a calculator. Keep in mind, however, that radicals can definitely show up on the No-calculator section of the test.

Getting to the Answer: Chances are that the test makers do not expect you to multiply decimals and then take a square root. Rather, the decimals are likely to have fairly common fraction equivalents that will multiply together nicely. Start with that:

$$\sqrt{0.75} \times \sqrt{0.8} = \sqrt{\frac{3}{4}} \times \sqrt{\frac{4}{5}} = \sqrt{\frac{3}{\cancel{4}} \times \frac{\cancel{4}}{5}} = \sqrt{\frac{3}{5}} = \frac{\sqrt{3}}{\sqrt{5}}$$

Don't forget—you're not allowed to leave a radical in the denominator of a fraction, so you need to rationalize the denominator. To do this, multiply the top and bottom of the fraction by the radical in the bottom. The result is $\frac{\sqrt{3}}{\sqrt{5}} \times \frac{\sqrt{5}}{\sqrt{5}} = \frac{\sqrt{15}}{5}$, which matches (B).

9. A

Difficulty: Medium

Category: Passport to Advanced Math / Exponents

Strategic Advice: You could rewrite the fraction exponent using a radical, find the largest perfect cube that divides into each factor, and bring the cube roots outside the radical. However, writing 27 as 3^3 and then using rules of exponents is most likely the faster route. Don't forget—when you raise an exponent to an exponent, you multiply the exponents.

Getting to the Answer:

$$(27x^6y^{12})^{\frac{1}{3}}$$
$$= 3^{3 \times \frac{1}{3}} x^{6 \times \frac{1}{3}} y^{12 \times \frac{1}{3}}$$
$$= 3x^2y^4$$

Choice (A) is correct.

10. A

Difficulty: Medium

Category: Passport to Advanced Math / Exponents

Strategic Advice: Solve equations containing radical expressions the same way you solve any other equation: isolate the variable using inverse operations. Try not to be concerned by how many parts there are to the equation in this question. Perform one inverse operation at a time, working your way toward getting the variable out of the radical and then by itself.

Getting to the Answer: Start by subtracting 8 from both sides of the equation, and then multiply by 3. Then, square both sides to remove the radical.

$$8 + \frac{\sqrt{2x+29}}{3} = 9$$
$$\frac{\sqrt{2x+29}}{3} = 1$$
$$\sqrt{2x+29} = 3$$
$$2x + 29 = 9$$

Now you have a simple linear equation that you can solve using more inverse operations: subtract 29 and divide by 2 to find that $x = -10$. Be careful—just because the equation started with a radical and the answer is negative, does not mean that *No solution* is the correct answer. If you plug -10 into the expression under the radical, the result is a positive number, which means -10 is a perfectly valid solution. Therefore, (A) is correct.

11. C

Difficulty: Medium

Category: Passport to Advanced Math / Exponents

Strategic Advice: Look for a common factor that can be divided out of the numerator and the denominator. If you find one, you can cancel it. It will save time if you look for the greatest common factor.

Getting to the Answer: Factor out the GCF of *both* the numerator and the denominator. Then cancel what you can. In this expression, the GCF is $3x^2y$.

$$\frac{12x^3y^2 - 9x^2y}{6x^4y + 18x^3y^3}$$

$$= \frac{3x^2y(4xy - 3)}{3x^2y(2x^2 + 6xy^2)}$$

$$= \frac{4xy - 3}{2x^2 + 6xy^2}$$

This matches (C).

12. B
Difficulty: Medium

Category: Passport to Advanced Math / Exponents

Strategic Advice: Look closely at the dividend and the divisor. The divisor, $5x$, can be divided into each term in the dividend evenly, which means you don't need to use polynomial long division. Just divide each term by $5x$ and leave the signs the same.

Getting to the Answer: You could divide each term mentally, but it may be safer to write each term over $5x$, and then use rules of exponents to simplify.

$$\frac{30x^3}{5x} + \frac{45x^2}{5x} - \frac{10x}{5x} = 6x^2 + 9x - 2$$

The question asks for the coefficient of x, so the correct answer is 9, which is (B).

13. D
Difficulty: Medium

Category: Passport to Advanced Math / Exponents

Strategic Advice: Just as with rational expressions, factoring out the GCF of the terms is a great way to start a question like this.

Getting to the Answer: The GCF of the terms under the radical is m^4n^2. Factor this out and see if you can take the square root of anything:

$$\sqrt{9m^5n^2 - m^4n^2} = \sqrt{m^4n^2(9m - 1)}$$
$$= m^2n\sqrt{9m - 1}$$

The result matches (D).

14. B
Difficulty: Medium

Category: Passport to Advanced Math / Exponents

Strategic Advice: This is another question that involves a science formula and, although interesting to learn about, may use up valuable time on Test Day. To save time, skim the first couple of sentences and look for the actual question near the end. Chances are that you'll either be plugging a value into the formula, or solving the formula for a specific variable.

Getting to the Answer: The question asks you to solve the equation for L. Use inverse operations to accomplish the task: divide both sides of the equation by 2π and then square both sides. You'll need to apply the exponent to all the terms on the left side of the equation, including the π:

$$T = 2\pi\sqrt{\frac{L}{g}}$$

$$\frac{T}{2\pi} = \sqrt{\frac{L}{g}}$$

$$\left(\frac{T}{2\pi}\right)^2 = \left(\sqrt{\frac{L}{g}}\right)^2$$

$$\frac{T^2}{4\pi^2} = \frac{L}{g}$$

Finally, multiply both sides by g to remove g from the denominator and isolate L.

$$L = \frac{gT^2}{4\pi^2}$$

The correct answer is (B).

15. D

Difficulty: Hard

Category: Passport to Advanced Math / Exponents

Strategic Advice: When adding and subtracting long polynomials, writing the problem vertically will help you stay organized.

Getting to the Answer: Multiply each term in the first expression by $\frac{3}{2}$ and each term in the second expression by –2. Then add the two polynomials by writing them vertically and combining like terms.

$$\frac{3}{2}A = \frac{3}{2}\left(4x^2 + 7x - 1\right) = 6x^2 + \frac{21}{2}x - \frac{3}{2}$$

$$-2B = -2\left(-x^2 - 5x + 3\right) = 2x^2 + 10x - 6$$

$$\begin{array}{r} 6x^2 + \dfrac{21}{2}x - \dfrac{3}{2} \\ + \ 2x^2 + \dfrac{20}{2}x - \dfrac{12}{2} \\ \hline 8x^2 + \dfrac{41}{2}x - \dfrac{15}{2} \end{array}$$

This means (D) is correct.

16. A

Difficulty: Hard

Category: Passport to Advanced Math / Exponents

Strategic Advice: It is not possible to add, subtract, multiply, or divide radicals that represent roots of different degrees (such as a square root and a cube root) when they are written in radical form. Instead, you must write the radicals using fraction exponents and then use rules of exponents to combine the terms. Keep in mind that this is a non-calculator question.

Getting to the Answer: Write each radical using a fraction exponent, and then use the rule $a^x \times a^y = a^{x+y}$ to answer the question.

$$\sqrt{2} \times \sqrt[4]{2} = 2^{\frac{1}{2}} \times 2^{\frac{1}{4}}$$
$$= 2^{\frac{1}{2}+\frac{1}{4}}$$
$$= 2^{\frac{2}{4}+\frac{1}{4}}$$
$$= 2^{\frac{3}{4}}$$

The answers are written in radical, so convert back to radicals using the saying "power over root." The result is $\sqrt[4]{2^3} = \sqrt[4]{8}$, which is (A).

17. 10/3

Difficulty: Hard

Category: Passport to Advanced Math / Exponents

Strategic Advice: Rewrite the radicals as fraction exponents: $\sqrt[3]{x} = x^{\frac{1}{3}}$ and $\sqrt{x} = x^{\frac{1}{2}}$.

Getting to the Answer: Write each factor in the expression in exponential form. Then use the rules of exponents to simplify the expression. Add the exponents of the factors that are being multiplied and subtract the exponent of the factor that is being divided:

$$\frac{\sqrt[3]{x} \cdot x^{\frac{5}{2}} \cdot x}{\sqrt{x}} = \frac{x^{\frac{1}{3}} \cdot x^{\frac{5}{2}} \cdot x^1}{x^{\frac{1}{2}}} = x^{\frac{1}{3}+\frac{5}{2}+\frac{1}{1}-\frac{1}{2}} = x^{\frac{2}{6}+\frac{15}{6}+\frac{6}{6}-\frac{3}{6}}$$

$$= x^{\frac{20}{6}} = x^{\frac{10}{3}}.$$

The question states that n is the power of x, so the value of n is $\frac{10}{3}$.

You can check your answer by choosing a value for x and plugging the original expression into your calculator and comparing it to the result when you plug the same value for x into the reduced expression.

18. 21

Difficulty: Hard

Category: Passport to Advanced Math / Exponents

Strategic Advice: The math itself is not difficult in this question. However, there are a lot of operations in the equation, so there will be a lot of steps to solving it. Be patient, carefully performing one step at a time.

Getting to the Answer: Solve this radical equation the same way you would solve any other equation: isolate the variable using inverse operations.

$$12 + \frac{3\sqrt{x-5}}{2} = 18 \qquad \text{Subtract 12.}$$

$$\frac{3\sqrt{x-5}}{2} = 6 \qquad \text{Multiply by 2.}$$

$$3\sqrt{x-5} = 12 \qquad \text{Divide by 3.}$$

$$\sqrt{x-5} = 4 \qquad \text{Square both sides.}$$

$$x - 5 = 16 \qquad \text{Add 5.}$$

$$x = 21$$

The correct answer is 21. This is a Grid-in question, so if you have time it wouldn't hurt to check your answer by plugging 21 back into the original equation.

CHAPTER 7

PREPARE

1. C
Difficulty: Easy

Category: Passport to Advanced Math / Functions & Function Notation

Strategic Advice: Ready your English-math translation skills for this question.

Getting to the Answer: Examine each piece of the question stem individually. "The cube of x" becomes x^3, and "the fourth root of the sum of three and the square of the product of two and x" becomes $\sqrt[4]{3+(2x)^2}$. The former is subtracted from the latter, so the right side of your inequality should be $\sqrt[4]{3+(2x)^2} - x^3$. The question states that this quantity is less than $f(x)$; after simplifying the radicand, you'll have $f(x) > \sqrt[4]{3+4x^2} - x^3$. (C) is correct.

2. B
Difficulty: Easy

Category: Passport to Advanced Math / Functions & Function Notation

Strategic Advice: Interpret each function's graph carefully to ensure you pick the correct points.

Getting to the Answer: Start with $h(0)$; according to the graph, $h(0) = 4$. Repeat with $g(x)$ ($= 8$) and $f(x)$ ($= 3$). Manipulate these values as instructed: $4 - 3(8 - 5) = 4 - 15 = -11$. (B) is correct.

3. A
Difficulty: Medium

Category: Passport to Advanced Math / Functions & Function Notation

Strategic Advice: Reduce the amount of work required by determining the y-intercept of the function.

Getting to the Answer: The table indicates that Clara had 21 votes on day 3, not at the start of the contest. This means that C and D are incorrect. To determine whether (A) or B is correct, pick a point to try in both functions.

$$
\begin{aligned}
\text{(A): } 35 &= 2 \times 4^2 + 3 \\
35 &= 2 \times 16 + 3 \\
35 &= 32 + 3 \\
35 &= 35 \\
\text{B: } 35 &= \frac{1}{2} \times 4^2 + 3 \\
35 &= \frac{1}{2} \times 16 + 3 \\
35 &= 8 + 3 \\
35 &\neq 11
\end{aligned}
$$

(A) is correct.

4. C
Difficulty: Medium

Category: Passport to Advanced Math / Functions & Function Notation

Strategic Advice: There's a lot going on in this question. Use the Kaplan Strategy for Translating English Into Math to help you keep everything organized.

Getting to the Answer: Variables have been defined for you, so there's no work to do there. Consider the functions one at a time. The function $g(x)$ represents 5% cash back on gasoline purchases up to $1,500, which translates to $g(x) = 0.05x$. A cardholder only gets 5% on purchases up to $1,500, so the function domain is restricted to $0 \leq x \leq 1,500$. Similarly, $e(x)$ represents 2% cash back. However, this is for purchases past $1,500, so the function must involve subtracting 1,500 from x. Multiplying the difference by 0.02 means $e(x) = 0.02(x - 1,500)$ with the domain restricted to $x > 1,500$. Only choice (C) contains both functions.

5. D

Difficulty: Easy

Category: Passport to Advanced Math / Functions & Function Notation

Strategic Advice: Read carefully; it's easy to make a mistake with such similar expressions in the numerator and denominator.

Getting to the Answer: Find the numerator and denominator separately:

$$p(5) = 5^2 - 4 \times 5 + 8 = 13$$
$$q(p(5)) = q(13) = 13 - 3 = 10$$
$$q(5) = 5 - 3 = 2$$
$$p(q(5)) = p(2) = 2^2 - 4 \times 2 + 8 = 4$$

Then combine properly:

$$\frac{q(p(5))}{p(q(5))} = \frac{10}{4} = 2.5$$

The correct answer is (D).

6. D

Difficulty: Medium

Category: Passport to Advanced Math / Functions & Function Notation

Strategic Advice: Think about the order in which the two functions must be computed to obtain Everett's pay.

Getting to the Answer: The question implies that Everett's commission depends on his sales over $4,000, which means your composition of functions should read $(c \circ e)(s)$. Because Everett's $1,000 base salary is independent of his sales, it should not be in the function argument (inside the parentheses with s). Therefore, the correct function is $(c \circ e)(s) + 1,000$, which is (D).

7. A

Difficulty: Medium

Category: Passport to Advanced Math / Functions & Function Notation

Strategic Advice: Read the transformation sequence carefully before selecting an answer.

Getting to the Answer: A horizontal compression requires the domain variable (x here) to have a coefficient greater than 1; eliminate D, which does not contain a coefficient greater than 1. A reflection about the x-axis (vertical) requires a negative sign before the function variable (j in this question). Eliminate C. An upward shift means the constant quantifying the shift must be outside the function argument parentheses. Only (A) contains all three transformations.

PRACTICE

8. C

Difficulty: Hard

Category: Passport to Advanced Math / Functions & Function Notation

Strategic Advice: Beware extraneous information; focus on what will get you to the answer.

Getting to the Answer: You're told the honeybee population decreases 35% each month; this means exponential decay is occurring, so use $y = x_0 (1 + r)^x$ as your function template. Set p as the honeybee population and t as the time in months; watch the sign of r. Your function should be $p(t) = (4.23 \times 10^8)(0.65)^t$. Now plug in the time in months:

$p(12) = (4.23 \times 10^8)(0.65)^{12} \approx 2{,}406{,}028$. The correct answer is (C).

9. C

Difficulty: Medium

Category: Passport to Advanced Math / Functions & Function Notation

Strategic Advice: Think critically: Once you realize that *b* follows *a*, you know that this composition of functions is really taking the reciprocal of *a*(*x*).

Getting to the Answer: Remember how to translate function notation into something useful: $(b \circ a)(x)$ means *b*(*x*) follows *a*(*x*) (in other words, *b*(*a*(*x*))). You can rewrite this as $\frac{1}{a(x)}$, which you should recognize as the reciprocal of *a*(*x*). This new function will be undefined anywhere that *a*(*x*) = 0. Looking at the graph, you can see that a(*x*) crosses the *x*-axis four times, making choice (C) correct.

PERFORM

10. B

Difficulty: Hard

Category: Passport to Advanced Math / Functions & Function Notation

Strategic Advice: Don't panic about this involving a trigonometric function; the standard transformation rules apply.

Getting to the Answer: The easiest transformation to identify is the –4 downward shift. Eliminate C and D, as neither contains this shift. Both A and (B) contain a vertical expansion, but the difference is subtle, so hone in on the transformed function's horizontal compression effected by the 2 in parentheses. Choice (B) has a compressed sine graph, so it is correct.

11. A

Difficulty: Hard

Category: Passport to Advanced Math / Functions & Function Notation

Strategic Advice: Determine how many prose pages Briana can type per minute, then assemble your function accordingly.

Getting to the Answer: Use the two given rates to determine Briana's typing rate in pages per minute. She types 45 words per minute, which becomes $\frac{45 \text{ words}}{1 \text{ min}} \times \frac{1 \text{ page}}{500 \text{ words}} = \frac{45 \text{ pages}}{500 \text{ min}} = \frac{9 \text{ pages}}{100 \text{ min}}$. Multiplying this rate by *m* gets you the number of pages typed after *m* minutes, which can then be subtracted from the starting page count (60) to get the number of pages Briana has left to type. The function should read $p(m) = 60 - \frac{9m}{100}$, which matches (A).

12. D

Difficulty: Medium

Category: Passport to Advanced Math / Functions & Function Notation

Strategic Advice: Use your knowledge of function increases and decreases.

Getting to the Answer: Examine the graph. A peak in fuel economy at 50 mph is obvious, but what else can be said? A closer look at the increase below 50 mph and the decrease below 50 mph reveals a critical detail: that the decreasing part of the graph is steeper than the increase. This means the rate of decrease is faster than the rate of increase. This corresponds to (D).

EXTRA PRACTICE

1. A

Difficulty: Easy

Category: Passport to Advanced Math / Functions & Function Notation

Strategic Advice: Understanding function notation will serve you well on Test Day. The notation $g(-2)$ means the value of the function when $x = -2$.

Getting to the Answer: Substitute -2 for x and simplify. Don't forget to use the correct order of operations as you work:

$$g(-2) = -2(-2)^2 + 7(-2) - 3$$
$$= -2(4) + (-14) - 3$$
$$= -8 - 14 - 3$$
$$= -25$$

Choice (A) is correct.

2. A

Difficulty: Easy

Category: Passport to Advanced Math / Functions & Function Notation

Strategic Advice: The notation $k(x)$ is read k of x and means the range value (output) of the function that corresponds to a given domain value (input). So $k(4)$ means the output value of the function when 4 is substituted for the input (x), and $k(1)$ means the output value of the function when 1 is substituted for the input (x).

Getting to the Answer: Substitute 4 and 1 into the function, one at a time, and then subtract the results.

$$k(4) = 5(4) + 2 = 20 + 2 = 22$$
$$k(1) = 5(1) + 2 = 5 + 2 = 7$$
$$22 - 7 = 15$$

Choice (A) is correct. Caution—this is not the same as subtracting $4 - 1$ and then substituting 3 into the function!

3. D

Difficulty: Medium

Category: Passport to Advanced Math / Functions & Function Notation

Strategic Advice: To determine the domain, look at the x-values. To determine the range, look at the y-values.

Getting to the Answer: For the domain, the graph is continuous (no holes or gaps in the graph) and has arrows on both sides, so the domain is all real numbers. This means you can eliminate A and B. For the range, the function's maximum (the vertex) is located at $(-3, 4)$, which means the highest possible y-value of $f(x)$ is 4. The graph is continuous and opens downward, so the range of the function is $y \leq 4$, which is the same as $f(x) \leq 4$, making (D) correct.

4. D

Difficulty: Medium

Category: Passport to Advanced Math / Functions & Function Notation

Strategic Advice: Draw a quick sketch of the equation (or graph it in your graphing calculator).

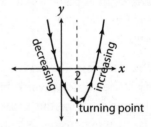

Getting to the Answer: Based on the equation, the graph is a parabola that opens upward with a vertex of $(2, -5)$. A parabola changes direction at the x-coordinate of its vertex. This is all the information you need to answer the question. You can immediately eliminate A and B. To choose between C and (D), take a closer look at the sketch. To the left of 2 (or $x < 2$), the parabola is decreasing, and to the right of 2 (or $x > 2$), it is increasing. This makes (D) correct.

5. B

Difficulty: Medium

Category: Passport to Advanced Math / Functions & Function Notation

Strategic Advice: When finding values associated with function notation, you almost always have to decide whether you're plugging something in for *x* or solving for *x*.

Getting to the Answer: In this question, you are given a range value (14), which means $f(x) = 14$, and you are asked for the corresponding domain value (*x*-value). This means you are solving for *x*, not substituting for *x*. Set the function equal to 14 and solve using inverse operations:

$$14 = \frac{x^2}{4} - 11$$
$$25 = \frac{x^2}{4}$$
$$100 = x^2$$
$$\pm 10 = x$$

Negative 10 is not one of the answer choices, so (B) is correct.

6. C

Difficulty: Medium

Category: Passport to Advanced Math / Functions & Function Notation

Strategic Advice: Use the properties of the absolute value function to quickly hone in on the right answer.

Getting to the Answer: The function graphed is the absolute value function, and you can see that all values in its range are positive. That makes the negative value in (C) impossible. Because you're looking for the statement that is NOT true, you can safely conclude that (C) is correct.

7. C

Difficulty: Medium

Category: Passport to Advanced Math / Functions & Function Notation

Strategic Advice: Piecewise functions look intimidating, but they are usually very simple functions—they're just written in pieces. Your job is to figure out which piece of the function you need to use to answer the question.

Getting to the Answer: The right-hand side of each piece of the function tells you what part of the domain (which *x*-values) goes with that particular expression. In this function, only values of *x* that are less than or equal to zero go with the top expression, values of *x* greater than zero and less than or equal to 3 go with the middle expression, and values of *x* that are greater than 3 go with the bottom expression. Because –3 is less than 0, plug it into the top expression and simplify:

$$f(-3) = (-3)^2 + 1$$
$$= 9 + 1$$
$$= 10$$

This matches (C).

8. D

Difficulty: Medium

Category: Passport to Advanced Math / Functions & Function Notation

Strategic Advice: Pay careful attention to the axis labels as you read the answer choices. Time is graphed on the *x*-axis, and distance is graphed on the *y*-axis.

Getting to the Answer: Compare each answer choice to the graph, eliminating false statements as you go.

Choice A: Carmel went to the library first, so the library (not the grocery store) is about 5 miles from his home. Eliminate this choice.

Choice B: Carmel traveled 7 miles away from his home (between $t = 0$ minutes and $t = 30$ minutes), but then also traveled 7 miles back (between $t = 45$ minutes and $t = 60$ minutes), so he traveled a total of 14 miles. Eliminate this choice.

Choice C: When Carmel reached the library, he was 5 miles from home; when he reached the grocery store, he was 7 miles from home. This means the grocery store must be 7 − 5 = 2 miles farther away. Eliminate this choice.

Choice (D) must be correct. Carmel is the same distance from home (5 miles) between $t = 15$ minutes and $t = 25$ minutes, so he spent 10 minutes at the library. He is stopped once again (at the grocery store) between $t = 30$ minutes and $t = 45$ minutes, so he spent 15 minutes at the grocery store.

9. C
Difficulty: Medium

Category: Passport to Advanced Math / Functions & Function Notation

Strategic Advice: Graphically, the notation $f(-2)$ means the *y*-value when *x* is −2. Pay careful attention to which graph is which. It may help to draw dots on the graph.

Getting to the Answer: Find $x = -2$ along the horizontal axis, trace up to the graph of $f(x)$, and draw a dot on the graph. Do the same for $g(2)$, as shown below:

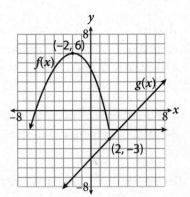

Now, read the *y*-coordinates from the graph and subtract: $f(-2)$ is 6 and $g(2)$ is −3, so $f(-2) + g(2) = 6 + (-3) = 3$, which is (C).

10. C
Difficulty: Medium

Category: Passport to Advanced Math / Functions & Function Notation

Strategic Advice: Transformations that are grouped with the *x* in a function shift the graph horizontally and therefore affect the *x*-coordinates of points on the graph. Transformations that are not grouped with the *x* shift the graph vertically and therefore affect the *y*-coordinates of points on the graph. Remember, horizontal shifts are always the reverse of what they look like. When working with multiple transformations, follow the same order of operations as always—parentheses first, then multiply and divide, then add and subtract.

Getting to the Answer: Start with the parentheses: $(x − 2)$. This shifts the graph right 2 units, so add 2 to the *x*-coordinate of the given point: $(5, 3) \rightarrow (5 + 2, 3) = (7, 3)$. Next, apply the negative in front of *g* because it represents multiplication. The negative is not grouped with the *x*, so multiply the *y*-coordinate by −1 to get $(7, 3(-1)) \rightarrow (7, -3)$. Finally, the +8 is not grouped with *x*, so add 8 to the *y*-coordinate: $(7, -3) \rightarrow (7, -3 + 8) = (7, 5)$, which matches (C).

You could also plot the point on a coordinate plane, perform the transformations (right 2, reflect vertically over the *x*-axis, and then up 8), to find the new point. The result will be the same.

11. A
Difficulty: Hard

Category: Passport to Advanced Math / Functions & Function Notation

Strategic Advice: The notation $(f \circ g)(x)$ indicates a composition of two functions that can also be written as $f(g(x))$ and is read "*f* of *g* of *x*." It means that the output when *x* is substituted into $g(x)$ becomes the input for $f(x)$.

Getting to the Answer: Substitute 6 for *x* in $g(x)$, simplify, and then substitute the result into $f(x)$:

$$g(6) = \frac{6}{4} - 1 = \frac{3}{2} - 1 = \frac{3}{2} - \frac{2}{2} = \frac{1}{2}$$

$$f\left(\frac{1}{2}\right) = \left(\frac{1}{2}\right)^2 + \frac{5}{2} = \frac{1}{4} + \frac{5}{2} = \frac{1}{4} + \frac{10}{4} = \frac{11}{4}$$

So $(f \circ g)(6) = \frac{11}{4} = 2.75$, making (A) the correct choice.

12. B
Difficulty: Hard

Category: Passport to Advanced Math / Functions & Function Notation

Strategic Advice: The key to answering this question is to have a conceptual understanding of function notation. Here, the input $(x + 2)$ has already been substituted and simplified in the given function. Your job is to determine what the function would have looked like had x been the input instead.

Getting to the Answer: To keep things organized, let $u = x + 2$, the old input. This means $x = u - 2$. Substitute this into p and simplify:

$$\begin{aligned}
p(u - 2) &= 3(u - 2)^2 + 4(u - 2) + 1 \\
&= 3(u^2 - 4u + 4) + 4u - 8 + 1 \\
&= 3u^2 - 12u + 12 + 4u - 8 + 1 \\
&= 3u^2 - 8u + 5
\end{aligned}$$

Because we defined x as $u - 2$, this means $p(u) = 3u^2 - 8u + 5$.

When working with function notation, you evaluate the function by substituting a given input value for the variable in the parentheses. Here, if the input value is x, then $p(x) = 3x^2 - 8x + 5$, which means (B) is correct.

13. 3.5 or 3.50
Difficulty: Medium

Category: Passport to Advanced Math / Functions & Function Notation

Strategic Advice: This is a fairly straightforward question, but be careful to check that you answered the right question (how much more profits *per unit* at a selling price of $25 than at $20).

Getting to the Answer: Start by evaluating the function at $x = 25$ and at $x = 20$. Make sure you follow the correct order of operations as you simplify.

$$\begin{aligned}
P(25) &= 150(25) - (25)^2 \\
&= 3{,}750 - 625 \\
&= 3{,}125 \\
P(20) &= 150(20) - (20)^2 \\
&= 3{,}000 - 400 \\
&= 2{,}600
\end{aligned}$$

The question asks how much more profit *per unit* the company makes, so find the difference in the amounts of profit and divide by the number of units (150) to get $\frac{3{,}125 - 2{,}600}{150} = \frac{525}{150} = \$3.50$, or 3.5.

14. 305

Difficulty: Medium

Category: Passport to Advanced Math / Functions & Function Notation

Strategic Advice: Always pay careful attention to what the variable in a function represents, especially in questions that deal with real-world scenarios. In this question, t does *not* represent the time, so don't find $C(5)$. Rather, you need to start by finding the number of hours that pass between 7 AM and 5 PM.

Getting to the Answer: Because there are 10 hours between 7 AM and 5 PM, evaluate the function at $t = 10$. Make sure you follow the correct order of operations as you simplify.

$$
\begin{aligned}
C(t) &= -0.0815t^4 + t^3 + 12t \\
C(10) &= -0.0815(10)^4 + (10)^3 + 12(10) \\
&= -0.0815(10{,}000) + 1{,}000 + 120 \\
&= -815 + 1{,}000 + 120 \\
&= 305
\end{aligned}
$$

CHAPTER 8

PREPARE

1. B
Difficulty: Easy

Category: Passport to Advanced Math / Quadratics

Strategic Advice: Whenever you see binomials, think FOIL. Here, no rearranging is necessary, so you can go right into it!

Getting to the Answer: FOIL the binomials $(6 - 5x)$ $(15x - 11)$: First, Outer, Inner, Last. First: $(6)(15x) = 90x$. Outer: $(6)(-11) = -66$. Inner: $(-5x)(15x) = -75x^2$. Last: $(-5x)(-11) = 55x$. Add all the terms together and combine like terms: $90x - 66 - 75x^2 + 55x = -75x^2 + 145x - 66$. The correct answer is (B)

2. C
Difficulty: Easy

Category: Passport to Advanced Math / Quadratics

Strategic Advice: Unless you are asked to match a graph, you should try to factor quadratics. Whenever you have a fraction containing quadratics, something will usually cancel out.

Getting to the Answer: To factor the numerator and denominator into binomials, you should first factor out a 3 in the denominator to make that quadratic a bit simpler. Then use the quadratic shortcuts on the numerator and denominator to reveal an $x - 5$ term that will cancel out:

$$\frac{x^2 - 10x + 25}{3x^2 - 75} = \frac{(x-5)(x-5)}{3(x^2 - 25)}$$

$$= \frac{(x-5)(x-5)}{3(x-5)(x+5)} = \frac{(x-5)}{3(x+5)}$$

The correct answer is (C).

3. D
Difficulty: Medium

Category: Passport to Advanced Math / Quadratics

Strategic Advice: When something doesn't factor cleanly, consider completing the square or using the quadratic formula.

Getting to the Answer: Factoring won't work here. However, the coefficient of x^2 is 1, so try completing the square:

$$x^2 + 2x - 5 = 0$$
$$x^2 + 2x = 5$$
$$\left(\frac{b}{2}\right)^2 = \left(\frac{2}{2}\right)^2 = 1^2 = 1$$
$$x^2 + 2x + 1 = 5 + 1$$
$$(x+1)^2 = 6$$
$$x + 1 = \pm\sqrt{6}$$
$$x = -1 \pm \sqrt{6}$$

Choice (D) matches one of the two possible values of x, so it's the correct answer.

4. C
Difficulty: Medium

Category: Passport to Advanced Math / Quadratics

Strategic Advice: The x-coordinates of a function are the values of x that make the function equal 0.

Getting to the Answer: Set the equation equal to zero. Direct factoring is impossible because the coefficient of x^2 isn't 1, but you can use the grouping technique. Identify two numbers whose product is ac and whose sum is b

$$3x^2 - 2x - 8 = 0$$
$$3x^2 - 6x + 4x - 8 = 0$$
$$3x(x - 2) + 4(x - 2) = 0$$
$$(3x + 4)(x - 2) = 0$$
$$(3x + 4) = 0 \text{ or } (x - 2) = 0$$
$$x = -\frac{4}{3} \text{ or } x = 2$$

The answer is (C).

5. B

Difficulty: Medium

Category: Passport to Advanced Math / Quadratics

Strategic Advice: Use your knowledge of parabolas to evaluate each choice systematically.

Getting to the Answer: Keep in mind that the question asks for the statement that's false, so eliminate the true choices as you go. The parabola opens downward, so the a term should be negative. Eliminate A. The parabola's vertex is in quadrant I, so h and k are both positive. That makes choice D true as well; eliminate it. The axis of symmetry is $x = h$, so $x = 3$. Choice B, however, claims that the axis of symmetry is $y = 3$—a common mistake. The line $y = 3$ is horizontal, and a horizontal line cannot be the axis of symmetry for *any* parabolic function. (B) is false and is therefore the correct answer.

C is a true statement because the line $g(x) = \dfrac{2x}{3}$ passes through the point (3, 2), which is indeed the vertex of $f(x)$.

6. C

Difficulty: Hard

Category: Passport to Advanced Math / Quadratics

Strategic Advice: When factoring, grouping, and completing the square are all unavailable, it's time to whip out the quadratic formula!

Getting to the Answer: Plug values carefully into the quadratic formula to solve for x.

$$2x^2 - 5x - 2 = 0$$

$$x = \frac{-b \pm \sqrt{b^2 - 4ac}}{2a}$$

$$x = \frac{-(-5) \pm \sqrt{(-5)^2 - 4(2)(-2)}}{2(2)}$$

$$x = \frac{5 \pm \sqrt{25 - (-16)}}{4}$$

$$x = \frac{5 \pm \sqrt{41}}{4}$$

$$x = \frac{5}{4} + \frac{\sqrt{41}}{4} \text{ or } x = \frac{5}{4} - \frac{\sqrt{41}}{4}$$

The answer is (C).

7. A

Difficulty: Hard

Category: Passport to Advanced Math / Quadratics

Strategic Advice: Most students see only the quadratic and start solving. Think about how the x-values can help you find the answer.

Getting to the Answer: First, rearrange to get the quadratic equal to zero.

$$\frac{1}{4}(4x^2 - 8x - k) = 30$$

$$x^2 - 2x - \frac{k}{4} = 30$$

$$x^2 - 2x - \frac{k}{4} - 30 = 0$$

Next, create binomials and FOIL.

$$(x - 7)(x + 5) = 0$$

$$x^2 - 2x - 35 = 0$$

Finally, set the two equations equal to each other and solve for k:

$$x^2 - 2x - \frac{k}{4} - 30 = x^2 - 2x - 35$$

$$-\frac{k}{4} = -5$$

$$-k = -20$$

$$k = 20$$

$$2k = 40$$

Here's the catch: you are not asked for k; you are asked for $2k$, which is 40. The answer is (A).

PRACTICE

8. D
Difficulty: Hard

Category: Passport to Advanced Math / Quadratics

Strategic Advice: Work through this systematically. Find the maximum height of the potato, then find the time it takes the potato to hit the ground.

Getting to the Answer: The x-coordinate of the vertex is given by $h = \dfrac{-b}{2a} = \dfrac{-224}{2(-16)} = 7$. Plug this into the function to get the y-coordinate: $k = y(7) = -16(7)^2 + 224(7) + 240 = 1{,}024$. Next, calculate how long it takes for the potato to hit the ground. This will occur when $y(t) = 0$. Plug in and factor to solve:

$$-16t^2 + 224t + 240 = 0$$
$$t^2 - 14(t) - 15 = 0$$
$$(t-15)(t+1) = 0$$
$$t = 15 \text{ or } t = -1$$

Since time can't be negative, $t = 15$. Don't forget that you were asked for the sum of the height and the time, not for either of the raw values. The sum of 15 and 1,024 is 1,039, choice (D).

9. B
Difficulty: Medium

Category: Passport to Advanced Math / Quadratics

Strategic Advice: Use number properties to avoid doing any actual math.

Getting to the Answer: If $ab > 0$, then a and b are either both positive or both negative. In the inequality $b^2ac < 0$, you can ignore the b^2 term because it will be positive regardless of the sign of b. This implies that either a or c is positive, and the other is negative. The x-intercepts are b and c. Since b has the same sign as a, while c has the opposite sign as a, it follows that b and c have opposite signs.

The correct answer must therefore be a function with one negative root and one positive root. Scan the functions to find the correct one. Ignore the complicated-looking numbers—all that matter are the signs! (B) is correct.

PERFORM

10. A
Difficulty: Hard

Category: Passport to Advanced Math / Quadratics

Strategic Advice: When a quadratic looks impossible, see if you can use one of the quadratic shortcuts. The presence of 4, 9, and 16—all perfect squares—is a big clue!

Getting to the Answer: Observe that $4x - 12\sqrt{x} + 9$ is an instance of the quadratic shortcut $(a-b)^2 = a^2 - 2ab + b^2$. Use the shortcut to factor the equation, then finish the problem with substitution.

$$4x - 12\sqrt{x} + 9 = 16$$
$$(2\sqrt{x} - 3)^2 = 16$$
$$2\sqrt{x} - 3 = 4$$

Now go after $10\sqrt{x} - 15 : 10\sqrt{x} - 15 = 5(2\sqrt{x} - 3) = 5(4) = 20$.

The correct answer is (A).

11. B
Difficulty: Medium

Category: Passport to Advanced Math / Quadratics

Strategic Advice: To find where two functions intersect, set them equal to each other, then solve.

Getting to the Answer: Neither of the functions is presented in standard form, so make this question a little easier by simplifying each one before setting them equal to each other.

$$f(x) = 3(x - 4)^2 + 4 = 3(x^2 - 8x + 16) + 4 = 3x^2$$
$$- 24x + 48 + 4 = 3x^2 - 24x + 52$$

$$g(x) = (x + 5)^2 + 2x - 135 = x^2 + 10x + 25 + 2x$$
$$- 135 = x^2 + 12x - 110$$

$$f(x) = g(x)$$
$$3x^2 - 24x + 52 = x^2 + 12x - 110$$
$$2x^2 - 36x + 162 = 0$$
$$x^2 - 18x + 81 = 0$$

Notice that this is a quadratic shortcut:

$$x^2 - 18x + 81 = (x - 9)^2 = 0$$
$$x = 9$$

Note that the question asks how many intersection points there are, *not* what the points are. Since there is only one solution for x, there must be only one point of intersection, which is (B). Don't waste time plugging 9 back in!

12. 2
Difficulty: Easy

Category: Passport to Advanced Math / Quadratics

Strategic Advice: An x-intercept of a function is a point at which the y-coordinate equals 0.

Getting to the Answer: Set the equation equal to zero, simplify, and factor.

$$g(x) = -2.5x^2 + 10x - 7.5$$
$$0 = -2.5x^2 + 10x - 7.5$$
$$0 = x^2 - 4x + 3$$
$$0 = (x - 1)(x - 3)$$
$$x = 1 \text{ or } 3$$

Recall that the question asks for the *difference* between the x-intercepts, not for the x-intercepts themselves. The difference between 3 and 1 is 2.

13. C
Difficulty: Medium

Category: Passport to Advanced Math / Quadratics

Strategic Advice: Fraction-laden equations are often simpler than they look; they still follow the same rules that any other equation does.

Getting to the Answer: An axis of symmetry splits the parabola in half and travels through the vertex. You have a formula to find h instantly. All you have to do is plug and chug to get your answer—just be careful with the fractions and negatives.

$$x = -\frac{b}{2a}$$

$$x = -17 \div 2\left(\frac{-11}{3}\right)$$

$$x = -17 \div \frac{-22}{3}$$

$$x = -17 \times \frac{-3}{22}$$

$$x = \frac{51}{22}$$

The correct answer is (C).

EXTRA PRACTICE

1. B

Difficulty: Easy

Category: Passport to Advanced Math / Quadratics

Strategic Advice: To multiply two binomials, distribute each term in the first set of parentheses to each term in the second set. You can also think FOIL.

Getting to the Answer: Multiply $2a$ by each term in the second factor and then multiply $5b$ by each term. Combine like terms if possible.

$$
\begin{aligned}
(2a+5b)(a-3b) &= 2a(a-3b)+5b(a-3b)\\
&= 2a(a)+2a(-3b)+5b(a)+5b(-3b)\\
&= 2a^2-6ab+5ab-15b^2\\
&= 2a^2-ab-15b^2
\end{aligned}
$$

Choice (B) is correct.

2. A

Difficulty: Easy

Category: Passport to Advanced Math / Quadratics

Strategic Advice: *Roots* are the same as *solutions* to an equation, so you need to solve the equation for x. Taking the square root of a quantity is the inverse operation of squaring it, and both sides of this equation are already perfect squares, so take their square roots. Then solve the resulting equations. Remember, there will be two equations to solve.

Getting to the Answer:

$$
\begin{aligned}
(x+3)^2 &= 49\\
\sqrt[2]{(x+3)^2} &= \pm\sqrt{49}\\
x+3 &= \pm7
\end{aligned}
$$

Now simplify each equation: $x + 3 = -7$, or $x = -10$; and $x + 3 = 7$, or $x = 4$, so (A) is correct.

If you didn't recognize that you could use square rooting to solve the equation, you could also expand the left side, then subtract 49, factor the resulting equation, and set the factors equal to 0. This is a perfectly fine way to solve the equation, but it takes considerably longer.

3. B

Difficulty: Easy

Category: Passport to Advanced Math / Quadratics

Strategic Advice: Use the factored form to find the x-intercepts and the standard form to find the y-intercept.

Getting to the Answer: Using the first equation, set each of the factors equal to 0 and solve for x to find that the x-intercepts are $-\dfrac{1}{2}$ and 5. This means you can eliminate A and D. From the standard form of the equation, you can see that the y-intercept is -5 because $0^2 - 3(0) - 5 = -5$, so (B) is correct.

4. C

Difficulty: Easy

Category: Passport to Advanced Math / Quadratics

Strategic Advice: Being able to make connections between equations and graphs is a valuable skill. The pieces of a quadratic equation written in standard form give you lots of information about its graph. For example, finding the value of $\dfrac{-b}{2a}$ (the quadratic formula without the radical part) tells you where the axis of symmetry occurs.

Getting to the Answer: This question is asking about c, which is the only constant term in the equation. If you substitute 0 for x, the equation becomes $y = a(0)^2 + b(0) + c$, or just $y = c$. This means the point $(0, c)$ will be on the graph, which is the y-intercept, making (C) correct.

5. A

Difficulty: Medium

Category: Passport to Advanced Math / Quadratics

Strategic Advice: When a question doesn't provide a lot of information to go on, it most likely involves something conceptual. In this question, you are being tested on whether you can relate a maximum value given in a real-world scenario to the vertex of a parabola and use that vertex to choose the corresponding quadratic equation.

Getting to the Answer: The answer choices all look very similar, so think logically to eliminate a couple. A rocket goes *up*, hits a maximum height, and then comes *down*. This tells you that the graph will be an upside-down parabola, which means the equation should have a negative sign in front. Eliminate C and D. To choose between A and B, you need to recall what the *vertex form* of a quadratic looks like and what it tells you. When a quadratic equation is written in the form $y = a(x - h)^2 + k$, the vertex of the graph is (h, k). The h tells you *where* the maximum (or minimum) occurs, and the k tells you *what* the maximum (or minimum) value is. Here, the maximum height of 34 feet occurs at 3 seconds, so k is 34 and h is 3. Substitute these values into vertex form to find that the correct equation is $y = -16(x - 3)^2 + 34$. Translate this to function language ($h(t) = y$ and $t = x$) to arrive at the answer: $h(t) = -16(t - 3)^2 + 34$, which is (A).

6. A

Difficulty: Medium

Category: Passport to Advanced Math / Quadratics

Strategic Advice: Use what you know about the different forms of a quadratic equation to choose the correct graph.

Getting to the Answer: The equation is given in standard form, so right away you know the y-intercept is the constant term (c), which is -8. This means you can eliminate B and C. The squared term in the equation has a positive coefficient (1), so the parabola must open upward. This means D can't be correct. The only remaining choice is (A), which is correct. You could also write the equation in factored form, $y = (x + 4)(x - 2)$, to see that the x-intercepts are -4 and 2, which also match the graph in (A).

7. A

Difficulty: Medium

Category: Passport to Advanced Math / Quadratics

Strategic Advice: When finding solutions to a quadratic equation, always start by rewriting the equation to make it equal 0 (unless both sides of the equation are already perfect squares). Then, take a peek at the answer choices—if they are all nice numbers, then factoring is probably the quickest method for solving the equation. If the answers include messy fractions or square roots, then using the quadratic formula may be a better choice.

Getting to the Answer: To make the equation equal 0, subtract 30 from both sides to get $x^2 - 7x - 30 = 0$. The answer choices are all integers, so factor the equation. Look for two numbers whose product is -30 and whose sum is -7. The two numbers are -10 and 3, so the factors are $(x - 10)$ and $(x + 3)$. Set each factor equal to 0 and solve to find that $x = 10$ and $x = -3$. The question states that $x > 0$, so x must equal 10. Before selecting an answer, don't forget to check that you answered the right question—the question asks for the value of $x - 5$, not just x, so the correct answer is $10 - 5 = 5$, which means (A) is correct.

If this question appeared in the calculator section of the test, you could also graph the equation in your graphing calculator and use the "zero" function to find the solutions.

8. C

Difficulty: Medium

Category: Passport to Advanced Math / Quadratics

Strategic Advice: Examine the graph—there are no gridlines and no numbers along the axes.

This means that arriving at the correct answer will require some thought.

Getting to the Answer: According to the graph, one *x*-intercept is to the left of the *y*-axis, and the other is to the right. This tells you that one value of *x* is positive, while the other is negative, so you can immediately eliminate D (both factors have the same sign). To choose between the remaining equations, find the *x*-intercepts by setting each factor equal to 0 and solving for *x*. In A, the *x*-intercepts are $\frac{1}{2}$ and –1, but that would mean that *e* is *twice* as far from the origin as *f*, not *half* as far, so eliminate A. In B, the *x*-intercepts are 1 and –2. Again, that would mean that *e* is twice as far from the origin as *f*, not half as far, so eliminate B. This means (C) must be correct. The *x*-intercepts are 1 and $-\frac{1}{2}$, which fits the criterion that *e* is half as far from the origin as *f*.

9. B

Difficulty: Medium

Category: Passport to Advanced Math / Quadratics

Strategic Advice: There are no coefficients (numbers) in the equation, so you'll need to think about how the values of *a*, *b*, and *c* affect the graph.

Getting to the Answer: Compare each statement to the graph to determine whether it is true, eliminating choices as you go. Remember, you are looking for the statement that is *not* true. The parabola opens upward, so the value of *a* must be positive, which means you can eliminate A because it *is* true (> 0 means positive). The value of *b* is the tricky one, so skip it for now, and consider C. When written in standard form, the value of *c* tells you the *y*-intercept. According to the graph, the *y*-intercept is below the *x*-axis and is therefore negative, so *c* < 0 is true. Eliminate C. Unfortunately, this means you'll need to consider B. Based on the equation alone, it is not easy to determine whether *b* is positive or negative, so you'll need to think outside the box. The trick for finding the *x*-coordinate of the vertex of a parabola

is to calculate $\frac{-b}{2a}$ (the quadratic formula without the radical part). In the graph, the *x*-coordinate of the vertex is 3, so set the formula equal to 3, solve for *b*, and see what happens.

$$\frac{-b}{2a} = \frac{3}{1}$$
$$-b = 6a$$
$$b = -6a$$

You have already determined that *a* is positive (because the parabola opens upward), so *b* must be negative. This means *b* is less than 0, not greater, making (B) correct.

10. C

Difficulty: Medium

Category: Passport to Advanced Math / Quadratics

Strategic Advice: Equations that are equivalent have the same solutions, so you are looking for the equation that is simply written in a different form. You could expand each of the equations in the answer choices, but unless you get lucky, this will use up quite a bit of time.

Getting to the Answer: The answer choices are written in vertex form, so use the method of completing the square to convert the equation in the question to the same form. First, write the equation in standard form: $y = x^2 + 6x - 40$. Move the 40 to the other side to temporarily get it out of the way. Then, complete the square on the right-hand side, by finding $\left(\frac{b}{2}\right)^2 = \left(\frac{6}{2}\right)^2 = 3^2 = 9$, and adding the result to both sides of the equation.

$$y = x^2 + 6x - 40$$
$$y + 40 = x^2 + 6x$$
$$y + 40 + 9 = x^2 + 6x + 9$$
$$y + 49 = x^2 + 6x + 9$$

Next, factor the right-hand side of the equation (which should be a perfect square trinomial) and rewrite it as a square.

$$y + 49 = (x + 3)(x + 3)$$
$$y + 49 = (x + 3)^2$$

Finally, solve for y to get $y = (x + 3)^2 - 49$, which makes (C) correct.

11. B
Difficulty: Medium

Category: Passport to Advanced Math / Quadratics

Strategic Advice: When a quadratic equation is written in the form $y = a(x - h)^2 + k$, the minimum value (or the maximum value if $a < 0$) is given by k, and the axis of symmetry is given by the equation $x = h$.

Getting to the Answer: The question states that the minimum of the parabola is 5, so look for an equation where k is 5. You can eliminate C and D because k is 3 in C and –3 in D. The question also states that the axis of symmetry is $x = -3$, so h must be –3. Be careful—this is tricky. The equation in A is not correct because the vertex form of a parabola has a negative before the h, so $(x - 3)$ would produce an axis of symmetry at $x = 3$, not –3. This means (B) is correct.

You could also graph each equation in your graphing calculator to see which one matches the criteria given in the question, but this is likely to use up valuable time on Test Day.

12. A
Difficulty: Medium

Category: Passport to Advanced Math / Quadratics

Strategic Advice: Even though one of the equations in this system isn't linear, you can still solve the system using substitution.

Getting to the Answer: You already know that y is equal to $2x$, so substitute $2x$ for y in the second equation. Don't forget that when you square $2x$, you must square both the coefficient and the variable. Also, be careful—there are a lot of 2s floating around, so pay careful attention as you plug in values.

$$2x^2 + 2y^2 = 240$$
$$x^2 + y^2 = 120$$
$$x^2 + (2x)^2 = 120$$
$$x^2 + 4x^2 = 120$$
$$5x^2 = 120$$
$$x^2 = 24$$

The question asks for the value of x^2, not x, so there is no need to take the square root of 24 to find the value of x. Choice (A) is correct.

13. B
Difficulty: Hard

Category: Passport to Advanced Math / Quadratics

Strategic Advice: Pay careful attention to what the question is asking. You are looking for a quadratic equation that produces a maximum value that is greater than the one shown in the graph. Take a peek at the answer choices—C and D are given in vertex form, so consider those first. If neither is correct, then you'll need to think about the question in a different way.

Getting to the Answer: The maximum value shown in the graph is about 56 or 57 feet. When a quadratic equation is written in vertex form, $y = a(x - h)^2 + k$, the maximum value is given by k, so check C and D first because they will be the easiest to compare to the graph. In C, k is 48, which is not greater than 56 or 57 and therefore not correct. In D, k is 52, which is also not greater than 56 or 57. This means either A or (B) must be correct. You now have two options—you could expand the equation in each answer choice and then complete the square to find the vertex, or you could expand the equations, find the x-coordinate of the vertex using the formula $x = \dfrac{-b}{2a}$, and then plug in the result to find the *y*-value. Completing the square usually takes a bit of time, so the second option is probably the quicker route to take. Expanding A, you get $h = -16t^2 + 48t$ with $a = -16$ and $b = 48$. The *x*-coordinate of the vertex is $\dfrac{-48}{2(-16)} = \dfrac{-48}{-32} = 1.5$. Substituting this back into the equation, the *y*-value of the vertex (which is the maximum value of the function) is $-16(1.5)^2 + 48(1.5) = 36$, which is not greater than 56 or 57, so (B) must be correct. Don't waste valuable time checking, but if you use the same strategy, you'll find that the maximum height of the equation in (B) is 81 feet.

14. 0

Difficulty: Medium

Category: Passport to Advanced Math / Quadratics

Strategic Advice: To find the roots of an equation, you need to set it equal to 0, factor it, and then solve. Whenever the leading coefficient is a fraction, factoring becomes very messy. Luckily, you can clear the fraction the same way you do when solving equations (multiply both sides of the equation by the denominator of the fraction).

Getting to the Answer:

$$0 = \frac{1}{3}x^2 - 2x + 3$$
$$3(0) = 3\left(\frac{1}{3}x^2 - 2x + 3\right)$$
$$0 = x^2 - 6x + 9$$
$$0 = (x - 3)(x - 3)$$

The equation only has one unique solution ($x = 3$), so the positive difference between the roots is actually 0.

15. 5

Difficulty: Hard

Category: Passport to Advanced Math / Quadratics

Strategic Advice: Before you plug –5 in for *x*, which creates messy numbers, factor the given equation.

Getting to the Answer:

$$x^2 + 2xk + k^2 = 0$$
$$(x + k)(x + k) = 0$$
$$(x + k)^2 = 0$$

Now plug in –5 for *x* and solve for *k*:

$$(-5 + k)^2 = 0$$
$$\sqrt[2]{(-5 + k)^2} = \pm\sqrt{0}$$
$$-5 + k = 0$$
$$k = 5$$

16. 6.5 or 13/2

Difficulty: Hard

Category: Passport to Advanced Math / Quadratics

Strategic Advice: This is a tough question with no real shortcuts. The highest power of *x* in the equation is 2, so the equation is quadratic. Writing quadratic equations can be tricky and time-consuming. If you know the roots, you can use factors to write the equation. If you don't know the roots, you need to create a system of equations to find the coefficients of the variable terms.

Getting to the Answer: You don't know the roots of this equation, so start with the point that has the nicest values (0, 2) and substitute them into the equation, $y = ax^2 + bx + c$.

$$2 = a(0)^2 + b(0) + c$$
$$2 = c$$

Now your equation looks like $y = ax^2 + bx + 2$. Next, use the other two points to create a system of two equations in two variables.

$$(-2, -10) \rightarrow -10 = a(-2)^2 + b(-2) + 2 \rightarrow -12 = 4a - 2b$$
$$(4, 14) \rightarrow 14 = a(4)^2 + b(4) + 2 \rightarrow 12 = 16a + 4b$$

You now have a system of equations to solve. None of the variables has a coefficient of 1, so use elimination to solve the system. If you multiply the top equation by 2, the *b*-terms will eliminate each other.

$$2[4a - 2b = -12] \rightarrow 8a - 4b = -24$$
$$16a + 4b = 12 \rightarrow \underline{16a + 4b = 12}$$
$$24a = -12$$
$$a = -\frac{1}{2}$$

Now, find b by substituting the value of a into either of the original equations. Using the bottom equation, you get this:

$$16\left(-\frac{1}{2}\right) + 4b = 12$$
$$-8 + 4b = 12$$
$$4b = 20$$
$$b = 5$$

The value of $a + b + c$ is $-\frac{1}{2} + 5 + 2 = 6\frac{1}{2}$. You can't enter a mixed number, so grid in your answer as the decimal number 6.5 or the improper fraction 13/2.

CHAPTER 9

PREPARE

1. D
Difficulty: Medium

Category: Additional Topics in Math / Geometry

Strategic Advice: Pay attention to which angles are formed by which transversal. Angles formed by different transversals are not necessarily related.

Getting to the Answer: The left transversal forms angles *a*, *b*, and *d*. From the figure you know *a* and *d* are corresponding (and therefore equal) angles. Together, angles *a* and *b* form a straight line, so they are supplementary; because *a* and *d* are equal, *b* and *d* are also supplementary. The other transversal forms *c* and *e*, which are supplementary. Consider angles *a*, *b*, and *d* as belonging to Group 1 and angles *c* and *e* as belonging to Group 2. None of the angles in Group 1 are necessarily equal, supplementary, or in any way related to any of the angles in Group 2 because they are formed by different transversals. For this reason, A, B, and C are incorrect, as they all try to relate angles from two different groups. That leaves (D), which is correct.

If you're not fully confident that (D) is correct, remember that *b* and *d* are supplementary, as are *c* and *e*. Therefore, $b + d = e + c = 180$. Rearrange the equation to yield $b + d - c = e$.

2. A
Difficulty: Medium

Category: Additional Topics in Math / Geometry

Strategic Advice: Draw a diagram to visualize the situation. If you don't immediately see any helpful angles or shapes, add additional lines.

Getting to the Answer: After drawing a diagram of Aundria and Annette's routes to the summit and labeling it with the information given, look for a way to uncover a right triangle with additional lines. Once complete, use the rectangle you created to fill in the lengths of the new segments. The completed diagram is shown below.

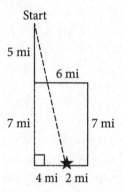

Use the Pythagorean theorem to calculate the distance Annette will travel:

$$(5+7)^2 + 4^2 = c^2$$
$$c^2 = 144 + 16 = 160$$
$$c = \sqrt{160} = 4\sqrt{10}$$

But you're not done yet! The question asks you to find the total distance the two women travel. Aundria travels $5 + 6 + 7 + 2 = 20$ mi; together, she and Annette will travel $20 + 4\sqrt{10}$ mi, which is approximately 32.65 mi. Choice (A) is correct.

3. 39
Difficulty: Easy

Category: Additional Topics in Math / Geometry

Strategic Advice: Draw a diagram to visualize the situation in the question.

Getting to the Answer: Start by drawing Uwe's field and the fence he plans to build:

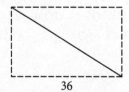

You know the length and the area of the field. Use these to find the width:

$$A = lw$$

$$540 = 36w$$

$$w = 15$$

Now you know that the fence is the hypotenuse of a right triangle with legs 15 and 36. Before turning to the Pythagorean theorem, look for a Pythagorean triplet to lessen the required work. Indeed, this is a 5-12-13 triangle multiplied by 3. Therefore, the hypotenuse—and meters of fence needed—is $13 \times 3 = 39$.

4. B
Difficulty: Medium

Category: Additional Topics in Math / Geometry

Strategic Advice: Don't panic if you don't see how to get the answer right away. Fill in the figure with what you know, and identify what else you can determine from there. You'll arrive at the answer in just a few steps.

Getting to the Answer: In $\triangle FDC$, only one angle is missing, so you can solve for it and fill it in: $m\angle DFC = 180° - 70° - 60° = 50°$. Because $\angle DFC$ and $\angle BFG$ are vertical angles, $m\angle BFG = m\angle DFC = 50°$. At this point, you have two of the three angles in $\triangle BFG$, so you can solve for the third: $m\angle FBG = 180° - 50° - 60° = 70°$. Because $\overline{AD}$ and $\overline{BC}$ are parallel, $\angle FBG$ and $\angle BAD$ are corresponding angles (and are therefore equal). You can now conclude that $\angle x = 70°$, which matches (B).

5. B
Difficulty: Easy

Category: Additional Topics in Math / Geometry

Strategic Advice: Look for simpler shapes, and determine what you know about those first.

Getting to the Answer: You're told that $\overline{AB} = 6$. Because $ABCD$ is a rectangle, $\overline{AB}$ must equal $\overline{DC}$, so $\overline{DC} = 6$. The question states that $\overline{FD} = \overline{DC}$, so $\overline{FD}$ is 6, too. You're told that the perimeter of rectangle $ABCD$ is 30. Thus, $30 = \overline{AB} + \overline{BC} + \overline{CD} + \overline{AD} = 6 + 6 + \overline{BC} + \overline{AD}$ and $\overline{BC} + \overline{AD} = 30 - 6 - 6 = 18$. Because $\overline{BC} = \overline{AD}$ and $9 + 9 = 18$, $\overline{BC}$ and $\overline{AD}$ must each equal 9. Use the Pythagorean theorem to find $\overline{FA}$:

$$6^2 + \overline{FA}^2 = 9^2$$

$$\overline{FA}^2 = 81 - 36$$

$$\overline{FA} = \sqrt{45}$$

Finally, simplify the radical to get your answer: $\sqrt{45} = \sqrt{9} \times \sqrt{5} = 3\sqrt{5}$. (B) is correct.

PRACTICE

6. C
Difficulty: Hard

Category: Additional Topics in Math / Geometry

Strategic Advice: Look for hidden special right triangles to help you find the answer, and add new information to your diagram as you find it.

Getting to the Answer: Start by finding $\angle ACD$ from the two given angles: $m\angle ACD = 180° - 15° - 30° = 135°$. Because $\angle ACB$ is supplementary to $\angle ACD$, $\angle ACB$ measures 45°. $\triangle ABC$ is a right triangle, so its missing angle ($\angle BAC$) is also 45°, making $\triangle ABC$ a 45-45-90 triangle. This means $\angle BAD$ is 60°; therefore, $\triangle ABD$ is a 30-60-90 triangle.

Knowing that you have two special right triangles will allow you to unlock the unknown side lengths. $\overline{AC}$ is the hypotenuse of the 45-45-90 triangle (side ratio: $x:x:x\sqrt{2}$), so $\overline{AB}$ and $\overline{BC}$ (the two legs) must be $2\sqrt{2}$ (solve the equation $4 = x\sqrt{2}$ to find this). $\overline{AB}$ is also the shorter leg of the 30-60-90 triangle (side ratio: $x:x\sqrt{3}:2x$), so $\overline{BD}$ (longer leg) is $2\sqrt{6}$, and $\overline{AD}$ (hypotenuse) is $4\sqrt{2}$. Don't stop just yet; remember which perimeter you need. Take the difference of $\overline{BD}$ and $\overline{BC}$ to determine $\overline{CD}$, which is $2\sqrt{6} - 2\sqrt{2}$. You now have all three sides of ΔACD, so add them together to get your answer: $P_{ACD} = 4 + (2\sqrt{6} - 2\sqrt{2}) + 4\sqrt{2}$. This simplifies to $4 + 2\sqrt{6} + 2\sqrt{2}$, making (C) correct.

The completed diagram is shown below.

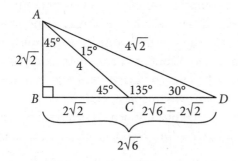

7. 100

Difficulty: Easy

Category: Additional Topics in Math / Geometry

Strategic Advice: Use your knowledge of supplementary and vertical angles to systematically solve for y and then x.

Getting to the Answer: Because supplementary angles sum to 180°, $2y + 4y = 180$. Simplification yields $y = 30$. Don't stop here: the question wants x, not y. Shift your focus to the vertical angles. The angle marked $4y$ is vertical to the one marked $x + 20$, so $4y = x + 20$. Plugging in 30 for y yields $x = 4(30) - 20 = 120 - 20 = 100$. The correct answer is 100.

8. 52

Difficulty: Medium

Category: Additional Topics in Math / Geometry

Strategic Advice: If the question doesn't give you a figure, draw one. Making a figure saves time and helps you steer clear of traps.

Getting to the Answer: First, draw a rectangle to represent the wall space. Next draw another rectangle inside the first to represent the TV. Label the diagram with the information the question provides.

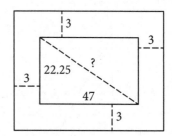

To find the dimensions of the TV, subtract 6 from the length and width of the wall space. Note that many students might erroneously subtract only 3 inches from each dimension, yielding TV dimensions of 25.2550. However, the space adds 3 inches on all four sides of the TV, so you should actually subtract 6 inches from the length and width of the wall space. Therefore, the correct TV dimensions are 22.25×47.

With the TV dimensions in hand, you can use the Pythagorean theorem to determine the size (a.k.a. the diagonal) of the largest TV that Whitney can fit in this wall space:

$$a^2 + b^2 = c^2$$

$$22.25^2 + 47^2 = c^2$$

$$495.0625 + 2{,}209 = c^2$$

$$2{,}704.0625 = c^2$$

$$52.001 \approx c$$

Grid in 52

PERFORM

9. D

Difficulty: Medium

Category: Additional Topics in Math / Geometry

Strategic Advice: Use the 30-60-90 triangle ratio, and don't forget to answer the question posed!

Getting to the Answer: The sides of a 30-60-90 triangle are in the ratio $x : x\sqrt{3} : 2x$, so label the triangle accordingly:

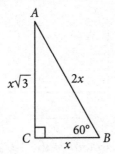

The area of a triangle is $A = \frac{1}{2}bh$, and you're told that the area of this triangle is $8\sqrt{3}$. Use this to solve for x:

$$8\sqrt{3} = \frac{1}{2}(x)(x\sqrt{3}) = \frac{1}{2}x^2\sqrt{3}$$

$$16 = x^2$$

$$x = 4$$

This matches A, but A is a trap! You just solved for x, which is the length of $\overline{CB}$. The question asks for the length of $\overline{AB}$, not $\overline{CB}$. Because $\overline{CB}$ is twice $\overline{AB}$, the correct answer is 8, which is (D).

10. 3/8 or .375

Difficulty: Hard

Category: Additional Topics in Math / Geometry

Strategic Advice: Three of the four squares have a smaller square within them. Take this into account when doing your calculations.

Getting to the Answer: The question states that each progressively larger square has a perimeter that is 4 cm greater than that of the previous square. Therefore, each progressively larger square will also have a side length that is 1 cm greater than that of the previous square. Use this fact to determine the area of each square; the following table summarizes the change in side length and area moving outward from the innermost square.

	S1 (innermost)	S2	S3	S4 (outermost)
Side length	1	2	3	4
Area	1	4	9	16

Next, determine the area of the white and black regions. When calculating these, remember to account for the area taken up by the square inscribed within. Square 1 contains 1 cm² white space, Square 2 contains $4 - 1 = 3$ cm² black space, Square 3 contains $9 - 4 = 5$ cm² white space, and Square 4 contains $16 - 9 = 7$ cm² black space. The question asks for the probability of randomly selecting a point in one of the white regions, which is $\frac{1+5}{16} = \frac{6}{16} = \frac{3}{8}$. Grid in $\frac{3}{8}$ or .375.

11. B

Difficulty: Medium

Category: Additional Topics in Math / Geometry

Strategic Advice: With complex figures, keep in mind that it might take more than one calculation or step to get to the answer.

Getting to the Answer: Given the area of $\triangle ABC$ and the length of the base AB, you can find its height, $CB : 150 = \frac{1}{2}(20)CB = 10CB \rightarrow CB = 15$. This means that $\triangle ABC$ is a 3-4-5 triangle with dimensions scaled up by a factor of 5, so the hypotenuse ($\overline{AC}$) must be $5 \times 5 = 25$. Next, turn your attention to the smaller triangle, $\triangle AGH$. You're told that the hypotenuse of this triangle, $\overline{AH}$, is 20. Because $\triangle ABC$ and $\triangle AGH$ are similar triangles, their corresponding sides must be proportional.

$$\frac{AH}{AC} = \frac{HG}{CB}$$

$$\frac{20}{25} = \frac{HG}{15}$$

$$300 = 25HG$$

$$\overline{HG} = 12$$

Choice (B) is the correct answer.

12. A

Difficulty: Hard

Category: Additional Topics in Math / Geometry

Strategic Advice: Extend the existing lines to reveal helpful hidden angles and triangles.

Getting to the Answer: Because j and k are parallel, the two other segments are actually transversals. Extend them to visualize the rest of the associated angles. We've labeled a few angles to aid in the explanation; you need not do the same on Test Day.

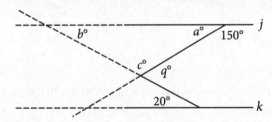

The angles marked $a°$ and 150° are supplementary, so $a = 180° - 150° = 30°$. The angles marked $b°$ and 20° are alternate interior angles (and therefore equal), so $b = 20$. Notice that the angles marked $a°$, $b°$, and $c°$ are all in the same triangle; consequently, their sum is 180°. Therefore, $c = 180 - 30 - 20 = 130$. Because the angles marked $c°$ and $q°$ are supplementary, $q = 180 - 130 = 50$. (A) is therefore correct.

EXTRA PRACTICE

1. C

Difficulty: Easy

Category: Additional Topics in Math / Geometry

Strategic Advice: Don't immediately assume you need to use trig to answer this question (although it is possible). Instead, keep in mind that the SAT is more likely to test your knowledge of right triangles, so start by determining whether triangle *ABC* is a right triangle.

Getting to the Answer: The sum of the angles of every triangle is 180 degrees. Subtract the angle measures given from 180 to find that angle *B* equals 180 − 51.5 − 38.5 = 90 degrees. This means the triangle is a right triangle. Because *B* is the right angle, side *AC* must be the hypotenuse. Use the Pythagorean theorem to find its length:

$$a^2 + b^2 = c^2$$

$$28^2 + 45^2 = c^2$$

$$784 + 2{,}025 = c^2$$

$$2{,}809 = c^2$$

$$53 = c$$

This makes (C) the correct answer.

2. B

Difficulty: Easy

Category: Additional Topics in Math / Geometry

Strategic Advice: The sum of the interior angle measures of every triangle is 180°. To figure out the value of *x*, begin by filling in the angle measures for the triangle.

Getting to the Answer: The angle vertical to the 48° angle is also 48°, and the angle supplementary to the 135° angle has a measure of 180° − 135° = 45°.

Now that you know two of the angles in the triangle, you can calculate the measure of the third angle, *y*, by subtracting from 180 to get 180 − 48 − 45 = 87°. The angle with measure *x*° is supplementary to angle *y*, so 87 + *x* = 180°. Thus, *x* = 93°, which means that *x* − *y* = 93 − 87 = 6, which is (B).

3. C

Difficulty: Easy

Category: Additional Topics in Math / Geometry

Strategic Advice: From the question, you know that the triangle formed by Earth, the moon, and the sun is a right triangle. This means you can use the Pythagorean theorem to find the missing side, which is the hypotenuse.

Getting to the Answer: You can divide both numbers by 1,000 to reduce the number of zeros and make them more manageable.

$$a^2 + b^2 = c^2$$

$$240^2 + 91{,}674^2 = c^2$$

$$57{,}600 + 8{,}404{,}122{,}276 = c^2$$

$$8{,}404{,}179{,}876 = c^2$$

$$91{,}674.31 = c$$

Don't forget to multiply the result by 1,000 (because you divided by 1,000 earlier). There are approximately 91,674,000 miles between Earth and the sun, which matches (C).

4. D

Difficulty: Easy

Category: Additional Topics in Math / Geometry

Strategic Advice: Two of the angles in the triangle have degree measures 30 and 90, which means the third angle must measure 60 degrees. This means you are dealing with a special right triangle and can use the 30-60-90 shortcut.

Getting to the Answer: In a 30-60-90 triangle, the sides are always in the ratio $x : x\sqrt{3} : 2x$ (short leg : long leg : hypotenuse). The only length you know is the long leg—the side represented by the ground and the width of the bottom two steps. The ramp is to be placed 8 feet, or 96 inches, from the bottom step, and the steps themselves account for an additional 20 inches, which means this leg of the triangle is 116 inches long. Use the ratio to determine that you need to divide by $\sqrt{3}$ to find the length of the shorter leg, and then multiply the result by 2 to find the length of the hypotenuse, which represents the ramp.

$$116 \div \sqrt{3} = 66.97$$
$$66.97 \times 2 = 133.95$$

The result is about 134 inches, which matches (D).

5. A

Difficulty: Medium

Category: Additional Topics in Math / Geometry

Strategic Advice: Start by translating from English into math. Because one leg of the triangle is three times as long as the other, let x and $3x$ represent the lengths.

Getting to the Answer: Use the Pythagorean theorem to find the hypotenuse.

$$a^2 + b^2 = c^2$$
$$x^2 + (3x)^2 = c^2$$
$$x^2 + 9x^2 = c^2$$
$$10x^2 = c^2$$
$$\sqrt{10x^2} = c$$

Although you can't find a numerical value for c, you do know that the number under the radical must be a multiple of 10, so (A) is correct.

6. A

Difficulty: Medium

Category: Additional Topics in Math / Geometry

Strategic Advice: Many geometry questions require adding lines to the figure given. If you're not sure where to get started on a question like this, see if you can add a line to make a right triangle or other familiar figure.

Getting to the Answer: Start by connecting the ranch to the campsite. Then draw in a horizontal line and a vertical line to form a right triangle.

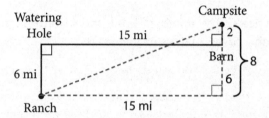

The length of one leg of the triangle is 15 miles, the distance from the watering hole to the barn. The length of the other leg is 6 + 2 = 8 miles, the distance from the ranch to the watering hole and then from the barn to the campsite. The two legs of the right triangle are 8 and 15. You might recognize the Pythagorean triplet, 8, 15, 17, but if you don't, you can always rely on the Pythagorean theorem:

$$8^2 + 15^2 = c^2$$
$$64 + 225 = c^2$$
$$289 = c^2$$
$$\sqrt{289} = \sqrt{c^2}$$
$$17 = c$$

The actual trail is 6 + 15 + 2 = 23 miles long. The direct route is 17 miles, so the direct route is 23 − 17 = 6 miles shorter, making (A) the correct answer.

7. B

Difficulty: Medium

Category: Additional Topics in Math / Geometry

Strategic Advice: Lengths that represent Pythagorean triplets form right triangles. Convert any fractional measurements or mixed units to inches so that you can look for Pythagorean triplets.

Getting to the Answer: Choice A is a Pythagorean triplet, so you can eliminate it right away. Don't let (B) fool you—3, 4, 5 is a Pythagorean triplet but $\frac{1}{3}, \frac{1}{4}, \frac{1}{5}$ is not. (If you're not convinced, try these numbers in the Pythagorean theorem).

Choice (B): $\frac{1}{3}$ foot = 4 inches, $\frac{1}{4}$ foot = 3 inches, and $\frac{1}{5}$ foot = 2.4 inches. Keep this choice for now.

Choice C: The numbers 9, 40, and 41 represent a Pythagorean triplet so eliminate this choice.

Choice D: $\frac{3}{4}$ foot = 9 inches, 1 foot = 12 inches, 15 inches = 15 inches. The numbers 9, 12, 15 are 3 times the numbers 3, 4, 5, so they represent a Pythagorean triplet Eliminate D.

This means (B) must be correct. You could also use the Pythagorean theorem to verify your answer.

8. D
Difficulty: Medium

Category: Additional Topics in Math / Geometry

Strategic Advice: Pay careful attention to labels on a diagram, including tick marks that indicate congruence.

Getting to the Answer: Because one angle of the triangle measures 90°, and the two legs are congruent (notice the tick marks), this is a 45-45-90 triangle. The side lengths of a 45-45-90 triangle are in the ratio $s:s:s\sqrt{2}$, where s represents the length of a leg and $s\sqrt{2}$ represents the length of the hypotenuse. (Don't forget—the formula page provides this information.) Don't be too hasty in choosing

your answer—it's not 7! Set up an equation using the ratio and the length of the side ($7\sqrt{2}$) to find h:

$$h = s\sqrt{2}$$
$$= 7\sqrt{2} \times \sqrt{2}$$
$$= 7\sqrt{4}$$
$$= 7(2)$$
$$= 14$$

The length of the hypotenuse is 14, so (D) is correct.

9. C
Difficulty: Medium

Category: Additional Topics in Math / Geometry

Strategic Advice: If you're not sure how to start a question like this, look for vertical angles and supplementary angles in the figure and fill in their measures. Remember, vertical angles have equal measures, supplementary angles add up to 180°, and the sum of the interior angles of a triangle is also 180°.

Getting to the Answer: Line L forms a right triangle with the x- and y-axes, so one of the interior angles of the triangle has a measure of 90°. You know that $\angle q = 140°$, and angles p and q form a straight line, which means they are supplementary. So $\angle p$ must equal 180° − 140° = 40°. One of the interior angles of the triangle is vertical to $\angle p$, so it also equals 40°. Now find the last angle measure inside the triangle by subtracting: 180° − 90° − 40° = 50°. This angle is supplementary to angle r, so $r = 180° − 50° = 130°$. This means that $\angle r - p° = 130° - 40° = 90°$, making (C) the correct choice.

10. B
Difficulty: Medium

Category: Additional Topics in Math / Geometry

Strategic Advice: Be on the lookout for Pythagorean triplets such as 3-4-5 right triangles, as well as multiples of Pythagorean triplets.

Getting to the Answer: You've been given two side lengths of a right triangle; the shorter leg ($\overline{OR}$, which is a radius of the circle) is 1.5, and the longer leg ($\overline{RQ}$) is 2. If you mentally double these values, you should recognize that triangle ORQ is a 3-4-5 right triangle in which the 3-4-5 ratio has been cut in half, resulting in side lengths of 1.5, 2, and 2.5. This means the length of $\overline{OQ}$ is 2.5. Segment OP is a radius, so it must be equal in length to $\overline{OR}$, which is 1.5. Because $\overline{PQ} = \overline{OQ} - \overline{OP}$, the length of $\overline{PQ}$ is 2.5 − 1.5 = 1, making (B) correct.

11. D

Difficulty: Medium

Category: Additional Topics in Math / Geometry

Strategic Advice: This question is fairly straightforward—use the Pythagorean theorem to find h. The tricky part is the algebra, so simplify each term carefully as you work through the solution.

Getting to the Answer: The sides $3d$, $5d$, and h form a right triangle, so plug these values into the Pythagorean theorem, and then solve for h. Be careful—when you square $3d$ and $5d$, you must square the coefficient and the variable.

$$a^2 + b^2 = c^2$$
$$(3d)^2 + (5d)^2 = h^2$$
$$9d^2 + 25d^2 = h^2$$
$$34d^2 = h^2$$
$$\sqrt{34d^2} = h$$
$$d\sqrt{34} = h$$

Choice (D) is correct.

12. B

Difficulty: Hard

Category: Additional Topics in Math / Geometry

Strategic Advice: Always look for 45-45-90 and 30-60-90 triangles on Test Day.

Getting to the Answer: First, find the measure of the missing angle in the triangle: 180 − 105 − 45 = 30 degrees. Now, draw the height of the triangle up from B to a point, D, on $\overline{AC}$; this creates two right triangles.

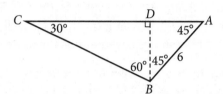

Triangle ABD is a 45-45-90 triangle, so its side lengths are in the ratio $s:s:s\sqrt{2}$. Because $\overline{AB}$ is the hypotenuse, set up an equation using the ratio of the sides:

$$6 = s\sqrt{2}$$
$$\frac{6}{\sqrt{2}} = s$$
$$\frac{6}{\sqrt{2}} \frac{\sqrt{2}}{\sqrt{2}} = s$$
$$\frac{6\sqrt{2}}{2} = s$$
$$3\sqrt{2} = s$$

Triangle BDC is a 30-60-90 triangle, so its side lengths are in the ratio of $x:x\sqrt{3}:2x$. You just found the dimensions of the shorter leg, $3\sqrt{2}$, so multiply it by $\sqrt{3}$ to find the length of the longer leg ($\sqrt{3} \times 3\sqrt{2} = 3\sqrt{6}$). Now, find the length of $\overline{AC}$, which is the base of the triangle, by adding $\overline{AD}$ to $\overline{DC}$: $3\sqrt{2} + 3\sqrt{6}$. Finally, use the area formula, $A = \frac{1}{2}bh$, to find the area of the whole triangle:

$$A = \frac{1}{2}(3\sqrt{2} + 3\sqrt{6})(3\sqrt{2})$$
$$= \frac{1}{2}(18 + 9\sqrt{12})$$
$$= \frac{1}{2}(18 + 18\sqrt{3})$$
$$= 9 + 9\sqrt{3}$$

Choice (B) is correct.

13. D

Difficulty: Hard

Category: Additional Topics in Math / Geometry

Strategic Advice: A thorough understanding of the most commonly tested triangles on the SAT, 30-60-90 and 45-45-90 special right triangles, will allow you to cruise through any questions that use them.

Getting to the Answer: Recall that the sides of a 30-60-90 triangle are in the ratio $x : x\sqrt{3} : 2x$. Because $\overline{QR} = 4$ and QRT is a 30-60-90 triangle, $\overline{QT} = 4\sqrt{3}$. The question tells you that T is the midpoint of $\overline{QS}$, so $\overline{QS} = 2(4\sqrt{3}) = 8\sqrt{3}$. The question is asking for the length of $\overline{RS}$, the hypotenuse of $\triangle QRS$, so use the Pythagorean theorem:

$$a^2 + b^2 = c^2$$
$$4^2 + (8\sqrt{3})^2 = c^2$$
$$16 + 192 = c^2$$
$$208 = c^2$$
$$\sqrt{208} = c$$
$$\sqrt{16 \times 13} = c$$
$$4\sqrt{13} = c$$

Choice (D) is correct.

Note that the SAT often puts answers to questions involving radicals in simplest form. Practice pulling out perfect squares.

14. D

Difficulty: Hard

Category: Additional Topics in Math / Geometry

Strategic Advice: You'll need to use several formulas to answer this question: area of a triangle, reverse FOIL (factoring), and the Pythagorean theorem. Be patient and take it one step at a time.

Getting to the Answer: In a right triangle, one leg is the base and the other is the height. Use x and $x + 3$ to represent the lengths of these two legs (because

the question states that one leg is 3 inches longer than the other). Use the area formula and set the equation equal to the given area:

$$35 = \frac{1}{2}(x)(x+3)$$
$$2(35) = \cancel{2}\left(\frac{1}{\cancel{2}}(x)(x+3)\right)$$
$$70 = (x)(x+3)$$
$$70 = x^2 + 3x$$

Now, subtract 70 to make the equation equal 0 and then factor it. The factors are $(x + 10)$ and $(x - 7)$, which means $x = -10$ and $x = 7$. Lengths cannot be negative, so the shorter leg must have a length of 7. This means the longer leg has a length of $7 + 3 = 10$. Now use the Pythagorean theorem to find the length of the hypotenuse.

$$a^2 + b^2 = c^2$$
$$7^2 + 10^2 = c^2$$
$$49 + 100 = c^2$$
$$149 = c^2$$
$$\sqrt{149} = \sqrt{c^2}$$
$$\sqrt{149} = c$$

Choice (D) is correct.

15. C

Difficulty: Hard

Category: Additional Topics in Math / Geometry

Strategic Advice: The two most useful geometry properties you can memorize are that the interior angles of a triangle and supplementary angles both sum to 180°.

Getting to the Answer: Remember, vertical angles formed by intersecting lines are congruent. This means the angle with the measure $90 - \dfrac{b}{2}$ is congruent to the interior angle of the triangle vertical to it. Likewise, the angle with the measure $90 - 3b$

is vertical to the other interior angle of the triangle. To find a in terms of b, set the sum of triangle DEF's angles equal to 180° and solve for a:

$$a + \left(90 - \frac{b}{2}\right) + (90 - 3b) = 180$$

$$a - \frac{b}{2} - 3b = 0$$

$$a = 3b + \frac{b}{2}$$

$$a = \frac{6b}{2} + \frac{b}{2}$$

$$a = \frac{7b}{2}$$

This matches (C).

16. 30
Difficulty: Medium

Category: Additional Topics in Math / Geometry

Strategic Advice: Write the given lengths of the sides as a ratio (shortest to longest), $1.5 : \frac{3\sqrt{3}}{2} : 3$. Try to manipulate this ratio so that it looks like one you're familiar with.

Getting to the Answer: Clear the fraction by doubling each part of the ratio to get $3 : 3\sqrt{3} : 6$. Notice that each part of the ratio is divisible by 3, so divide a 3 out. The result is $1 : \sqrt{3} : 2$, which should look very familiar by now. The triangle is a 30-60-90 triangle, which means the measure of the smallest angle is 30 degrees.

17. 28
Difficulty: Medium

Category: Additional Topics in Math / Geometry

Strategic Advice: Whenever you see a right triangle with whole number dimensions, you can bet you are probably going to use the Pythagorean theorem.

Getting to the Answer: Use the Pythagorean theorem to find the length of the diagonal shown in the figure.

$$a^2 + b^2 = c^2$$

$$42^2 + 56^2 = c^2$$

$$1{,}764 + 3{,}136 = c^2$$

$$4{,}900 = c^2$$

$$\sqrt{4{,}900} = \sqrt{c^2}$$

$$70 = c$$

The length of the sidewalk is 70 feet. Now, divide by 5 to get $70 \div 5 = 14$, but be careful—this is not the answer. The college plans to put the lights on *both* sides of the sidewalk, so they actually need $14 \times 2 = 28$ lights.

18. 2
Difficulty: Medium

Category: Additional Topics in Math / Geometry

Strategic Advice: The triangle shown is not pretty. Sketch in a line directly down from Z and directly across from X until the two lines meet to form a right triangle. Call this point W.

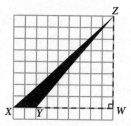

Getting to the Answer: The area of a triangle can be found using the formula $A = \frac{1}{2}bh$. Let $\overline{XY}$ be the base. It spans 2 squares on the grid, which measure $\frac{1}{2}$ centimeter each, so $\overline{XY} = 1$. Now, the height is $\overline{ZW}$. Count the number of units: there are 8, which means the height of the triangle is 4 units. Substitute these numbers into the area formula and simplify: $A = \frac{1}{2}(1)(4) = 2$ square centimeters.

19. 170

Difficulty: Medium

Category: Additional Topics in Math / Geometry

Strategic Advice: When there doesn't seem to be much information to go on in a question, look for information that might be hidden, such as the presence of a 30-60-90 triangle.

Getting to the Answer: The bearing of 120°, as shown in the figure, means 120° east of north. The bearing extends into the second quadrant. Each quadrant is 90°, which means the angle created by the bearing in the second quadrant is 120° − 90° = 30°. This means the angle inside the triangle is 90° − 30° = 60°. Hence, the triangle is a 30-60-90 triangle, which has side lengths in the ratio $x : x\sqrt{3} : 2x$. You know the longer leg, 295, so divide by $\sqrt{3}$ to find the length of the shorter leg, which represents the distance between Bismarck and Pierre: $295 \div \sqrt{3} = 170.318$, which rounds to 170 miles.

20. 51

Difficulty: Hard

Category: Additional Topics in Math / Geometry

Strategic Advice: You can often use the information you found in the first part of an extended response question to solve the second part.

Getting to the Answer: To find the amount of time the plane was in the air, you'll need to know how far it had flown. In the previous question, you found the length of the shorter side of the triangle, 170 miles. The airplane's path is represented by the hypotenuse of the triangle. To find its length, use the Pythagorean theorem or simply multiply the length of the shorter leg by 2 (because it's a 30-60-90 triangle) to get 170 × 2 = 340 miles. Now, use the formula Distance = Rate × Time and solve for time:

$$340 = 400t$$
$$\frac{340}{400} = t$$
$$0.85 = t$$

Be careful—this isn't the answer! The rate was given in miles per hour, so the plane had been in the air 0.85 hours, which is equal to 0.85 × 60 = 51 minutes.

CHAPTER 10

PREPARE

1. B

Difficulty: Medium

Category: Reading / Global

Strategic Advice: Review your Passage Map to find the general connection among the paragraphs. Be careful to stay within the scope of the passage.

Getting to the Answer: The passage begins with poems of the "earliest Greeks" and ends with the poetry of the "heroic age." The author attributes the differences in the poetry to the changes in Greek society between those two times. The author's tone is informational, offering judgment on the poetry of the different periods. Predict that the main purpose is to discuss how societal changes affected poetry. Choice (B) matches this prediction.

PRACTICE

The following passage discusses facts and speculation about a spy during the American Revolution.

Although he may not have been the first American spy, when Captain Nathan Hale uttered his famous final words, "I only regret that I have but one
Line life to lose for my country," he likely ensured that
5 he would long be remembered as the first patriotic martyr of the American Revolution. *Even today,* Hale's story serves as an inspiration for others who have chosen to enter the often deadly and thankless profession of covert intelligence gathering. *Yet,* as
10 it seems clear that the sacrifice Hale made in the autumn of 1776 will long be valued, relatively little is actually known about his fateful mission.

NH = Am. spy during Rev. War.

mission details unknown

Born in Connecticut in 1755 as the sixth child of Richard Hale, a prosperous farmer, Nathan's
15 childhood and education were rather accelerated. Nathan was only 14 years old when he entered Yale University as a freshman, just 18 when he graduated as one of the top students in his class, and not yet 20 when he enlisted in the militia in 1774. With
20 the whole country abuzz from military movements and with many joining the separatist cause, Nathan quickly became involved in the military organization of his hometown. By the time news of the first battles of the war reached Connecticut in 1775, historical
25 records indicate that Hale had become an outspoken leader of the independence movement. His subsequent commissioning as an officer in the Connecticut regiment is well documented, *but* it is the events of 1776, when Hale began his secret mission,
30 that are largely unknown.

bkgd & educ

military bkgd: CT Reg

It is known that Hale was indeed a spy and that he had been a member of the Knowlton Rangers, a small group of elite soldiers operating under what was called a "detached command," taking orders
35 directly from General George Washington. Historians also believe that it was Hale who accompanied a young sergeant named Stephen Hempstead on a mission involving Washington's Long Island forces. *But,* perhaps due to chaos in New York City created
40 by the great fires that had been set in September of 1776, the precise details of Hale's mission and capture are unclear. Historical accounts pick up the story when he was taken before the commanding British General and, after honestly providing his
45 rank and name, was immediately condemned to death by hanging. There was no formal trial, but, according to the British, the papers Hale had on his person were damning enough, and the next morning he was hanged in an apple orchard in the middle
50 of Manhattan. *Yet, despite* the uncertainty surrounding Hale's story of espionage, a clear and undisputed written record verifies the young martyr's final words, for which he will likely be forever remembered and admired.

elite unit of soldiers: KR

mission still unclear

executed by Brit.

2. D

Difficulty: Medium

Category: Reading / Detail

Strategic Advice: Look at your Passage Map to find the important details you noted.

Getting to the Answer: Your Passage Map should note that paragraph 2 details Hale's military background. Review that paragraph to find the details of Hale's commission. In the last sentence, the author writes that Hale received a commission in the Connecticut regiment, or (D).

3. C

Difficulty: Medium

Category: Reading / Global

Strategic Advice: To answer a Global question, use your Passage Map to summarize the passage.

Getting to the Answer: Overall, the passage presents Hale and his history in a positive tone. In the first paragraph, the author states that Hale continues to be an inspiration, and in the final paragraph, the author suggests that there are good reasons Hale is remembered and admired. Predict that the author's purpose is to describe Hale in a positive way. Choice (C) matches this prediction. Be careful. While we'd like to know more about Hale's secret mission to New York, that detail is still unknown, making A out-of-scope and incorrect.

PERFORM

This passage discusses the cane toad's introduction to and effect on the Australian environment.

The cane toad, a large, brightly colored amphibian that can weigh more than a pound, was <u>first introduced to the Australian continent by the sugar-</u>
Line <u>cane industry</u>. The cane toad was a known predator
5 of the <u>cane beetle</u>, which had been devouring the sugarcane crops since the early 1900s. Australian farmers thought that by importing these toads from their <u>native habitats in the Americas</u>, they could use the toads effectively to feast on pests like the
10 cane beetle and eradicate the growing insect threat. So, in 1935, roughly 100 cane toads were carefully packed into crates and shipped to Australia. Upon their toads' arrival, the cane farmers eagerly brought them to a pond <u>in the northeast province of Queensland.</u>
15 Before long, the <u>female cane toads</u> had laid hundreds of thousands of eggs in elongated, gelatinous strings, and the farmers waited for their new predators to be born. As the eggs hatched, the pond became filled with great clouds of squirming,
20 wriggling tadpoles that, upon reaching maturity, were taken to the sugarcane fields and turned loose. The situation that resulted from this <u>fateful release,</u> however, did not coincide with the farmers' plan. In fact, the introduction of cane toads into the wild
25 in Australia has since been deemed <u>nothing short of an ecological disaster.</u>

Easily numbering well into the millions—<u>an exact figure has been impossible to calculate</u>—the cane toads soon dominated the landscape in
30 Queensland. Following their release, some of the toads descended as planned on the sugarcane crops and began to eat the beetles. However, they soon lost interest in their new habitat. For one thing, the mature cane beetles could fly away from their
35 predators, forcing these slow, fat toads to work very hard for their food. In addition, the fields were hot and dry and provided little sleeping shelter for the newcomers, who generally prefer wet shade. These adverse conditions were not severe enough
40 to kill off the toads, but instead the toads began to look elsewhere for food and shelter. Nearby towns, full of lush gardens and well-watered lawns, were extremely inviting, and soon the <u>toads had overrun entire residential areas.</u> They covered the lawns,
45 filled the gardens, found shelter under flowerpots or on porches, and even began to eat bowls of food left outside for pets like cats and dogs.

Today, the people of Queensland <u>hunt cane toads as if they were mosquitoes.</u> But the toads
50 continue to spread south and west through Aus-

Margin notes:

why Aus. farmers brought c.t.

toads released into fields

turned into disaster

A LOT of toads

c.t. ate other things, moved to lawns and gardens

toad takeover

today = c.t. hunted

tralia in staggering numbers. As for the sugarcane industry, just five years after the release of the toads, an effective insecticide spray became available, and the cane beetles were easily exterminated. Scien-
55 tists as well as the Australian government, however, continue to grapple with the cane toad problem.

4. D

Difficulty: Medium

Category: Reading / Detail

Strategic Advice: When presented with an EXCEPT question, use your Passage Map to locate the details in the answer choices. Eliminate an answer choice when you find its referenced detail.

Getting to the Answer: The first paragraph describes the reason the cane toad was introduced. Eliminate A. Paragraph 2 tells you that the toads bred rapidly and successfully; eliminate B. The last sentence in paragraph 2 calls the introduction of the cane toad "an ecological disaster" (line 26), so you can eliminate C. Thus, (D) is correct.

5. B

Difficulty: Hard

Category: Reading / Inference

Strategic Advice: Use your Passage Map to narrow the range of possible answers and paraphrase what the author would agree with.

Getting to the Answer: The passage describes the cause of a problem: the introduction of the cane toad. The passage then describes the effects of that introduction: a huge environmental disaster. Predict that the author would agree that the new species harmed the environment. You can eliminate answer choices that go beyond the scope of this prediction. The author's main focus is on the cause of the problem and the negative effect that resulted. Choice (B) is correct.

EXTRA PRACTICE

The following passage describes the discovery of gold in California and the effects of that discovery on the United States.

topic = CA gold in 1940s

    People around the world unanimously agree that gold is a valuable mineral. Gold has been seen as a precious commodity by many cultures throughout
Line time, and Americans of the 1840s were no different.
5 When James W. Marshall, a carpenter and sawmill owner, discovered a gold nugget in the American River, California was forever changed. News of his discovery attracted thousands of immigrants from other parts of California, as well as other places around the United
10 States and the world.

    In the Sierra Nevada, a mountain range that runs 400 miles through California, years of erosion caused by rainfall and the downhill flow of mountain streams

how CA & gold came to be

loosened pieces of gold that had been embedded in
15 the solid rock formed over 100 million years ago. California is largely made of quartz previously found at the bottom of the Pacific Ocean. Underwater volcanoes melted the quartz into magma and pushed it up towards the surface, sometimes forming islands. Due to the
20 movements of the Earth's tectonic plates, these islands were pushed together and against the West Coast. This movement and accumulation of land over millions of years formed the area known as California. The gold that was dispersed across the sea floor became
25 concentrated and redistributed throughout the veins of quartz in the Sierra Nevada Mountains.

    Marshall's discovery was quickly verified and publicized by the New York Herald in August of 1848. Current California residents of the time were able to
30 get to the gold fields first. Soon after, President James Polk confirmed the discovery in an address to Congress. His address prompted many Americans to move west, as well as other fortune-seekers from around the world to immigrate to the United States. This influx of people

pop. explosion

35 caused California's population to increase, as well as experience a change in demographics. The particular geologic makeup made California the prime location for mining gold. The Northern California city of San

Francisco grew from 1,000 people in 1848 to more than
40 20,000 people in just two years. Because of the rapid population increase, the United States government incorporated the territory into the Union. California became the Union's 31st state in 1850, though it had only been acquired from Mexico two short years before. This was the fastest any new territory has ever been given statehood in the history of the United States.

why CA became state

    Americans from places east of California migrated via two very long and often dangerous paths. Some endured a six-month boat voyage, which departed from
50 New York City and sailed south as far as the tip of South America before heading north to California. The trip was so perilous that most Americans relocating to California opted to travel the famous Oregon Trail. Riding in covered wagons through dangerous conditions, trav-
55 elers who opted to move by land also had a six-month trip to endure. By 1850, the sheer number of people attempting the voyage inspired the creation of the Panama Railway. Built specifically to reduce travel time to California, the first transcontinental railroad, decreased
60 the length of the trip by several months.

2 ways to CA

    Forty-Niners came to California from many different countries around the globe, including China, Germany, Mexico, Turkey, France, and Ireland. The largest group of people to successfully
65 immigrate to California from abroad was the Chinese. Many did not intend to settle in the United States, but instead planned to return home with their fortunes. While many did so, when gold grew scarce and the Chinese Exclusion Act was
70 passed in 1882, prohibiting Chinese immigration for 10 years, many immigrants instead put down roots in California. The result was the most ethnically diverse state in the Union by the middle of the 19th century.

not just Amer.

75   Though the gold in California didn't last long after its discovery, the effects that it had on the population, including the number of people in the state, their ethnicities, and the way they travelled, have lasted to the modern day.

CA gold effects → today

Percent Population Change, 1850–1860

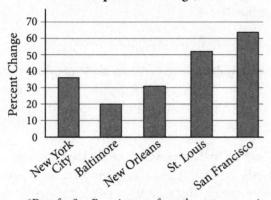

*Data for San Francisco are from the state census in 1852. The 1850 census data were destroyed in a fire.

Data from the *United States Bureau of the Census*.

1. B

Difficulty: Medium

Category: Reading / Rhetoric

Strategic Advice: Look at your notes for the second paragraph. Why does the author include it?

Getting to the Answer: The passage provides geological information to make a point about why gold was so easily mined in California. Choice (B) correctly identifies this information.

2. A

Difficulty: Easy

Category: Reading / Detail

Strategic Advice: One main cause of migration is listed in the passage. Review your notes to find the answer.

Getting to the Answer: The passage states that President Polk's "address to Congress … prompted many Americans to move west" (lines 31-32). Choice (A) conveys this meaning.

3. D

Difficulty: Medium

Category: Reading / Vocab-in-Context

Strategic Advice: Read the referenced line and the sentences around it. Then, use context clues to determine the word's meaning.

Getting to the Answer: The passage suggests that there was an overwhelming increase in population. Choice (D), "rush," conveys this meaning.

4. D

Difficulty: Hard

Category: Reading / Inference

Strategic Advice: Note what the passage states about California's statehood: California entered into the Union despite a surprising fact.

Getting to the Answer: The passage states that "California became the Union's 31st state in 1850, though it had only been acquired from Mexico two short years before" (lines 42-44). It can be inferred, then, that most states had spent longer as territories before being admitted into the Union. Choice (D) is correct.

5. C

Difficulty: Medium

Category: Reading / Command of Evidence

Strategic Advice: Carefully reread the part of the passage that addresses statehood. Identify the specific claims it makes.

Getting to the Answer: The passage states that the United States incorporated California "though it had only been acquired from Mexico two short years before" (lines 43-44). Choice (C) is correct because it explicitly identifies what was unusual about California's statehood process.

6. D

Difficulty: Medium

Category: Reading / Inference

Strategic Advice: Skim quickly to find the information describing the cause stated in the question. Then, read closely to locate the effects of that cause.

Getting to the Answer: The passage states explicitly that the creation of the Panama Railway was built in response to the needs of migrants to California. Choice (D) is correct.

7. C

Difficulty: Hard

Category: Reading / Inference

Strategic Advice: Determine what the passage states about immigrant groups. Consider what can be concluded with certainty about them.

Getting to the Answer: The passage notes that California was very ethnically diverse by the middle of the 19th century. This suggests that immigrants to California came from more places than did immigrants to other states. Choice (C) is correct.

8. D

Difficulty: Medium

Category: Reading / Command of Evidence

Strategic Advice: Review your answer to the previous question. Look for information about California immigration from the passage.

Getting to the Answer: The passage states that California was "the most ethnically diverse state in the Union by the middle of the 19th century" (lines 72-74). This provides evidence for the assertion that immigrants to California came from more nations than did immigrants to other states. Choice (D), therefore, provides the strongest evidence and is correct.

9. C

Difficulty: Easy

Category: Reading / Vocab-in-Context

Strategic Advice: Consider the structure of the sentence. What is the relationship between the nature of the voyage and the choice to travel the Oregon Trail?

Getting to the Answer: The passage states that both routes to California were "very long and often dangerous" (line 48). "Perilous," therefore, is likely to mean "dangerous." Choice (C) is correct.

10. C

Difficulty: Hard

Category: Reading / Rhetoric

Strategic Advice: Review each paragraph and try to identify its main point. Then, assess the answer choices.

Getting to the Answer: The initial paragraphs discuss why gold is important and why it was concentrated in California. It then analyzes the effects of its discovery there. Choice (C) accurately assesses the structure of the passage.

11. A

Difficulty: Medium

Category: Reading / Synthesis

Strategic Advice: Read the chart carefully. Pay particular attention to what the *y*-axis represents.

Getting to the Answer: The population change of all cities for the period from 1850 to 1860 was positive. In other words, all cities gained population, though some gained more than others. Choice (A) is correct, as it correctly identifies that all cities gained in population during this period.

CHAPTER 11

PREPARE

1. D

Difficulty: Easy

Category: Reading / Global

Strategic Advice: After you read a passage, use your Passage Map to quickly paraphrase the author's reason for writing the passage. Keep your focus on the passage as a whole, not one specific part.

Getting to the Answer: The author describes how his introduction to the alphabet initiated changes in his mistress and her treatment of him. He continues to describe how he secretly continued to learn to read, despite the likely consequences if he were discovered. Predict that the main purpose is to describe a process undertaken by Douglass. Choice (D) matches this prediction.

2. B

Difficulty: Medium

Category: Reading / Inference

Strategic Advice: The phrase "strongly suggests" and the cited text indicate that this is an Inference question about an explicit cause-and-effect relationship. Determine whether the cited lines act as the cause or effect and predict what the missing part of the relationship is.

Getting to the Answer: The cited statement informs the reader that slavery caused injury to both Douglass and his mistress; this is the effect. Rephrase the question stem: What was the cause of slavery's injurious effect on the mistress? In the sentences following the cited portion, Douglass describes a variety of good qualities his mistress possessed when he first met her. Douglass then relates how, as a result of owning slaves, her positive qualities were

replaced by negative qualities. Predict that Douglass's mistress started out as a good person, and owning slaves turned her into a bad person. Choice (B) matches this prediction.

3. B

Difficulty: Medium

Category: Reading / Command of Evidence

Strategic Advice: Answering Command of Evidence questions correctly depends on your answer to the previous question. Use the prediction you made to answer the previous question to form your prediction for this question.

Getting to the Answer: To answer the previous question, you predicted that Douglass's mistress started out as a good person and turned into a bad person. This question asks you to provide evidence that she turned into a bad person. Choice (B) conveys how the mistress changed for the worse.

PRACTICE

The following passage explains the challenges facing a population of trees and possible solutions.

Today, oaks are plagued with problems. There is lack of regeneration in populations of certain species. Pests such as the acorn weevil and the filbert

Line worm eat away at acorns and prevent germination.
5 By undermining the root systems of seedlings and saplings, ground squirrels, gophers, and other small mammals often prevent these young plants from reaching tree size. Severe diseases, such as sudden oak death, kill many adult oaks. Many mature oaks
10 are having a tough time with fire suppression. In the past, with light surface fires, the oaks had been able to maintain a stronghold where other plants were not able to compete and died out. Now oaks are being toppled by trees that have a higher toler-
15 ance for shade and are not fire-resistant; earlier such trees would have been killed when Native Americans set fires.

oak problems: pests & disease, other trees

Given all of these challenges, the "old-growth"
Line oaks—the large old valley oaks, Garry oaks, coast
20 live oaks, and canyon live oaks that have huge girth
and large canopies—may become a thing of the
past. These oaks in particular are important because
there are often more terrestrial vertebrates living
in mature oak stands than in seedling and sapling
25 areas. This prevalence of animals occurs because
the large crowns of such oaks provide cover and
feeding sites for a large variety of wildlife.

oaks may die out

The University of California has embarked on an
ambitious and necessary research program called
30 the Integrated Hardwood Range Management
Program to explore the significant causes of oak
decline and offer varied solutions. These include
investigating the use of grassing regimes that are
compatible with oak seedling establishment, reveg-
35 etating sites with native grasses to facilitate better
germination of oak seedlings, documenting insects
and pathogens that attack oaks, and exploring the
ways that native people managed oaks in the past.
Scientists at the Pacific Northwest Research Station
40 in Olympia, Washington, and at Redwood National
Park in northern California are reintroducing the
burning practices of Native Americans. When
used in Garry oak ecosystems, fires keep Douglas
firs from encroaching on the oaks and promote
45 the growth of wildflowers that are important food
plants. Further investigations about these fire
practices may be essential in figuring out how to
maintain oaks in the western landscape today, given
that the fires address many of the factors that are
50 now causing oak decline—from how to eliminate
insect pests of acorns to how to maintain an open
structure in oak groves.

research into problems & solutions

Nat. Am. approach

Ecological restoration, the traditional approach
to woodland maintenance, refers to humans
55 intervening on a very limited time scale to bring
back plants and animals known to have historically
existed in an area. The decline of oaks, one of the
most significant plants to Native Americans, shows
us that humans may play an integral part in the
60 restoration of oak areas. While animals such as jays
have been recognized as crucial partners in oak

ecol rest = limited human intervention

well-being, human actions through the eons may
also have been key to the oaks' flourishing.

new view: humans may help

Sudden oak death, for example, although of
65 exotic origin, may be curtailed locally by thinning
around coastal oaks and tan oaks and setting light
surface fires, simulating ancient fire management
practices of Native Americans. Indigenous shrubs
and trees that grow in association with oaks
70 are hosts to the sudden oak death pathogen. By
limiting the growth of these shrubs, burning that
mimics earlier Native American ways may reduce
opportunities for disease agents to jump from
other plants to oak trees. With a more open envi-
75 ronment, it may be harder for sudden oak death to
spread.

sudden oak death

The oak landscapes that we inherited, which
still bear the marks of former Native American
interactions, demand a new kind of restoration that
80 complements other forms of ecological restoration.
This new kind of restoration could be called
ethnobotanical restoration, defined as reestablishing the historic plant communities of a given area
and restoring indigenous harvesting, vegetation
85 management, and cultivation practices (seedbearing, burning, pruning, sowing, tilling, and weeding)
necessary to maintain these communities in the
long term.

ethnobot. rest = uses humans

Thus, this kind of restoration is not only about
90 restoring plants but also about restoring the human
place within nature. Ethnobotanical restoration is
viewed not as a process that can be completed but
rather as a continuous interaction between people
and plants, as both of their fates are intertwined in
95 a region. Using oaks (through harvesting acorns
and making products from all parts of the tree) and
human intervention (by thinning tree populations
and lighting light fires) may offer us ways to beneficially coexist while improving the long-term health
100 and well-being of the remarkable oak.

restore human role = help the oak

4. C

Difficulty: Medium

Category: Reading / Global

Strategic Advice: Even when you can't make a specific prediction, summarize the author's central idea by reviewing your Passage Map.

Getting to the Answer: The author begins by listing the problems plaguing oak trees and continues by describing possible solutions to each of the problems. Common to each of the solutions is the requirement that humans actively participate in an ongoing process. The author concludes the passage by describing this kind of participation as "ethnobotanical restoration" (lines 81–82). Predict that humans need to participate actively in efforts to restore oaks. Choice (C) matches this prediction.

5. B

Difficulty: Medium

Category: Reading / Detail

Strategic Advice: Use your Passage Map to locate cited phrases. Rephrase what each phrase means.

Getting to the Answer: The author describes ecological restoration as a process that is completed in a very short time and ethnobotanical restoration as a process that seeks to restore ongoing human interaction with plant communities. Choice (B) is correct.

6. B

Difficulty: Easy

Category: Reading / Command of Evidence

Strategic Advice: To answer this question, use the prediction you made to answer the previous question.

Getting to the Answer: To answer the previous question, you needed to recognize that the main difference between the two types of restoration is that while ecological restoration takes place over a short period of time and can be completed, ethnobotanical restoration requires long-term involvement by humans in the natural process of maintaining historic plant communities. Choice (D) is correct.

PERFORM

The following passage details findings from different eras of prenatal screening and the methods and experiments those findings prompted.

Screening newborns for rare genetic diseases is a relatively new practice that began approximately forty years ago. Prior to the advent of screening,
Line biomedical researchers and health professionals
5 were preoccupied with the most prominent causes of newborn mortality, such as diarrheal diseases, influenza, and other infectious diseases. By 1960, however, the infant mortality rate had dropped to less than three percent of live births from over
10 ten percent fifty years earlier. The declining rate was due, in part, to the widespread use of antibiotics; the development of vaccines, particularly the Salk and Sabin polio vaccines; improved nutrition; better education; and generally im-
15 proved sanitary practices. As infant mortality rates dropped, attention shifted to the etiology of rare diseases. The first major milestone in this focus shift occurred in 1962, when President Kennedy announced that the federal government would
20 begin exploring the problem of mental disability— until then, a largely ignored issue. He created the President's Panel on Mental Retardation to lead this exploration.

During roughly the same time period, a major
25 scientific breakthrough in the study of phenylke- tonuria, or PKU, was underway. In 1934, Dr. Asbjorn Folling of Norway first described

early yrs, docs focused on common killers of newborns

success- look at @ rare diseases

JFK → mental disability prg.

found
cause of
PKU

the condition when he observed that some of his
mentally disabled patients had phenylpyruvic acid
30 in their urine, a finding indicative of a deficiency in
the enzyme that converts phenylalanine to tyrosine,
a necessary component for protein synthesis. When
this transformation does not occur, phenylalanine
accumulates in the blood. High levels of phenylala-
35 nine are toxic to the developing brain of an infant

high &
low phen.
cause
problems

and cause mental retardation. At the time, the preventive strategy was to reduce phenylalanine levels
in the patient's diet. This approach had one serious
drawback, though. Phenylalanine is an essential
40 amino acid necessary for proper growth, so deficiencies in it may also lead to mental retardation.

Despite this risk, the younger siblings of children
with PKU were given diets low in phenylalanine
from a very early age. The results were somewhat

possible
sol'n: phen-
free formula

45 encouraging and, in light of the beneficial evidence
from this special diet, two therapeutically promising research initiatives were launched. One was to
devise a source of protein free of phenylalanine. The
outcome was the infant formula Lofenalac, which is
50 still in use today. The other initiative was aimed at
developing a method for detecting high phenylalanine levels before damage to the developing brain
could occur.

Dr. Robert Guthrie led the second initiative,
55 which yielded a breakthrough in the early 1960s.
He developed a test to detect PKU before it became
clinically symptomatic. The test consisted of a

possible
sol'n: early
detection

culture of *Bacillus subtilis* and B-2-thienylalanine,
which inhibits the growth of the bacteria. Once
60 a blood sample from the newborn was added to
this culture, the bacteria would leach the phenyl-

Dr G found
test

alanine from the blood spot, overcome the inhibition caused by the B-2-thienylalanine, and grow.
Bacterial growth beyond a normal range indicated
65 elevated levels of phenylalanine and thus the presence of PKU in the newborn.

The test was not perfect. Over the next few years,
it produced quite a few false positives, and some

some
problems
w/ test...

children unnecessarily received low phenylala-
70 nine diets. To compound the problem, there was
uncertainty about the amount of phenylalanine to

cut from the diet; as a result, some healthy children
developed mental disabilities because of the treatment. Nevertheless, PKU screening was generally
75 considered a success, and spurred questions about
whether other diseases might be prevented through
early detection. After further study, it became clear
that they could. By the late 1960s, newborn screening for rare genetic diseases had become a perma-
80 nent part of infant health care in the United States.

overall =
very useful

other
screenings

7. C
Difficulty: Medium

Category: Reading / Inference

Strategic Advice: The phrase "most strongly suggests" and the clue word "prior" indicate that this is an Inference question asking about an explicit relationship. Review your Passage Map to understand how the author connects certain ideas to each other.

Getting to the Answer: The word "prior" and the cited lines indicate that the relationship is sequential. First, the low phenylalanine diet, which was implemented despite its risks, proved beneficial. Then, the research initiatives began because of the benefits associated with the diet. Predict that the diet was prescribed in spite of those negative outcomes. Choice (C) matches this prediction.

8. D
Difficulty: Medium

Category: Reading / Command of Evidence

Strategic Advice: When answering a Command of Evidence question, find the cited lines that most closely support the prediction you made to answer the previous question.

Getting to the Answer: You predicted that the diet was prescribed in spite of the drawbacks. Compare each of the answer choices to your prediction. Only (D) describes the drawbacks associated with the special diet.

9. B

Difficulty: Medium

Category: Reading / Global

Strategic Advice: Use your Passage Map to quickly summarize the passage. Maintain focus on the general context of each paragraph. Concentrate on the central ideas in each paragraph, not on specific details.

Getting to the Answer: The author introduces the passage by discussing the practice of screening newborns and concludes the passage by describing genetic screening as "a permanent part of infant health care" (lines 79–80). Throughout the passage, the author focuses on the process that brought about the use of genetic screening. Choice (B) is correct.

10. D

Difficulty: Easy

Category: Reading / Detail

Strategic Advice: "According to the passage" indicates that this is a Detail question. Use your Passage Map to locate the referenced details.

Getting to the Answer: Locate each referenced detail and determine why the author included that detail. Choice A is mentioned as a contributor to the decline in the infant mortality rate and can be eliminated. Eliminate B because Lofenalac was developed to treat PKU. Eliminate C because it discusses problems with the test. Choice (D) is correct because the general success of the test showed the potential of screening tests.

11. D

Difficulty: Medium

Category: Reading / Command of Evidence

Strategic Advice: To answer a Command of Evidence question, find the cited lines that most closely support the answer choice you selected in the previous question.

Getting to the Answer: Return to the place in the passage that provided the answer to the previous question. Check to see if one of the answer choices to this question includes the detail you found for the previous question. Choice (D) is correct.

EXTRA PRACTICE

This passage describes how tree farms, widely thought to offer little support to wildlife, became home to a rare species of birds.

As our environment changes over time, <u>certain species thrive while others become rarer.</u> One such species is the small, difficult-to-find Swainson's
Line warbler. Scientists struggle to estimate the popula-
5 tion of this songbird because it is challenging to track. America's foremost wildlife artist, <u>John James Audubon,</u> attempted to describe the bird in the 1830s. Even then, it was considered uncommon. Some of the other birds studied by Audubon have
10 already become extinct, including the ivory-billed woodpecker. Others, such as the Allen's hummingbird, the spotted owl, and the osprey, are at increased risk of extinction due to their habitats disappearing. Against all odds, the Swainson's
15 warbler has held on by changing where it spends its summer seasons.

The Swainson's warbler has been at risk for extinction due to the specificity of its needs. During breeding season, summer, the bird tradition-
20 ally spends time in the southeastern United States forests and lowlands. It then migrates to subtropical locations in the winter, seeking the dry forests of Jamaica or other evergreen forests in Mexico and Cuba. The low population has been attributed to
25 the loss of these habitats due to the gradual conversion of hardwood forests into farmland, reservoirs, and urban or suburban areas. With numbers as low as 90,000 worldwide, the prognosis for the continued survival of the bird <u>has been bleak.</u>
30 Scientists have been studying the birds across the southern United States for more than two decades, but attempts to conserve the species have fallen short due to a lack of understanding of their true habitat needs. Scientists tried to shift the Swainson's
35 warbler to national forests, public refuges, and private sanctuaries, but success was limited. Recently, though, researchers found that the population is increasing. Since the 1990s, Swainson's warblers

have been doing what scientists attempted to do for
40 them: the birds have created new breeding grounds for themselves by moving into industrial pine plantations that have been planted in ten different states.

Millions of acres of industrial pine forests have been planted since the 1920s. Some of these planta-
45 tions are even located in the same areas that Swainson's warblers used to use for breeding grounds before the area's natural forests disappeared. With trees cut every 25 to 35 years, these plantations support a $200 billion industry that produces wood-
50 based goods from housing lumber to notebook paper. The pine plantations were once thought by scientists to offer little support to any wildlife. They do not make ideal habitats due to the even spacing of planted rows and the lack of diversity in tree
55 species. These plantations, though, happen to <u>offer the Swainson's warbler two of the things they most require</u> from their habitats.

When the pines at these tree farms reach about 20 feet high, they hit the one specific stage of
60 growth that appeals to the birds. This height creates high-density undergrowth that the birds rely on for protection during their breeding season. This point of the pine development best mimics the bird's traditional habitat. Before deforestation occurred in
65 the Southeastern United States, Swainson's warblers lived in thickets of cane or areas with dense vines and tangled undergrowth. At the pine plantations, the habitat lasts for about seven to eight years before the trees grow too tall to provide the birds the
70 coverage that they seek. The birds move on once the tangled undergrowth they prefer disappears.

The Swainson's warbler's secondary requirement that pine plantations can easily provide is space. A single breeding pair of the species requires between
75 10 and 20 acres of land. This large amount of space is one of the reasons why the species was so vulnerable to deforestation.

Today pine plantations occupy some 40 million acres in the southern United States. Not all of
80 these acres are usable to the birds, though. When the cutting cycles and the amount of time the trees offer the type of undergrowth desirable to the Swainson's

Margin notes:

SW = uncommon, hard to track

Aud. studied SW

why SW = vulnerable

habitats disappearing

need to truly understand habitat

birds made their own new habitat

SW uses pine plantations used in industry

ideal conditions for birds → undergrowth

birds need space → acres

only some plantations = useful

warblers are considered, it is estimated that approximately 10 million acres of pine plantations are available to the birds at one time.

These numbers suggest that pine plantations will become the Swainson's warbler's primary habitat over time. The species owes its continued existence to its ability to adapt. While other species of warbler have disappeared entirely due to the clearing of natural forests, the Swainson's warbler has remained flexible, shifting its behavior to ensure its own preservation.

pine will become primary habitat

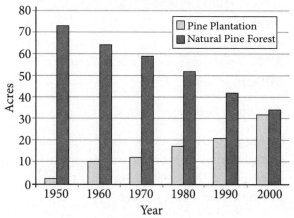

Planted vs. Natural Pine Forests in the Southern U.S.

Adapted from *United States Geological Survey, Land Cover Trends Project.*

1. C

Difficulty: Medium

Category: Reading / Global

Strategic Advice: Think about the central idea of the passage. Eliminate answer choices such as A and D that contain supporting details for the central idea. The correct answer will be an idea that is supported by all of the details in the passage.

Getting to the Answer: This passage is mostly about how the Swainson's warbler population has begun to recover after its natural habitat was reduced by deforestation. Choice (C) is correct.

2. C

Difficulty: Hard

Category: Reading / Rhetoric

Strategic Advice: Review your notes for the first paragraph. Consider the central idea of the paragraph and how it relates to the central idea of the passage. Select the answer choice that most accurately describes the purpose this sentence serves in the passage.

Getting to the Answer: The author mentions these other species of birds to give examples of other animals that are at risk because their habitats have been destroyed, which matches (C).

3. C

Difficulty: Medium

Category: Reading / Inference

Strategic Advice: Review your paragraph 3 notes. How did scientists attempt to preserve the population of the Swainson's warbler? The correct answer should paraphrase your own idea.

Getting to the Answer: In lines 30–36 of paragraph 3, the author explains that previous attempts at conservation have been unsuccessful because scientists did not understand what the birds need in a habitat. This matches (C).

4. C

Difficulty: Medium

Category: Reading / Command of Evidence

Strategic Advice: Locate each of the answer choices in the passage. The correct answer should provide direct support for the answer to the previous question.

Getting to the Answer: In paragraph 3, the author describes why previous conservation efforts by scientists have failed. Choice (C) is correct.

5. D

Difficulty: Medium

Category: Reading / Vocab-in-Context

Strategic Advice: Replace "conversion" in the sentence with each of the answer choices. Consider which word makes the most sense in context.

Getting to the Answer: In this sentence, "transformation" can replace "conversion" without changing the overall meaning. Choice (D) is correct.

6. A

Difficulty: Hard

Category: Reading / Inference

Strategic Advice: Look for the answer choice that is directly supported by the evidence in the text. Eliminate answer choices that are related to the main topic but go too far, such as D.

Getting to the Answer: In paragraph 1, the author discusses the risk of extinction of other birds due to a decrease in their habitats. Choice (A) is correct because it is most directly supported by the evidence in the passage.

7. B

Difficulty: Medium

Category: Reading / Command of Evidence

Strategic Advice: Use your reasoning for answering the previous question to figure out where in the passage the best evidence for that answer will come from.

Getting to the Answer: The details in paragraph 1 provide the most direct support for the idea that more birds will become extinct if their habitats continue to disappear. Choice (B) is correct.

8. D

Difficulty: Easy

Category: Reading / Global

Strategic Advice: Consider the central idea of the passage and the message conveyed by the information included. Select the answer that most closely explains what the author wants to relate to the reader.

Getting to the Answer: This passage is mostly about how the Swainson's warbler has adapted after losing much of its natural habitat. The author's purpose is to explain how this happened, (D).

9. C

Difficulty: Hard

Category: Reading / Inference

Strategic Advice: Think about the process undertaken in each of the answer choices and compare it to the Swainson's warbler's migrating to a new, man-made habitat.

Getting to the Answer: The migration of the Swainson's warbler to pine forests planted by humans is most similar to aquatic animals making new homes from shipwrecks. In both instances, animals have taken something created by humans and made it into a home. Choice (C) is correct.

10. A

Difficulty: Medium

Category: Reading / Vocab-in-Context

Strategic Advice: Eliminate answer choices such as B and D that are synonyms for "point" but do not make sense in context.

Getting to the Answer: In this sentence, the author is describing the stage of development that most closely resembles the bird's natural habitat. This matches (A).

11. A

Difficulty: Medium

Category: Reading / Synthesis

Strategic Advice: Consider only the information presented in the graph. The correct answer will be directly supported by the data.

Getting to the Answer: The graph shows that over the decade, the number of acres of pine plantations has grown steadily while that of natural pine forests has declined. The conclusion that the number of acres of pine plantations could soon surpass that of natural pine forests is supported by the data presented in the graph. Choice (A) is correct.

CHAPTER 12

PREPARE

1. C

Difficulty: Medium

Category: Reading / Inference

Strategic Advice: When you see the phrase "which choice best describes" and the question stem provides both sides of the relationship, look for the answer choice that joins the two sides correctly.

Getting to the Answer: Locate the discussion regarding the insurgents and the government. Paraphrase what each side wanted. Predict that the insurgents wanted more slavery while the government wanted slavery to remain unchanged. Choice (C) matches your prediction.

2. C

Difficulty: Medium

Category: Reading / Vocab-in-Context

Strategic Advice: When you see the phrase "most nearly means" and a cited line, predict a word to substitute for the word in question.

Getting to the Answer: Read the sentence without "interest" and determine the author's intended meaning. Predict that the slave-owning states felt they had a right to own slaves. Choice (C) expresses the same idea.

3. B

Difficulty: Hard

Category: Reading / Inference

Strategic Advice: A relationship clue word in the question stem indicates that you should ask how items are related to each other.

Getting to the Answer: The question stem describes an unanticipated result and asks you to identify the cause. Read around the cited lines until you understand what the cause was. Earlier in the paragraph, Lincoln claims that the cause of the war was slavery, later stating that neither side thought slavery "might cease" (line 40). Predict that the referenced result is the end of slavery, (B).

PRACTICE

The following passage is an excerpt from the preface of Moll Flanders *(1722) by Daniel Defoe.*

The world is so taken up of late with novels and romances, that <u>it will be hard for a private history to be taken for genuine</u>, where the names and other
Line circumstances of the person are concealed, and on
5 this account we must be content to leave the reader to pass his own opinion upon the ensuing sheet, and take it just as he pleases.

The author is here <u>supposed to be</u> writing <u>her own history</u>, and in the very beginning of her
10 account she gives the reasons why she thinks fit to conceal her true name, after which there is no occasion to say any more about that.

It is true that the <u>original of this story is put into new words</u>, and the style of the famous lady we here
15 speak of is a little altered; particularly she is made to tell her own tale in modester words than she told it at first, the copy which came first to hand having been written in language more like one still in Newgate than one grown penitent and humble, as
20 she afterwards pretends to be.

The pen employed in finishing her story, and making it <u>what you now see it to be</u>, has had no little difficulty to put it into a dress fit to be seen, and to make it speak language fit to be read. When
25 a woman debauched from her youth, nay, even being the offspring of debauchery and vice, comes to give an account of all her vicious practices, and even to descend to the particular occasions and circumstances by which she ran through in threescore
30 years, an author must be hard put to wrap it up so

auth. to reader: story might not seem true

MF = autobio but not real ID

writing style altered to be tamer

MF story = dark

clean as not to give room, especially for <u>vicious</u> <u>readers</u>, to turn it to his disadvantage.

All possible care, (however,) has been taken to give no lewd ideas, no immodest turns in the new

35 dressing up of this story; no, not to the worst parts of her expressions. <u>To this purpose</u> some of the vicious part of her life, which could not be modestly told, is quite left out, and several other parts are very much shortened. What is left 'tis hoped will

40 not offend the chastest reader or the modest hearer; and as the best use is made even of the worst story, the moral 'tis hoped will keep the reader serious, even where the story might incline him to be otherwise. <u>To give the history of a wicked life</u> repented

45 of, necessarily requires that the wicked part should be make as wicked as the real history of it will bear, to illustrate and give a beauty to the penitent part, which is certainly the best and brightest, if related with equal spirit and life.

50 (But) as this work is <u>chiefly recommended to</u> <u>those who know how to read it</u>, and how to make the good uses of it which the story all along recommends to them, so it is to be hoped that such readers will be more pleased with the moral than the

55 fable, with the application than with the relation, and with the end of the writer than with the life of the person written of.

There is in this story <u>abundance of delightful</u> <u>incidents, and all of them usefully applied.</u> There is

60 an agreeable turn artfully given them in the relating, that naturally instructs the reader, either one way or other. The first part of her lewd life with the young gentleman at Colchester has so many happy turns given it to expose the crime, and warn all

65 whose circumstances are adapted to it, of the ruinous end of such things, and the foolish, thoughtless, and abhorred conduct of both the parties, that it abundantly atones for all the lively description she gives of her folly and wickedness.

70 Upon this foundation this book is recommended to the reader as a work from every part of which something may be learned, and some just and religious inference is drawn, by which the reader will have something of instruction, if he pleases to

75 make use of it.

MF = changed ways later in life

auth's request: focus on how MF is good

how lewdness can be beneficial

reader should learn from MF's story

4. D
Difficulty: Medium

Category: Reading / Inference

Strategic Advice: The phrase "According to the passage" and a relationship clue word indicate that you should ask yourself how items are being related.

Getting to the Answer: The clue word "because" suggests that this is a cause-and-effect relationship. Find the reference to the narrator's concern and reread the section. Predict that the recent popularity of novels encourages readers to believe what they read is fictional. This prediction matches (D).

5. C
Difficulty: Medium

Category: Reading / Inference

Strategic Advice: Open-ended Inference questions about relationships (explicit or implicit) require you to describe the relationship in your own words.

Getting to the Answer: Because the question stem is essentially asking about why the narrator wrote the story described in the passage and not the passage itself, focus on what the narrator says about the purpose of the story. By paraphrasing the narrator's intent stated in the final paragraph, you can predict that the narrator thinks readers can learn good things from the story. Choice (C) matches this prediction.

6. B
Difficulty: Medium

Category: Reading / Vocab-in-Context

Strategic Advice: When answering Vocab-in-Context questions, focus on synonyms for the word in question, not on a specific definition.

Getting to the Answer: Read the sentence without "usefully applied" and ask what the narrator is trying to convey. Throughout the passage, the narrator returns to the idea that the story is written not to relate "wicked" tales but to provide readers with an opportunity to learn from the lessons found in the story. Predict that the narrator is reaffirming the purpose for writing such stories. Choice (B) matches your prediction.

PERFORM

The following passage is about the role chemistry plays in archeology.

Demonstrating that chemistry sometimes can inform history, researchers from the National Institute of Standards and Technology (NIST), Colorado
Line College and Mount Saint Mary's University in
5 Emmitsburg, Maryland, have shown that sensitive nondestructive evaluation (NDE) techniques can be used to determine the elemental composition of ancient coins, even coins that generally have been considered too corroded for such methods. Along
10 the way, the researchers' analysis of coins minted in ancient Judea has raised new questions about who ruled the area while giving insight into trading patterns and industry in the region.

Elemental and isotope analysis of the metals in
15 ancient artifacts sometimes can pinpoint the places where the metal was mined, because ores in a given region often have a unique composition. This can be combined with historical records of when mines in the area were operating to determine when the
20 coin was likely struck. The results not only help date the coin, but also offer insight into trade and power relationships in the region.

To compare the effectiveness of various nondestructive analytical methods with destructive
25 methods often used to determine the age and origin of ancient coins, the group studied coins minted by Kings Herod Agrippa I and Herod Agrippa II in what is modern day Palestine and Israel, during a biblically and historically significant period.

30 The vast numbers of a particular coin, a prutah, found in the archaeological record has led scholars to disagree about when they were struck and by whom. The provenance of the coin is important because it is used to establish dates for places and
35 events in the early years of Christianity and the onset of the Jewish War (66-70 CE) against the Romans and the Diaspora that followed.

To better establish whether the coins were minted by Agrippa I (41-45 CE) or Agrippa II
40 (after 61 CE), the team performed X-ray fluorescence and lead isotope analysis to fingerprint the ores used in the production of the coins. These NDE methods are not commonly used on corroded coins because the corrosion can affect the
45 results—in some cases making it difficult to get a result at all. The team showed that these problems could be overcome using polarizing optics and powerful new software for X-ray fluorescence analysis, combined with careful calibration of
50 the mass spectrometer using Standard Reference Materials from NIST.

The lead isotope analysis, performed at NIST, showed that the coins that had been attributed to Agrippa I were indeed from that era. More interest-
55 ingly, however, the group found that the copper from which the coins were made most likely came from mines that scholars thought hadn't been opened until a century later.

"All the archaeological evidence has thus far
60 suggested that the Romans had moved into Arabia in the second century CE," says Nathan Bower of Colorado College. "What this analysis shows is that the Romans may have reached the region earlier or found that these mines had already been
65 opened. Either way, our findings suggest that the Romans had a much closer relationship with this particular region than scholars had previously thought."

To follow up on their research, the group is
70 planning to perform more tests to determine if the mines in question may have been operating even earlier than their recent findings suggest.

Margin notes:

chemistry (NDE) → new q's abt. history

chem. shows where metal is from

chem + history → insight into trade & power

study to determine non-destructive vs destructive analysis

scholars disagree abt. coin's origin

origin = used to establish timeline

method used in research

corrosion affects results

solution to corrosion issues

results of the research: mines existed earlier than they thought

quote abt findings: Romans & region coins minted in

next steps in research

7. A

Difficulty: Medium

Category: Reading / Vocab-in-Context

Strategic Advice: Remember to avoid common meanings when answering Vocab-in-Context questions.

Getting to the Answer: Read the sentence without "struck" and rephrase what the author means. Predict that the author is referring to when the coins were minted. Choice (A) is correct.

8. D

Difficulty: Medium

Category: Reading / Inference

Strategic Advice: To answer Inference questions that are not about specific parts of the passage, find the author's thesis and look for the answer choice that is consistent with it.

Getting to the Answer: Use your Passage Map to locate the thesis. The author states in the first sentence that science can help us learn about history. Lead isotope analysis is presented as an example of how science "can inform" (lines 1-2) history. In the first paragraph, the author states that this analysis has raised questions and in paragraph 6, the author indicates that the analysis answered questions about when the analyzed coins were made. Therefore, (D) is correct.

9. D

Difficulty: Medium

Category: Reading / Inference

Strategic Advice: The phrase "according to the passage" and a relationship keyword in the question stem signal an Inference question.

Getting to the Answer: The relationship keyword "because" indicates a cause-and-effect relationship, so identify why the researchers chose the coin in question. Predict that if the scientists' technique could help answer historian's questions, then historians would recognize the value of the technique. Choice (D) is correct.

10. A

Difficulty: Easy

Category: Reading / Vocab-in-Context

Strategic Advice: The phrase "most nearly means" and a cited line indicate a Vocab-in-Context question.

Getting to the Answer: Read the sentence without "establish" and think of a synonym that can replace it. Predict that because scientists wanted to determine facts through their research, they wanted to determine who made the coins. Choice (A) matches your prediction.

EXTRA PRACTICE

The following passage is adapted from Around the World in Eighty Days *by Jules Verne.*

usual routine

Phileas Fogg, having shut the door of his house at half-past eleven, and having put his right foot before his left five hundred and seventy-five times,

Line and his left foot before his right five hundred and

5 seventy-six times, reached the Reform Club. He repaired at once to the dining-room and took his place at the <u>habitual table</u>, the cover of which had already been laid for him. A flunkey handed him an uncut Times, which he proceeded to cut with a

PF = creature of habit

10 skill which betrayed <u>familiarity</u> with this delicate operation. The perusal of this paper absorbed Phileas Fogg until a quarter before four, whilst the Standard, his next task, occupied him till the dinner hour. <u>Dinner passed as breakfast had done</u>,

day in the life of PF

15 and Mr. Fogg re-appeared in the reading-room and sat down to the Pall Mall[1] at twenty minutes before six. Half an hour later several members of the Reform came in and drew up to the fireplace.

PF's friends

They were Mr. Fogg's usual partners at whist[2]:

20 Andrew Stuart, an engineer; John Sullivan and Samuel Fallentin, bankers; Thomas Flanagan, a brewer; and Gauthier Ralph, one of the Directors of the Bank of England.

"Well, Ralph," said Thomas Flanagan, "what

25 about <u>that robbery?</u>"

recent robbery @ bank

"Oh," replied Stuart, "the Bank will lose the money."

"On the contrary," broke in Ralph, "I hope we may put our hands on the robber. Skillful detectives

30 have been sent to all the principal ports of America and the Continent, and he'll be a clever fellow if he slips through their fingers."

"But have you got the robber's description?" asked Stuart.

35 "In the first place, <u>he is no robber at all</u>," re-turned Ralph, positively.

"What! a fellow who makes off with fifty-five thousand pounds, no robber?"

"No."

40 "Perhaps he's a manufacturer, then."

"<u>The Daily Telegraph says that he is a gentleman</u>."

robber = unusual

It was Phileas Fogg, whose head now emerged from behind his newspapers, who made this

45 remark. A package of banknotes, to the value of fifty-five thousand pounds, had been taken from the principal cashier's table, that functionary being at the moment engaged in registering the receipt of three shillings and sixpence. Let it be observed that

details about robbery

50 the Bank of England reposes a touching confidence in the honesty of the public. There are neither guards nor gratings to protect its treasures; gold, silver, banknotes are freely exposed, at the mercy of the first comer. A keen observer of English customs

55 relates that, being in one of the rooms of the Bank one day, he had the curiosity to examine a gold in-got weighing some seven or eight pounds. He took it up, scrutinised it, passed it to his neighbour, he to the next man, and so on until the ingot, going from

60 hand to hand, was transferred to the end of a dark entry; nor did it return to its place for half an hour. Meanwhile, the cashier had not so much as raised his head. But in the present instance things had not gone so smoothly. The package of notes not being

65 found when five o'clock sounded from the ponder-ous clock in the "drawing office," the amount was passed to the account of profit and loss.

There were <u>real grounds for supposing</u>, as the Daily Telegraph said, that <u>the thief did not belong</u>

newspaper → thief = unusual, not common criminal

70 <u>to a professional band</u>. On the day of the robbery a well-dressed gentleman of polished manners, and with a well-to-do air, had been observed going to and fro in the paying room where the crime was committed. A description of him was easily pro-

75 cured and sent to the detectives; and some hopeful spirits, of whom Ralph was one, did not despair of his apprehension. The papers and clubs were full of the affair, and everywhere people were discuss-ing the probabilities of a successful pursuit; and the

80 Reform Club was especially agitated, several of its members being Bank officials.

Ralph would not concede that the work of the detectives was likely to be in vain, for he thought that the prize offered would greatly stimulate their

different opin-ions on robbery being solved

85 zeal and activity. But Stuart was far from sharing

this confidence; and, as they placed themselves at the whist-table, they continued to argue the matter.

Stuart → thief will escape

90   "I maintain," said Stuart, "<u>that the chances are in favour of the thief, who must be a shrewd fellow</u>."

    "Well, but where can he fly to?" asked Ralph. "No country is safe for him."

    "Pshaw!"

    "Where could he go, then?"

PF → world not big anymore

95   "Oh, I don't know that. <u>The world is big enough</u>."

    "It was once," said Phileas Fogg, in a low tone.

¹ Pall Mall: a street in the city of Westminster, London
² Whist: a trick-taking card game. Modern derivatives include Hearts and Spades

1. D
Difficulty: Medium

Category: Reading / Vocab-in-Context

Strategic Advice: Locate context clues to help determine the meaning of the word. Predict a meaning for the word and then match it to the closest answer choice.

Getting to the Answer: The sentence describes Fogg arriving at the club and going to his usual table. A good prediction might be "went." Be careful of answer choices that offer alternate meanings for the target word. Look for the nearest match in the answers. Choice (D) fits with the tone and context of the sentence.

2. C
Difficulty: Medium

Category: Reading / Inference

Strategic Advice: Review the descriptions of Phileas Fogg and his actions in your Passage Map. Summarize what the beginning of the passage says about Fogg.

Getting to the Answer: Paragraph 1 describes Fogg counting out his steps on his way to the club. Upon arriving at the club, Fogg goes to his

"habitual table" (line 7) and performs a routine series of actions. Choice (C) is correct, as the details in paragraph 1 depict a man who likes to keep to a set routine.

3. A
Difficulty: Medium

Category: Reading / Command of Evidence

Strategic Advice: Review your answer to the previous question. Locate the answer choice that directly supports the conclusion you drew to answer the previous question.

Getting to the Answer: Choice (A) is correct. It provides the best support for the idea that Phileas Fogg is a man of habit and routine. The word "habitual" (line 7) and the fact that his table was prepared ahead of time for him suggest that Fogg followed this routine regularly.

4. A
Difficulty: Medium

Category: Reading / Inference

Strategic Advice: Review the answer choices. Skim your Passage Map for evidence that would prove one of the answer choices.

Getting to the Answer: Fogg reads the newspaper at the beginning of the passage. He chimes in with a comment on the robbery the other men are discussing based on the information he learned in the paper. Therefore, (A) is correct.

5. D
Difficulty: Easy

Category: Reading / Command of Evidence

Strategic Advice: Review your answer to the previous question. Decide which lines of text show Fogg's understanding of current events.

Getting to the Answer: Choice (D) is correct. In these lines, Fogg interjects with additional information about a crime that is a current event.

6. B

Difficulty: Medium

Category: Reading / Detail

Strategic Advice: Locate the portion of the text that discusses the bank. Draw a logical conclusion about the Bank of England based on the text and predict an answer.

Getting to the Answer: The passage describes the lack of security measures at the bank that led to a theft in broad daylight. The text references a lack of guards or protective gratings. Choice (B) is correct.

7. A

Difficulty: Easy

Category: Reading / Vocab-in-Context

Strategic Advice: Find context clues in the target sentence. Predict the meaning of the word and look for a match in the answer choices.

Getting to the Answer: "Functionary" (line 47) refers back to the "principal cashier" (line 47) mentioned earlier in the sentence. Pay attention to the tone and specific context clues to help you choose between two related answer choices such as "official" and "servant." Choice (A) is correct; it provides a suitably neutral word that could substitute for "principal cashier."

8. C

Difficulty: Medium

Category: Reading / Inference

Strategic Advice: Find the part of the passage that describes the thief. Locate sentences that focus on a description of the suspect.

Summarize the details in a one-sentence description.

Getting to the Answer: Lines 70-74 ("On the day ... crime was committed") describe the suspect as a gentleman. Choice (C) is correct because the passage suggests that the police do not believe the man to be a professional thief due to the description of his appearance and demeanor.

9. B

Difficulty: Hard

Category: Reading / Rhetoric

Strategic Advice: Reread the cited line. Concentrate on how the sentence impacts the text surrounding it.

Getting to the Answer: Examining the surrounding text shows that this comment occurs during a discussion about the thief being on the run. Fogg has silently listened to the conversation to this point, but now quietly interjects. This suggests that Fogg will have more to say about the topic; (B) is correct.

10. C

Difficulty: Hard

Category: Reading / Rhetoric

Strategic Advice: Think about the passage as a whole. Use one sentence to predict the purpose of this passage. Make sure the tone of the answer choice matches the tone of the passage.

Getting to the Answer: The excerpt provides a brief character sketch of Phileas Fogg and establishes the dynamics of his friendships at the Reform Club. Choice (C) is correct; it accurately identifies the purpose of the excerpt.

CHAPTER 13

PREPARE

1. C

Difficulty: Medium

Category: Reading / Rhetoric

Strategic Advice: Use your Passage Map to summarize the author's tone and purpose. Look for key words that indicate the author's opinion.

Getting to the Answer: A good summary of the author's tone and purpose would be: "Do the solar constant and sunspots affect Earth's weather? Research suggests that they do, but does not explain how. Although questions remain, scientists think the data could be useful." The tone of the passage is informative, and key words are used to illustrate the connections between the data collected and the scientific understanding gained. Predict that the author's purpose is to inform the reader about an aspect of scientific research and the results of that research. Choice (C) is correct.

2. B

Difficulty: Medium

Category: Reading / Rhetoric

Strategic Advice: To answer questions about the role of a cited section in the context of the entire passage, focus on how the cited section helps the author achieve his overall purpose for writing the passage.

Getting to the Answer: Review your Passage Map notes for paragraph 8. The author explains that the scientists don't fully understand their findings. The author uses the questions in the paragraph to illustrate the areas of the research that the scientists don't understand. Choice (B) is correct.

3. B

Difficulty: Easy

Category: Reading / Rhetoric

Strategic Advice: Questions about the purpose of a particular phrase are really asking about how that phrase helps the author achieve his or her overall purpose.

Getting to the Answer: Think about the cited phrase in the context of the author's purpose to inform the reader about solar constant research and its potential applications. Predict that even without a full understanding of the interactions between solar cycles and Earth's climate, the solar constant research might soon have practical uses. Choice (B) is correct.

PRACTICE

The following is an excerpt from The Woman in White, *a novel by Wilkie Collins published in 1859 and considered to be one of the first novels of the mystery genre.*

(Pesca's) face and manner, on the evening when we confronted each other at my mother's gate, were more than sufficient to inform me that <u>something</u>
Line <u>extraordinary had happened</u>. It was quite useless,
5 however, to ask him for an immediate explanation. I could only conjecture, while he was dragging me in by both hands, that, knowing my habits, he had come to the cottage to make sure of meeting me that night and that <u>he had some news to tell of an</u>
10 <u>unusually agreeable kind.</u>

We both bounced into the parlor in a highly abrupt and undignified manner. My mother sat by the open window laughing and fanning herself. Pesca was one of her especial favorites, and his
15 wildest eccentricities were always pardonable in her eyes. From the first moment she found out that the little Professor was deeply and gratefully attached to her son, she opened her heart to him unreservedly and took <u>all his puzzling foreign peculiarities</u> for

*P's face →
smthg
happened*

*Mom accepts
P's oddities*

P = prof?

S does not accept P bc of propriety

elders = more excited by new things; youth = unaffected

kids = too well raised?

Mom acted younger than sis w/ P

M&P – great news! Excited!

S obsessed with cup

20 granted, without so much as attempting to understand any one of them.

My sister Sarah, with all the advantages of youth,
was, strangely enough, less pliable. She did full
justice to Pesca's excellent qualities of heart, but
25 she could not accept him implicitly, as my mother
accepted him, for my sake. Her insular notions of
propriety rose in perpetual revolt against Pesca's
constitutional contempt for appearances, and she
was always more or less undisguisedly astonished
30 at her mother's familiarity with the eccentric little
foreigner. I have observed, not only in my sister's
case, but in the instances of others, that <u>we of the
young generation are nowhere near as hearty and
impulsive as some of our elders</u>. I constantly see
35 old people flushed and excited by the prospect of
some anticipated pleasure which altogether fails to
ruffle the tranquility of their serene grandchildren.
Are we, I wonder, quite such genuine boys and girls
now as our seniors were in their time? Has the great
40 advance in education taken rather too long a stride,
and are we in these modern days just the least trifle
in the world too well brought up?

Without attempting to answer those questions
decisively, I may at least record that I never saw my
45 mother and my sister together in Pesca's society
without finding my mother much the younger
woman of the two. On this occasion, (for example,)
while the old lady was laughing heartily over the
boyish manner in which we tumbled into the par-
50 lor, Sarah was perturbedly picking up the broken
pieces of a teacup, which the Professor had knocked
off the table in his precipitate advance to meet me
at the door.

"I don't know what would have happened,
55 Walter," said my mother, "if you had delayed much
longer. Pesca has been half mad with impatience,
and I have been half mad with curiosity. The Professor has brought some wonderful news with him,
in which he says you are concerned, and he has
60 cruelly refused to give us the smallest hint of it till
his friend Walter appeared."

"Very provoking: it spoils the set," murmured
Sarah to herself, mournfully absorbed over the
ruins of the broken cup.

P addresses group

P jests

P needs drawing master to travel

P volunteers someone

65 While these words were being spoken, Pesca,
<u>happily and fussily unconscious</u> of the irrepa-
rable wrong which the crockery had suffered at
his hands, was dragging a large arm-chair to the
opposite end of the room, so as to command us all
70 three, in the character of a public speaker addressing an audience. Having turned the chair with its
back towards us, he jumped into it on his knees and
<u>excitedly addressed his small congregation</u> of three
from an impromptu pulpit.

75 "Now, my good dears," began Pesca, "listen to
me. The time has come—I recite my good news—
I speak at last."

"Hear, hear," said my mother, humoring the joke.

"The next thing he will break, Mamma," whis-
80 pered Sarah, "will be the back of the best arm-chair."

"Among the fine London Houses where I teach
the language of my native country," said Pesca, "is
one, mighty fine, in the big place called Portland.
The golden Papa there, the mighty merchant, says 'I
85 have got a letter from my friend, the Mister, and he
wants a recommend from me, of a drawing-master,
to go down to his house in the country. Perhaps you
know of a drawing master that I can recommend?'

"I address myself to the mighty merchant, and
90 I say, '"Dear sir, I have the man! The first and foremost drawing-master of the world!"'

4. C
Difficulty: Medium

Category: Reading / Rhetoric

Strategic Advice: Use your Passage Map to
identify how this paragraph helps the narrator
achieve his overall purpose for the passage.

Getting to the Answer: This paragraph provides context for the rest of the passage. The
narrator describes Pesca's expressive nature, his
understanding of Pesca, and the reason for the
subsequent events in the passage. Predict that
this paragraph sets the stage for understanding
how Pesca's character will impact the rest of
the story. Choice (C) matches your prediction.

5. A

Difficulty: Medium

Category: Reading / Rhetoric

Strategic Advice: To understand why a narrator chooses a particular word or phrase, focus on the author's purpose for writing the passage. The cited section will work to accomplish that purpose.

Getting to the Answer: Throughout the paragraph, the narrator describes why his mother finds Pesca so pleasing. This introductory wording sets the stage by describing Pesca as undignified. This feature of his personality is a great match for (A).

6. D

Difficulty: Medium

Category: Reading / Rhetoric

Strategic Advice: Focus on how the narrator sees the characters and events to understand the author's point of view.

Getting to the Answer: U.S. and World Literature passages focus on the relationships between main characters. Here, the main characters are the narrator, his mother, his sister, and Pesca. The narrator doesn't describe the interaction between the two women, focusing instead on the reaction that each woman has to Pesca's actions. Predict that the author wants to create a sketch of each woman by using those different responses. Choice (D) is correct.

PERFORM

The following is adapted from Helen Keller's address to the American Association to Promote the Teaching of Speech to the Deaf at Mt. Airy, Philadelphia, Pennsylvania (July 8, 1896).

If you knew all the joy I feel in being able to speak to you today, I think you would have some

Line idea of the value of speech to the deaf, and you would understand why I want every little deaf
5 child in all this great world to have an opportunity to learn to speak. I know that much has been said and written on this subject, and that there is a wide difference of opinion among teachers of the deaf in regard to oral instruction. It seems very strange to
10 me that there should be this difference of opinion; I cannot understand how any one interested in our education can fail to appreciate the satisfaction we feel in being able to express our thoughts in living words. Why I use speech constantly, and I cannot
15 begin to tell you how much pleasure it gives me to do so. Of course I know that it is not always easy for strangers to understand me, but it will be by and by; and in the meantime I have the unspeakable happiness of knowing that my family and friends
20 rejoice in my ability to speak. My little sister and baby brother love to have me tell them stories in the long summer evenings when I am at home; and my mother and teacher often ask me to read to them from my favourite books. I also discuss the politi-
25 cal situation with my dear father, and we decide the most perplexing questions quite as satisfactorily to ourselves as if I could see and hear. So you see what a blessing speech is to me. It brings me into closer and tenderer relationship with those I love, and
30 makes it possible for me to enjoy the sweet companionship of a great many persons from whom I should be entirely cut off if I could not talk.

I can remember the time before I learned to speak, and how I used to struggle to express my
35 thoughts by means of the manual alphabet—how my thoughts used to beat against my fingertips like little birds striving to gain their freedom, until one day Miss Fuller opened wide the prison-door and let them escape. I wonder if she remembers how
40 eagerly and gladly they spread their wings and flew away. Of course, it was not easy at first to fly. The speech-wings were weak and broken, and had lost all the grace and beauty that had once been theirs; indeed, nothing was left save the impulse to fly,
45 but that was something. One can never consent to creep when one feels an impulse to soar. But,

HK → joy of speech, shared with deaf

all want ability to speak

uses speech to tell stories, read, argue, etc.

cut off from world until Ms F showed speech

struggled at first

hard to not succeed; kept trying

nevertheless, it seemed to me sometimes that I could never use my speech wings as God intended I should use them; there were so many difficulties
50 in the way, so many discouragements; but I kept on trying, knowing that patience and perseverance would win in the end. And while I worked, I built the most beautiful air-castles, and dreamed dreams, the pleasantest of which was of the time when I
55 should talk like other people; and the thought of the pleasure it would give my mother to hear my voice once more, sweetened every effort and made every failure an incentive to try harder the next time. So I want to say to those who are trying to

those struggling to speak: it gets better.

60 learn to speak and those who are teaching them: Be of good cheer. Do not think of today's failures, but of the success that may come tomorrow. You have set yourselves a difficult task, but you will succeed if you persevere; and you will find a joy in over-
65 coming obstacles—a delight in climbing rugged paths, which you would perhaps never know if you did not sometime slip backward—if the road was always smooth and pleasant. Remember, no effort that we make to attain something beautiful is ever

results will be worth it

70 lost. Sometime, somewhere, somehow we shall find that which we seek. We shall speak, yes, and sing, too, as God intended we should speak and sing.

7. A

Difficulty: Medium

Category: Reading / Rhetoric

Strategic Advice: Review your Passage Map and identify the author's purpose for writing the passage. Ask how the cited phrase helps the author achieve that purpose.

Getting to the Answer: This passage focuses on the author's experience of overcoming the obstacles between her and the ability to speak, the results that her success made possible, and her belief that others should have the same opportunity. By showing how difficult expression was before she could speak, the author emphasizes the benefits she received because she fought so hard. Predict that the phrase

highlights how hard expressing herself was before she could speak. Choice (A) matches your prediction.

8. C

Difficulty: Medium

Category: Reading / Rhetoric

Strategic Advice: To answer questions about an author's point of view, use your Passage Map to summarize the author's purpose for writing the passage. Ask who would express that point of view.

Getting to the Answer: In the first paragraph, the author describes a difference of opinion among teachers who work with deaf students and then states her position on the issue. She thinks that other deaf people should have the chance to learn to speak. Additionally, she makes it clear that she is not an outside observer of a disability, but someone who struggled to overcome adversity. Predict that the author seeks to ensure that other deaf people have access to the same oral instruction that she received. Choice (C) is correct.

9. B

Difficulty: Medium

Category: Reading / Rhetoric

Strategic Advice: Review your Passage Map and identify the author's purpose not only for the overall passage but also for the cited section.

Getting to the Answer: The author begins the passage by stating her position: All deaf children should have the opportunity to learn to speak. She then acknowledges that not everyone shares that opinion. To persuade those who disagree with her, she provides specific examples from her own experience to support her position and to sway those who disagree. Choice (B) is correct.

EXTRA PRACTICE

The following passage explores the <u>history and impact of public higher education</u> in the United States.

Every year, hundreds of thousands of students graduate from U.S. public universities. Many of the largest and most elite schools in the nation fall into
Line the category of public, or state, institutions. Unlike
5 private universities, which generally operate independently from any government influence, public higher education was established through government legislation and is sustained through state or federal involvement in various ways. <u>A look into</u>
10 <u>the history of U.S. public higher education can shed light on the changing ideals of the American story over the past century and a half.</u>

America's earliest higher-education institutions, like Harvard, were initially developed by and for
15 clergy, or church workers. For 17th-century Puritans in America, church leadership was of utmost importance. At that time, clergy was the main profession for which college degrees were offered. But during the 18th and 19th centuries, paralleling
20 the onset of secular (and increasingly scientifically inclined) modern thought, the nation and government acknowledged the <u>need for broader higher education opportunities</u>. Philosophers and politicians alike were aware that well-educated citizens
25 were a vital element of a functional democracy. A better-informed voting population could secure a better political future. (Moreover,) with aims to advance the fields of technology and agriculture through higher education, legislators anticipated
30 potential economic improvements nationwide as well. It was in the nation's best interest to make college more accessible.

In 1862, <u>President Lincoln</u> signed the <u>Morill Land-Grant Act.</u> This was, in many ways, the force
35 behind the public university system. The Morill Act ensured that public land would be set aside for the establishment of universities across the country. The coming decades saw a massive increase in the opening of universities in the nation. Hundreds
40 of U.S. public universities began to operate. These schools received federal and state support, offered practical, accessible education, and sought, originally, to advance the fields of agriculture and mechanics. Soon these schools offered wide variet-
45 ies of subjects and specialties. These universities would be operated by their respective states, but all would adhere to certain broad federal regulations.

At the time, the government was seeking to mend racial injustices through legislation. To
50 this effect, a <u>second land act</u> was passed in 1890 in hopes of inhibiting discrimination in public universities. While at the time this did not quite accomplish the intended openness and diversity, <u>it paved the way for the culture of diversity</u> the
55 American university system enjoys today. Many public universities are now richly diverse, with regulations in place to accept students of any race, ethnicity, or socioeconomic status. In a similar vein, women—once a minority in colleges—increasingly
60 gained a strong presence in U.S. universities over the past 150 years. Women actually surpassed men in overall U.S. college attendance around the turn of the 21st century.

Since the legislation of the 19th-century, public
65 universities have undergone <u>momentous growth</u>. The system has evolved to address and accommodate the nuances of 20th- and 21st-century American culture and development. Offering to in-state students some of the most affordable degree
70 programs in higher education, these schools have now graduated millions of undergraduate and graduate students. Public universities also manage the majority of the nation's government-funded academic research initiatives. Featuring some of the
75 most competitive athletic programs in the world, as well as elite scholarship and arts programs, the U.S. public universities' <u>accomplishments seem boundless</u>. With schools in Alaska, Hawaii, and even U.S. territories like Puerto Rico and Guam, public
80 university impact reaches the farthest corners and populations of the nation. The state school system

[Margin annotations:]
public colleges → tied closely to gov't & USA

early schools = religious

wanting to advance in tech. prompted public univ.

Lincoln & M L-G Act → public land for univ.

2nd act later pushed for diversity

growth in schools; affordable

gov't research, athletics, and more

impact on others

has been formative for American culture, philoso-phy, economics, medicine, politics, and much more.

85 The eminence of the U.S. public university net-work stretches beyond the United States. Students travel from across the globe to study at the top pro-grams. Cutting-edge schools like the University of Virginia (UVA) and University of California at Los Angeles (UCLA) receive continual international

attracts global attention

90 attention for their accomplishments in scholarship and research. Programs, faculty, and students from these schools participate in the global conversation in significant ways, working toward a better future for the planet.

95 Given those early visions for a more robustly educated voting population, the enormity of

reflect values of U.S. identity

the system that the Morill Act launched is remarkable. U.S. public universities have both shaped and employed many of America's greatest

100 thinkers. Considering their timeline and their accomplishments, these schools seem to reflect the post–Civil War history of diversity, liberty, creativity, and equal opportunity that in many ways distinguishes the American cultural identity.

1. C
Difficulty: Hard

Category: Reading / Rhetoric

Strategic Advice: The correct answer will reflect a specific position supported in both the second paragraph and the passage as a whole.

Getting to the Answer: The author is citing politi-cal and economic reasons to explain why the gov-ernment "acknowledged the need" (line 22) for educated citizens. Choice (C) is correct.

2. B
Difficulty: Medium

Category: Reading / Command of Evidence

Strategic Advice: The correct choice should support your answer to the previous question. Consider which choice best shows a clear rela-tionship to your answer.

Getting to the Answer: Choice (B) is correct because it explicitly states that the government saw the "need for broader higher education opportunities" (lines 22–23).

3. A
Difficulty: Medium

Category: Reading / Rhetoric

Strategic Advice: Summarize the paragraph and think about what the author would want the reader to know after reading it.

Getting to the Answer: The Morill Act was an early example of the federal government's desire to increase enrollment at public universi-ties. Choice (A) is correct.

4. B
Difficulty: Medium

Category: Reading / Rhetoric

Strategic Advice: The author's choice of words is deliberate. Read the sentence carefully and think about what the author is suggesting when he uses the word "accessible."

Getting to the Answer: The passage notes that public universities received federal and state support. This means the universities could then function at a lower cost and could enable more students to attend. Choice (B) is correct.

5. D
Difficulty: Easy

Category: Reading / Vocab-in-Context

Strategic Advice: Use context clues to help you predict the meaning of the word as it is used in the sentence.

Getting to the Answer: The last sentence in paragraph 3 contrasts the fact that although universities would be operated by states, they would still need to follow, or comply with, federal regulations because they received federal support. Choice (D) is correct.

6. C

Difficulty: Hard

Category: Reading / Rhetoric

Strategic Advice: A central theme of the passage is that expansion of public universities has impacted American culture. Consider which of these pieces of evidence best supports that theme.

Getting to the Answer: In paragraph 4, the author describes how public universities have gradually become more diverse, offering educational opportunities to many people who would not have otherwise had them in previous years. This has had a significant impact on American culture. Choice (C) is correct.

7. C

Difficulty: Medium

Category: Reading / Rhetoric

Strategic Advice: Think about why the author would want to include this fact. Look for the answer that is accurately reflected in the context of the paragraph.

Getting to the Answer: The paragraph's central idea is that the student populations of public universities have grown increasingly diverse. Choice (C) is correct because it provides support for this idea.

8. B

Difficulty: Easy

Category: Reading / Command of Evidence

Strategic Advice: Look for the choice that offers support for the answer to the previous question. There should be a clear relationship between the correct choice and the previous answer.

Getting to the Answer: Choice (B) clearly states that public universities are diverse today, even though the 1890 Land Act did not increase diversity when it was passed. This corresponds to the answer to the previous question.

9. D

Difficulty: Easy

Category: Reading / Vocab-in-Context

Strategic Advice: Predict the meaning of the word with context clues from the sentence and paragraph. Use each choice in the sentence to figure out which one makes the most sense.

Getting to the Answer: The second sentence of paragraph 5 states that the public university system "has evolved," which implies it has done so in response to change or variations in American culture over time. Choice (D) is correct.

10. C

Difficulty: Hard

Category: Reading / Rhetoric

Strategic Advice: Consider what the passage is about overall and what the author wants the reader to learn, rather than an idea that is mentioned only in passing or in support of the passage's purpose.

Getting to the Answer: The author has written a brief history of public higher education in the United States. In both the introduction and conclusion, the author connects the evolution of the public university system with generally accepted ideals and cultural values, such as diversity and liberty. Choice (C) is correct.

11. B

Difficulty: Medium

Category: Reading / Rhetoric

Strategic Advice: Consider the central idea of the passage that you identified in a previous question and the central idea in the fifth paragraph.

Getting to the Answer: The passage is primarily about the way in which U.S. higher education has reflected American cultural identity. Federal legislation often reflects the values of the nation as a whole. The fifth paragraph summarizes some contemporary examples of previous legislative efforts. Choice (B) is correct.

CHAPTER 14

PREPARE

1. B

Difficulty: Medium

Category: Reading / Rhetoric

Strategic Advice: Review your Passage Map to understand how the focus shifts over the course of the passage. Restate in one or two words what the focus is in the beginning of the passage and what the focus is at the end of the passage.

Getting to the Answer: The passage is written from the point of view of Pamela, who expresses her fear of the master in the beginning of the passage. By the middle of the passage, her fear has transformed into disrespectful anger at her master's actions. Predict that Pamela starts out afraid, but then loses her fear and respect for the master. Choice (B) matches your prediction.

2. A

Difficulty: Hard

Category: Reading / Rhetoric

Strategic Advice: In a U.S. and World Literature passage, identify what the characters think of each other and what they think about themselves.

Getting to the Answer: This question asks you to infer what Pamela thinks. For most of the passage, Pamela is subservient to her master; she asks for forgiveness and calls him "Your Honour" in line 18. However, in the final paragraph, Pamela defends herself. She says to her master that he has done her "the greatest harm in the world" (lines 46–47) because he has taught her "to forget herself, and what belongs to" (lines 47–48) her. Therefore, while Pamela recognizes the economic discrepancies that exist between

her and her master, she still likely believes that servants and masters do not differ in their basic human rights. Choice (A) is correct.

PRACTICE

The following passage was written (on the last night of 1849) by Florence Nightingale. She was not only a pioneer in the profession of nursing but also one of the first European women to travel to Egypt (1849-1850) and keep a detailed journal of her letters and reflections of her journey.

My Dear People,

Yes, I think your imagination has hardly followed me through the place where I have been
Line spending the last night of the old year. Did you
5 listen to it passing away and think of me? Where
do you think I heard it sigh out its soul? In the dim
unearthly colonnades of Karnak, which stood and
watched it, motionless, silent, and awful, as they had
done for thousands of years, to whom, no doubt,
10 thousands of years seem but as a day. Would that
I could call up Karnak before your eyes for one
moment, but it "is beyond expression."

No one could trust themselves with their
imagination alone there. Gigantic shadows spring
15 upon every side; "the dead are stirred up for thee to
meet thee at thy coming, even the chief ones of the
earth," and they look out from among the columns,
and you feel as terror-stricken to be there, miserable intruder, among these mighty dead, as if you
20 had awakened the angel of the Last Day. Imagine six
columns on either side, of which the last is almost
out of sight, though they stand very near each other,
while you look up to the stars from between them,
as you would from a deep narrow gorge in the Alps,
25 and then, passing through 160 of these, ranged in
eight aisles on either side, the end choked up with
heaps of rubbish, this rubbish consisting of stones
twenty and thirty feet long, so that it looks like a
mountain fallen to ruin, not a temple. How art thou
30 fallen from heaven, oh Lucifer, son of the morning!
He did exalt his throne above the stars of God; for

Imagination near Karnak?

K = impossible to describe

Imagination runs wild → fear

details of Karnak = temple

I looked through a colonnade, and under the roof
saw the deep blue sky and star shining brightly; and
as you look upon these mighty ruins, a voice seems
35 continually saying to you, And seekest thou good
things for thyself? Seek them not, for is there ought
like this ruin? One wonders that people come back
from Egypt and live lives as they did before.

trip to Egy. changes you

Yet Karnak by starlight is not to me painful: we
40 had seen Luxor in the sunshine. I had expected
the temples of Thebes to be solemn, but Luxor was
fearful. Rows of painted columns, propylae, colossi,
and—built up in the Holy Place—mud [not even
huts, but] unroofed enclosures chalked out, or
45 rather mudded out, for families, with their one oven
and broken earthen vessel; and, squatting on the
ground among the painted hieroglyphs, creatures
with large nose-rings, the children's eyes streaming
with matter, on which the mothers let the flies rest,
50 because "it is good for them," without an attempt to
drive them off; tattooed men on the ground, with
camels feeding out of their laps, and nothing but a
few doura stalks strewed for their beds;—I cannot describe the impression it makes: it is as if one
55 were steering towards the sun, the glorious Eastern
sun, arrayed in its golden clouds, and were to find,
on nearing it, that it were full—instead of glorified
beings as one expected—of a race of dwarf cannibals, stained with blood and dressed in bones. The
60 contrast could not be more terrible than the savages
of the Present in the temples of the Past at Luxor.

FN does not find K painful

describes people as different; does not approve

But Karnak by starlight is peace; not peace and
joy, but peace—solemn peace. You feel like spirits
revisiting your former world, strange and fallen to
65 ruins; but it has done its work, and there is nothing
agonizing about it. Egypt should have no sun and
no day, no human beings. It should always be seen
in solitude and by night; one eternal night it should
have, like Job's, and let the stars of the twilight be its
70 lamps; neither let it see the dawning of the day.

K = peaceful, spirits

at one with solitude at night

3. B

Difficulty: Easy

Category: Reading / Rhetoric

Strategic Advice: Questions about why an author includes a section in a passage require you to identify how it fits into the passage as a whole.

Getting to the Answer: The author concentrates, throughout the passage, on how much Egypt has affected her. The cited section is not so much about the lack of effect Egypt has had on the other people mentioned, but more about the great effect Egypt has had on the author. Choice (B) is correct.

4. C

Difficulty: Medium

Category: Reading / Rhetoric

Strategic Advice: Authors often use contrast to make a point or strengthen an argument. Reread around the cited lines and paraphrase the main points the author makes about the ideas being contrasted.

Getting to the Answer: To answer this question, you must compare the author's experiences in Karnak and Luxor. The author describes Karnak in lofty, ethereal language filled with references to the eternal. The author expects to find the same thing in Luxor—"I had expected the temples of Thebes to be solemn…" (lines 40–41)—but finds something completely different: "but Luxor was fearful" (lines 41–42). Predict that the comparison between the two cities highlights the author's negative reaction to the conditions at Luxor. Choice (C) matches your prediction.

5. A

Difficulty: Medium

Category: Reading / Rhetoric

Strategic Advice: Questions concerning the overall structure of a text require you to think about how the author presents the central ideas and builds the main argument.

Getting to the Answer: Review your Passage Map and look for patterns in how the author expresses the important ideas in the passage. In the second paragraph, the author shifts between the real and the imagined: "Gigantic shadows spring up on every side … 'the dead are stirred up for thee to meet…'" (lines 14–16). This shift between the real and the imagined continues in the third paragraph: "Rows of painted … golden clouds" (lines 42-56). Predict that the author mixes real descriptions with imaginative descriptions, which matches (A).

6. B

Difficulty: Medium

Category: Reading / Rhetoric

Strategic Advice: When a question gives you a "Yes, because" or "No, because" option, answer the question in two steps. First, determine whether the answer is "Yes" or "No" and eliminate the other two choices. Second, answer the "because" part of the question.

Getting to the Answer: Read around the cited claim and determine whether the evidence supports it. Review your notes about the third paragraph. The details that the author includes about Luxor provide adequate support for the claim she makes. Eliminate C and D. To answer the "because" question, paraphrase the support the author provided for the claim: Conditions seemed dire. Choice (B) is correct.

PERFORM

This passage explores the <u>differences in perception between humans and owls</u>.

It's not difficult to believe that humans and animals perceive the world in different ways. As humans, (sight) is the sense with which we <u>primarily interpret</u> the
Line information around us, and other senses are gener-
5 ally subordinate. Our sense of survival is fortunately not dependent on our acute senses, or we would surely starve to death or be hunted into extinction. Owls, (however,) are masters of their senses, making such optimal use of their biological strengths that
10 we, by comparison, can best be described as wearing blindfolds and earplugs. Were an owl to attempt to hunt with our limited senses, it would most likely call us the lesser species, and possibly initiate attempts to label us as endangered.
15   As evidenced by our expression "owl-eyed," owls are known for their acute vision and all-seeing nature. (Surprisingly, however,) owls have <u>a more limited range of view than humans</u>. Whereas a human can see 180 degrees without turning his or
20 her head, an owl can only see 110 degrees under the same conditions. Owls have extremely well-developed eyes, but their structure is such that they are fixed in one position: an owl can look nowhere but straight ahead. They are farsighted, prevented
25 from seeing clearly anything within a few inches of their eyes; the popular image of a cartoon owl with reading glasses is not far removed from truth. <u>Despite these limitations, however, owls maximize their advantages</u>. Their sensitive eyes are very
30 effective at collecting and processing light, making them <u>efficient night hunters</u>. They can turn their heads almost completely around and nearly upside down, capitalizing on this range of movement to <u>see over their own shoulders and directly</u>
35 <u>beneath themselves</u>. They optimize their farsightedness to spot the minute movements of prey at great distances. With regard to <u>auditory efficiency</u>, owls, like humans, hear a limited range of audible sounds. Within that range, (however,) they have

humans use sight

owls use all senses

acute vision, but have to turn their heads

eyes = fixed & farsighted

process light, night hunters

can turn their heads all around

limited sounds, but better at hearing many frequencies

40 acute hearing at certain frequencies, helping them detect diminutive movements in the undergrowth. Some nocturnal species, such as the barn owl, have asymmetrical ear openings and disc-like facial feathers to facilitate the channeling and interpreta-

45 tion of sounds. They aggregate sensory information instantaneously to produce a mental map of their surroundings and location of possible prey.

Like owls, we use our senses to map the world around us, but there the similarities end. We cannot

owls make complex map

50 understand the complex means by which the owl's hearing and sight work conjunctively to detect the subtle shifting of snow or leaves that signals food. The comparison itself is ludicrous, in fact, because our means for survival are so different: humans do

55 not live solitary lives, constantly alert to the movement of prey that determines whether we live or die. We do not think in the same way, if thought is

need to think this way bc solitary

even the right concept: we interpret information using extremely different cerebral processes, and we

60 can't know whether owls are even consciously aware of the complex workings of their brains. When I sit in the forest and study my environment, my world is interpreted with language. The owl's world is— well, it's impossible to tell, isn't it?

65 The owl may see the same forest we see, but

aware of forest in different way than humans

he is aware of it in a completely different way. I admire the foliage and the rustling leaves, and listen to birdsong. He hears the soft rustle of a leaf and knows that a chipmunk moves thirty feet off to our

70 right, directly underneath the poplar tree. I can say that the owl thinks about the chipmunk, but not how, for I don't have the correct mental processes to describe the complex interpretations of sensory detail into impulse and action; I am governed by

75 words instead of instinct.

7. D

Difficulty: Medium

Category: Reading / Rhetoric

Strategic Advice: Use your Passage Map to answer questions concerning the central argument in a passage. Review the first paragraph

to determine the author's thesis. Think about what must be true for the claim to be correct.

Getting to the Answer: The author begins with the claim that "humans and animals perceive the world in different ways" (lines 1–2). Predict that the assumption must have to do with how our brains work in different ways, which matches (D).

8. C

Difficulty: Medium

Category: Reading / Rhetoric

Strategic Advice: To answer a Rhetoric question that asks about support for a claim, use your Passage Map to locate the claims the author makes and the support the author provides. Make a general prediction about the claims the author supports and then find the answer choice that matches.

Getting to the Answer: The author claims that owls and humans have adapted to their environments in different ways. Since this question asks about owls, focus on the claims the author makes about them. Predict that the author provides support for the claim that owls have effectively adapted to their environment. In the second paragraph, the author provides several examples of ways owls successfully adapted. Choice (C) is correct.

9. D

Difficulty: Easy

Category: Reading / Rhetoric

Strategic Advice: When you see the phrase "in order to" and a cited line, identify how the cited detail fits into the overall structure of the passage.

Getting to the Answer: Overall, the passage compares the differences between the sensory adaptations of owls and humans. Read around the cited line and paraphrase why the author mentions barn owls. Predict that barn owl hearing is an example of how owls have adapted to improve their ability to hunt. Choice (D) matches your prediction.

10. A

Difficulty: Medium

Category: Reading / Rhetoric

Strategic Advice: Review your Passage Map, focusing on how the author presents the information in the passage.

Getting to the Answer: In paragraph 1, the author compares human perception to that of other animals, specifically owls. The author then discusses different ways in which owls and humans use their respective sensory apparatuses. Predict that the passage is structured by comparing the differences between how owls and humans perceive the world. Choice (A) is correct.

EXTRA PRACTICE

This passage is adapted from Carrie Chapman Catt's 1917 "Address to the United States Congress." Catt served as president of the National American Woman Suffrage Association; the closing arguments of her speech are excerpted below.

aud = congress

Your party platforms have pledged woman suffrage. Then why not be honest, frank friends of our cause, adopt it in reality as your own,

auth: give suff. now

Line make it a party program and "fight with us"? As
5 a party measure—a measure of all parties—why not put the amendment through Congress and the Legislatures? We shall all be better friends, we shall have a happier nation, we women will be free to support loyally the party of our choice, and we shall
10 be far prouder of our history.

"There is one thing mightier than kings and armies"—aye, than Congresses and political parties—"the power of an idea when its time has come to move." The time for woman suffrage has come.
15 The woman's hour has struck. If parties prefer to postpone action longer and thus do battle with this idea, they challenge the inevitable. The idea will not

ideas > parties

perish; the party which opposes it may. Every delay, every trick, every political dishonesty from now
20 on will antagonize the women of the land more and more, and when the party or parties which have so delayed woman suffrage finally let it come,

give suffrage or lose votes

their sincerity will be doubted and their appeal to the new voters will be met with suspicion. This is
25 the psychology of the situation. Can you afford the risk? Think it over.

We know you will meet opposition. There are a few "woman haters" left, a few "old males of the tribe," as Vance Thompson calls them, whose duty

haters gonna hate!

30 they believe it to be to keep women in the places they have carefully picked out for them. Treitschke, made world famous by war literature, said some years ago: "Germany, which knows all about Germany and France, knows far better what is good
35 for Alsace-Lorraine than that miserable people can

possibly know." A few American Treitschkes we have who know better than women what is good for them. There are women, too ... But the world does

America will not wait for haters to catch up

not wait for such as these, nor does Liberty pause to
40 heed the plaint of men and women with a grouch. She does not wait for those who have a special interest to serve, nor a selfish reason for depriving other people of freedom. Holding her torch aloft, Liberty is pointing the way onward and upward and
45 saying to America, "Come."

To you the supporters of our cause, in Senate and House, and the number is large, the suffragists of the nation express their grateful thanks. This

thanks suffragists for their work

address is not meant for you. We are more truly
50 appreciative of all you have done than any words can express. We ask you to make a last, hard fight for the amendment during the present session. Since last we asked a vote on this amendment your position has been fortified by the addition
55 to suffrage territory of Great Britain, Canada, and New York.

Some of you have been too indifferent to give more than casual attention to this question. It is worthy of your immediate consideration—a ques-

suffrage = major issue

60 tion big enough to engage the attention of our Allies in war time, is too big a question for you to neglect ...

Gentlemen, we hereby petition you, our only designated representatives, to redress our griev-
65 ances by the immediate passage of the influence to

call to action

secure its ratification in your own state, in order that the women of our nation may be endowed with political freedom that our nation may resume its world leadership in democracy.
70 Woman suffrage is coming—you know it. Will

suff. will happen with or without gov't

you, Honorable Senators and Members of the House of Representatives, help or hinder it?

1. C

Difficulty: Medium

Category: Reading / Rhetoric

Strategic Advice: The correct answer will be clearly stated within the text and will reflect the tone and intent of the author.

Getting to the Answer: The introduction to the passage states that Carrie Chapman Catt speaks on behalf of the National American Woman Suffrage Association. In the first paragraph, she asks lawmakers to support a constitutional amendment. The context of the surrounding paragraph makes clear that the amendment would grant women suffrage, rendering (C) correct.

2. D

Difficulty: Easy

Category: Reading / Detail

Strategic Advice: The correct answer will clearly restate—or have the same meaning as—the excerpted line.

Getting to the Answer: The excerpted line states, "Woman suffrage is coming" (line 70), which means that women will gain the right to vote, eventually, as expressed in (D).

3. A

Difficulty: Medium

Category: Reading / Inference

Strategic Advice: The correct answer will reflect the underlying or implied meaning of the excerpted line and the context of the surrounding text.

Getting to the Answer: The excerpted line states that suffrage will happen and women will gain the vote. It goes on to explain that as voters, women will not trust those who practiced

dishonest and devious tactics (as expressed in the previous line). The concluding lines of the paragraph suggest a threat to the politicians' power. Taken together, these lines imply that women voters, when they gain the vote, will not vote for politicians who opposed their right to suffrage, as stated in (A).

4. D

Difficulty: Medium

Category: Reading / Vocab-in-Context

Strategic Advice: The correct answer will correctly replace the original word and retain the meaning of the original sentence.

Getting to the Answer: The text states that Catt and her supporters want congressional lawmakers to "redress our grievances" (lines 64–65), meaning to set right—or to remedy—the ills committed against women. Choice (D) reflects this meaning.

5. D

Difficulty: Hard

Category: Reading / Rhetoric

Strategic Advice: The correct answer will relate directly to the meaning of the question that Catt poses and to the main purpose of the passage as a whole.

Getting to the Answer: Catt's speech aims to win support for a constitutional amendment granting woman suffrage. Throughout the speech, she tries to persuade lawmakers to choose suffrage. She concludes by asking lawmakers whether they will help or hinder suffrage. Her final question puts responsibility on each lawmaker for his personal, individual choice on the matter, making (D) correct.

6. B

Difficulty: Medium

Category: Reading / Vocab-in-Context

Strategic Advice: The correct answer will reflect the specific meaning of the word in context of the surrounding sentence and text.

Getting to the Answer: The text states that "Every delay, every trick, every political dishonesty from now on will antagonize the women of the land more and more" (lines 18–21). The surrounding text suggests that women will only become more resolved to their purpose as a result of delay, as well as more angry—or bitter—with politicians who forestall them, making (B) correct.

7. B

Difficulty: Medium

Category: Reading / Rhetoric

Strategic Advice: The correct answer will be supported by evidence within the text.

Getting to the Answer: Catt acknowledges that opposition to woman suffrage remains, but she dismisses the opposition as "woman haters" (line 28) and "old males of the tribe" (lines 28–29), suggesting that they are dated and ineffectual. She goes on to state that the world will not slow down for this opposition and that the cause of liberty will continue, implying that suffrage will happen despite the opposition. The suggestion is that suffrage is unavoidable, as stated in (B). In the previous paragraph, Catt also refers to suffrage as "inevitable" (line 17).

8. C

Difficulty: Medium

Category: Reading / Command of Evidence

Strategic Advice: The correct answer will provide evidence, either in reasoning or in fact, to support the claim in the answer to the previous question.

Getting to the Answer: The answer to the previous question asserts that woman suffrage is inevitable. Evidence to support this claim would show that suffrage is advancing, as demonstrated by (C).

9. D

Difficulty: Medium

Category: Reading / Inference

Strategic Advice: The correct answer will reflect the implied meaning of the excerpted line without assuming too much or distorting the context of the text.

Getting to the Answer: The excerpted line states that once women have the political freedom granted by suffrage, then the nation will resume its leadership in democracy. The implication is that the nation is not a leader in democracy as long as it denies women the right to vote. Therefore, (D) is correct.

10. C

Difficulty: Easy

Category: Reading / Rhetoric

Strategic Advice: The correct answer will reflect both the position of the author and the purpose expressed in the text.

Getting to the Answer: In the passage, Catt gives a speech in which she appeals to legislators to enact a constitutional amendment, or legislative reform, to grant women suffrage. She is speaking as a political activist. The correct answer is (C).

11. D

Difficulty: Medium

Category: Reading / Command of Evidence

Strategic Advice: The correct answer will provide evidence, either in reasoning or in fact, to support the specific position of the answer to the previous question.

Getting to the Answer: The answer to the previous question states that Catt is an activist appealing for legislative reform. Choice (D) is correct because in this line Catt, directly appeals to legislators to secure passage of the reform to which she refers earlier in the speech.

CHAPTER 15

PREPARE

1. C

Difficulty: Medium

Category: Reading / Synthesis

Strategic Advice: To find similarities between paired passages, keep in mind the central idea, topic, and scope of each passage.

Getting to the Answer: Both passages focus on crime and society. Although the authors don't agree on how a society should deal with the issue of crime, they both argue that the issue needs to be addressed. Choice (C) is correct.

2. B

Difficulty: Medium

Category: Reading / Synthesis

Strategic Advice: Use the question stem to identify which parts of the two passages you're being asked to compare or contrast.

Getting to the Answer: Summarize what each author concludes. The author of Passage 1 suggests that strict standards must be upheld. The author of Passage 2 argues that addressing the root causes of crime will provide better societal outcomes. Predict that better education can help reduce crime. Choice (B) matches that prediction.

3. A

Difficulty: Easy

Category: Reading / Synthesis

Strategic Advice: Read the question closely. Identify how the question stem asks you to combine the information in the passage and the graphic.

Getting to the Answer: Because you are asked to infer a trend in the data based on Passage 2, paraphrase what the author of Passage 2 thinks would happen if the root causes of crime were addressed. Predict that the author thinks that greater educational opportunities would reduce crime. Applying that prediction to the graphic suggests that the percentage of high school dropouts in inmate populations would decrease. Choice (A) is correct.

PRACTICE

Passage 1 describes how scientists study stem cells and possible uses. Passage 2 discusses the potential risks of stem cell research.

Passage 1

Stem cells truly are science's miracle cure. These undifferentiated cells have not yet chosen what type of cell to become, and can be nudged into becom-
Line ing whatever type of cell is needed to help a sick
5 patient. Stem cells can be used to replace damaged cells in a person who has a degenerative disease or a serious injury.

Scientists obtain stem cells primarily from discarded embryos. True, they can also be obtained
10 from the blood or organs from healthy adults, but these stem cells, while showing some usefulness, are not as adaptable as embryonic stem cells. Embryonic stem cells are incredibly helpful and can mean a revolutionary change in quality of life for patients
15 suffering from debilitating diseases such as Parkinson's or Alzheimer's. Someday, stem cells could even eliminate the need for human test subjects in drug tests. Without the use of embryonic stem cells, though, that could take an immeasurably longer
20 amount of time to become a reality.

With stem cell research, the benefits for living, breathing, sentient people outweigh any debate regarding the origins of the cells themselves. In this age of scientific enlightenment, we must always ask
25 ourselves: What action can best benefit humanity? By answering, we clearly see that stem cell research must continue.

how SCs work, why powerful

embryonic > adult SCs

w/o emb. SCs, research = slower

SC research should continue

Passage 2

ethics of emb. SC use → how far is too far?

We stand at an important crossroads in scientific progress. We have the capability now to improve humanity in ways never thought possible, (but) at what cost? At what point must progress bow before conscience? Just because we can, is it true that we should?

Stem cell research has the potential to be an enormous boon to the medical industry. The advance of diseases can be assuaged or halted completely through this remarkable new medicine.

ethics easy to disregard

(But) scientists assault the dignity of life when they use embryonic stem cells for their work. By taking cells from discarded embryos, we begin treading on a slippery slope. It is all too easy to transition from using discarded embryos to creating embryos solely for the purpose of stem cell medicine.

auth. op.: emb. made just for research = bad

Since stem cells can be obtained from healthy adults with no cost to life, this is the path on which we should be progressing. These stem cells, safely obtained, can have a significant positive impact on the lives of patients.

use adult SCs instead

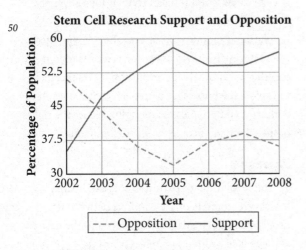

Stem Cell Research Support and Opposition

4. C

Difficulty: Medium

Category: Reading / Synthesis

Strategic Advice: Synthesis questions ask you to find similarities and differences between paired passages. Compare the different points of view, focusing on how the authors agree and disagree.

Getting to the Answer: This question asks you to identify the way in which the authors think alike. To find the correct answer, compare your summaries of the passages. The author of Passage 1 maintains that stem cell research can provide benefits and recommends using stem cells regardless of the source. The author of Passage 2 agrees that stem cell research can provide benefits but argues that using adult stem cells is the course to follow. Both authors agree that stem cell research has benefits. Choice (C) is correct.

5. D

Difficulty: Hard

Category: Reading / Synthesis

Strategic Advice: To make a strong prediction when faced with a general question, focus on the central idea, topic, and scope of each passage.

Getting to the Answer: Harder Synthesis questions will require you to identify not only how the authors agree or disagree but also why they agree or disagree. What these authors disagree on is easy to identify: They disagree about which type of stem cells should be used in the research. Now, ask why they disagree. The author of Passage 1 thinks that the benefits are defined solely by the physical improvements possible, and the author of Passage 2 thinks that the benefits of stem cell research must be considered in terms of the moral as well as the physical results. Choice (D) is correct.

6. C

Difficulty: Medium

Category: Reading / Synthesis

Strategic Advice: Look for trends in the data. Evaluate the categories and time frames mentioned in the answer choices.

Getting to the Answer: This question asks you to compare changes in data between two categories—support for and opposition to—over different time periods. Count the number of squares up or down each line moves as it moves two squares over. Compare the changes on the graph to the changes described in each answer choice and eliminate answer choices that don't match. When you check the time frame of 2005 to 2007, note that opposition to stem cell research increased about one full square, and support for stem cell research decreased about one half of a square. This matches the changes in the data described in (C).

PERFORM

The following passages reflect on the Machnovschina, an anarchist peasant uprising in the Ukraine active from approximately 1917 to 1922 under the leadership of Nestor Makhno. During their brief and turbulent history, the Makhnovshchina (also known as Makhnovists) fought against the Central Powers, the White Army, and the Red Army, their sometimes ally that eventually turned on them and defeated them. The first passage discusses the relationship between the Makhnovists and their supporters, while the second discusses the differences between the Makhnovists on the outskirts of the emerging Soviet Union and the Bolsheviks who controlled it.

Passage 1

Even had the Ukrainian civilians wanted to ignore the sectarianism of their time and remain neutral, they did not have that luxury—the turmoil
Line was too absolute, the excitement and terror of
5 revolutionary upheaval too absolutely compelling.

Even for the most isolated of peasants, political impartiality was impossible. From the beginning, there was a bond among revolutionary intellectuals, civilians, and military leaders.

10 The causes of civil unrest compounded. Adding to the burden of uncounted years of economic and political subjugation under a quasi-feudal system[1] was the added pressure of an invading Austro-Hungarian army. Meanwhile, Russia was in a state
15 of chaos, and the Bolsheviks[2] were rapidly consolidating power in a system that promised equality and the rule of the proletariat. There was no central authority to organize them (Russia had all but given up the Ukraine to the invading Central Powers[3]),
20 and the traditional power of the rich landlords had collapsed with the Czarist government. There was no status quo and no safe choice.

Faced with this state of affairs, many Ukrainian peasants chose to organize themselves within
25 the Makhnovshchina. Educated in the field and trained behind the plow, they were now charged with the task of organizing and defending a new society under conditions of tremendous adversity. Although the Makhnovshchina was an anarchist,
30 revolutionary movement, it was one that emerged out of necessity. It was a way for peasants to join together for mutual aid, revolutionary intellectuals to explore the possibility of a society without central authority, and generals to attempt to secure the rights
35 of the Ukrainian people to self-determination.

Passage 2

The revolutionary period in Russian history is a classic example of the conflicts between the programs of dogmatic, rigid leaders and the desires and needs of ordinary people. One of the best
40 examples of this is the struggle between the Bolsheviks and the Makhnovshchina. Not only did the word "revolution" mean very different things to the Kremlin[4] bureaucrats and the Ukrainian partisans, but the reality of the revolution was very different
45 as well. This fact was noted by one anonymous soldier who, beginning his career as a Kremlin

Margin notes:
from beg.: bond among diff people

many causes of civil unrest

A-H army invasion

Bolsh. organizing but no central auth.

Uk. peasants → Makh.

anarchist but necessary

Makh vs Bolsh

diff. in theory (accepted vs debated)

guard, eventually became a member of the Makhnovist army. He noted that "conditions could not
have been more different between the two camps.
50 In the one, decisions were based on the political
theories of Marx[5] and Lenin,[6] theories which were
never doubted or questioned in the least. In the
other, theories were even more important—debated
vigorously and openly—but only after the day's
55 work had been done and the important decisions
had been made based on the needs of the community for food, freedom, and self-defense."

Bolsh. propaganda

Although the Kremlin's approach might seem
like harmless intellectualism, it had disastrous con-
60 sequences that the anonymous soldier couldn't have
forseen. As the Bolshevik Party gained increasing
power, it began to control the official view of events
with a systematic paranoia unprecedented in history. If the events differed from the official view, the

either w/ or against Bolsh.

65 events themselves (and those who participated in
them) were deemed the enemy.

The wartime writings of Leon Trotsky[7] are the
best indication of this trend. He alternately characterized
the Makhnovists as heroes and traitors depending
70 on the current needs of the Bolsheviks. When he
required Makhnovists to fight alongside the Red

ex. of prop.: LT changed tack based on Makh. actions

Army[8], he portrayed them as courageous heroes
and valiant fighters, but when he did not, they suddenly became traitors and enemies of the revolu-
75 tion. In 1920, as the Makhnovshchina and the Red
Army united to fight against a powerful White
Army[9] campaign, Trotsky wrote:

"The working class of the Ukraine can never, and
especially not in conditions of tremendous military
80 danger, allow particular units sometimes to fight in

LT → quote

our ranks and sometimes to stab us in the back.[+]
Waging war against the world's exploiters, the
workers' and peasants' Red Army says: 'Who is not

all or nothing

with me is against me, and whoever is with me is to
85 remain in my ranks and not leave them till the end.'"

Uk. parti-sans → neg portrayal; Makh. only loyal if respect for Red Army

The Ukranian partisans, even as peasants and
workmen, were painted as the servants of foreign
aristocrats bent on undermining the revolution. Even though Bolshevik presence had been
90 weak in the Ukraine, Trotsky still saw fit to portray

himself as the representative of "the working class
of the Ukraine" and the Makhnovists as loyal to the
working class only to the degree that they recognized Red Army authority.

[1] Serfdom had only been abolished in 1861, and many traces of
it remained.
[2] The Bolsheviks were the Communist party that established the
Soviet Union.
[3] The Central Powers were Germany, Austria-Hungary, the
Ottoman Empire, and Bulgaria. During World War I (which
took place from 1914 to 1918), they were fighting against the
Allies—France, Russia, Great Britain, and the United States.
During the period in question, the Austro-Hungarian Army
was occupying much of the Ukraine.
[4] The Russian capital building which, at the time, was occupied
by the Bolshevik Party
[5] Karl Marx, the ideological founder of Communism
[6] Vladimir Ilyich Lenin, the leader of the Bolsheviks
[7] Leon Trotsky, one of the leaders of the Bolsheviks
[8] The Bolshevik Army
[9] A conservative army opposed to the revolutionary movements
in Russia
[+] The previous alliance between the Makhnovshchina and the
Red Army had been broken when the Bolsheviks attacked and
devastated the unsuspecting anarchists in a surprise attack.

**Proportion of Seats in the Russian
Constituent Assembly, 1918**

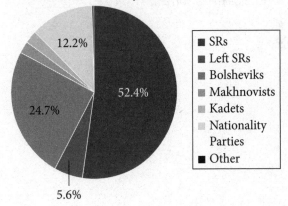

7. C

Difficulty: Medium

Category: Reading / Synthesis

Strategic Advice: To answer Synthesis questions, focus on the similarities and differences
between the passages. Identify what the authors
agree and disagree on.

Getting to the Answer: This question stem asks what the author of Passage 2 thinks about a promise made by the Bolsheviks. Review your Passage Map to determine that the author of Passage 2 holds a negative view of the Bolsheviks. Predict that the author of Passage 2 would view the Bolsheviks' promise in a negative light. Choice (C) is correct.

8. D

Difficulty: Medium

Category: Reading / Synthesis

Strategic Advice: Synthesis questions that ask what the authors agree on require you to identify the similarities in each author's purpose for writing the passage.

Getting to the Answer: Although each passage focuses on a different aspect of the Makhnovischina, they both describe the Makhnovischina as a group formed to provide mutual aid, intellectual freedom, and military defense. Choice (D) is correct.

9. A

Difficulty: Hard

Category: Reading / Synthesis

Strategic Advice: Read the question stem closely to identify what it asks you to look for.

Getting to the Answer: Because the question stem asks what can be inferred by looking at Passage 2 and the data in the pie chart in tandem, base your interpretation of that data on the negative viewpoint that the author of Passage 2 expresses regarding the Bolsheviks. Predict that the author thinks that the Bolsheviks gained power at the expense of others. When the data in the pie chart are viewed from that perspective, it can be inferred that the Bolsheviks were stronger than their proportion of seats on the assembly would suggest. Choice (A) is correct.

EXTRA PRACTICE

Passage 1 is about how scientists use radioisotopes to date artifacts and remains. Passage 2 discusses the varying problems with radioactive contaminants.

Passage 1

Archaeologists often rely on measuring the amounts of different atoms present in an item from a site to determine its age. The identity of an atom
Line depends on how many protons it has in its nucleus;
5 for example, all carbon atoms have 6 protons. Each atom of an element, however, can have a differ-ent number of neutrons, so there can be several versions, or isotopes, of each element. Scientists name the isotopes by the total number of protons
10 plus neutrons. For example, a carbon atom with 6 neutrons is carbon-12 while a carbon atom with 7 neutrons is carbon-13.

Some combinations of protons and neutrons are not stable and will change over time. For example,
15 carbon-14, which has 6 protons and 8 neutrons, will slowly change into nitrogen-14, with 7 protons and 7 neutrons. Scientists can directly measure the amount of carbon-12 and carbon-14 in a sample or they can use radiation measurements to calculate these
20 amounts. Each atom of carbon-14 that changes to nitrogen-14 emits radiation. Scientists can measure the rate of emission and use that to calculate the total amount of carbon-14 present in a sample.

Carbon-14 atoms are formed in the atmosphere
25 at the same rate at which they decay. Therefore the ratio of carbon-12 to carbon-14 atoms in the atmosphere is constant. Living plants and animals have the same ratio of carbon-12 to carbon-14 in their tissues because they are constantly taking in
30 carbon in the form of food or carbon dioxide. After the plant or animal dies, however it stops taking in carbon and so the amount of carbon-14 atoms in its tissues starts to decrease at a predictable rate.

By measuring the ratio of carbon-12 to carbon-14
35 in a bone, for example a scientist can determine how long the animal the bone came from has been dead. To determine an object's age this way is called "car-

bon-14 dating." Carbon-14 dating can be performed on any material made by a living organism, such as
40 wood or paper from trees or bones and skin from animals. Materials with ages up to about 50,000 years old can be dated. By finding the age of several objects found at different depths at an archeological dig, the archeologists can then make a timeline for the layers
45 of the site. Objects in the same layer will be about the same age. By using carbon dating for a few objects in a layer, archeologists know the age of other objects in that layer, even if the layer itself cannot be carbon dated.

Passage 2

50 Radioactive materials contain unstable atoms that decay, releasing energy in the form of radiation. The radiation can be harmful to living tissue because it can penetrate into cells and damage their DNA. If an explosion or a leak at a nuclear power plant releases
55 large amounts of radioactive materials, the sur-rounding area could be hazardous until the amount of radioactive material drops back to normal levels. The amount of danger from the radiation and the amount of time until the areas are safe again depend on
60 how fast the materials emit radiation.

Scientists use the "half-life" of a material to indicate how quickly it decays. The half-life of a material is the amount of time it takes for half of a sample of that material to decay. A mate-
65 rial with a short half-life decays more quickly than a material with a long half-life. For example iodine-131 and cesium-137 can both be released as a result of an accident at a nuclear power plant. Iodine-131 decays rapidly, with a half-life of 8 days.
70 Cesium-137, however decays more slowly, with a half-life of 30 years.

If an accident releases iodine-131, therefore it is a short-term concern. The amount of radiation emitted will be high but will drop rapidly. After
75 two months, less than one percent of the original iodine-131 will remain. An accidental release of cesium-137, however, is a long-term concern. The amount of radiation emitted at first will be low but will drop slowly. It will take about 200 years

definition of isotope & examples

all atoms of one element have same # protons, diff. # neutrons

ways to measure decay

carb-14 atom decay = predictable

how carb-14 dating is used → timelines based on layers

why radiation = harmful

danger depends rate of rad. release

half-life use and definition

half-life = faster decay

cesium-137 = bigger concern than iodine-131

80 for the amount of cesium-137 remaining to drop below one percent. The total amount of radiation emitted in both cases will be the same, for the same amount of initial material. <u>The difference lies in whether the radiation is all released rapidly at high</u>
85 <u>levels in a short time, or is released slowly at low levels, over a long time span.</u>

danger comes down to how fast rad. is released

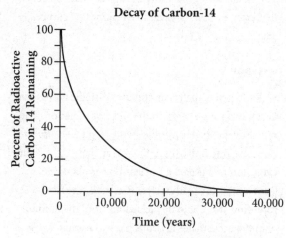

Decay of Carbon-14

This data is from the *Journal of Research of the National Bureau of Standards*, Vol. 64, No. 4, April 1951, pp. 328 – 333.

1. C

Difficulty: Hard

Category: Reading / Inference

Strategic Advice: Use your Passage Map to find a description of what materials can be dated using carbon-14 dating. Pay close attention to your notes for paragraph 4.

Getting to the Answer: In paragraph 4, the author states that carbon-14 dating can be used on materials made by a living organism. An arrowhead made from a bone is constructed of such material, (C).

2. D

Difficulty: Hard

Category: Reading / Command of Evidence

Strategic Advice: Locate each of the answer choices in the passage. The correct answer should provide direct support for the answer to the previous question.

Getting to the Answer: In paragraph 4, the author describes the process for carbon-14 dating. Choice (D) is correct because this sentence provides a direct description of the materials that can be dated using carbon-14 dating.

3. B

Difficulty: Medium

Category: Reading / Vocab-in-Context

Strategic Advice: Replace "decay" in the sentence with each of the answer choices. Consider which word makes the most sense in context.

Getting to the Answer: The previous paragraph discusses how scientists measure the rate of emission to calculate the amount of carbon-14 in a sample. "Emission" means release; therefore, the amount of carbon-14 is becoming smaller if the atoms are releasing it. In this sentence, therefore, "decay" most nearly means to decrease, which matches "deteriorate," (B).

4. C

Difficulty: Easy

Category: Reading / Inference

Strategic Advice: Look at your notes for paragraph 3. Summarize the ratio of carbon-12 to carbon-14 in living tissue in your own words. Look for the answer choice that most closely matches your prediction.

Getting to the Answer: In paragraph 3, the author explains that the ratio of carbon-12 to carbon-14 is constant. Choice (C) is correct.

5. C

Difficulty: Medium

Category: Reading / Command of Evidence

Strategic Advice: Review what part of the passage you used to predict an answer for the previous question.

Getting to the Answer: In paragraph 3, the author explains why the rate of carbon-12 to carbon-14 remains constant in the tissues of living plants and animals. Choice (C) is correct.

6. B

Difficulty: Medium

Category: Reading / Detail

Strategic Advice: Read around the cited lines. The author directly states why a release of iodine-131 is not cause for long-term concern.

Getting to the Answer: In paragraph 3, the author explains that the initial release of radiation from an accident involving iodine-131 will be high, but the level of radiation will drop quickly. Choice (B) is correct.

7. C

Difficulty: Medium

Category: Reading / Detail

Strategic Advice: Use your Passage Map to find the information about how exposure to radiation affects living tissue.

Getting to the Answer: In paragraph 1, the author explains that radiation is harmful to living tissue because it can cause damage to the cells' DNA, which matches (C).

8. A

Difficulty: Easy

Category: Reading / Vocab-in-Context

Strategic Advice: Eliminate answer choices such as B and C that are synonyms for "original" but do not make sense in context. Select the word that can replace "original" in the sentence without changing the meaning of the sentence.

Getting to the Answer: The previous paragraph explains how scientists use "half-life" to determine how quickly material decays. If the material is decaying, then "original" refers to the first, or earliest, material. Choice (A) is correct.

9. D

Difficulty: Medium

Category: Reading / Detail

Strategic Advice: Review your notes for the first part of Passage 2. Try to put into your own words how scientists use half-life calculations of radioactive materials. Look for the answer that most closely matches your idea.

Getting to the Answer: In paragraph 1, the author explains that the level of danger posed by radiation released during a nuclear accident depends on how quickly radiation is released. In paragraph 2, the author discusses how the half-life of radioactive material is used to determine how long a material will emit radiation. Choice (D) is correct because it most clearly paraphrases the information in the passage about how scientists use half-life calculations.

10. A

Difficulty: Hard

Category: Reading / Synthesis

Strategic Advice: The central idea will be supported by all of the evidence presented in both passages. Avoid answers such as B and C that are supported only by the evidence in one passage.

Getting to the Answer: Choice (A) is correct because this statement is a generalization about the study of physics supported by both passages: Passage 1 discusses the application of atomic and nuclear physics in archeology while Passage 2 details how scientists apply atomic and nuclear physics to studies of radioactivity.

11. A

Difficulty: Hard

Category: Reading / Synthesis

Strategic Advice: Consider the information in the passages about half-life and how it relates to the data presented in the chart.

Getting to the Answer: The definition of "half-life" is given in Passage 2. The half-life of a material is the amount of time it takes for half of that material to decay. The graph shows that about 50 percent of carbon-14 remains after 5,400 years. Choice (A) is correct.

CHAPTER 16

PREPARE

1. C

Difficulty: Medium

Category: Writing & Language / Effective Language Use

Strategic Advice: Be alert to sudden changes in tone and style within a passage. Describe the style in a word or two and look for the answer choice that is most similar.

Getting to the Answer: The overall tone of this passage can be described as formal. Reread the underlined segment. The shift to the second person pronoun makes the tone in the underlined section much less formal. Plug in the remaining choices to find the answer choice that matches the formal tone in the rest of the passage. Choice (C) matches well.

2. D

Difficulty: Medium

Category: Writing & Language / Quantitative

Strategic Advice: Look for trends in the data. Compare the categories that the answer choices mention.

Getting to the Answer: This question asks you to compare changes in data on two pie charts. Make sure to note which chart represents which year. Note the change in each of the answer choices. Eliminate choices that are incorrect. Eliminate A because the percent of a budget spent on food has dropped, not risen. Eliminate B because the percent of a budget spent on healthcare has risen, not dropped. Choice C can be eliminated because the percent of a budget spent on food has dropped more than the percent of a budget spent on transportation. Choice (D) is correct.

PRACTICE

3. C

Difficulty: Medium

Category: Writing & Language / Effective Language Use

Strategic Advice: Consider how you would refer to a number in a different context. Would you say you fell in love "hundred days" ago?

Getting to the Answer: "Hundred" refers to a digit (ones digit, tens digit, hundreds digit, etc.), whereas "one hundred" is an actual number. In order to begin the sentence in an idiomatically correct way, it is necessary to use the full number, "one hundred." Choice (C) matches well.

4. C

Difficulty: Medium

Category: Writing & Language / Sentence Formation

Strategic Advice: If there is no obvious error in the underlined segment, keep reading until you can identify the issue.

Getting to the Answer: The underlined portion is correctly used as the subject of an independent clause. However, because the clause after the comma is also independent, the sentence is a run-on. Since you are not given the option to fix the comma splice, look for the answer choice that makes the first clause dependent without introducing another error. Choice (C) correctly subordinates the first clause by beginning the sentence with "when."

5. B
Difficulty: Easy

Category: Writing & Language / Usage

Strategic Advice: Subjects and verbs must agree in person and number. Singular third person subjects take singular third person verbs, and plural third person subjects take plural third person verbs. The closest noun to an underlined verb may not be its subject.

Getting to the Answer: Read around the underlined portion until you can identify the subject of the underlined verb. Remember, a noun that is the object of a preposition cannot be the subject of a sentence. In this sentence, the subject is the plural noun "components" and needs a plural verb. Choice (B) is correct.

PERFORM

6. B
Difficulty: Medium

Category: Writing & Language / Effective Language Use

Strategic Advice: Using two words that mean the same thing is redundant. Look for the answer choice that creates the most concise sentence.

Getting to the Answer: As written, the sentence uses a compound predicate made up of "fascinated and intrigued." Because both words convey the same idea, namely that scientists found Jupiter to be very interesting, using one is sufficient. Choice (B) concisely conveys the idea.

7. D
Difficulty: Medium

Category: Writing & Language / Sentence Formation

Strategic Advice: Read around an underlined period and check to make sure that each clause forms a complete sentence.

Getting to the Answer: Because the second clause is a fragment, it needs to be properly connected to the previous sentence with either subordination or punctuation. Choice B provides punctuation that corrects the fragment but does not form an effective sentence. Since the information in the second clause explains why the moons of Jupiter provided evidence for a theory, the second clause needs to be combined with the previous sentence. Choice (D) joins the clause to the sentence.

8. D
Difficulty: Easy

Category: Writing & Language / Sentence Formation

Strategic Advice: Compare underlined verbs with related verbs. Related verbs forms need to be parallel.

Getting to the Answer: The verbs "completed" and "collected" form a compound predicate and need to be parallel in form. As written, the underlined section unnecessarily reintroduces the subject. Join the two verbs without punctuation. Choice (D) is correct.

9. C
Difficulty: Easy

Category: Writing & Language / Development

Strategic Advice: If you have the option to omit a sentence, think carefully about the author's topic. If the underlined portion strays from the topic, omit it.

Getting to the Answer: The author's topic is Jupiter. The underlined portion adds information about *Pioneer 10* that is irrelevant to the topic. Choice (C) correctly omits the sentence for this reason.

10. B

Difficulty: Medium

Category: Writing & Language / Effective Language Use

Strategic Advice: If an underlined segment does not contain a grammatical error, check for other kinds of errors tested on the SAT.

Getting to the Answer: As written, the underlined portion is a complete sentence. Reread that sentence in the context of the following sentence. They sound choppy together and create a wordiness issue. Because the underlined sentence provides information about Jupiter, it can be incorporated into the next sentence. Choice (B) forms a modifying phrase that effectively introduces the subject of the sentence.

11. D

Difficulty: Medium

Category: Writing & Language / Usage

Strategic Advice: Related nouns must be consistent in number. Check other nouns around an underlined noun to make sure they agree.

Getting to the Answer: The underlined noun is related to the noun phrase "number of probes." Because there was more than one probe, there was more than one measurement. Choice (D) correctly makes the underlined noun plural.

12. C

Difficulty: Medium

Category: Writing & Language / Quantitative

Strategic Advice: When you see a question with an infographic, remember to use the Kaplan Method for Infographics.

Getting to the Answer: The sentence to which the underlined portion belongs is comparing Earth's rotational speed to that of Jupiter's. The relevant information is how much faster Jupiter rotates. Look in the third column of the table for that data. Compare the information you find with the answer choices. Choice (C) provides accurate and relevant information.

13. D

Difficulty: Medium

Category: Writing & Language / Usage

Strategic Advice: A pronoun's antecedent must be clear and unambiguous. Always identify the antecedent of an underlined pronoun.

Getting to the Answer: The underlined possessive pronoun could refer to a number of things: our diameter, Earth's diameter, and Earth's rotational speed. Reread the sentence to determine what the author means. The sentence compares the diameter of Jupiter to the diameter of Earth. Look for the answer choice that makes that comparison clear. Choice (D) is correct.

EXTRA PRACTICE

1. C
Difficulty: Easy

Category: Writing & Language / Effective Language Use

Strategic Advice: Watch out for choices, like B, which are extremely wordy. It is better to be as direct and simple as possible.

Getting to the Answer: Additional adjectives do not add more meaning to this content. Choice (C) is the most concise and effective way of stating the information in the passage.

2. A
Difficulty: Medium

Category: Writing & Language / Punctuation

Strategic Advice: Study the words in a series and see where a comma might need to be inserted or eliminated.

Getting to the Answer: Recall that the SAT requires lists of three to have commas after the first two items in the list, not just after the first item. Choice (A) is correct.

3. D
Difficulty: Hard

Category: Writing & Language / Development

Strategic Advice: To find the best answer choice, look for the sentence that has the most relevant details presented in a clear and concise way.

Getting to the Answer: Choice (D) has the most relevant details about what the Pony Express was like when it was at its peak.

4. C
Difficulty: Medium

Category: Writing & Language / Sentence Formation

Strategic Advice: Be careful of inappropriate transition words when relating sentences to one another.

Getting to the Answer: Choice (C) divides the two thoughts into two complete sentences by adding a period and capitalizing the first word of the second sentence.

5. A
Difficulty: Easy

Category: Writing & Language / Effective Language Use

Strategic Advice: The context of the sentence suggests which word would have the correct connotation. Check each word to see how it fits with the context.

Getting to the Answer: Only (A) fits with the context of the sentence. The other choices are unlikely.

6. B
Difficulty: Medium

Category: Writing & Language / Sentence Formation

Strategic Advice: Verbs within a sentence should be parallel. Check to see if this is true here.

Getting to the Answer: The correct choice, (B), has all the verbs in the same form.

7. A

Difficulty: Hard

Category: Writing & Language / Development

Strategic Advice: To find the central idea of a paragraph, identify important details and summarize them in a sentence. Then, find the choice that is the closest to your summary. Do not choose a detail rather than a central idea.

Getting to the Answer: The paragraph mostly discusses the challenges riders faced, so (A) most accurately sums up the central idea of the paragraph.

8. B

Difficulty: Medium

Category: Writing & Language / Organization

Strategic Advice: Look for the relationship between this sentence and the previous one. This will help you choose the appropriate transition word. Read the word into the sentence to ensure that it makes sense.

Getting to the Answer: Choice (B) shows the relationship between the two sentences by emphasizing that the riders could overcome these challenges.

9. B

Difficulty: Medium

Category: Writing & Language / Quantitative

Strategic Advice: The graphic gives specific information about when events relating to the Pony Express took place. Interpret it to choose the correct answer choice.

Getting to the Answer: Choice (B) is the only one that accurately reflects the information in the timeline.

10. C

Difficulty: Medium

Category: Writing & Language / Effective Language Use

Strategic Advice: The context of the sentence suggests which word would have the best fit. Check each word to see how it fits with the context.

Getting to the Answer: Choice (C) best fits the context of the sentence.

11. D

Difficulty: Medium

Category: Writing & Language / Effective Language Use

Strategic Advice: Watch out for answer choices that may have incorrect transition words.

Getting to the Answer: Choice (D) joins the sentences concisely and correctly by using the conjunction "and."

CHAPTER 17

PREPARE

1. A
Difficulty: Medium

Category: Writing & Language / Development

Strategic Advice: Carefully consider sentences that seem to be making a claim that is central to the passage. Select the answer choice that matches the evidence that the author provides in the rest of the passage.

Getting to the Answer: After the first paragraph, the author explains how Dr. Marshall's findings fundamentally changed how the medical community understands ulcers. The underlined segment is correct as written because it accurately depicts Marshall as a disrupting force in the field. Choice (A) is correct.

2. B
Difficulty: Hard

Category: Writing & Language / Development

Strategic Advice: Sentences containing supporting details need to contribute to the author's central idea. Consider the context of the underlined section and select the answer choice that best advances the development of the author's argument.

Getting to the Answer: Choice (B) is correct. It develops the author's narrative by elaborating on how Dr. Marshall was outside of the mainstream of his field early in his career.

3. B
Difficulty: Hard

Category: Writing & Language / Development

Strategic Advice: Supporting details should confirm the central idea and not contradict specifics that are mentioned elsewhere. Look for the answer choice that assists the reader's understanding of the passage and is also in agreement with previously mentioned points.

Getting to the Answer: Choice (B) is correct because it links the current paragraph to the following paragraph, which mentions Dr. Marshall's experiments with an important type of bacteria. The other answer choices are either off-topic or conflict with details found elsewhere in the passage.

4. D
Difficulty: Easy

Category: Writing & Language / Development

Strategic Advice: The last sentence in a passage often serves to recap what the author has said up to that point, acting as a summarization of the central idea. It should not conflict with the rest of the passage or go off-topic.

Getting to the Answer: Choice (D) is correct because it accurately summarizes the accomplishments of Dr. Marshall as described in the passage.

PRACTICE

5. D
Difficulty: Medium

Category: Writing & Language / Development

Strategic Advice: Scrutinize details of densely factual passages to make sure they are on-topic and do not conflict with other details or the central idea.

Getting to the Answer: This passage is concerned with the details of human skin and explaining the properties and purposes of skin. Choice (D) abides by the author's narrative for the passage and is therefore correct.

6. A

Difficulty: Medium

Category: Writing & Language / Development

Strategic Advice: Pick the answer choice that is in line with the author's central idea and tone.

Getting to the Answer: In this passage, the author explains how the skin is essential to life by listing its various properties and processes for keeping the body in healthy operation. The underlined section is in line with the author's overall effort. Choice (A) is correct.

7. C

Difficulty: Medium

Category: Writing & Language / Development

Strategic Advice: Make sure details in the underlined section are relevant to the topic. Even if a detail matches the tone of the passage (in this case, strictly fact-based), it might not be relevant to the central idea.

Getting to the Answer: Most of the answer choices for this question sound legitimate and even factually correct. However, only (C) keeps the focus on the human skin and its characteristics, so it is correct. Remember, the focus of the paragraph is on the defensive functions of the skin, not on how those functions work at a cellular level. You also know that immediate medical attention is too extreme for any instance of skin breaking (small cuts, etc.).

8. A

Difficulty: Medium

Category: Writing & Language / Development

Strategic Advice: Concluding sentences often reassert or summarize the author's central idea; therefore, they cannot fundamentally conflict with the author's assertions.

Getting to the Answer: In this passage, the author has made clear that the skin is a very important organ that protects the body from a variety of illnesses and disorders, as well as from physical harm. Choice (A) is correct, as it ties preceding points and details together into a coherent conclusion for the author's argument.

PERFORM

9. A

Difficulty: Medium

Category: Writing & Language / Development

Strategic Advice: Scrutinize the answer choices for how they relate to the author's central ideas as well as how they potentially conflict with details that come later in the passage.

Getting to the Answer: Choice (A) is correct because—without going off-topic or conflicting with later details—it elaborates on the idea that Polk followed in Jackson's footsteps.

10. C

Difficulty: Easy

Category: Writing & Language / Development

Strategic Advice: Pay close attention to long lists of evidence to make sure that each component is in line with the central idea and context of the sentence.

Getting to the Answer: Choice (C) is correct because it is the only answer choice that both stays focused on matters of policy (as the first part of the sentence mentions) and supports the thesis that Polk and Jackson were in agreement on most points of public policy.

11. D

Difficulty: Easy

Category: Writing & Language / Development

Strategic Advice: The first sentence of a paragraph sets the paragraph's tone and purpose. Pay attention to what the other sentences of the paragraph are describing and pick the answer choice that is the best introduction for those details.

Getting to the Answer: This paragraph is concerned with explaining the chronology of Polk's early life. Choice (D) is correct because it states the place and date of Polk's birth, making it a logical introduction to the following sentences.

12. D

Difficulty: Medium

Category: Writing & Language / Development

Strategic Advice: Supporting details fit the context of the paragraph and do not contradict details found elsewhere in the passage. Select the answer choice that satisfies these guidelines.

Getting to the Answer: This paragraph is narrowly concerned with Polk's origins and early political career. Choice (D) fits the context and does not contradict later details.

13. C

Difficulty: Medium

Category: Writing & Language / Development

Strategic Advice: A paragraph's final sentence ideally guides the paragraph's central idea to a conclusion and remains linked to the central idea of the passage.

Getting to the Answer: Choice (C) is correct because it is the most effective conclusion for a paragraph tasked with explaining Polk's early political career. Choice (C) also makes a clear connection to the following paragraph, helping the narrative flow.

14. B

Difficulty: Medium

Category: Writing & Language / Development

Strategic Advice: Remember that supporting evidence needs to focus on and contribute to the central idea.

Getting to the Answer: The author's intent is to introduce the two main candidates in the 1844 election, leading to the following sentence that discusses their opinions of expansionism. Choice (B) is correct because it stays focused on the paragraph's topic and contributes to the argument that Polk recognized popular support for expansionism that other candidates overlooked or ignored.

15. A

Difficulty: Medium

Category: Writing & Language / Development

Strategic Advice: Examine details and parenthetical asides for relevance to the central idea. The goal is to make sure that no contradictions are being introduced into the narrative.

Getting to the Answer: No change is necessary because the underlined section touches on two central themes of the passage: Polk's support for expansionist policies and his Jacksonian view of America. Choice (A) is correct.

16. B

Difficulty: Hard

Category: Writing & Language / Development

Strategic Advice: Pay close attention to a paragraph's first sentence. It should set the stage for details to follow and also be in line with the passage's central idea.

Getting to the Answer: As alluded to in the first paragraph and explained clearly in the final paragraph, Polk did much to expand the borders of the United States. He even supported war with Mexico to gain territory. Choice (B) is correct.

EXTRA PRACTICE

1. A

Difficulty: Medium

Category: Writing & Language / Development

Strategic Advice: Reread the paragraph to determine which answer choice best introduces the main point.

Getting to the Answer: The correct choice, (A), is the only one that accurately explains how the career is now popular and helpful but had to develop over time after a shift in health care needs.

2. D

Difficulty: Easy

Category: Writing & Language / Development

Strategic Advice: Reread the sentence and determine which answer choice creates the most focused sentence.

Getting to the Answer: The additional comments about the school's quality and programs are unnecessary. Choice (D) creates the most focused sentence.

3. B

Difficulty: Medium

Category: Writing & Language / Effective Language Use

Strategic Advice: Look for nearby context clues and use what you know of each answer choice's definition to determine which word most accurately reflects the intention of the sentence.

Getting to the Answer: The intention of the sentence is to state that students should acquire new hands-on medical knowledge through work experience. The word with the definition that best describes this acquisition is "accrue," (B).

4. B

Difficulty: Easy

Category: Writing & Language / Effective Language Use

Strategic Advice: Read the entire sentence for context clues and determine which answer choice creates a logical sentence without wordiness or redundancies.

Getting to the Answer: Because it eliminates wordiness, and because the word "programs" is used later in the same sentence, (B) is correct.

5. D

Difficulty: Medium

Category: Writing & Language / Effective Language Use

Strategic Advice: Find context clues and determine which answer choice creates a logical sentence without wordiness or redundancies.

Getting to the Answer: Because there is still an exam to pass before these individuals became PAs, and because the repetition of the words "graduates" and "graduation" is redundant, (D) is the correct answer.

6. D

Difficulty: Medium

Category: Writing & Language / Organization

Strategic Advice: Review the answer choices to determine which creates a paragraph with the best logical progression of ideas.

Getting to the Answer: The paragraph discusses the steps a student must take in order to become a PA and does not discuss maintaining one's license until the end, as it is something someone does only after becoming a PA. Choice (D) is correct.

7. C

Difficulty: Medium

Category: Writing & Language / Effective Language Use

Strategic Advice: Use context clues to determine which answer choice best fits the context of the sentence and paragraph while conveying the author's intended meaning.

Getting to the Answer: The sentence suggests that doctors work alone while PAs work under supervision. The word with the definition that best describes a doctor's unsupervised work is "autonomously," (C).

8. A

Difficulty: Medium

Category: Writing & Language / Organization

Strategic Advice: Decide which answer choice offers the best transition for an accurate flow of ideas.

Getting to the Answer: Choice (A) offers the best transition in order to summarize why the previous information is important and to show the positive effects PAs have on the health care team.

9. C

Difficulty: Hard

Category: Writing & Language / Shifts in Construction

Strategic Advice: Evaluate whether the subject or object of the sentence is referred to by the pronoun and then determine which answer choice creates a logical and grammatically sound sentence.

Getting to the Answer: It is the PA who works under a physician, and because the pronoun refers to the object of the sentence, physicians, the appropriate pronoun to use in this situation is "whom." Therefore, (C) is correct.

10. B

Difficulty: Medium

Category: Writing & Language / Effective Language Use

Strategic Advice: Reread the paragraph and decide which answer choice maintains the style and tone of the author's voice.

Getting to the Answer: The author has not yet referenced him or herself, the reader, or any third party for an opinion in this passage. This makes the consistent tone found in (B) correct.

11. D

Difficulty: Medium

Category: Writing & Language / Development

Strategic Advice: Review the paragraph to determine which claim made by the author is lacking details or support evidence that would strengthen the author's case.

Getting to the Answer: The second sentence in the paragraph is the only one in which the author makes a claim based on projections, but the author fails to use specific figures. Adding these figures would strengthen this claim, thus (D) is correct.

Answers & Explanations

CHAPTER 18

PREPARE

1. B

Difficulty: Medium

Category: Writing & Language / Effective Language Use

Strategic Advice: To answer a Precision question, reread the sentence containing the underlined word and determine what meaning the author wants to convey.

Getting to the Answer: In this sentence, the author contrasts imaginative readers who are able to enjoy ancient mythology with ordinary readers who are consumed by their everyday worries. "Prosaic" means ordinary. Choice (B) is correct.

2. D

Difficulty: Easy

Category: Writing & Language / Effective Language Use

Strategic Advice: Using two words with essentially the same meaning in the same sentence is redundant and creates a concision error.

Getting to the Answer: Because "understand" and "comprehend" have the same meaning, the correct answer will eliminate one of those words. Choice (D) is the only answer choice that does so and is therefore correct.

3. A

Difficulty: Medium

Category: Writing & Language / Effective Language Use

Strategic Advice: When answering a Style and Tone question, you will sometimes need to read the entire passage or paragraph before selecting the correct answer.

Getting to the Answer: This underlined portion is correct as written. The purpose of this paragraph is to suggest that the modern story mirrors modern life. In sentence 2, the author describes the modern story as having "complexity and ambivalence." By repeating the same phrase to describe the modern reader's life, the author has matched the style and tone to the purpose of the paragraph. Choice (A) is correct.

4. C

Difficulty: Hard

Category: Writing & Language / Effective Language Use

Strategic Advice: Remember that syntax errors do not necessarily indicate that a sentence is grammatically incorrect.

Getting to the Answer: The question stem asks you which of the answer choices most effectively combines the two sentences. Choice (C) does this by turning the second sentence into a modifying phrase that provides information about the action in the independent clause.

PRACTICE

5. D

Difficulty: Hard

Category: Writing & Language / Effective Language Use

Strategic Advice: Make sure the order in which words and phrases are written makes sense logically.

Getting to the Answer: As written, this sentence is hard to follow. The author is trying to emphasize the information that men also served as nurses during the Civil War. Choice (D) is correct because it is the only answer choice with grammatically and logically correct syntax.

6. B

Difficulty: Medium

Category: Writing & Language / Effective Language Use

Strategic Advice: Even if an underlined word or phrase sounds correct, analyze its meaning—both literal and figurative—to ensure it is appropriate in context.

Getting to the Answer: While it is easy to interpret a meaning from the underlined phrase "major victories," that meaning does not convey the author's intention. The phrase "major victories" suggests that of all the accomplishments of this organization, excluding men was one of the most important. Reread the sentences before and after the underlined phrase to understand that what the author means to convey is the idea that this exclusion occurred early in the history of the nurses' organization. Choice (B) corrects this error by explaining that this exclusion was one of the early victories within a series of accomplishments.

7. C

Difficulty: Easy

Category: Writing & Language / Effective Language Use

Strategic Advice: Avoid the temptation to use more words than necessary. The SAT requires concision; avoid wordiness and redundancy.

Getting to the Answer: As written, the underlined segment is redundant: "denied admission to" and "excluded from" have the same meaning. Look for the most succinct way to convey the author's intended meaning. Choice (C) is correct.

8. B

Difficulty: Medium

Category: Writing & Language / Effective Language Use

Strategic Advice: Style and Tone errors are nuanced—pay attention to the details in the sentences surrounding the underlined word or phrase.

Getting to the Answer: As written, the underlined portion does not match the style and tone of the passage because it includes the author's opinion while the rest of the passage offers no judgment on any of the situations discussed. Choice (B) correctly maintains the objective tone of the passage by omitting any subjective viewpoints.

PERFORM

9. B

Difficulty: Medium

Category: Writing & Language / Effective Language Use

Strategic Advice: Questions about the author's word choice require you to determine the author's intended meaning within the context of the sentence.

Getting to the Answer: Read the sentence to understand the context in which the underlined word, "imagine," is used. The author uses "imagine" to describe how certain groups portray the risks associated with genetically modified organisms. Because the author views these groups as the opposition, the word needs to convey a sense of resistance to the truth. As written, the sentence conveys too benign of a meaning. Choice (B) is correct.

10. D

Difficulty: Easy

Category: Writing & Language / Effective Language Use

Strategic Advice: A sentence is redundant when two words that mean the same thing are used to express one idea.

Getting to the Answer: "Interfere" and "tamper" have the same meaning and are used to express a single idea about intentionally changing nature. The correct answer will eliminate one of those words. Choice (D) is correct.

11. B

Difficulty: Medium

Category: Writing & Language / Effective Language Use

Strategic Advice: Do not automatically select the shortest answer choice when presented with a Concision question. The correct answer choice must fully convey the author's intended meaning.

Getting to the Answer: As written, the underlined segment is the shortest answer choice, but it is difficult to determine exactly which group of people "we" refers to. Choice (B) is correct because it specifies the range of people included in "we" most concisely.

12. B

Difficulty: Hard

Category: Writing & Language / Effective Language Use

Strategic Advice: Syntax questions often require you to recognize that grammatically correct sentence structure alone may not produce the most effective writing.

Getting to the Answer: Although the sentences are grammatically correct as written, the question stem asks which of the answer choices most effectively combines the two sentences. Because the second sentence provides additional information about the "certain bird species" mentioned in the first sentence, use the relative pronoun "that" to indicate which species could be affected by the decline in the insect population. Choice (B) is correct.

13. D

Difficulty: Medium

Category: Writing & Language / Effective Language Use

Strategic Advice: Auxiliary verbs, like the underlined "will," add functional or grammatical meaning like expressing tense, voice, or emphasis to the clause in which they appear. When an auxiliary verb is underlined, make sure it fits the context of the paragraph or passage.

Getting to the Answer: Throughout the paragraph, the author uses the auxiliary verb "could" to indicate that the possibility exists to complete the described actions—"could lead" and "could have." Nothing in the paragraph suggests that the author has shifted from conjecture (indicated by "could") to either certainty ("will" and "would") or necessity ("must"). Choice (D) is correct.

14. A

Difficulty: Medium

Category: Writing & Language / Effective Language Use

Strategic Advice: When an entire sentence is underlined, check for a syntax error.

Getting to the Answer: This sentence is correct as written. The author arranges the parts of the sentence in the most logical order by introducing the topic ("actual impact"), describing what is being impacted, and drawing a conclusion about the topic. Choice (A) is correct.

15. A

Difficulty: Medium

Category: Writing & Language / Effective Language Use

Strategic Advice: To answer Word Choice questions, reread the sentence containing the underlined word or phrase to determine the author's intended meaning.

Getting to the Answer: Determine that the underlined phrase "essential fallacy" provides information about the basis for the argument discussed in this sentence. Rephrase the sentence as: the argument is based on a false idea. Choice (A) is correct.

16. D

Difficulty: Medium

Category: Writing & Language / Effective Language Use

Strategic Advice: When answering a Style and Tone question, you will sometimes need to read the entire passage or paragraph before selecting the correct answer.

Getting to the Answer: In the first three paragraphs, the author focuses on the negative aspects of genetically modified organisms. In the fourth paragraph, he dismisses the counter argument raised by advocates for genetically modified organisms. The tone in the final paragraph becomes strident and accusatory. The final sentence must match this tone in order to effectively conclude the paragraph and the passage. Choice (D) is correct because it suggests that the stakes for the planet are enormous and our misplaced trust would have dire consequences.

EXTRA PRACTICE

1. B

Difficulty: Medium

Category: Writing & Language / Punctuation

Strategic Advice: Read the sentence to determine how the list within it should be formatted. If it is more of an aside than a direct part of the sentence's main structure, the list should be set off by punctuation.

Getting to the Answer: As the sentence is written, its many commas are confusing. Because there is a list in the sentence, the commas within that list should remain. However, the list of poetic forms is not directly related to the rest of the sentence, so this should be clarified with punctuation. Dashes are the best way to mark this as a separate thought. Choice (B) correctly adds dashes to both the beginning and end of the list.

2. A

Difficulty: Easy

Category: Writing & Language / Effective Language Use

Strategic Advice: Determine what the sentence is saying about the history of the haiku. Is "complex" the most accurate way to describe it?

Getting to the Answer: The passage describes the many forms and many centuries that comprise the history of haiku. Choice (A), "complex," perfectly describes the long, rich, and detailed history of the poetic form.

3. A

Difficulty: Hard

Category: Writing & Language / Development

Strategic Advice: Determine which answer choice makes the most sense as an introduction to this paragraph. Consider what the purpose of the paragraph is and locate a sentence among the answer choices that encapsulates that idea.

Getting to the Answer: The purpose of this paragraph, based on its other sentences, is to explain the history of haiku and how its structure has changed over time. Choice (A) is the only answer choice related to these ideas. While the other answer choices may briefly mention the structure of haiku or its history, they all focus on other aspects of haiku—its entertainment value, the difficulty of understanding its rules, or the challenge of writing it.

4. B

Difficulty: Easy

Category: Writing & Language / Development

Strategic Advice: Determine the purpose of this sentence within the passage.

Getting to the Answer: While it is interesting for the audience to know that "hokku" eventually became "haiku," the sentence's placement in the passage is not optimal. The next sentence returns the discussion to the hokku form. In addition, readers encounter another explanation of the name "haiku" later, in paragraph 5. Choice (B) is correct because the sentence should be omitted from paragraph 2.

5. C

Difficulty: Medium

Category: Writing & Language / Organization

Strategic Advice: Consider the information presented by the rest of the paragraph to determine what "alternating turns" refers to.

Getting to the Answer: Sentence 7 describes the specifics of different word games introduced in sentence 5, so it makes sense that it would follow sentence 5. Choice (C) is correct.

6. C

Difficulty: Easy

Category: Writing & Language / Organization

Strategic Advice: Make sure that this sentence clearly and precisely transitions from the topic of the previous paragraph to the topic of this paragraph.

Getting to the Answer: As currently written, the first sentence does not make a clear connection to the preceding paragraph. By making the discussion of time more precise, the beginning of this paragraph flows better from the previous paragraph. The reader understands more clearly how the details in each paragraph connect. Choice (C) is correct.

7. D

Difficulty: Medium

Category: Writing & Language / Effective Language Use

Strategic Advice: Determine the purpose of sharing this information with readers. The tone of the sentence should be suited to its purpose.

Getting to the Answer: The paragraph is a straightforward piece of informative writing. The original sentence and C are both too casual for the rest of the passage, while B is too formal and wordy. Choice (D) correctly communicates the information of this sentence with the right level of formality.

8. D

Difficulty: Hard

Category: Writing & Language / Development

Strategic Advice: Find the answer choice that clearly supports the topic sentence of the paragraph while elegantly tying into the next sentence.

Getting to the Answer: The topic sentence of this paragraph emphasizes the themes in Basho's work and how haiku became associated with nature and the seasons. Choice (D) provides examples of possible subjects of Basho haikus and is therefore correct.

9. C

Difficulty: Hard

Category: Writing & Language / Effective Language Use

Strategic Advice: Consider what the sentence is communicating and if any words can be eliminated to say the same thing more concisely.

Getting to the Answer: The sentence uses too many words to communicate its point. By combining ideas and eliminating wordiness, the sentence can flow more smoothly. Choice (C) is correct because it maintains the sentence's meaning and uses fewer words to do so.

10. B

Difficulty: Medium

Category: Writing & Language / Effective Language Use

Strategic Advice: Consider the precise relationship between Shiki and the other poets mentioned. The correct answer choice will describe his effect on them.

Getting to the Answer: It seems clear that Shiki's work was an influence on cummings and Pound. While "helped" and "aided" both generally suggest that his effect on them was positive, "inspired" is more accurate. Shiki had left his mark, and the other poets learned from him. Choice (B) is correct.

11. D

Difficulty: Medium

Category: Writing & Language / Effective Language Use

Strategic Advice: Read the sentence and determine whether its thoughts are joined logically. The correct conjunction will make clear the relationship between the thoughts.

Getting to the Answer: The two parts of the sentence are directly related; the writers are "taken with the brevity of the form" because of what it provides them. Neither the sentence as it is written nor choices B or C express this relationship. Choice (D) correctly combines the sentence while maintaining the relationship between the two clauses.

CHAPTER 19

PREPARE

1. C
Difficulty: Medium

Category: Writing & Language / Usage

Strategic Advice: Phrases that include the words *most* or *more*, or include adjectives that end in *-er* or *-est*, are points of comparison. Make sure the construction of the comparison is grammatically correct as well as appropriate for the sentence's context.

Getting to the Answer: If the sentence were explicitly comparing two directors, the current construction would be appropriate. When comparing three or more people, the superlative "most important" is correct. If an author does not specify the number of people or things in a group, assume that it is more than two and use the superlative. Choice (C) is correct because it uses the correct superlative construction.

2. B
Difficulty: Hard

Category: Writing & Language / Usage

Strategic Advice: Whenever an idea or topic is referred to by synonymous nouns in different parts of the same sentence, make sure that those nouns are in agreement.

Getting to the Answer: The underlined section is a synonym for a previously mentioned plural noun ("films"). While "work" can refer to a body of productions much like the singular form of "film" can, the author's intention is to use the plural form of the noun. Choice (B) is correct because it is in agreement with "films."

3. C
Difficulty: Medium

Category: Writing & Language / Usage

Strategic Advice: If the underlined section is a pronoun, make sure that it does not create ambiguity or confusion for the reader. If the pronoun's antecedent is unclear, consider replacing it with a noun.

Getting to the Answer: The use of "him" in this location can confuse the reader: Is the author referring to Kurosawa, one of the samurai, or someone else? Given that the author is describing the conception of the lead characters from the film *Seven Samurai*, we can be certain that the underlined section is referring to the characters' creator, Kurosawa. Choice (C) is correct.

4. A
Difficulty: Easy

Category: Writing & Language / Usage

Strategic Advice: An idiom is a combination of words that must be used together to convey either a figurative or literal meaning. Make sure that idioms used in the passage are appropriate for the context and are in agreement with the author's central ideas.

Getting to the Answer: The author is making the point that critics of Kurosawa made two contentions simultaneously—they charged he was both unoriginal and too Westernized. The current construction of "neither...nor" is both grammatically correct and appropriate for the context. Choice (A) is correct.

PRACTICE

5. B
Difficulty: Medium

Category: Writing & Language / Usage

Strategic Advice: Make sure that comparisons use the correct construction that is aligned with the central idea and context of the passage.

Getting to the Answer: The author is making a comparison involving all North American animals—definitely a group larger than two. A superlative construction is appropriate, but it also needs to align with the thesis that the opossum is a very unusual animal. Choice (B) is correct because it is grammatically correct and fits the author's central idea.

6. D
Difficulty: Medium

Category: Writing & Language / Usage

Strategic Advice: When a pronoun is the subject of a sentence, make sure that its antecedent is clear. If it is not clear to which noun the pronoun is referring, then replace the pronoun.

Getting to the Answer: The current construction of the sentence creates an ambiguity: does "It" refer to the opossum or the kangaroo? Since the passage describes the characteristics of the opossum, this sentence should be about that animal as well. Choice (D) is correct because it makes the sentence's subject clear to the reader.

7. C
Difficulty: Medium

Category: Writing & Language / Usage

Strategic Advice: Make sure that the proper prepositions are being used in the passage.

Getting to the Answer: The preposition "in" is incorrect given the context. The author is describing "limitations *on* the amount of food... that can be stored..." Choice (C) is correct. If idioms are tricky, think of an analogous situation. A computer's limited warranty has limitations *on* the kinds of things you can do with it. It doesn't have limitations *in* those things.

8. C
Difficulty: Easy

Category: Writing & Language / Usage

Strategic Advice: Review a pronoun's antecedent to make sure there is agreement throughout the sentence or section.

Getting to the Answer: Early in this sentence, the author establishes the singular possessive form ("the opossum's") as the antecedent of the pronoun in the underlined section. Also, except for an earlier section that discusses "the female opossum," the author uses the non-gendered pronoun "it" when referring to the animal. Choice (C) is correct because it is singular, possessive, and non-gendered.

PERFORM

9. A
Difficulty: Medium

Category: Writing & Language / Usage

Strategic Advice: Read the sentence in its entirety to make sure there is no subject-verb disagreement.

Getting to the Answer: The verb in the underlined section, "were," appears after the parenthetical remark set aside by dashes. The current version of the subject, "blimps," is in agreement with the verb. No change is necessary; (A) is correct.

10. B

Difficulty: Medium

Category: Writing & Language / Usage

Strategic Advice: Make sure that comparisons are in the appropriate format—comparative when comparing two things, superlative when comparing three or more things.

Getting to the Answer: In the previous sentence, the author states that the *Hindenburg* was "one of a kind." The ship was unique out of all airships, making superlative descriptions appropriate. Given the superlative construction and the author's focus on the ship's dimensions, (B) is correct because the reader can infer that the *Hindenburg* was the "largest" airship of its time.

11. C

Difficulty: Medium

Category: Writing & Language / Usage

Strategic Advice: Complex sentences can often benefit from the use of pronouns, reducing wordiness and repetition. That said, make sure that the use of a pronoun will not introduce ambiguity into the sentence.

Getting to the Answer: In a complicated sentence including multiple nouns, it is often better to avoid pronouns to preserve the clarity of the author's claims. Choice (C) is correct.

12. B

Difficulty: Hard

Category: Writing & Language / Usage

Strategic Advice: Check to see if the underlined section is part of an idiomatic expression, such as *either...or*.

Getting to the Answer: The sentence contains the first half of the idiomatic combination *not only...but also*. The use of "and" in this context is incorrect. Choice (B), "but also," is correct.

13. B

Difficulty: Easy

Category: Writing & Language / Usage

Strategic Advice: Pay attention to commonly confused words, such as *except* and *accept*, to make sure that careless mistakes do not go unaddressed in a passage.

Getting to the Answer: "It's" is a contraction of "it is" and is incorrect in this context. The sentence requires the singular possessive pronoun, "its." Choice (B) is correct.

14. C

Difficulty: Medium

Category: Writing & Language / Usage

Strategic Advice: Make sure the underlined section is using the appropriate prepositions.

Getting to the Answer: If the verb "rest" refers to a direct object, the preposition "on" is required. Choice (C) is correct because it correctly constructs the idiom.

15. D

Difficulty: Easy

Category: Writing & Language / Usage

Strategic Advice: Examine the use of nouns that are used as synonyms within the same sentence. They should agree in number, and their shared meaning should either be easily understood or previously explained by the author.

Getting to the Answer: At this point in the passage, the author has already established that "balloon" is a synonym for "blimp" and "airship." The underlined section is therefore the correct term, but it disagrees in number with the rest of the sentence in which the associated noun ("airship") is singular. Choice (D) is correct because it is in numerical agreement with the previous noun.

16. B

Difficulty: Easy

Category: Writing & Language / Usage

Strategic Advice: Examine the sentence's use of pronouns for agreement with antecedents.

Getting to the Answer: The sentence's use of "their" as a possessive pronoun conflicts with the antecedent "the airship" which is singular. Choice (B) is correct because it is a singular, possessive pronoun in agreement with its antecedent.

EXTRA PRACTICE

1. B

Difficulty: Medium

Category: Writing & Language / Sentence Formation

Strategic Advice: Compare the two parts of the sentence. Is the second part a subordinate or coordinate clause?

Getting to the Answer: "Since" is a conjunction used between subordinating ideas. These two clauses are coordinating and require a coordinating conjunction meaning "in addition to." Choice (B) is correct.

2. D

Difficulty: Medium

Category: Writing & Language / Effective Language Use

Strategic Advice: Analyze how the underlined word is used in the sentence. Test each answer choice to see if it improves the overall clarity of the text.

Getting to the Answer: The opening sentences of the passage are about how the cold weather makes starting cars difficult. When used as a verb, "credit" means to have faith in something. Choice (D), "blame," means to hold responsible, and is correct.

3. D

Difficulty: Hard

Category: Writing & Language / Organization

Strategic Advice: Review how the content of sentence 3 is related to the entire paragraph. Recall that transitions help the reader understand logical relationships between ideas. What words in sentence 3 signal a transition?

Getting to the Answer: Sentence 4 explains what happens when the number of electrons increases. Because sentence 3 further develops the explanation of what happens when the number of electrons decreases, the transition "likewise" is a clue that it should follow sentence 4. Choice (D) is correct.

4. A

Difficulty: Hard

Category: Writing & Language / Development

Strategic Advice: Identify the key details in the paragraph. Then, summarize them to find the central idea.

Getting to the Answer: All of the sentences in this paragraph describe how a battery is constructed and works. Choice (A) is correct.

5. D

Difficulty: Easy

Category: Writing & Language / Punctuation

Strategic Advice: Determine if the items listed need to be treated as a series.

Getting to the Answer: Since there are only two items, no commas are needed. Choice (D) is correct.

6. C

Difficulty: Easy

Category: Writing & Language / Usage

Strategic Advice: Determine the tense and the number of the subject. Then, predict the verb form that matches.

Getting to the Answer: Since "lead oxide" is singular and the paragraph is written in present tense, (C) is correct.

7. C

Difficulty: Medium

Category: Writing & Language / Effective Language Use

Strategic Advice: Establish how the underlined word is used in the sentence; consider the connotations and denotations of the answer choices. Remember that the correct term should reflect the scientific subject matter.

Getting to the Answer: "Boundary" is a term meaning a limitation. "Circuit," a noun, is the scientific term that means circumference or course. Choice (C) is correct.

8. B

Difficulty: Hard

Category: Writing & Language / Development

Strategic Advice: Closely examine the topic sentence and the supporting details; identify the central idea of the paragraph.

Getting to the Answer: Choice (B) is the only option that adds supporting information about how a current flows through a battery charger.

9. D

Difficulty: Medium

Category: Writing & Language / Effective Language Use

Strategic Advice: Look at how the word is used in the sentence; analyze its grammatical function. Use context clues to determine which choice is correct.

Getting to the Answer: "Practicality" is an adverb meaning in a practical manner; "probability" is a noun meaning likelihood. Choice (D) is correct.

10. A

Difficulty: Medium

Category: Writing & Language / Usage

Strategic Advice: Test all of the answer choices. Recall that contractions represent two words combined as one.

Getting to the Answer: The contraction "it's" is short for *it is* and is inappropriate here. Choice (A) is correct.

11. A

Difficulty: Hard

Category: Writing & Language / Quantitative

Strategic Advice: Study the graph carefully and consider how its data points connect to the content of the passage.

Getting to the Answer: The overall graph trend suggests that battery performance peaks at moderate temperatures, suffers slightly at higher temperatures, and declines greatly at lower ones. The lowest point of the *x*-axis indicates a temperature of approximately 30°F. At this temperature, for example, a battery-operated car can travel a distance of approximately 20 miles as shown on the *y*-axis, as opposed to peak performance of more than 40 miles. Since cold temperatures adversely affect the battery performance of an electric car, (A) is correct.

CHAPTER 20

EXTRA PRACTICE

Adapted from "Freedom or Death," a speech delivered by Emmeline Pankhurst on November 13, 1913, in Hartford, Connecticut

Mrs. Hepburn, ladies and gentlemen:

Tonight I am not here to advocate woman suffrage. American suffragists can do that very well for themselves. <u>I am here as a soldier who has temporarily left the field of battle in order to explain what civil war is like when civil war is waged by women.</u> I am here as a person who, according to the law courts of my country, it has been decided, is of no value to the community at all: and I am adjudged because of my life to be a dangerous person.

(Now,) first of all I want to make you understand the <u>inevitableness of revolution and civil war, even on the part of women</u>, when you reach a certain stage in the development of a community's life. It is quite easy for you to understand the desirability of revolution <u>if I were a man</u>. If an Irish revolutionary had addressed this meeting, and many have addressed meetings all over the United States during the last twenty or thirty years, it would not be necessary for that revolutionary to explain the need of revolution beyond saying that the people of his country were denied—and by people, meaning men—were denied the right of self-government. That would explain the whole situation. <u>If I were a man</u> and I said to you, "I come from a country which professes to have representative institutions and (yet) denies me, a taxpayer, an inhabitant of the country, representative rights," you would at once understand that that human being, being a man, was justified in the adoption of revolutionary methods to get representative institutions. (But) since I am a woman it is <u>necessary in the twentieth century to explain why women have adopted revolutionary methods in order to win the rights of citizenship.</u>

You see, (in spite of) a good deal that we hear about revolutionary methods not being necessary for American women, we women, in trying to make our case clear, always have to make as part of our argument, and urge upon men in our audience the fact—a very simple fact—that women are human beings. <u>I want to put a few political arguments before you—not arguments for the suffrage, because I said when I opened, I didn't mean to do that—but arguments for the adoption of militant methods in order to win political rights.</u>

(Suppose) the men of Hartford had a grievance, and they laid that grievance before their legislature, and the legislature obstinately refused to listen

purpose

war metaphor

hypothetical

must do this bc woman

kinds of arguments for ev.

more hypothet.

to them, or to remove their grievance, what would be the proper and the constitutional and the practical way of getting their grievance removed? Well, <u>it is perfectly obvious</u> at the next general election, when the legislature is elected, <u>the men of Hartford would turn out that legislature and elect a new one: entirely change the personnel of an obstinate legislature.</u>

(But) let the men of Hartford <u>imagine</u> that they were not in the position of being voters at all, that they were governed without their consent being obtained, that the legislature turned an absolutely deaf ear to their demands, what would the men of Hartford do then? They couldn't vote the legislature out. They would have to make a <u>choice of two evils</u>: they would either have to <u>submit indefinitely to an unjust state of affairs</u>, or they would have <u>to rise up and adopt some of the antiquated means by which men in the past got their grievances remedied</u>. We know what happened when <u>your forefathers</u> decided that they must have representation for taxation, many, many years ago. When they felt they couldn't wait any longer, when they laid all the arguments before an obstinate British government that they could think of, and when their arguments were absolutely disregarded, when every other means had failed, they began by the tea party at Boston, and they went on until they had won the independence of the United States of America. <u>That is what happened in the old days.</u>

<u>It is perfectly evident to any</u> (logical mind) that when you have got the vote, you can get out of any legislature whatever you want, (or) if you cannot get it, you can send them about their business and choose other people who will be more attentive to your demands, (But) it is clear to the meanest intelligence that if you have not got the vote, you must either submit to laws just or unjust, administration just or unjust, or <u>the time inevitably comes when you will revolt against that injustice and use violent means to put an end to it.</u>

effects of men not having rights

ex. of Am. Rev.

war = inevitable

Sample Student Response #1

Emmeline Pankhurst is a militant suffragist, but she has not come to Hartford, Connecticut, to speak about suffrage. No, she makes that clear with the first line of her speech. Pankhurst does not want to explain why woman suffrage is just and necessary; she has come to explain why *the way* that she and her fellow suffragists fight for suffrage is just and necessary. To Pankhurst, the battle for woman suffrage is a civil war, and she is a soldier in that war ready to justify not her cause but her methods, not her ideas but her strategies, not her goals but her tactics. Pankhurst claims that the government, by denying women the vote to begin with, has left them with only protest and revolt as a means to win political change. She positions her speech as a defense of her methods, but as such, it also affirms her cause.

From the start, Pankhurst excites interest by claiming that the fight for woman suffrage is not merely a difference of opinion but a battle. She is not a reformer, an activist, or an ideologue. She is a soldier! She couches her argument in terms that demand the attention and the empathy of men and woman alike. After all, the United States is rooted in a history of revolution and civil war. Pankhurst draws a comparison with Irish revolutionaries as well. Anyone familiar with global events in of the late 19th and early 20th century would know that Irish revolutionaries were actively appealing to sympathies abroad, especially among Americans. In drawing this comparison, Pankhurst not only equates woman suffrage with political revolutions but also equates women with men, the underlying principle of the woman suffrage movement. She claims that if she were a male revolutionary, no one would doubt the right of her methods; it is only because she is a female revolutionary that there is any question. Furthermore, she makes clear that the battle itself is for "the rights of citizenship." By this rhetoric, she makes clear that suffrage is something to which women are entitled as citizens. This means that to deny woman suffrage is to deny them as citizens. She goes on to argue that the issue in question is not only suffrage but also women's status as human beings. To deny women suffrage is not just to deny them citizenship but to deny them humanity. Pankhurst appeals to her audience's higher emotions and sense of right, and weaves justification of her desired reform into her defense of the means to win that reform.

Pankhurst shifts back to defense of militant protest tactics, and reminds the audience that she is not there to discuss suffrage. In this way, she placates members of the audience who might question suffrage while again assuming the merit of suffrage. The end is just. She has only to justify her means. Pankhurst brings home the comparison to the *men* of Hartford. They are citizens with rights under their government. If they objected to the governance of their leaders, what would they *do*? Why, they would "turn out that legislature and elect a new one," of course! That's how political matters are resolved in democratic society. But what if they could not? Pankhurst argues that the men of Hartford, if denied their political rights as citizens, would do what their forebears had done. Here, she makes another emotional appeal by focusing on the heart of America. When denied their rights, the American revolutionaries used militant forms of protest, as demonstrated in the Boston Tea Party. When that failed, they took up arms and declared their independence. As Pankhurst explains, the political revolutionaries of the past had to choose between "two evils": submitting to "an unjust state of affairs" or rising up and using "antiquated means by which men in the past got their grievances remedied." Pankhurst appeals to the morality of her audience by making clear that she considers violent methods unpleasant. The implication is that she and the suffragists have been denied the preferred nonviolent solutions by being denied the vote. Again, Pankhurst skillfully weaves an argument for suffrage into her defense of the tactics to win suffrage.

Pankhurst concludes by reaffirming her underlying assumption—that suffrage is just and necessary. "It is perfectly evident to any logical mind," she says, suggesting that reason itself is on the side of the suffragists. She explains that when you have the vote, you don't need to use other protest methods—violent or otherwise; however, when you cannot take part in government in a legitimate way, then you must either submit or revolt. Pankhurst ties together the stated purpose of her speech with the underlying purpose. Submission is not an option. Their cause is just; therefore, their means, the only means open to the suffragists, is just. Throughout her speech, Pankhurst defends suffragists' militant activism, but in so doing, she justifies the cause of that activism. After all, if women had the vote, they would not need to revolt. To win revolutionary change, suffragists must adopt revolutions means. Pankhurst's argument feeds on itself, and the act of assumption becomes an act of persuasion.

Reading—4: The writer thoroughly understands the source text as evidenced by her use of para-phrases of Pankhurst's speech as well as direct quotations. She accurately summarizes Pankhurst's central idea (*Pankhurst does not want to explain why woman suffrage is just and necessary; she has come to explain why* the way *that she and her fellow suffragists fight for suffrage is just and necessary*) in the introduction and also cites many details and examples that support Pankhurst's purpose, explaining how these details interrelate with Pankhurst's central argument. This response demon-strates thorough comprehension of the source text.

Analysis—2: This response offers limited analysis of the source text and therefore partial understanding of the analytical task. In the second body paragraph, the writer lists different features of Pankhurst's speech (such as historical examples and appealing to the *audience's higher emotions and sense of right*), but does not expand on how these features contribute to or advance Pankhurst's central argument. Rather than an analysis of how Pankhurst persuades her audience that violent and nonviolent protest tactics are necessary to gain political rights for women, this response is more a summary of Pankhurst's speech.

Writing—3: The writer demonstrates effective use and control of standard written English in this mostly cohesive response. She includes her own central claim in the introduction (*To Pankhurst, the battle for woman suffrage is a civil war, and she is a soldier in that war ready to justify not her cause but her methods, not her ideas but her strategies, not her goals but her tactics*) and uses a variety of sentence structures. The two body paragraphs could be better organized—each seems like a hodgepodge of separate points rather than a cohesive, in-depth exploration of one feature of Pankhurst's argu-ment, detracting from a coherent progression of ideas. While the overall style and tone is objective, the writer does deviate from formal writing at times: *Anyone familiar with global events in of the late 19th and early 20th century would know that Irish revolutionaries were actively appealing to sympathies abroad, especially among Americans.* Overall, the writing in this response is proficient.

Sample Student Response #2

Emmeline Pankhurst does appear in Hartford, Connecticut, to speak about suffrage. From the start of her speech, she makes clear that she does not want to explain why woman suffrage is necessary. Rather, she means to explain why the way that she and her fellow suffragists fight for suffrage is necessary. Pankhurst looks at the battle for woman suffrage as a civil war. She calls herself a soldier sent to explain her tactics in the war, not the importance of her side in the war. In her speech, Pankhurst explains that she and the suffragists must use violent means to win change because it is the only means open to them. She asserts that they cannot win reform any other way precisely because suffrage is denied to them. In this way, she uses her defense of her methods to actually justify the underlying cause—suffrage for women.

Pankhurst grabs her audience's attention by calling woman suffrage not just a political debate but a civil war. In the same way, she makes herself more than a reformer or an activist; she declares herself a soldier. In this way, she gets men and woman to listen to what she has to say. Her references to revolution and civil war also call up America's own history, rooted in political revolt. In addition to this comparison, she compares the struggle of suffragists with that of Irish revolutionaries. Not only is the woman suffrage movement a political revolution, she seems to say, but also women (revolutionary and otherwise) are equal with men. If she were a man, she says no one would doubt her right to revolt, but because she's a woman, she and her fellow suffragists have to explain themselves.

Pankhurst also claims that the struggle for suffrage is really a fight for "the rights of citizenship." She implies that by denying women the right to vote, the government is denying them citizenships. In using this rhetoric, she makes the idea that suffrage is something to which women are entitled as citizens clear. This means that to deny woman suffrage is to deny them as citizens. She goes on to say "that women are human beings," making the debate over suffrage also a denial of women's humanity. By doing this, Pankhurst tries to appeal to her audience's emotions and sympathies. She begins by talking about the way she works for political change, but by calling attention to the battle and to women as citizens and humans, she really makes the case for suffrage itself.

Finally, Pankhurst ties it all together in her final paragraph. She even suggests that reason itself is on her side by stating that it's "perfectly evident to any logical mind" and "clear to the meanest intelligence" that if you can vote, you can change government peacefully, while if you can't vote, you have to resort to other means. For this reason, using even violent means of protest and revolt to win suffrage is just. Pankhurst concludes by claiming that her tactics are needed precisely because women can't vote. This argument rests on the assumption that woman suffrage itself is right and necessary, and in a circular kind of way, ends up defending suffrage as well as the tactics to win suffrage.

Reading—2: This writer demonstrates some comprehension of the source text. He shortly relates an overview of Pankhurst's central purpose (*she does not want to explain why woman suffrage is necessary*). However, the writer does not go beyond what can be interpreted from Pankhurst's speech and misunderstands some important details. There is very little textual evidence used in the response.

Analysis—2: This writer demonstrates a partial understanding of the analytical task, offering a limited analysis of the source text. He is able to identify pieces of evidence Pankhurst uses, but is ineffective in explaining their importance in regard to the central argument. Also, the lack of direct quotations or paraphrases from the text leaves much of the writer's analysis unsubstantiated. There is also a lack of focus on the features of the text most relevant to furthering Pankhurst's central argument.

Writing—2: This response has little cohesion and demonstrates limited skill in the use and control of standard written English. Rather than using the introduction and conclusion as touchstones of the response, the writer merely uses the four paragraphs (including the two body paragraphs) to describe Pankhurst's argument as it unfolds. There is limited progression of ideas within paragraphs but this progression is absent from the overall response. The sentence structures utilized are repetitive and the style and tone are nowhere near as formal and objective as they should be. While there are some careless grammatical and spelling errors, they do not detract from the author's intended meaning.